CAREER GUIDANCE: A HANDBOOK OF METHODS

ROBERT E. CAMPBELL
The Ohio State University

GARRY R. WALZ
The University of Michigan

JULIET V. MILLER
The University of Michigan

SARA FINN KRIGER
Ohio Department of Mental Health and Mental Retardation

CHARLES E. MERRILL PUBLISHING COMPANY
A Bell & Howell Company
Columbus, Ohio

THE MERRILL SERIES
IN CAREER PROGRAMS

Editorial Board: Director, Robert Taylor, The Ohio State University; Theodore Cote, Temple University; Aleene Cross, University of Georgia; Louise Keller, University of Northern Colorado; Mary Klaurens, University of Minnesota; Wilbur Miller, University of Missouri; Carl Schaefer, Rutgers — The State University; Robert Warmbrod, The Ohio State University.

Published by
Charles E. Merrill Publishing Company
A Bell & Howell Company
Columbus, Ohio 43216

Copyright © 1973 by The Center for Vocational and Technical Education, The Ohio State University. All rights reserved. No part of this book may be reproduced in any form, electronic or mechanical, including photocopy, recording, or any information storage and retrieval system, without permission in writing from the publisher.

Copyright is claimed until September 1978. Thereafter all portions of this book covered by this copyright will be in the public domain.

The text was developed under a grant from the U. S. Office of Education, Department of Health, Education, and Welfare. However the opinions and other content do not necessarily reflect the position of policy of the agency, and no official endorsement should be inferred.

International Standard Book Number: 0-675-08894-1

Library of Congress Catalog Card Number: 73-83286

2 3 4 5 6 — 78 77 76 75 74

Printed in the United States of America

PREFACE

Within the past decade, there have been many career guidance innovations and developments designed to assist guidance personnel in upgrading their services and programs. Despite the mushrooming of innovative guidance methods, the authors were struck by the lack of a single source that organized, codified, and synthesized these innovations. During the 1969 Las Vegas American Personnel and Guidance Association's annual meeting, the senior authors (Walz and Campbell) outlined a basic plan to remedy this situation, i.e. a sourcebook of guidance methods. The senior authors represented a merger of two critical national resource centers for the substance of the book, namely, The Center for Vocational and Technical Education at The Ohio State University which houses an Education Resource Information Center Clearinghouse for Vocational and Technical Education, and the Education Resource Information Center Clearinghouse for Counseling and Personnel Services at the University of Michigan. The initial national search of career guidance methods was both overwhelming and disappointing.

Although two thousand methods were identified, many of these represented duplications and incomplete methods, and emphasized significant gaps. At the same time, however, many promising methods emerged. As our initial screening and review progressed so did the shape of the book. We became increasingly convinced that it would take a great deal of time and tedious effort, but would definitely provide a much needed contribution to guidance. Interested colleagues maintained our moral courage and persuaded us not to abandon what at times seemed a hopeless task. The continual reappraisal of our substantive base, our concerns for the needs of guidance practitioners, and our desire to publish a viable book led us through numerous revisions. The present volume which describes over six hundred current methods will open vistas for the dedicated practitioner who is concerned with improving his guidance program. It will also be helpful as a textbook for training guidance personnel at all levels since it allows the student to scan quickly the parameters of methods as well as examine specific approaches in depth.

The methods will vary in the degree to which each has been subjected to evaluation, since the authors found it impossible to evaluate each. In some instances, there has been rigorous evaluation whereas in others, virtually none. Typically this is cited by the method innovator. In other instances, some methods are still in developmental stages and are subsequently being evaluated. We would encourage the reader to write to method developers if more information is desired on this matter. There are many excellent methods described in this book which are worthy of implementation, but we feel that it is the responsibility of the reader to make his own judgments as to utility of each for his program. We are sure that practitioners will want to modify a method to suit their program constraints and needs, since it is very unlikely that any given method will be an exact fit, and we personally feel that practitioners should have this latitude. Probably what is more critical is that the book is heuristic and provides a stimulant for upgrading archaic programs. Hopefully, the methods will alert the reader to ideas and trigger new ones.

Needless to say, many have contributed to the development and completion of this handbook. First of all our hats go off to the tireless efforts over the years of the project staff which included consultants, reviewers, writers, diggers, and secretaries. Hence, appreciation should be extended to Marvin Barbulla, Henry Borow, J. Eugene Bottoms, Christine Brose, Susan Carlson, Edward P. Dworkin, Norman C. Gysbers, Lorraine S. Hansen, Dorothy P. Jackson, Carol Jaslow, George Leonard, Bill E. Lovelace, Paul B. Leiter, Phillip A. Perrone, and Edwin Whitfield.

A second group of behind-the-scenes contributors were for the most part administrative in that they helped set the stage and supported us with operational matters which are critical to any publication, e.g. budgets, copyright procedures, editing, coordination of personnel and production

Preface

scheduling. This group included The Center for Vocational and Technical Education staff: Robert E. Taylor, the Director, Edward J. Morrison, Associate Director for Research, and Joel H. Magisos, Associate Director for Information Services; and the Merrill editorial staff, Beverly Kolz and Connie Bates, for their insightful suggestions.

Probably the most critical to the production of the book were the many method developers who unselfishly contributed voluminous reports from which we were able to identify guidance methods. Although they are too numerous to mention here they are all cited within the text and deserve special praise for their creativity and painstaking efforts in generating new frontiers for guidance. With an undertaking as large as this, it is inevitable, despite our thorough searching, to overlook some excellent methods. This was not intentional, but simply a lack of communication. If this occurred to you, we offer our apologies and encourage you to alert us to the oversight.

Finally we would like to acknowledge the U.S. Office of Education for their willingness to support this project and for their wisdom in establishing the very valuable Education Resource Information Center clearinghouses without which this book could not have become a reality.

The authors

CONTENTS

1   **Introduction**   **1**

Structure of the Handbook, 3; Strategies for Using the Handbook, 7.

2   **Educational Level Considerations Relating to Career Guidance**   **13**

Introduction, 13; Educational Level: Elementary, 16; Method Applications, 20; Educational Level: Junior High School, 22; Method Applications, 27; Educational Level: High School, 30; Method Applications, 35; Educational Level: Post-High School, 38; Method Applications, 43.

3   **Population Subgroups for Whom Special Guidance Procedures Are Desirable**   **45**

Introduction, 45; Potential Dropouts, 48; Method Applications, 50; Slow

Learners, 51; Method Applications, 53; Underachievers, 53; Method Applications, 56; Disadvantaged, 56; Method Applications, 59; Rural Youth, 60; Method Applications, 64; Mexican American Youth, 65; Method Applications, 67; Women, 68; Method Applications, 70; Handicapped Youth, 71; Method Applications, 74.

4 Types of Career Guidance Methods 75

Factors Affecting the Selection of Methods, 76; Method Type: Behavioral Techniques, 77; Method Applications, 81; Method Type: Computer-Assisted Guidance, 81; Method Applications, 85; Method Type: Educational Media, 87; Method Applications, 90; Method Type: Group Procedures, 92; Method Applications, 96; Method Type: Information Retrieval Systems, 98; Method Applications, 101; Method Type: Simulation Gaming, 102; Method Applications, 106; Method Type: Career Relevant Curricula, 107; Method Applications, 111; Method Type: Work Experience Programs, 114; Method Applications, 119.

5 Designing Career Guidance Approaches 121

Designing Career Guidance Approaches, 122; Career Guidance Approaches, 123; Approach: Career Information Systems, 123; Approach: Developmental Programs, 128; Approach: Involving Parents in Their Child's Career Development, 131; Approach: Manpower and Economic Education, 135; Approach: Mobile Career Guidance Services, 139; Approach:

Contents

Teaching Decision Making, 143; Approach: Special Curricula to Motivate Career Exploration, 146; Approach: Using Models to Learn Vocational Behaviors, 150; Approach: Simulation to Facilitate Vocational Exploration and Decision Making, 154; Approach: Vocational Exploration Through Media and Classroom Activities, 160.

6 Guidelines for Career Guidance Program Development — 167

Introduction, 167; Exemplary Programs, 169; Do You Share These Concerns?, 185; Some Basic Characteristics of Effective Career Guidance Programs, 186; Implementing Career Guidance Programs, 195.

7 Career Guidance: Where We Are and What We Need — 201

Where We Are, 201; Images of the Future: What We Need, 206; Conclusion, 211.

8 Compendium of Career Guidance Methods — 213

Method Abstracts, 215; Abstract Method Index, 377; Availability of Methods, 380.

References — 395

Index — 415

Contents

Teaching Decision Making, 143; Approach: Special Curricula to Motivate Career Exploration, 146; Approach: Using Models to Learn Vocational Behaviors, 150; Approach: Simulation to Facilitate Vocational Exploration and Decision Making, 154; Approach: Vocational Exploration Through Media and Classroom Activities, 160.

6 Guidelines for Career Guidance Program Development — 167

Introduction, 167; Exemplary Programs, 169; Do You Share These Concerns?, 185; Some Basic Characteristics of Effective Career Guidance Programs, 186; Implementing Career Guidance Programs, 195.

7 Career Guidance: Where We Are and What We Need — 201

Where We Are, 201; Images of the Future: What We Need, 206; Conclusion, 211.

8 Compendium of Career Guidance Methods — 213

Method Abstracts, 215; Abstract Method Index, 377; Availability of Methods, 380.

References — 395

Index — 415

Chapter 1 INTRODUCTION

Without a doubt, there is an increasing demand for innovative methods to facilitate career development. Those charged with the responsibility for career guidance, such as teachers and counselors, are constantly searching for more effective ways of fulfilling their mission. The job of developing career guidance programs is not an easy one. It necessitates providing comprehensive programs for all students at all educational levels and, quite often, this needs to be accomplished with limited staff and resources. Although a major task of developing career guidance programs involves conceptualizing program goals and objectives, perhaps a more difficult task is the selection of appropriate methods for achieving the objectives.

For the purpose of this handbook, the term method is being used collectively to include *all* techniques and approaches for achieving specific career guidance objectives. However, methods differ from programs and systems. The latter imply broader strategies for implementing a total program and mission, e.g., procedures used to achieve seventh-grade occupational exploration would be viewed as methods, whereas the entire junior high school career guidance effort would be described as a total program or system involving the integration of many individual methods.

In order to maintain a dynamic career guidance program, the guidance counselor must keep abreast of a substantial body of professional literature. (In this handbook, the term guidance counselor is being used synonymously with other terms such as career guidance counselor, counselor and vocational guidance counselor to represent a professional person who is primarily responsible for assisting students with their career development.) Within the past decade, there has been a staggering number of innovations and developments in career guidance methods. Our computerized search in 1969 identified approximately 2000 methods which had been developed during the sixties. In addition to federal funding, four overlapping trends have stimulated the generation of new methods: theoretical advancements, technological innovation, new emphases in the guidance movement, and broader societal changes.

Theoretical advancements, e.g., conceptual framework for vocational development, have been proposed primarily by Super and his colleagues (Osipow 1968) and have triggered related work on vocational developmental tasks and the measurement of vocational maturity. In addition to proposing macro frameworks, there has been much attention directed toward micro facets of the total process of development, such as developmental transition points, vocational-decision making, occupational mobility, worker adjustment, and occupational exploration. A recent article by Hall (1971) provides a fresh perspective for viewing careers over the life span and suggests many additional substantive areas for proposing microtheory. A similar broad perspective has been offered by Campbell (1969) under the rubric of vocational ecology.

A second trend which has generated new guidance methods has been that of *technological innovation,* such as increased use of computers, multi-media, and simulation techniques. In 1969, Tiedeman estimated that at least fourteen different computer-based vocational guidance models were developed during the late sixties. Advances in hardware have encouraged creative marriages with career guidance approaches, such as video-tape occupational information and programmed learning.

Changing emphases in *the practice of guidance* represents a third trend which has influenced method design. These include emphasis on program accountability and evaluation, systems approaches, behavioral objectives, and K-14 developmental approaches. Most of these require the integration of multiple methods for total program design. The fourth trend is manifested by *changing societal forces,* such as the women's liberation movement, disadvantaged groups, and youth cults.

Each of these trends has had considerable impact on the mushrooming of career guidance methods. Trying to keep up with the new methods in these areas is difficult enough because of their vast number, but the problem is further compounded by the observation that the average

Introduction

counselor does not have easy access to a large portion of the literature concerning these methods. Much is published in limited quantity as project reports and may take several years before they appear in a professional journal, and even these may be scattered in many journals.

To date there is no one source where method innovations are organized, codified, and synthesized. A critical need exists at this time for a handbook of career guidance methods that has practical applications for schools and employment centers. The purpose of this handbook is to fulfill this need by:

1. Describing important and potentially useful methods applicable to career guidance that are currently in practice or in the experimental/developmental stage.
2. Organizing these methods according to selected criteria, e.g., type of student population for whom methods are intended, educational level, and nature of methods.
3. Providing a conceptual framework for the selection of methods which are appropriate for meeting specific guidance goals with specific student populations.
4. Presenting a number of distinct guidance approaches and providing information about the specific steps needed to design applications of these approaches for a particular guidance setting.
5. Providing models and procedural guidelines for developing a total career guidance program.
6. Identifying gaps and discrepancies in career guidance methods and generating potentially useful methods when possible.

Structure of the Handbook

A handbook is designed to allow quick access to information needed to solve highly specific problems. Unlike many books, it is not intended to be read from cover to cover. Rather, it is designed to enable the reader to look up many different points according to his particular need at a given time. A cookbook is a common example of a handbook. If someone is looking for an interesting dessert recipe, they would not start at the beginning of the book where the appetizer recipes are found. When using any handbook, it is necessary first to understand the basic structure of the handbook so that those sections which are most relevant can be easily located. The Career Guidance Handbook contains the following sections.

METHODS ACCORDING TO EDUCATIONAL LEVEL

It is quite possible that a counselor or teacher would want to identify all career guidance methods which are appropriate for a particular age group. If a program is being designed for elementary school students, it is probably not necessary to survey all high school programs, since many of the methods used with older students are not appropriate for elementary students. Chapter 2 classifies career guidance methods according to four educational levels: (a) elementary, (b) junior high, (c) high school, and (d) post high school. In addition to listing examples of methods which have been used with each of these four levels, this section also presents information which is needed when designing new or modifying existing methods for these four groups. Included for each of the four levels is information about the need for career guidance, specific career guidance goals, and characteristics of the students which determine the appropriateness of various methods.

METHODS ACCORDING TO SPECIAL POPULATION

Recently there has been considerable discussion about the needs of special student groups for career guidance. Although a school may have a basic career guidance program, the staff may decide that the program is not effective with all students. Therefore, they may decide to design special career guidance experiences for such groups as girls, disadvantaged or handicapped. Chapter 3 lists methods according to their appropriate use with eight special student groups: (a) potential dropouts, (b) slow learners, (c) underachievers, (d) disadvantaged, (e) rural youth, (f) Mexican-American youth, (g) women, and (h) handicapped. In addition to listing methods, the section also presents information which is needed when designing methods for these groups. Included for each student group is a definition of the special group, research information describing characteristics of the group, and major considerations related to designing methods for the group.

METHODS ACCORDING TO METHOD TYPE

There is a wide variety of career guidance methods. When surveying methods, the counselor or teacher may be overwhelmed by the vast numbers available. However, it is possible to categorize individual methods into method types and then look at the basic effectiveness of the type for meeting career guidance goals. Chapter 4 presents career guidance methods according to eight method types: (a) behavioral approaches,

Introduction

(b) computer-assisted counseling, (c) educational media, (d) group procedures, (e) information systems, (f) simulation gaming, (g) vocationally relevant curriculum, and (h) work experience programs. In addition to listing methods which belong in each group, this section also presents information which is needed when designing these method types. Included for each of the eight method types is a description of the basic method, its characteristics, and a description of variations of methods which fall within the type.

DESIGNING CAREER GUIDANCE APPROACHES

Chapters 2 through 4 are intended to help counselors and teachers to quickly survey and understand the wide variety of career guidance methods which are currently available. Chapter 5 includes specific information needed to design, implement and evaluate a number of career guidance approaches. Ten specific career guidance approaches, which are combinations of guidance activities which lead to the development of specific student behaviors, are identified and described: (a) career information systems to communicate localized educational and occupational opportunities, (b) developmental programs to facilitate early and continuous influence on vocational development, (c) developmental programs to involve parents in their child's vocational development, (d) manpower and economic education as a basis for understanding the world of work, (e) mobile career guidance services, (f) special curricula to motivate career exploration, (g) means of teaching decision making, (h) use of models to learn vocational behaviors, (i) simulation to facilitate vocational exploration and decision making, and (j) vocational exploration through media and classroom activities.

The chapter specifically focuses on: (a) presenting examples of how other schools have used these approaches, (b) helping teachers and counselors to decide whether the approach is appropriate for their students, (c) providing the basic principles which underlie the approach, and (d) describing concrete steps which are required to design, implement, evaluate and revise an application of the approach for a specific guidance program.

GUIDELINES FOR PROGRAM DEVELOPMENT

Although previous chapters have described a plethora of individual career guidance methods, a total program is more than a random collection of individual methods. It should be designed to incorporate multiple methods to achieve a unified program mission. The purpose of chapter 6 is to provide practical guidelines for developing comprehensive career guidance programs.

Programs represent a functional organization of guidance methods and services. They are broader in scope than individual methods and should reflect the total conceptual framework of the purpose, goals and/or objectives. Chapter 6 outlines program guidelines stemming from two basic considerations: (1) organizational-administrative management, and (2) student vocational development. The chapter elaborates on these two basic considerations by brief descriptions of exemplary program models and the examination of critical program elements, such as program accountability, design, and maximizing resources.

STATUS OF CAREER GUIDANCE METHODS

Chapter 7 provides a "state of the art" summary of career guidance methods. As such, it discusses gaps in available methods and prospects for the future, evaluation of current practices, the need for developing mechanisms for sharing innovative methods, and problems in career guidance roles and the implementation of new methods. For the most part, the chapter places more emphasis on "what should be" rather than what exists, stressing futuristic trends and new images as they relate to career guidance.

CAREER GUIDANCE RESOURCE BANK

A major step in developing this handbook was to survey all existing career guidance programs and practices in the United States. This survey was accomplished by using several information sources. First, a computer search of the Educational Resources Information Center (ERIC) files was completed. This provided information about career guidance programs and practices which have been developed through both federal funding and local educational units and individuals throughout the country. Also, a comprehensive search of journals, doctoral dissertations and books was conducted. These search procedures resulted in the identification of several hundred career guidance methods. Chapter 8 provides a resource bank which lists in alphabetical order by author all materials identified describing career guidance methods. The information for each entry includes a complete reference, an abstract or annotation in most cases, and information about how to obtain the report.

Due to the magnitude of the task of producing this handbook, several limitations had to be imposed to achieve the task within a reasonable time. While the career guidance resource bank does represent a national

Introduction

survey and each method was screened for its potential value, it was beyond the scope of the project to *evaluate* each method. This would have involved an excessively lengthy time period which was not manageable for the authors. Hence, the authors cannot place a "Good Housekeeping Seal of Approval" on every method. However, it should be pointed out that the methods reported in Chapter 8 vary as to their state of valid field testing, i.e., some project investigators reported complete validation whereas others reported field testing to some degree, and still others reported virtually nothing. It is the authors' position that despite the absence of field testing of each method, the central concern is that guidance practitioners become alert to innovative approaches which might be used in their programs. In instances where a method is selected for use, and no rigorous field testing is available, it is highly recommended that the practitioners treat the method as an experimental field test before casting it in bronze for their program.

With a few exceptions, methods describing individual counseling, tests, and occupational literature were omitted from the handbook. The authors felt that while these methods were important, they have been typically reviewed in other sources, such as Buros' *Mental Measurements Yearbook* (1961) and/or Baer and Roeber (1964), Hoppock (1967), Hopke (1967), etc. The reader should note that there are some methods which tangentially cover these topics by a broader approach, e.g., Project VIEW embraces a package of occupational information rather than a single method which focuses on only one occupation and/or career.

In addition to single guidance methods, the authors have also included reviews of multiple methods. For example, Budke (1971) published a review and synthesis of occupational exploration methods, and Lockett and Davenport (1971) published a review of vocational education for the urban disadvantaged.

Strategies for Using the Handbook

There are several ways of using this handbook. How it will be used depends on the needs of the teacher or counselor at the particular time he is using it. Three main strategies for using it are: (a) to get a broad overview of the existing programs and practices in career guidance, (b) to gain specific information about either certain types of student groups or particular career guidance methods, and (c) to gain direct assistance in developing career guidance programs and practices.

BROAD OVERVIEW OF EXISTING PRACTICES

There are times when counselors or teachers may want to survey the wide range of career guidance methods, e.g., when updating one's general understanding of the field, wanting to test the comprehensiveness of one's information about methods, or wanting an overview of an unfamiliar educational area. For the individual who wants this broad overview there are three main sections which can help him achieve this goal. The section presenting methods by method type and the one on designing career guidance approaches describe many methods and will help the reader to develop a framework for understanding all methods. Also, a quick scanning of the resource bank would help to alert the reader to the wide variety of existing methods.

SPECIFIC INFORMATION ABOUT TYPES OF STUDENTS AND METHODS

The process of career guidance program development probably occurs in two ways. First, the counselor and/or teacher may be concerned because existing career guidance activities are not meeting the needs of particular students. For example, they may feel that while much is being done for the college-bound student, little is being done to help the non-college-bound student with career planning. They may realize that while the existing career guidance program is helping some students, others, such as girls or disadvantaged students, are not receiving adequate career planning assistance. Another possibility is the guidance staff might feel the existing junior high and high school programs need the support of early elementary school career guidance experiences.

All of these possibilities represent guidance needs. When such needs become pressing, guidance staffs are faced with the problem of identifying needed program goals and designing new career guidance activities. The two chapters which present methods by educational level and by special population are designed to help career guidance workers to translate their vague concerns about program adequacy into specific program goals and to identify methods which have been used by others to meet these goals.

Another way in which career guidance program development can occur is by either increased interest on the part of the staff or increased facilities in the school which facilitate the use of a particular career guidance method. It may be that several counselors have just returned from a conference where they participated in some group experiences and are convinced that the use of group procedures can strengthen their own guidance program. Or perhaps, the school system has just installed a

Introduction

computer system for use in student accounting and record keeping, and the guidance staff feels that the system should also include a career exploration system for use by students. It may be that for some time the guidance staff has felt that a career guidance curriculum for use with junior high school students would help facilitate the vocational development of all students. Now, through funding under the Vocational Education Act, there is the opportunity to develop such a program.

Chapters 4 and 5 can help the user to find specific information about a particular career guidance method. This information is designed to help the reader better understand the methods, thus allowing him to decide whether it is appropriate for the goals of his guidance program and whether it can be adapted for use in his school.

ASSISTANCE IN DESIGNING CAREER GUIDANCE PROGRAMS

A major problem faced by career guidance workers is finding information about how to design, implement and evaluate career guidance approaches and programs. It is quite easy to find information which tells what others are doing in career guidance, but this information seldom includes the specific steps which are needed if another school is to implement the same guidance approach. This may be one reason why it is so difficult for counselors and teachers to find the time in their busy schedules to plan and implement new programs.

A major goal of this handbook is to provide the information needed to design, implement, evaluate and revise career guidance procedures. There are several questions which are basic to this program development process, and these provide a framework for development. The questions include:

1. What are the characteristics and needs of the students which the program will serve?
2. Based on these students' needs, what are appropriate goals for the program?
3. What career guidance methods are available which can potentially meet these program goals?
4. Of the available methods, which are most appropriate for the program goals and the staff and resources of a particular school?
5. Having selected the most appropriate method, how will it be adapted to a particular school situation?
6. What types of supportive guidance services are needed in addition to the new method?

7. Exactly what procedures will be used to implement the method? How will staff be trained? How will it be communicated to students, administration and parents?
8. How will the effectiveness of the new guidance program be evaluated?

These eight basic program development questions can provide a basis for either individual career guidance workers or total guidance staffs as they develop new career guidance programs and practices for their schools. In any design effort, specific answers should be developed for each of these eight questions before the new program is initiated. Specifically, the handbook can be used to develop these plans in the following way:

Step 1: Describe characteristics and needs of the students which the program will serve. The sections of the handbook which classify methods by educational level and by special population contain generalizations about student needs which have been derived from a wide variety of research studies. These sections can help in the development of statements of student needs. They also provide basic information and references to other information sources which can be consulted to further refine need statements.

Step 2: Develop program goals derived from descriptions of student needs. The two sections mentioned above also suggest specific program goals which other writers have indicated as being appropriate for specific student needs. These are stated rather generally. However, it is suggested that once general goals have been identified, the guidance staff translate these into specific behavioral objectives for the program. These behavioral objectives will be helpful as the program is communicated to others, methods are selected, student behavior resulting from the program is assessed, and the effectiveness of the program is evaluated.

Step 3: Survey career guidance methods. After student needs have been identified and program goals have been established, the next step in program design is to survey broadly all available career guidance methods which potentially can meet the objectives of the program. Useful for this comprehensive overview of available methods are the section which presents methods by method cluster, the section on designing career guidance methods, and the resource bank.

Step 4: Select appropriate methods. After a broad search has been conducted, it will be necessary to limit the list of available methods

Introduction 11

and, finally, to select those methods which are most appropriate for the specific school setting and student population. When narrowing the range of methods, the following questions can be helpful:

1. How successful is the method for promoting the type of learning desired?
2. How effective is one method when compared to others which are also appropriate?
3. Rather than just one method, are there several different ones that can be effectively combined?
4. Does the school staff have the skills needed to use the method?
5. Does the school have the other resources, i.e., equipment and materials, needed for use of the method?
6. Is the method compatible with the existing guidance program, or will it require large-scale changes?

The section of the handbook which presents methods by method cluster attempts to compare methods in terms of learning effectiveness and can, therefore, provide a first step in evaluating methods. The section on designing career guidance approaches describes combinations of methods and patterns of resources needed to implement these approaches. It also can provide other types of information needed for method selection.

Step 5: Adapt the method to a particular school situation. Although it is possible to identify methods which are potentially able to meet problem objectives, it is still necessary to design a specific application of the methods which is appropriate for a particular school setting. The easiest way to design new method applications is to build on the developmental efforts of others. Once a particular method has been selected, it is suggested that an inventory be made of all of the applications which others have developed of the method. These basic models are presented in the chapters on methods by method type and on designing career guidance approaches.

As these models are studied, it is suggested that they be evaluated in terms of the ease with which they could be adapted in a particular school situation. Such questions should be asked as: Have they been used with students similar in age and background to our school? Have they been successfully used to meet goals similar to our program? Have they developed specific materials and procedures which could be used in our school? Once the most appropriate program models have been selected, they can be modified as necessary to fit a particular school setting.

Step 6: Design supportive services. From reviewing the experiences of others as they develop new career guidance methods, it is clear that methods often fail not because the method is weak but because the counseling services which accompany the method are weak. For example, great expense may go into designing a computer-assisted counseling system, and the basic system may be sound in that it presents current, accurate and appropriate occupational-educational information for the students using the system; however, such a system may well fail to meet program goals if the staff is not available to train students in the use of the system and not enough counselor time is allotted for follow-up counseling interviews to help students to use the information in career planning.

The chapter on designing career guidance approaches provides information not only on the approach itself but on the types of supportive guidance services which others have found necessary to the success of the method. After teachers and counselors have designed a specific application of a method for their school, they will want to plan carefully the exact nature of the supportive services which will be used in conjunction with the method.

Step 7: Design evaluation procedures. Increasingly, writers are stressing the importance of designing evaluation procedures prior to initiating new career guidance programs. Too often evaluation is an afterthought, and therefore, important evaluation information is not collected. From reviewing career guidance programs, three types of evaluations emerge.

First, it is important to evaluate the specific method application. For example, if the "Life Career Game" is being used with a group of elementary school students, the materials and the procedures used to play the game need to be evaluated to determine if they are appropriate for this particular group of students. A second evaluation consideration is the effectiveness of the total guidance experience. Continuing the "Life Career Game" example, while the materials and procedures of the game may be very appropriate, the supportive guidance activities, i.e., classroom discussions, group counseling sessions, etc., may not be effective in helping students to relate what they have learned from the game to their own vocational planning. Finally, any career guidance program is designed to help facilitate the development of specific vocational planning behavior in the students for which it is designed.

One last type of evaluation is the extent to which, as a result of the guidance experience, the students are exhibiting these desired behaviors. The sections of the handbook on designing career guidance approaches and career guidance programs both provide information which is needed to design evaluation procedures.

Chapter 2 EDUCATIONAL LEVEL CONSIDERATIONS RELATING TO CAREER GUIDANCE

In this chapter, career guidance methods have been classified according to the four major educational levels within the American school system: Elementary school (grades K-6), Junior High School (grades 7-9), Senior High School (grades 10-12) and Post-High School (grades 13 and over). These subsections are used as the framework for classifying methods.

Introduction

The rationale for classifying career guidance methods by educational level stems from both practical and theoretical considerations. In American society, career guidance is available primarily within the school system and where it is available, it is usually provided by one or more career guidance counselors or by teachers or other personnel who act in this capacity. In spite of the differences in programs, services, facilities and goals, a career guidance counselor operates within the confines and structural context of the school system. Thus, a counselor is typically in charge of career guidance and counseling for one educational level. Grouping methods by this way eliminates the need for the counselor to weed through methods applicable to other educational levels and facilitates scanning a given grade range for possible overlaps or deficiencies. It also helps the counselor quickly to familiarize and orient himself to some of the variables which are deemed important for a particular grade level grouping.

A classification by educational level recognizes that, at any level, individual differences exist in terms of vocational development, vocational maturity and readiness for a particular approach to career guidance. Super (1957), Super and Overstreet (1960) and Crites (1969) define vocational maturity as the degree to which an individual becomes oriented to the world of work, seeks vocational information, is aware of the need to make a decision and can recognize the direction of his vocational preference. Other elements in vocational maturity include the wisdom of the vocational choice, and so on.

By definition, the concept of vocational maturity is normative in nature. The process by which an individual develops vocational maturity varies among individuals, as well as within individuals, at different stages of physical maturity. Classifying methods according to grade levels allows the counselor to become aware of methods that are generally applicable to students of a certain level, and also to be able to utilize an alternative approach with those students who are of a particular grade level but are above or below the normative standard in their vocational maturity.

The concept of vocational maturity stems from a theoretical framework which is related to another dimension associated with classifying methods by educational or grade levels. At least two theories of career development, those of Super and Ginzberg, Ginsburg, Axelrad and Herma, have emphasized the developmental, sequential nature of the process of vocational preference and choice (Osipow 1968). Super (1957), in particular, believes that the process of vocational development follows the basic principles governing human development in general. He describes vocational development as a series of tasks which the individual has to accomplish for each age level, and without the completion of these, he cannot satisfactorily progress to the next developmental stage. Two of these tasks are crystallization (focusing on a vocational preference in a certain direction) and specification (narrowing down the preference to a specific area).

Ginzberg, Ginsburg, Axelrad and Herma (1951) view the process as consisting of three major stages. During the Fantasy stage (ages 4-11), a child moves from a play orientation to a work orientation. Next he advances to the Tentative stage (ages 11-18) where his interests and values with regard to work are formed. Then, during the Realistic stage (ages 18-22), interests and preferences crystallize and choices become specific.

Educational Level Considerations 15

These conceptualizations of career development clearly indicate expectations exist for the stage of vocational development a child should reach by a certain age. These expectations, conceptualized as normative and flexible, are incorporated within the concept of vocational maturity. However, it is also possible to specify possible behavioral outcomes which are to be expected from the student at each grade level. The counselor would then be guided by a list of behavioral objectives, i.e., statements which describe observable expected performance which students should be capable of at the conclusion of a particular learning unit. This concept would not be inconsistent with the differential readiness of individual students at different ages, since outcomes could be varied and tailored to the individual. This is noted by Campbell et al. (1971) who, based upon theory and research in the area of career development, have identified behavioral objectives representing four major dimensions of vocational behavior for the senior high school grade levels. These are: (a) knowledge of self, (b) knowledge of the world of work, (c) vocational planning skills and resources, and (d) attitudes, values and motivation toward work.

A similar framework of behavioral objectives, based on the same conceptual scheme, could have been identified for grade levels K-6. However, from both a theoretical and a practical point of view, the specification of behavioral objectives for early grade levels would have been a difficult task, and a task beyond the scope of this publication, due to insufficient information. Most theory, research and career guidance methods are limited to higher educational levels, with a concentration on late junior high school and senior high school.

By classifying methods by educational level, the authors also attempt to emphasize the idea that, since career development appears to be a systematic, developmental (i.e., progress over time) process, career guidance programs in the school need also to be built on the principle of systematic, orderly progress. Organizing programs which would start with simple goals, and systematically progress through higher degrees of sophistication and eventually lead to career choice, could well be accomplished through the educational level approach. Establishing a network of methods suitable for students at different grade levels would facilitate incorporating both continuity and systematic progression into school-wide programs of career guidance. It would also eliminate duplication of effort on one hand, and lack of career guidance for the younger student population on the other.

In this chapter, career guidance methods are grouped according to their applicability to one or more of the four educational levels described earlier. Each section is presented in five main parts, each pertaining to the particular level being discussed: (a) the rationale for career guidance, (b) the career guidance goals appropriate, (c) considerations in designing methods for career guidance, (d) implications for career guidance, and (e) a listing of applicable methods.

Educational Level: Elementary

RATIONALE FOR CAREER GUIDANCE

Recently, developmental psychology and vocational development theory have had increasing impact on school guidance programs. Therefore, guidance has become the process of assisting human development from childhood through adulthood. Van Hoose (1969) has summarized this development as follows:

1. Human development is a highly complex and personal process.
2. The individual is always in a state of growing and developing.
3. The development of an individual involves academic, emotional, and physical aspects which are interrelated.
4. Most elementary children have the potential for healthy development.

Because of the nature of human development, early childhood experiences have a great impact on subsequent development. Based on this premise, there has been considerable effort to develop elementary guidance programs.

Basic to both human development in general and vocational development specifically is the concept of developmental tasks. Havighurst (1962) has described developmental tasks as tasks which arise at or about a certain period in the life of an individual. Success with one task results in a greater probability of success with future tasks. Guidance may be viewed as helping students to master developmental tasks. Whereas classroom instructional activities are designed to help the process of mastery through the learning of basic skills, guidance activities are designed to facilitate total development. Van Hoose (1969) suggests that guidance can "help the child learn to view himself realistically and to develop a positive attitude toward himself and the world around him."

Grams (1966) also stresses the idea that development is an on-going process and that guidance should be designed to facilitate total development. He further stresses the importance of early learning experiences. He proposes the following assumption about learning:

1. It is continuous.
2. Important learning occurs before school entry.
3. During the first three years of school, significant learning which is basic to building an adequate personality occurs.
4. Psychological health is related to effectiveness as a learner.
5. Learning is influenced by personal values and by perceptions of self and others.

The increasing emphasis on the developmental aspects of guidance have been specifically related to career guidance. Hansen (1969) summarizes the research on vocational development by indicating that elementary school students (a) have a knowledge of the prestige rankings of occupations, (b) tentatively choose higher level occupations, and (c) limit their range of vocational choices. These findings indicate that if young children do not receive help in the vocational development process, they may develop unrealistic, limited occupational goals.

GOALS OF CAREER GUIDANCE

With the increased stress on career guidance as a process which facilitates vocational development, career guidance has moved from the basic objective of information dissemination to include several broader goals. Whitfield (1968) suggests that:

> Effective elementary school guidance must provide a general foundation for the respect of all human endeavor and an understanding of the relationship of all learning, the interdependence of all work, and the relationship of abilities, interests, and other personal characteristics to the requirements needed in a variety of human activities of which work is one. (p. 91)

Bugg (1969) has suggested two broad types of career guidance services are needed in the elementary school: (a) counseling for self-understanding and personal development, and (b) a well-formulated program of broad, general occupational information that serves as the foundation for later career decisions.

The goal of self-understanding has been described in a variety of ways and has several aspects. Hansen (1969) suggests the goal of assisting in developing a positive self-concept. Career guidance activities should help students to better understand their interests, abilities and values. Another goal related to self-understanding involves the development of a willingness and ability to take responsibility for self (Hill 1968, Cottingham 1967). Closely related to this feeling of self-responsibility are skills which enable the individual to plan and direct his life, specifically problem solving and decision making. Still another guidance objective closely related to self-understanding is the understanding of others. Cottingham (1967) suggests that guidance should facilitate the social development of pupils by helping them to understand human behavior and interpersonal relationships.

In summary, self-related goals of career guidance in the elementary school include (a) understanding of self in terms of interests, abilities and skills, (b) skill in those processes needed to assume reponsibility for self, e.g., decision making and problem solving, and (c) understanding of others and ability to form healthy interpersonal relationships.

Another set of goals for career guidance in the elementary school relates to acquainting the student with the world of work. Several writers (Thompson 1969, Hansen 1969) have suggested three major sub-goals related to knowledge of the world of work. First is to develop a healthy attitude toward work and a respect for the importance of all types of work performed in society. A second goal is to stimulate interest in several occupations. At the elementary level, students need to explore a variety of occupations and to expand their knowledge of occupational areas. Finally, a career guidance program must help students to become aware of the changing world of work. Because the nature of occupations change, it is quite possible that occupations explored at the elementary level will become obsolete; therefore, students need to develop a flexible attitude toward jobs and work.

CONSIDERATIONS IN DESIGNING CAREER GUIDANCE METHODS

In designing career guidance activities for elementary school guidance programs, one needs to consider a number of things about the nature of the elementary student as a learner. Four major considerations include:

1. For elementary students, a major way of learning is through imitating the behavior of others.
2. Verbal skills are not highly developed in children; therefore, learning is enhanced if there is opportunity for physical activity.
3. Elementary school children are able to understand only those concepts which are represented in their immediate perceptual field.

Educational Level Considerations

4. Elementary school children need the opportunity to explore the vocational world rather than make definite choices.

Children use role modeling as a basis for the development of their own behavior; therefore a major instructional technique for career guidance is the use of a variety of such models of behavior. Rather than having students read about occupations, it is important to have them interact with individuals in various occupations. The presentation of a variety of role models helps to communicate to the child the idea that there are a number of occupational roles. Typically, a child's role models are limited to those people in his immediate environment, e.g., parents. Career guidance activities might well be designed to provide a number of models from outside his immediate environment, thus broadening his vocational perceptions.

A major trend in career guidance in the elementary school is the use of action-oriented methods. Since children do not have high verbal and reading skills, methods which rely on reading or extensive discussion probably will not be motivating nor will they facilitate learning. But a number of effective methods have been developed which allow high activity in play-type experiences, including dramatics, role playing, games, and simulation. It appears that through these types of activity, elementary students can effectively explore the occupational world.

A major generalization from recent research on the nature of cognitive development in children is that younger children can only think in terms of their immediate perceptual field; they cannot think in abstractions. Also quite limited is their ability to relate one experience to another and to generalize common elements. Therefore, it is not effective to design learning experiences which rely on a child being able to draw on information which he has not experienced. If children are to understand various occupational possibilities, they need to experience concrete examples of specific occupational behaviors.

Elementary school children need exploratory experiences which broaden their understanding of themselves and the occupational world. Typically, these students do not understand the occupational world, do not perceive their surrounding environment in occupational terms and have stereotyped ideas of the nature of a few selected occupations. Elementary career guidance experiences, therefore, should concentrate on expanding the child's view of the world of work and on helping him to interpret his individual characteristics in vocational terms.

IMPLICATIONS FOR CAREER GUIDANCE

1. Since vocational development is a continuous process extending throughout an individual's life, it is important to initiate early childhood

career guidance experiences which will facilitate this process. Many writers have suggested that vocational development will occur regardless of whether or not there are early interventions, but the adequacy of this development can be influenced by early guidance interventions.

2. Several basic elementary career guidance goals for which there is high consensus include helping the individual to (a) interpret his personal characteristics in terms of their relationship to possible vocational roles, (b) understand the variety of occupational possibilities which exist in society, (c) develop an appreciation for all types of work, and (d) understand the changing nature of the occupational world.

3. Children learn new behaviors by imitating the behavior of others in their immediate environment. A major career guidance technique for the elementary level is to bring into the child's world adults who provide models of behavior.

4. Elementary children are highly motivated by action-oriented learning experiences. For this reason, verbally oriented counseling techniques which are used with older populations are not appropriate for the elementary level. Such techniques as games, dramatics, role playing and simulation are more motivating and result in greater learning.

5. The cognitive development level of young children does not permit them to think in abstractions or generalize from one situation to another; therefore, career guidance methods must be designed to enable these students to learn through direct experiences.

6. Elementary students typically have a narrow view of the occupational world, have stereotyped views of a few occupations and no knowledge of others, and aspire to high level occupations. This indicates that these students need exploratory, broadening experiences which enable them to understand the occupational world more accurately.

METHOD APPLICATIONS*

Abington School District. Career development activities.

Atlanta Board of Education. Formulation of models for preparing occupational materials for pupils from various socioeconomic levels in grades 3–8.

Bank, I. M. Children explore careerland through vocational role models.

Brown, J. A. and MacDougall, M. A. Computerized simulated games: a socialization tool for child guidance.

---

*These can be found in chapter 8 (alphabetically listed).

Educational Level Considerations

Frank, R. L. and Matthes, W. A. Strategies for implementation of guidance in the elementary school.

Goff, W. H. Vocational guidance in elementary schools.

Goodson, E. Occupational information materials in selected elementary and middle schools.

Gueder, B., ed. Handbook for elementary school guidance.

Hoeltzel, K. E. Paper presented at the workshop on the development of guidelines for planning career development programs K-12 in Ohio.

Laws, L. Elementary guide for career development grades 1–6.

Leonard, G. E. Developmental career guidance in action, the first year.

Leonard, G. E. and Stephens, E. Elementary school employment service.

Leonard, G. E. Vocational planning and career behavior, a report on the developmental career guidance project.

Martin, A. M. A multimedia approach to communicating occupational information to non-college youth. Interim technical report.

Miller, W. R. and Blankenbaker, E. K. Annotated bibliography of publications and reports of research dealing with the interpretation of the world of work to elementary children.

Mitchell, E. F. et al. A comprehensive orientation to the world of work through industrial arts and vocational education (grades 1–12).

Monroe School District 103. An exemplary cooperative in elementary school guidance for small school districts.

New Jersey State Education Department. The world of work: increasing the vocational awareness of elementary school children.

New York State Education Department. Elementary school guidance.

Newton, G. E. A report of the elementary school guidance project—Centennial and Irving Schools.

Ohlsen, M. M. Counseling children in groups.

Oklahoma State Department of Education. A guide for developmental vocational guidance.

Oklahoma State Department of Education. A guide for elementary guidance and counseling in Oklahoma schools.

Palo Alto Unified School District. Conference summary—from theory to practice. The description and demonstration of a guidance program in one district K–12.

Pennsylvania Advancement School. Group counseling for urban schools: a handbook.

Pettit, M. L. and Robinson, H. G. A study of methods designed to improve the relationships between parents' attitudes and the underachievement of their elementary school children.

Ploughman, T. L. Project: Pontiac vocational career development program: evaluation report.

Pruitt, A. S. Teacher involvement in the curriculum and career guidance.

Rector, W. H. and Shaw, M. C. Group counseling with parents: feasibility reactions, and interrelationships. Monograph number 5.

Rose, S. D. A behavioral approach to group treatment of children.

San Diego Unified School District. Supplementary educational services—instructional television educational experience development and distribution.

Shirts, R. G. Career simulation for sixth-grade pupils.

Shirts, R. G. Life career game, players manual.

Texas Board of Education. Texas occupational orientation program.

Todd, R. D. and Todd, K. P. A prospectus for the development of a career development and technology program for elementary school children.

Usitalo, R. J. Elementary counseling and guidance. A second year's report on the operation of a laboratory.

Whitfield, E. A. Vocational guidance in the elementary school: integration or fragmentation?

Educational Level: Junior High School

RATIONALE FOR CAREER GUIDANCE

Since vocational development is a continuous process, it is important to provide continuous career guidance experiences throughout the school years which will assist in this developmental process. This rationale has stimulated recent thinking about the nature of vocational guidance activities and goals which are most appropriate for junior high school students. However, to clearly understand the rationale underlying these junior high school programs, it is necessary to examine the nature of the junior high school and its students. O'Dell (1968, p. 2) suggests three major goals of junior high school education:

1. Continued development, refinement and strengthening of basic skills and knowledge, and teaching how these skills and knowledge may be applied to the world of work.
2. Adequate preparation of pupils for subsequent educational experiences and for critical educational and vocational decision making.

Educational Level Considerations

3. Gradual transition from the educational environment of the elementary school to that of the senior high school.

The major function of the junior high school, then, is to help students to explore various learning areas with an emphasis on future planning and goal setting.

Also important to planning career guidance experiences is an understanding of the nature of the junior high school students. Johnson et al. (1961) describe these students as being in a transitional role between childhood and adolescence. Some of their major characteristics include: (a) students will be at quite different levels of development, with boys usually lagging behind girls, (b) individual students will be changing very rapidly during this period, and (c) students will have ambivalent feelings about whether they want to be treated as children or adults. These characteristics point to the fact that within the total group, as well as within the individual, there will be great fluctuation in behavior.

Walker (1960) suggests eight characteristics of this student group and relates these to guidance needs:

1. They are relatively unstable and capricious; therefore need the stability and consistency of relationships with understanding adults as found in a counseling relationship.
2. They lack first-hand knowledge of the 'real' world; therefore need experiences that will supply this knowledge both directly and vicariously.
3. They have lacked opportunity to test their capacities in a variety of demanding situations; therefore need opportunities to explore and try out their emerging potentials.
4. They tend to lack the security of self-confidence; therefore need successful experiences which will tend to build self-assurance into the developing personality.
5. They have developed many questions, even anxieties, about themselves and their place in the scheme of things; therefore need an array of relationships, both adult and peer, and experiences which will enhance their search for answers.
6. They find heterosexual relations very unsatisfactory because of maturational differences between girls and boys at these ages; therefore need sensitive adult guidance in thinking through the concerns and anxieties that develop from this condition.
7. They are characterized by rather hostile attitudes toward many restrictions which as children they accepted; therefore they need opportunities to release or manage these hostilities in a nonpunitive and understanding atmosphere.
8. They have as yet failed to develop a sense of identity; therefore they need a wide variety of experiences which will help them

become more aware of who they are, how they relate to others, and how their peers perceive them. (p. 4)

Vocational development research has focused on specific aspects of vocational development in junior high school students. This research has also supported the appropriateness of general goals for junior high career guidance. In discussing the implications of research on the vocational maturity of ninth-grade boys for vocational guidance practices, Super (1960) suggests:

> Education in the ninth grade should be so organized as to make available experiences which foster a planful approach to developmental tasks, to arouse an awareness of the need to make pre-occupational and occupational choices, and to orient adolescents to the kinds and sequences of choices which they will be called upon to make and to the factors which they should consider in making these choices. It should not require the making of definitive, directional, educational and occupational choices in this grade. (p. 158)

GOALS OF CAREER GUIDANCE

A number of writers have discussed the major goals which are appropriate for junior high school career guidance programs (Hudak et al. 1967, Oklahoma State Department 1968, Albracht et al. 1968, Bottoms and Cleere 1969). The general nature of these goals parallel the basic goals previously described for junior high school education. Junior high school is a time when students can begin realistically to explore the relationship between their characteristics and the nature of various types of occupations, to learn the processes involved in planning and implementing occupational goals, and to develop a tentative plan for their own future.

Bottoms and Cleere (1969) report an extensive model for a basic program for vocational exploration in the junior high school. Included in this model are a number of specific behavioral objectives for such programs, presented under the following general categories:

1. *Self and relationships with others:* understanding of student's own aptitudes and interests, and understanding of human development and individual differences.
2. *The world of work:* the multi-dimensional aspects of work; the structure of the world of work; the relationship between changing demands for jobs and needed work skills; employment trends; employers' expectations; relationships between school activities and career development; and the realities of requirements of work.

3. *Education and training:* the use of vocational information resources and available training programs; the concept of entry occupations; and how to study and take tests.
4. *Economic education:* basic concepts of production, distribution and consumption; the general economic structure; reasons why people work; the social significance of work; and principles of money management.
5. *Employability skills:* the value of education and job-hunting techniques.
6. *Decision-making process:* components of the process; awareness of educational and vocational information resources and how to use them; resources available to assist in vocational planning; and understanding of the career development process.

Junior high school career guidance is designed to provide linkage between the elementary school, where students explore themselves and the occupational world in terms of their immediate environment and broaden perceptions about occupational possibilities, and the high school, where students need to narrow and tentatively select vocational and educational directions.

Specific goals for such junior high programs include: (a) the opportunity to explore clusters of educational and occupational possibilities and to begin to relate these to interests and abilities, (b) the opportunity to learn specific vocationally and educationally related skills, such as study skills and job-seeking behavior, and (c) the opportunity to become aware of the types of information and processes needed for effective planning and decision making.

CONSIDERATIONS IN DESIGNING CAREER GUIDANCE METHODS

There are a number of basic considerations which are important in the development and utilization of career guidance methods for junior high school programs. It is important to remember that the student population is very diverse in terms of individual development. Therefore, it is difficult to generalize about the specific types of methods which are most effective for all junior high school students. For students at a lower developmental level, some of the considerations suggested in the section on elementary guidance may be more appropriate.

A first major factor to be considered in the use of methods is abstractions versus concreteness. Bottoms and Cleere (1969) suggest an abstract-concrete continuum which includes the following levels from most abstract to most concrete:

1. Verbal symbols (i.e., written materials)
2. Records, radio, pictures, and/or filmstrips
3. Motion pictures
4. Television
5. Exhibits
6. Field trips
7. Demonstrations
8. Dramatized experiences
9. Simulated experiences
10. Direct purposeful experiences

Most junior high methods tend to be more concrete than abstract since students are just developing effective verbal and abstract reasoning skills and, therefore, tend to learn best from concrete, directly experienced activities.

Another major characteristic of effective junior high methods is that they allow for the expression and exploration of feelings and attitudes. Pre-adolescence is a time of uncertainty and of ambivalent feelings. For this reason, O'Dell (1968) suggests that counseling is an extremely important component of junior high guidance programs and should be available to all students. Drews (1965) suggests that the communication of occupational information should allow for the expression of feelings and reactions to the information.

Another important consideration suggested by Drews (1965) is the extent to which specific vocational guidance approaches are interrelated and clearly specify the learning to occur. This is a trend in many of the more thoroughly developed career guidance programs. It is important for career guidance experiences to be integrated so that students see continuity and interrelationship among the experiences. Also, many programs are designed with specific behavioral outcomes which are intended to result from the use of the methods. These outcomes can be communicated to students so that they are aware of the purpose of the learning activity.

IMPLICATIONS FOR CAREER GUIDANCE

1. The junior high school experience is seen as a transitional experience which helps students to move from the general skill acquisition of

Educational Level Considerations

the elementary school to the more specific preparation for adult life which occurs in the high school.

2. Junior high school students are also in a stage of transition from childhood to adolescence which results in rapid change within individual students and considerable variance in the developmental level of individuals within the total group. Individual differences are predominant at this period.

3. Career guidance objectives for the junior high school include: (a) exploring the relationship between student characteristics and occupational and educational requirements, (b) learning the processes involved in planning and implementing occupational goals, (c) learning general educationally and vocationally related behaviors, and (d) beginning to develop tentative plans for the future.

4. Concrete, action-oriented methods are particularly effective with junior high school students since they are just developing abstract verbal skills. Methods may be viewed on an abstract-concrete continuum. The developmental level of specific junior high groups will determine how concrete the methods need to be.

5. The junior high age is one characterized by rapid growth and change which results in intense feelings. For this reason, career guidance methods should allow for the expression and exploration of these feelings.

METHOD APPLICATIONS*

Abington School District. Career development activities.

Adams County Board of Education. Vocational guidance program for slow learners.

Albracht, J. et al. Using existing vocational programs for providing exploratory experiences.

Atlanta Board of Education. Formulation of models for preparing occupational materials for pupils from various socioeconomic levels in grades 3-8.

Barbula, P. M. and Isaac, S. W. Career simulation for adolescent pupils. Final report.

Baugh, D. S. and Martin, W. E. Total career capability for all.

Bottoms, G. and Cleere, W. R. A one-week institute to develop objectives and models for a continuous exploratory program related to the world of work from junior high through senior high school.

---

*These can be found in chapter 8 (alphabetically listed).

Budke, W. E. Review and synthesis of information on occupational exploration.

Cincinnati Public Schools. Man: his life and work. A career orientation manual for teachers of seventh- and eighth-grade social studies.

Circle, D. F. et al. The career information service. A guide to its development and use.

Cohn, B. et al. The effects of group counseling on school adjustment of underachieving junior high school boys who demonstrate acting-out behavior.

College Entrance Examination Board. Deciding, A decision-making program for students.

Colorado State University. Occupational education program. Image of the world of work. Description and analysis of teacher orientation activities (August 1968).

Colorado State University. Occupational education programs; image of the world of work, volume III. Lesson plans: resource file.

Darcy, R. L. An experimental junior high school course in occupational opportunities and labor market processes. Final report.

Drier, H. N. and Jepsen, D. A. The use of television and video-tape compared to researching printed career information as a means of assisting rural ninth grade youth career-decision-making process.

Gelatt, H. B. A decision-making approach to guidance.

Goodson, S. Occupational information materials in selected elementary and middle schools.

Hansen, L. S. Career guidance practices in school and community.

Hoeltzel, K. E. et al. Papers presented at the workshop on the development of guidelines for planning career development programs K-12 in Ohio.

Hudak, V. M. and Butler, F. C. Development and evaluation of an experimental curriculum for the New Quincy (Mass.) vocational-technical school, development and tryout of a junior high school student vocational plan, ninth quarterly technical report.

Jackson, J. S. et al. Evaluation of the career development laboratory: Sayre junior high school.

Krumboltz, J. D. et al. Vocational problem-solving experiences for stimulating career exploration and interest: Phase II. Final report.

Leonard, R. S. Vocational guidance in junior high: One school's answer.

Lockwood, O. et al. Four worlds: An approach to occupational guidance.

Lux, D. G. and Ray, W. World of Manufacturing: industrial arts curriculum project.

Educational Level Considerations

Lux, D. G. and Ray, W. World of Construction: industrial arts curriculum project.

Madison Junior High School. Madison area project. Suggested typical content outline for junior high school group guidance. Appendix E.

Martin, A. M. A multimedia approach to communicating occupational information to noncollege youth. Technical report.

Martin, A. M. A multimedia approach to communicating occupational information to noncollege youth. Interim technical report.

Minneapolis Public Schools. World of work: Grade 9. Teacher's guide for the school year 1967–1968.

Mitchell, E. F. et al. A comprehensive orientation to the world of work through industrial arts and vocational education (grades 1–12).

Muskegon Public Schools. The effect of additional counseling on the able student's vocational and educational planning. A report of the Muskegon guidance project.

Niles Community Schools. Occupational education for all students.

Oklahoma State Department of Education. A guide for developmental vocational guidance. Grades K–12.

Oklahoma Vocational Research Coordinating Unit. A guide for teachers of a course in career exploration, grades 8–10.

Oregon State Department of Education. Guide to structure and articulation of occupational education programs (grades 7–12 and post-high school).

Oregon State Department of Education. Teacher's guide to: Self understanding through occupational exploration (SUTOE).

Palo Alto Unified School District. Conference summary — from theory to practice. The description and demonstration of guidance program in one district K–12.

Pennsylvania Advancement School. Group counseling for urban schools: a handbook.

Rowe, F. A. Foundation for a seventh-grade guidance unit: an analysis of the developmental level of the seventh-grade student and nationally current occupational guidance classes.

San Diego Unified School District. Supplementary educational services — instructional television educational experience development and distribution.

School Districts of Cochise County. Pilot program (demonstration project) of an experimental method for providing occupational education to youth in small schools.

Segel, D. and Ruble, R. A. The Lincoln project: A study of the educational program of a junior high school in a transitional neighborhood: A report of the Lincoln guidance research project.

Sherman, V. S. Trial and testing of an experimental guidance curriculum. Final report.

Sturges, J. C. et al. A comparison of two methods of providing information to ninth-grade students about the world of work.

Texas Board of Education. Texas occupational orientation program.

Thompson, A. S. et al. The educational and career exploration system: field trial and evaluation in Montclair High School.

Todd, V. E. and Bates, Z. Development of a junior high school instrument for appraising social readiness for employment.

Tunker, J. A. Pre-high school vocational group guidance for potential dropouts and noncollege-bound youth.

Ullery, J. W. and O'Brien, R. K. Testing of the guidance program. Project ABLE; development and evaluation of an experimental curriculum for the New Quincy (Mass.)

Utah State University. Proposal for a mobile assisted career exploration unit.

Washington Township Board of Education. Adventures in occupations.

Weaver, C. E. Orientation to work for the students in the junior high school.

Wilson, E. H. A task-oriented course in decision making. (Information system for vocational decision, project report number 7).

Yinger, J. M. et al. Middle start: supportive interventions for higher education among students of disadvantaged backgrounds.

Educational Level: High School

RATIONALE FOR CAREER GUIDANCE

The high school years, ranging from the tenth to the twelfth grades, are the richest years in terms of emphasis. This is reflected in theories of career development, the number of methods developed for this group, and in the concern that both private and public agencies show regarding the career development of high school students.

This emphasis stems from several conditions which are unique to the high school level. In American society, as in most other western cultures, graduation from high school signifies the completion of an educational, as well as a developmental-maturational, unit. At the end of this unit the individual is expected to assume the responsibility for deciding the di-

Educational Level Considerations

rection of his future personal and vocational life. During high school reality becomes closer to the individual in many ways: There is a need for serious planning and making important decisions; there is a need to assess values and isolate interests. In addition, the individual experiences pressure from his parents, the school, potential employers, his peers and other sources, all of which impinge on him in multiple directions.

The immediacy of needs, the multiplicity of potential directions to choose from, and the forcefulness of pressures exerted upon the individual during his high school years can result in productive, meaningful and wise decisions on one hand, or confusion and distress on the other (Super et al. 1967). From the point of view of both the individual and of society, it is at the high school level that career guidance assumes a significant and unique role. This role is not confined to assisting the students in making vocational decisions that will lead to productive careers; it also involves assessing the usefulness of our educational programs in terms of preparing youth for facing life and being able to become productive individuals within their society. Marland (1971) has recently called to the attention of educators the false dichotomy between things academic and things vocational, which now characterizes our educational system during the high school years. He has called for a balancing of academic curricula with vocational programs. Career guidance counselors in the high school can detect deficiencies or imbalances in educational programs, as well as contribute to their improvement through developing appropriate procedures and techniques.

GOALS OF CAREER GUIDANCE

Due to the complexity of our economy as well as our environment, both physical and social, a high school student who is awaiting graduation can be seen as standing at a multi-directional crossroads. Both our labor market and our educational system offer a multiplicity of avenues, opportunities and options. Individuals, on the other hand, possess varied interests, preferences, abilities and values, the combination of which may be suitable for a variety of occupations (Super 1957). Consequently, the primary goals of career guidance at the high school level are:

1. Supplying students with information which will inform them of the various options open to them upon graduation, e.g., further schooling, apprenticeship programs, work opportunities, etc.
2. Training students to locate and use such information on their own, e.g., inform students of periodic issues of government

bulletins on employment opportunities, school catalogues, and where these may be found.
3. Training students to interpret and evaluate occupational or educational information.
4. Helping each student to become aware of his interests, needs, abilities and values, especially as these relate to his future life.

Another important goal of career guidance is teaching the student to make decisions, or providing him with opportunities for decision making. This goal involves both short- and long-range benefits. Although the most immediate need at the high school level is that of making a specific decision about where to go next, the practice involved in making such a decision can be advantageous for making later decisions. The student becomes aware of the need to investigate and weigh information before embarking on a certain program of action. This long-term benefit also relates to another major goal of career guidance — assisting students in acquiring both information and practice which will eventually result in long-term planning. Both our labor market and our technology are undergoing almost continuous development and change. Thus, it has become increasingly necessary to plan not for a single career, but rather for a series of positions within one's work-span. The ability to plan for the future can be seen as an important "tool" for the individual, especially at the high school level, when the first phase of a career is imminent.

Career guidance at the high school level also has as its goal assessing the needs of both the labor market and the individual, and arranging conditions which will facilitate the meshing of the two. One such condition is directing the individual toward gaining work experiences which will increase his knowledge of the labor market and its requirements, and will also facilitate his decision making regarding employment. Another such condition is initiating programs at school which will provide such experience. This goal is in line with Marland's (1971) idea of balancing the academic education with vocational education. This also could be done through work-study programs and other innovative arrangements.

The goals of career guidance in the high school have their basis in theoretical views of career development (explained in the beginning of this chapter). They also have practical elements, in that they go beyond the individual and take into consideration current forces and requirements within our society which have a bearing on the individual. Overall, giving consideration to the combination of both internal elements (individual ability, needs, etc.) and external elements (societal forces) establishes the basic goal of career guidance, i.e., giving the student a "sense of agency," an awareness that he is an active agent in determining the course of his own career (Tiedeman 1967).

CONSIDERATIONS IN DESIGNING CAREER GUIDANCE METHODS

In designing career guidance methods for the high school level, two kinds of factors related to this age need to be considered: (a) *developmental-maturational factors*, i.e., what are students at this level able to do, how abstractly can they be expected to think, and what skills do they possess that would maximize their gains from methods designed especially for them; (b) *need-press factors*, i.e., what are the needs of individuals at this age, especially as these correspond to the tasks they are expected to perform and the pressures that are put upon them from external sources.

Developmentally and maturationally, the high school student possesses adequate verbal and conceptual skills. Therefore, learning can be achieved through different methods. This constitutes an advantage for designing career guidance methods by minimizing potential limitations in design and applicability so that highly complex methods can be utilized. It also broadens the range of methods potentially suitable for this age.

In terms of need-press factors, certain considerations must be taken into account: With the abundance of occupational and educational information on one hand, and the need of the student at this age to acquire and evaluate information and make a decision regarding a future direction on the other, career guidance methods can be designed to facilitate these tasks. Methods can aid students in obtaining information that would otherwise not be apparent and therefore available, to the student. They also could be designed to assist him in locating relevant information in the future, in evaluating this information in terms of his needs, and guide him in making sound decisions. This is especially relevant since grades 10-12 have the potential of leading toward multiple and varied tracts. Students who reach this grade level may: (a) drop out of school prematurely, (b) plan to continue their education in college, (c) plan to acquire some kind of post-high school training other than college, or (d) plan to graduate from high school and work.

Therefore, methods for this age group need to be designed to help the individual in exploring himself and becoming aware of his needs, abilities, interests and values, especially as these relate to deciding on a future direction. For example, upon reexamination of their educational needs, school dropouts might want to reenter the educational system to upgrade their occupational status.

Methods also need to be designed that would help the high school student to deal with the external pressures that are directed toward him from various sources. These methods could attack the situation in two ways: One way would be to help the individual deal with the emotional aspect of the pressure, i.e., his feelings of frustration, helplessness, insecurity, and so on. Another way would be to focus on certain aspects of career guidance that would eliminate, rather than alleviate, the pressures. Thus, career guidance methods that would put an emphasis on placement, i.e., going one step further than the high school and helping the student to reach into the world of work, would eliminate the frustration of looking for a job. Methods could also be designed to help the student acquire non-technical skills, employability skills such as interview skills, adjustment to supervision, peer relations and so on.

Such methods could potentially facilitate work adjustment and increase satisfaction with the position. They would also make the transition from school to work a smoother process. Garbin et al. (1970) have recently called attention to the adjustment problems of youth making this transition. Their research into this area also points out the need for methods which would help the student to bridge the gap between two different ways of life, school and work.

IMPLICATIONS FOR CAREER GUIDANCE

1. During the high school years, the individual is confronted with the reality of having to make decisions which would determine the course of his future life. He experiences internal, as well as external, pressures which impinge on him in multiple directions.

2. At this stage career guidance has a unique and significant role in that it can prepare the student for dealing with these pressures effectively.

3. Since the high school student's verbal and conceptual skills are greatly developed, career guidance can proceed along multiple and complex dimensions; it can facilitate exploration, evaluation of opportunities and decision making.

4. Career guidance can also assist the individual in becoming aware of himself now and of his potential in the future. It can help him to deal effectively with pressures that stem from his internal frustration, and with pressures that originate in the external environment.

5. A significant contribution of career guidance is helping the student to bridge the gap between school and work. Eliminating the problems associated with this transition could be achieved through focusing on such methods as placement, teaching non-technical skills and counseling.

6. At this grade level, at least four major future directions are possible: dropping out, college, post-high school training, and work after graduation. Career guidance can assist in clarifying the advantages of these avenues so that effective decisions can be made.

METHOD APPLICATIONS*

Akron-Summit County Public Schools Placement Department.

Albracht, J., et al. Using existing programs for providing exploratory experiences.

Bancroft, J. & Lawson, W. H. Project NOTIFY — Needed occupational television instruction for youth.

Birnbaum, R. Influencing college attendance plans.

Boocock, S. S. The life career game.

Budke, W. E. Review and synthesis of information on occupational exploration.

Bureau of Employment Security. Counselors desk aid — eighteen basic vocational directions — summary information.

Bureau of Employment Security. Selected characteristics of occupations (physical demands, working conditions, training time) A supplement to the D.O.T.

Bureau of Labor Statistics. Occupational outlook handbook 1966–67.

Campbell, G. C. The organization and implementation of an occupational information service program in the high school.

Career Information Center. The career information center, A working model.

Chancey, G. E. Career development unit — Job interview.

Chicago Urban League. Jobs now, a project to find employment for 3000 young men and women.

Circle, D. F., et al. The career information service. A guide to its development and use.

Civil Service Commission. Job briefs, selected federal jobs, duties, qualification requirements, sample test questions.

Green, L. F. A report of the Oakland guidance project: A demonstration project to study and refine counseling procedures for employment.

---

*These can be found in chapter 8 (alphabetically listed).

Gutsch, K. U. & Logan, R. H. Newspapers as a means of disseminating occupational information.

Hamilton, J. A. Video group social models, group stimulus materials and client characteristics in vocational counseling.

Hansen, L. S. Description of an emerging developmental career guidance program at Marshall-University High School utilizing volunteer paraprofessionals.

Harkness Center. Multi-occupations at Harkness Center. Progress report #1.

Harris, J. Computerized vocational information system (CVIS) project.

Houston Vocational Guidance Project. A high school job placement program.

Hollis, J. & Hollis, L. Personalizing information processes.

Iadipoli, M. V. Projects for group guidance.

Impellitteri, J. T. The computer as an aid to instruction and guidance in the school.

Indiana Career Resource Center. Resource of systems for vocational planning.

Krumboltz, J. D. & Schroeder, W. W. Promoting career planning through reinforcement.

Krumboltz, J. D. Vocational problem-solving experiences for stimulating career exploration and interest, phase II. Final report.

Martin, A. M. A multimedia approach to communicating occupational information to non-college youth.

McGovern, L. & Hansen, L. S. National vocational guidance week: A post mortem.

McBride, C. A. The Cleveland job development service.

Michigan Community Schools. Occupational education for all students.

Michigan State Department of Education. A vertically integrated occupational curriculum for schools in Michigan.

Mihalka, J. A. Job hunting course.

Miller, C. H. A pilot project for vocational guidance in economically under- areas.

Mullen, M. J. A volunteer program in vocational information and career guidance for secondary schools.

Munger, D. The occupational information speakers bureau.

New Hampshire State Department of Education. An annotated bibliography of resources in the fields of vocational-technical education and vocational guidance.

Educational Level Considerations

New Jersey State Department of Education. Teachers guide for a model program on introduction to vocations.

Office of Education. World of work curriculum PM 400–7. Instructors manual.

Oklahoma State Department of Education. A guide for vocational development. K–12.

Oregon State Department of Education. Guide to structure and articulation of occupational education programs. (Grades 7 through 12 and post-high school).

Osipow, S. H. & Alderfer, R. D. The effects of the vocationally oriented speech course on the vocational planning behavior of high school students.

Overs, R. P. & Deutsch, E. C. Sociological studies of occupations abstracts.

Palo Alto Unified School District. Conference summary — from theory to practice. The description and demonstration of a guidance program in one district K–12.

Peterson, N. D. A pilot project in vocational guidance, placement, and work experience for youth for whom existing work experiences are not appropriate.

Presidents Council on Youth Opportunity. Manual for youth coordinators.

Reinhart, B. A. Toward a vocational student information system: A progress report.

Schauble, P. A. Emotional simulation in personal counseling.

Tennyson, W. W. and Meyer, W. G. Pilot training project for teachers of distribution and marketing, focusing on responsibilities for career development.

Tuckman, B. A study of curriculums for occupational preparation and education.

U.S. Department of Health, Education and Welfare, Office of Education. The career information center — a working model.

Utah Research Coordinating Unit for Vocational and Technical Education. VIEW: Vocational information for education and work.

Varenhorst, B. B. Innovative tool for group counseling: The life career game.

Weiss, D. J. Computer-assisted synthesis of psychometric data in vocational counseling.

Wilmington Public Schools. Closed circuit TV — a tool for guidance.

Winefordner, D. W. Orienting students to the world of work using the data-people-things conceptual framework and the Ohio vocational interest survey.

Young, E. Counseling without offices: Guidance in a new context.

Educational Level: Post-High School

RATIONALE FOR CAREER GUIDANCE

Individuals who have completed high school present a variety of needs and circumstances for career guidance. Previously, career guidance was confined within the high school and culminated with graduation at the twelfth grade. This concentration stemmed from the belief that by the twelfth grade most students have gone through a certain amount of exploration, have narrowed or specified the range of their vocational interests and have made at least a preliminary vocational decision.

Recently, however, through the work of vocational development theorists and researchers in career guidance, more light has been shed on the need for career guidance beyond the high school level.

Super et al. (1967) conducted a ten-year longitudinal study of vocational development from junior high school until the middle twenties. They found that a large proportion of the subjects studied (about one-third) floundered during the post-high school years. In addition, the study revealed that subjects averaged six moves from one employment to another during the seven-year span from leaving high school until age twenty-five.

Based upon Project Talent findings (Flanagan et al. 1962), Cooley and Lohnes (1968) report that vocational plans tend to stabilize considerably *after* high school graduation. This would suggest that the first year out of high school as a time of significant reality-testing and development of commitment.

Garbin et al. (1970) have found that individuals who enter the world of work following their high school years encounter work adjustment problems that interfere with their progress both vocationally and personally.

In addition, individuals who are at a level beyond high school may well have delayed their vocational decisions to a later date and are, therefore, in need of career guidance. This would apply to students who are enrolled at a junior college in hope of obtaining career training, as well as to those who plan to transfer to a four-year college. Youths of the age range of grades 13-14 who are not enrolled in a formal educational or vocational program are searching for a suitable position. Great need thus exists for career guidance for youths in grades 13-14.

GOALS OF CAREER GUIDANCE

The period beyond high school is characterized by a multiplicity of individual needs and circumstances on one hand, and a multiplicity of

Educational Level Considerations

potential avenues to pursue on the other. It becomes clear, then, that the goals of career guidance at the post-high school level must themselves be varied to fit the needs of a varied population.

A significant part of the population in grades 13-14 consists of individuals who are pursuing a training program. Of these, some may plan to enroll in a four-year college at the end of the fourteenth grade. To an extent, these individuals have delayed their career planning beyond the high school level and may well be searching for some specificity in their future direction. For these individuals, the major goal of career guidance becomes that of availing them of information regarding educational programs, teaching them how to seek and gather information on their own and how to evaluate this information when it becomes available. Most importantly, they need practice in decision making that will help them in the immediate future as well as at a later date. Decision making may be a particular weakness for this group since they may have used the junior college as a means of prolonging their exploration and deferring their decision making.

Another segment of this population is composed of those students whose intentions are to obtain some kind of vocational training. For them, the goals of career guidance also focus on helping them to explore their abilities, and their needs and the avenues open to them, leading to practice in career decisions.

Those individuals who are in the labor market, whether they graduated, dropped out of school prematurely or completed their training, comprise a large population for whom career guidance can be a great asset. Research indicates (Fleishman 1963, Ley 1966) that young employees often fail on their jobs mainly because of the absence of non-technical skills. Garbin et al. (1970) identified several problems associated with poor work adjustment of young employees, such as: lack of information and contacts relative to job qualifications and job placement, and lack of experience or desired attitudes in dealing with peers, supervision, and the work environment in general.

Career guidance beyond the high school level has as its major goals not only facilitating the identification of specific areas of interest and ability, and bringing about the ability to make decisions, but identifying and teaching those non-technical skills (such as interviewing) which are required for work adjustment; providing placement assistance and contacts; and helping youth plan the course of their vocational life, i.e., think in terms of a career rather than in terms of one position.

For some individuals, the particular need at this stage is for updating and upgrading their education or their training, either for purposes of keeping up with new trends or in order to qualify for a higher position. In addition, an important goal of career guidance at this age involves those individuals who have made at least one unsuccessful job try-out.

Career guidance can then help the individual to evaluate his previous experience objectively, help him to gain some skills that will prevent the same experience in the future, and direct him to an area which will prove more suitable for his abilities and needs and where he could make a more significant contribution.

CONSIDERATIONS IN DESIGNING CAREER GUIDANCE METHODS

Grades 13-14 present a special situation from a career guidance point of view. Therefore, designing career guidance methods for this grade level involves taking certain factors into consideration.

The main factor to be taken into account is the varied nature of the population at this grade level range. Individuals in need of career guidance may be: (a) enrolled in an educational or training program, (b) holding a position within the framework of the labor market, (c) actively looking for a specific position, and (d) indecisive about the direction toward which to channel their energies. The varied nature of this population requires careful assessment of the special characteristics and needs of its members. In addition, it emphasizes the need for establishing differential goals, not only for different members of the population, but also as circumstances change at different times throughout an individual's career. A flexible, modifiable approach to career guidance at this level is essential.

The importance of guidance at this grade level has been recently empirically highlighted in a study by Garbin and Vaughn (1971). This study surveyed approximately 5000 students in vocational-technical programs at 60 different community-junior colleges located throughout the United States. Although the survey embraced many aspects of junior colleges, several of the survey's conclusions are especially relevant for guidance:

> (1) Summary data revealed that the personnel in the high schools from which the community college students graduated had relatively little impact upon certain of their career decisions. Most striking are the results on the relatively limited number of respondents who maintained they were influenced by the guidance counselor regarding program source and program selection. The small percentage of students who said the vocational education teacher was the most important influence in choice of program is also noteworthy. (p. 175)
> (2) Since the students did not share a basic homogeneity in certain characteristics, the position advanced by some writers (Jacob,

Educational Level Considerations

1957; Eddy, 1959) is not supported. Instead, the findings concur with the results reported by Rose (1963), which also dispelled the myth of student unanimity. As a consequence, any program of study, counseling perspective, or administrative philosophy must not "lump together" community college vocational students and view them as a homogeneous group. Such stereotypical orientation will only further camouflage each student's unique and individualistic qualities. It will be deleterious to the quality of his educational experience which should be devoted primarily to developing his uniqueness and individuality to the fullest potential. (p. 187)

(3) The findings of this research agree with other studies (Medsker and Trent, 1955; Shawl, 1966) which indicate large percentages of students attend junior college because of its proximity to their homes. About two out of 10 respondents in the present sample considered "close to home" as the most important reason why they were attending their present college; the same ratio resulted from the students' mean evaluations of a variety of possible factors as to three levels of relative importance. "Low cost" was identified by roughly the same proportion of students using either measuring procedure. For many respondents, "low cost" and "close to home" would be highly related factors; they take on added importance when it is considered that one-third of the sample were "self-supporting." Furthermore, two-thirds of the subjects were employed on at least a part-time basis while attending college. (p. 187)

(4) It is commonplace knowledge that the geographical mobility rate in the United States is extremely high. In fact, approximately one out of five families move each year. Considering the extent of geographical mobility, it may be advisable for community colleges to offer occupational training required by the labor market of a much broader economic or market area, rather than restricting the skills taught to those required primarily for entry into locally important occupations (Thornton, 1960). This would lessen the negative effects of geographical mobility, which tends to be concentrated for a given segment of the population, within a particular economic or labor market area. This recommendation assumes greater pertinency when data on the respondents future community orientation are recalled. In reference to the question, "Do you intend to remain in this community?" the responses were almost equally divided among "no," "yes," and "not sure". (p. 189)

Another major consideration in the design of methods for this population is the immediacy of the problem. Many of the youths who seek career guidance at this level have prolonged their period of exploration and have delayed the need to make a vocational decision by enrolling in a formal educational program. Others, who underwent some kind of vocational training and have held a position without satisfactory results, can be thought of as having had their initial vocational trial. For both these groups, and for those who are looking for a position, career guidance becomes a very immediate need.

Related to the urgency factor in career guidance is the importance of providing placement services for this group. Focusing on placement as an integral part of career guidance can eliminate or decrease the frustration and disappointment involved in the process of looking for, and being placed in, a position, especially the first one. Ideally, placement would involve some kind of follow-up or other kinds of supportive services to make the integration within the economic milieu a smooth process.

Perhaps the Cornell Study, which is surveying the placement services of New York State two-year colleges (directed by Hedlund 1972), will shed more light on the design of junior college placement services. The survey includes collecting information on the training experience and role of placement personnel, the needs of the students being served, placement facilities, services, goals, and the examination of linkages with educational programs. Also being examined are placement success rates and problems, mechanisms for employer contact, relationships with the community, and the use of labor market information.

Many youths in the age range of grades 13–14 are not enrolled in a formal educational or training program and, therefore, are not part of a setting where career guidance is provided. In designing career guidance methods, this situation needs to be taken into account. Methods need to be designed which could be applied to community or neighborhood settings. In addition, methods are needed to coordinate existing community resources and encourage their use by youths in need of career guidance.

IMPLICATIONS FOR CAREER GUIDANCE

1. A great need exists for career guidance in grades 13-14. This need stems from the variety of potential future directions which are available to students and also from the fact that many individuals at this level are still undecided about their interests and needs and lack certain skills which are essential for work adjustment.

2. Individuals in need of career guidance at the post-high school level comprise a varied population in terms of needs, characteristics, age, goals and the setting in which they are found. Career guidance approaches need to be both flexible and varied to fit this population.

Educational Level Considerations

3. The population in need of career guidance at this stage may well include women at various stages of life who plan to enter or to return to the job market and are in need of career guidance.

4. Long range career planning, including retraining and upgrading one's education or training, is important at this stage.

5. At this level, the need for career guidance is characterized by immediacy and urgency. Career guidance can be both exploratory (when no job try-out has been made) or remedial (when an unsuccessful job try-out has been made).

6. At this level, placement, as an integral part of career guidance, should be focused on in order to facilitate integration within the economic milieu.

7. Career guidance beyond high school has the unique role of reaching into the community, offering services within the neighborhood setting and coordinating existing programs.

METHOD APPLICATIONS*

Boocock, S. S. The life career game.
Bureau of Employment Security. Counselors desk aid — eighteen basic vocational directions — summary information.
Bureau of Employment Security. Selected characteristics of occupations (Physical demands, working conditions, training time) A supplement to the D.O.T.
Bureau of Labor Statistics. Occupational outlook handbook 1966–1967.
Chicago Urban League. Jobs now, a project to find employment for 3000 young men and women, etc.
Civil Service Commission. Job briefs, selected federal jobs, duties, qualification requirements, sample test questions.
Ewing, T. N. and Gilbert, W. M. An investigation of the importance of the personal relationship in teaching machine procedures.
Garrison, T. G. Vocational guidance manual for counselors, teachers, and educators.
Gutsch, K. U. and Logan, R. H. Newspapers as a means of disseminating occupational information.
Harding, F. D. What can happen when there are enough counselors: One approach at a two-year technical institute.
Harkness Center. Multi-occupations at Harkness Center. Progress report #1.
Hollis, J. and Hollis, L. Personalizing information processes.

---

*These can be found in chapter 8 (alphabetically listed).

Hoyt, K. B. The specialty oriented student research program: A five year report.

Michigan State Department of Education. A vertically integrated occupational curriculum for schools in Michigan.

Odle, G. S. The student information center as an educational resource.

Office of Education. World of work curriculum PM 400–7, instructors manual.

Oregon State Department of Education. Guide to structure and articulation of occupational education programs.

Overs, R. P. and Deutsch, E. C. Sociological studies of occupations abstracts.

Presidents Council on Youth Opportunity. Manual for youth coordinators.

Pucel, D. J. and Nelson, H. F. Project mini-score: Some preliminary implications for vocational guidance.

Reinhart, B. A. Toward a vocational student information system: A progress report.

Schauble, P. G. Emotional simulation in personal counseling.

Weiss, D. J. Computer-assisted synthesis of psychometric data in vocational counseling.

Wilkinson, R. D. Student campus employees.

Witherspoon, F. D. Group guidance in junior college — A frame of reference.

Woody, R. H. Vocational counseling with behavioral techniques.

Chapter 3 POPULATION SUBGROUPS FOR WHOM SPECIAL GUIDANCE PROCEDURES ARE DESIRABLE

Introduction

In this chapter career guidance methods have been classified according to the special population for which they have been found useful. The term "special population" is defined as *a group of individuals who seek career guidance, but possess at least one unique characteristic in terms of needs or problems which presents a special problem for career guidance.* Examples of different characteristics include (a) ethnic or cultural background, (b) learning ability and motivation, (c) economic or social status in society, and (d) geographic location. Classification of methods by special population stems from the following considerations.

INDIVIDUAL DIFFERENCES

Individual differences in ability, potential, background, need, and opportunities exist within any group of people. Recognition of this requires differential treatment which is designed and tailored to fit these differences and, thus, maximizes the effects of the treatment given to them. Although the concept of individual differences ultimately implies the uniqueness of each individual (and the requirement of a unique treatment or method for each individual), there exist certain classes of differences which are common to a group of individuals and which differentiate them from other groups. Classifying methods according to their applicability to such groups provides us with a technique which maximizes the potential utility of the methods, but at the same time is more economical and practical than devising individualized methods. Thus, classifying methods in this manner is seen as a way of meeting the requirements of individual differences and narrowing the range of methods for each group, thus sharpening their usefulness.

UNIQUE GOALS

Related to the existence of individual differences is the existence of unique goals for each group. Whereas a guidance objective for one group might be to increase the group's exploratory behavior, an objective for a second group might well be to facilitate its members' decision-making skills, and so on. Thus, a classification of methods by special population is seen as a way of providing a unique population with the most appropriate avenues for reaching its specific goals.

LIMITING AND MODIFYING METHODS

Regretfully, there are gaps in the availability of methods for specific groups within the total population. However, by classifying existing methods by population there is the possibility of being able to apply a method which has proved successful with one special population to a similar population for which a specific method is not yet available. For example, if a method is needed for use with Japanese American children, a method which has proved successful with Spanish American children might be tried, recognizing the underlying cultural background of both groups which differentiates them from the general population. Related to this, a classification by population might be of use when a guidance office or agency prefers to modify an existing method and apply it to a specific population. In this case, the relevant principles can be extracted from the methods which specifically apply to this population, and then can be used to modify the existing method.

SIZE AND COST

The inquiries and research undertaken by a guidance office or agency prior to the adoption of a new program for a specific population might well include considerations of both size and cost. "Size" refers to the

Special Career Guidance Procedures 47

size of the group required for an effective program, the facilities involved, and so on; "cost" refers to the expenditure in equipment, manpower, time and money involved in putting a method into practice. By referring to the various methods applicable to one population, an estimate can then be made for any similar program, without having to conduct feasibility studies and spend valuable time and effort.

UNIQUE METHODS

The methods which are presented in this volume were categorized according to their specific applicability to one or more of the eight special populations discerned. These eight populations can subsequently be grouped according to some common factor that they possess. Thus, achievement and motivational problems emerge as a factor underlying three special population groups, i.e., underachievers, potential dropouts and slow learners. Disadvantaged blacks, Spanish Americans and rural youth can be grouped under a cultural-ethnic-racial factor. However, the special populations of women and physically handicapped do not fall under any common factor for grouping and stand alone as special populations.

Several points of importance relevant to the classification of methods by special population stand out and should be taken into consideration by the reader. Methods were selected following an extensive review of literature and material. In the views of the writers, they represent the best available methods for a particular population group. However, it should be kept in mind that considerable gaps exist in terms of the availability and specificity of guidance methods. Although methods are classified according to the special population for which they were designed, these methods might well apply to other special populations, but concrete evidence as to their potential applicability is lacking. Thus, in attempting to establish a guidance program within a school or an agency system, the reader should feel at liberty to take the guidelines presented in this section, and modify and supplement them to develop an improved product which would fit the specific needs of a certain unique population group. Apart from the methods themselves, which are tools and a main source of guidance for the counselor, the reader will find useful the section which contains research generalizations.

There is a definition of each population in clear and specific terms. Clarifying the nature of, and defining, the population involved is an important step in identifying sources of problems and understanding the background, limitations and unique needs of members of a special population. A clear definition is particularly important in view of stereotypes, misuse and indiscriminate use of terms in literature and everyday life.

The body of the section dealing with research generalizations contains findings, speculations and attempts at dealing with various problems, all relative to the special population under consideration. The information presented, and implications from it, are gathered in such a manner as to increase the reader's familiarity with, and understanding of, the background, characteristics and needs of the special population. In addition, recommendations and new developments in the area of fulfilling these needs are also presented.

This chapter provides general guidelines and an orientation for the reader, in order to maximize his ability to evaluate the methods available, to apply or modify them to his own needs, and to develop new methods in order to fill gaps which currently exist and to fulfill the needs of members of a special population.

Potential Dropouts

WHO ARE DROPOUTS?

Schreiber (1967) defined the term dropout as "a pupil who leaves school, for any reason except death, before graduation or completion of a program of studies and without transferring to another school" (p. 4). Only in part does this definition reflect the problems and consequences attached to the event of dropping out of school.

It is widely asserted that the potential dropout can not learn and is alienated from school (Schasre and Wallach 1965). Whereas this might raise questions with regard to the causes within the educational system or the educational setting, from a career guidance point of view our interest lies in obtaining information about how a dropout functions in the occupational world so that we can preserve or redirect the human talent and train or guide potential dropouts to become productive members of society.

WHAT DOES RESEARCH SAY?

Most of the data relevant to the problems of potential dropouts are more descriptive in nature than predictive or remedial (Wages, Thomas and Kuvlesky 1969, Miller 1963). In most of the literature available, the school dropout emerges as a critical problem to American education and American society (Schreiber 1965, Cervantes 1965), resulting from the increase in our society's emphasis on education and achievement. But, apart from being a social outcast, the dropout finds himself at a disadvantage both vocationally and occupationally. Cervantes (1965) points

Special Career Guidance Procedures

out that the economy is limited in its ability to absorb the dropout, since he typically enters the labor market with no skills. In addition, many employers are reluctant to hire a dropout, even if he does have some skills or can be rapidly trained. Miller (1963) showed that the overwhelming majority of those who drop out are capable of doing school work, in spite of the widely asserted opinion that the prospective dropout cannot learn and is alienated from school.

The actual number of students who leave school before graduation (and usually at the ninth grade) has been estimated to be between one-third and two-fifths of all youth, with the southern states having a disproportionate percentage. While the majority come from working class and farm families, Miller (1963) estimates that about one-fourth of the dropouts in Syracuse, New York, came from white-collar families, particularly those in marginal occupational positions.

Financial difficulty and dissatisfaction with the school *per se* emerge in many studies as the most salient reasons for leaving school (Bowman and Matthews 1960, Chaloupka 1958, Moore 1954). However, Brian (1963) lists some administrative and supervisory practices which contribute to the dropout problem, including allowing pupils to drop out at the age limit as a way to solve the case of "problem pupils"; closing the school doors on returnees who previously dropped out of school; failing to provide curricular adaptations for teenage low achievers who are not academically or vocationally inclined; and assigning too many problem pupils to a class and the school counselor.

Whatever the reasons which precipitate dropping out of either high school or college, statistics are available which reflect trends in the occupational world and give an indication as to the conditions and obstacles the dropout will confront upon leaving school. Thus, Schiffman's (1962) data show that, in 1961, the percentage of unemployment among dropouts was 26.8 as compared with 17.9 among graduates. In 1962 the U.S. Bureau of Labor Statistics showed the strong relationship between the kinds of jobs people hold and their education, with the concentration of dropouts being in farm, service, and operative occupations.

Gallington (1966, 1965) gives basic criteria for identifying potential high school dropouts. These criteria include objective measures such as, intellectual measures, achievement records and home and family statistics; and subjective measures such as, attitudes toward people, attitude toward school, and personal ambitions and drive.

IMPLICATIONS FOR CAREER GUIDANCE

The implications that the above facts and speculations bear for guidance and particularly for vocational guidance usually revolve around two core approaches: (a) encourage the dropout to return to complete his formal education through high school, or (b) direct the dropout to skill training that will enable him to compete in the labor market (National Committee for Children and Youth 1961, Schasre and Wallach 1965).

These approaches appear to oversimplify a complex problem, since, in most cases, the potential dropout is experiencing adjustment problems and a frustrating history of educational failure. Therefore, methods should incorporate specialized counseling services to deal with the debilitating aspects of the student's career development as part of the total career guidance program for the student.

METHOD APPLICATIONS*

Albracht, J. et al. Using existing vocational programs for providing exploratory experiences.

Anderson, C. M. Project 13.

Bureau of Employment Security. Selected characteristics of occupations (physical demands, working conditions, training time). A supplement to the D. O. T.

Bureau of Employment Security. Counselors desk aid — eighteen basic vocational directions — summary.

Chicago Urban League. Jobs Now, a project to find employment for 3,000 young men and women.

Darcy, R. L. An experimental junior high school course in occupational opportunities and labor market processes.

Green, L. F. A report of the Oakland guidance project; a demonstration project to study and refine counseling procedures for employment.

Leonard, G. E. Developmental career guidance in action, the first year.

Leubling, H. E. Counseling with dropouts: a three year study.

Martin, A. M. A multimedia approach to communicating occupational information to non-college youth. Technical report.

Office of Education. World of work curriculum (PM 400-7). Instructors manual. Job Corps.

Lorber, F. & Schrank, R. The Bloomingdale project, report of a demonstration on-the-job training program.

Sullivan, H. J. The effects of selected film and counseling experiences on capable girl's attitudes toward college.

New York State Education Department. Developing work-study programs for potential dropouts — a manual STEP: the school to employment program.

Wilkinson, R. D. Student campus employees.

Witherspoon, F. D. Group guidance in junior college — a frame of reference.

---

*These can be found in chapter 8 (alphabetically listed).

Slow Learners

WHO ARE THE SLOW LEARNERS?

Intellectually, slow learners are those children whose IQ scores are included in the lowest quartile of the population, ranging between 50 and 80. They have a maximum mental growth ranging between 11 years and 13 years, 6 months (Johnson 1963, Crawford and Cross 1967), and they comprise a special population for education and guidance because they not only fall below the average in intellectual capacity but often exhibit problem behavior and special educational, social and vocational needs.

Slow learners, sometimes referred to as "educable mentally retarded," compose the largest group of mentally retarded persons. Among the general school population, 15 to 18 percent can be considered slow learners. Johnson (1963) estimates that about one-fourth of them come from adequate homes and are making a reasonable, if difficult, adjustment to life. Typical of the slow learner is his limited rate and level of development. He is unable to "keep up" with the rest of his class or peer group, especially in his rate of academic growth. He starts late and continues to fall behind; this appears to be true in both skill and content areas.

WHAT DOES RESEARCH SAY?

The special characteristics of the slow learner and the problems that they present have attracted interest but have stimulated only very little systematic investigation. The majority of the literature relevant to the slow learner and his needs treats the problem as primarily academic, as part of the school and its curriculum. Johnson (1963) asserts that curricula have become stereotyped to the detriment of children who do not fit into the "average" or "normal" part of the population; seldom has a curriculum been designed specifically for the slow learner, despite the diversity of courses available at the secondary level. More recently, however, some constructive attempts have been made to deal with the problem, and these too are primarily educational in nature. For example, Baumgartner (1965) advocates building a total educational program for this group, and others (Sutton 1967, Ohio Department of Education 1961) have designed more specific curricula for them. Most states have departments of special education which include programs for slow learners.

In spite of the tendency to emphasize techniques of bridging the educational gap between the average child and the slow learner, and to overlook the potential importance of vocational guidance with this population, several techniques recommended within the educational field might well have implications for career guidance and the development of career guidance methods that will reach this group and suit their needs. Thus, Riessman (1966) delineates some of the characteristics of the slow learner and their implications for the development of new programs. He observes that the slow learner cannot understand a concept unless he performs some physical movement (e.g., using his hands, jumping) in connection with the idea. Therefore, it is imperative that programs include games, actions, role playing, films and materials. He also recommends that emphasis be shifted from a concentration on the child's deficits and past to the child's positive strengths and his present and future.

Jeffrey (1967) describes a program based on reinforcement and the shaping of behavior in preparation for a specialized program of vocational and academic training. Sutton (1967) devised a program with the aim of improving the job placement opportunities of slow learners. The program included special education, orientation to business and industry, establishment of a job placement service for enrolled terminal students, and the development of procedures and instruments capable of identifying jobs suitable for this group. Crawford and Cross (1967) have developed what they call a "realistic" approach toward meeting the needs of the slow learners in high school. They incorporated a work-study program in the special-education curriculum and found it effective in providing the slow learner with a practical, realistic experience in preparation for adulthood.

IMPLICATIONS FOR CAREER GUIDANCE

In spite of the paucity of research in this area, especially as it relates to the needs of this group from a career guidance point of view, a picture emerges of the slow-learning child and young adult as an individual with limited skills and capacities, with special needs and special characteristics for which specialized methods of guidance, both educational and vocational, must be devised:

1. Methods must take into account not only these individuals' slow rate and limited level of intellectual development, but also the social-psychological implications of being "slow" in an environment where academic acceleration and achievement are prized.

2. Methods must consider the fact that the slow learner may well have to be specifically taught many social and work skills which the normal child obtains through incidental learning.

3. The availability of job environments into which slow learners could comfortably fit, and the need for specialized personnel to implement new methods, are additional considerations which should not be overlooked when attempting to help the slow learner to become a productive member of society.

METHOD APPLICATIONS*

Anderson, C. M. Project 13.

Beedy, V. et al. A prevocational and social adjustment program for educable adolescents: A pilot project.

Geteles, F. et al. A cooperative vocational pattern for in-school mentally retarded youth.

Kendall, M. A trip to the Statler-Hilton Hotel.

McPherson, H. & Stevens, T. M. Developing a work experience program for slow learning youth: a report of a three year extension and improvement project.

Martin, A. M. A multimedia approach to communicating occupational information to non-college youth. Technical report.

Underachievers

WHO ARE THE UNDERACHIEVERS?

Intuitively, the term underachievement suggests that a student is not functioning as well as he or she could. Also suggested are a waste in existing human talent and inefficiency in utilizing or directing this talent. These bear implications for career guidance and merit the classification of this group as a special population, with unique characteristics and needs.

However, as Kornrich (1965) points out, intuitive definitions of underachievement are simplistic and misleading in nature. Underachievement implies discrepancies between actual and predicted performance. Not only do different definitions vary in the precision with which they specify this discrepancy, but the concept itself is broad, relying on our current means of prediction, which in themselves are imperfect and limited in scope (Thorndike 1963). The term underachievement has become a "catchall" for a wide variety of educational limitations (Aubrey 1970). Whereas the problems involved with discrepant and diverse definitions should be borne in mind, there still exists

---

*These can be found in chapter 8 (alphabetically listed).

a body of literature which is relevant to, and useful in, understanding and dealing with underachievers from a career guidance point of view.

WHAT DOES RESEARCH SAY?

Fine (1967) states that the term "underachievers" usually denotes students who rank in the top third in intellectual ability but whose performance is dramatically below that level. Raph, Goldberg and Passow (1966) point out that underachievement emerges as a problem at the secondary school level.

Several studies attempt to relate various factors to academic underachievement. Chance (1961) found that children whose mothers favored earlier independence training made less adequate school progress in both reading and arithmetic relative to their intellectual ability than children whose mothers favored later independence training. Coleman (1960) links academic achievement among adolescents to the social and value system of which they are a part. A social system in which academic achievement is not highly valued will include fewer people whose actual intelligence and achievement is high. Fink (1962a, 1962b) postulated a relationship between concept of self and academic underachievement and obtained data from observation in clinical practice of school psychology to confirm his hypothesis that an inadequate self-concept is related to low academic achievement, based on grade point average. Results were more conclusive for boys than for girls. Studies investigating a multitude of factors contributing to underachievement are summarized by Gowan (1960). These include: frustrated emotional needs and value conflicts (Broedel, Ohlsen and Proff 1958) poor study habits (Westfall 1958) and additional factors relating to parental and cultural influence. Roth and Meyersberg (1963) see underachievement as a syndrome involving anxiety, hopelessness and frustration, and urge recognition of the dynamic processes involved in underachievement.

Only a very few objective studies are available in the area of occupational and vocational choices of underachieving high school students. Gowan (1957), surveying the dynamics of underachievement, concluded that the orientation of an underachieving student is more toward immediate occupational choices; he does not appear to see very far ahead in terms of educational and vocational choice. In addition, members of this population have vague occupational and academic choices. Broedel et al. (1958) also found remoteness of goals to be characteristic of this group, and Armstrong (1955) found that underachievers' interests were not in line with goals set for them by others.

Armstrong (1955) also compared normal achievers with underachievers and found that the latter showed more high scores on the

Special Career Guidance Procedures

Outdoor, Persuasive, Literary and Musical scales in the Kuder Preference Record Manual, while normal achievers had high scores on the Occupational, Scientific, Social Service and Clerical scales. Frankel (1960) and Phelps (1957) found that underachievers were less interested in school and less active and interested in future educational goals than normal achievers. This group also was found to have lower vocational aspirations and to experience problems in the areas of post-high school plans, school adjustment and family relationships, and attitudes toward themselves (Portland Public Schools 1959).

Ozoglu (1964) found underachievers' occupational choices to be out of line with their scholastic ability, interest, and achievement. There was little agreement on occupational choice between the underachiever and his parents. On the other hand, Ozoglu found that underachievers who receive interpretation of test scores from a counselor move toward more appropriate occupational choices than those who obtain test interpretations by other methods in the school. Both individual and group counseling was found effective in achieving emotional growth (Broedel et al. 1960) and adjustment (Baymur and Patterson 1960).

However, according to Gowan (1955), counseling the underachiever presents a number of problems: Underachievers tend to be self-sufficient and unsociable and, therefore, are harder to reach; they also tend to have less exposure to the normal socializing effects of their peers due to lack of contact. Aubrey (1970) suggests that the bulk of students placed in the "underachiever" category are erroneously labeled and sees the role of the counselor as assisting them best by working with the adults making these mistaken judgments. Earlier Drasgow (1957) had seen the role of the counselor as helping the underachiever to divorce himself from an alien curriculum and discover an appropriate one.

IMPLICATIONS FOR CAREER GUIDANCE

From the above, a picture emerges of the underachiever as an individual whose characteristics and needs are different from the average student population. From a vocational guidance point of view, the discrepancy between ability and achievement, his negative attitude, and the vagueness or inappropriateness of his vocational interests, plans, and choices, presents a challenge to the counselor. The challenge lies not only with regard to the underachiever himself, but also with regard to societal expectations and emphasis on achievement as a measure of a person's worth. The task of the guidance counselor is therefore multidimensional:

1. He can attempt to inspire the underachiever to reach higher levels of achievement.

2. He can arouse the underachiever's interests in a certain vocational area and increase his exploratory behavior in search of relevant vocational and occupational information.
3. He can provide counseling for better adjustment and more positive self-concept and explore and strengthen those traits and behaviors in which the individual does achieve and succeed.

Methods of vocational guidance, if specifically designed for this population, become a highly useful tool in the hand of the counselor and teacher. In addition, the counselor, bearing in mind the ambiguity and implications of the concept of underachievement itself, should attempt to design new methods that will aid specific individuals.

In developing new approaches, the notion of differential treatment should be considered. From reviewing the research on underachievement it appears evident that no single treatment approach, such as study skills or group counseling, is effective for all underachievers. There are different types of underachievers and treatment should be geared to the individual.

METHOD APPLICATIONS*

Boocock, S. S. The life career game.

Martin, A. M. A multimedia approach to communicating occupational information to non-college youth. Technical report.

Witherspoon, F. D. Group guidance in junior college—a frame of reference.

Disadvantaged

WHO ARE THE DISADVANTAGED?

The term "disadvantaged," as it is currently used, is a broad term which encompasses cultural, educational, environmental, economic, physical, social and psychological deprivation. The multidimensionality of the term reflects the multidimensionality of the problem on one hand, and the complexity of dealing with this problem effectively on the other. Although different population groups may possess handicaps similar to those mentioned above (e.g., cultural or physical handicaps), it is the cumulative nature of various dimensions of deprivation which necessitates the classification of the "disadvantaged" as a special, unique population in terms of characteristics and needs, particularly as these apply to career guidance.

---

*These can be found in chapter 8 (alphabetically listed).

Special Career Guidance Procedures

The disadvantaged youth has come to the awareness of writers and researchers only in recent years, so systematic research studies are limited (Duncan and Gazda 1967). But even in spite of the heterogeneity of the group, certain characteristics common to disadvantaged youth have been recognized.

WHAT DOES RESEARCH SAY?

In the educational realm, Riessman (1962) has found a high frequency of school failure, a lack of educational tradition in the home and inadequate motivation to be characteristic of this group. Shaw (1963) also found a high dropout rate; Brazziel and Gordon (1963) found insufficient language skills as typical. Riessman (1962) further specifies the special pattern of communication of the deprived child:

1. Physical and visual rather than aural
2. Content-centered rather than form-centered
3. Externally oriented rather than introspective
4. Problem-centered rather than abstract-centered
5. Inductive rather than deductive
6. Spatial rather than temporal
7. Slow, careful, patient, persevering (in areas of importance) rather than quick, clever, facile, flexible. (p. 73)

Anderson (1966) describes the perception of disadvantaged youth with regard to education and/or the school. He found these youths to feel rejected and not part of the school body and to see learning as irrelevant to their own aspirations. The disadvantageousness of these youths in the educational realm is reinforced by what Vontress (1963) called the "demoralizing" school atmosphere, services, facilities and attitudes among which these students are expected to learn.

In the personal realm, disadvantaged youths have been characterized as possessing an inadequate or negative self-concept (Dela-Dora 1963, Riessman 1962, Brazziel and Gordon 1963, Brown 1966). Inadequate self-concepts were found frequently among disadvantaged elementary and high school students (Soares and Soares 1969). Roussève (1963) describes disadvantaged youths as having childhoods without much love.

In the vocational realm, education, personal conditions and characteristics have a multiplicative effect. The negative self-concept of this population group necessarily determines their vocational aspiration level and their perception as to what kinds of areas are open to them. In addition, their high dropout rate and poor learning and verbal skills in general further minimize their likelihood of being hired for gainful employment. Mathis (1969) sees the aptitude barrier, i.e., the inability of disadvantaged youths to pass aptitude screening instruments such as the General Aptitude Test Battery used by the U.S. Employment Service, as the principal factor which keeps the disadvantaged from the world of work. He further states that performance level tests would be more adequate and appropriate measures of the ability and potential of this group.

Recent and more systematic research in this area has resulted in encouraging findings. Campbell et al. (1969) investigated the vocational development of disadvantaged junior high school students in four communities located in various regions in the U. S. In the area of educational-vocational planning, the authors found that, generally, most non-disadvantaged males expected to complete four years of college work, while disadvantaged students were split evenly between expecting to graduate from college and expecting to graduate from high school. In addition, it was found that disadvantaged youth do give a considerable amount of thought to both scholastic plans and future jobs. On the other hand, disadvantaged students scored lower on a vocational maturity scale than non-disadvantaged students.

IMPLICATIONS FOR CAREER GUIDANCE

Findings and considerations presented above with respect to the educational, personal and vocational realms have direct implication for career guidance.

1. The educational and cognitive handicaps of this group emphasize the need to find methods for education and vocational guidance that minimize the need for verbal and abstract skills. Riessman (1966) suggests the use of role playing, films, and other materials which could be manipulated by physical, rather than cognitive, means. Wagner (1967) describes a method based on demonstrations and limited verbal responses as useful for teaching concepts in science. Boocock (1967) advocates the use of game models in teaching students how to become aware of themselves as human systems in relation to their environments.

2. In the personal area, Calia (1966) and Duncan and Gazda (1963) see counseling as having the potential of helping the disadvantaged youth to develop a more adequate self-concept and increasing his motivation to become a productive member of society and to overcome the conditions which define him as disadvantaged. However, Calia (1966) emphasized the need to reformulate the counselor's role by using action-oriented talk, improving environmental resources and so on in order to fit the needs of this group.

Special Career Guidance Procedures

3. Within the vocational realm, Campbell et al. (1969) see their finding (that the disadvantaged student views the school as an opportunity to prepare for a productive and satisfying life despite his previously acquired handicap) as a challenge to the school to provide these youths with opportunities to accomplish their expectations.

In all these areas (Gordon 1969), the career guidance counselor, whether he is associated with a school system or a community development agency, emerges as a vital element in dealing with this population and in acting as an agent of change in transforming disadvantaged youth into productive members of society.

METHOD APPLICATIONS*

Anderson, C. M. Project 13.

Atlanta Board of Education. Formulation of models for preparing occupational materials for pupils from various socioeconomic levels in grades 3-8.

Delta County Joint School District 50. Development of social and occupational perception in rural areas.

Feck, V. What vocational education teachers and counselors should know about urban disadvantaged.

Fishman, J. R. et al. Training for new careers.

Glassman, A. I. et al. Summer work-study program on urban problems for secondary school youth from inner-city communities.

Goldstein, G. (ed.) College bound: a directory of special programs and financial aid for minority group students.

Green, L. F. A report of the Oakland guidance project: A demonstration project to study and refine counseling procedures for employment.

Hansen, L. S. Description of an emerging developmental career guidance program at Marshall-University High School utilizing volunteer paraprofessionals.

Landers, J. Higher horizons program.

Leonard, G. E. Vocational planning and career behavior: A report on the developmental career guidance project.

Leonard, G. E. Developmental career guidance in action, the first year.

Leonard, G. E. & Stephens, E. Elementary school employment service.

Letson, J. W. Formulation of models for preparing occupational materials for pupils from various socioeconomic levels in grades 3-8.

---

*These can be found in chapter 8 (alphabetically listed).

Leubling, H. E. Counseling with dropouts: A three year study.

Litzinger, W. & Visser, C. Closing the vocational counseling realities gap.

Los Angeles County Superintendent of Schools. Portraits: the literature of minorities: an annotated bibliography of literature by and about four ethnic groups in the United States for grades 7–12.

Martin, A. M. A multimedia approach to communicating occupational information to non-college youth. Technical report.

Mink, O. G. & Kaplan, B. A. (eds.) America's problem youth: education and guidance of the disadvantaged.

Mitchell, H. Counseling black students: a model in response to the need for relevant counselor training programs.

Osipow, S. H. & Alderfer, R. D. The effects of the vocationally oriented speech course on the vocational planning behavior of high school students.

Schauble, P. G. Emotional simulation in personal counseling.

Segel, D. & Ruble, R. A. The Lincoln project: A study of the educational program of a junior high school in a transitional neighborhood.

Research Coordinating Unit for Vocational and Technical Education. V.I.E.W. Vocational information for education and work.

Winborn, R. & Martinson, W. Innovation in guidance: A mobile counseling center.

Zimpel, L. (ed.) The disadvantaged worker: readings in developing minority manpower.

Zweilbelson, I. Guiding parents and motivating talented students who live in low-rent neighborhoods.

Rural Youth

WHO ARE RURAL YOUTH?

Although an overwhelming proportion of the population of the United States lives in sprawling urban areas, a substantial proportion, approximately forty million, lives in rural areas. Rural families are scattered in small villages, town and hamlets throughout the country. The combination of factors specific to rural settings, such as geographic isolation, limited occupational exposure, declining job opportunities, and massive migration to urban centers presents unique problems in providing a sound education and career guidance to rural youth.

Special Career Guidance Procedures 61

WHAT DOES RESEARCH SAY?

Studies dealing with the vocational development and career planning of rural youth include investigations of vocational aspirations, migration and mobility, occupational training and general education, vocational guidance and employment. A summary of these studies and their implications for career guidance are described below.

The severe decline of farm-related job opportunities has taken a heavy toll on the rural economy. The Manpower Report of the President (1968) reported that since World War II there has been a 50 percent decline in the number of persons employed in agricultural occupations. Advancements in farming technology have reduced the farm labor need. In 1961 one farmer produced enough food for twenty-six persons whereas in 1940 his efforts had fed only eleven persons (Griessman and Densley 1970). This job decline has had the greatest employment affect on farm laborers, farm foremen and farm youth.

Farm laborers and farm foremen have one of the highest migration rates from farm to non-farm jobs; farm youth also have a very high migration rate, especially during the early years of labor force participation. Bishop (1967) points out that young adults who have relatively little invested in farming and who have a longer period of prospective employment in which to recoup the costs of migration are much more prone to transfer to non-farm occupations. In contrast, farm operators (owners) are much less likely to migrate since they are older, have larger investments in farms and farm skills and have fewer alternative opportunities (Bishop 1970).

The recent development of off-farm occupations such as agribusiness has helped the rural economy somewhat. Off-farm occupations provide supportive services for farmers and include such activities as the manufacture and distribution of farm supplies and the marketing of agricultural products. Estimates place about 6 million workers in manufacturing and distributing and 10 million in marketing (Griessman and Densley 1970).

Poor employment prospects in rural America have resulted in massive migration to the cities. The base farm population declined rapidly, from 31 million in 1920 to approximately 10 million in 1969 (Bishop 1970). Many migrants are inadequately prepared to cope with the shift to the metropolis; few have job skills to compete in the urban labor market, and in most instances little advanced planning has been involved in the move. Jobs are typically obtained through personal contacts such as family or friends. Marsh (1967) found that the planning period was "one month or less for about one-third of the moves reported; alternatives were not even considered in two-thirds of them; and, in over half of the cases, family heads who relocated consulted no more than one source of job information."

IMPLICATIONS FOR CAREER GUIDANCE

The decline in rural job opportunities, massive migration to the cities, and the trend toward off-farm occupations has important implications for education and career guidance. Educational reform is needed which will prepare residents to become employable whether they remain in rural areas either as farmers or in off-farm positions or migrate to the city. Educational programs should stress not only job-skill training but instruction in career planning. Areas which have heavy migration to the cities might want to consider offering courses which better prepare their residents for migration. Migratory instruction could be combined logically with career planning and give attention to common family problems, such as installment buying, placement services, health care and housing. There are a number of agencies who provide service to migrants, such as the Urban League, but too often migrants are unaware of their existence.

Griessman and Densley (1970), in the review of education for rural areas, point out that rural schools are more traditional and resist change more than urban schools. They also remind the outside observer that rural schools often have to operate with limited financial, personnel and facility resources. Many geographically isolated schools are too small to provide the kind of quality comprehensive program needed by their students.

The joint-area vocational school concept provided by the Vocational Education Act of 1963 has been a great help to rural education. The area school concept provided federal and state assistance in establishing a training center to serve multiple school districts concurrently. The area schools help to fill a void by offering educational programs which member schools normally could not provide independently. In most cases, students take courses at both their parent school and the area school. Several states have developed program models for providing student personnel services in area schools (Bottoms 1967, Petry 1969). The models provide guidelines for student personnel services, e.g., career exploration, admission to programs and job placement.

The Western States Small Schools Project (Merrell 1970) is another example of educational reform in rural education. The experimental project is designed to improve the career preparation of youth who at-

Special Career Guidance Procedures 63

tend small, rural schools by developing and evaluating an integrated career development curriculum. It pays special attention to enhancing the career opportunities of rural youth who choose to leave the rural setting for gainful employment.

The occupational aspirations of rural youth have been the subject of a number of studies (Anderson 1944, Buck and Bible 1961, Burchinal 1961, Cowhig 1960, Slocum 1956, Sewell and Orenstein 1965). Although it is difficult to generalize as to the aspirations of all rural youth from these studies due to differences in sampling, methodology, and how each investigator defines his criteria, Kuvlesky (1970) suggests the following summary:

> The accumulated research evidence clearly indicates that most rural youth *do not* have low level job and educational aspirations and expectations at present—personally, I doubt that they ever did. Whatever was true in the past, it is abundantly clear from recent research across the country that rural youth generally have very high job and educational aspirations and expectations. Recent analyses of regional data collected from several states in the South clearly support this generalization. Rural youth predominantly prefer and to a large extent expect employment in professional or semi-professional and technical types of jobs. In reference to educational attainment, the vast majority of rural youth desire college level education and almost all desire at least formal vocational training or junior college after high school completion. There is a tendency for aggregate deflection from college goals toward anticipation of post high school vocational training. Currently, evidence from both the South and Northwest indicate that few rural youth either desire or expect to farm—this has obvious implications for the need to continue Vocational-Agriculture programs for local high schools.
>
> While it is true that urban youth tend to have higher level status projections than rural youth, this should not be interpreted to mean that rural youth have low level status projections, for it is abundantly clear that the rural/urban differentials are much less important than the similarly high aspiration and expectations held by most youth. Differences by race in the South and by social class across the nation are of a similar nature. Certainly class, race, and ethnic differentials exist — the disadvantaged youth tend to hold lower level goals and anticipated attainments. Still the majority of even the most disadvantaged youth, the rural Negro in the South and Mexican American rural youth of the Southwest, desire high prestige job attainments and college level education.
>
> In conclusion, most rural youth, regardless of class or race, are like most other youth in holding high ambitions for attainment. At the same time, it should not be overlooked that sizeable minorities

of disadvantaged rural youth, perhaps much more than other types of youth, have relatively low level aspirations. Obviously any program of guidance or vocationnal training established to help these youth will have to take these differences into account — the same programs are not likely to work effectively for both the very ambitious and the unambitious.

Griessman and Densley (1970), in their extensive review of studies dealing with counseling and student personnel services for rural youth, offer the following conclusions:

1. Students in rural areas have limited contact with the industrial world and as a result have a narrowed vision of vocational opportunities.

2. One-half of the rural schools do not have full-time guidance counselors.

3. Comprehensive guidance services are needed which emphasize occupational exploration and planning, placement, and follow-up of graduates.

4. Surveys have shown that rural youth do not want to migrate, but are forced to for improved employment opportunities.

5. Programs should provide maximum individual involvement and personal development to enhance accurate self-concepts.

METHOD APPLICATIONS*

Agan, R. J. et al. The development and demonstration of a coordinated and integrated program of occupational information, selection, and preparation in a secondary school. Final report.

Danner, R. Showcase for vocational guidance and occupational education.

Delta County Joint School District 50. Development of social and occupational perception in rural areas.

Digneo, E. H. & Shaya, T. Career selection education program, 1965–1968 report.

Drier, H. N. and Jepsen, D. A. The use of television and video tape compared to researching printed career information as a means of assisting rural 9th grade youth career decision making process.

Hansen, S. L. Description of an emerging developmental career guidance program at Marshall-University High School utilizing volunteer paraprofessionals.

Leonard, G. E. Vocational planning and career behavior: A report on the developmental career guidance project.

---

*These can be found in chapter 8 (alphabetically listed).

Special Career Guidance Procedures 65

Martin, A. M. A multimedia approach to communicating occupational information to non-college youth. Technical report.

Mawby, R. G. Adult educational programs and parents' roles in career plans of rural youth.

Peterson, N. D. A pilot project in vocational guidance, placement, and work experience for youth for whom existing work experiences are not appropriate.

School Districts of Cochise County. Pilot program (demonstration project) of an experimental method for providing occupational education to youth in small schools.

Washington Township Board of Education. Adventures in occupations.

Walker, R. W. What vocational education teachers should know about disadvantaged youth in rural areas.

Winborn, R. & Martinson, W. Innovation in guidance: A mobile counseling center.

Mexican-American Youth

WHO ARE MEXICAN-AMERICAN YOUTH?

Youths of Mexican descent comprise a special population for career guidance due to several reasons. Being of Mexican descent, they are subjected to the conditions of dual cultural influence and cultural shift, and as such, experience difficulty because of differences in language, status and tradition. Somora (1964) contends that people of Mexican descent are the slowest immigrant group to become assimilated into the majority culture.

The traditional culture of Mexican people, which provides the background for the cultural backbone of Mexican immigrants, and which is passed orally from generation to generation, is typified by strong family ties; the family is the focus of social identifications. Roles, both social and occupational, of male and female members of the family and the extended family are rigidly specified and followed (Burma 1944).

WHAT DOES RESEARCH SAY?

People of Mexican descent comprise the third largest minority group in the U. S. (Simpson 1958). A sizeable proportion of these have the status of a socio-economically disadvantaged group in the U. S.: Being unskilled in any trade or profession, they predominantly occupy positions as farm hands; they live in rural, underdeveloped areas and under poor physical and economic conditions. They represent one of the most disadvantaged minorities in our society (Rowan 1968). Current conditions and the cultural shift which brings with it both differences and uncertainty with regard to values probably account for Ulibarri's (1968) finding of personality disorganization among this group. Personality disorganization is expressed in the Mexican-American self-image, diffusion of values, alcoholism, vandalism and drug addiction. However, the population is young, the median age being twenty. Twenty-one percent of the population are teenagers. From the standpoint of guidance, this high proportion becomes of interest, especially if we consider some educational and occupational research findings.

Madsen (1964) relates that because of the status and role definition of women, male children are more likely to go to and complete school than girls. However, because American schools are so different in terms of goals and traditions, Mexican-American parents do not value so highly education in general for their children.

Since the average family is subjected to frequent moves due to seasonal work, the children's education is frequently interrupted. Educational research has shown that, on the average, Mexican-American students score lower than Caucasians on standardized intelligence tests. A number of studies using Stanford-Binet Intelligence Tests have shown the average IQ score of Mexican-American youth to be markedly below the mean, leading to an assumption that these children have poor scholastic ability (Hill 1936, Coers 1935, Cook 1955); however, as pointed out by Jensen (1961), differences in language, value systems and norms render such conclusions questionable and misleading. According to the 1960 U. S. Census, probably only 12 percent of the Spanish-speaking population in Texas, where one of the largest concentrations of this group exists, had graduated from high school (U. S. Department of H.E.W. 1966). The dropout rate among Mexican-American youth is high even compared with other minority groups (Wages 1969).

More along the occupational line, Kuvlesky (1969) found that Mexican-American youths maintained a much stronger intensity of desire for their educational-vocational goals than Negroes or Caucasians. But their goals were also lower than the other two groups. In the past, social scientists have not been greatly concerned with the occupational goals and achievements of Mexican-Americans in general. Recently, however, there are some indications regarding the occupational expectation of Mexican-American youths. Heller (1967) found that only 4 percent of high school seniors expected to be in unskilled or semi-skilled occupations, as compared to 42 percent among their fathers. Thirty-five percent aspired to professional positions while only 2 percent of their fathers

Special Career Guidance Procedures 67

held such positions. In spite of the finding that the overall aspiration level of Mexican-American youth is lower than Caucasians, Heller finds a trend among Mexican-American youth to have goals and values exceeding those of their fathers and approaching those of the majority of youth.

IMPLICATIONS FOR CAREER GUIDANCE

From a vocational guidance perspective, these research generalizations point out the needs of this special population.

1. Methods are needed that will point the way toward overcoming barriers of both culture and society.
2. Programs which are both remedial and instructive with regard to values and conditions of American society and the implications and consequences of dropping out would aid not only youths but also their parents.
3. It is imperative for counselors to recognize the uniqueness of this group and to initiate programs and research studies which would broaden our understanding of Mexican-American youths.

METHOD APPLICATIONS*

Bridgford, C. Teaching about minorities: an annotated bibliography on blacks, chicanos, and indians.

Franklin County Board of Education, Georgia. Operation DIRECT.

Gordon, J. E., et al. Role modeling and role playing in employability development agencies.

Hansen, L. S. Description of an emerging developmental career guidance program at Marshall-University High School utilizing volunteer paraprofessionals.

High School District A. Pilot project mobile vocational guidance services.

Lelevier, B., Jr. A portfolio of outstanding Americans of Mexican descent.

Leonard, G. E. Vocational planning and career behavior: A report on the developmental career guidance project.

Martin, A. M. A multimedia approach to communicating occupational information to non-college youth. Technical report.

Rivera, F. A Mexican American source book with study guideline.

Ulibarri, S. R. Learn, amigo, learn.

Zwielbelson, I. Guiding parents and motivating talented students who live in low-rent neighborhoods.

---

*These can be found in chapter 8 (alphabetically listed).

Women

WHO ARE WOMEN?

Recent attention given to the status of women in our society points out women have in various aspects of life and work, problems which justify the classification of women as a special population with regard to career guidance.

WHAT DOES RESEARCH SAY?

Status is one of the most important and encompassing of all realities in the life of women in America. In general, the status of the modern woman in our society is affected by both internal and external factors. External factors include the effect of a persistent stereotype in our society. This stereotype implies that women are in some respect inferior when compared to man. This belief is prevalent in both men and women (Fernberger 1948, Sheriffs and Jarrett 1953) and presents an obstacle for any woman who does not see herself as such or who attempts to break this barrier and achieve independence and identity. In addition, society has ignored women as individuals with the result that they have the social status of a minority group. As pointed out by Hacker (1951), women are subject to discrimination (e.g., in job availability and remuneration), there is a degree of social distance between them and the superior group (men) and they encounter the same problems and resistance in attempting to enter jobs as a minority group member.

Theoretically, women are given a choice of roles, such as homemaker, a career-woman or a combination of two. However, society emphasizes the intrinsic value of the homemaking role for women (Beilin and Werner 1957) and looks down on working women (Glenn 1959). This situation is precipitated by external, societal forces and standards and is transmitted through individual child-rearing attitudes and practices. In turn, it brings about an internal conflict within women; not only do women have a conflict of roles, a confusion with regard to their identity, and a dissatisfaction and frustration resulting from their inability to determine and control their own future, but the discontinuity which characterizes the life pattern of women, i.e., the existence of separate periods which are respectively devoted to education, premarital work, managing a family, and work after their children have grown, give women little chance to develop a consistent concept of themselves as individuals (Lewis 1968).

Occupationally, it should be pointed out that, in general, a woman's employment is not accepted by her husband as a substitute for household

Special Career Guidance Procedures

responsibility; so a working woman actually plays a dual role, and most women regard financial needs as their reason for working (Women's Bureau 1952). In addition, women face such drawbacks as reluctance of employers to hire them, although women's "quit rates" are more stable than men's over a period of time (Wells 1955). Career women, if they are working wives or working mothers, are subject to criticism from many sides.

In general, theories of career development, having been conceived and tested on the basis of research with male subjects, have not been found applicable to women. This shortcoming has contributed to the general neglect of theorists, researchers and counselors concerning the problems of career development of women. Recently, however, Kriger (1972) has completed a theoretical research study with results bearing direct counseling and theoretical implications for a new conceptualization of career development of women.

Studying the applicability of Roe's theory to women, Kriger found that women's career choice was significantly related to a woman's perception of her mother's child-rearing attitudes. Thus, homemakers perceived their mothers as having been relatively restrictive in their child-rearing attitudes; on the other hand, career women, whether they were employed in male-dominated or female-dominated occupations, perceived their mothers as having been relatively permissive in their child-rearing attitudes.

In the same study, Kriger (1972) also found highly significant differences in the level of achievement motivation among three groups of women. Homemakers were the least achievement motivated, career women in female-dominated occupations came second, and career women in male-dominated occupations were most achievement motivated.

The new conceptualization of career development of women suggested by the author implies that both girls and women should be encouraged to first choose between a homemaking role or a career role as a primary occupational choice. Only after this choice is made should they be encouraged to make a secondary occupational choice, i.e., choose a specific occupational field and level within that field. The first career choice is seen as a function of the child-rearing practices that the girl was subjected to as a child, whereas the secondary career choice is a function of a girl's level of achievement motivation.

IMPLICATIONS FOR CAREER GUIDANCE

In consideration of (1) the fact that 35 percent of all women in this country of working age are in the labor force at any given time, (2) the prediction that this figure will increase in the future (Women's Bureau

1963), and (3) the fact that nearly 40 percent of the entire work force in the U. S. is made up of women (U. S. Department of Labor, 1970), the implications for career guidance of women are threefold:

1. Guidance counselors are required to be aware of the physical, social-psychological and occupational meanings of being a woman in our society, so that they can better prepare their female clients to deal with these situations.

2. Guidance counselors, especially if they deal with young female clients, can use methods and programs specifically designed for the special needs of women; they can also assist them in facing and making decisions, e.g., vocational, marriage-career choices, etc., and in planning for the future. Planning for the future can be done in such a way that women will be able to overcome obstacles which presently block their potential advancement. Lewis (1968) cites the failure on the part of persons guiding girls to recognize some fundamental differences between the developmental patterns of males and females as hampering girls in their educational and vocational planning.

3. It is the responsibility of guidance counselors, among others, to affect social change and to work toward restoration of equality and individuality of women.

4. In view of the implication of a new conceptualization of the career development of women, guidance counselors could encourage clients to first make a primary career choice, i.e, decide between homemaking and a career; only then should they be encouraged to make a secondary career choice, i.e., a more specific decision concerning the occupational field, and level within that field, that they would like to pursue.

METHOD APPLICATIONS*

Berry, J. Counseling for women's roles in the 80's.
Berry, J. et al. Counseling girls and women—awareness analysis, action.
Epstein, C. F. Woman's place; options and limits in professional careers.
Fishman, J. R. et al. Training for new careers.
Hansen, L. S. Description of an emerging developmental career guidance program at Marshall-University High School utilizing volunteer paraprofessionals.
Hansen, L. S. A learning opportunities package.
Hedges, J. N. Future jobs for high school girls.

---

*These can be found in chapter 8 (alphabetically listed).

Special Career Guidance Procedures

Impellitteri, J. T. Exploration with a computer assisted occupational system.

Krumboltz, J. D. et al. Vocational problem-solving experiences for stimulating career exploration and interest, phase II. Final report.

Miller, C. H. A pilot project for vocational counseling in economically underdeveloped areas.

Osipow, S. H. and Alderfer, R. D. The effects of the vocationally oriented speech course on the vocational planning behavior of high school students.

Sullivan, H. J. The effects of selected film and counseling experiences on capable girls' attitudes toward college.

Terlin, R. Job finding techniques for mature women.

Vetter, L. and Sethney, B. Planning ahead for the world of work.

Yabroff, W. W. An experiment in teaching decision-making.

Handicapped Youth

WHO ARE THE HANDICAPPED?

As it is currently used, the term "handicapped" denotes the existence of a deficiency, without specifying its nature or location. However, writers in this area (Angel 1969, Arthur 1967) maintain that a handicap should be defined only in relation to the particular requirement of a specific task. Thus, among the general classification of handicapped persons are the mentally retarded, deaf, speech and hearing impaired, visually handicapped, seriously emotionally disturbed, crippled and multihandicapped and those with learning disabilities (U. S. Department of H.E.W. 1969). The diversity in the nature and degree of handicap underscores the need of this group for career guidance and justifies their classification as a special population. This section will limit its consideration to the physically handicapped, in order to avoid overlap with other special population groups that are treated elsewhere (e.g., slow learners, underachievers, etc.).

WHAT DOES RESEARCH SAY?

Disabled or handicapped persons were legally recognized by the 1943 Vocational Rehabilitation Law which provided states with funds for services for them. In 1954 an amendment to that law was issued which extended the range of services, facilities and provisions for disabled persons. In 1965 another milestone was reached when amendments were issued which provided for expanded programs and training opportunities for the disabled and for the preparation of professional personnel associated with this population (U.S. Department of H.E.W. 1969, Eshelman 1966, Roberts 1965).

These and subsequent legislations resulted in attempts to understand the problems of the handicapped and to aid them in overcoming their disability. The attempts to understand the problems presented and faced by the handicapped person have resulted in the recognition that problems are multidimensional. Thus, the person with a disability not only has a physical impairment which narrows the range of tasks that he can perform; he also frequently faces psychological problems stemming from the emotional impact of his disability, the fear of becoming dependent on others and lack of self-confidence. In addition, he faces the problem of negative social attitudes toward his disability, ostracism and a failure on the part of society to recognize his merits and his potential for making a contribution in some area of life (Angel 1969, Arthur 1967).

Attempts to aid the handicapped person in overcoming his disability have been made in several dimensions: (a) Provisions have been made by national, state and private agencies to supply medical, surgical, psychiatric and hospital care, and funding for ancillary services to reduce or remove the disability (Eshelman 1966). (b) Special workshops and similar settings have been established for training, retraining and employing the handicapped (Frank 1967; U. S. Department of Labor 1967, Stubbins and Hadley, 1967). Angel (1969) presents a thorough description and analysis of the problems and specific needs of persons with different handicaps, where they can find help, their employment and training possibilities and other helpful hints on how to secure a position. Jaffee, Day and Adams (1964) present an analysis of the disabled worker in the labor market at large, especially when the disability is inflicted after the person has been a part of the labor market. (c) Recently there has been a surge in the attention given to disability problems of children. In 1965, 20 percent of the persons rehabilitated by the state-federal rehabilitation programs were below the age of twenty (Eshelman 1966), which only mildly reflects the percentage of children among the total number of disabled persons in the U. S. With the establishment of private agencies for research and assistance to crippled, blind, and other handicapped children, more scientific knowledge is currently available about their special problems and needs, and it is this knowledge that is particularly relevant to the role of career guidance.

Bender and Silver (1948) and Cruickshank (1955) have pointed out that brain-injured children often develop an inadequate and frequently disturbed concept of body image. Disorders in perception, distractability

Special Career Guidance Procedures

and other psychological characteristics are also typical of this group (Cruickshank 1961). It is also recognized that handicapped children are subjected to negative attitudes by their peers and even their parents, which further reinforce their own lack of self-confidence.

More specific to the role of career guidance and the career guidance counselor are recent developments in the following three areas.

1. *Classification and identification of handicap.* Love (1967) discusses the background of identification techniques for exceptionalities in children and parental attitudes toward their handicapped children. Rappaport (1965) reports on considerations of differences in diagnosis of brain-damaged children.

2. *Innovations in educational programs which are specifically designed for children with different handicaps.* Cruickshank (1961) developed a special teaching method for brain-injured children. The Council for Exceptional Children (1969) presents abstracts of innovations in reading methods and teaching techniques for handicapped children. The Arkansas State Department of Education (1969) issues statements concerning the philosophy of special education classes, steps in setting up programs, and program standards for educational and vocational training in home economics.

3. *Counseling.* The Wichita Unified School District (1969) reports improvement in academic growth, skill areas and attitudes of children who were given psychological services and therapy as an adjunct to medical and educational programs at a diagnostic and resource center for special education. An important supportive service included in the program was parental counseling.

IMPLICATIONS FOR CAREER GUIDANCE

The information presented above has several implications for vocational guidance in general, and the vocational guidance counselor in particular.

1. The availability of workshops is encouraging in that it provides the vocational counselor with a setting where the severely handicapped can be placed. On the other hand, recent developments in educational programs specifically designed for the handicapped, and the utility of counseling for this population underscores the more active role a counselor can play in maximizing the vocational productivity of the handicapped child and fostering the development of his potentials.

2. In addition to educational and personal counseling of the child, the counselor can aid in counseling his parents, so that the social and family environment of the child is ameliorated. Hewett (1970) has recently described the problems and anxieties of everyday family life with handicapped children.

3. An area which appears to be overlooked in both past and recent research on the handicapped is vocational development and career guidance. Kinnane and Suziedelis (1966) found handicapped adults and young adults to have different work values and the latter to be affected by interpersonal concerns. The authors emphasize the need for further study and attention to providing handicapped workers with a clearer understanding of the satisfaction they seek from work to make occupational choice more in line with values. The importance of vocational guidance with handicapped children can not be overemphasized. If the handicapped child is to become a productive member of society, it is necessary to understand his needs and problems, devise methods of teaching him to overcome these, and direct him to an occupation which suits his needs and makes the best of his potential.

METHOD APPLICATIONS*

Garrison, T. G. Vocational guidance manual for counselors, teachers, and educators.

Harkness Center. Multi-occupations at Harkness Center. Progress report #1.

Manus, G. I. and Manus, M. Educational and vocational guidance for the handicapped student.

Martin, A. M. A multimedia approach to communicating occupational information to non-college youth. Technical report.

Rothstein, H. J. Problems and issues in the counseling of the disabled disadvantaged patient.

Schauble, P. G. Emotional simulation in personal counseling, etc., speech presented at A.P.G.A.

Truax, C. B. The use of supportive personnel in rehabilitation counseling: Process and outcome—Arkansas Rehabilitation Research and Training Center.

---

*These can be found in chapter 8 (alphabetically listed).

Chapter 4 TYPES OF CAREER GUIDANCE METHODS

This section provides a basis for the understanding and selection of various types of vocational guidance methods, presented by method types. A method is a procedure or technique which is used by one individual (e.g., teacher or counselor) to facilitate the learning or behavior change of another. The authors have grouped the methods according to shared characteristics so that the general nature of the learning process involved may be better understood. Eight basic career guidance method types are discussed in this chapter: (a) behavioral approaches, (b) computer-assisted counseling, (c) educational media, (d) group procedures, (e) information systems, (f) simulation gaming, (g) vocationally relevant curriculum, and (h) work-experience programs.

Under each type are presented (a) definition of the method type, (b) a description of the characteristics of the method type, (c) specific types of methods included in the type, and (d) implications of this information for career guidance. This information is presented so that the user may better understand the nature of the learning process involved with various educational methods, the ways in which these methods might be applied to the area of career guidance and the direct relevance which these methods have for specific program needs.

Factors Affecting the Selection of Methods

There are a number of educational methods which are available for use in career guidance programs. Recently, there have been many new applications of these methods to the field. Both counselors and teachers may well have heard about these applications, and be interested in evaluating the appropriateness of such methods for their own career guidance program. When utilizing these methods, the following factors need to be considered.

Learning Objectives. Before deciding on any one specific career guidance method, it is first necessary to specify the objectives which one hopes to meet through the application of the method. Career guidance programs are designed to facilitate the vocational development of individual students. Therefore, it is important to state exactly which behaviors are to be learned. Once these have been described, they provide criteria for the selection of methods.

Learning Potential of the Method. Once learning objectives have been developed, it is possible to examine methods in terms of their potential for facilitating the type of learning which is desired. The development of educational methods is usually based on specific learning principles. Each method is effective in facilitating some types of learning; however, not all methods are equally effective for all types of learning with all students. It is important to study the research on the effectiveness of methods in order to select the most appropriate methods for any given learning objective. This section attempts to provide this type of information.

Relative Advantage Compared to Other Methods. Research indicates that often several methods are equally effective in facilitating specific types of learning; therefore, when selecting a method, it is not always necessary or possible to select the one most appropriate method. Often it will be possible to find two or more methods which will be equally effective. Once the number of available methods has been narrowed, other criteria can be applied.

Combination of Methods. An interesting research finding is that often a combination of methods is more effective than any one method used individually. The important consideration here is that the methods be compatible and enhance one another. When designing career guidance procedures, it is important to consider ways in which methods might be combined to increase motivation and learning effectiveness.

Types of Career Guidance Methods 77

Available Expertise. Once objectives have been stated and a limited number of appropriate methods have been identified, still other things must be considered in order to make the final selection of methods. These include a number of feasibility issues. First, it is important to select a method which can be used by the available staff. This means that, all other factors being equal, a method should be selected either because someone on the existing staff has the expertise needed to use the method or because other resource people are readily available.

Available Resources. In addition to staffing, other resource considerations are important in the selection of a method. Educational methods require specific facilities and equipment which are often quite costly. One possible rule for selecting a method is that, if the facilities are already available and the method is as effective as others, then the method should be selected. For example, if television equipment is available, then this method of disseminating information would be selected over other possibilities. If no appropriate facilities are available, then another principle to follow is to select methods which have multiple uses.

Compatibility with Existing Program. Change is often difficult to initiate and maintain. This is because a change in one part of a program may require subsequent changes in other parts of the program. When selecting a method, it is important to consider the impact of the acceptance of that method on other parts of the career guidance program. In general, it is preferable to select those methods which are most compatible with the existing program either because less change is needed or because those changes which are required have a favorable impact on the program.

Method Type: Behavioral Techniques

DEFINITION

Krumboltz (1968) has offered the following definition of counseling:

> Counseling consists of whatever ethical activities a counselor undertakes in an effort to help the client engage in those types of behavior which will lead to the resolution of the client's problem. (p. 120)

This definition is basic to behavioral counseling which utilizes a number of behavioral techniques, employed by the counselor and others, to help change the client's behavior. These behavior modification techniques include a number of principles related to the field of learning, but emphasize the specific objectives of clinical treatment and behavior change (Ullmann and Krasner 1965).

CHARACTERISTICS

Behavioral counseling is based on the premise that behavior is learned. Hosford (1969) suggests that behavior results from the interaction of an individual with his environment. The specific types of behaviors which an individual develops are a result of the frequency and types of reinforcements received in other similar situations. Maladaptive behavior is learned in much the same way that other behavior is learned. Central to behavioral counseling is the concern with observable behavior rather than inferences about the internal state of the client. Franks and Susskind (1968) state that behavior is the result of the impact of stimuli on the individual rather than of psychodynamic processes within the individual.

The need for counseling arises when the client desires to modify existing behavior which is maladaptive, or to develop new behaviors. Ivey (1969) describes the goal of behavioral counseling as giving individuals a maximum choice of alternatives for their own behavior. In order to insure this goal, the client must be provided with effective ways of learning new behaviors. Osipow and Walsh (1970a) indicate that the goal is "the development of some skill which will enable the client to be more effective or the elimination of some undesirable response sequence" (p. 6).

Basic to behavioral counseling is the definition of roles for the client and the counselor. The role of the client is to determine the goals of counseling. That is, it is his responsibility to specify the new types of behavior he wants to learn. The role of the counselor is to use his skills to meet the client's goals (Woody 1968).

The counselor takes an experimental stance. The goals of counseling, which have been stated by the client, become the desired outcomes of counseling. The success of counseling depends on the extent to which these outcomes have materialized. Evaluation of these outcomes is possible because they have been stated in terms of specific behaviors. This evaluation process provides a basis for the counselor to assess the effectiveness of specific counseling procedures for producing specific behavioral outcomes (Krumboltz and Thoresen 1969). Behavioral counseling then allows the application of a number of types of behavioral techniques. These methods are based on research in the field of learning.

SPECIFIC BEHAVIORAL TECHNIQUES

A number of behavioral techniques have been developed; however, most of them belong to three broad categories: (a) reinforcement, (b) social modeling, and (c) counterconditioning.

Reinforcement. Reinforcement techniques are based on the premise that, if a behavior is followed by a rewarding response from the environment, the probability that the behavior will occur again is increased (Skinner 1953). Also basic to this approach is the distinction between primary reinforcers (e.g., food) which have great impact on early childhood behavior, and secondary reinforcers (e.g., praise, money or grades) which have a greater impact as the individual matures (Hosford 1969).

Reinforcement techniques usually make use of secondary reinforcers to promote learning of the desired behavior. Use of these techniques require the selection of specific reinforcers which will be effective in producing a specific behavior with a particular client. These techniques are most effective for strengthening behaviors which are already familiar to the client.

Krumboltz and Thoresen (1969) provide some basic considerations which govern the selection of reinforcers: (a) Not all reinforcers have the same meaning to all people. (b) Reinforcers can lose their effectiveness with use. (c) Reinforcers often must come from individuals other than the counselor.

Social Modeling. "Social modeling involves the use of real or symbolic models who demonstrate the desired behavior that a client wishes to acquire" (Hosford 1969, p. 12). The individual learns the behavior by viewing another person performing the behavior rather than through direct experience. This approach is basically one of learning by imitation. It is most effective when the client is learning new, complex patterns of behavior.

The basic types of modeling include the use of either live models or symbolic models. Live models are real people who exhibit the desired behavior. When using these, problems can arise because it is difficult to predict the exact nature of the behavior which the model will exhibit and because the behavior of the model may be influenced by the response of the client (Krumboltz and Thoresen 1969). When selecting live models, it is important to consider the characteristics of the model. Research indicates it is most effective to select (a) models of the same sex as the client, (b) models whom the client perceives as being of high status, (c) peers as they have high social power for the client, and (d) models who are similar to the client (Hosford 1969).

Symbolic models are models which have been developed through recordings, films, video-tapes, etc. These models allow for greater control than live models; they can be made appropriate for specific clients, can be void of negative characteristics and can be used both at any time or any number of times.

Counterconditioning. Counterconditioning methods are sometimes used when the goal of counseling is to learn appropriate behavior in response to anxiety-producing situations. Woody (1968) describes this method as one in which "a hierarchy of fear-producing situations is developed. Then gradually, through imaginary or actual experiencing of the threatening situations, the person becomes desensitized to it" (p. 99). The basis of this approach is encouraging the client to respond to the anxiety-producing stimulus in a non-anxious way, i.e., by relaxing, thus weakening the bond between the anxiety and the eliciting stimuli (Hosford 1969).

IMPLICATIONS FOR CAREER GUIDANCE

1. Behavioral counseling assumes that behavior is learned through the interaction of the individual with his environment. This generalization would apply to vocational behavior; therefore, vocational behavior can be facilitated by the application of learning principles to vocational counseling activities.

2. Behavioral counseling stresses the importance of evaluating the effectiveness of counseling procedures in terms of client behavior. Therefore, effective vocational counseling is that counseling which successfully produces those vocationally relevant behaviors which the client has specified, e.g., information seeking, specific job skills, or decision making.

3. One behavioral approach is the use of reinforcement, in which the desired behavior is rewarded. This technique can be used in vocational counseling when the desired behavior is already familiar to the client, e.g., seeking occupational information.

4. Modeling is a behavioral approach in which learning occurs through imitation of the behavior of another, as in interviewing people from various occupations. This technique actually is used rather extensively in career guidance whether it be in the form of career days, visits to various occupational settings, or interviews with members of occupational groups. A study of the theory and research related to modeling can help to develop sound principles for the development of such career guidance procedures. This technique is most appropriate for learning new complex behaviors.

5. A final behavioral technique is counterconditioning which is helpful in reducing anxiety. Although this method does not have as much

Types of Career Guidance Methods

potential as reinforcement and modeling for use in career guidance, it might be used to reduce anxiety related to certain vocational behaviors, e.g., job interviews.

METHOD APPLICATIONS*

Bank, I. M. Children explore careerland through vocational role-models.

Baron, R. M. et al. The role of social reinforcement parameters in improving trainee task performance and self-image.

Bertcher, H. et al. Role modeling and role playing: a manual for vocational development and employment agencies.

Council for Exceptional Children. Behavior modification and related procedures.

Gordon, J. E. et al. Role modeling and role playing in employability development agencies.

Hamilton, J. A. Video group social models, group stimulus materials and client characteristics in vocational counseling.

Krumboltz, J. D. et al. Nonverbal factors in the effectiveness of models in counseling.

Krumboltz, J. D. and Schroeder, W. W. Promoting career planning through reinforcement.

Krumboltz, J. D. et al. A study to determine how counseling procedures can be used to help students make decisions and plans more effectively.

Paniagua, L. and Jackson, V. C. Role play in new career training.

Rose, S. D. A behavioral approach to group treatment of children.

Schauble, P. G. Emotional simulation in personal counseling.

Snellgrove, C. E. The effects of counselor reinforcement on a student's negative responses.

Summers, R. Methods and techniques for improving the educational aspirational level of senior high school students.

Thoresen, C. E. et al. Behavioral school counseling: A demonstration of the Stanford career planning project.

Woody, R. H. Vocational counseling with behavioral techniques.

Method Type: Computer-Assisted Guidance

DEFINITION

Computer-assisted guidance is an application of the computer to guidance, which is closely related to computer-assisted instruction.

---

*These can be found in chapter 8 (alphabetically listed).

Impellitteri (1967) describes computer-assisted instruction as: "An individualized instruction whereby a computer by means of some student-subject matter interface equipment elicits student responses to questions it presents, processes those responses, and based upon some decisions model proceeds to other materials in the programmed sequence" (p. 2). This process allows greater individualization of learning because the computer is capable of auditing student responses and presenting the most appropriate materials for that student's particular level of learning (Tiedeman 1969).

CHARACTERISTICS

Individualization of instruction and counseling is an educational goal which is difficult to obtain because it demands that large amounts of information be processed. This includes information which is related to the nature of the learner and his progress, and to the subject matter which is being learned (Cooley 1968). This individualization process is central to guidance. A major goal of counseling is to help students to process information related to life decisions.

Roberts (1967) suggests that implementation of this goal is difficult because (a) There are large amounts of data involved. (b) Students spend limited time with counselors. (c) The decision-making process is not clearly understood. (d) The role of the counselor in this process is not clear. (e) There are a limited number of trained counselors. He concludes that: "It would appear that modern computer technology with direct accessing could offer relief with respect to the general problem of storing and accessing the rather prodigious quantity and types of data required in making 'intelligent' social decisions" (p. 2).

Computer-assisted instruction is designed to comply with some of the basic conditions required for effective learning. Hansen (1968) summarizes these necessary learning conditions: (a) The attention of the student is focused on the learning task because he is in dialogue with the computer and learning proceeds at an appropriate pace for him. (b) The materials presented are appropriate for the level of learning of the individual student because the computer can allow for individual selection of content. (c) The student receives immediate feedback about the appropriateness of his responses. (d) Periodic review of learning which focuses on individual student needs is possible. (e) On-going evaluation of learning can be built into the system.

A review of the research on computer-assisted instruction indicates that this method (a) is as effective as other instructional methods, (b) can adjust to individual student differences with regard to learning

Types of Career Guidance Methods

sequence, depth and mode of materials, and rate of progress, (c) can record and manipulate a wide variety of learning data about the student during instruction, and (d) can integrate and control a wide variety of audio-visual aids in learning. Research also indicates that through time sharing, a large number of students can use the system simultaneously, a broad range of learning areas can be programmed, and students seem to react positively to this form of learning (Bundy 1968).

Suppes (1967) indicates that in addition to the advantage of being able to individualize instruction through the use of the computer, this method provides other educational benefits. First, it can enable educational personnel to perform more meaningful roles because the amount of time used for record keeping and the teaching of standard skills is reduced. Secondly, data about styles of learning can be collected which can facilitate a clearer understanding of the nature of the learning process.

SPECIFIC COMPUTER-ASSISTED GUIDANCE SYSTEMS

There are many applications of computers to the field of guidance. Although these various computer systems are quite different, it is possible to classify them according to three types: (a) information-processing systems, (b) tutorial systems, and (c) dialogue systems.

Information-Processing Systems. Although all computer systems are based on information processing, there are some systems which serve *only* this function. These systems process information which is then disseminated to the student by the counselor (Loughary 1968, 1970). Veldman and Menaker (1968) describe three types of information processing systems: (a) test-report generation systems which score tests and produce profiles of scores across a number of scales, (b) verbal data systems which are capable of interpreting the content of sentence completion instruments, story-telling tasks or interviews, and (c) statistical prediction systems which analyze multivariate data which provide a basis for the prediction of outcomes of individual decisions. In addition to information about individuals, these systems can process information about the environment such as educational and occupational information.

Tutorial Systems. These systems are used by students. They are "designed to go beyond information processing, and replace counselors in performing different tasks" (Loughary 1970, p. 185). Zinn (1970) suggests that in these systems the "system developer," who designs the tutorial system, defines objectives, describes subject matter in considerable detail, and provides drills which facilitate learning. These systems can be compared to the interaction of a student with a tutor (Suppes 1968). The systems are designed to provide instruction in predetermined areas, but the mode of instruction can be varied according to the needs of the individual student.

The primary function of these systems in guidance is to facilitate decision making through the dissemination of relevant information about self and environment. Veldman and Menaker (1968) suggest that: "The computer program is written to include a fund of knowledge about various options open to the client, and is also designed to question him about his preferences, abilities, etc., with regard to the available options" (p. 171). These systems, therefore, perform the simple information-gathering and disseminating tasks which are usually performed by the counselor.

Dialogue Systems. It is important to note that dialogue systems are really a goal for the future and do not currently exist. Such systems would be designed so that the nature of the interaction between the computer and the student could be similar to that which typically exists between the student and the counselor. There would be several characteristics of such a system. First, it would allow the student to speak and would be able to recognize and respond to these spoken comments (Suppes 1968). Secondly, the system would not require a standardized mode of response from the client; rather it would be able to comprehend various types of responses and would question, clarify and interpret these responses. It would elicit information from the client and utilize it in the interaction (Veldman and Menaker 1968).

Another characteristic of such a system is that it would be highly personalized. Loughary (1970) suggests that: "The system would offer personal decision-making and planning assistance to an individual over a considerable period of time" (p. 191). It would also allow the individual to try out decisions in simulated situations, thus evaluating possible outcomes prior to acting in real life situations (Loughary 1970, Zinn 1970).

Although these systems will not exist for some time, they do provide criteria for the development of all systems. The goal of system development should be to have the system as sensitive to individual needs as the current technology allows.

IMPLICATIONS FOR CAREER GUIDANCE

1. For students to make sound vocational and educational decisions, it is important to have relevant information about self, and about educational and occupational possibilities. This means that large amounts of information must be collected, stored and made available upon demand. The computer can be an effective tool for storing and manipulating this information.

Types of Career Guidance Methods

2. Although the decision-making process may be similar for all students, the actual vocational and educational decisions made are highly individual. Therefore, different students require quite different types of information. Computer-assisted guidance is designed to allow for individualized instruction. That is, the student can specify his exact information needs and receive only relevant information.

3. Typically, the information dissemination function consumes a large amount of counselor time. Once the information has been disseminated, the counselor has little time to help the student utilize the information in vocational decision making. In computer-assisted guidance, the information dissemination function is performed by the computer, thus freeing the counselor for other counseling activities.

4. In some computer guidance systems, the student is also provided assistance in the decision-making process. He is given a structure for making decisions, encouraged to consider various alternatives, and given feedback on the probable outcomes of various decisions. When used in this way, the computer is actually giving instruction in decision making.

5. It is important to realize that computer-assisted guidance systems are now in the developmental stages. Such systems are being used by only a few students on an experimental basis. However, they do hold promise as a career guidance method and, therefore, school systems should keep informed about recent developments and consider ways of implementing such systems in the future.

METHOD APPLICATIONS*

Bailey, L. J. (ed.) Facilitating career development: an annotated bibliography.

Bartlesville Public Schools. Readings in computer based guidance.

Baruch, R. Computer assisted systems in guidance and education.

Bohn, M. J. et al. The education and career exploration system.

Brown, J. A. and MacDougall, M. A. Computerized simulated games: a socialization tool for child guidance.

Cogswell, J. F. et al. The design of a man-machine counseling system.

Cogswell, J. F. and Estavan, D. P. Explorations in computer assisted counseling.

Cogswell, J. F. et al. Exploratory study of information—processing, procedures and computer based technology in vocational counseling. Final report.

Friesen, D. D. The validation of an automated counseling system.

Friesen, J. D. Computer based systems in guidance and counseling.

Hallworth, H. J. et al. A computer assisted vocational counseling system.

---

*These can be found in chapter 8 (alphabetically listed).

Hansen, L. S. et al. Career guidance practices in school and community.

Harris, J. Computerized vocational information system project.

Harvard University. Annual report. Information system for vocational decisions.

Helm, C. Computer simulation techniques for research on guidance problems.

Impellitteri, J. T. The computer as an aid to instruction and guidance in the school.

Impellitteri, J. T. The development and evaluation of a pilot computer assisted occupational guidance program. Final report.

Impellitteri, J. T. Exploration with a computer assisted occupational information system.

Interactive computer system will help students make career decisions.

Johnson, D. and Burham, R. Computer based guidance system.

Kellogg, F. Computer-based job matching systems: An exploration of the state of the art and the proposed nationwide matching system.

Loughary, J. W. and Tondow, M. Computers as substitute counselors: Some possibilities.

Loughary, J. W. Man-machine systems in education.

Myers, R. A., Lindeman, R. H., Forrest, D. J., and Super, D. E. Preliminary report: Assessment of the first year of use of the educational and career exploration system in secondary schools of Genessee County, Michigan.

National Vocational Guidance Association, Commission on Computer-Assisted Guidance Systems.

Roberts, T. L. and Frederick, F. J. Computer assisted counseling. Progress report number 1.

Roberts, T. L. et al. Software documentation for the Bartlesville Public Schools: Part one.

Roman, R. A. Implementation of a career decision game on a time shared computer: an exploration of its value in a simulated guidance environment.

Smith, T. W. Development of a research-based and computer-assisted guidance system.

Super, D. E. Using computers in guidance: An experiment in a secondary school.

Thompson, A. S. et al. The educational and career exploration system: field trial and evaluation in Montclair High School.

Tiedeman, D. V. Economic, educational, and personal implications of implementing computerized guidance information systems.

Tiedeman, D. (Ed.) Eighth invitational conference on systems under construction for career education and development, report of proceedings.

Tiedeman, D. V. et al. An information system for vocational decisions. Sixth quarterly report.

Weiss, D. J. Computer-assisted synthesis of psychometric data in vocational counseling.

Willowbrook High School. A report on project CVIS (computerized vocational information system).

Youst, D. B. The Rochester career guidance project.

Method Type: Educational Media

DEFINITION

A medium is any device or equipment which is used to transmit information between two people. Rossi and Biddle (1966) indicate that "It is the use to which the device is put which makes it a medium" (p. 3). For example, a television set is a medium only when it is used to transmit information between a sender and a receiver. Media may consist of a single device or may be comprised of a combination of devices. Media become educational media when they are used by one person to influence the learning of another. Gagne (1965) states this another way when he suggests that instructional media "refer to the various kinds of components of the learning environment that generate stimulation to the learner" (p. 271).

CHARACTERISTICS

There are a variety of educational media, including written materials, films, tape recordings, television and programmed instructional materials. A considerable amount of research has been conducted on the effectiveness of each. It is possible to generalize that each of these media can be used effectively to influence learning. Chu and Schramm (1968) indicate that two major questions concerning the use of any medium are: Is it appropriate? How can it be used effectively? They further suggest that educational media are most effective when (a) they are an integral part of the instructional program, (b) the media developer and the teacher work together, (c) they are carefully introduced to the system, and (d) they are applied to a large enough educational problem to justify the effort.

Although media differ, there are some general characteristics which all media share, one being that communication through the use of media is typically one-way communication (Havelock 1969). This means that the message comes from the sender via the medium and the receiver has little or no opportunity to either alter the nature of the message or to provide feedback to the sender. His only choices are to receive the message or to ignore it. Therefore, it is essential that the message is appropriate for the specific needs of the receiver.

Media can be classified according to several dimensions. Rossi and Biddle (1966) describe these general characteristics as: (a) whether or not literacy is required to use the medium, (b) which sense modality is used, i.e., hearing and/or seeing, (c) whether it is static (e.g., slides) or dynamic (e.g., films), (d) the extent to which the medium is controlled by the sender and the receiver, (e) whether it is used by a group or an individual, (f) the amount of cost per user, and (g) the mechanical techniques employed. These characteristics can provide a basis for evaluating the effectiveness of any medium for a given educational use with a given user group.

The acceptance of educational media will be influenced not only by the appropriateness of their use for a specific educational goal, but also by other factors within the school system. It is quite possible that several media will be equally effective so other criteria for selection might include (a) cost, (b) the extent to which it has multiple use, (c) the extent to which school staff can understand and control it, (d) the extent to which it supports rather than displaces existing practices, and (e) the nature of student response to the medium.

It may be that selection of one medium over another is not always the goal. Havelock (1969) stresses the idea that, "generally a combination of media is more effective than any one used singly if the characteristics of the selected media complement one another" (ch. 9, p. 3).

SPECIFIC TYPES OF MEDIA

Although there are many varieties of educational media, the authors are only describing four major types: (a) written materials, (b) audio media, (c) audio-visual media, and (d) programmed instructional materials.

Written Materials. Written materials are probably the most commonly used medium. Gagne (1965) states that: "Assuming that the student possesses the necessary prerequisite knowledge, instruction by means of a book is usually a remarkably rapid and efficient process" (p. 276). However, there are some major problems with this medium. First,

Types of Career Guidance Methods

the user may not be able to use the written materials either because he cannot read or because he is not motivated to do so. Research indicates that written materials are most often used by people of high educational achievement and high socio-economic status (Schramm 1962). Basically, written materials are quite useful for disseminating information but they are not as successful in arousing interest (Havelock 1969).

Audio Media. These media include radio and recordings. They allow for wide dissemination of information, do not require literacy and can be used effectively to stimulate interest in the message. A comparison needs to be made between these media and audio-visual media. Audio media have the advantage of being less expensive. Chu and Schramm (1968) say "The effects of visual images upon learning do not seem to be uniformly beneficial" (p. 166). If the learning task is manual or deals with concepts which are not familiar to the learner, then visual images are helpful. Otherwise, media such as recordings and radio may be equally effective.

Audio-Visual Media. These media include films and television and therefore are dynamic. Gagne (1965) indicates that: "Each can display events, rather than simply objects, and also sequences of events" (p. 280). Another characteristic of these media is that they provide continuity of action. If action is important to the learning task, then these media are more effective than still, visual media, i.e., slides (Chu and Schramm 1968). There seems to be no difference in the effectiveness of films and television. The advantages of one over the other depend on such factors as cost and ease of use. Television tends to cost more, but it is more flexible because it allows for revision of the message. Also, it can be adapted to enable two-way communication between the user and the sender.

Programmed Instructional Materials. Programmed instructional materials can use any one or combination of the educational media previously described. Programmed instruction refers to the way in which media are used. These materials are self-instructional and have the following characteristics: (a) They involve small sequential learning steps. (b) The learner actively responds to the message. (c) The learner can move at his own pace. (d) Feedback is provided on the accuracy of the learner's response. (e) Correct responses are reinforced. (f) A record of student responses is recorded for future use by the student or the teacher (Trow 1963). Research indicates that programmed instruction is a very effective learning technique. The principles underlying this method can provide a basis for the effective use of educational media.

IMPLICATIONS FOR CAREER GUIDANCE

1. Information dissemination is an important career guidance activity. Educational media are designed to transmit effectively information to the learner, thus facilitating the learning process; therefore, it is possible to use media, rather than the counselor, to disseminate information.

2. It is important to remember that media do not allow user feedback and clarification as readily as human interaction. If media are used, it is important to either build in this two-way flow of information or to allow for follow-up by guidance personnel.

3. Educational media have different characteristics. Which medium is used must be determined by an analysis of the nature of the information to be communicated and the nature of the user.

4. Written materials are most often used to communicate occupational information. However, this may be quite inappropriate since it requires that the user be literate. Of all educational media written materials are the least motivating.

5. Media which are either audio and/or visual, e.g., tape recordings, radio, television and films, are more effective in increasing student motivation for use. Media which are only audio are effective if the material presented is familiar to the student. However, if the information is new, media which are both audio and visual are preferable. Since students are seldom familiar with the nature of various occupations, audio-visual media might be more appropriate for communicating occupational information.

6. Usually a combination of media is more effective than any one medium used separately. This indicates that methods of communicating occupational and educational information might combine various media, i.e., written materials in conjunction with visual materials.

METHOD APPLICATIONS*

Atlanta Board of Education. Formulation of models for preparing occupational materials for pupils from various socioeconomic levels in grades three through eight.

Bancroft, J. and Lawson, W. H. Project NOTIFY — needed occupational television instruction for youth.

Beachley, C. Careers via closed circuit television.

Birnbaum, R. Influencing college attendance plans.

---

*These can be found in chapter 8 (alphabetically listed).

Types of Career Guidance Methods

Briggs, L. J. and Norris, E. L. Techniques for selection and presenting occupational information to high school students.

Drews, E. M. The effectiveness of special training with audio-visuals in changing aspirations in intellectually superior students.

Drier, H. N. and Jepsen, D. A. The use of television and video tape compared to researching printed career information as a means of assisting rural 9th grade youth career decision making process.

Ewing, T. N. and Gilbert, W. M. An investigation of the importance of the personal relationship and associated factors in teaching machine procedures.

Ganschow, L. H. et al. Stimulating educational information-seeking and changes in student attitude toward vocational education by videotape and film presentations.

Goodson, S. Occupational information materials in selected elementary and middle schools.

Guidance Associates. Guidance Catalogue. Volume 11.

Kagan, N. Multimedia in guidance and counseling.

Laramore, D. Jobs on film.

Martin, A. M. A multimedia approach to communicating occupational information to noncollege youth. Interim technical report.

Martin, A. M. A multimedia approach to communicating occupational information to noncollege youth. Technical report.

McDaniels, C. How to develop better career films.

Minneapolis Public Schools. World of work: Grade nine.

Muro, J. J. Evaluation of a comprehensive guidance and counseling service for rural Maine communities.

National Institutes of Health. Graduate, then what — jobs in health. A report on the use of radio as a recruitment tool for the health occupations.

Ryan, C. W. and Whitman, R. A. Video aides in school counseling — some practical innovations.

San Diego Unified School District. Supplementary educational — instructional television educational experience development and distribution.

Stogdill, R. M. and Bailey, W. R. Changing response of vocational students to supervision: the use of motion pictures and group discussions.

Sullivan, H. J. The effects of selected film and counseling experiences on capable girls' attitudes toward college.

Tonkin, W. J. Vocational guidance through videotaping and television.

Walsh, G. A. A study of new and dramatic approaches to vocational guidance through the use of exhibits and displays.

Wilmington Public Schools. Closed circuit TV — a tool for guidance.

Method Type: Group Procedures

DEFINITION

Group procedures encompass a large number of situations in which a leader, i.e., teacher or counselor, interacts with more than one student. Group procedures range from large classroom instruction to small-group therapy sessions. Goldman (1962) suggests that group procedures may be classified along two dimensions: content and process. Content relates to the nature of the information being dealt with in the group, i.e., subject matter, school-related information or non-school-related information. Process refers to the nature of the interaction between the group leader and the group members, i.e., leader-controlled, group controlled, or leader and group members in cooperation with one another.

Another dimension, suggested by Cox and Herr (1968), is the technique or method used by the leader. Although group procedures vary considerably, it is possible to analyze each group procedure in terms of the content, process and technique involved.

CHARACTERISTICS

Group procedures include procedures which are used with groups of students rather than individuals. Therefore, group dynamics are central to understanding the nature of these group procedures. A group consists of a number of members who are, "aware of their dependence on each other to accomplish a goal and accept their responsibility to each other in the process" (Lifton 1967, p. 25). Groups can be described in terms of a number of characteristics including: (a) size of the group, (b) the nature of the group leadership, (c) goals or reasons for the group existing, and (d) norms or acceptable modes of member behavior.

Because a group is a combination of individuals who share goals and norms of behavior, it provides certain learning conditions. Demsch (1968) describes some generalizations about the nature of learning in groups: (a) The group allows members to learn about interpersonal relationships. (b) The leader acts as a role model for the members. (c) The group can support behavior change in individual members. (d) The group provides a reality situation in which members can experiment with new behaviors. (e) Group members can help each other to perceive reality more accurately. (f) The group allows members to make positive contributions to others.

Combs et al. (1963) describes the advantages of group counseling, which can be generalized to several types of group procedures: (a) It

Types of Career Guidance Methods

spreads the effect of the counselor to a number of students. (b) It is less threatening to students since it involves other members of their peer group. (c) It utilizes the social setting and peer identification in learning. (d) The counselor provides a role model. (e) Group procedures often encourage the student to seek individual assistance.

There are a number of considerations which are important in planning and designing group procedures. These have been summarized by a number of writers (Dye 1968, Combs et al. 1963, Cohn 1967). The first consideration relates to the selection of group members. Typically, students are selected for a group because they have common interests and concerns. Stated another way, they have shared learning goals. Beyond this consideration, it is difficult to generalize about other criteria for the selection of members. Research does not indicate whether heterogeneous or homogeneous grouping is most effective. Frequently group members are selected because they are similar in age, grade level and/or developmental level. Another consideration in the selection of members is whether or not participation is voluntary or involuntary. Either is possible, but which stance is taken will have a subsequent impact on the nature of the group interaction. A final consideration is the size of the group. The number of members to be selected for the group will depend on the goals of the group and on the nature of the group procedures which will be used (Dye 1968).

Once the group members have been selected and the group has been formed, a number of other considerations arise. These include: (a) What physical setting is needed for group meetings? (b) How long will group meetings last? (c) Exactly what group procedures will be used? (d) What leadership style will be used? and (e) How long will the group continue to exist? (Combs et al. 1963). Although these questions must be answered, it is quite possible that the group itself will be actively involved in making these decisions.

TYPES OF GROUP PROCEDURES

There are a variety of techniques which can be used with groups. Many educational methods can be applied; however, there are four major types of group situations which are commonly used in education and have direct relevance to career guidance. These include: (a) large group instruction, (b) group guidance, (c) group counseling, and (d) group therapy.

Large Group Instruction. Large group instruction is frequently used in education. It can be particularly useful for disseminating information. Shaw and Wurstein (1965) indicate that this method also can employ various educational media in the communication of information, thus freeing counselor time. If the goal of the group is to communicate information to large groups of students, this method is very appropriate. As Cox and Herr (1968) indicate: "To repeat this information over and over again in individual sessions is gross ineconomy" (p. 12). It is important to realize, however, that large group procedures do not allow for group interaction or for individual group members to clarify the information by questioning the leader.

Group Guidance. Group guidance is distinguished from large group instruction in that it involves a small group of students and provides the opportunity for interaction among the group members. Usually group guidance is instructional or informative in nature.

> The group approach is utilized because several students share a common need for information which the counselor can provide. The content is typically school or career-related. During an initial phase, the counselor and/or members of the group present information. This may be followed by a period of discussion and exchange of ideas, reactions, and attitudes which are primarily intellectual. (Dye 1968, p. 4)

Vocational decision-making requires the consideration of information about both self and environment. Cox and Herr (1968) suggest that while large group instruction may be effective for communicating information about the environment, the group guidance situation is more effective for communicating information about self. They suggest that: "If the small group is the proper size, each member will be able to be heard as often as his needs require. If the counselor is disseminating information, he can find out at any time whether his information is being received and correctly interpreted" (p. 16).

Group Counseling. Group counseling has been defined by Mahler (1969) as:

> The process of using group interaction to facilitate deeper self-understanding and self-acceptance. The concerns and problems encountered are centered in the developmental growth tasks of members rather than on pathological blocks and distortions of reality. (p. 11)

It is important to differentiate between group counseling and group guidance. Dye (1968) suggests that whereas group guidance is intended to be instructional, group counseling deals with self. "The purpose is to increase each member's awareness and understanding of personal and interpersonal processes" (p. 4).

Types of Career Guidance Methods

Gazda (1970) suggests that group guidance and group counseling differ in the following ways: (a) Group guidance is intended for all students whereas group counseling is intended for students with temporary problems which require more than information. (b) Group guidance is only indirectly concerned with attitudes and behaviors whereas group counseling actively attempts to modify them through effective involvement. (c) Group guidance procedures can be used with large groups whereas group counseling procedures, which rely heavily on group interaction, can only be used with small groups.

Group counseling, then, uses small groups to help students to learn about themselves and to develop new behaviors and attitudes. These groups focus on the problems of individual group members and on the interaction of the members It is assumed, however, that members' problems are normal developmental problems. The counselor plays a less active role than in group guidance.

Group Therapy. Several writers have discussed the differences between group counseling and group therapy (Lifton 1967; Gazda 1968, 1970; Cox and Herr 1968; and Mahler 1969). Group therapy is a group procedure designed for use with clients who have severe emotional problems. It is a form of psychotherapy which is (a) long-term in duration, (b) designed to produce personality change, and (c) conducted by a therapist with considerable psychological training (Cox and Herr 1968).

Usually group therapy is not conducted in the school situation. However, Tolor and Griffin (1969) suggest that in some cases it would be appropriate to do so because the client would be able to recall more vividly school experiences and because the therapist could have more ready access to school personnel for consultation. Also, Cox and Herr (1968) suggest that some of the methods more frequently associated with group therapy, e.g., play therapy and psychodrama, might be applied to normal developmental problems in group counseling situations.

Implications for Career Guidance

1. Group procedures enable group interaction among peers and between students and the counselor which facilitates learning, particularly learning about self. This type of learning situation can be used effectively to facilitate vocational exploration.

2. Large group instruction and group guidance procedures are particularly effective when the learning goal is the dissemination of information, i.e., occupational information. Through using groups to disseminate information, counselor time is released for other types of

counseling activities. To provide for clarification of the information through interaction, it is suggested that group size be limited and that the leadership style used by the counselor be democratic in nature.

3. Some students may have negative attitudes about themselves which inhibit their vocational development and limit the extent to which they are willing to consider vocational possibilities. Group counseling procedures are particularly appropriate for use with these students. These procedures focus on individual group members and encourage the exploration of feelings about self and others.

4. Group therapy is usually limited to use with clients who have severe emotional problems. Although this group procedure is seldom used in the school setting, career guidance personnel should be aware of this procedure and be able to refer students for therapy when personality problems are affecting vocational development.

5. Although large group instruction, group guidance, group counseling, and group therapy have been described as distinct group approaches, they use many of the same methods and might be thought of as a continuum rather than as distinct categories. Any group procedure might combine various elements of these four types depending on the career guidance goals.

METHOD APPLICATIONS*

Aughinbaugh, L. A. Group versus individual counseling: A junior college study. Final report.

Bates, M. Test of group counseling.

Cohn, B. et al. The effects of group counseling on school adjustment of underachieving junior high school boys who demonstrate acting-out behavior.

Flowers, S. H. A project to demonstrate the effectiveness of unstructured group counseling in developing in disabled persons insights and positive attitudes.

Hansen, J. and Cramer, S. Group guidance and counseling in the schools.

Hoffnung, R. T. and Mills, R. B. Situational group counseling with disadvantaged youth.

Hoppock, R. How to conduct an occupational group conference with an alumnus.

Houston vocational guidance project.

Iadipaoli, M. V. Projects for group guidance.

Jeffs, G. A. et al. Group counseling and personal development.

---

*These can be found in chapter 8 (alphabetically listed).

Types of Career Guidance Methods

Kemp, C. G. Foundations of group counseling.

Kemp, C. G. (Ed.) Perspectives on the group process: A foundation for counseling with groups.

Madison Area Project. Suggested typical context outline for junior high school group guidance. Appendix E.

Mahler, C. A. Group counseling in the schools.

Mahler, C. A. and Caldwell, E. Group counseling in secondary schools.

Mezzano, J. Group counseling with low-motivated male high school students: Comparative effects of two uses in counselor time.

Mihalka, J. A. Job hunting course.

Muskegon Guidance Project. The effect of additional counseling on the able student's vocational and educational planning.

New York State Education Department. Planning models for group counseling.

Ofman, W. Evaluation of a group counseling procedure.

Ohlsen, M. M. Counseling children in groups.

Ohlsen, M. M. and Proff, F. C. Response patterns associated with group counseling.

Oregon State Department of Education. Group guidance in Oregon secondary schools.

Pennsylvania Advancement School. Group counseling for urban schools: a handbook.

Rector, W. H. and Shaw, M. C. Group counseling with parents: Feasibility reactions, and interrelationships.

Stetter, R. A group guidance technique for classroom teachers.

Shaw, M. C. and Tuel, J. K. Guidance research in action: Group counseling with parents. Monograph 2.

Sloan, N. E. Personnel services review. Series 3: Human resources in the guidance program, family counseling.

Stogdill, R. M. and Bailey, W.R. Changing response of vocational students to supervision: the use of motion pictures and group discussions.

University of Texas. Student's personal adjustment to work, suggested plans for group discussions in vocational industrial education. Volume II.

Vocational Guidance Service. Career guidance through groups. A job placement and group vocational guidance program for high school youth.

Weals, R. and Johnson, E. Doubled and vulnerable: A sociodrama on vocational decision making.

Witherspoon, F. D. Group guidance in junior college: A frame of reference.

Method Type: Information Retrieval Systems

DEFINITION

An information retrieval system is any system designed to facilitate the, "total process of gathering, analyzing, indexing, filing and making available information using human and/or hardware to carry out this process" (Gulick 1968, p. 255). The traditional library is probably the most familiar type of information system. However, information retrieval systems may differ from this model in terms of: (a) the type of information stored, (b) the form in which it is stored, and (c) the classification system which is used to retrieve the information.

CHARACTERISTICS

Information retrieval systems are designed to disseminate information to students. Any information system involves several aspects of information handling including: (a) what type of information the system contains, (b) how the information is identified and collected, (c) how the information is classified within the system, (d) how the information is stored, and (e) how the user retrieves the information (Miller 1970).

A major consideration in system development are the resources which will be used to perform these processes. These resources can include a number of people, such as those who produce the information, design the system, help others to use the system, and use the system themselves. Other resources include nonhuman resources such as computers, audio-visual equipment, specialized retrieval equipment, and micro-form viewing equipment.

There are some basic considerations which underlie the development of all information retrieval systems. First, it is important that the system not only transmit information to the user, but also that it allow the user to give feedback on how useful the system is for him (Havelock and Benne 1967). Many systems have failed because there is little opportunity for this user feedback. Secondly, information systems should be designed not only to desseminate information but also to help the user to learn how to use the information effectively (Tiedeman 1968). It is assumed that the information will help the students to develop new behaviors or make decisions. However, without an understanding of how to use the information, this may not occur. Another important factor relates to the nature of the information in the system. It is essential that the information is relevant to the needs and characteristics of the intended users (Hoffer 1968).

TYPES OF INFORMATION RETRIEVAL SYSTEMS

Currently there are a number of information retrieval systems which are relevant to guidance. These include: (a) educational development and planning systems, (b) locally oriented occupational information systems, (c) information systems to facilitate vocational decision making, and (d) information systems for staff training and program development.

Educational Development and Planning Systems. This type of system contains such information about students as test scores, grades, personal characteristics, etc. These systems are designed for use by both educational staff and by students. Ellis (1968) suggests that they provide a basis for: "Student self-appraisal and future planning, parental understanding and cooperation, effective teaching and counseling, and need-centered curriculum development" (p. 106). Frequently, these systems are state-wide. Benson (1969) suggests that such systems should contain information about the nature of the students as they enter and move through the educational system as well as information about the nature of educational programs in which they participate. This would enable analysis of the effectiveness of educational programs for particular students.

Locally Oriented Occupational Information Systems. These systems are designed to communicate general and local occupational information to students for use in vocational planning and placement. They are often developed by large educational units such as county or state departments of education. These information systems are particularly relevant for those students who are not planning to attend college, since these students need information about training possibilities in the local area (Hoyt 1968). Typically, these systems stress information about occupations for which there is high local demand. The following criteria are used for selecting occupations: (a) shortage and heavy demand occupations, (b) occupations for which education is available in the local area, and (c) occupations which are open to high school and two-year college graduates and school leavers (DuBato 1968).

Such systems are usually designed to develop master information services which can be offered to a number of schools in the same locality (Whitfield 1968a). These services are based on the assumption that: "The tasks of acquiring, classifying, evaluating, storing and disseminating information have become so complex as to preclude their being carried out effectively by individual school counselors as part of their on-the-job activities (Kroll 1967, p. 14).

Information Systems to Facilitate Vocational Decision Making. These systems focus on providing the student with information about self, educational opportunities, and the world of work, and on helping him develop skills in effective vocational decision making. They are usually computer-based, thus allowing not only the retrieval of information for student use, but also the monitoring of the nature of the student's interaction with the information. In the most sophisticated of these systems, the student's interaction with the computer includes training and assistance in the process of decision making. Although most of these systems are currently in experimental stages, they are indicative of the future trend in information systems (Miller 1970).

Information Systems for Staff Training and Program Development.
These systems contain information about current educational programs, practices and research. They are intended to be used by career guidance personnel rather than students. Examples are the Educational Resources Information Center (ERIC), sponsored by the U.S. Office of Education (Burchinal 1967), and the School Research Information Service (SRIS), operated by Phi Delta Kappa.

The goals of these systems include collecting, abstracting, indexing and making available materials describing current educational research and practice. These materials are announced through a series of publications which enable counselors to keep informed about current educational developments. These large national systems can help the individual to search quickly for highly specific information. Also, it is possible for local schools to develop professional information centers which allow the staff access to information needed for program development (Miller 1970).

IMPLICATIONS FOR CAREER GUIDANCE

1. For students to make sound vocational and educational decisions, it is important to have relevant information about self and educational and occupational possibilities. Information retrieval systems provide a systematic way to collect, process, store and disseminate such information for student use.

2. Since these systems are capable of performing the information dissemination function, a greater amount of counselor time can be spent in helping students and in consulting with parents and school personnel about students.

3. Information retrieval systems provide a model for information services which can be developed at the regional level, i.e., county or state level. One application is the development of systems of locally relevant educational and vocational information which can be utilized by all schools in the area.

4. Another application is the development of a regional student information system. Such a system provides information which students can use in vocational decision making and school personnel can use in making the school curriculum more vocationally relevant.

5. Finally, there are existing national information systems which provide information about current educational research and programs. Such systems can be used by career guidance personnel to facilitate the development of career guidance programs and procedures.

METHOD APPLICATIONS*

Agan, R. J. et al. The development and demonstration of a coordinated and integrated program of occupational information.

California State Department of Education. A proposed system for reporting job placement follow-through data.

Circle, D. F. et al. The career information service: A guide to its development and use.

College Entrance Examination Board. Comparative guidance and placement program (CGP).

DuBato, G. S. A feasibility study to investigate the structure and operation of a model occupational information dissemination unit which would operate between the New York state employment service and the New York education department.

DuBato, G. S. VOGUE: a demonstration system of occupational information for career guidance.

Ellis, B. W. and Swan, R. (Ed.) NVGA bibliography of current career information: 1969.

Gerstein, M. and Hoover, R. VIEW — Vocational information for education and work.

Harvard University. Annual report: Information system for vocational decisions.

Hollis, J. and Hollis, L. Personalizing information processes.

Hoyt, K. B. The specialty oriented student research program: A five-year report.

Isaacson, L. E. Career information in counseling and teaching.

Jackson, J. S. et al. Evaluation of the career development laboratory.

Jones, G. B. Using project TALENT to improve vocational guidance.

Letson, J. W. Formulation of models for preparing occupational materials for pupils from various socio-economic levels in grades three through eight.

---

*These can be found in chapter 8 (alphabetically listed).

Lindquist, E. F. et al. Education information project.

Mullen, M. J. A volunteer program in vocational information and career guidance for secondary schools.

National Center for Career Information Services.

Odle, S. G. The student information center as an education reserve.

Pierson, G. N. et al. A regional career information center, development and process, 1967.

Reinhart, B. A. Toward a vocational student information system: A progress report.

Ritter, R. Project VISION: An approach to a model system of occupational employment information.

Smith, G. C. Counselor's guide to manpower information.

State University of New York. A demonstration system of occupational information for career guidance. Final report.

Tiedeman, D. V. et al. An information system for vocational decisions. Sixth quarterly report.

Viernstein, M. C. The extension of Holland's occupational classification to all occupations in the Dictionary of Occupational Titles.

Whitfield, E. A. and Glaeser, G. A. Project VIEW: History and development.

Whitfield, E. A. and Glaeser, G. A. A demonstration of a regional career information center: The VIEW system. A summary of research results 1967-1968.

Willowbrook High School. A report on project CVIS (computerized vocational information systems).

Youst, D. B. A comprehensive micro-image file for occupational information.

Method Type: Simulation Gaming

DEFINITION

Simulation gaming, when used as a teaching device, is the process of providing experiences which parallel real life situations and involve the participant in such activities as: (a) seeking and obtaining information; (b) decision making; and (c) acting on feedback received as a result of a specific decision strategy. Simulation gaming, therefore, enables the individual to test out a real situation; to investigate the extent to which the real situation is satisfying to him, i.e., a specific occupation; to learn

Types of Career Guidance Methods

which skills and learnings may be required in the situation; to apply specific skills and learnings to a situation; and to see the effects which specific skills, strategies and decisions have on a given situation (Kersch 1970).

CHARACTERISTICS

Games and play seem to be a natural activity of man. Children devote a considerable amount of time to play. Boocock (1968a) reviews previous thinking about the role of games in a child's life and suggests that games (a) provide an opportunity for children to learn behaviors which are needed in adult life, (b) are attractive to children and capture their interest and commitment, (c) provide a view of the surrounding environment and society, and (d) facilitate the socialization of children. She further suggests that once the role of games is clear "A logical next step in the sequence would be in a sense to reverse the process, i.e., to design and use specific games to produce desired learning and/or socialization" (p. 61).

Coleman (1968a) describes the nature of the learning process which occurs through simulation gaming. First, simulation gaming produces motivation for learning since the student is able to formulate goals through the game which make the learning of new information more relevant for him. Secondly, simulation gaming enables the learner to understand which types of actions are necessary to obtain his desired goal. Finally, because the learner is able to set goals and determine those actions related to the goal, he is able to develop a basis for the selection of relevant information.

Abt (1968) suggests that simulation gaming involves three types of learning: (a) facts expressed in the game context, (b) processes simulated by the game, and (c) relative costs and benefits, risks and potential rewards of alternative strategies of decision making. This method is motivating because it draws on the student's life experiences and is effective in helping the student to develop problem-solving approaches which can be utilized in his real life.

Simulation gaming presents a non-threatening environment in which the student can take an experimental stance. Kersch (1970) indicates that the student is able to take time to practice new behaviors, to explore various alternatives, and to make mistakes without real pressures and consequences.

Simulation gaming combines elements from both simulation games into one method. Coleman (1968a) lists the following essential properties of simulation gaming: (a) its basic elements are players or actors, each striving to achieve his goal. (b) It is limited to a small, fixed set of players. (c) Its rules limit the range and define the nature of legitimate actions of the players. (d) Through the rules, it establishes the basic order, sequence and structure within which the actions take place. (e) It is delimited in time as well as scope, with an end defined by the rules. (f) Its rules constitute a temporary suspension of some of the ordinary activities of life and rules of behavior.

Abt (1968) suggests that games may emphasize skills (e.g., chess or tennis), chance (e.g., dice or roulette), reality, or fantasy. Simulation games usually emphasize reality by allowing the student to experience real world situations which are beyond the student's direct experience. Simulation games, then, are gamelike in that they have specific rules, goals to be reached and a specific number of players involved. They are simulated in the sense that they involve real life situations which allow the students to practice behaviors and skills which will be needed at some future point in their lives.

TYPES OF SIMULATION GAMES

Two types of simulation games which have direct relevance for facilitating the vocational development of students are social interaction games and individual skill games.

Social Interaction Games. Social interaction games are those games which enable the learner to understand better the nature of the interaction between himself and the environment in which he lives. Coleman (1968b) defines a social simulation game as, "consisting of a player or players acting in a social environment. By its very definition, it is concerned principally with that part of the individual's environment that consists of other people, groups, and organizations" (p. 30).

Through playing these social simulation games, the student has an opportunity to explore the nature of a social environment through (a) possible roles he and others might play, (b) norms of behavior in that environment, and (c) strategies which enable him to exert control on the environment (Schild 1968).

An example of this social simulation game is the "Life Career Game" (Barbula 1967, Varenhorst 1968, 1969) which provides students with an opportunity to try out their decision-making approaches on a fictitious student in order to assess the consequences of their planning in the school achievement and the vocational development of that student (Barbula 1967). This game is played by teams of students who plan the life of an imaginary student by making decisions about how he will allocate his time to various activities over an eight-year period:

Types of Career Guidance Methods

Players are then fed back the consequences of these decisions in the form of scores or game points which are indications of the relative satisfaction of the life being planned. Thus the decision for each succeeding year must take into consideration the consequences of decisions made in the preceding years. Scoring of the game is based on the probability tables and data that have been compiled from analyses of current national statistics related to career planning. Thus, through the scoring, students are introduced to facts recording operating principles of our society (Varenhorst 1968, p. 308).

Individual Skill Simulations. These allow the student to understand and acquire behaviors which he will need in the future. A logical application of this type of simulation is in the exploration and/or learning of occupational behaviors. While exploring various occupational possibilities, it is important for the student to have the opportunity to understand the nature of work involved in various occupations. As Krumboltz (1969) indicates: "Young people seldom have the opportunity to solve the types of problems faced by people in many occupations. Young people may observe employed persons at their work, but even then they see only the manifestations of the job, not the problem-solving process itself" (p. 293). In response to this need, Krumboltz has developed job simulation kits which are designed to give young people the opportunity to solve simple but realistic problems similar to those solved by members of various occupations (Johnson 1968, Krumboltz and Sheppard 1969, Krumboltz 1967a, 1967b).

Individual skill simulations place less emphasis on the interaction of one player with another. Rather, they provide a simulated situation in which the individual may practice skills and behaviors which directly parallel those required in a real life situation. Usually, these simulation games provide a model of the behavior, allow the individual to practice the behavior, and then provide feedback on his performance.

IMPLICATIONS FOR CAREER GUIDANCE

1. Information about the nature of various occupations is a necessary element of vocational planning. Simulation gaming is one method which can be used to provide this information.

2. The use of simulated occupational experiences allows for greater control of the way in which the occupation is being described. When interviews with people in the occupation are used, there is the danger that the information will be biased.

3. The use of simulated occupational experiences enables the student to experience the nature of the work activity by solving occupa-

tional problems. Therefore, simulation is a possible alternative to work experience as a method of career exploration and occupational training.

4. Simulation can also be used to help the student to explore various alternatives prior to making final choices. Because he is able to experience these alternatives, he feels that choice is a reality.

5. Simulation seems to be at least as effective in facilitating learning as other educational methods and seems to be more effective in increasing the motivation to learn. Although educational and vocational planning is important, the student does not always understand the importance of such activity. Simulation gaming can be used to help motivate students to become actively involved in the vocational decision-making process.

6. Vocational development is a process which continues throughout life. Recently, there has been increasing emphasis on vocational guidance activities at the elementary school level. Since games are a natural activity of young children, simulation gaming would seem to hold considerable promise as a method appropriate for this age group.

METHOD APPLICATIONS*

Bailey, L. J. (ed.) Facilitating career development: an annotated bibliography.

Barbula, P. M. and Isaac, S. W. Career simulation for adolescent pupils. Final report.

Boocock, S. S. The life career game.

Boocock, S. S. and Schild, E. O. Simulation games in learning.

Brown, J. A. and MacDougall, M. A. Computerized simulated games: a socialization tool for child guidance.

Cohen, K. C. Effects of the 'consumer game' on learning and attitudes of selected seventh grade students in a target-area school.

Helm, C. Computer simulation techniques for research on guidance problems.

Johnson, R. G. Simulated occupational problems in encouraging career exploration.

Johnson, R. G. Job simulations to promote vocational interests.

Jones, G. B. and Krumboltz, J. D. Stimulating vocational exploration through film-mediated problems.

Kersch, S. F. Personnel services review. Series I: Innovations in the training and supervision of counselor, simulation gaming.

Krumboltz, J. D. et al. Vocational problem-solving experiences for stimulating career exploration and interest: Phase II. Final report.

---

*These can be found in chapter 8 (alphabetically listed).

Krumboltz, J. D. Vocational problem-solving experiences for stimulating career exploration and interest: Phase II. Mid-project report.

Krumboltz, J. D. et al. Vocational problem-solving experiences for stimulating career exploration and interest: Final report.

Nelson, D. E. An experimental evaluation of methods of teaching students to consider alternative problem solutions.

Nelson, D. E. and Krumboltz, J. D. Encouraging career exploration through "simulated work" and "vocational detective" experiences.

Patten, R. J. and Lawrence, L. S. Enthusiasm, interest, and learning. The results of a game training, a study of simulation at the University of Colorado.

Roberts, R. L. and Keahey, S. P. Gaming for vocational awareness: A systems approach.

Roman, R. A. Implementation of a career decision game on a time shared computer: an exploration of its value in a simulated guidance environment.

Schauble, P. G. Emotional simulation in personal counseling.

Shirts, R. G. Career simulation for sixth grade pupils.

Varenhorst, B. B. Innovative tool for group counseling: The life career game.

Varenhorst, B. B. Information regarding the use of the life career game in the Palo Alto Unified School District guidance program.

Wigderson, H. The name of the game — simulation. Research brief #4.

Method Type: Career Relevant Curricula

DEFINITION

School curriculum refers to the nature of the information which is learned by students in the classroom situation. In recent years, there has been considerable research on the nature of vocational development which indicates ways in which the classroom situation might be used to facilitate the vocational development of students. However, it can be generalized that "While vocational development and career planning are valid and inescapable concerns of education, contemporary principles and concepts of vocational guidance have not been effectively incorporated within the school curriculum" (Ashcraft 1966, p. i). Career relevant curricula include any curriculum which in some way attempts to relate the nature of the information being learned to either the present or future vocational life of the student.

CHARACTERISTICS

Career guidance can be defined broadly to include all educational experiences which help students to make and implement vocational decisions. Several writers (Winefordner 1968, Pruitt 1969) suggest that all school experiences in some way affect the vocational development of students. Often, however, this impact may be negative rather than positive because there has not been a conscious effort to relate learning experiences to vocational development. Pruitt (1969) suggests that:

> Given the involuntary nature of career development and the extensiveness of teacher-student contact, it seems reasonable that teachers should use the vehicle of their contacts — the curriculum and instruction — for the purpose of assisting career development in a constructive way.

Tennyson (1965) suggests that: "A distinctive contribution which each teacher can make to the vocational development of his students is to show the application of his subject to the life environment of the present and the future" (p. 13). Specifically, he can help the student to (a) understand the occupational possibilities which grow out of a particular subject matter, (b) understand the relationship between occupational requirements and the education needed to meet these requirements, and (c) respect the various types of work which are related to the subject matter.

There is a need for counselors and teachers to cooperate in finding ways to make the instructional program career relevant for students. Three possible types of collaboration are: (a) Counselors can utilize instructional and administrative resources to assist and implement the decisions of pupils. (b) Teachers can help counselors disseminate vocationally related information to students. (c) Counselors can help teachers by providing data about students which can be used as a basis for curriculum development (Odgers 1966).

Basically, then, there seems to be agreement in the field that the school curriculum can be used to enhance the vocational development of students. To achieve this goal, it is necessary for counselors and teachers to cooperate in the development of curriculum. Also, it is necessary to use systematic methods for developing such curricula. As Woods (1966) has suggested: "Most would agree that the sporadic dissemination of information and an occasional conference of interested educators will not accomplish this goal" (p. 151).

Several writers (Bushnell 1970, Ryan 1969, Campbell 1968, and Woods 1966) have suggested the application of the systems approach to the development of guidance programs and curricula. Using this ap-

Types of Career Guidance Methods

proach, the following steps are suggested as necessary to the curriculum development process: (a) assess what has been done by others in the past, (b) state specific career development objectives, (c) identify available approaches for meeting objectives, (d) select one approach and develop curricular materials, (e) test the materials on a limited number of students, (f) revise materials, (g) disseminate for broad use, and (h) devise a system for on-going evaluation (Woods 1966).

TYPES OF VOCATIONALLY RELEVANT CURRICULA

There are three broad categories of curriculum applications which are quite distinct. These include: (a) developmental career guidance curricula, (b) special career guidance curricula, and (c) career-relevant school curricula.

Developmental Career Guidance Curricula. Recent research and theory have indicated that career development is an on-going process which continues from early childhood throughout life. Based on this concept, new guidance programs are being developed which provide planned, coordinated guidance experiences to facilitate the vocational development of children from kindergarten through twelfth grade. Leonard (1968b) has suggested that:

> Because developmental career guidance is an on-going process, stress is given to development aspects of career knowledge: Aspiration, Choice, and Planning. Stress is also given to the ever changing nature of preparation for adult life. Furthermore, there is an emphasis on guidance and counseling based upon our knowledge of developmental patterns of people. Guidance thus oriented is conceived of as dynamic, contiguous with growth stages, relevant to the world of work, and integrative of old and new experiences. (p. 31)

These developmental programs have several shared characteristics. First, they have developed behavioral objectives which are appropriate for various age and grade levels. Secondly, they have developed a series of planned guidance experiences and curricular materials which are designed to meet these objectives. Finally, they stress cooperation between the guidance staff and teachers, and have developed extensive in-service training programs to facilitate the implementation of the program.

Special Career Guidance Curricula. Another application of curricula to the field of career guidance is the special career guidance curriculum. These curricula are not necessarily longitudinal in nature. Rather, they stress the development of special curriculum materials to help to facilitate specific vocationally related behaviors. Such applications are often based on the concept that decision making and planning are essential skills which are needed for vocational development (Gelatt 1968, Sherman 1967, Wilson 1967). They are comprised of specially designed and tested curriculum materials which are intended to help students to learn these skills and behaviors.

These curricula are designed to teach skills which typically have not been taught systematically through the instructional program. Wilson (1967) suggests that outcomes of this learning might include (a) the learning of the language of the process of decision making, (b) practicing decision making under the supervision of a teacher or counselor, and (c) making explicit one's own criteria for choices. Sherman (1967) stresses the importance of integrating affective learning with cognitive learning. Such efforts are an attempt to clarify the content of guidance and develop new curriculum materials to communicate this content to students.

Career Relevant School Curriculum. The previously described types of curriculum have stressed content which is directly related to vocational development, i.e., information about self and the world of work. Another application of curriculum to guidance is the career relevant school curriculum. Here the stress is on helping students to see relationships between the basic school curriculum, i.e., science, mathematics, etc., and future occupational experiences. The premise here is that teachers can play a vital role in making all learning relate to the real life experiences of the student. Pruitt (1969) suggests that through the general school curriculum, students can learn which competencies are needed for success in specific occupational fields, and which personal preferences they have for various occupational possibilities.

Tennyson (1965) also recognizes the need for relating school experiences to occupational possibilities and suggests various methods which might be used to accomplish this. He notes that both the instructional and guidance staffs must cooperate to make school curriculum career relevant. In the past, not all educators have seen this as an appropriate goal. If it is to be achieved, it will require agreement among all school staff and definite plans for implementation. Major steps are now being made to facilitate the development of vocationally relevant curricula. The career education thrust has added impetus to this. Of particular interest are the current efforts by the U.S. Office of Education to develop four basic Comprehensive Career Education Models.

IMPLICATIONS FOR CAREER GUIDANCE

1. There are several ways in which the school curriculum can be designed to facilitate vocational development. Regardless of which way

Types of Career Guidance Methods

is used, implementation depends largely on cooperation between the guidance staff and the instructional staff.

2. The school curriculum is a major vehicle through which learning occurs in the school. Although there are other guidance procedures, use of the curriculum for facilitating vocational development is needed if all students are to be reached.

3. One possible application of the curriculum to career guidance is the use of developmental, longitudinal guidance programs which are designed to help students explore, choose and implement vocational plans. These programs provide guidance experiences from kindergarten through twelfth grade. Specific objectives are developed by grade level and special curricula are designed to meet these objectives.

4. It is becoming clear that vocational development involves the development of specific behaviors and skills, i.e., decision making. Research is clarifying the nature of these specific skills so that it is now possible to design special guidance curricula to teach these skills.

5. All school experiences have some type of impact on vocational development. Students' understanding of occupations is largely a result of the school experience. For this reason, there is a need to consider the nature of the impact of the total educational curriculum on vocational development. Teachers and counselors need to work together to find ways of making the curriculum career relevant.

6. As with the development of other types of curriculum, it is important that career relevant curricula be carefully designed, implemented and evaluated. This process includes the statement of objectives, exploration of alternative approaches, selection of approach to be used, development of curriculum materials, field testing, revision, implementation and on-going evaluation.

METHOD APPLICATIONS*

Abington School District. Career development activities. Grades 5, 6, 7.

Agan, R. J. et al. The development and demonstration of a coordinated and integrated program of occupational information, selection, and preparation in a secondary school.

Albract, J. et al. Using existing vocational programs for providing exploratory experiences.

Alschuler, A. How to develop achievement motivation: a course manual for teachers.

Bailey, L. J. (ed.) Facilitating career development: an annotated bibliography.

Bush, D. O. et al. Between education and work: The image of the world of work.

---

*These can be found in chapter 8 (alphabetically listed).

California State Advisory Council on Vocational Education and Technical Training. Feasibility study of career ladder curriculum and guidance and counseling.

Case Western Reserve University. A working curriculum paper on technology and the world of work and careers.

Chancey, G. E. Career development unit job interview.

Cincinnati Public Schools. Man: his life and work. A career orientation manual for teachers of seventh and eighth grade social studies.

College Entrance Examination Board. Deciding, A decision-making program for students.

Darcy, R. L. An experimental junior high school course in occupational opportunities and labor market processes.

Dunn, J. A. The 1970 PLAN guidance program.

Dunn, J. A. Project PLAN: Guidance through the instructional process.

Flanagan, J. C. Project PLAN: The basic role of guidance in individualizing education.

Gelatt, H. B. A decision-making approach to guidance.

Geteles, F. et al. A cooperative vocational pattern for in-school mentally retarded youth.

Greater Hartford Chamber of Commerce. Project inspire: vocational guidance institute.

Grossmont Union High School District. Studies in success: A promising approach to the vocational guidance of average high school students.

Hamilton, J. A. and Jones, G. B. Integrating and evaluating career information in a developmental guidance program.

Hamilton, J. A. and Webster, W. J. Occupational information as an integral strand in the PLAN social studies curriculum.

Hamilton, J. A. and Jones, G. B. Individualizing educational and vocational guidance designing a prototype program.

Hansen, Lorraine (Sunny) A Learning Opportunities Package.

Hansen, L. S. et al. Career guidance practices in school and community.

Hilverda, E. and Slocum, W. L. Vocational guidance through the curriculum in a small rural school system.

Horyna, L. L. et al. Working, learning and career planning: A cooperative approach to human resource development.

Houston vocational guidance project.

Jones, G. B. and Nelson, D. E. Elements of a comprehensive guidance system integrated into the instructional process.

Leonard, G. E. Developmental career guidance in action. The first year.

Types of Career Guidance Methods

Leonard, G. E. et al. The developmental career guidance project: An interim report.

Leonard, G. E. Vocational planning and career behavior. A report of the developmental career guidance project.

Lockwood, O. et al. Four worlds: An approach to occupational guidance.

Melnotte, J. M. The application of project TALENT and project PLAN to goal-oriented curriculum.

Mihalka, J. A. Job hunting course.

Miller, W. R. and Blankenbaker, E. K. Annotated bibliography of publications and reports of research dealing with the interpretation of the world of work to elementary children.

Miller, C. H. A pilot project in vocational counseling in economically underdeveloped areas.

Minneapolis Public Schools. World of work: Grade nine. Teacher's guide for the school year 1967-1968.

Minnesota University. Suggested teaching-learning approaches for career development in the curriculum.

Mitchell, E. F. et al. A comprehensive orientation to the world of work through industrial arts and vocational education (grades 1-12).

New Jersey State Department of Education. Teacher's guide for a model program on introduction to vocations.

New Jersey State Education Department. The world of work: Increasing the vocational awareness of elementary school children.

Office of Education. World of work curriculum: Instructor's manual.

Oklahoma State Department of Education. A guide for developmental vocational guidance. Grades K-12.

Oklahoma Vocational Research Coordinating Unit. A guide for teachers of a course in career exploration, grades 8-9-10.

Oregon State Department of Education. Teacher's guide to: Self understanding through occupational exploration.

Osipow, S. H. and Alderfer, R. D. The effects of a vocationally oriented speech course on the vocational planning behavior of high school students.

Palo Alto Unified School District. Conference summary — from theory to practice: The description and demonstration of a guidance program in one district, K-12.

Ploughman, T. L. Project: Pontiac vocational career development program; evaluation report.

Pruitt, A. S. Teacher involvement in the curriculum and career guidance.

Rhodes, J. A. Vocational education and guidance: A system for the seventies.

Rowe, F. A. Foundation for a seventh grade guidance unit: an analysis of the development level of the seventh grade student and nationally current occupational guidance classes.

Ryan, T. A. Effect of an integrated instructional counseling program to improve vocational decision-making of community college youth.

Saskatchewan New Start, Inc. Life skills: a course in applied problem solving.

Sherman, V. S. Guidance curriculum for increased self understanding and motivation for career planning.

Sherman, V. S. Guidance curriculum for increased self understanding and motivation for career planning. Appendix.

Sherman, V. S. Trial and testing of an experimental guidance curriculum.

Sturges, J. C. Assisting vocational development through a unit in civics: A comparison of two techniques.

Sturges, J. C. et al. A comparison of two methods of providing information to ninth grade students about the world of work.

Stutz, R. C. Development and evaluation of an integrated career development curriculum.

Taylor, J. E., Montague, E. K. and Michaels, E. R. An occupational clustering system and curriculum implications for the comprehensive career education model.

Tennyson, W. W. et al. The teacher's role in career development.

Texas Board of Education. Texas occupational orientation Program.

Todd, R. D. & Todd, K. P. A prospectus for the development of a career-development and technology program for elementary school children.

Vetter, L. & Sethney, B. J. Planning ahead for the world of work: research report abstract, teacher manual, student materials.

Warren, M. A. et al. Generalizations related to concepts important for your orientation to the world of work.

Wilson, E. H. A task oriented course in decision-making.

Method Type: Work Experience Programs

DEFINITION

Many career guidance procedures are designed to help students to explore information about themselves and the world of work in order to make tentative occupational choices. The testing of these choices in a real work situation in order to explore their appropriateness for the individual is another guidance goal. Work experience programs are one possible method of facilitating this reality testing. Bishop (1969) defines work experience programs as:

> An organized group of learning experiences in school and in the work world for developing personal adjustment, personality stability, individual pupil motivation, and a desire to develop individual potential with respect to assimilation into the social and economic structure. (p. 93)

In standards which were developed for the work experience program for Los Angeles, California (1960), work experience is seen as:

> A practical activity in the production or distribution of services or goods, carried out under normal working conditions, in commerce, business, industry, and in professional or institutional fields. It is intended to further civic or occupational competence in youth. p. 1)

The work experience concept is undergoing major reevaluation at the present time. New career education concepts indicate the need for work experience to be available to all students as part of the on-going educational process. In response to this goal, many new work experience models are emerging.

CHARACTERISTICS

The rationale underlying work experience programs is that students need the opportunity to test vocational choices prior to actual entry into an occupational field. Several benefits are derived from such experience. First, the student is able to develop certain work-related habits and skills, e.g., work skills, responsibility to job, meeting adults involved in work, etc. Huffman (1967) suggests that specific learnings include (a) learning skills under actual conditions of employment, (b) gaining technical and related information which will enable learner to work successfully in his chosen occupation, and (c) adjustment to the work situation including acceptance of responsibility, relationships with other workers and acceptance of supervision.

Another benefit of work experience is that it enables the student to see the relationship between school and work. Bishop (1969) has suggested that a major goal of work experience programs should be to "develop a realistic understanding of the relationships between the world of work and education which assists the individual in becoming a contributing member of society" (p. 93). Subgoals related to this major objective are (a) to select an educational program appropriate for career objectives, (b) to relate interests, aptitudes, abilities and aspirations to occupational goals, and (c) to appreciate the value of an education. Although work experience often occurs late in the school experience, such goals indicate a need for providing early work experience as an assistance to curriculum selection.

Recently there has been increasing emphasis on finding ways of retaining special types of student, e.g., potential dropouts or disadvantaged, in the school situation. Several writers (Peterson 1967, Detroit Public Schools 1967, Nixon 1966) have suggested that work experience programs might successfully increase the motivation for learning in such students. Such programs potentially can increase motivation by (a) increasing feelings of self-worth, (b) helping students to see the relevance of school for future goals, (c) helping students to find the financial assistance needed to remain in school, and (d) developing specific occupational skills.

Programs designed to give students the opportunity to test occupational alternatives in either real or simulated work situations are potentially beneficial. However, unless such programs are carefully designed and implemented, a number of difficulties may arise (McCracken 1969, Hamburger 1967). One possible weakness of such programs is that the occupational experiences which are offered are not relevant to the students. The experience may be very narrow, i.e., the student may be involved in the more routine tasks connected with the occupation, or the experience may be related to occupations which are not congruent with the student's interest and abilities.

Another possible problem is that the occupations for which training is offered may not be high-demand occupations. If this is the case, the student may well be unable to find employment in the occupation which he has selected and for which he has trained. A final problem is that negative attitudes toward the occupation may develop not because of the nature of the occupation itself but because of the relationship between the people in the work experience situation and the student.

TYPES OF WORK EXPERIENCE PROGRAMS

Traditionally, work experience programs have been cooperative education-type programs in which students split their time between school attendance and work. Recently, newer types of work experience programs have been developed. Four major types of work experience programs are (a) cooperative education programs, (b) work-study programs, (c) volunteer work experience programs, and (d) simulated work experience programs.

Cooperative Education Programs. Schill (1966) describes cooperative education programs as programs in which the student "works part-time and studies in a formal classroom setting part-time" (p. 1). He distinguishes this type of program from work-study programs by indicating that in work-study programs students receive pay for the time spent in the work setting. Huffman (1967) does not make this distinction. He does, however, stress the complementary aspect between school curriculum and employment setting; the learning which occurs on the job should relate to that which occurs within the school. This is accomplished by using school personnel, i.e., cooperative education coordinators and counselors, to help students to interpret their on-the-job experience. He also stresses the importance of using an advisory committee to bring joint planning to bear on school and community vocational problems.

Work-Study Programs. Recent federal legislation has provided funding for work experience programs. Nixon (1966) provides a review of funding which is available through such acts as the Economic Opportunity Act, the Vocational Education Act, and the Manpower Development Training Act. Schill (1966), in a national survey of work-study and cooperative education programs, found that work-study programs are usually designed for special populations, e.g., disadvantaged, dropouts and/or unemployed. They also are more apt to be administered in non-secondary school settings, e.g., junior college, technical or vocational schools or specially established centers. Although the goals of work-study programs are similar to cooperative education programs, newer training designs are often used because of the special resources available for such programs.

Volunteer Work Experience Programs. Another type of work experience program is the volunteer program, which tends to be less formal in design than work-study or cooperative education programs. Traditionally, school clubs, e.g., future teachers or future nurses, have provided such volunteer experiences. More recently, manpower shortages in such fields as health services occupations have created an impetus for the further development of such programs. Usually volunteer work experience is quite extraneous to the school experience, i.e., it takes place after school hours and there is no real attempt to coordinate it with school experiences. Only recently have some programs been initiated which offer school credit for volunteer service and which have evaluated the impact of such experiences on vocational development (Arffa 1966).

Simulated Work Experience Programs. A major problem with real work experience is that it is difficult to provide the student with a variety of experiences that are related to his special abilities and interests. Often work experience programs have been criticized for creating negative attitudes toward work (McCracken 1969, Hamburger 1967). An alternative to real work experiences is simulated work experience.

The technique of simulation has been used in several work experience programs (Detroit Public Schools 1967, Bitter 1966, Krumboltz 1969). Bitter (1966) suggests that simulated experiences are particularly effective with students who have work adjustment problems which make it difficult for them to perform in the real work setting. Also, simulated experiences can allow the student to experiment with a number of different types of occupations, thus broadening his occupational aspirations (Detroit Public Schools 1967). Finally, it has been suggested that the value of work experience is often contaminated because of the negative feelings of those employed in the work setting. Simulation can provide the opportunity to understand the nature of an occupation without being influenced by others in the work setting.

IMPLICATIONS FOR CAREER GUIDANCE

1. Work experience programs can potentially help students to explore vocational possibilities, expand vocational aspirations and make tentative vocational choices. However, there is no assurance that such programs will accomplish such goals. Career guidance personnel will need to work closely with vocational education staffs and community employers to insure the development of work experience programs which contribute to the vocational development of students participating in such programs.

2. Work experience programs have been particularly effective in motivating special types of students, e.g., disadvantaged, potential dropouts, and/or handicapped. Such programs seem to increase the students' feelings of worth and help them to see school experiences as relevant to their own lives. Also, considerable federal support for such programs has stimulated a number of training designs which potentially can be applied to other programs.

3. There are several different types of work experience programs which provide students with an opportunity to work in real work settings. These include cooperative education programs, work-study programs and volunteer programs. Unless carefully planned, these programs may have the disadvantages of: (a) providing a limited view of only one occupation and only the more routine activities associated with that occupation, (b) creating negative rather than positive attitudes toward work because of poor relationships with people in the work setting or the negative attitudes of individual workers, and (c) lacking relationship with the school experience.

Types of Career Guidance Methods 119

4. Simulated work experiences can be designed to control some of the negative aspects of real work experience. However, some have argued that the real work experience is more effective in helping the student learn some work-related behaviors, e.g., punctuality, relationships with fellow workers and ability to take supervision.

5. Work experience traditionally has been provided at the high school level. If carefully designed, work experience can facilitate vocational exploration and, therefore, might be a method appropriate for the junior high school level. Such exploratory work experience can help prepare students to make sound curriculum choices.

METHOD APPLICATIONS

Arffa, M. S. Influence of volunteer experience on career choice.

Barzelay, R. Giving summer jobs a new dimension.

Benjamin, G. E. Significant job success factors found in work-study programs in five major New York state cities.

Boggs, G. E. A comparative analysis of the impact of various types of curricula on the vocational success of school dropouts.

Boyer, M. A. Cooperative work-experience education programs in junior colleges.

Bunda, R. and Mezzano, J. A study of the effects of a work experience program on performance of potential dropouts.

Burchill, G. W. Work-study programs for alienated youth.

Chaffee, E. and Kelly, R. E. A work experience education and employment placement program. A guide.

Council for Exceptional Children. Vocational education and work study programs.

Detroit Public Schools. Evaluation of the project in-school youth work training program for fourteen and fifteen year old youth.

Fielstra, C. Work experience education program in Santa Barbara county high school districts. Report of an evaluative study.

Flicker, B. A school and work program in an adult manpower setting for potential dropouts needing educational redirection.

Gentile, F. D. and Houseman, R. A development project in self and home employment for the homebound.

Geteles, F. et al. A cooperative vocational pattern for in-school mentally retarded youth.

---

*These can be found in chapter 8 (alphabetically listed).

Glassman, A. I. et al. Summer work-study program on urban problems for secondary school youth from inner-city communities. Final report.

Goldhammer, K. et al. Career oriented relevant education.

Hamburger, M. The significance of work experience in adolescent development.

Institute for Educational Development. "Partnership" high schools: The search for new ways to cooperate.

Jobs Now Project. Jobs now project — second year.

Joseph, M. P. et al. Work opportunity center for Minneapolis, Minnesota.

Lorber, F. and Schrank, R. The Bloomingdale project. Report of a demonstration on-the-job training program.

Madison Joint School District No. 8. Prevocational thrust in general education.

McPherson, H. and Stephens, R. M. Developing a work-experience program for slow learning youth.

Miller, K. L. Adapting the WIN employability orientation program to the needs of a medium-sized community.

Mitchell, F. H. Implementing a vocational guidance program.

New York State Education Department. Guided occupational training: A vocational work experience program for intellectually limited and educationally handicapped students.

Oregon State Department of Education. Guide to structure and articulation of occupational education programs.

Peterson, N. D. A pilot project in vocational guidance, placement, and work experience for youth for whom existing work experiences are not appropriate.

Summers, R. Methods and techniques for improving the educational aspirational level of senior high school students.

Walker, M. B. The remunerative work experience program.

Wayne State University. Project PIT: A summer industrial work experience and occupational guidance program.

Chapter 5 DESIGNING CAREER GUIDANCE APPROACHES

Practicing counselors have contacts with students daily. Through these contacts they develop an understanding of the career guidance needs of these students. Also, through reading professional literature, talking with colleagues and attending professional meetings, they become aware of career guidance methods which are being used by others throughout the country. The goal of this chapter is to provide a framework for translating the needs of students into guidance goals and for designing tailored career guidance approaches which can help implement these guidance goals. These approaches are defined as combinations of guidance activities which lead to the development of specific student behaviors.

Previously in this handbook, information has been presented on vocational development at various grade levels, needs of special populations and characteristics of guidance methods. This chapter focuses on (a) presenting specific guidance approaches which have been developed by others to meet special student needs, (b) helping the reader to determine whether the approach would meet the needs of his own student group, (c) providing the basic principles which govern the use of the approach, and (d) providing concrete steps needed to design, implement, evaluate and revise an application of the approach for a specific guidance program.

Designing Career Guidance Approaches

DO YOU SHARE THESE CONCERNS?

Each approach is introduced by suggesting specific types of student needs which the approach can meet. The reader needs to determine the extent to which the needs parallel the ones he has encountered in his own experiences with students. This will help to decide whether the approach is appropriate for use within a specific career guidance program. Not all of the approaches will be appropriate.

THE APPROACH AS APPLIED BY OTHERS

If the approach seems to be appropriate then the reader should survey examples of how other schools have developed and applied the approach. These applications are intended to help the reader to understand the approach more clearly and to suggest possible program models which might be modified for his school setting.

SOME BASIC PRINCIPLES

Although any guidance approach may have many different applications, there are some basic principles underlying each approach which should govern the development of any specific applications. These principles can provide a framework for evaluating the soundness of any particular application.

HOW TO DESIGN AND IMPLEMENT THE APPROACH

Understanding the nature of a guidance approach and exploring the ways in which others have used the approach is only a first step in designing and implementing the approach for a guidance program. Concrete steps are necessary. This section provides concrete suggestions and focuses on three major areas. First, suggestions are given for designing the approach, e.g., how simulation can be used to learn decision making. Information is provided which relates to planning materials, staffing, modification of existing resources, etc. Secondly, suggestions are given for implementing the guidance approach into on-going guidance and instructional activities. This includes training of staff, supportive classroom and guidance activities and initiating use of the approach. Finally, suggestions are given for evaluating the program. This includes collecting data about changes in student behavior, staff and student attitudes

Designing Career Guidance Approaches

toward the approach and workability of the approach. In addition to suggestions about how to evaluate the approach, information is given about possible revisions which might be made to strengthen the approach.

Career Guidance Approaches

This chapter includes specific design information about ten career guidance approaches. These approaches have been selected because (a) there are high quality examples of applications of the approach available, (b) specific information is available about how to design the approach, and (c) the approach can be used widely by a number of schools either because expensive equipment and resources are not required, or because schools have already completed the expensive developmental work and are willing to share materials with other schools. The approaches included in the chapter are:

1. Career information systems to communicate localized educational and occupational opportunities.
2. Developmental programs to facilitate early and continuous influence on career development.
3. Involving parents in their child's career development.
4. Manpower and economic education as a basis for understanding the world of work.
5. Mobile career guidance services.
6. Special curricula to motivate career exploration.
7. Teaching decision making.
8. Using models to learn vocational behaviors.
9. Using simulation to facilitate vocational exploration and decision making.
10. Vocational exploration through media and classroom activities.

Approach: Career Information Systems

DO YOU SHARE THESE CONCERNS?

Although one has studied general aspects of occupational information and its use in career planning, there still is difficulty in helping students to find current information about specific training opportunities.

Follow-up studies of recent high school graduates indicate that students do not feel as if they receive enough help in understanding training opportunities which are open in their local area. As a result, many are now working in jobs which hold little interest for them.

Recently a number of school districts have developed localized career information systems which (a) collect current information about local educational and occupational opportunities, (b) effectively communicate this information to students, (c) provide supportive counseling and guidance services to help students to make educational-vocational plans based on the information, and (d) provide in-service training to counselors and teachers to better prepare them to work with these systems.

THE APPROACH AS DEVELOPED BY OTHERS

The following are examples of career information systems, which can provide models for the development of other systems. In some cases, they have already been used successfully by other school systems.

Project VIEW. Project VIEW (Vital Information for Education and Work) is conducted by the San Diego County Career Information Center and serves a student population of approximately 30,000 in thirty secondary schools in San Diego County. Career information is produced for all occupations which require less than a baccalaureate degree and for which training is available and local job opportunities exist. This information, presently covering approximately 200 occupations, is disseminated to the schools participating in the project.

The basic dissemination tool is a data processing card containing a microfilm of four pages of information placed into an aperture in the card. The occupational briefs (VIEW scripts) consist of two cards on a given job. One card contains four pages of information applicable statewide while the second card contains three to four pages of local area information. The microfilm aperture cards can be used in standard microfilm readers and/or reader-printers which allow a student to print out a hard copy of the materials. The aperture cards are key punched to provide data processing capabilities for filing and retrieving the cards.

In summary, Project VIEW collects, organizes, and synthesizes various types of information. VIEW packages the data in a compact form so that a counselor is not crowded out of his office space by hundreds of publications, catalogs, and occupational briefs. The VIEW system makes the initial career investigation step easier for students and counselors by providing compact easy-to-read information on jobs, financial aids and colleges in a form that is readily accessible and continually updated. The

VIEW system has been widely disseminated and has been used as a model by several state and county educational units. A National VIEW Center is being established at the present time. For further information contact Dr. Edwin Whitfield, Guidance Coordinator, Department of Education, San Diego County, San Diego, California 92111 (Whitfield and Glaeser 1968).

Newton Public Schools. Some Massachusetts schools have developed a model for the development and use of a complete career information service. There are three major elements in this service including: (a) the career information library, (b) the job placement service, and (c) the follow-up service. These three services were combined into the career guidance resource center which provides a focal point for a variety of career guidance activities including counseling, information dissemination, and community liaison work. A comprehensive guide to the development of a career information service, which provides complete directions for developing a similar service in other schools, has been developed. The basic document cited in the bibliography contains this complete guide (Circle 1968).

The Specialty-Oriented Student Research Program (SOS).
This program, developed at the University of Iowa, is aimed at the collection, analysis and dissemination of new knowledge which allows counselors to better guide students headed toward trade, technical, or business school settings at the post-high school level. This program is concerned with the following areas: (a) the nature of the specialty-oriented student, (b) appraisal procedure, (c) educational-occupational information, and (d) counseling procedures. A major part of the program has been the development of the SOS Guidance Research Information Booklets.

These booklets present data collected from students both during training and six months after training. Each booklet presents information for a particular curricular major in a specific type of specialty institution. Major purposes of the booklets are to: (a) help students to develop a better basis for thinking about themselves in terms of their post-high school educational and vocational plans, (b) help students to orient their thinking with respect to questions which may be important to ask concerning post-high school training, and (c) serve as an aid in decision making for students considering training at one or more of the specific schools represented by the research findings. Further information is available from Dr. Kenneth Hoyt, College of Education, University of Maryland, College Park, Maryland 20742.

BASIC PRINCIPLES

When using information systems which have been developed by others or designing new systems, it is important to remember the following principles:

1. These career information systems are developed to provide specific, current information about *local and regional* educational and occupational opportunities.
2. Collection, synthesis and analysis of the information, and the development of special materials to communicate the information to students is completed by a *regional educational unit*, i.e., intermediate school district or county unit.
3. *Standardized procedures* are developed which allow for easy data collection and easy-to-duplicate, compact systems which can be provided to a number of counseling programs throughout the regional area.
4. As with all new practices, *special training procedures* for counselors, teachers and students are needed to insure proper use of these systems.
5. *Follow-up studies* of students who have used the materials are needed to provide information for revision of the materials and for selection of new types of information to be added to the system.

DESIGNING AND IMPLEMENTING CAREER INFORMATION SYSTEMS

Establish Educational Unit Responsible for System Development.
These systems require a considerable amount of time and resources to develop; therefore, it is necessary to have a large unit responsible for overall development. Such units as large city school districts, intermediate school districts or county school systems are possible. Also, it is necessary to consider funding opportunities. Other such systems have been developed through funding from the Vocational Education Act and from the Elementary and Secondary Education Act.

Assess Career Information Needs.
A first step in the development of the system is the assessment of the information needs of students who will be seeking either employment or training opportunities in the local area after high school graduation. Specific procedures for assessing students' needs which have been used by others are questionnaires and special advisory panels consisting of teachers, counselors and students.

Designing Career Guidance Approaches

Design the Information System. The next step is to design the information system. Rather than developing a totally new system, it is possible to use an existing system as a model. Several other districts have adapted the San Diego VIEW System for use in their local area.

When designing a system it is important to consider several factors such as: (a) special types of written materials which will be developed to communicate the information, (b) the form in which the system will be disseminated, and (c) basic costs of equipment needed to use the system. The system should be in a form which is compact, allows for reproduction of materials by students, and is easy to update. When considering costs, the price of equipment needed by each school using the system should be considered.

Select and Collect Specific Information. To collect the information, it is necessary to survey local, post-high school training institutions. When gathering this information, it is suggested that students be interviewed to determine questions which they have about training institutions. The program is a possible reference for these student-oriented concerns. In Project VIEW, it was found that it was important to analyze training opportunities and identify duplicate types of programs which may have different curriculum titles. Once the training opportunities have been surveyed, it is important to match these opportunities against local job market demands. Also, in addition to this highly specific local information, it is possible to include general occupational information in the system.

Develop Information System Materials. Possible information which might be included in these occupational information materials include: (a) the nature of the occupation, (b) worker characteristics, (c) training needed, (d) information about local training opportunities, and (e) local individuals in the occupations who are willing to talk with students. It is also important to make the materials motivating by using language which can be understood by the students and by using pictures and other graphics. Once the basic materials have been developed, they need to be reproduced and distributed to the participating schools.

Trial and Test of Materials on a Limited Basis. Before all of the materials for the system are developed, it is suggested that the materials be tested on a limited basis. A few schools might be selected as field test sites. Once materials have been developed on a few occupations, teachers, counselors and students in these schools can use the materials and react to them. Based on information from this trial, revisions can be made in the basic format and procedures, and the total body of materials for the system can be completed.

Train Counselors and Students. Students need special instruction in the use of information systems. It is possible to develop self-instructional materials such as film strips or programmed instructional materials to help students to use the system effectively. Teachers and counselors also need instruction both in the use of the system and in the nature of the current local occupational picture. Others have found that teachers and counselors often are not familiar with the educational-occupational information which is most important to those students who will be seeking entry occupations or short-term training after high school. In-service training workshops for teachers and counselors can help better to prepare them to work with these students in vocational decision making.

Student Follow-up. It is important to follow-up students who have used the system while they are in training institutions and when they have entered a job. This follow-up should collect information which will help evaluate the extent to which the system has helped students develop accurate perceptions of occupations and make satisfying choices. Also, the information can help counselors better to understand choice patterns of students, and provide a basis for evaluation and updating of the system materials.

Approach: Developmental Programs

DO YOU SHARE THESE CONCERNS?

High school students usually express a concern about making post-high school decisions related to educational and vocational planning. However, they do not seem prepared to make these choices. Often both students and their parents say that they wish they were better prepared to make decisions.

> You are a junior high school counselor and are responsible for planning career guidance experiences for the students in your school. You have already designed some experiences which you think might be helpful to students. However, as you attend local counselor meetings, you realize that there are several counselors in your system who are also responsible for other programs at the elementary and high school level. All of you recognize a strong need for help in coordinating career guidance efforts throughout your school system.

A number of state and regional groups have recently initiated developmental vocational guidance programs for all levels, kindergarten through twelfth grade, which: (a) provide both general and specific guidance objectives for all school levels, (b) suggest guidance activities, (c) help local school systems to design developmental programs for their own system, and (d) provide training and consultation to local schools.

THE APPROACH AS DEVELOPED BY OTHERS

The Developmental Career Guidance Program. In the Detroit public schools, this program is a developmental program specifically for inner-city youth. Its goals are to: (a) broaden the occupational perceptions of these youth, (b) encourage them to plan for the future, and (c) provide more adequate role models. Experimental schools were used in the program representing kindergarten through twelfth-grade settings. Special training programs were held for teams of guidance staff from these schools, and later, consultation help was also provided within the school setting.

A major emphasis was on total involvement of parents and community, which was made possible through assistance from paraprofessional personnel. Activities include (a) counseling, (b) dissemination of information, (c) activities to broaden student's perceptions of the world of work, (d) work with parents to involve them in their child's vocational development, (e) work with the community to gain neighborhood support, (f) professional consultation for the guidance staffs in participating schools, and (g) overall coordination to insure smooth articulation within the program (Leonard 1969).

The Oklahoma State Department of Education. Oklahoma schools have developed a guide for the development of vocational guidance programs, kindergarten through twelfth grade. This guide presents (a) specific and general objectives, (b) suggested guidance activities for meeting the objectives, and (c) suggested learning resource materials. This information is presented for each of four levels: kindergarten through third grade, fourth through sixth grade, seventh through ninth grade and tenth through twelfth grade. This guide does not suggest any one particular program but rather gives a framework by providing the objectives and various ways of meeting the objectives. Final selection of actual program components is left to the local school depending on the resources and staff available.

Other states are currently involved in the development of similar guides for the design and implementation of developmental career guidance programs. The document cited in the bibliography is the complete Oklahoma guide (Oklahoma State Department of Education 1968).

BASIC PRINCIPLES

When designing developmental programs, it is important to remember the following principles:

1. Career development is a continuous process and, therefore, it is important to initiate career guidance activities at the elementary

level and to *coordinate these guidance activities from the kindergarten through twelfth grade.*
2. A first step in such coordination is to *develop guidance objectives* for career guidance programs kindergarten through twelfth grade.
3. Once these objectives have been developed, it is possible to *suggest a number of guidance activities which can meet a particular objective.* Which of these activities will be used by a particular school will depend on the resources of the school.
4. Although it is ultimately the responsibility of the local school system to design a developmental career guidance program appropriate for that system, *regional and state educational units can play a leadership role* in stimulating program development. These larger units can develop basic guidance objectives, suggest a variety of guidance activities and resources, and provide consultation and training to counselors in local schools.

DESIGNING AND IMPLEMENTING DEVELOPMENTAL GUIDANCE PROGRAMS

Establish Unit Responsibility for the Program Suggestion and Planning Phase. The design and implementation of a developmental guidance program is a major task. To facilitate the development of such programs at the local level it is helpful to have larger educational units responsible for providing major guidance and suggestion. Often state departments of education assume this responsibility. Also, regional educational units, training institutions and professional associations can cooperate in these efforts. Probably a task force representing these groups in addition to representatives from local schools, i.e., counselors and vocational education teachers, could be established to develop program development guidelines.

Survey Efforts of Other States and Groups. Producing a program development guide which suggests vocational guidance objectives and activities for kindergarten through twelfth grade is a task which need not be repeated by each state or regional group. Once the groups responsible for the development of such a guide have been established, it would be fruitful to explore the efforts of other similar groups. Certainly basic program objectives can apply nationally to all students and, in many cases, the suggested activities can also be used. The efforts of other groups can be modified to meet special needs as the planning groups feel it is necessary. After a thorough search of available program development information has been completed, the final evaluation and selection of information to be included in the program development guide can be made.

Designing Career Guidance Approaches

Disseminate Program Development Information to Counselors and Teachers in Local Schools. Once the basic framework for developmental career guidance programs has been developed, major efforts are needed to disseminate this information to guidance staffs in local schools. A number of procedures are possible including the development of written program development guides, special workshops to help guidance personnel design programs for their own school setting, and consultation with individual school systems.

Marshall Local Resources to Support Developmental Programs. Those school systems which have been successful in designing and implementing developmental career guidance programs have found that such programs require the support of a large number of people in the local area such as community resource groups, school personnel, parent groups and students. A first step is to form a team representing these groups and guidance personnel from various schools in the system. This group can be responsible for designing specific programs and coordinating efforts at various school levels throughout the system.

A second step is to communicate the nature of the program to specific schools and to identify a number of resource people who can help implement the program. Developmental programs will need large staffs. Other programs have solved the staffing need by using such personnel as paraprofessionals, students and community volunteers in addition to the regular school staff.

Implement Program in Local School. Once the kindergarten through twelfth grade program has been designed for the entire system and staffing for local schools has been completed, program implementation can begin. Other developmental programs have found that it is highly desirable to have on-going consultation, training and coordination as the program progresses. It will be necessary for at least one representative from each school, a team if possible, to meet periodically with outside resource people and with other guidance staffs within the system to evaluate the progress of the program, to initiate new program ideas and to discuss articulation problems within the program.

Approach: Involving Parents in Their Child's Career Development

DO YOU SHARE THESE CONCERNS?

You have been working with a group of junior high school students to help them in vocational exploration activities. However, there seems to be little feeling on the part of the students that they have a voice in their own career decisions. Some students indicate that their parents are anxious to have them enter specific careers.

You have been working with a group of disadvantaged students to help them plan for further training after high school. However, they feel that they neither have the ability nor can they afford to participate in post-high school educational experiences.

The previous examples illustrate the type of impact that parents can have on the vocational development of students. When designing career guidance programs, it is important to remember that the vocational development of students can be strengthened by helping parents to (a) understand the need for planning for future educational training possibilities, (b) understand the nature of the vocational development process, and (c) realize the importance of allowing the student to exercise freedom of choice in vocational decision making.

THE APPROACH AS DEVELOPED BY OTHERS

Muskegon, Michigan. The Muskegon public schools developed a program to strengthen the educational and vocational development of able students. In addition to group and individual counseling with students, a major emphasis was placed on working with parents. Home visits were made prior to the opening of school to strengthen communication between home and school. Also, phone communication with parents throughout the year was encouraged. Special meetings were held with parents to discuss problems common to all parents of adolescents. This parent involvement facilitated parent support of the child's vocational development by (a) increasing the parents' awareness of and planning for support of the child's future education, and (b) allowing the child greater voice in career planning discussions (Muskegon Public Schools 1965).

The Developmental Career Guidance Project. Initiated in Detroit, Michigan, this program uses career development as a framework for the development of a guidance program for inner-city youth. Goals of the program were (a) to broaden the perception of inner-city youth regarding occupational opportunities, (b) to help overcome their lack of planning for the future, and (c) to provide better role models. A major aspect of the program was the recognition that parents are an important "significant other" in the life of the child and influence the child's perception of himself. Two major emphases in working with parents were to inform them of educational and vocational training opportunities and

Designing Career Guidance Approaches

ways or means of taking advantage of these, and to help parents find the best ways and means of helping their children develop in a healthy fashion (Leonard 1968a).

Three-Year Study. Parents of first, seventh, and ninth graders were invited to participate in small group discussions. It was emphasized that this would not be a lecture series, but a discussion group focusing upon concerns parents have about their growing children. At the ninth-grade level, the focus was on educational and vocational decision making. The group leaders or counselors were representative of the various pupil personnel specialties. Data were collected in six school districts based upon the experiences of 38 counselors and 53 parent counseling groups. An analysis of the parent post-series reaction sheet showed a highly positive attitude of parents participating in group counseling. This attitude was strengthened after a second year of counseling in the same district. An analysis of the written "counselor reactions to specific groups" (CRSG) showed that counselor responses became more positive the longer parents remained in their respective groups (Rector and Shaw, 1966).

BASIC PRINCIPLES

There are several basic principles which need to be considered when designing programs for parent counseling and consultation:

1. The nature of the parent-child relationship is one of the major variables related to achievement. It is important to remember that the effect of *parent behavior can either support or negate* basic career guidance efforts.
2. Parents are *concerned about their child's vocational development* and seem to react favorably to the opportunity to share their feelings and problems with other parents, and to receive information which can help them better understand their own children.
3. Past programs indicate that parent groups respond better to more *didactic and directive group sessions* in which they have the opportunity to both gain information and to share the information with other parents.
4. Effective ways are needed to open the *channels of communication* between parents and the school so that they feel comfortable in the home-school relationship. School personnel can facilitate this by home visits and by using the common bond of being a parent and/or family member.

DESIGNING AND IMPLEMENTING A PARENT INVOLVEMENT PROGRAM

Set Goals. When designing a parent involvement program, it is important to clearly specify the area of focus for the program. Usually, it is recommended that the focus be on specific aspects of child behavior which will help the parent to better understand his own child. Possible areas related to career development are (a) the nature of the decision-making process, (b) the importance of both the child and the parent planning for future educational-vocational goals, and (c) the nature of career development, including what might be expected of children at various educational levels.

Nature of the Program. Some major considerations concerning the nature of the program include (a) the size of parent groups, (b) the criteria for selection of members, (c) the length and scheduling of the program, and (d) on-going services for parents. The size will depend on the goals of programs. Usually quite small groups (under twenty) are more conducive to group discussion and interaction between parents. Sessions usually last between one to two hours. These may meet weekly or perhaps other arrangements will be necessary.

Parents probably should be consulted to determine the best scheduling pattern for a particular group. A pattern which has been used in some groups is to have weekly sessions for six weeks with the option to continue for another six to eight weeks if parents desire. An essential aspect of a parent involvement program is the provision for on-going, individual services to parents as they request them. These services include counseling and phone communication.

Staffing the Program. These programs are usually staffed by counselors and/or other pupil personnel specialists. Although it is possible to have one counselor per group, usually there are at least two staff members per group. A successful model has been to have co-counselors with one being male and the other female. Another possible source of staff is paraprofessionals. Use of paraprofessionals can enable more home visits, thus helping to bridge the gap between home and school. Since parent group sessions usually need to be held at night, it is important to consider allowing staff release time during the day to compensate for a heavy evening schedule.

Types of Activities. Typically, parent groups center on information-giving and group-discussion activities. They are not usually designed to be group counseling or therapy sessions. However, time should be allowed for group members to interact and to share concerns related to their child's vocational development and planning. Usually, parents come with the expectation of receiving a "lecture," so special activities will need to be designed to encourage discussion and interaction. In addition to group discussions, other possible activities are field trips to occupational and educational institutions, outside speakers, and use of those materials which are being used with students.

Initiating the Program. Contacting parents to invite them to participate in the program is a major consideration. Home visits are probably most effective but require a considerable amount of time and staff. Other alternatives are phone calls and/or letters. Some type of orientation is also important. A major goal during orientation is to gain commitment from parents for continuing participation. Research indicates that those parents who have the most favorable attitudes toward parent programs also have attended a greater number of meetings. In the initial meeting, it might be possible to get written commitment from parents. Subsequently, parents might be contacted if they do not attend meetings to try to encourage them to return.

Evaluation of Program. A first evaluation step is to seek parents' reactions to the program, including such information as how enjoyable it was, how much they feel they learned and how helpful it was in suggesting ways of working with their own child. A second type of evaluation is the extent to which the parent program resulted in changes in student attitudes and behaviors—for example, increases in the desire of the student to plan for his vocational and educational future or increases in the extent to which the student feels he has a voice at home in making his own decisions.

Approach: Manpower and Economic Education

DO YOU SHARE THESE CONCERNS?

When exploring the world of work with elementary school students, it is usually found that they have no understanding of the nature of work, the importance of work in society and the basic principles of economics. Therefore, work does not seem important to them and they have difficulty thinking in terms of work.

In talking with recent high school graduates, one often finds that generally they are not prepared to participate successfully in the labor force. This is partially because they lack a general understanding of work-related concepts such as work satisfaction, methods of seeking employment, the impact of technology on occupations or basic personal economic management.

Although both specific skill training and personalized career guidance are important, economic and manpower education increasingly is being viewed as an important educational experience for all school students. In order to think vocationally, it is necessary to understand the basic economic system which supports the various occupational possibilities which are open in society. Economic and manpower education programs promote this general understanding by communicating information about (a) basic principles of economics, (b) the effects of technology on the change nature of the labor market, (c) economic and non-economic dimensions of work, (d) various occupational opportunities in the United States, and (e) the effects of manpower and economic information on personal career decision making.

THE APPROACH AS DEVELOPED BY OTHERS

Several complete manpower and economic education curricula have been developed which can be used and/or adapted for use in other school settings.

A major curriculum has been developed for use with junior high school students to help them to acquire an understanding of the economic process and the role of work in the life of men and women, and further explain how young people can enhance their future employability by their own knowledge, skills, motivation and behavior patterns. The course consists of seventy-five separate lessons. Each lesson contains (a) a concise abstract outlining the central topic or theme to be studied, (b) the core of the lesson including questions to be answered in writing or class discussions by students (statistical data is provided in charts, tables, and the text itself to enable the student to test assertions or conclusions against significant empirical facts), and (c) a summary paragraph which recapitulates and emphasizes the most essential understandings that students should have learned from the lesson.

Student and teacher materials for the course may be purchased from the Joint Council on Economic Education, 1212 Avenue of the Americas, New York, New York 10036. Also, a semester-long television series of forty-six twenty-minute shows to use in conjunction with the curriculum materials has been developed. Information about this series is available from Mr. Lee Reaves, Director, Arkansas Educational Television Commission, 350 South Donaphey Street, Conway, Arkansas 72032. Further information about the entire curriculum is available from Phillip Powell, Director, Center for Economic Education, Henderson State College, Arkadelphia, Arkansas 71923 (Darcy 1968).

The Joint Council on Economic Education. Working with the Minneapolis public schools, the council developed guidelines and suggested goals and experiences for a component on economic education to be included in an elementary school social studies program. Basic economic learnings suggested include: (a) The economy is concerned with the problems of deciding how to make the best use of resources to satisfy human wants. (b) Production and consumption are functions of any economic system. (c) In America, competition in a market is the system whereby consumer and producer goods and services are allocated. (d) The federal government helps to regulate the system and participates in the allocation of goods and services through its spending. (e) Economic growth depends on the quality and quantity of productive resources. (f) Money is a medium of exchange, a measure for comparing all economic goods and a store of value. (g) Specialization leads to interdependency locally and internationally. (h) Other nations have the same basic economic considerations.

These principles are communicated to kindergarten children in terms of home and school; to first graders in terms of home and neighborhood; to second graders in terms of neighborhood; to third graders in terms of city — past and present; to fourth graders in terms of state; to fifth graders in terms of nation and to sixth graders in terms of Western Hemisphere. The basic document cited in the bibliography is the actual handbook for elementary school teachers (Joint Council on Economic Education 1967).

Project PROBE. This is a complete program in economic education developed for grades K-12 in the state of New York. Two basic teachers' guides have been developed: One for grades K-6 and the other for grades 7-12. These guides are a series of inquiry plans for the systematic development of learning and thinking skills. The materials for each grade level include: (a) a summary of the plans, justification of them, identification of the concepts and content that the students will explore, and an outline of the instructional strategy; (b) a statement of the objectives of each topic concerning skill development and the level of performance expected at the close of a planned activity; and (c) a description of strategy including specific activities, questions which should be used, and learning events or situations for the year. The two basic documents cited in the bibliography are the actual handbooks for teachers (Elliott et al. 1970).

SOME BASIC PRINCIPLES

When using manpower and economic education programs, the following principles are important.

1. Manpower and economic information are increasingly being viewed as an *essential school learning* which is necessary for effective adult living.
2. Basic manpower and economic information can be introduced as a *separate curriculum* or *incorporated* as part of another school subject, such as social studies.
3. Basic designs are available for teaching manpower and economic education at *all levels, kindergarten through twelfth grade*. It has been recommended that economic education begin at the elementary level.
4. Manpower and economic education can help to prepare youth to become more successful workers, and can help them to understand the importance of individual career planning. This, however, is not an automatic process. Special *coordination between economic education and career guidance programs* is needed.

COORDINATING ECONOMIC EDUCATION AND CAREER GUIDANCE PROGRAMS

Development of manpower and economic education curricula is a major effort, and several existing curricula are available. The major responsibilities of guidance personnel in the development and implementation of manpower and economic education include the following.

Stimulate Interest in Starting Manpower and Economic Education Programs. These programs are important for students, kindergarten through twelfth grade. If such programs are not already available in a particular school, guidance personnel might work actively with social studies teachers to stimulate interest and support adoption of such programs.

Insure the Development of Effective Economic Behaviors. Manpower and economic education can deal with the economic system in an abstract, theoretical way or it can help students to develop effective economic behaviors, e.g., occupational behaviors, vocational planning behaviors, personal economic management behaviors. If such a program is to facilitate career development, it must promote these personal behaviors. Guidance personnel should be concerned with consulting with others about curriculum and learning experiences to insure such learning.

Relate Economic Education to Vocational Guidance Opportunities. Much of the information gained from economic and manpower

Designing Career Guidance Approaches

education programs can help students to realize the importance of personal vocational planning. However, this personal planning needs to be supported by career guidance opportunities. Guidance personnel should develop guidance opportunities which are provided in conjunction with economic education.

Approach: Mobile Career Guidance Services

DO YOU SHARE THESE CONCERNS?

You are working in a rural area or small school district. You are aware of the needs of your students for career guidance but have limited resources for providing such services.

You are working in a school setting which offers vocational guidance and education services to post-high school students. It is difficult to find effective ways of communicating the nature of these programs to out-of-school youth and encouraging them to enter these programs.

You are responsible for guidance services in a rural school district. A major problem in providing these services is lack of available counseling staff and inability to reach the existing staff for in-service training activities.

Mobile education services enable a variety of educational services to be provided in small, rural school districts. Use of these mobile services in career guidance allows (a) increased counseling services for students in hard-to-reach areas, (b) increased staff training for these areas, and (c) availability of career guidance resources, i.e., occupational information, which the individual school could not afford.

THE APPROACH AS DEVELOPED BY OTHERS

Several school districts or combinations of a number of districts have developed mobile career guidance services.

County Program in Indiana. A mobile counseling center staffed by four counselors was developed to serve high school students in four counties in southern Indiana. The operation is a 10′x40′ trailer equipped with three counseling offices, testing cubicle and educational-occupational reading area, plus a reception and psychometric area. It is self-contained except for the electrical supply for the heating, air conditioning and lighting system. The mobile center travels the four Indiana counties giving a full range of guidance programs not only to the students of the area but to teachers and parents as well (Winborn and Martinson 1967).

Havre, Montana. Havre High School District A developed a mobile center to provide vocational guidance services to high school students in six counties. The mobile center visits each high school in the six-county area for a specified number of days depending on the school enrollment. During each visit, the center's guidance counselor organizes students to visit the center in small groups based on vocational interests. Each group is exposed to group counseling and occupational information using various media. Each student then has a chance to meet individually with the counselor. For further information contact Havre High School District A, 727 Second Avenue, Havre, Montana 59501 (Havre High School District, Montana).

Carnesville, Georgia. The Franklin County Board of Education in Carnesville developed mobile student-personnel teams to serve a four-county area. Emphasis was placed on providing guidance and counseling services to K-3 students in scattered small schools. Five teams were formed, each composed of an elementary counselor and a paraprofessional working in conjunction with the classroom teacher. The counselor worked in a classroom on a scheduled basis to identify (a) children with learning difficulties or motivational problems, and (b) students with social adjustment problems, especially those caused by cultural dissonance. Counselors sought to develop in teachers an increased sensitivity to classroom dynamics and to aid teachers in the administration and interpretation of sociometric devices. For further information contact Franklin County Board of Education, Route 3, Danielson, Georgia 30633 (Franklin County Schools, Georgia).

San Pablo, California. Contra Costa College is using a mobile unit for community outreach activity. The unit is staffed by one counselor and one paraprofessional, and activity is concentrated in the area of the district which has the largest disadvantaged population. Purposes of the unit are to (a) extend counseling services to the community, (b) reach potential students who would not otherwise receive counseling services, (c) bridge the communication gap between college and community, (d) encourage educational-vocational decision making, (e) strengthen the image of the college in the community, and (f) encourage youth to attend the college (Gordon 1970).

Designing Career Guidance Approaches

SOME BASIC PRINCIPLES

Basic principles underlying the use of mobile career guidance services are:

1. These services are designed for *hard-to-reach populations*. This can include both students who live in geographically isolated areas or students who are culturally isolated within large communities.
2. When designing mobile services the emphasis should be on *services* rather than *mobility*. While quite elaborate physical units can be designed, it should be remembered that the quality of services is influenced more by the nature of staff than by the nature of the mobile unit. Resources purchased for the mobile unit, i.e. media and materials, should be directly related to the services being offered.
3. Mobile services should be viewed as a means of *strengthening existing services* rather than a substitute for them. Since it is impossible for mobile services to remain at one location on a continuous basis, it is important to use these resources as a means of training existing staff to provide these continuing services.
4. Many mobile educational services have used *paraprofessionals* to help to staff the units. They prove useful in providing clerical help and basic guidance services, thus freeing professional time for counseling and consultation.

DESIGNING AND IMPLEMENTING A MOBILE CAREER GUIDANCE SERVICE

Set Goals. It is impossible for a mobile unit to meet all needs for all people; therefore, it is important to designate the specific goals and the target population. A first decision is which students will be served. Services may be provided for all students, or for those with special problems which cannot be serviced by the local school. Another consideration is whether services will be offered directly to students, or whether the mobile staff will consult with and train local staff to strengthen local services to students.

Staffing. A number of staffing patterns have been used in mobile units. There is usually a basic professional staff consisting of counselors and/or other pupil personnel specialists, but supportive help is usually needed. In some cases, paraprofessionals have been used, including college student volunteers and people from the local community. Also, consultants from other institutions, such as counselor educators and state department of education personnel, have been used.

Physical Facilities. Designing and selecting the actual mobile unit is a rather complex task. A good strategy is to collaborate with others who have mobile service units. However, some basic considerations can be mentioned. First, the basic mobile unit is usually a self-propelled mobile home. Others have found that these units are easy to maneuver and, in the long run, are lower in cost. Secondly, based on the services to be provided, the staff must decide how to sub-divide the basic unit. Some possible sub-areas include a counseling area, an information area and a testing area. It is also important to have an attractive physical appearance to insure a motivating learning climate. A final consideration is the resources, i.e., basic materials and media supplies, which will be contained within the unit. Again, these should be necessary to the services being offered. However, it is also suggested that these resources be designed to allow for flexibility in case the unit is used for other services.

Coordinate Services with Schools. Mobile services are at any one school location for a very short period of time. Therefore, it is important to carefully coordinate mobile services with the existing school programs. First, it is important to communicate the nature of the mobile services to school staffs and students prior to visiting the school. This orientation before arrival is crucial if the local school is to make maximum use of the mobile services. Secondly, it is necessary to develop a master schedule for the use of the mobile services. Two ways in which scheduling decisions have been made by others is on the basis of need by the local school and on the basis of student enrollment numbers. Finally, it is important to provide follow-up supportive services and consultation to school staff after the mobile unit has left the school. Since a major use of mobile units is to strengthen the existing school program through consultation and training, this follow-up is essential if any lasting change is to occur.

Evaluation. There are several types of evaluation which are possible. A first level of evaluation would be to collect statistics on the number and type of services provided to various individuals within the schools visited. Secondly, a follow-up can be done to gain information about the nature of the school program after the mobile unit has left. Finally, an ultimate evaluation would be to collect information about the adequacy of the educational-vocational plans of students in the schools which have been visited.

Approach: Teaching Decision Making

DO YOU SHARE THESE CONCERNS?

As you work with students to help them to develop post-high school educational plans, you feel it would be helpful to have information about how other students from your school have achieved in various colleges and universities in your state.

Although you have conducted follow-up studies of recent graduates from your high school, you would like to find some way of organizing the information gained from these studies in a format which could be easily used by you and by students currently in your school.

Deciding. The *Deciding* program, which is a course of study to teach students how to make decisions, is currently available from the College Entrance Examination Board. This decision-making curriculum was developed by H.B. Gelatt, Barbara Varenhorst and Richard Carey based on several years of experience in a guidance program oriented toward decision making in Palo Alto, California. Designed for students in junior and senior high schools, the program is a course of study in developing decision-making skills that can serve as a basis for a school-wide decision-making curriculum, as a major component in the guidance program, or as part of subject areas such as English, social studies and health education. The curriculum emphasized the role of values, information and strategies in the decision-making process and helped students to understand various applications of the decision-making process to their own life decisions.

Although no two students are alike, they may be quite similar in terms of a number of characteristics, e.g., interests, ability, past grades. Therefore, it can be helpful for students to have information about how other students similar to themselves have performed in various educational institutions.

Recently, several programs have been developed which help students to learn to make decisions by (a) helping them to understand the process of decision making, (b) helping them to develop their own framework for decision making, (c) providing experience tables indicating the probability of success in various choice alternatives, and (d) giving them an opportunity to practice the process of decision making.

THE APPROACH AS DEVELOPED BY OTHERS

Newton, Massachusetts. A task-oriented course in decision making was developed as part of the Information System for Vocational Decisions and was used with ninth graders in Newton, Massachusetts. The need of ninth graders to make course selections for the tenth grade was used as a basis for teaching the basic process of decision making. A booklet entitled "You, the Decider" was developed for use by students, and teachers were trained to help students to use the booklet and to help them to learn decision-making skills. Three main goals of the programs included: (a) learning the language of the process of decision making, (b) practicing decision making under supervision, and (c) developing and communicating a personal criteria for choice. Included in the booklet are experience tables indicating how ninth-grade students with specific grade averages in specific subjects, e.g., English, had done in similar tenth-grade subjects. The document cited in the bibliography contains the booklet, "You, the Decider" and examples of experience tables (Wilson 1967).

Project MINI-SCORE. This is a six-year project conducted by the University of Minnesota to identify criteria which are useful to counselors and others in counseling post-high school vocational-technical students as they select specific vocational-technical curricula. The project has four phases: (a) testing of applicants to area vocational-technical schools, resulting in data on the personal characteristics, ability, interests, values, aptitudes and level of vocational development; (b) follow-up after testing to see if applicant is admitted to technical school, and if so, whether he completes training; (c) another follow-up twelve months after completion of training to determine current employment status; and (d) analysis of data and development of expectancy tables and test-instrument norms applicable to all major vocational-technical curriculum areas with suggestions for using this information in counseling (Pucel 1968).

SOME BASIC PRINCIPLES

When designing decision-making programs, the following principles should be considered:

1. Sound decision making requires reliable information about *various options and about chances of success in these options.*
2. Follow-up studies of past students provide data for the development of *experience or expectancy tables* for use by, and/or with, current students.

3. These tables at best can only give students an indication of how they might perform in the same situation and, therefore, *data should be presented in general, simplified terms* which can be easily understood by students.
4. These tables can easily be interpreted by both students and school staff as giving answers about how a student will perform. It is essential that these *tables be used only in conjunction with other guidance activities* such as basic courses in decision making and/or individual counseling.
5. It is also important to note that a student must realize that such tables are based on his current status, i.e., ninth-grade grade point average. What he does in future years will alter the nature of the alternatives and probabilities for success in various alternatives. Therefore, it is suggested that use of such information be part of an *on-going guidance experience* which provides help for students at a variety of choice points throughout his school experience.

DESIGNING AND IMPLEMENTING DECISION-MAKING GUIDANCE EXPERIENCES

Design Guidance Goals. Instruction in decision making which utilizes expectancy tables is intended not only to help students to make specific choices which are needed at a particular time in their life, but also, more importantly, to help them to learn the process of decision making so they may use the process throughout their life. Both the Palo Alto program and the Newton program can be used as a model for describing basic decision-making skills which can be taught through this type of guidance experience. To teach the process, it is necessary to identify a number of choices which students must make and use these as opportunities for basic instruction in decision making, e.g., choice of high school curriculum, choice of post-high school training institution, etc. It has been recommended that decision-making training be an on-going guidance experience available to students at several points throughout junior high and senior high school.

Identify and Collect Information Needed for Decision Making. Expectancy tables are based on information collected from previous students after they have implemented their specific educational and occupational choices. Specific information which will be collected through follow-up studies depends on the goals of the guidance program. However, some areas of information which might be considered include (a) high school grades, (b) nature of post-high school educational institution attended, (c) educational achievement in these institutions,

(d) success in specific school curricula, and (e) initial job placement. Grades, or school achievement, is only one possible type of information. It is preferable to collect multiple types of information including personal characteristics, interests, abilities and vocational maturity.

Design Guidance Experience. There are several possible ways of providing decision-making instruction. Some schools have used basic materials in conjunction with classroom activities in on-going courses, e.g., social studies. In other cases, self-instructional materials have been developed which enable the student to work individually. Ultimately, it is possible to develop computer-assisted instructional systems which contain both instructional elements and the data needed for specific decisions. The Information System for Vocational Decisions at Harvard is an example of such a computer system. It is possible to use self-instructional methods to introduce the basic decision-making process and to enable students to make tentative decisions. However, it is important to provide some type of opportunity for the student to discuss his choice and his basis for choice with a counselor or teacher either individually or in a group.

Evaluate and Revise Program. First, it is important to design the program initially so that there is provision for on-going data collection. If students are using follow-up information as one component in the decision-making process, it is essential that the information be current and accurate. Actual evaluation of the decision-making program might include two types of information. First, students who have used the decision-making process to make one choice, i.e., high school curriculum, should be able to apply the process to another type of choice, i.e., post-high school training. A second type of evaluation relates to the extent to which students are both satisfied with, and successful in, their choices.

Approach: Special Curricula to Motivate Career Exploration

DO YOU SHARE THESE CONCERNS?

Although it is important to provide an opportunity for all students to engage in vocational exploration activities, it is not possible to encourage such activity through the one-to-one counseling relationship.

Teachers have expressed a willingness to have a component related to career planning in their classes but they express a need for direction in terms of what the goals of such a program should be and what instructional materials would be used.

Designing Career Guidance Approaches

A number of vocational exploration curricula have been developed which (a) encourage exploration of self in relationship to the world of work, (b) provide specific learning objectives, (c) give specific classroom activities, and (d) provide instruction about specific teaching procedures which might be used. These curricula to motivate career exploration are a possible response to the need for all students to have the opportunity to learn and practice vocational exploration skills.

THE APPROACH AS DEVELOPED BY OTHERS

Oregon State Department of Education. Oregon schools have a one-year course entitled "Self Understanding Through Occupational Exploration," designed to assist ninth graders with educational and career planning. Its aims are to enable students to (a) gain knowledge and understanding of possible future goals and job opportunities, (b) develop social skills in applying for work via application and job interviews, (c) gain understanding of employers' viewpoints and requirements, (d) broaden his knowledge of the general economic structure as related to labor force needs, (e) understand the importance of opportunities offered through high school and post-high school training programs, and (f) assess his own strengths and weaknesses. The course, individually tailored, includes evaluation of goals via investigation, idea exchanges in groups, role playing, interviewing, letter writing, reporting, visitations, speakers, films, appropriate research exercises and testing. The document cited in the bibliography is the complete teacher's guide and curriculum (Oregon State Department of Education 1968).

New Jersey State Department of Education. New Jersey schools have a curriculum entitled "Introduction to Vocations," which coordinates those areas of school closely allied to the world of work, e.g. vocational guidance, industrial education, business education and home economics. The curriculum consists of a number of units with each unit being organized according to basic concepts, objectives, suggested time allotment, class discussion topics and activities, learning experiences and references. Major units include (a) Introduction, (b) Understanding yourself, (c) The economics of industry, (d) Exploring mechanical operations, (e) Exploring science laboratory occupations, (f) Exploring occupations related to home economics, (g) Exploring the business world, and (h) Evaluating your experiences and planning ahead (New Jersey State Department of Education 1968).

Abington School District, Pennsylvania. This school district has developed "Career Development Activities" for grades 5–7. These learning experiences center on a different theme for each year: (a) Grade

5 — "How Our Interests Develop and Their Importance in Our Lives," (b) Grade 6 — "Changes That Are Taking Place, Decisions Which Are Made, and How They Affect Our Lives," and (c) Grade 7 — "Our Values and Their Influence on Our Decisions and Our Lives." Specific learning objectives and experiences were developed along with specific instructions for teachers. These learning experiences draw on innovations in methodology: simulation, gaming, role playing, problem solving, decision making, dramatics and guest speakers. A conscious effort was made to avoid learning activities which are didactic in nature and also to avoid learning about specific jobs. The major goal of the curriculum is to help students to understand the process through which career decisions are made. The document cited in the bibliography contains the complete curriculum giving specific learning activities and teacher instructions (Abington School District, 1968).

SOME BASIC PRINCIPLES

When designing special curricula, the following should be considered:

1. There are *basic vocational exploration skills* which can be learned by students. These involve skills related to self-understanding and understanding of the world of work.
2. If all students are to learn to apply these skills to their own vocational planning, *some method in addition to one-to-one counseling* must be used.
3. It is possible to specify these exploratory skills and *design curricula* which will enable large numbers of students to learn and practice these skills.
4. A vocational exploration curriculum needs to be *carefully designed* and should include (a) learning objectives, (b) suggested learning activities, (c) suggested instructional methods.
5. Such curricula can maintain an *individualized, guidance point of view*, allowing for group discussion, individualized activities, active involvement in learning, etc.

DESIGNING AND IMPLEMENTING A VOCATIONAL EXPLORATION CURRICULUM

Select the Intended Population. Most special vocational exploration curricula are designed for a specific group of students. In some cases, they are designed for only one grade and in others for several grades. If the curriculum is to be comprehensive and include complete materials

Designing Career Guidance Approaches

for use with students, it is probably wise to limit the scope of the program to one or two grades.

Maintain a Guidance Point of View. Because vocational exploration curricula are designed for use with groups of students does not mean that they cannot be individualized. Some suggestions which others have used for keeping these curricula guidance-oriented include (a) encourage group discussion, (b) design for active participation by students through such activities as role playing and field trips, (c) individualize the curriculum by suggesting alternative assignments based on students' interests and needs, (d) make the learning situation non-graded if possible, and (e) allow an opportunity for student reaction to the learning experience.

Develop the Curriculum Materials. Using both teachers and counselors to develop the materials seems to be most effective. An approach used by others is to first determine the learning goals of the program. After these have been established, a survey can be conducted to identify possible learning activities and resources which have been developed by others. Once these learning activities have been identified, they can be selected and/or modified in terms of the specific learning objectives. Finally, once the objectives and suggested activities have been developed, it is important to develop specific instructional directions to insure effective use by teachers. Throughout the development of the curriculum, the goals should be to make the program very specific so that it may be used directly by teachers as a curriculum guide.

Plan for the Implementation of the Curriculum. There are several ways in which vocational exploration curricula can be implemented into the school program. Three possibilities include: (a) It can be incorporated as a part of a large curriculum sequence, e.g., into a social studies or vocational education program. (b) It can be offered as a separate course offering using team staffing of counselors and teachers. (c) It can be a self-instructional program which allows students to work by themselves with the opportunity for follow-up interviews with the counseling staff.

Communicate Program to Involved Persons. The success of vocational guidance curricula depends largely on the extent to which involved groups understand the nature and goals of these programs. There are four major groups which should be informed about the program. First, teachers need to thoroughly understand the curriculum and to be trained in effective use of the curriculum. Secondly, students need to know what to expect from the program and how it might be useful to them in the future. Through communicating with parents about the program, it is possible to gain their support and help them to become involved in their children's vocational development. Finally, these curricula usually rely heavily on community support. Since they are action-oriented and frequently include guest speakers and field trips, it is important to inform the community about the goals of the program and ways in which community members can participate in the program.

Initiate Use of the Curriculum. Once the curriculum goals and materials have been developed and teachers have been trained, the program can be initiated. A major consideration at this time is to establish definite procedures for coordination between the teaching and guidance staff. Guidance personnel can lend support both through clarifying for teachers the nature of the learning activities and through offering supportive individual or small group counseling services to students. Another important step in initiating the program is to build in a definite procedure for seeking student and teacher response to the curriculum. This can be done through classroom observation, written response or through interviewing selected participants.

Evaluate and Revise Curriculum. Three major evaluation areas include (a) workability of the program, i.e., are the materials effective, are instructional procedures clear; (b) reactions of both students and teachers to program, i.e., do they find it worthwhile, interesting, and motivating; and (c) changes in student behavior, i.e., can they illustrate exploratory behavior and can they apply this behavior to their own personal planning.

Approach: Using Models to Learn Vocational Behaviors

DO YOU SHARE THESE CONCERNS?

You are counseling a number of twelfth graders who will be seeking employment after they graduate. They seem to be quite afraid of interviewing for jobs and not sure how to look for jobs.

You have been working with a group of students trying to encourage them to explore various occupational clusters. However, they seem unable to seek and use information in their vocational planning.

You are working with a group of students who are involved in work experience programs. They are having some difficulty in their relationship with their supervisor on the job. You would like to help them to find ways of improving the relationship.

Designing Career Guidance Approaches

For all of these students, some type of career guidance experience is needed which will (a) help them learn the exact nature of successful vocational behavior, (b) motivate them to use these behaviors, (c) provide an opportunity to practice these behaviors, and (d) allow them to try out the behaviors in real-life situations.

THE APPROACH AS DEVELOPED BY OTHERS

A career guidance approach which can meet these student needs is the use of social modeling to teach vocational behaviors. Examples of this approach which have been developed are the following.

Social Skill Seminar. Northern Systems Company developed this program to help disadvantaged job trainees to develop successful on-the-job social behaviors. This is a role-playing situation in which the trainees observe a prepared sociodrama. The steps in the process include: (a) An initial sociodrama portrays a trainee within a specific situation striving for a personal goal. (b) The trainee behavior is inappropriate and does not lead to goal attainment. (c) The observers visualize themselves in the same situation and experience the role model's lack of success. (d) A group discussion focuses on the behavior of the role model. (e) Another sociodrama is conducted with the role model using appropriate behaviors and obtaining personal goals (Harrison 1971).

Group Counseling. Group counseling sessions were conducted using social models as a stimulus to evaluate high school students' ability to seek and process career information. Before the program began, students were asked to answer the question, "If you were watching a group of students your age present a panel discussion on some topic, what are the characteristics of a student which would make you want to pay particular attention to him?" After the characteristics of effective models were identified, four fifteen-minute video-taped sessions were developed using students as models. These tapes showed a group counseling session in which the students were using effective vocational-information-seeking and information-processing behaviors. Group counseling sessions focused on viewing these tapes, then discussing the behaviors which had been seen and, finally, practicing these behaviors (Hamilton 1969).

SOME BASIC PRINCIPLES

Social modeling is an approach which allows the student to see someone else perform the behavior to be learned and then discuss and practice the behavior in a counseling setting. When designing an application of this approach for a specific program, it is important to remember the following principles:

1. The behavior learned is one which the *student recognizes a need* to develop. The vocational behaviors should be selected because the student has expressed a desire to learn these behaviors.
2. Models should *clearly present the behavior* to be learned, thus allowing the student to understand and imitate the behavior. Effective models are those individuals who are admired by the student and who are somewhat similar to him.
3. Once the student has seen the behavior as used by the model, he needs an opportunity to *practice and perfect the behavior* in a non-threatening situation.
4. The ultimate goal is to use effective vocational behaviors in real life situations. Therefore, the student, once he understands the behavior and has practiced it, needs an opportunity to *use the behavior in a real situation*, i.e., in an actual job interview.

DESIGNING AND IMPLEMENTING A SOCIAL MODELING EXPERIENCE

Identify and Describe the Behavior. Modeling is designed to help students learn specific behaviors, e.g., how to seek occupational information, how to participate in group counseling, or how to communicate with a supervisor on the job. A first step in designing the modeling experience is to identify and describe the behaviors which are needed by the students by both asking students to identify vocational behaviors which they feel they need to develop and by using counselor experience with a number of students to identify behaviors which other students have needed help with in the past.

Select Models to be Used. Modeling is based on the idea that students will imitate the behaviors of those whom they admire, e.g., the child imitating his parent's behaviors. Therefore, it is necessary to select models who are respected by the student. Appropriate models must be people who have characteristics which make them likable to the students. Also, they should be like the students in terms of such characteristics as sex, age, social status, etc. One way of selecting model characteristics is to have the students describe the type of person whom they most respect and like, and then select people who have these characteristics. It is important to note that models are usually people who are unknown to the client, e.g., students from other schools, people from various occupations, etc.

Design Presentation of Model. Modeling does not require that the model actually be physically present in the counseling situation or even that the model be a living person. Real people can be used as models

Designing Career Guidance Approaches

and their behavior can be presented through films, tape recordings, and video-tape recordings. If real people are used, it is important to work with them carefully to be certain that they are using the desired behavior and that the behaviors are clearly presented. These real modeling applications may be easier to develop, but it is sometimes difficult to control the exact nature of the behavior being shown. Another type of modeling centers on creating behavior models which are not real people. For example, it is possible to coach an individual in the desired behavior and then have him role play the behavior. These created models can be presented on film or video tape. Also, it is possible to develop a structured role-play situation in which the students themselves role play the desired behavior.

Whether live or created models are used, it is important that the exact behavior is clearly presented in such a way that the students both recognize and understand it. Several steps can be taken to insure this. First, it is possible to have cues within the modeling situation which indicate that the behavior is being used. For example, if the model is illustrating effective information-seeking behaviors, the situation might present a counseling interview in which a student is talking with a counselor. When he suggests appropriate information-seeking activities, the counselor might reinforce the behavior with positive comments. Such cues as this help the viewer to understand the behavior. Also, it is important to present the behavior in steps which can be absorbed by the students. If the behavior is quite complex, several modeling situations might be used with each one communicating one aspect of the behavior.

Prepare Students for Modeling Experience. The students must recognize the importance and relevance of the behaviors presented in the modeling situation. Therefore, it is important to integrate the use of modeling in an on-going guidance experience. Students might be selected for guidance groups based on common characteristics or a shared need for learning new behaviors. Prior to presenting the models, the group might focus on the need for the new behavior and possible uses of the behavior in their life situation.

Present and Clarify the New Behavior. After students recognize the need and relevance of the new behaviors, the modeling situation can be used. After the model has been presented, the students need an opportunity to discuss and clarify the nature of the behaviors. This can be done through either discussing the behavior or by having the students role play the behavior to test their understanding. It is most effective to actually give students an opportunity to test and practice the new behavior in the guidance situation.

Plan for Real-Life Application of the Behavior. A final stage in the use of modeling is to help the students to try the new behavior in a real-life situation. Each student is assisted in applying the new behavior and evaluating how effective the behavior was. This trial can be structured within the guidance setting. For example, each group member might outline a plan for trying the new behavior, actually use the behavior outside the group situation and then evaluate the effectiveness of the behavior in the group.

Evaluate the Experience. The final evaluation of the modeling experience is the extent to which the student can use the new behavior. Evaluation includes several levels, such as first talking with students to get their reactions to the experience and check their understanding of the behavior. A second step would be to have the student use the behavior in the guidance situation and, finally, have the student use the behavior in situations outside the counseling setting.

Revise the Modeling Situation. If evaluation indicates that the behavior was not clearly communicated and that the students are not able to use the behavior in real situations, then it is necessary to revise the modeling situation. Several types of revision are possible. First, it may be that the model who was used did not appeal to the students, and therefore, the students did not want to acquire the new behavior. If this is so, then new models might be selected. It may also be that the students found the model appealing but the behavior was not clearly specified in the model situation. In this case, the same model might revise the modeling experience either through using more cues to indicate when the behavior is being used or through breaking the behavior into smaller segments so that the students can more readily identify the exact nature of the behavior. A final type of revision might be in the way the modeling situation is introduced into the guidance experience. It might be that students do understand the nature of the behavior but that they do not see its relevance for themselves or have not had sufficient opportunity to practice and perfect the behavior in the guidance situation.

Approach: Simulation to Facilitate Vocational Exploration and Decision Making

DO YOU SHARE THESE CONCERNS?

You have been working with a group of potential dropouts. The goal has been to help them to select vocational curricula which will

Designing Career Guidance Approaches

encourage them to remain in school. However, they have shown little or no interest in the information you have presented.

When counseling students in future educational and vocational planning, you have noticed that they are very hesitant to discuss their personal feelings about themselves and their perceptions of the world of work.

As you talk with students, it has become clear that they have a vague interest in planning for the future. However, for them the adult world is unknown and seems complex; therefore, they are having difficulty in their planning attempts.

For all these students, some type of experience is needed which will (a) help them to develop an accurate understanding of the world of education and work, (b) provide a non-threatening opportunity to explore this world, (c) stimulate their interest in planning for the future, and (d) motivate them to adopt an information-seeking stance.

THE APPROACH AS DEVELOPED BY OTHERS

If the students need this type of experience, a guidance approach which utilizes simulated experiences to acquaint students with the world of work and motivate them in further vocational-educational planning might be considered. Although it is possible that a guidance staff might develop simulated experiences, it must be noted that the development and testing of these experiences takes considerable time. Therefore, a more feasible use of simulation is to start with materials developed by others and possibly modify these for a particular school setting and student population. Two examples of simulation which are commercially available are presented below.

Job Experience Kits. These have been designed to give students the opportunity to solve problems typical of a particular occupation. About twenty occupational kits are now available, most for low-entry jobs, e.g., accountant, salesperson, X-ray technician and truckdriver. Each kit has a similar format. After a motivational introduction on the importance of the occupation, the student is presented with a problem and the information he will need to solve it. The problems are representative of those actually faced by the people in the various occupations and are presented in a realistic manner. Materials meet the following criteria: (a) Vocabulary used can be comprehended by 95 percent of high school students. (b) The problems are intrinsically interesting to students. (c) About 75 percent of the students can solve the problems within fifty minutes. (d) Representatives of the particular occupations have judged the problems to be typical of their occupation (Krumboltz 1967a). Kits are available from Science Research Associates, Test and Guidance Marketing, 259 East Erie St., Chicago, Illinois 60611.

Life Career Game. This game simulates certain features of the "labor" market, the "education" market, and the "marriage" market, as they now operate in the United States and as projections indicate they will function in the future. By playing, students gain an understanding of these institutions and some advance experience in planning for their own future. Participants learn (a) how the life cycles of men and women are patterned, including the kinds of career decisions that persons in our society must make at various points in their lives; (b) the way in which decisions about occupations, education, family life and the use of leisure time are interrelated (e.g., a person's education affects what kinds of jobs he can obtain and the kind of person he marries, and the decisions a person makes at one point of his life affect his opportunities at later points); (c) what factors affect a person's success and satisfaction with his education, job, marriage, and free time; (d) what kinds of educational and occupational opportunities are open to individuals with varying sets of personal characteristics, and how to locate and use reference materials which contain this type of information.

The game can be played by any number of teams, each consisting of two to four players. Each team works with a profile or case history of a fictitious person (usually a student about the age of the players). The game is organized into rounds or decision periods, each of which represents one year in the life of this person. A game runs for a designated number of rounds.

During each decision period, players plan their person's schedule of activities for a typical week, allocating his time among school, studying, a job, family responsibilities and leisure time activities. In addition, for certain activities — a job, or higher education — a person must make some kind of formal application and be accepted.

When players have made their decisions about the person for a given year, scores are computed. The scoring tables and spinners are based upon U.S. Census and other national survey data. They show what this person, given his character, past experiences and present efforts, would probably achieve in the areas of education, occupation, family life and leisure. The winner is the team which accumulates the highest score (Barbula 1967, Boocock 1967, Varenhorst 1968). The game is available from Western Publishing Company, School and Library Department, 150 Parish Drive, Wayne, New Jersey.

Designing Career Guidance Approaches

SOME BASIC PRINCIPLES

When using simulated experiences which have been developed by others or designing new experiences, it is important to remember the following principles:

1. Simulated experiences are intended to be *motivating and enjoyable* for students. They have the "fun" quality of games which holds the interest of participants. Students seem to react very favorably to simulated experiences and, therefore, the teacher and/or counselor who is supervising the simulated experience should support this enjoyable atmosphere.
2. Simulated experiences represent *real environments*. While some games represent a fantasy world, simulation relies on an accurate, current picture of the real world. When either designing new experience or using those developed by others, it is essential to evaluate the information presented through the simulated experience in terms of its appropriateness for the population with which it is used.
3. Simulated experiences can be viewed as *non-threatening substitutes for real experience*. Through these experiences, students can understand various roles possible in society, the complexity of decisions and the tasks involved in various occupations. This experience allows students to role play the life of another without having to commit himself to selecting that role. When supervising students in these experiences, the teacher and/or counselor should encourage this experimental stance rather than force commitment to a particular role.
4. The simulated experiences previously described are designed to help students to *learn the process of information seeking and decision making*. They provide a model of behavior which is applied within the game to the life of another individual. After the simulated experience, it is necesary to provide other experience, i.e., occupational materials or group counseling sessions, to allow students to apply this model to their own lives.

DESIGNING AND IMPLEMENTING SIMULATION EXPERIENCES

Identify Student Characteristics. The two simulated experiences which have been described are appropriate for use with junior high and senior high school students. In some cases, they have been modified for use in the elementary school. It has also been found that they can be used with a heterogeneous group, e.g., gifted students and underachievers. However, it is important to test the materials on students before final selection.

Identify Materials Available. Two simulated experiences have been described. The *Life Career Game* has been modified by some schools to fit special needs of their particular student group (Barbula 1967, Varenhorst 1968). The *Job Experience Kits* are designed primarily to introduce entry jobs and presently are limited to twenty occupations. As an initial step, these materials could be used in their present forms on an experimental level. However, in time, they might be modified and used as models for the development of new simulated experiences.

Design of the Simulated Experience. Although a simulated experience which has been developed by others may be used, there is some flexibility in terms of the way in which it is used. For example, in the *Life Career Game*, it is possible to vary the number of fictitious people used, i.e., all teams use the same person or teams use different people. Another possibility is to expand certain parts of these experiences into role-playing sessions or to introduce additional facts and information.

Design Game Setting and Environment. Simulated experiences have been used by others both in special guidance settings in which students leave the classroom to participate or as an integral classroom experience. Either may be used but the classroom experience may be easier to schedule. The most effective setting seems to be a self-contained setting in which all individuals are actively involved in the experience. This is important because there needs to be freedom for group discussion and emotional reaction from students (e.g., when one class was playing the *Life Career Game*, a team applied for a child and the total class cheered when they received it).

A final consideration in the game setting is the availability of supplemental resources. Since these experiences motivate further information seeking, it is helpful to have educational-occupational information materials present during the experience so students may act immediately to seek information of interest to them.

Design Post-Simulation Guidance Activities. These experiences naturally lead into further information seeking and planning activities. Some possible follow-up guidance activities which have been used by others include testing, supplemental information sources, role playing and group counseling. Some type of follow-up counseling activity, either group or individual, seems particularly appropriate since through the

Designing Career Guidance Approaches

game the students have formed peer relationships, have developed a shared experience with other students and can talk first about the fictitious person in the game rather than about themselves.

Train Teachers and/or Counselors to Direct Activities. As is true in all games, it is important that someone be available to direct the activity who is thoroughly familiar with the actions required in the game and the rules of play. The most effective way of training staff to perform this role is to have them actually participate in the simulated experience. Also, it is possible to develop supplementary written materials which describe such information as (a) materials needed, (b) the basic organization of the experience, (c) how to start the experience, (d) rules for play, (e) when the experience is completed, and (f) supplemental activities to be used both in conjunction with and after the experience.

Evaluate Students' Comprehension and Ability to Use Simulated Materials. For these experiences to be successful it is first necessary that students be able to read the written instructions and complete the basic simulated activities. Close observation during the experience can provide useful data about the extent to which the experiences are appropriate for a particular student group. If the experiences seem too difficult, they may be modified through supplementary verbal instructions, simplified written instructions or different team composition.

Evaluate Information Gained Through Experience. These experiences are designed not only to motivate further action but also to facilitate specific learning. Therefore, it is possible to evaluate specific learning which has occurred during the game. Such an evaluation is important since further guidance activities are based on these game learnings.

Evaluate Post-Game Behavior. These experiences are designed to teach information seeking, decision making and planning behaviors which can be applied by the student to his own vocational-educational planning. The ultimate test of the effectiveness of these experiences is the extent to which the student is willing and able to apply these skills to his own life. Through follow-up interviews and guidance activities, it is possible to determine how the student is using the skills he has developed in the simulated experience.

Revise Guidance Experience. Based on the preceding types of evaluation data, it is possible to evaluate the effectiveness of the guidance experience and, subsequently, revise the experience. Major areas of consideration are: (a) Are the simulated materials appropriate for these students? (b) Were the materials used in a way which was appropriate for the students? (c) Was the setting supportive of intended learnings? (d) Did post-simulation guidance activities support the application of learnings of the game? These questions can help to determine what part of the application needs to be modified.

Approach: Vocational Exploration Through Media and Classroom Activities

DO YOU SHARE THESE CONCERNS?

After talking with several students in your elementary school you realize that, although they know their father goes to "work" each day, they have little understanding of what work is.

John is a tenth grader who wants to be an engineer. However, he cannot explain what an engineer does and can think of no other occupations which interest him.

After a series of interviews with junior high school students, it is clear that few of them are able to suggest vocational areas which interest them, and few have made any attempt to seek information about various occupations.

For all of these students, some type of vocational exploration activity is needed to (a) encourage them to think vocationally, (b) broaden their perception of the world of work, (c) help them to check their understanding of the world of work against reality, (d) help them to discover broad areas of work which interest them, and (e) motivate them to seek further information about the world of work.

THE APPROACH AS DEVELOPED BY OTHERS

If students need this type of experience, a guidance approach which utilizes some type of educational media to present information about occupational clusters and classroom activities to stimulate vocational exploration might be considered. Examples of this approach which have been developed by others are the following.

Video tape. In order to provide information about entry jobs in a number of job clusters (e.g., secretarial, food retailing, automotive technology), a video tape was presented to high school students to commu-

Designing Career Guidance Approaches

nicate information about the job cluster, encourage them to remain in school and to motivate them to think about job training. Disadvantaged minority groups responded particularly well to these tapes (Bancroft 1966).

Television Series. Minneapolis Public Schools developed a series entitled "World of Work" to be used in the classroom to present information about occupational areas, to stimulate further exploration of the world of work and to provide a basis for program planning. Specific teacher guides were developed for each television program which suggested activities to be done prior to, during, and after the television program (Minneapolis Public Schools 1968).

Team teaching. Team teaching and various types of media were reported by Lockwood, et al. to encourage vocational exploration with gifted students. The "Four Worlds" program introduced students to the natural, technological, aesthetic and human worlds through classroom discussion and use of media. The goals of this exploration were to broaden students' understanding of the world of work, of the infinite possibilities open to them in these four areas of human endeavor, and of the excitement and challenge available through work (Lockwood et al. 1968).

SOME BASIC PRINCIPLES

These are only a few possible applications of this approach. When designing an application of this approach for a specific program, it is important to remember the following principles:

1. The information presented should be about broad *occupational clusters* rather than specific occupations. There are many ways to cluster occupations including by interest area, job families or level of training.
2. The goal is to provide *broad information* about shared characteristics of occupations within a cluster. Highly specific information about a single occupation should be avoided since it narrows rather than broadens the student's perceptions and results in early occupational choice.
3. The *message must be appropriate* for the particular student group. A number of media can be used to communicate information about occupational clusters, e.g., television, video tape, tape recordings, films, etc. More important than which media are used is the type of message which is presented. It should be

motivating, geared to the student's experience and vocabulary level, and accurate.

4. It is essential that the *student be involved* in the media. Using media for educational-vocational purposes should be selected because of student need, and specific activities for involving the student before, during and after the media experience must be developed.

5. Media should be *used in conjunction with other activities.* Media transmits a message to the student; however, it is essential that the student then have the opportunity to clarify the message and develop further plans for exploration based on the message. These steps require teacher and counselor intervention.

DESIGNING AND IMPLEMENTING CLASSROOM EXPERIENCES

Identify Teachers and Classroom Situations. This approach requires cooperation from teachers. It is important to look at the school situation and identify which teachers have an interest in vocational development and which curricular areas might appropriately include vocational exploration experiences. At this point the goal is to stimulate interest in such an approach, not necessarily to get commitment from specific individuals.

Identify Available Media Equipment and Expertise. In designing a specific application of this approach, it is best to begin with what is available in a specific school situation. It is possible to use many different types of media; there is not one medium that is definitely superior to the others. Therefore, media selection will depend primarily on those resources which are available. The guidance staff will specify what will be communicated through the media, but the development of the specific materials will need to be done by someone who has expertise in the specific media which are selected.

Select Students Who Can Be Resources. This approach is designed for use with students; therefore, it is important to identify students who can help in the development of materials. A resource group of students will be able to suggest areas of interest, respond to specific materials and even help in the development of materials.

Survey Available Community Resources. Representatives from various occupational clusters in the community are a valuable resource for the development of this approach. These individuals can provide information about the local occupational scene, can be used in media

Designing Career Guidance Approaches

presentations as occupational models, and can help with follow-up activities such as classroom visitations.

Identify Media Applications Developed by Others. Rather than developing new media materials, it is possible to modify materials which have been developed for use in other schools. Before any decisions are made, it is important to survey what others have done.

Select and Coordinate a Resource Group. Based on a survey of available resources, it is possible to select a resource group to help in the design of the applications. This group might include teachers, community resource people, students, counselors and media experts.

Identify the Needs of Students. The nature of these materials will depend on the nature of the students for which they are intended. Major factors to be considered include the students' (a) level of vocational development, (b) current experience level, (c) current vocabulary level, and (d) level of readiness for such information.

Once these factors have been identified, it is possible to develop a working criteria which states specifically what type of information is needed and how it should be presented. For example, if working with a group of elementary students, it might be decided that the content should show occupations related by the type of activities a worker performs. Since the students have had little opportunity to see people at work and have rather limited verbal skills, the materials should show people performing work activities, be audio-visual rather than written, and explain the information in a vocabulary related to the students own experiences.

Specify the Information Content. Crucial to this approach is the emphasis on broad information about common elements of occupations. The goal is not to present information about a larger number of specific occupations, but to broadly cover general occupational areas. If time and resources are limited, it is possible to select only a few clusters. Most applications of this approach focus on five to ten occupational clusters. Exactly how the occupations are clustered depends on the students' needs. Some clusters which have been used by others are by (a) job activity for elementary students, (b) relationship to school curriculum for junior high students, and (c) emphasis on entry occupations for non-college bound high school students.

Specify How the Information Should Be Presented. Once the content of the materials has been specified, the next step is to design exactly how the information will be communicated. As other schools have developed applications, they have focused on the following questions: (a) How can we use occupational models to communicate the information? (b) How long should the experience be, based on the attention span of the students? (c) What vocabulary will be comprehended by the students? (d) What experiences will they be able to relate to? (e) In what sequence should the information be presented? (f) How can continuity between sessions be insured?

Select Media and Coordinate Material Development. Based on the survey of available resources, the inventory of student needs and the criteria for content and format, it is possible to design the specific applications. This process calls for evaluating the appropriateness of available materials and media for the specific message and format needed for the student group. Once a combination of media to be used has been selected, the development of the materials can begin. The guidance staff can coordinate this development using media developers, teachers, community resource people and students.

Design and Describe Classroom Activities. Schools which have used this approach successfully have written teachers' guides for use of the materials. These should include (a) information about what will be presented in the materials, (b) suggested activities which will prepare the students to use the media, (c) activities which will involve the students in using the media (e.g., questions to think about while viewing video-tape presentations), (d) suggested areas of discussion after using the materials to insure clarification of the information presented, and (e) further vocational exploration activities.

Train Teachers to Use These Materials. It is the responsibility of the guidance staff to train teachers in the use of the media materials and to prepare them for leading subsequent classroom activities. The success of this approach relies greatly on the teachers' classroom behavior.

Specify Available Follow-up Counseling Services. This approach depends on cooperation between counselors and teachers. Therefore, it is important to communicate specific ways in which the counselor can help both within the classroom and through follow-up counseling services with individuals or groups of students.

Evaluate Media Materials. A first step in evaluation is to seek student reactions to the media materials. This can be done in several ways, e.g., interviewing students, using a dialogue system which allows the student to respond periodically as he uses the materials, and seeking student reactions to the materials.

Evaluate Teacher and Student Reaction. In addition to evaluating the specific media materials, it is important to get student and teacher reactions to the total experience. From teachers, information might focus on ease of use, appropriateness of suggested activities for students and their attitudes toward using the approach in their classroom. From students, information might focus on interest in materials, level of understanding of the information and motivation to further exploration.

Stimulate Exploratory Behavior. The goal of this approach is to motivate students to explore the world of work and to broaden their perceptions of work. Therefore, final evaluation must be based on the extent to which the specific approach has stimulated this behavior. This evaluation might focus on such factors as students seeking further help from the teacher or counselor, or their willingness to engage in further suggested exploratory activities.

Chapter 6 GUIDELINES FOR CAREER GUIDANCE PROGRAM DEVELOPMENT

Introduction

Although previous chapters have described a plethora of individual career guidance methods, little has been said about total career guidance programing. A total program is more than a random collection of individual methods; it systematically incorporates multiple methods to achieve a unified mission.

The purpose of this chapter is to provide practical guidelines for developing total career guidance programs. Programs differ from methods in that they are frameworks of guidance services rather than the vehicles of guidance itself. Methods are defined as the means of carrying out specific guidance objectives. They are techniques and utilize a variety of materials and tools in order to help a student to achieve his guidance goals or fulfill his guidance needs. Programs, on the other hand, are broader in scope. They are systems which incorporate specific methods administratively, organizationally and in accordance with broad theoretical principles.

The rationale for examining total guidance programing stems from two major considerations: Organizational-administrative management and student development.

ORGANIZATIONAL-ADMINISTRATIVE MANAGEMENT

The benefits to any guidance program which are derived from establishing a systematic organizational-administrative framework are several: (a) The existence of one total program which encompasses a variety of services for a variety of populations has a minimizing effect on both cost and space. Equipment, time and space can be made to work more effectively if they are organized into a unit, under one major structure. (b) Related to this minimizing effect is the extra benefit of avoiding duplication of services; duplication of materials and efforts can lead to both waste and frustration on the part of guidance counselors as well as the student. (c) Under one total framework of career guidance, the tasks of hiring, training and maintaining personnel become more simplified and more effective, in that individuals' specialized capabilities and skills can be applied to the program as a whole rather than be confined to fragmented services. (d) When career guidance services are organized into a whole, the evaluation of these services can be built into the program itself and can be conducted more effectively. Since services are structured to guide the individual from grades K to 12, the completion of each phase of guidance becomes a built-in evaluation checkpoint, in that a student is not able to advance to the next phase without adequate mastery of the preceding one. This, then, presents the opportunity for evaluating the student's progress, as well as the effectiveness of various phases of the program, and of instituting changes in the programs or remedial work for the student as necessary. Theoretically, this would result in a highly viable and productive program.

STUDENT DEVELOPMENT

The main idea underlying this consideration is that guidance is a continuous, developmental process. This conceptualization follows not only from the basic principles of physical development leading to progressive stages of maturity, but also from more recent theoretical formulations of the progressive, developmental nature of vocational interests, career planning and career choice.

Comprehensive career guidance programs have within them elements that are consistent with this developmental approach: (a) The basic element in a total program is that of continuity. Services are organized in a manner that provides students with a timely and orderly continuous set of phases, all planned, organized and coordinated as parts of a bigger whole. (b) Related to continuity is the idea that progressive stages of guidance can be based on previous learning or in accordance with the present level of learning; thus, being more appropriate for the recipients

Guidelines for Career Guidance Program Development 169

of guidance. This also allows the incorporation of career guidance elements into the curriculum itself. (c) In keeping with the developmental factor, the availability of a whole career guidance program also allows for the establishment of goals for each stage and the ability to carry them out more easily than if services were provided unsystematically or haphazardly. In a comprehensive program, goals that are unique for each grade level can be established and based on the particular needs of students at this level, or adapted and modified when change is needed. This also adds an element of viability and flexibility to any aspect of career guidance services. (d) In an organized system of services, i.e., a career guidance program, individuals with differential rates of vocational development can be assisted more efficiently and proceed according to their own pace. This eliminates premature advancement to higher stages in the guidance program, or the embarrassment of falling behind the class "norm".

In summary, the benefits of instituting whole programs of career guidance can be appreciated from both an organizational and developmental point of view. Based on the considerations enumerated above, this chapter elaborates on the development of programs of career guidance. The following section contains descriptions of five career guidance programs that are now in existence or at various stages of development or implementation. These are (a) Self Understanding Through Occupational Exploration (SUTOE) for junior high school programs (Oregon Board of Education 1969); (b) The Systems Approach: An Emerging Behavioral Model for Career Guidance (BMCG) for senior high school programs (Campbell et al. 1971); (c) Student Personnel Services in Georgia's Area Vocational-Technical Schools (SPS) (Bottoms 1967); (d) The Developmental Career Guidance Project, Detroit (DCGP) for elementary school programs (Leonard 1968); and (e) The Comprehensive Career Guidance Program (CCGS) for K-12 programs (Jones et al., 1971).

These programs serve as models and are followed by an enumeration and elaboration of the significant characteristics of effective programs. The purpose of this chapter is to provide some practical as well as conceptual guidelines for setting up programs within a school.

Exemplary Programs

SUTOE

Based upon the idea that all citizens are eventually faced with a variety of occupational choices, SUTOE is a classroom approach designed to help

junior high school students explore themselves in relation to occupations.
SUTOE attempts to present information about career exploration in a systematic way. The program is based on a set of underlying basic assumptions:

1. All students should have an opportunity to explore the broad total of the world of work.
2. All students should have opportunity to develop a self-concept.
3. All students should have experiences in meaningful decision making, and in accepting responsibility for their own decisions.
4. The junior high school years are a time of high potential for developing an awareness of relevant factors to be considered in decision making.
5. Career choice and its implementation is a developmental process.
6. A challenging experience-centered course that stimulates creative individualism is valid for junior high students in that they become more aware of both strengths and weaknesses, and reflect more positive interests.
7. A program that provides opportunity for acquiring self-understanding *and* knowledge of the world of work, will contribute much toward helping youth prepare for their place in a complex socio-economic world of reality.
8. More adequate educational goals and tentative career choices may be established by students, as a result of the experiences provided through an organized classroom approach.

The program is built as a course of study divided into units. Each unit focuses on the fulfillment of a set of specific timespan. This program attacks the problems involved in inadequate vocational guidance by offering a broad and comprehensive approach. Separate units fit into a whole, advancing systematically from one stage of knowledge and development to the next. These units and their respective objectives are represented below.

Approximate
Weeks per UNIT

6   I PUPIL INVOLVEMENT IN *SUTOE*

   Objective 1. The student will write about his tentative occupational plans.
              2. The students will know the purpose of the course, its general content, the methods to be used, and specific requirements.
              3. The students and the teacher will establish an effective working relationship.

4. The student will gain knowledge about our economic system and its manpower needs as it relates to the individual.
5. The student will become familiar with occupational classifications and clusters.
6. The student will know resources for later in-depth study of occupations.
7. The student can relate self-understanding to a tentative occupational choice.

4   II SELF APPRAISAL AND SELF UNDERSTANDING

Objective
1. The student will become aware of the terminology used for self-understanding and job selection.
2. The student will gather for his own use all possible information about himself.
3. Each student will compile a profile of himself which will help him assess his strengths and weaknesses.
4. The student will plan experiences, both inside and outside the school, which will help him capitalize on his strengths and strengthen his weaknesses.

4   III RELATING SCHOOL TO OCCUPATIONAL PLANNING

Objective
1. The student will relate the value of his present studies to future occupational opportunities.
2. The student will be able to relate the skills, knowledge, attitudes and habits of at least one elective course to salable skills in a future job.
3. The student develops or reviews, through individual or group conferences with counselors, his educational plan for high school.
4. The student will analyze and reinforce skills he has developed or needs to develop to be successful at being a student (his present occupation).

6   IV THE INDIVIDUAL'S ROLE IN THE ECONOMIC SYSTEM

Objective
1. The student will become acquainted with the concepts related to production, distribution and consumption, which are essential to understanding our economic system.
2. The student will explore the need for a healthy economy, as it relates to himself.
3. The student will examine aspects of business operation.
4. The student will realize the role of government in our economic system.
5. The student will investigate his role as a consumer.

4   V PREPARING STUDENTS FOR IN-DEPTH CAREER STUDY INTRODUCTION TO UNITS VI, VII, AND VIII

Objective
1. The student will learn to interpret the *DOT* numerical coding system and to use the *DOT* system in finding and filing occupational information.

2. The student will organize for in-depth study of selected occupations by identifying individual preferences for research in relation to *Data, People,* and *Things.*
3. The student will learn the appropriate research activities for gathering and evaluating occupational information.

2   VI   EXPLORING JOBS PRIMARILY INVOLVING WORK WITH *DATA* (IDEAS, SYMBOLS)

Objective
1. The student will gain a general understanding of the relationship of *Data* work with our economic system.
2. The student will identify and explore specific requirements and skills needed for working with data as a primary function.
3. The student will investigate changes taking place in this field of work and compare the opportunities in data work with those in other facets of employment.
4. The student will evaluate personal interests in this category in relation to other knowledge of self.

2   VII   EXPLORING JOBS PRIMARILY INVOLVING WORK WITH *PEOPLE* (ANIMALS)

Objective
1. The student will gain a general knowledge of the relationship of careers involving working with people to the economic system.
2. The student will identify and explore specific requirements and skills needed for working with people as a primary function.
3. The student will investigate changes taking place in this field of work and compare the opportunities in jobs working with people to those in other facets of employment.
4. The student will evaluate personal interests in this category in relation to other knowledge of self.

2   VIII   EXPLORING JOBS PRIMARILY INVOLVING WORK WITH *THINGS* (OBJECTIVES, MATERIALS)

Objective
1. The student will gain a general knowledge of the relationships of careers involving working with things in the economic system.
2. The student will identify and explore specific requirements and skills needed for working with things as a primary function.
3. The student will investigate changes taking place in this field of work and compare the opportunities in jobs working with things to those in other facets of employment.
4. The student will evaluate personal interests in this category in relation to other knowledge of self.

5   IX   EVALUATING EXPERIENCES AND PLANNING AHEAD

Objective
1. Each student will review his future educational needs and reassess occupational opportunities.
2. Each student will clarify his understanding of regulations and agencies controlling or affecting workers.
3. The student will know effective resources and techniques for locating and acquiring jobs.

Guidelines for Career Guidance Program Development

  4. The student will identify factors involved in holding and succeeding in a job.
  5. The student is able to identify guidance resources which will assist persons whose educational plans require change.

1   X   FINAL COURSE EVALUATION AND RECOMMENDATIONS
  Objective   1. The students and teacher evaluate individual and group progress and react to the *SUTOE* experience.
        2. The instructor will seek cooperation for follow-up studies at the high school and post-high school level.

In order to achieve its goals, SUTOE utilizes a variety of resources, techniques and materials as part of the course. These include field trips, games, role playing, guest speakers, school library or school guidance center, testing, work experience, job placement and more.

The program involves periodic evaluation of students' progress in meeting specific unit objectives. In addition, the overall achievement during the year with respect to the broad goals of the course, and the course itself, are also evaluated. Suggestions for implementation of this evaluation and of each unit are included in the program.

BMCG

The behavioral model for career guidance (BMCG) was developed for senior high school programs on the premise that, if guidance programs are to be effective, they must be systematically designed to achieve stated objectives. In accordance with this premise, the BMCG was built using a systems approach as a base. This approach can be defined as the selection of elements, relationships and procedures to achieve a specific purpose (Hare 1967). The primary advantage of using "systems" is to increase the likelihood that a given goal will be achieved. Systems models facilitate the management and monitoring of a program by insuring a flow from start to finish. They also identify alternative methods for achieving a goal, creating a searching attitude and insuring the success of the program by building such mechanisms as feedback and monitoring into the system.

The model is intended to have utility for a variety of persons such as practicing counselors, pupil personnel, administrators, state departments of vocational education and counselor educators. To insure utility, the authors have incorporated several features, such as (a) flexible use of the model to allow use in different settings, (b) an atlas of useful resources, and (c) procedural guidelines, i.e., step-by-step modifiable outlines intended as guides to program planners. In most instances, the guides can be modified as dictated by circumstances and needs of the local situation.

The most basic feature of this model, apart from the fact that it utilizes the systems approach, is that it is built upon the identification and implementation of behavioral objectives. A behavioral objective is a statement which describes an observable kind of useful performance which successful students will be capable of performing at the conclusion of a particular learning unit. The objective is stated in terms of a student's expected performance which can be observed and evaluated, thus allowing for an evaluation of the effectiveness of the guidance procedures themselves.

The four basic elements and criteria of behavioral objectives are:

1. Expected student performance
2. Content of the learning to be achieved
3. Evaluative criteria to assess the performance
4. The student's opportunity to demonstrate behavior.

The behavioral model consists of ten procedural phases derived from four basic components. These components are:

1. Specifying program objectives
2. Generating alternative methods
3. Designing program evaluation
4. Implementing planned change.

The ten phases are outlined below:

I. *Context Evaluation*

Context evaluation: An evaluation which defines the environment in which change is to occur, depicts unmet student needs and identifies problems which result in needs not being met. It includes determining what needs exist in the guidance program.

II. *Assigning Program Goal Priorities*

Program goal: A statement of goals which is a collection of words or symbols describing general intentions (Ryan 1963).

III. *The Translation of Goals to Student Behavioral Objectives*

Behavioral objective: A statement which describes an observable kind of useful performance which successful students will be capable of performing at the conclusion of a particular learning unit.

Guidelines for Career Guidance Program Development

IV. *Input Evaluation: Selection of Methods*

Input evaluation: An evaluation which determines alternative methods of carrying out a problem or objective.

Method: Is institutionally centered and is assumed to be an administrative function, e.g., group guidance, program modification, testing and occupational information. In the systems model each method is the broader compilation of specific means or techniques for accomplishing guidance objectives.

V. *Input Evaluation: Selection of Techniques*

Input evaluation: An evaluation which determines alternative methods of carrying out a problem or objective.

Technique: A specific means or relationship that is adopted by an institutional agent to facilitate learning for a defined body of participants in a specific situation. In the systems model, institutional agents would be the guidance staff or the faculty. The "participants" would be the clients or students. The "specific situation" in the model refers to the educational sites. Techniques refer to the means of obtaining the client's involvement in a learning situation, e.g., written autobiographies, reading pamphlets, books and visiting work settings.

VI. *Diffusion: Trial Implementation*

Diffusion: A stage in the change process concerned with the dissemination and demonstration of innovative ideas on a trial basis.

VII. *Process Evaluation*

Process evaluation: An evaluation which determines how a technique on trial is progressing. Its objective is to detect or predict defects in procedural design.

VIII. *Product Evaluation*

Product evaluation: An evaluation which measures and interprets actual (student performance) attainments during, and at the end of, a project cycle.

IX. *Adoption*

Adoption: A stage in the change process concerned with the final adaptation of an innovation to the local situation.

X. *Recycling*

Recycling: Refers to the circular movement of the systems approach. It is the linkage point between the adoption phase and the context evaluation. A system is not a static process with a beginning and an ending, but rather an on-going process that continually follows through the nine phases previously mentioned.

Each phase contains a number of expected outcomes which can be adapted incrementally within the constraints of the school's program.

In summary, the Behavioral Model for Career Guidance is a complex, yet flexible, system which can be applied at many levels of career guidance in order to improve their services. The basic model is not restricted to career guidance and has utility for other aspects of the educational system.

The model is currently being field-tested in five school districts as part of the Ohio State University's Center for Vocational and Technical Education project entitled "Operation Guidance". Upon completion of the field test (1974), a complete self-instructional seven-module package will be available for school personnel. The seven-module package will enable school personnel (e.g., counselors, student personnel directors, teachers and administrators) to plan, design, implement and evaluate a total career guidance program.

SPS

The total guidance program which has been adopted by the Georgia educational system is an example of a program which has been carefully tailored to fit the characteristics of the school system and the needs of the students.

For over a decade, Georgia has been developing an extensive network of area vocational-technical schools in order to meet the urgent need for highly trained workers and the growing number of individuals who need vocational training in order to enter the world of work. However, many of the trainees have neither the commitment nor the abilities to pursue a given occupational field. In order to bridge the gap between the potential workers and the world of work, an extensive program of student personnel services was developed.

From the start, the Student Personnel Services (SPS) program was conceived as a comprehensive and systematic network of services. Its development proceeded in two phases. In Phase I, the ideas of area school administrators, instructors, student personnel specialists and students were solicited with regard to the student personnel services needed in the area schools. In Phase II, resources from local, state and national levels were mobilized for the development and implementation of the student personnel services program. These services were built around the objectives and problems existing specifically in vocational-technical schools.

The student personnel services and activities are based on the premise that the student has decisions that he must make in pursuit of his destiny. The primary goal of SPS is to assist a student in making those

TABLE I

Goals of Student Personnel Services in Area Vocational-Technical Schools

Before Enrollment	During Enrollment	Leaving School and Entering Employment
1. He accepts vocational-technical concept.	1. He understands school policies as applicable for himself.	1. He accepts responsibility for making plans for the transition from school to employment.
2. He perceives a vocational-technical specialty as valuable to him.	2. He develops positive attitudes toward himself, school, program, prospective employer, and vocational-technical training.	2. He identifies with the world of work in the specialty for which trained.

3. He explores problems which may be obstacles to enrolling but which he plans to solve.
  a. Financial
  b. Transportation
  c. Program
  d. Housing
  e. Physical
	3. He develops good interpersonal relationships with fellow students, instructors, and outside public.	3. He enters appropriate post school occupation—who it is and what he has to offer.

4. He relates his experiences and aptitudes to the vocational-technical curriculum.	4. When information is needed in order to further clarify his vocational direction, he judges his present knowledge, defines gaps in it, finds sources, selects information he sees as pertinent, and incorporates the new knowledge.	
5. He relates himself to a specific course.		
6. He selects a specific program and completes the admissions process of making application, taking entrance tests, having interviews, making a deposit, and registering for classes.		

educational-occupational decisions needed in order to successfully move into, and out of, the area schools, and to make progress while enrolled. Specific goals are summarized in Table I on page 177. The student personnel worker thus functions to assist students in clarifying their assets, the range of their choices and the availability of opportunities whereby realistic decisions may be made.

The Student Personnel Services are based on several interrelated, operating principles:

1. The student services function in area schools is predicated upon a commitment to students.
2. Student personnel specialists are the prime advocates of treating the individual student as a worthwhile person.
3. Student personnel work is based on the principle of involving the area school student in planning for his future as well as for his present.
4. The student personnel specialist provides accurate, quality and specific information to students concerning themselves and the job structure.
5. Student personnel work is based upon the individual differences of the area school student.
6. The student personnel specialist establishes a constructive working relationship with those in and out of the area school who can assist him in achieving the goals of the student personnel services program.

Two main approaches are used by the student personnel specialist in order to accomplish the goal of SPS: through direct and indirect help. Examples of direct help would be counseling, providing relevant information to the student himself, group guidance activities aimed at developing skills in getting a job or orientation to the school, and so on.

The indirect approach is based on influencing the environment in which the student lives, works and studies. Examples of indirect methods include (a) creating and distributing printed materials, such as catalogues, brochures, records, etc., to high school counselors; (b) working with instructors on committees such as pre-admission, admissions, guidance, etc.; and (c) working with other student personnel workers.

The implementation of an effective SPS program proceeds along several lines:

1. Pre-admission information aimed at overcoming personal doubts and stereotyped attitudes toward vocational education or occupational opportunities are prepared and disseminated.

Guidelines for Career Guidance Program Development 179

2. Clear-cut admission strategies and policies are formulated that assist in evaluating a student's abilities, values and desires in terms of school offerings and limitations, and in terms of making decisions.
3. A well developed system of keeping student records is also established.
4. Counseling services are offered prior, during and after enrollment.
5. An organized and systematic "information service" for the enrolled student is developed. This is aimed at orienting the student to the school's purposes, objectives, policies, etc., and at developing positive and realistic attitudes.
6. A job placement service is considered essential to SPS. It provides the student with the personal skills and attitudes needed to enter into, and adjust to, the world of work.
7. Evaluation and follow-up programs are designed as part of the total SPS program. Their purpose is to collect data in order to evaluate and improve programs.

In conclusion, the total program of SPS is seen as an effective instrument, or means, through which emphasis is maintained on the needs of the individual as he progresses from a potential worker to an employed and skilled worker.

DCGP

The Developmental Career Guidance Project (DCGP) is a comprehensive program developed in 1964 under the direction of George Leonard. The program is geared to the needs of selected inner-city youth, and is based on a variety of activities which utilize the facilities and involvement of both the school and community.

The developers of the program see developmental career guidance as an on-going process and conceive guidance as a dynamic process, one that is contiguous with growth stages and relevant to the real world of work. Guidance is related to events in the classroom, in the home and within the peer group. Work was selected as the focus of guidance since it relates, either directly or indirectly, to almost any aspect of life, e.g., physical, social, educational and so on. Therefore, within the program, stress is given to developmental aspects of career knowledge, aspirations, choice and planning, as these relate to growing boys and girls, especially culturally disadvantaged youngsters who have special needs (see Chapter 3).

The main objective of the DCG program is to increase the awareness of students about all phases of work. It is designed to gradually and systematically add work knowledge and experience to whatever base exists in the young child as he enters school. Another objective is to help every child to develop a realistic and functional awareness of himself as a worthwhile human being who will sooner or later enter the world of work. Focus is placed on individual potential, attitudes, values, skills, aspirations, perceptions, relationships, self-image and the like. A third objective is to inform, involve and coordinate all significant others, those who mold the personality of each child. Special emphasis is placed on the interaction between groups and among group members, and effective communication skills are considered essential. Another built-in objective is the systematic evaluation of the program through the analysis of student attitudes, plans and progress.

Within a school, the project is carried out by a guidance team, consisting of a guidance consultant, a career community aide and student assistants. This team, as well as the principals, teachers, project staff directors and special consultants, work with students and their parents.

The guidance project consists of a variety of activities, including (a) individual and group counseling, (b) dissemination of information in classes and as a general school activity, (c) broadening of perceptions through field trips and speakers, (d) informing and advising parents, (e) community work, mainly initiating and maintaining a close liaison with community agencies and neighborhood organizations in order to utilize and coordinate efforts and services, and (f) consultation services for the students, school staff, parents, community and industry. Other activities are specifically designed to insure that the project is carried out smoothly and effectively, to maintain a flexible "flow" of activities and to make the program viable and effective.

For purposes of evaluating the effectiveness of the progress of individuals who participate in the program, certain instruments were designed as part of the project. The survey technique is utilized in order to gain information about students at various grade levels. In addition, faculty attitudes and perceptions are also surveyed in order to gain some knowledge about their reactions to, and perceptions and attitudes of, the program and its operation.

Prior to the development of the DCGP, a considerable amount of thought, planning and discussion was solicited from resource personnel and consultants. These preliminary efforts are indicative of the complexity of the process of program invention and development, and of the necessity for careful thinking out, planning and development before implementation occurs. In terms of both development and implementation this program also demonstrates a deliberate attempt to maximize available and potential resources in order to render the program effective and beneficial.

CCGS

The CCGS employs a systematic approach to develop and evaluate guidance-oriented objectives and related instructional and counseling experiences for youth (K-12). Instructional and counseling procedures include providing students with information about the requirements for (and the probable consequences of) selecting a wide variety of alternatives, with opportunities to assess their talents in relation to these alternatives, and with assistance in formulating their educational and life goals in light of this information. Since it is believed that the most efficient and personally satisfying learning and development results from goal-directed behavior, the main purpose of the CCGS is to help youth to assess their multipotentialities and limitations, to discover their needs, to formulate goals and related objectives, and to work toward realization of these goals and objectives with increasing ability to constructively manage their own behavior.

The systematic approach used in the development, implementation and evaluation of objective-based programs in the CCGS involved five types of activities which are described below:

I. *Identification of Youth Development Needs and Related Objectives.* A comprehensive guidance system must define the various subpopulations comprising the total range of students, specify the desired terminal competencies of individual youths in these varied groups, identify the current status (entry level) of these competencies among the youth, and formulate meaningful "needs" statements which (a) describe the extent and nature of the discrepancies between these entry and terminal levels, and (b) can be translated into explicitly stated objectives.

II. *Classification of Objectives by Commonalities.* Needs statements translated into meaningful behavioral objectives should constitute a rather extensive data bank of guidelines for guidance and counseling activities and should delineate the alternative types of assistance available for students. To expedite student comprehension of the available alternatives and to foster improved administrative efficiency in the development and evaluation of programs, the data bank of objectives should be organized in a meaningful fashion. A preliminary investigation of varied information sources, as well as analyses of successful guidance programs and guidance-related research projects, has produced the following grouping of student needs and objectives by *content*.

Vocational:	Behaviors related to exploring and making decisions concerning both opportunities in the world of work and personal characteristics related to such opportunities.
Educational:	Behaviors required for exploring, making decisions concerning, and pursuing the amount and kind of education and training one wants during school and throughout the rest of his life.
Personal-Social	Intrapersonal competencies needed to function effectively as an independent person and interpersonal behaviors needed in small group situations, including two-person relationships. Behaviors applicable to various settings including home and classroom.
Academic-Learning	Behaviors involved in handling varied learning tasks more effectively and efficiently. Learning how to learn in varied settings, not just in the formal classroom.
Citizenship:	Behaviors differentiated from those in the social behavior area because they are appropriate to secondary (e.g., government) rather than primary (e.g., family) social groups and systems.
Leisure:	Behaviors connected with the exploration and utilization of leisure, cultural and recreational pursuits.

III. *Specification of Alternative Strategies.* The third activity in the systematic approach to the development and evaluation of CCGS programs involves the exploration and selection of suitable learning experiences for youth and their parents. Clear statements of priority needs and related objectives permit creativity in the selection and investigation of a wide range of possible instructional, counseling and evaluational approaches. The project staff attempts to: (1) compile a body of techniques and procedures which can be used in implementing direct and indirect intervention strategies. *Direct interventions* are defined as learning activities employed directly with students, and include activities such as orientation, personal assessment, personal choice and personal problem-solving skills. *Indirect interventions* are defined as those implemented by technological or human resources around the student in order to assist him in protecting and fostering the development of his individuality. Five interventions are specified: aspects of the educational setting, school personnel, community resources, research and evaluation; (2) evaluate the effectiveness of some of the currently available techniques and procedures; and (3) conduct developmental work where suitable strategies have not been available.

These developmental efforts have resulted in the design of a variety of instructional-counseling strategies which cover all seven of the direct intervention components, as well as four of the six content areas of student needs, i.e., educational, vocational, personal-social, and academic-learning. Such efforts have not exhausted the range of possible strategies but have permitted empirical comparisons of the relative effectiveness of several alternate approaches.

IV. *Implementation of Selected Strategies.* Individualized learning units have been designed to present learning opportunities to youth and their parents through selected instructional and counseling strategies. Each unit contains (a) statements of measurable objectives expressed in terms of desired youth outcomes, (b) suggestions of materials and resources each youth might use and procedures he might follow in order to achieve each objective, and (c) references to an evaluation procedure or instrument which will help each youth to determine whether or not he has met each objective. Units have the advantage of being useful in separate guidance classes, individual counseling sessions, group counseling or guidance experiences, or being integrated with other instructional materials and procedures in conventional curriculum areas.

To organize units into programs for each CCGS direct intervention component, a central theme of "each student as a problem solver" has been employed. That is, each program attempts to help youth to apply problem-solving skills to formulate and pursue personal goals and plans in each of the six areas of behaviors. The following diagram briefly illustrates the personal problem-solving skills around which all CCGS instructional-counseling (i.e., direct intervention) experiences have been organized. Each skill outlined has been defined in terms of more detailed student behaviors described in the project report.

SUMMARY OF PERSONAL PROBLEM-SOLVING SKILLS

Planning Emphasis:	Perceiving and defining problem
	Gathering and evaluating information
Decision-Making Emphasis:	Considering multiple alternatives and their related consequences
	Selecting alternate solutions and plans
Implementing/Managing Emphasis:	Implementing plans
	Analyzing product/process

V. *Evaluation of Selected Strategies.* The fifth activity in the systematic design and improvement of CCGS components involves evaluation, feedback and correction tasks leading to the validation of successful strategies, improvement of partially successful strategies and development of more appropriate ones. This activity necessitates the development of tests and performance standards for measuring a student's attainment of objectives (i.e., anticipated learning effects). To assist in the evaluation of CCGS direct intervention program outcomes, two major types of instruments have been used: (a) guidance proficiency tests (i.e., end-of-unit tests focusing on knowledge, attitudinal and overt behavioral outcomes) and (b) guidance survey tests assessing achievement and attitudes across three or four units or across complete programs.

Several field studies were conducted to evaluate the effects of CCGS programs; to collect assessments of youth, parent, and school personnel reactions to guidance units; and to make informal examinations of programs' unanticipated side effects. CCGS direct intervention programs which were investigated in this manner included: (a) Orientation-In, (b) Personal and Social Development, (c) Effective Personal Problem Solving, and (d) Educational and Vocational Goal Formulation. The results of these formative evaluation efforts furnished corrective feedback which was used to make modifications both in products and in procedures developed and employed in previous activities.

The ultimate aim of the CCGS is a comprehensive data bank of behavorial objectives, each keyed to a variety of appropriate instructional, counseling, and evaluational materials and procedures available for student, parent, counselor and teacher use. For the direct intervention CCGS components, the ultimate desired outcome is an exhaustive catalog of empirically validated instructional and counseling strategies keyed to behavorial objectives and cross-indexed with: (a) type of student need and problem (i.e., a need for which a youth desires assistance), (b) student characteristics which have been demonstrated to be associated with the effectiveness of a strategy (c) situational conditions under which an effective strategy is employed, and (d) characteristics of the individual(s) administering a strategy.

With such a catalog, guidance personnel should be better able to individualize guidance services and, hopefully, help education in general adjustment to the separate needs of each student. Because of the varied and ever-changing nature of student characteristics and needs, it is acknowledged that the variety of strategies investigated for possible incorporation into this catalog will have to extend well beyond that considered in the final project report. In addition, continued advances must be made in the specification and improvement of decision rules for the selection of strategies from this catalog.

In addition to the five program models cited above, the reader might also examine the new and emerging U.S.O.E.-sponsored career education

Guidelines for Career Guidance Program Development 185

models (e.g., school-based, industry-based, home-based and residential school-based models). Most of these are very extensive total school reorganization type models incorporating a guidance program component. Several suggested references are Goldhammer and Taylor (1972) and Tiedeman (1972).

Do You Share These Concerns?

1. Does your guidance service operate on the basis of *no* clearly established student objectives derived from theoretical findings and information?
2. Does your school provide guidance services that are inadequate to meet student needs, inappropriate for your particular student population and inefficient in terms of fulfilling guidance objectives?
3. Do the guidance services provided in your school or school system consist of the accumulation of isolated guidance methods that are not part of a total framework of guidance services?
4. Do you find students, teachers and others in your school poorly informed about the guidance program, how it works, what it offers, and why it is offered?
5. Are you troubled by lack of financial or manpower resources due to the fact that your growing needs demand constant expansion, and yet no systematic centralization of your resources exists?
6. Do you find that your services do not offer the student a continuous, systematic, and developmentally oriented guidance experience that he can build on at each successive grade?
7. Do you feel that your guidance program is inefficient because your school does not own expensive equipment?

These, and other related concerns, point out several problems in existing guidance services. A basic problem is that, traditionally, career guidance has been service-oriented rather than student-oriented. In other words, guidance has been operationally defined as "what guidance counselors can do", rather than "what students need in order to attain a certain level of vocational or personal maturity". Only recently has more emphasis been placed on student needs and student development. But, even with this awareness, other problems exist. These center around the disorganization in, and lack of, planning of guidance programs as a unified system. Typically, innovations in the field are introduced and incorporated into guidance programs in a piecemeal fashion. Guidance programs face problems similar to those faced by schools themselves of the pressures of constantly growing needs, and changing political, social, educational and economic conditions. These, in turn, determine the needs of students, and the nature of facilities and order of priorities of guidance programs.

Another factor which has an effect on the qualitative standard of guidance programs is the awareness of the public in general, and students in particular, to the problems and functions of guidance. When awareness is heightened, support is more available, and vice versa. In addition, theoretical and technological developments in the field of guidance constitute a press on guidance programs toward continual modification and change, thus decreasing the degree of stability of these programs.

The solution to this multidimensional problem is in amalgamating guidance services into total guidance programs. Guidance programs can then be designed to include built-in features which minimize, if not totally eliminate, potential problems of the sort described above.

The purpose of this chapter is to enumerate and illustrate the features and characteristics which are considered essential components of any effective guidance program. These characteristics can then serve as guidelines for the development or modification of such programs within the context of school or community.

Some Basic Characteristics of Effective Career Guidance Programs

Total career guidance programs previously have been defined as unified systems of guidance services which envelop isolated elements of career guidance in a school or a school system and incorporate them into a complex, multidimensional whole. As was emphasized earlier, both organizational and developmental advantages are derived from the use of total career guidance programs.

TRANSLATION OF THEORY AND RESEARCH TO PROGRAMS

Career guidance programs should be built on a theory of career development. The function of a theory is to provide formulations and ideas concerning the process, pattern and dynamics of the career development of individuals. A theory, by definition, (Crites 1969, Osipow 1968) helps us in organizing and integrating present knowledge in the area; generates interest and research; leads to the formulation and testing of hypotheses and to the collection of data; and helps us to predict events and, on the basis of findings, confirm or modify expectations with regard to career development.

The benefits derived from using theory as a basis for total career guidance programs are several: (a) A theory provides us with principles about career development, thus facilitating clarification of program and student objectives and ways of implementing these objectives. (b) Building programs upon theoretical principles facilitates the evaluation of the effectiveness of the program through expectations for students derived from the theory. (c) A program built on a theoretical base is also likely to be more comprehensive and more progressive and consistent in terms of its application to students at various grade levels.

In attempting to translate career development theories into career guidance programs, the first task is asking the following questions and seeking the answers:

1. What are the theoretical principles that have been brought forth thus far?
2. How sound are these principles, i.e., are they supported by research findings? Do they lead to generalization about career development?
3. Have these principles been applied to career guidance? If so, in what way, and what were the results of this application?
4. What principles are most suited to the particular program in question, and what implications would they have for setting up this program?

In seeking some of the answers to these questions, the reader can refer to previous chapters in this handbook, and through these, to other references. Chapters 2 and 3 are of particular relevance to this characteristic. Laws' (1970) model, The Elementary Guide for Career Development, is an example of the incorporation of theoretical principles to career guidance. The guide was developed on the idea proposed by current career theorists, such as Ginzberg, Super, Tiedeman and others, that career choice is a long-range, gradual, process essentially involving the acquisition of self-understanding and knowledge of the world of work. The program, therefore, was constructed in order to lay the groundwork for this knowledge early in life, and continue until such time as the individual has become relatively self-reliant and autonomous with regard to his work life.

PROGRAM MISSION AND ACCOUNTABILITY

Total career guidance programs are complex systems organized toward the achievement of pre-determined goals. Therefore, an important principle in building career guidance programs is the clarification of goals. Goals, in turn, would determine the nature of the program and the way one would go about setting it up. The questions related to mission and accountability of the program are:

1. What are the needs of our population? (This is determined by the nature of the student population, the geographic location, socio-economic considerations, needs of the community, etc.)
2. How can we translate these needs into specific and clear program goals?
3. Are these goals realistic? Are they adequate? Can they be carried out? And what kind of program would be needed in order to meet these goals?
4. Do we have the means to accomplish the goals? Do the goals justify the expenditure involved?

Some answers to these questions will be found in chapters 2 and 3. However, the mission of every program should be based on information that is specific, rather than general. Each population is unique since it is made up of elements that are determined by the particular psychological, situational, social and temporal factors that prevail. Thus, although generalizations can serve as guidelines for setting up programs, needs must be appraised individually for each population for which a program is being considered. A concern for mission and accountability necessitates the building of a program which is student-oriented and caters to students' needs, rather than service-oriented to fit the skills and practices of counselors.

The behavorial approach to career guidance is an example of a program that has incorporated within its design the careful consideration of goals in very specific terms. Goals are specified as behavorial objectives and thus allow for easier implementation and for built-in evaluation of the program.

PROGRAM DESIGN

Total career guidance programs must be carefully planned and designed before they can be implemented. Because of the availability of several theoretical principles, an array of potential goals, and a multitude

Guidelines for Career Guidance Program Development 189

of ways of implementing these goals, careful planning and design of a program is essential. Planning can be thought of as "custom-tailoring" of the program to fit the needs of the school. It is not only a task which is preliminary to the building of a program, but also a continuous, ongoing process which is carried out while the program itself is in existence.

The questions to be asked when implementing a program are:

1. Given certain theoretical principles in career guidance, and a number of specific goals, what kinds of programs need be designed (e.g., a program which conveys career guidance through curriculum units; a program built solely on dissemination of relevant information and counseling, etc.)?
2. What are the possible ways of implementing such a program? Can it be implemented in several stages? Can it be adapted to the current school context? Would changes and additions to staff and equipment be necessary? Are there similar existing programs that can be used as models? Do we need to bring in consultants for planning? etc.

Chapters 4, 5 and 8 present an array of methods which are grouped and clustered in terms of their types and their application to career guidance goals. The information presented in these chapters will provide the reader with the broad range of methods that are currently available and which could be incorporated into career guidance programs. In addition, the principles inherent in these methods would also constitute a source of ideas for program planners from which they could draw.

SUTOE (Oregon Board of Education 1969) and DCGP (Leonard 1968) are examples of programs that have been carefully planned and designed to meet the needs of students and the facilities available to the school.

PROCEDURAL PARSIMONY

Depending on the nature and needs of the school or school system, programs will be designed in varying degrees of complexity. By definition, however, any program will encompass a number of components, which together will render it a unique whole. The design and implementation of programs is often a gradual process; thus, various components of the total program should be added progressively as the program evolves, depending on needs and resources.

Procedural parsimony demands that careful selectivity be exercised in adding components to the program core. The benefits of selectivity are both quantitative and qualitative. From a quantitative point of view, selectivity would restrict randomly adding components that duplicate the function of other components and, thus, render the program too cumbersome and/or redundant. From a qualitative point of view, selectivity insures the inclusion of components that are considered to be superior to other elements in terms of fulfilling the needs of the program.

Basic questions for consideration in this area are:

1. What type of components does the total program require at its current stage of implementation?
2. What components are available to fulfill specific program needs? Are other existing program components capable of fulfilling the same need?
3. Which components would best fulfill the need and best suit the existing structure of the program?

The reader would again find it useful to refer to chapters 4, 5 and 8 and examine the evaluative comments that are included throughout the handbook. These would provide relevant information regarding the use and applicability of individual methods, presenting both alternative methods which may be substituted for existing ones and a range of different methods which are designed to achieve the same vocational or behavioral goal. This information permits selective consideration of methods and the gradual addition of effective components to the program core.

The BMCG (Campbell et al.) is designed to systematically select and progressively add program components to fit the particular needs of the school.

VIABILITY AND FLEXIBILITY

Two essential characteristics for any program are *viability*, i.e., workability and potential for successful implementation and adoption of a program to become an integral part of the school guidance services; and *flexibility*, i.e., adaptability to changing needs and changing conditions, and quality that allows keeping up with the time, the introduction of new techniques and the elimination of ineffective ones, etc.

The breadth, scope and magnitude of total career guidance programs can, at times, result in models or systems that are too monumental to work effectively or too rigid to allow for change. It is specifically for this reason that both viability and flexibility need to be made integral features of a program. The investment of time, money and effort demand a full return from the final product. A full return would be possible only if programs were both viable and flexible.

Designers and evaluators of programs should ask themselves the following questions:

1. Is the program in question such that it can be incorporated into the school system and become a useful part of it?
2. Are there any components in the program that are too complex to be mastered by the staff in the time available for training? Are they too complicated, too expensive, or require facilities and skills that are beyond the means of the school?
3. In the future, when conditions change, would the program be usable? Would it lend itself to innovations in the field, to changes in manpower and to changes in student needs?

Chapters 4, 5 and 8 provide the reader with a source of ideas and information regarding methods and approaches that, when incorporated within a total career guidance program, may add flexible and viable elements to it. In addition, the characteristics of viability and flexibility stem from the attitude and alertness of the people involved in the program as well as with components of the program itself. Kroll (1971) believes that counselors "must learn how to diagnose situational and organizational deficiencies." Kroll also alleges that in providing services, school counselors often have tended to limit themselves to inflexible, single role models or a set of operating procedures. Therefore, when changes in programs did occur, they take place within a static framework of assumptions and values; the end result has been the perpetuation of traditional programs that reflect little of the community environment and context of student needs. Thus, an attempt should be made to render the program flexible, viable and useful from the start, and to make appropriate changes when student needs dictate such changes.

Programs such as Georgia's area vocational schools (Bottoms 1966, 1967) Developmental Career Guidance Project (Leonard 1968) and the Behavioral Model for Career Guidance (Campbell et al. 1971) have incorporated within their frameworks elements that insure flexibility and viability.

MAXIMIZING RESOURCES

The inherent idea in the development of total career guidance programs is that they will embrace isolated elements of guidance services and pool these together in order to maximize the total effect of career guidance.

The uniqueness and effectiveness of any career guidance program are determined by how many and how well various resources are tapped and utilized. The term "resources" is not limited to financial means or manpower. It extends to printed materials, other agents or agencies in the community, and to innovative ideas and suggestions. "Maximizing" refers to: (a) making the most of what exists, and (b) being innovative, imaginative and resourceful in order to identify and incorporate additional resources that will add to the effectiveness of the program without creating a need for additional expenditures.

An example of maximizing would be convincing members of volunteer organizations to adopt a facet of the program, e.g., putting on a "Career Day" as their project for the year. Organizers of the program would benefit through gaining this additional help, and members of the volunteer organization would feel that they had done their share in helping students and community. B'nai B'rith and other civic volunteer organizations throughout the country have available to them resources and assistance which are relevant to projects in career guidance. The DCGP (Leonard 1968) is an example of a program where the developers effectively maximized community resources.

Chapters 4, 5 and 8 would be useful in giving the reader an overview of the kinds of resources potentially available to him. These include films, computers, publications, gaming techniques, volunteers and community agencies. In attempting to maximize resources, one should be encouraged to exercise his imagination to the fullest by investigating and then utilizing the services, facilities, manpower and ideas which are, or may become, available to him with a little effort and determination.

CONTINUITY FROM GRADES K–14

Ideally, total career guidance programs should be flexible and broad enough to encompass the needs of students from grades K–14. Designing program continuity and breadth is the feature that differentiates systematic career guidance programs from a random collection of career guidance methods.

This continuity has developmental advantages, i.e., career guidance becomes progressively more complex and appropriate with advancement in stages of student development; also, it allows students to receive guidance whenever they, as individuals, are developmentally ready for it, rather than being subjected to guidance based on others' expectations or readiness as derived from normative data.

In addition, there is an organizational advantage, in that continuity minimizes waste in time, money and resources and tends to maximize the effectiveness of a program.

The reader will find chapters 2 and 3 particularly relevant to the issue of continuity. In addition, many of the methods compiled in chapter 8 and clustered in chapters 4 and 5 are based on principles that can be applied in keeping with the continuity criterion. Ideas from other methods can be utilized in order to construct programs or build parts of programs so that these will provide students with a continuous, systematic and orderly guidance experience toward career development.

This concept also applies to establishing continuity and consistency in personnel and policy. Conflicting advice, suggestions and recommendations will confuse teachers, counselors and administrators, and will minimize student benefits. A systematic program should minimize communication problems due to its clarity of goals, methods and responsibilities.

Very few career guidance programs have attempted to incorporate continuity into their structure. However, the Behavioral Model for Career Guidance (Campbell et al. 1971) is flexible and general enough in structure that it can be applied to any grade level.

CREDIBILITY

Credibility is one characteristic which is related to the acceptance of the program. The image of the program in the eyes of others, the degree of credibility it arouses, and ultimately, the degree to which it is used, are important elements in the success of the program. Students, teachers, parents, agents in the community and the developers of the program themselves must believe in the effectiveness of the program before they will rely upon it. Since beliefs and attitudes about the usefulness of the program are liable to emerge regardless of factual data, it is the responsibility of those in charge to create a positive, yet realistic, image so that the program will be accepted and used.

Ways of creating such an image are through (a) printed materials, (b) lectures and demonstrations, (c) results of evaluative studies, (d) interest in the program, and (e) a spirit of enthusiasm about its use and usefulness.

In creating informational and promotional materials, the principle should be to foster understanding to overcome ignorance about the program. Promotional materials should supplement direct personal contact in order to gain acceptance for the program. The functions and characteristics of the program should be discussed in the community;

public and professional groups should be informed about what is being done and why; and community leaders and other relevant individuals should be involved in the planning, implementation and promotional stages of the program. Parents, community citizens and students should be invited for tours and demonstrations. Their reactions can serve as a gauge of the degree of acceptance, as well as a community forum for improving and supporting the program.

EVALUATION

Probably the most important characteristic of any effective program is the provision for its periodic evaluation. The questions which must be asked in regard to evaluation are:

1. Is the program effective? Does it do what it is set up to do? Does it help students to meet their needs? Does it do so at a manageable cost? Is it worthwhile?
2. Are specific elements in the program equally effective, or are some of these redundant and ineffective?
3. Does the program contain built-in phases for evaluation, modification and change?
4. Is the program effective in terms of individual student performances at particular stages, its use by the school in general and its consequence for the career development of students and for the needs of the community?

Throughout the handbook, an attempt was made to alert the reader to the need for evaluating methods and practices in terms of their potential in fulfilling goals. The reader may find it helpful to refer to the evaluative summaries within each chapter in order to get an idea about the importance of periodic evaluation of elements within programs and of total programs.

The Behavioral Model for Career Guidance, SUTOE, Georgia's Student Personnel Services, CCGS, and DCGP are examples of programs that have incorporated evaluation checkpoints to determine the success and usefulness of the program.

Dworkin and Walz (Chapter 13, "An Evaluation Model for Guidance" in Cook, D. *Guidance for Education in Revolution*, 1971, pp. 314-21) advocate that program evaluation should be viewed as continuous and should be kept in mind throughout the program. They suggest six steps (or types) of evaluation. These are:

1. *Individual Input Evaluation:*
    "The major purposes of Individual Input evaluation are to

identify the career needs of those individuals we wish to assist, and to delineate problems underlying these needs."

2. *Environmental Input Evaluation:*
"Environmental Input evaluation allows the program developer to describe the environment, the unmet needs of the environment, and problems underlying these needs."

3. *Objective Evaluation:*
"Objectives for career guidance programs must be specified and ranked in terms of priority. Objectives should be based on information generated from the previous two evaluation activities."

4. *Setting Evaluation:*
"Setting evaluation allows us to identify the most appropriate setting(s) in which to implement career guidance objectives in whole or part; and to identify strategies for dealing with constraints associated with the selected setting(s)."

5. *Process Evaluation:*
"Process evaluation is needed to identify and develop appropriate methods for accomplishing the career guidance objectives; and to identify and monitor on a continual basis the potential sources of failure (and success) in the program. Methods refer both to the topics and subject matter treated, e.g., job descriptions, test results, and educational information; and the various ways of organizing and disseminating information to individuals, e.g., computers and tape recorders (hardware); and role playing, modeling and field trips (software)."

6. *Product Evaluation:*
"Product evaluation allows us to assess the effectiveness of the entire career guidance program after it has run full cycle, i.e., to relate outcomes to methods, setting, objectives, and environment and individual input in order to measure and interpret outcomes of the career guidance program."

Implementing Career Guidance Programs

The main focus throughout this chapter has been the idea that career guidance services should be organized into career guidance programs. Earlier sections of this chapter enumerated the concerns shared by many guidance counselors and administrators with regard to career guidance, illuminated some of the benefits of career guidance programming and illustrated the characteristics of effective career guidance programs.

Implementation is another significant part of instituting career guidance programs. As the term connotes, implementation is the process of completing — insuring the carrying out and actual fulfillment of the program. It is an essential element to the performance and execution of career guidance programs.

The main component of the implementation process involves people, and more specifically, students, their parents, their teachers, school administrators and personnel, school counselors, school boards and members of the community at large.

The degree and form of involvement of these people in a career guidance program are varied. Some are developers of programs and constitute a source of innovative ideas based on previous experience and research; others are "economists", who estimate costs of equipment, space, time, etc. Still others are "trainers," concerned with teaching counselors and teachers how the program operates. Other people serve as "salesmen", their task being to insure that programs are adopted by school boards or other bodies; then there are the "buyers" who are willing to institute the program in their school and try it out. Students are "consumers" or receptors of the products of a guidance program, and teachers and counselors are "givers" or "operators" of the program. Parents and the community at large are "supporters"; they contribute financial, moral and other forms of help and support so that the program can become a success.

Although it is recognized that each category of people involved in a career guidance program plays an essential part in the total process of implementing a program and perpetuating its operation, it is difficult to quantify their role and contribution, and to construct a "formula" for program implementation. This difficulty stems from the individualized nature of each program. Programs are designed in accordance with needs, which are individual and unique for each school district or even each school. So are resources, means, manpower and environmental conditions unique as well as other factors that have a bearing on implementation. For this reason, the implementation of a program demands as much innovation, planning and effort as the conceptual development of a program itself.

Specific guidelines for implementing career guidance programs are not readily available in current literature. On the other hand, some sources in the area of guidance in general are available which may be of assistance in instituting career guidance programs. The reader may choose to consult literature which is classified in library catalogues under the heading of "Organization and Administration of Guidance." Riccio and Quaranta (1968) present information regarding the establishment of

Guidelines for Career Guidance Program Development

guidance programs in secondary schools and specifically deal with the role of guidance in the educational setting; types of students one may encounter within this setting; the selection, role and requirement for preparation of counselors; and some general elements relevant to implementation of guidance services, such as organizational patterns and cost.

Campbell et al. (1971, pp. 132-133) developed a checklist of practical considerations in selecting career guidance methods and techniques as part of program implementation. The purpose of the checklist was to assist school staff in assessing the practicality of adopting a given method or technique. The rating scale-type checklist embraces the following method considerations:

Magnitude	Staff
Completeness	Training
Complexity	Social setting
Convenience	Equipment and
Flexibility	Materials
Distinctiveness	Time
Replicability	Space
Interaction with	Formal rules
other programs	Community
Readiness	Administration
Cost	Student
Content	

Zeran and Riccio (1962) present a more elaborate guide for implementation. They describe in detail the kind of information needed and the way to go about obtaining it with regard to the analysis of the individual. In addition, they categorize types of information services which should be offered by a guidance service, what the objectives of information services are, how to obtain materials and how best to disseminate it. This is particularly relevant to career guidance, where information materials are a significant tool for aiding the counselor. Placement and follow-up of the individual, both educationally and vocationally, are described, as well as organizational patterns and practices, and the physical facilities needed for guidance.

Peters and Shertzer (1963) provide another useful source for ideas on program implementation. A chapter entitled "Budget, Facilities and Public Support for Guidance" gives information regarding cost estimation; budgeting; average cost of guidance programs in schools of various size populations; sources of financial support; needs and procedures for strengthening public support; needs and cost of physical facilities; and the like. In addition, they include accounts of guidance programs in action which are useful examples of how total guidance programs are organized.

In implementing individualized career guidance programs, many of the considerations relevant to guidance services in general will be necessary. The particular factors affecting the implementation of each program will depend on the specific nature of the program, the nature of the community, budget and facilities, historical factors such as the kind of career guidance services previously available, the extent to which manpower can be utilized, and the degree of emphasis that is given to career guidance in relation to total guidance services. With developments in career guidance methods such as those described in previous chapters, and with increasing realization of the needs of students, career guidance should occupy a growing part of total guidance services. This realization will also reflect itself in larger budgets, more specialized training for counselors and more effective programs.

A total career guidance program begins with an idea, progresses through stages of the development of, and research on, that idea, and culminates with implementation, i.e., when the program is adopted by a school system and instituted as part of the guidance framework. After implementation, a new, continuous cycle begins, characterized by innovative ideas, research, development and change, designed to keep the program functional and effective.

The success of a total program of career guidance depends on several factors. Powell (1971), in relating his experiences in thinking through, developing and carrying out such a program, believes that communication, cooperation and coordination are the most essential elements. To these should be added such factors as organization, leadership and commitment on the part of all concerned through the stages of development, implementation, evaluation and change.

To increase the probability of effective implementation of an innovation, Dworkin and Walz (Cook 1971) have outlined three step-by-step strategies for the adoption and implementation of a program innovation. The three strategies are based upon the work of Havelock (1969) and are intended for three different administrative levels of adoption.

The first is called the *Problem Solving Orientation* and can best be used at the local level, e.g., individual school or school system. Its tactics include T-group, sensitivity training, reflection, authentic feedback, role playing, the derivation conference, survey feedback, and brain storming. The second is entitled the *Social Interaction Orientation* intended for the regional level, e.g., intermediate school district. Tactics include mass media dissemination, the "county agent", the salesman, prestige suggestion, and opinion leadership utilization. Thirdly is the *Research, Development, and Diffusion Strategic Orientation,* best used at the national level where financial, personnel and time constraints are minimal. Suggested tactics are experienced demonstrations, research evaluation of adoption success and failure, user-need surveys, successive approximation, translation and packaging for diffusion.

All of the above emphasize the use or importance of a "change agent", i.e., the initiator and carrier of the innovation to the practitioner. His role is vitally important in that he provides the link between research and practice and maintains the momentum for change. In other words, he is the "ball carrier" or "the spark" who is primarily responsible for program change. In many instances he has to orchestrate a whole host of variables (participants, facilities, finances, etc.) which are critical to achieving change.

Above all, career guidance should be set up as an organized whole, as a system of guidance characterized by relatedness of goals and comprehensiveness of approach. Only as a whole can it effectively and economically recognize, plan for and deal with the present and future needs of students, take advantage of present resources and increase the effectiveness of future services.

Chapter 7 CAREER GUIDANCE—WHERE WE ARE AND WHAT WE NEED

The opportunity to review, describe and catalogue the available career guidance methods has provided us with an unusual opportunity — being able to gain perspective with regard to what has been developed and what remains to be done. Among the more useful outcomes of our work may well be the opportunity to consider the evident strengths among the career guidance methods and procedures, and the ability to identify gaps, suggesting a working direction for bringing about improved programs of career development and career guidance for students and adults. In this chapter, then the intent will be to survey where we are and to make specific suggestions and recommendations as to what we should be doing on both local and national levels to improve the development of and the delivery on career guidance practices and programs.

Where We Are

An overall impression gained from the available career guidance programs and practices is that in the last two decades we have made considerable gains in quantity if not in quality.

The practicing counselor today is presented with either a large choice of available resources and materials, developed from public funds and, therefore, available at a limited cost, or extensive materials developed commercially and commanding a considerable price.

Counselors may, in their consideration of materials to be used, be confronted by the fact that urgency, rather than importance, has frequently been a motivator in the development of those materials. Many areas for which they might most require resources may be quite lacking in them, whereas other areas may offer an abundance because producers seemingly develop new resources without specific knowledge of what has been developed previously. It is important, however, that we not assume too negative an attitude regarding what is available. If one has any doubts as to the utility of available resources, he should consider the magnitude of the task of planning and implementing a career development/career guidance program were he unable to use any of those resources. Clearly, the task would be one involving demands upon counselors to which very few would be able to respond effectively, given the limitations of their time and resources. It is clear that counselors must be very judicious in their selection and use of available materials, without regard for either their availability or visibility as sufficient evidence of their quality or desirability.

Developing this handbook has afforded the authors the unique opportunity of assessing the current trends and shortcomings of guidance methods. Our observations are as follows:

1. *Placement is almost entirely neglected in the career development and guidance literature.* Counselors, at all levels, wishing to find specific information on practices and programs for use in developing placement programs, would be extremely hard-pressed to find what might be useful to them in their own program development. While placement is a concept frequently alluded to and discussed as a necessary emphasis within a comprehensive program, few generators of career guidance resources have responded to the development of specific resources and programs. This is obviously an important gap, especially when one considers that increasing emphasis is being placed on providing the same placement services to those entering the world of work as is available to those entering higher education. It may also suggest that counselors are more concerned with the intellectual aspects of career development than they are with the followthrough, where ideas and plans are actualized and carried through into employment or work-study programs. Whatever the motivating cause, counselors wishing to develop effective placement programs will have to look beyond the available career guidance literature for imaginative models and examples which they can adopt to their own areas of concern.

2. *Career guidance practices and programs for unique populations are sparse and tend to be at the theoretical level rather than at the practical level.* Population subgroups, such as minority group members, women and the handicapped, present special career guidance needs. Both the appropriateness of the existing objectives and goals, as well as the relevance of the resources and practices used, call for special attention. In fact, the generic comprehensive guidance program with a career guidance emphasis will probably be comprehensive only for those students who are middle-class whites and who hold the culturally endorsed middle-class aspirations and motivations. Individuals of diverse cultural and socioeconomic backgrounds, desiring fuller participation in the opportunities in our society, find that the available resources are quite inadequate to their needs. There is, of course, the real danger that counselors who are responsive to the special needs of unique populations may, in finding a paucity of available resources, be tempted to utilize what already exists, rationalizing that resources developed essentially for existing male, middle-class populations are readily adaptable to all. Prior to the creation of more relevant and appropriate resources, counselors ought to give high priority to the development of more interactive career guidance methods, and design purposeful experiences which will assist in reaching those goals appropriate for unique populations.

3. *Career guidance resources are typically described in general terms and seldom contain specific information necessary to someone considering their adoption and use in their own programs.* After identifying what appears to be an appropriate resource, many counselors may be dismayed to find, when they obtain the basic resource document, that the information provided is insufficient to allow them to make judgments as to the effectiveness of such resources for their situations. Specific information, such as likely costs in terms of needed materials and resources, and space and equipment needs, demands likely to be placed on the management, and actual implementation procedures are seldom provided. Lacking specific information as to what was done, to whom, with what objectives in mind, and with what outcomes, counselors can only guess at the outcomes probable from their own use of the resource. In addition, they may have only vague notions as to what the resource will require in the investment of training and implementation time, as well as in physical resources, if the new career guidance approach is going to work successfully.

4. *There are only limited methods described or published for students at the post high school level.* As seen by the resource generators, career development and career guidance is primarily a concern to be addressed at the pre- and high school level. This is in contradiction to what we know about the critical stages in career development and the

experiences of young people as they leave high school and enter the world of work. For many, post-high school years are years of further exploration, trial and consolidation of plans. The availability of additional assistance to youth in the refinement of their choices and plans would seem to be a high priority objective for counselors. Clearly an important need is not being adequately met.

5. *The predominant emphasis is on describing and presenting methods which relate to the needs of individual counselors or single schools.* To a great extent, career guidance literature emphasizes the role of individual counselors or single school systems and ignores the importance of linkages between counselors in a programmatic sense, and the larger linkages among schools within a system and among systems within a state. Any goal as pervasive as career development requires systematic and planned consideration of the need for mutual reinforcement of linkages between those individuals and agencies which may play a role in the career development of given individuals. Unfortunately, guidance resources frequently have involved the delivery of career guidance almost solely from the work an individual counselor is doing within an individual school, in isolation from prior or subsequent schooling on the part of the student. There is little consideration of the importance of community input and the role of community agents in groups, in a more macro and systematic way of planning for the full utilization of those persons and resources which may be of assistance to individuals in career development.

6. *The roles of "significant others" in career guidance planning and decision making, and the means to include them in career guidance equations have been treated only minimally.* In many ways, the counselor's greatest contribution in the career development process may occur as a result of his skill in orchestrating the wide variety of human and material resources which can be of assistance to both young people and adults in their career development. However, if counselors are to do this, there must be greater consideration within the literature of how parents, teachers, representatives of business and industry, chambers of commerce and labor unions are included in the career development process. To date, the formal literature has been rather silent in this area, leading counselors to emphasize the use of packaged materials which assist individuals primarily at the informational level. While information is necessarily an important component of the career development process, there are real dangers in too heavy a reliance on informational resources. The materials not only can become outdated, but may very likely deal in abstractions, lacking the "guts" of significant interactions with people and places. Admittedly, it is difficult to combine people and physical resources in a meaningful and coherent plan of experiences. Unfortunately, counselors

will obtain little help from the literature, but they nonetheless must attend to the problem if they are going to be able to develop meaningful career development programs.

7. *Means are limited for the storing and sharing of preferred practices.* Counselors have only limited sources to which they can currently turn for information on the availability of career guidance practices and programs appropriate for specific goals and objectives. Likewise, there are very few means by which counselors can share career guidance innovations which they themselves have developed. This need to share is important, as it can lead to improvements in career guidance programs, as well as provide feedback to the program developer regarding experiences of others using the newly developed ideas and materials. This handbook will clearly fill part of this gap by providing a readily available resource that counselors can use. (Subsequent up-dates will work to insure its timeliness.) Ongoing programs devoted to developing counselor resources, such as those presented at the ERIC Center on Counseling and Personnel Services at the University of Michigan and the ERIC Center for Vocational-Technical Education at Ohio State University, will provide ready sources of current and evaluated career development and career guidance information.

8. *Implementation and adoption concerns have not regularly been addressed.* Perhaps one of the most useful kinds of information that a potential "innovation adopter" can use is the experience of previous adopters as to the response of a system to an innovation, and analyses and suggestions relating to adoptions which could be used to facilitate adoption and implementation in similar and dissimilar situations. The almost total lack of this kind of information suggests that many of the generators think that career guidance methods are adopted purely on the basis of their own virtues — a point of view which experience would hardly support. Perhaps one of the most necessary kinds of information relates to the specific experience of an author or generator in implementing his innovation within a given situation. This information should be provided in such detail that if the author has implemented the innovation in a single setting, the potential adopter can still make inferences relevant to his own situation.

9. *Conceptually, congruent practices and programs are few.* It is only very recently that we have noted the development of programs and practices built around an explicit theoretical rationale so that there is consistency and relevance between practices and procedures within the program. To a large extent, programs which have been presented are a patchwork of available resources, and they differ considerably in the extent to which the different resources are congruent and appropriate

to reaching specified goals and objectives of the program. The recent advent of comprehensively developed programs, where each of the practices and procedures relate to an explicit rationale and objective of the program, is a development which should lead to considerably improved programs.

10. *Training designs and renewal opportunities need considerably greater attention and development.* A major need within our career guidance literature is to speak not only of the "usable" physical resources but also of training needs and how counselors and other individuals can become more knowledgeable about emerging innovations and their use in career guidance. Many counselor education programs assign low priority to the career development area, and it is apparent from interaction with counselors that there is considerable disparity in the theoretical understanding and the actual action skills held by practicing counselors in the career development/career guidance area. Therefore, many counselors, as they are pressed to place greater priority on career guidance, will feel the need for self-help designs and resources which will enable them not only to update their current skills but also to develop new ones in the career guidance area. Certainly we need a great deal of emphasis here on the means by which we can assist counselors to be more impactful in the career guidance area with an emphasis on both pre-service and in-service training designs.

Images of the Future: What We Need

In this section we will give consideration to what the future is likely to demand in the way of career guidance practices and programs, and some specific recommendations as to how we can best respond to the future in the sense of new content and new delivery systems for career guidance. The following list is by no means exhaustive and is intended to stimulate the reader's thinking about possible directions and needs for the future. The critical question is, How can we be more responsive to futuristic trends by generating innovative guidance services?

1. *Paramount in the consideration of the development of innovative career guidance procedures is the need to give appropriate recognition to the changes in life styles and socio-economic conditions within our society.* It is clear that the position work occupies in our life and the way today's youth respond to the idea of career and vocation are changing; therefore, career guidance procedures must be responsive to the

increasingly evident shift in values. Overgrowing geographical mobility, greater emphasis on service occupations and the increasing likelihood of frequent job changes place a premium on the individual's ability to plan for and enter into a wide variety of occupations during his lifetime. It is likely that today's youngster may experience not the three occupations of which we spoke only a few years ago, but perhaps ten or twelve. This, then, makes career guidance a continuous process whereby an individual must be reviewing his present opportunities and plans, while consciously planning and preparing for new opportunities in the future. Increased occupational fluidity will place major emphasis on the individual's capacity to acquire information on occupations, both current and emergent, and to orient his behavior towards new opportunities.

2. *There is a particular need for more fully involving parents in the career decision-making and planning process.* To a large extent, parents presently mirror existing social values which place a preeminent emphasis on college attendance. Such parental reinforcement, based frequently on inadequate information and job stereotyping, may seriously interfere with the wise decision making of a young person regarding future opportunities. More importantly, parents are in a position to impart meaningful information and experiences to young people which can be relevant to them in their decision making. Therefore, they should be seen as active partners in the career planning equation and should have opportunities for further development of their own knowledge and expertise with regard to career planning. It is likely that the future will see greater opportunity for parents to be involved with young people on matters relating to career planning and with thinking about and planning for their own careers. Thus, it is anticipated that parents can and should be vital elements in career development, and we should appropriately respond to this by helping them to acquire the knowledge and skills needed to assist the young in making viable career plans and decisions.

3. *Hardware and educational technology will play an important, albeit limited, role in future career guidance programs.* The advantages of computer-assisted counseling and the use of a variety of multimedia resources are many, but for every advantage there are invariably disadvantages. Care must be given to an appropriate analysis of the trade-off between advantages and disadvantages. In a review of the impact of educational technology upon guidance, Walz (1970) emphasized how technology can be hindering to program development and called for a balanced and integrated approach. It is undoubtedly true that, even without additional investments in hardware, considerable advances can be made in both the content and delivery of career guidance. For many schools and large systems the more judicious investment of resources

may lie in the development of new programs and forms of training for upgrading the skills and knowledge of those who will be participating in the career guidance program. Further research and development of the hardware can more appropriately be left to research laboratories and to those systems able to obtain extensive outside funding so they may undertake experimental programs to determine the efficacy of the differential use of technology under a variety of actual operating conditions.

It is likely that the future will see a considerable increase in the utilization of technology in career guidance. Technology should be adopted only as the most effective approach to a given objective and not as an end in itself. In his review of the present state of technology, Walz (1970) suggests that heavy investments in technology may very well work as a deterent to further innovation because programs may have such heavy investments in a given system in terms of technology and hardware that they are unable to adopt and utilize promising new developments which would outmode and displace the existing equipment.

4. *Career guidance is evolving in the direction of a free-form approach with greater consideration given to outreach and extension programs which go beyond the school walls and years and are responsive to students in those environments where they are faced with making career occupation decisions and plans.* Students need the kind of career guidance which provides not merely theoretical knowledge but experience and practical knowledge of specific occupations. In addition, each individual needs assistance in relating his earlier choices and ongoing experiences to what he wishes for the future. The future may bring a situation where the individual has a continuing relationship with his counselor, much as is true with a family physician. An individual might look upon his counselor as one who, because of his intimate knowledge and experience of the client's concerns and experiences, can assist him, not only in a narrow point of time but throughout his life. It is probable that, as we move toward the community-learning-center concept, with centralization of learning facilities for the entire community (where educational opportunities are available day and night, throughout the year), career guidance will move from a specific service available only in the day school to a community service. In turn, career guidance would take full advantage of community resources in terms of providing information and opportunities for interaction with individuals skillful in the planning process and versed in technical knowledge about different occupations.

5. *New means of disseminating and sharing preferred practices and innovations in career guidance will be developed.* The future will see increased emphasis upon the means for communication regarding specific practices and procedures which are responsive to given needs and objec-

tives. In particular, the development of information systems and on-going communications devices will be of assistance to counselors who wish to update and renew their information and skill in career development areas. The development of the "Counselor Six-Pack" by the Counseling and Personnel Services Information Center is illustrative of the emergence of functional information systems which are responsive to the particular needs of a group of practicing professionals. This system includes six basic informational components: 1) a mass-media announcement sheet (CAPS/Capsule) describing new products and developments in the system; 2) a monthly news sheet (*Communique*) translating new research practices and programs in the field into action terms, usable by and readily adoptable for counselors; 3) a magazine (*Impact*) designed to promote innovation and change in counseling, and concerned with identifying the new issues and developments relevant to counseling, guidance and student services, as well as assisting counselors to acquire and use new resources in their programs; 4) a series of analyses papers (*Synthesis*) which delve, in depth, into particular areas of need and interest for counselors; 5) an intensive bibliography and search system (*Access*) which enables the user to undertake searches which identify all the relevant resources in an area of need; and 6) *The Little Annual*, a means for reviewing all available resources, practices and programs in high priority areas for a given year. The "Counselor Six-Pack" is an example of how counselor informational needs will be responded to in an organized fashion and will work towards utilization of the most relevant rather than the most available information.

6. *The role of the counselor as a change agent will be expanded.* A major responsibility of the counselor is to provide the opportunity for change in an individual and to stimulate change in societal structures and attitudes. Particularly counselors not only need to be concerned with how the individual perceives his environment and responds to it, but to show leadership in responding to those societal conditions which limit the full expression of an individual's talents and uniqueness.

For instance, the counselor may find it necessary to examine the opportunity structure as a way of ensuring that an individual may realize his occupational opportunities. Counselors will also become increasingly involved in stimulating social change in such areas as identifying problems for the public; disseminating information on the difficulties in utilization of particular procedures; assuming leadership in community affairs; engaging the cooperation of students, parents and fellow faculty members; and leading concentrated community action programs and working through educational legislative liaison bodies to bring about desirable legislative action. The action sphere of the counselor role is clearly moving beyond that of the school walls, and if he is to be responsive to the expectations of others, he will have to define his field of action as broader than that of the counseling interview.

7. *There will be continued interest in research on career development and the outcomes of specific career guidance interventions.* It is doubtful, at least in the immediate future, that research will be seen as a panacea for the problems confronting counselors, but it may be seen as a source of information basic to the selection and evaluation of individual programs. It is likely that there will be increased emphasis on evaluating programs and practices, and providing a form of accountability to students and the public relative to the objectives and outcomes of those various programs and practices. Counselors will undoubtedly be anxious to conduct more program and system research emphasizing the outcomes which occur in terms of individual behavior which results from understanding in a planned program of career development/career guidance experiences. Innovations in career guidance will probably contain, as part of the package, information on adoption and implementation. Counselors will place greater emphasis on how specific practices, as well as complete programs, can be operationalized in given settings. Counselors will become the teachers of other counselors to a far greater extent than ever before. The teachers, in particular, will become a group for whom special training experiences will need to be provided. Counselors will likely assume increasing responsibility for both the design and operation of training programs which seek to expand and disseminate the base of knowledge, as well as the skills necessary to initiate community-wide career education and career guidance programs.

8. *There will be an increasingly wide emphasis on system-wide planning and community participation.* The need for students to have integrated career development experiences in order that they may see continuity and an inter-relationship between their levels of schooling and experience will lead to greater community involvement in the planning and delivery of career guidance. There will be new feedback devices which will assist students to understand more adequately their own levels of development with regard to particular career development tasks. The demarkations between elementary school and middle school and senior high school will blur, as will those between school and work itself. Increasingly, people involved in school and work will function cooperatively in planning and operating programs designed to assist students and adults in the acquisition of better self-understandings of their skills and value systems, and how these may be expressed occupationally.

9. *There will be an increasing emphasis upon agency in programs for students and adults.* A major operational objective of programs will

be to instill in students and adults a sense of their control over their own destinies and the feeling that they are in a position to plan and control their own career development. The stress will be upon assisting individuals to act in their own self interests, to be more fully aware of the diagnostic procedures and the planning strategies which will enable them more fully to reach their goals.

10. *There must be increased emphasis upon necessary skills to deal with future shock.* The future will require individuals who possess, in addition to technical occupational skills, the capacity to learn rapidly, to relate and communicate with others, to serve as teacher and leader, to diagnose situations and determine appropriate behavior, and to handle conflicts. Such behaviors as these will become instrumental in determining an individual's ability not only to pursue a given occupation but also to perform effectively in that occupation. These are human skills that must become a part of the career development process if an individual is to work productively and satisfactorily in the emerging occupational world.

11. *More flexible and responsive organizational structures will be developed.* Career guidance programs will continue to develop as the needs for systematic programming become evident. New forms of organization which stress spontaneity, focus upon specific problems and outcomes and encourage broad participation in decision making will become the rule, in contrast to the static and role-oriented organizations of the present. In particular, organizations will be developed which emphasize responsiveness towards what the students need rather than to what the counselors can do. These new organizations will focus on the need for responsiveness to basic goals and objectives, while encouraging initiative and individual creativity on the part of those within the system, thereby enabling them to interface in ways necessary to bring about particular outcomes. However, these interfaces would be fluid — meeting needs, responding to those needs and permitting new groups to organize to meet still newer needs.

Conclusion

It is apparent that individuals today are faced with increasing opportunities and broadened means by which those opportunities may be realized. To be responsive to this, counselors will need to be organized in ways which emphasize more rapid and more pointed responses. Counselors, themselves, will increasingly understand the importance of linkages with others as well as the desire to involve the individual himself as an active participant in the design, conduct and evaluation of his learning experiences. Hopefully, the process will blur the line between counselor and client and will encourage many communities of learners who assemble because of a mutually shared desire to learn more about a given need or interest. Participation in such communities will occur as a function of skill and experience of those participating. In such settings, counselors will be seen as helpful and highly desirable participants, not because they carry the title "counselor," but because their expertise on human behavior, career development processes and environmental information, and their genuineness and humanness as individuals recommend them.

Chapter 8 COMPENDIUM OF CAREER GUIDANCE METHODS

The previous chapters of this handbook have been designed to provide a framework for the selection and use of career guidance methods. This chapter is a comprehensive resource bank of specific career guidance methods which have been developed for use in actual programs. This compendium is intended to provide a comprehensive listing of resources which describe methods which might be utilized within career guidance programs.

These methods were identified through a comprehensive search of the ERIC system and of the professional book and journal literature. There are 643 resumes, including all materials identified through June 1972.

The compendium consists of three major sections: (1) the Resume Section, (2) the Methods Index, and (3) the Availability of Materials Section. The Resume Section contains an abstracted listing of 643 methods arranged alphabetically by author. For each method, a complete bibliographic citation is given including the ERIC Document Number, if the document is available through the ERIC System.

The Subject Index arranges the methods by subject areas. A list of about seventy-five index terms are used. All of the terms except those preceded by an asterisk are ERIC descriptors and can be used to update the method compendium by an on-going search of the ERIC system.

Each index term in the Subject Index is followed by a numerical listing of those resumes which relate to the term. Once the reader has identified references by number, the actual resume can be found in the Resume Section where the methods appear in numerical order.

Finally, the Availability Section describes where ERIC documents may be obtained. This section describes how the reader may order single copies for his personal files from the ERIC Document Reproduction Service and where in his geographic area there is a complete ERIC collection available for his use.

METHOD ABSTRACTS

1. Abe, C. & Holland, J. L. Students with different vocational choices. A description of college freshmen, II. Iowa City: American College Testing Program, 1965. (ED 013 457)

    The American college survey was used to assess 12,432 college freshmen from 31 institutions on 43 scales. For each vocation selected by 10 or more students, the mean and standard deviation were computed for 117 student characteristics. The vocations were categorized into 13 areas, and summaries of student characteristics in each area were prepared. The descriptions of students seeking different vocations imply that/ (1) students seek vocations which are appropriate for their interests, values, and special talents, (2) vocational decisions depend upon many student characteristics, (3) the report may be valuable to students who cannot use the services of guidance workers, and (4) there is probably a close association between the choice of major field and choice of vocation. The present study may be limited by the fact that the students are aspirants, rather than employees, in the various vocations. Further research efforts are planned to/ (1) develop psychological classification schemes, (2) learn how students who persist in a field differ from those who leave it, (3) determine the predictive validities of the assessment devices used in this study, and (4) determine the influence of college climates upon a student's vocational choice. This document is an ACT Research Report, No. 4, June 1965.

2. Abington School District. Career development activities. Grades 5, 6, 7. Abington, Pa.: ASD, 1968. (ED 022 219)

    Curriculum materials for use in the vocational guidance of students in grades five, six, and seven are presented. These materials are based on several vocational development theories. The goal is the utilization of learning activities in the classroom to show students the processes through which career decisions may be made.

3. Adams County Board of Education. Vocational guidance program for slow learners. Gettysburg: ACBE. (ES 002 240)

Work experience programs will be developed for slow-learning and mentally retarded high school students in a four-county area. Discrete programs will be offered by each county, and a coordinating council will be established to guide county planning groups. In the first county's program, a coordinator/counselor will be engaged to—(1) conduct individual guidance counseling and group vocational guidance classes to instill a sense of good work habits and attitudes, (2) supervise the work experience programs and follow up on student placements, and (3) guide research and curriculum development activities which are attuned to the needs of special-education students. Students participating in the work experience programs will spend one-half day in school and one-half day at a training station in the community. Student work assignments will be rotated every 6 weeks. Parental approval will be mandatory for student participation in work experience programs, and students will be pretested for work readiness. The programs in the other counties will be similar in nature and will each have a counselor/coordinator as project leader. In some areas, students will spend one or two years in a workshop situation within the school and will receive training in such skills as appliance repair, building maintenance, and auto repair. Approximately 1,764 students, grades 7–12, will be served. For further information, contact Kenneth L. Tyson, 149 Carlisle St., Gettysburg, Pennsylvania 17325. (717) 334-2168.

4. Agan, R. J. (et al.) Commonalities in occupations; general related vocational information for exploratory experiences in occupations. Paola, Kan.: Paola High School; Manhattan: Kansas State University, 1968. (VT 026 292)

The objectives of this study were: (1) to develop and organize a coordinated program of vocational education which would include occupational information, selection, and preparation in the secondary school, (2) to use both individual and team-teaching techniques in the program, and (3) to give guidance in self-assessment by the students relative to their choice of a vocation. Paola High School was selected as the pilot center. Surveys were conducted to identify employment opportunities and the competencies required for 500 local occupations. On the basis of these surveys, instructional materials were developed for the junior year, "Commonalities in Occupations," and for the senior year, "Experiences in Occupations." These materials are included in Appendix A (VT 006 932). Data collection was by personal interviews and by questionnaires completed by graduating seniors. Within the 1967–68 junior class, 50 percent were enrolled in "Commonalities in Occupations." Eighty-five percent of students completing both years of the interdisciplinary program planned to work for the same employer in some capacity. Thirty-seven percent attended college and 26 percent attended trade school. Of those attending college or trade school, 82 percent used their senior year experience to finance education expenses. (CH)

5. Agan, R. J. (et al.) The development and demonstration of a coordinated and integrated program of occupational information, selection, and preparation in a secondary school. Final report. Appendix A. Manhattan: Kansas State University; Paola, Kan.: Paola High School, Pilot Project Instructional Team, 1968. (ED 022 962)

These instructional materials ("Commonalities in Occupations," 11th year and "Experiences in Occupations," 12th year) are for teacher use in conducting interdisciplinary occupational education courses for high school juniors and seniors. The development of these materials followed 3 years of pilot experimentation by a team of teachers engaged in an interdisciplinary approach to vocational education. Some of the content objectives are (1) to provide occupational information, selection, and preparation, (2) to identify common and differential aspects of vocation subjects and (3) to give guidance in self-assessment by students. Some units are (1) Occupational Commonalities Orientation, (2) Observation and Evaluation, and (3) Human Relations: Employer-Employee Relations. The material is designed for presentation by the teacher and each course covers an academic year. Students should be high school juniors and seniors with vocational education as either an interest or an occupational objective. The document is mimeographed and illustrated with drawings, charts, tables, and graphs. A descriptive report related to these materials is ED 022 961.

6. Akamine, T. & Heiner, H. G. Development of an experimental forced-choice occupational preference inventory. Report number

23. Final report. Olympia: Washington State Coordinating Council for Occupational Education; Pullman: Washington State University, 1968. (ED 022 959)

The purpose of this study was to develop an inventory which would (1) help pupils analyze their occupational interests, and (2) inform teachers, counselors, and curriculum planners about pupils' attitudes toward relatively specific elements of work such as acts, tools, materials, environments and human relationships generally associated with work in building trades, office, automobile service, health aid, and retail occupations. A prototype inventory developed by Heiner, Garlington and Whipple was revised and tested with 92 Caucasian and 81 Negro ninth grade pupils in two Tacoma, Washington junior high schools. Results indicate that the instrument does set the stage for guidance. Further research could focus on (1) refinement of items on the present inventory, (2) addition of other occupational categories, and (3) empirical studies to ascertain the validity, reliability, and distribution of responses.

7. Akron-Summit County Placement Project. Akron, Ohio: Akron and Summit County Public Schools, 1972. (Raymond A. Wasil, Director)

The Akron-Summit County Job Placement Department provides services for the nineteen high schools ranging from inner city to county suburbs. Its primary function is to facilitate the placement of disadvantaged in-school youth and dropouts into the world of work. Services to these young people are available for a period of one year after exiting from school. Five field offices within the nineteen high schools are manned by the placement specialists. The central office is located at the Summit County Board of Education.

Placement Specialists were trained by the department Director who originated the project.

By using federal government criteria, youth in the schools are identified as disadvantaged by the placement specialists. Group pre-employment clinics are conducted for in-school youth and job hunting clinics for those who have exited from school. Individual job counseling is constantly taking place. Contacts are made and maintained with business and industry. Youth are placed as job openings occur or are developed. Follow-ups are conducted on placements. Currently, in the nineteen high schools, over 6,500 youths, both in-school and out, are eligible for our services.

Publications in the areas of "Model for Implementation of School Placement," "Model for Conducting Pre-Employment Clinics and Job Hunting Clinics," and a model titled "Data Processing Techniques and Procedures for Placement and Guidance," have been developed. In little over a year, over 2,700 disadvantaged youth have been placed in job openings.

The techniques, procedures, and materials which have been developed for use with the disadvantaged, can be used with vocational or college bound students.

For more information, write: Mr. Raymond A. Wasil, Director, Akron-Summit County Public Schools Placement Project, Akron and Summit County Public Schools, 80 W. Center Street, Akron, Ohio 44308.

8. Albracht, J. (et al.) Using existing vocational programs for providing exploratory experiences. Carrollton: West Georgia College, 1968. (ED 027 432)

This program of exploring occupations seeks to use existing vocational programs to help the upper junior high and high school student: (1) understand himself in relation to various occupational roles, (2) plan for achieving his occupational goal, (3) show an awareness of himself as a productive citizen, and (4) learn of the available community opportunities related to existing vocational programs. Existing programs which might be used are shop or laboratory-type classes or cooperative part-time programs. Four phases of activities which may be used for these exploratory experiences are orientation, exploration, applied experiences, and evaluation and follow-up. Examples detailed for these general activities include the following: (1) filmstrips and discussions, (2) observation of shop and laboratory, of on-the-job observation, and field trips, (3) progress reports, participation in voluntary service organizations, and interviews, and (4) post tests, membership in organizations, and participation in work experience programs.

9. Alexander, K. The high achievement program. Anaheim, Cal.: Anaheim City School District, 1963. (ED 001 278)

Enrichment of the existing curriculum to encourage individual capabilities was conducted in the 4th, 5th, and 6th grades.

Three types of children chosen were: those who have keen insight into the ways other people are thinking and feeling; those who are best at organizing and solving the problems of technology, mechanics, or social situations; and those who like to get at the reasons behind things and categorize. The children were selected and parents notified by letter. An orientation meeting was held for the parents, teachers and principals.

Three types of enrichment programs discussed were: vertical-topics taught at higher grade levels, horizontal-utilizing grade level concepts in a wide variety of situations, supplemental-use of units not generally encountered in the regular course of study. The teacher was asked to use any of these to provide a program that would delve deeply into his fields of special interest.

Special materials used such as films and filmstrips, tape recorders and overhead projectors are listed and explained. A list of Special Activities include: classroom visits from medical professionals, television personnel, electronic personnel and government officials, special trips to study astronomy or zoology in a tide pool, and writing a full length novel.

The teachers' qualifications are discussed, such as graduate work and broad cultural background. The most important attribute would be ability to teach the child to think and challenge his own thinking.

An evaluation of the program shows that it achieved its objectives to some degree and expanded the students' as well as the teaching staffs' knowledge.

10. Allington Corporation. Occupations for you, part two. Alexandria, Va.: AC, 1968. (ED 029 940)

Described here in extensive detail is the second year of a talent development summer high school at Yale University. A compensatory program was provided for 117 underachieving Negro and white boys, judged to have unrealized intellectual potential, who came from both urban and rural areas. The report discusses the students, teachers, tutors, and administrative staff. The curriculum and course content as well as other features of the program are presented. Appendixes offer additional relevant information.

11. Alschuler, A. (et al.) Achievement motivation development project. Cambridge, Mass.: Harvard University, 1969. (ED 029 139)

Two objectives of this project were: (1) to discover what specific methods of arousing motivation are most effective for particular groups, and (2) to prepare instructional materials which will make the prototype achievement motivation course and motivational climates available to a wider number of educators. Attention is given to the methods (inputs) for arousing motives and ways of evaluating whether a motive has been aroused (yields). There are two general types of inputs: course inputs and environmental inputs. Course inputs may be placed in four groups: (1) teaching the achievement syndrome, (2) fostering goal setting, (3) providing cognitive supports, and (4) providing group supports. Environmental inputs are the opportunities and specific external cues for motives. Motivation is studied relative to potential high school dropouts, increases through structure and climate, and yields through individualized instruction. A related document is VT 008 366.

12. Alschuler, A. How to develop achievement motivation: a course manual for teachers. Interim report. Cambridge, Mass.: Achievement Motivation Development Project, 1969. (ED 029 967)

This teacher's manual grows out of a major research project that is attempting to discover the most effective methods of increasing motivation of the adolescent. The methods under study are combined into special courses that are given in schools by teachers, not in laboratories by research scientists nor in clinics by psychotherapists. "Psychological education" is described as a new educational movement of which the achievement motivation course is a part. The history, goals, methods, and rationale for this movement are discussed in some detail. Also, a fairly detailed course outline is provided to suggest how one course was put together. Chapter 2 is a set of instructions and suggestions put together to allow potential motivation course teachers to experience a course themselves. Chapter 3 builds on this experience by providing a review of the research on achievement motivation. Chapter 4 is a detailed, down-to-earth description of what goes in an achievement motivation course for students. The appendixes include an array of games, case studies, and role plays for achievement motivation courses.

13. Altman, J. W. What kinds of occupational information do students need? 1966 (ED 018 580)

Results of studies suggest that students not only need occupational information, they need more and better information to support their objectives of career choice, career planning and development, and development and application of vocational capabilities. A proposed comprehensive structure for needed occupational information is based on a continuum which reaches backward in time from a skilled worker on the job toward the cradle. It encompasses the stages (1) journeyman capability which needs knowledge about the tasks and contexts which define the job as well as practice in realistic applications, (2) neophyte capability which needs practice on selected tasks or partial tasks sequences with extrapolation and generalization to the fuller job context, (3) general vocational capability which includes general preparation for later specific vocational training, and a continual feedback of reality-testing information about tentative career choices and plans, (4) career planning capability which requires some kind of structure or map pointing out varieties of jobs, student self-information, and student application of information, and (5) vocational awareness which needs an identification of the components and institutions of a working society and the economic, political, and philosophical lines which govern them, a clarification of how work-roles grow out of these institutional roles, and a meaningful concept of the working world as an evolutionary rather than a static system. A bibliography is included. This speech was to be delivered at the Occupational Information and Vocational Guidance Conference (Pittsburgh, March 11–13, 1966).

14. Anderson, C. Project 13. Minneapolis, Minn.: Minneapolis Public Schools, 1966. (ED 010 779)

A program in low-income areas in Minneapolis provided the services of high school counselors to graduates and dropouts by (1) offering vocational guidance to unemployed graduates and actively assisting in job placement, (2) encouraging the return of dropouts to school and assisting in their readjustment to academic life, (3) organizing data on clients for use in current and future studies, including curriculum reforms, and (4) organizing a separate summer program to induce dropouts to resume schooling. Response to the program was encouraging, with the counselors making nearly 3,000 individual contacts in the initial 6-month period.

15. Arffa, M. S. The influence of volunteer experience on career choice. *The Vocational Guidance Quarterly,* 1966, 14(4), 287–289.

The present paper proposes to explore the influence of volunteer experience in a psychiatric hospital on the career choice of high school and college students. Specifically, this study attempts to discover (1) what changes, if any, occur in the career choice of students after an experience; (2) the direction of these changes; and (3) the extent to which these changes can be attributed to the volunteer experience.

The results of this study do not support the general conclusion that volunteer experience in a psychiatric hospital, *ipso facto,* directly influences a change in occupational choice *per se.* It is suggested that most student volunteers may make vocational decisions before volunteering and the experience tends to maintain or verify their choice rather than change it.

16. Arnold, W. Vocational technical and continuing education in Pennsylvania. A systems approach to state-local program planning. Harrisburg: Pennsylvania Research Coordinating Unit for Vocational Education, 1969. (ED 032 431)

The Pennsylvania Vocational Education Study was planned primarily as a pragmatic overview and analysis of vocational, technical, and continuing education for the years 1964–1968, with a goal of determining its achievements, deficiencies, and direction in the light of priority needs. Recommendations and conclusions were derived from data relating to: (1) a 5-year analysis of enrollments and expenditures in vocational-technical and continuing education, (2) economic trends, (3) occupational training agencies, programs, and output of graduates, (4) a description of a systems approach to vocational and technical education program-planning, (5) reporting procedures and financial aid policies, (6) teacher education and certification, (7) vocational guidance services, and (8) special problems of Philadelphia and Pittsburgh. Major recommendations were for: (1) expansion of post-secondary vocational and technical education, (2) increased funding and emphasis on adult education, (3) overcoming deficiencies in health occupations, technical education, and special needs programs for the socio-economic disadvantaged, (4) development of an organized systematic planning procedure, (5) modernization of financial aid policies and reporting procedures, and (6) improvement in communication patterns between state and local levels.

17. Ash, L. C. Expanding role for vocational and technical education. *Counselor Education and Supervision,* 1967, 6(2), 84–90.

The focal point of vocational and technical education has changed tremendously since a few years ago when our deepest concern was for the discovery and education of the gifted whose abilities would contribute to the development and advancement of our increasingly technological society. More recently, we have discovered that efforts along this line were not enough to create and preserve a strong nation. Each member of our society has a unique contribution to make, and only as we prepare him to make his contribution by helping him to develop occupational skills and suitable attitudes toward his work, can we hope to realize the full potential of our people.

Guidance counselors are a recognized source of specific information concerning occupations and ways of entering into them. Our perception of the need for all persons to be prepared for the world of work—so as to function at the optimum of their ability—can lead those whom we would counsel to develop understandings and abilities, thereby enabling them to become effective members of society.

One source of this preparation is vocational education which instructs in skills needed for gainful employment. It is conducted as a part of a program designed to fit individuals for work as semi-skilled or skilled workers or technicians.

Vocational education has an important function in the implementation of the manpower policy of the United States. In passing the Employment Act of 1946, the Congress declared it to be a continuing responsibility of the federal government "to promote maximum employment, production, and purchasing power." The President stated in his 1965 Economic Report that "We have made notable progress toward the Employment Act's central goal of ... useful employment opportunities, including self-employment, for those able ... willing and seeking to work and ... maximum employment, production, and purchasing power." Vocational education provides the training and retraining opportunities for those who are "able and wanting to work."

18. Ashcraft, K. B. (Ed.) Implementing career development theory and research through the curriculum. Report of a conference sponsored by the National Vocational Guidance Association, August, 1966. (ED 010 182)

A final report has been prepared on a conference concerning vocational development and career planning. Following a planning session, those individuals who had been identified as prominent innovators in selected topic areas were invited to participate in the conference. Participants prepared papers for distribution prior to the conference and made presentations at the conference. Following each presentation, the attendees broke into small discussion groups which had the definitive assignment of developing implementing procedures. The report included reproductions of the papers presented and the following summaries— (1) curricular implications for career development, (2) implications for counselor education, (3) implications for research, and (4) summary of the discussion sessions.

19. Astin, H. S. Career development during the high school years. *Journal of Counseling Psychology,* 1967, 14, 94–98.

This study, utilizing the Project TALENT Data Bank, was designed to assess the career expectations of 650 male high school seniors on the basis of their personal characteristics when they were in the 9th grade and of selected environmental characteristics of the schools attended. The student's measured interests and expressed career choice at the 9th-grade level were the best predictors of career outcomes at the 12th-grade level. The discriminating power of the test battery improved by adding selected environmental characteristics of the high schools attended by Ss. The major occupational groups in this study could be characterized by the unique personality orientations of Ss aspiring to them.

20. Atlanta Board of Education. Formulation of models for preparing occupational materials for pupils from various socioeconomic levels in grades three through eight. Atlanta, Ga.: ABE. (ES 001 578)

Occupational information will be developed for elementary students from various socioeconomic levels in a demonstration program for a metropolitan area. The materials will be disseminated in forms suitable for the grade and cognitive level of students so they will—(1) gain knowledge of several aspects of themselves and of the various occupations, and (2) be motivated to remain in high school and to seek additional training in either vocational-technical or college programs, or (3) be motivated to seek vocational training if they feel compelled to drop out of high school education. During the demonstration program students in nine schools will be involved in the development of materials on 100 clusters of occupations. The materials will be disseminated in four other schools, and three additional schools will be selected for control purposes. Media used for dissemination will include the printed word, television, and interviews or dialogs on discs to be played in juke boxes prominently located at school facilities. Dissemination will be continued over a period of 3 years to ascertain changes in the behavior of students. Conceptual models will be formulated, based on student responses, to be used in preparing additional materials. Approximately 5,327 students, grades 3–8, will participate in the demonstration program. For further information, contact John W. Letson, Superintendent, 224 Central Ave., Southwest, Atlanta, Georgia 30303. (404) 522-3381.

21. Aughinbaugh, L. A. Group versus individual counseling: a junior college study. Final report. Sacramento, Cal.: American River Junior College, 1968. (ED 027 893)

Increases in junior college enrollment, coupled with a shortage of qualified guidance personnel, have forced many colleges to rely more heavily on group than on individual counseling for students. In the fall of 1965, students entering American River College were randomly assigned to either group or individual sessions, or not assigned, and these groups were compared over a two-year period in persistence, academic achievement, goal motivation, student attitude change, and counselor evaluation of students' growth in self-understanding. An analysis of covariance showed that students counseled individually were rated significantly higher by their counselors in growth in self-understanding, and students counseled in groups had a significantly more positive attitude toward counseling. Although there were no significant differences between these groups in persistance, academic achievement, or goal motivation, when they were compared to students not assigned to either group or individual counseling sessions, they were significantly higher in these three areas. It was concluded that, regardless of method, when special attention is paid to counseling, students benefit.

22. Bailey, J. A. Career development concepts: significance and utility. *Personnel and Guidance Journal,* 1968, 47(1), 24–28.

Trustees of four appropriate professional associations determined the relative value of significant career-development concepts from a pre-selected list. Comparisons among the trustee groups are made, composite data are reported, suggestions for using the rank-ordered concepts in research as an external criterion are provided, and ideas for incorporating the concepts as topics for group guidance classes are given.

23. Bailey, L. J., Ed. Facilitating career development: an annotated bibliography. Final report. Springfield: Illinois State Board of Vocational Education and Rehabilitation, Vocational and Technical Education Division; Carbondale: Southern Illinois University, 1970. (ED 042 217)

This annotated bibliography presents abstracts of publications which focus on finding new directions for implementing career practices within the classroom.

It is limited to programs, practices, and techniques which are operational or have demonstrated potential for enhancing the process of career development. The emphasis is on relevance and applicability for comprehensive programs of occupational and career guidance. Chapter 1 is concerned with theoretical implications, applications, and a survey of computer based guidance systems. Chapter II summarizes many new models and techniques for guidance which view vocational behavior as a developmental process rather than as an event. The material in Chapter III deals with career development conferences and Chapter IV describes examples of programs designed to realize the ultimate criteria of a vocationally mature individual. Chapter V discusses career exploration achieved vicariously via games, simulation practices and guidance kits which encourage student activity and involvement. The intent of Chapter VI is to summarize recently developed instruments for measuring vocational behavior and Chapter VII illustrates the preponderance of approaches for providing occupational information and orientation.

24. Baltimore Public Schools. Vocational education systems for the 1970's. Baltimore: BPS. (ES 002 451)

Vocational education will be the focus of curriculum study in an urban school system which will participate in the ES '70 Network. The ES '70 Network will include 17 demonstration schools throughout the country, and in each school a complete systems analysis will be conducted on a selected portion of the secondary curriculum. In all participating schools, desired behavioral changes will be identified for the total subject offering and for the courses within the subject offering. Specific Performance Objectives (SPO) will then be developed for each course. The SPO's will be analyzed for contingent or higher articular relationships so that criterion behaviors may be sequenced. At the target school, performance objectives will be developed for vocational education, concentrating on experiences in machine shop, printing, stenography, and electricity. Teams will be formed from the industrial arts teaching staff to develop the SPO's within an assigned cluster. Once identified, the behavioral objectives will be arranged in accordance with the various types of learning, as defined by Gagne. Review and integration milestones will be established for the various teams. Continuing training will be provided to the staff in terms of new instructional materials, exchange of information with network schools, and information seminars provided by consultants. Workshops will be conducted in conjunction with other schools engaged in the ES '70 Network. Approximately 83,663 students, grades 7-12, will be served. For further information, contact Sidney Chernack, 3 East 25th St., Baltimore, Maryland 21218. (301) 467-4000.

25. Bancroft, J. & Lawson, W. H. Project Notify—needed occupational television instruction for youth. San Bernardino: San Bernardino Valley College, 1966. (ED 010 641)

An evaluation was made of the effectiveness of video tapes as a means of disseminating occupational information to high school students. After criteria for selection were determined, seven occupational areas were chosen for presentation by video tape. The television programs were designed to identify entry level jobs in the occupational areas covered, which were secretarial work, food retailing, department store retailing, automotive technology, lodging and food services, financial institution employment, and law enforcement. The population of the study consisted of 11th- and 12th-grade students in eight senior high schools. To determine the effectiveness of the program, a followup study was conducted by use of inventory questionnaires. A majority of the students had a very favorable reaction to the tapes, indicating that television in the classroom is an effective medium for providing occupational information. Student evaluations given in interviews 2 months after broadcast agreed closely with evaluations made immediately following broadcast. In the order of amount of help given, with "high" listed first, the programs were ranked—(1) those that presented clear development of facts, (2) those that encouraged students to remain in school, and (3) those that motivated students to think about matters specifically related to job planning. Programs that acquainted students with available job possibilities were considered beneficial, with most benefit being gained by disadvantaged minority students.

26. Bank, I. M. Children explore careerland through vocational role-models. *Vocational Guidance Quarterly,* 1969, 17(4), 284–288.

During the elementary school years, it would appear that boys and girls are in need of experiences which can provide maximal opportunity for vocational inquiry. A broader base for vocational choice can be developed during these formative years in the lives of elementary school students. The counselor can be instrumental in building an expanded careerland in which they are exposed to the world of work and workers at an early age. The individual's choice of alternatives in his future years of development may be enhanced by the effectiveness of exposures during these formative years.

27. Barbula, P. M. & Isaac, S. W. Career simulation for adolescent pupils. Final report. San Diego, Cal.: San Diego County Department of Education, 1967. (ED 016 268)

The purpose of this study was to assess student acquisition of knowledge about vocations after participation in a career simulation game and to determine attitudinal change toward vocational concepts. Data was collected through a pre-test and a post-test. A sample of sixth- and eighth-grade students was drawn for the treatment and the control groups. The treatment groups participated in the career simulation game while the control groups received the usual curriculum program. No statistically significant differences were found between the groups on a 10-item questionnaire on vocational insightfulness. A general trend to increase hours of study on the post-tests was evident for the treatment groups, although no statistically significant patterns were found. The negative results may be due to insensitive instrumentation. The investigators believe that further developmental work is indicated to explore simulation as a method of teaching career development principles to adolescents.

28. Barnette, W. L. & McCall, J. N. Validation of the Minnesota Vocational Interest Inventory for vocational high school boys, part I. Buffalo: University of the State of New York, 1963. (ED 003 260)

An investigation was made of the Minnesota Vocational Interest Inventory (MVII) patterns and vocational enrollment to aid in the selection and counseling of students. Over 1,000 high school boys in the 9th and 12th grades were tested. A variety of variables were tested including ethnic distribution. The MVII was found valid in some areas and lacking in others. The suggested changes for the MVII are to lower the technical vocabulary level and to eliminate the keys irrelevant to vocational curriculums.

29. Bartlesville Public Schools. Readings in computer based guidance. The Bartlesville system. Bartlesville, Okla.: BPS, 1970. (ED 042 223)

The document contains six papers which deal with the need for change in guidance and counseling due to the overwhelming amount of data which is insufficiently processed by conventional manual systems. Included in these papers are discussions on when these changes should occur and the nature of their alterations. The reports consider some of the ways in which the computer can be successfully used to provide needed support. These areas include: (1) information storage and retrieval; (2) diagnosis; (3) instructional gaming, and (4) synthetic confrontation therapy. The following topics are covered: (1) computer based gaming, a systems approach to vocational instruction; (2) synthetic confrontation therapy; (3) diagnosis and prediction; (4) a survey of two information languages for counselor applications; (5) gaming for vocational awareness; and (6) computer diagnostics.

30. Baruch, R. Computer-assisted systems in guidance and education: report of an invitational conference on the implications for the practice and education of counselors. Cambridge, Mass.: Graduate School of Education, Harvard University, 1969. (ED 040 598)

Four computer assisted systems, demonstrated for a conference on the implications of computer assisted instruction (CAI) for the practice and education of counselors, are described in this report. The systems are introduced in a first part, and include the Information System for Vocational Decisions (ISVD), the Educational and Career Exploration System (ECES), the Program for Learning in Accordance with Needs (PLAN), and the Interactive Learning System (ILS). Each system is then compared with the others using excerpts from the reaction papers of the participants, and further discussion of CAI is presented with topics focusing on the issues, the potential, implications, and recommendations.

31. Barzelay, R. Giving summer jobs a new dimension. *Manpower,* 1970, 2(5), 21–24.

    Summer jobs for youth are fine. They enable many poor youngsters to make a badly needed contribution to the family finances. For those in less stringent financial straits, summer work keeps otherwise idle hands busy and supplies a modest amount of cash for entertainment, clothing and other wants that might go unsatisfied.
    But is that enough? A few years ago General Foods decided that summer jobs could do much more. With intelligent effort, they could be a means of giving young people a truer picture of the business world. Meaningful jobs might also encourage students to remain in high school and seek a better future through a college education—especially if financial assistance were made available as an added inducement.

32. Bates, M. Test of group counseling. *Personnel and Guidance Journal,* 46, 749–753.

    High school students were counseled in groups designed around either a "traditional" or an "accelerated interaction" format. The efficiency of each approach in achieving the goals of guidance in education was studied. Group counseling appeared to be a useful counseling tool if organized on a weekly basis.

33. Baugh, S. & Martin, W. E. Total career capability for all. A career-development program model. Indiana: Fort Wayne Community Schools, 1970. (ED 044 719)

    A comprehensive career development program model is presented. It attempts to provide total career capability for all and has the following process objectives: (1) provide students with experiences and information that present occupational dimensions accurately; (2) provide appropriate situations at different levels so that all youth may have an opportunity to make decisions, to discuss and examine the decision-making process, and to understand the basis for judging the quality of one's decision; (3) manage and modify environmental factors to insure maximizing the impact on accomplishing career development objectives; (4) use both direct and indirect contacts with students in multiplying the students' perception of present and potential alternatives; (5) coordinate a comprehensive placement service; and (6) communicate to the student a respect for all work and of the importance of all work to society. The model is divided into four parts—elementary, junior high, secondary, and post secondary—and a career development model is given for each level and a flow chart.

34. Beachley, C. Careers via closed circuit television. *Vocational Guidance Quarterly,* 1959, 7, 67–70.

    High school counselors, assisted by classroom teachers and specialists working on topics pertinent to their phase of education formulated plans for an experimental five-year program of telecasts over closed circuit television including such fields as: personal problems, curriculum choices, and occupational information. After completing more than 100 of these telecasts in Washington County, Maryland, it was possible to assess the value of the program and speculate on the future of television as a means of dealing with careers and related occupational information. A description of the approaches and techniques used in developing the career telecasts is provided in addition to an evaluation of these telecasts.

35. Beam, H. E. & Clary, J. R. Introduction to vocations. Teacher's guide. Raleigh: North Carolina State University, 1968.

    Introduction to Vocation is a model program designed to correlate the necessary academic knowledge of high school students with exploratory manipulative experiences in selected areas of work. It is designed to provide youth an opportunity for appraising their own developing potentials.

The program is primarily aimed at non-college-bound students who will terminate their formal education before completing high school. The objective of the program is to (1) stimulate critical thinking concerning occupational choice; (2) to positively affect the vocational choice; (3) to broaden the base for vocational education offerings in the State of New Jersey. More specifically, the program helps develop proper attitudes toward and understanding of the world of work and to teach students to appraise their individual and unique interests, aptitudes, abilities and skills in relation to a variety of current and future vocational opportunities.

36. Beedy, V. (et al.). A prevocational and social adjustment program for educable retarded adolescents: a pilot project. Milwaukee media for rehabilitation research reports. Number 10. Milwaukee, Wis.: Curative Workshop of Milwaukee; Wisconsin University, 1971. (ED 046 041)

The primary object of this project was to provide a program encompassing vocationally-oriented enrichment activities for the educable retarded adolescent, whose retardation can be defined in terms of the following developmental areas: (1) educational; (2) mental; (3) social; and (4) vocational. Included in this report are sections on: (1) an introduction including a description of activities; (2) vocational adjustment which discusses role playing, counseling, films, interests, and tours; (3) educational adjustment which discusses teaching units on several subjects, classroom procedures, and choosing a curriculum; (4) social adjustment which discusses parents' attitudes and vocational goals, parents' evaluation of the program, and results; and (5) evaluation of the project, by client, parent and staff.

37. Beima, J. R. (Comp.) Occupation analysis as a basis for vocational education curriculum change. Juneau: Alaska State Department of Education, Division of Vocational Education, 1965. (ED 023 792)

The objectives of the survey were to identify the types of employment available for each population area in Alaska and to determine the occupational goals of high school students in the state, in order to provide a basis for evaluation of vocational education curricula. Of 15,308 high school students enrolled the first week of the 1966–67 school year, 14,581 students reported their father's occupation, mother's occupation, and their own vocational goal. Findings were: (1) 91 percent of the students' parents were employed in non-professional occupations, but only 25 percent of the students were receiving non-professional training to fill these existing jobs, (2) 75 percent of the students were receiving pre-college training required to fill 9 percent of the jobs, (3) 6,639 students reported their parents employed in areas utilizing skills learned in trade and industrial education, but only 2.8 percent of the students were receiving training in this area, (4) 5,099 students reported their mothers as full-time homemakers, and (5) 4,460 students reported their parents employed in areas related to business. The father's occupation, mother's occupation, and the student's vocational goal are tabulated.

38. Benjamin, G. E. Significant job success factors found in work study programs in five major New York state cities. Syracuse: Syracuse University, New York Division of Special Education and Rehabilitation, 1967.

The purpose of the study was to identify aspects found in secondary school vocational study programs that seem to be closely related to graduates' job success. Five variables relating to the work-study programs and four variables relating to job success were used as criteria in determining which graduates had been the most occupationally successful. Data were received from a random 20 percent of 246 of the graduates who participated in the vocational work-study programs in five major city school districts. Of the 20 hypotheses tested, only 2 were found to be significant at the .05 level of confidence: (1) The students' grade point averages will have a positive relationship to the "Dictionary of Occupational Titles" classification of graduates' jobs, and (2) Assignment of students to work-study job stations related to their major field will be related to the proportion of students' time employed after graduation. Some of the findings relating to the programs were: (1) Approximately 76 percent of the sample felt the program had helped them since graduation, (2) Approximately 80 percent felt they did better in school work while in the program, (3) Only 21 percent of the males and 70 percent of the females were placed in work-study program situations complimenting and extending their vocational programs, and (4) Relative minor emphasis was given to the guidance function of the 5 work-study programs. Data relating to employment revealed that (1) About 69 percent had a job when they left school upon graduation and an additional 12 percent found jobs within 30 days, (2) Approximately 82 percent were earning more than $1.51 per hour, and (3) The graduates' success on the job related to placement in jobs for which they had received specific training. A summary of the study is given in VT 005 269.

39. Berry, J. Counseling girls and women—awareness, analysis, action. Kansas City: Missouri University; Missouri State Department of Labor and Industrial Relations, 1966a. (ED 018 558)

Objectives of this guide to be used in an inservice training program are—(1) to alert counselors to specialized needs of girls and women, (2) to provide a readable source of background materials, (3) to develop appreciation of the role of the employment service in counseling girls and women, and (4) to create an awareness of research in the area of women's role in society. The perceptive counselor attempts to alert girls and women to social change and its impact on women's lives, future-oriented opportunities, and a life planning approach. The latter involves planning for multiple roles during different periods of their life. Women's employment falls into three general patterns—the constant employee, the in-and-out employee, and the novice. Attitudes are changing toward women's roles, and they now have to choose a career or home or both. Recent trends in education show that the more education a woman has, the greater are the chances that she will be working. New fields are opening for women with education. Continuing education is available to more people with different backgrounds. A annotated bibliography is included.

40. Berry, J. Counseling for women's roles in the 1980's. In M. R. Smith (Ed.) *Guidance-personnel work: future tense.* New York: Teachers College Press, Columbia University, 1966b. Chapter 10.

The increasing momentum of research on women's roles, education, and career accomplishments and an appreciation of the rapidity of social change suggest the exploration of male attitudes concerning women's roles, life planning approach appropriate for the 1980's, possible life patterns, and counselor training for advising girls and women. Little study has been made of the attitudes of husbands, employers, and educators toward the variety of life patterns and choices for women but there is some slight indication that younger men take a more sympathetic view toward wives' continuing education. Counseling for girls and women should encompass the educational, vocational, avocational, community, and family aspects of the total life span. Life patterns for women in the 1980's will include such activities as community service, continuing education, specialized professional work, or conducting of a business endeavor. Training for counselors of women might be incorporated in a specialized course, seminar, or workshop combined with supervised experience.

41. Bertcher, H. (et al.) Role modeling and role playing: a manual for vocational development and employment agencies. Ann Arbor, Mich.: Manpower Science Services, Inc., 1971. (ED 053 350)

This project investigated two major areas: (1) ways in which social science research and employment agency experience could be molded so as to make practical knowledge available to these agencies, and (2) ways of convincing employment agencies to use this knowledge. The manual resulting from the investigation focuses on role modeling and role playing because both have potential in improving the employability of disadvantaged persons. Both also have been used widely in experimental and demonstration projects. The intent of this manual is to serve as a direct and practical tool to employment agencies serving disadvantaged persons. It is also directed to counselors, coaches, community aides, crew chiefs, vocational instructors, and basic education instructors.

42. Bienenstok, T. & Sayres, W. C. Project ABLE—an appraisal. Albany: The University of the State of New York, 1964. (ED 001 522)

Project ABLE was established in 1961 in New York to identify and encourage high ability pupils from culturally deprived groups and low-socio-economic backgrounds. Local projects were established in sixteen districts with the backing of state funds, operating on elementary, junior and senior high school levels. Average costs per pupil varied considerably. The program is under general supervision of the Bureau of Guidance.

A typical ABLE project consists of three phases: 1) intensive remedial and cultural enrichment activities; 2) in-service sensitivity training for school personnel to acquaint them with the characteristics of culturally deprived children; and 3) expanded guidance and counseling service for both pupils and parents. Practices such as summer programs and new instructional techniques are described. The outcomes so far are positive. Most impressive is a perceptible change in school attitudes toward these children. Overall improvement of the students in educational aspirations, scholastic performance, school attendance, and classroom behavior indicate that continuation of the program is fully justified.

Issues and problems which developed in the program are described. The concepts of cultural deprivation and potential ability need to be clarified in relation to the purposes of the program. The program practices need to be related to the particular character of cultural deprivation. Instructional materials need to be developed which have more meaningful links with the world of these children. With the assistance of the state, a detailed evaluation of the various projects should be undertaken in order to satisfactorily resolve the kinds of problems in the report.

43. Bienenstok, T. & Sayres, W. C. STEP—school to employment program. An appraisal. Albany: the University of the State of New York, 1964. (ED 001 438)

Included is an analysis of a work-study demonstration program for potential dropouts from New York high schools. The findings are based on data and information gathered from many sources, all of which are connected with the program. The attempt is to place potential dropouts in part-time employment with either private employers or with public organizations. The purpose is to teach them good work habits and help them achieve successful adjustment to the demands of adulthood. An effort is made to encourage students to return to school on a full time basis.

Students are referred to STEP by guidance personnel or teachers. A teacher-counselor works closely with each student in an attempt to gain his confidence and provide at least the understanding friend with whom he can freely discuss his problems. Thus far, program cost has averaged $400 per year per student. Several criticisms of the program are presented and analyzed. The major problem lies with the choice of students to be placed in the p.ogram. If those at the bottom of the scale are chosen exclusively, it is difficult to produce results adequate to justify the expenditures of the program. If only the potentially "successful" students are chosen, one wonders if perhaps these students would not have progressed successfully without the help of the program.

44. Bigge, J. & Sandefur, J. T. An exploratory study of the effects of bibliotherapy on the behavioral pattern of adolescents. Emporia: Kansas State Teachers College, 1965. (ED 003 677)

The extent to which a planned program of reading could significantly influence the behavior of a selected group of adolescents was studied. Efforts were made to design the study in such a way that the investigators could determine whether significant differences existed in the areas of personality, personal problems, achievement, attendance, and discipline between two groups of students, one of which had been subjected to bibliotherapy while the other had served as a control group. The degree of change between the experimental group and the control group in personality was assessed by administering pre- and post-tests of the junior-senior high school personality questionnaire, in achievement by SRA Achievement Series, in personal and social problems by the Mooney Problem Check List, and in behavioral problems by the Haggerty-Olson-Wickman Behavior Rating Schedules. Significant change was evidenced in achievement between students who received bibliotherapy and those students who did not. A longitudinal study was proposed.

45. Bingham, W. C. Counseling services for unemployed youth. New York: New York University, Center for the Study of Unemployed Youth, 1967. (VT 004 213)

   Young people with serious unemployment problems are found most frequently among the youth who have suffered the most serious developmental deficiencies. Some problems of vocational behavior of the unemployed are examined, and an approach to the solution of those problems through counseling is explored. Focus is on the identification of those counseling tasks that can only be performed by the relatively untrained. Counseling techniques include: (1) be informed, (2) be committed, (3) listen and be responsive, (4) know your limitations, (5) plan each interview, (6) keep records, (7) be in the right place, (8) focus on discrepancies, (9) manipulate the environment, and (10) avoid overinvolvement. Group counseling versus individual counseling as well as issues, problems, and the writer's personal preferences for the selection and preparation of counselors below the professional level are presented.

46. Birnbaum, R. The effectiveness of two information dissemination programs in changing the orientation of middle-achievement high school students towards community college attendance. New York: Columbia University, 1967.

   The purpose of the study was to determine the effectiveness of two information dissemination programs in influencing middle-achievement students to consider community college attendance, and in increasing both the amount of accurate information they possessed and their positive attitudes towards these colleges.

47. Birnbaum, R. Influencing college attendance. *Personnel and Guidance Journal,* 1968, 46(8), 786–789.

   This study compared the effectiveness of a filmstrip with that of a filmstrip-and-counseling program in influencing the college attendance plans of high school juniors. The results indicate the importance of personal counseling compared with the sole use of mass media in efforts to influence post-high school plans.

48. Black, F. P. Attitude changes of vocational educators after attending a three-week workshop in vocational-technical education research. Cheyenne: Wyoming Research Coordinating Unit in Vocational-Technical Educations; Wyoming State Department of Education, 1969. (ED 027 431)

   To evaluate changes of attitude by vocational educators during a summer workshop in educational research, statistical data was obtained from a sample of four school administrators and 12 vocational education teachers who attended the workshop. Chi-square analysis and a Z test were utilized in evaluating attitude changes based on a pre- and a post-test. Some findings were: (1) A chi-square analysis revealed little significant differences between the pre-test mean score and the post-test mean score, and (3) vocational educators had a favorable outlook on the role of research in their field following the workshop.

49. Blocker, C. E. & Anthony, D. M. Social status and prestige in the selection of a program of study in the community-junior college. *Personnel and Guidance Journal,* 1968, 46(10), 1005–9.

   This study examines the relative emphasis placed upon social status and prestige in the selection of an occupation and program of study by students in the community-junior college.

50. Bloomberg, C. M. Job training for dropouts. *American Journal of Orthopsychiatry,* 1967, 37(4), 779–787.

   Account of a project to train unemployed high school dropouts as aides for preschool centers. Group process and outcome are detailed in terms of the course

51. Boggs, G. E. A comparative analysis of the impact of various types of curricula on the vocational success of school dropouts. Washington, D.C.: Office of Manpower Policy, Evaluation and Research (DOL), 1967. (ED 022 062)

The purpose of this dissertation, submitted to Oklahoma State University, was to investigate vocational success differences in four groups of subjects at the Manpower Development and Training Act School Dropout Rehabilitation Program in Oklahoma City in 1965. An *ex post facto* design involved 162 subjects in three curriculums (combination, vocation, or academic); 40 of these had dropped out or did not start the program and served as a control group. The subjects had to be (1) unemployed or underemployed school dropouts, (2) between the ages of 17–22, (3) out of school at least 1 year, and (4) judged capable of completing the program. Vocational success measures taken at 6-month and 1-year intervals after training were (1) entry into the labor market, (2) employment status, (3) number of jobs held, (4) number of days employed, (5) weekly wages, (6) job performance, and (7) job satisfaction. Results significant at the .05 level were: (1) The ratio of subjects entering the labor market to subjects not entering was greater for the vocational group than for the control group, (2) The ratios of employed to unemployed were greater for the combination and vocational groups than for the control group, (3) Combination, vocational, and academic groups were employed more days than the control group, and (4) The combination and vocational groups were employed more days than the academic group.

52. Bohn, M. J. (et al.) The educational and career exploration system: field trial and evaluation. New York: New York Teachers College, Columbia University, 1970. (ED 038 661)

The results of a field test of a computer-assisted counseling system, conducted in a suburban high school are presented. Three questions were asked: (1) does the education and career exploration system function adequately? (2) does it effect students' vocational development? and (3) what reactions does it elicit from students, parents, counselors, and teachers? The system, designed to provide the student with information concerning his educational and occupational choices for use in post high school plans, has three programs: (1) introduction and vocational orientation; (2) educational orientation and (3) post high school educational search. The subjects were: (1) black and white; (2) male and female; and (3) college and non-college bound. An experimental group consisting of students who had used the system and a control group who were not exposed to the system were randomly selected. Results indicate that the system experience leads to higher vocational maturity. Also, it was used equally by black and white students and by college and non-college bound students. Male students used the system more frequently than female students. Generally, the students were positive about their experience with the system, as were their parents. The counselors agreed on the potential contributions of the system but urged the use of other occupational materials.

53. Bolvin, J. & Lindvall, C. M. The project for individually prescribed instruction. The Oakleaf project. Pittsburgh, Pa.: Pittsburgh University, Learning Research and Development Center, 1966. (ED 010 522)

The Oakleaf project was a cooperative study of the problems involved in making provision for individual differences within the context of regular school operations. The Oakleaf Elementary School in suburban Pittsburgh was used as a laboratory for the development and trial of a program for individually prescribed instruction (IPI). The IPI procedure consisted of analyses of pupil progress at certain sequential steps in learning and the development of personal prescriptions to specify the learning experiences required to meet the individual needs of each student. Students participated in the IPI program for less than one-half hour each school day. During the rest of the day, the students engaged in study in the conventional manner. Three basic content areas were used with the program—reading. mathematics, and science. At the time of this report, the study effort was still in progress and no conclusions were presented. Possible research studies to be undertaken in the future as part of this continuing project were outlined.

Related reports are ED 010 205 through ED 010 211 and ED 010 519 through ED 010 523.

54. Bonfield, J. Development and validation of an identification scale for high ability dropouts. *Vocational Guidance Quarterly,* 1968, 16(3), 177–180.

The purpose of this study was to develop a dropout identification scale using responses to the MVII which differentiates dropouts from persisters. The scale was to be used to identify male students of above average mental ability who are potential school dropouts. Reliable identification would enable school personnel to implement more effective counseling programs to help the potential dropout remain in school or make a more adequate transition to the world of work.

55. Boocock, S. S. The life career game. *Personnel and Guidance Journal,* 1967, 46(4), 328-335.

Vocational counseling of adolescents is difficult because it requires their evaluation of situations that are unfamiliar and unimportant to many of them. Games with simulated environments are presented as one means of overcoming the discrepancy between the adolescent and the adult world. An example of such a game, in which students plan the life of a fictitious student and receive "feedback" on the possible consequences of their decisions is described. Field testing with the game indicates that it can arouse student interest, communicate factual information about career decision-making, and give young people a realistic, if vicarious, experience of certain aspects of adult life.

56. Boocock, S. S. & Schild, E. O. (Eds.) Simulation games in learning. Beverly Hills, Cal.: Sage Publications, Inc., 1966. (ED 026 857)

Simulation games serve many functions, but the important one to educators is that they present the student player with a real-life situation allowing him to use his knowledge and abilities while discovering decision-making skills for himself. To provide a basic reference on simulation gaming, essays on various aspects of games were collected from people responsible for the development of the technique. The rationale for the use of games in education is found in examining how social processes can be simulated and what educational objectives can be presented in this way. The potential impact that games can have is indicated in examples from research, including results from single game sessions showing effects on factual knowledge, attitudes, and strategies and results of longer games that were compared to conventional methods. The parameters influencing the effectiveness of games include learner characteristics: age, social status, intensity of participation, personal predispositions, and achievement level, as well as characteristics of game advisors. Other parameters are the way that a game is administered and whether competition is individual or group oriented. Finally, the effect of the future on the use of games is considered. A listing of centers working on educational games and a selective bibliography is appended.

57. Borow, H. Occupational information in guidance practice viewed in the perspective of vocational development theory and research. 1966. (ED 014 736)

Systematic examination of the counselee as a purposive, goal-seeking, learning organism is advocated. When occupational information is given to a counselee, it is filtered through psychological sets, attitudes, preconceptions, and defenses. Vocational guidance must selectively borrow from related behavioral sciences. Since 1950, a reconceptualization of guidance has taken place. Children acquire value systems which influence their choice of occupations. Junior high students have limited and questionable information about occupations and are not ready for counseling about specific vocational choices. Work has little meaning for disadvantaged youth. American youth is estranged from occupational life, and develops biases against work fields. Improved occupational information usage may include—(1) elementary counseling, (2) orientation to work in elementary school, and (3) experimental work on the effect of attitudes and emotional states on perception. (This document was presented at the Conference on Occupational Information and Vocational Guidance, Pittsburgh, Pennsylvania, March 11–13, 1966).

Compendium of Abstracted Methods 231

58. Bosdell, B. J. Evaluation of counseling treatments with underachieving high school students. Grand Forks: North Dakota University, 1962. (ED 003 061)

Counseling treatment methods were evaluated to determine their effectiveness in improving academic and personal adjustment of underachieving high school students. The participants included over 200 measured underachievers from grades 10-12 and 16 counselors. The students were randomly assigned to one of five treatment conditions—(1) individual counseling, (2) group counseling, (3) small group study skills instruction, (4) individual and group counseling combination, and (5) a control condition of no treatment. To assess changes occurring by each condition, several measuring instruments were used. An analysis of variance was employed to evaluate treatment effects. Significant differences were indicated on the effectiveness of different treatments. Students in the individual counseling and study skill groups improved more than those in the other groups in grade point average and study habits. On the criterion of personality change, there were no significant differences between treatments. A need for high school counselors to fit treatments to goals and needs of individual students was indicated.

59. Bottoms, G. & Cleere, W. R. A one-week institute to develop objectives and models for a continuous exploratory program related to the world of work from junior high through senior high school. Carrollton: West Georgia College, 1969. (ED 036 651)

The purpose of this conference was to develop models for conducting systematic and sequential exploratory experiences for junior and senior high school students which would lead to satisfactory job placement. The participants at the conference tried to identify behavioral objectives expected of the student as a result of the proposed program, develop a model for both large city and rural schools, and aid representatives of the various states in setting up a plan for their own states.

60. Bottoms, J. E. & Otto, F. L. Developing a program of student personnel services for area vocational-technical schools. Final report. Volumes I and II. Atlanta, Georgia State Department of Education, Division of Vocational Education; Washington, D.C.: Office of Education (DHEW), 1968. (ED 027 435)

This report presents the results of a developmental project which was conducted during 1966 and 1967 to plan and implement a program of student personnel services in Georgia's 25 post-secondary vocational-technical schools. In this report, student personnel services were defined as those services which aid the student to: (1) perceive realistically his own potentialities, values, and interests, (2) understand those educational and occupational opportunities available to him after program completion, (3) organize his information to a plan of action, and (4) implement the decisions made. Within the context of this study, student personnel services were divided into seven major areas: Preadmissions, Admissions, Records, Counseling, Information, Job Placement, and Evaluation. A follow-up program was designed to provide data which will: (1) assist student personnel specialists to determine which services need strengthening, (2) help administrators to determine instructional and curricular needs in the total school program, and (3) provide occupational information to potential area school students.

61. Bown, O. H. (et al.) Perceptions by adolescents of various procedural approaches used in filmed counseling sessions. Austin: Texas University, 1966. (ED 010 619)

Subjects (398) in the ninth and 12th grades, both male and female, were asked to rate initial, filmed counseling sessions as if they were the counselee. Five different counseling approaches were used in the filmed sessions—(1) advice giving—the counselor advises the client on a program of action, (2) questioning—the counselor poses a question to the client prior to each client response, (3) reflection of feeling—the counselor responds with feeling appropriate to the content of client responses, (4) supporting—the counselor attempts to convey to the client that the client has "what it takes" to work a problem out, and (5) information giving—the counselor provides information of a specific relevant nature to the client. After completing the "Westcott Problem Solving Scale," the subjects were divided into four cognitive groups, based upon their scores on the instrument's two dimensions—(1) the amount of information required or demanded for solving the problems and (2) the degree of success in solution of the problems. The groups were thus low demand-high success, low demand-low success, high demand-high success, and high demand-low success. Analysis of data obtained from counselor rating and counselor ranking forms (completed by all subjects after viewing the filmed sessions) yielded information concerning the preferences and rejections of the counseling approaches among the four cognitive groups. All four groups tended to prefer the advice giving approach and to reject the reflection of feeling approach. Both high demand groups also preferred the supporting approach. The questioning approach was rejected by all the males. All females except the high demand-low success group rejected the information-giving approach. Younger subjects tended to rate both the advice-giving and supporting approaches higher than older subjects.

62. Boyer, M. A. Cooperative work-experience education programs in junior colleges. Los Angeles: California University, ERIC Clearinghouse for Junior College Information; Washington, D.C.: American Association of Junior Colleges, 1970. (ED 042 455)

The combination of course work and related work experience into educational programs at the junior college level represents an attempt by these institutions to meet the changing requirements of today's employers. This Research Review looks at a few aspects of their programs. To begin with, the values of these programs are viewed from the standpoint of students, college, employer, and community. Next, the promotional responsibilities of both the program's advisory committee and the individual program coordinator are investigated, followed by a look at various program arrangements. The wide variety of program possibilities becomes evident as one views Rock Valley College's (Illinois) cooperative technical program with 40 local industries, the College of San Mateo's (California) teacher-assistant training program, and the potential benefits of combining a college education with the traditional police cadet training system. Significant areas of difficulty reported by colleges include student supervision, relevance of work experience to course work, scheduling conflicts, financial remuneration, and placement. Looking toward the future, San Mateo and Orange Coast Junior College Districts in California have received federal and private support to provide a national demonstration model for junior college cooperative education.

63. Boynton, R. E. New models and techniques in career guidance. Pittsburgh, Pa.: Pittsburgh University, 1966. (ED 012 936)

A model for a career guidance system that appears to effect positive change for students, schools, and the community is presented. There are four phases to the model, one for each year the student is in high school. The student's skills, aptitudes, interests, intelligence, and achievements are determined at initial fact gathering sessions. This information is stored in a computer. The student may obtain information from the computer about grades, courses taken, and college acceptance. The counselor receives a copy of all such sessions. Students are assigned by the computer to discussion groups which focus on the selection of occupational objectives. Career seminars provide students with opportunities to talk with representatives of careers in which they have an interest. Where feasible, senior year students are given work experience opportunities. This type of approach appears meaningful for students who are not college oriented. The use of a systems approach, peer groups for counseling, and community resources seems to operate effectively in preparing students to take their place in the economic life of a community.

64. Boys Club of New York. A suggested guidance program for combating school dropouts. New York: The Boy's Club of New York. (ED 001 735)

The problem of school dropouts was caused by consistent failure to achieve in regular school work, grade retention, reading retardation, and poor self-image. The Club's staff would help solve this problem through reaching, directing, and counseling boys in the area of health, compatibility, respect, staying in school, planning educational goals, and developing skills that could be used in adult life. The objective was to provide the group leaders with a more definite program for guidance.

During the season it would be advisable for the leader to talk to each individual boy about his future plans at least once; similar meetings should be held at the end of the season. From May to September, staff members should be required to study the record card of all boys in the Club. Also outlined topics of discussions might be prepared in advance and made available to the leader every month. Educational or vocational films or lectures could be scheduled one evening a month, or quarterly. During the year at least two seminars, each extending over a two-day or three-day period, should be held. Competitive essay and skit tournaments should be held, with education as one of the themes. *The Boys Club Record,* a monthly publication written by and for the boys, was found to be a good medium for reaching all boys.

65. Bradley, R. W., and Smith, R. D. Studies and projects to improve vocational guidance services. *Vocational Guidance Quarterly,* 1971, 19(4), 281–288.

In spite of the fact that the university has traditionally been the center of research, school counselors can make significant and unique contributions to the improvement of guidance and counseling by designing and conducting research studies relevant to their own schools [10]. Counselor educators have been encouraging prospective counselors to engage in research projects while in graduate school and to continue these applications with their own students when on the job. This paper covers types of vocationally related research and projects that practicing counselors would like to see done followed by some suggestions for potential application of these topics.

66. Brenner, M. H. Use of high school data to predict work performance. *Journal of Applied Psychology,* 1968, 52, 29–30.

For a sample of high school graduates employed in an aircraft plant, teachers' work habits and cooperation ratings, absenteeism, and grade-point data were obtained from high school transcripts and related to work-performance criteria of supervisory ratings, absenteeism, and tardiness records. Significant relationships were obtained between the high school predictors and the work-performance criteria.

67. Bridgford, C. Teaching about minorities: an annotated bibliography on blacks, chicanos, and indians. Boulder, Colo.: ERIC Clearinghouse for Social Studies/Social Science Education, 1971. (ED 049 970)

This annotated bibliography was prepared for the kindergarten through ninth grade social studies teacher and student for the purpose of ethnic studies. Although some of the references are to works of fiction and poetry, most of the entries are intended to give the teacher and the student a background in the heritage of the appropriate group, teaching methods, or both. Several of the entries are bibliographies themselves in order to give the reader avenues to other works. Both print and non-print materials are included along with a few copyrighted works. However, most are materials of limited circulation such as curriculum guides, position papers, and conference proceedings.

68. Briggs, L. J. (et al.) Instructional media: a procedure for the design of multi-media instruction, a critical review of research, and suggestions for future research. Pittsburgh, Pa.: American Institute for Research in Behavioral Sciences, 1967. (ED 024 278)

Based on the theses that all media have usefulness, that effectiveness is greatest when media selection is grounded on a systematic analysis of instructional objectives, and that educational specialists have a rightful function in the selection, packaging, and utilization of instructional sequences in all media, an analytical procedure was developed which constitutes a basis for matching media with educational objectives. Using this procedure, educational personnel who are responsible for the conduct of instruction would also be responsible for choosing the medium in which it would be programed. The choice would normally occur at the time of the original design of the curriculum. The analysis involves the use of the most dependable and generalizable knowledge available concerning the conditions of instruction required for each type of learning. In applying the procedure, the behavioral objectives for the course or unit are stated. The type of learning involved for each objective is identified. A media program is developed which lists instructional events, identifies characteristics of required stimuli, and states acceptable media options. The media options are then scanned for frequently occurring media. The medium in which the instruction should be packaged is assigned. And finally, specifications for the materials are written.

69. Briggs, L. J. & Norris, E. L. Techniques for selection the presenting occupational information to high school students. Planning and development of research programs in selected areas of vocational education, volume I. Pittsburgh: American Institute for Research in Behavioral Sciences, 1966. (ED 010 623)

As an initial step toward improvement in selecting and developing types of occupational information needed by high school students, as well as improvement of the format by which such information is presented, an experimental draft of occupational information materials was prepared and evaluated. These pilot materials were designed for use in career planning for one particular job family, the secretarial vocations. Three booklets were prepared, entitled "Women's Place in Today's World of Work," "Entry Jobs Leading to the Position of Secretary," and "What It's Like to be a Secretary." In addition, these booklets correspond respectively to student needs at three different stages of individual development— (1) the need to realistically perceive the place of both sexes in relation to the working world, (2) the need for awareness of the wide range of job families which one might enter, and (3) the need to select a specific educational or training program for a particular entry job in which one is interested. After a brief tryout of the materials (interviewing and testing selected students), the booklets were revised to improve their format of presentation. Additional research was recommended for identifying improved content and techniques to be used in presenting similar occupational information about other jobs or other job families. Related reports are ED 010 624 through ED 010 626.

70. Brown, D. Attitudes of school personnel toward the teacher's role in the guidance program. *Vocational Guidance Quarterly,* 1966, 14(4), 259–262.

The purpose of this study was to determine whether or not differences in attitudes existed among teachers, guidance workers and principals, in teachers participating in various guidance functions.

71. Brown, J. A. & MacDougall, M. A. Computerized simulated games: a socialized tool for child guidance. Charlottesville: Virginia University, 1971. (ED 048 608)

This paper describes a computer-controlled simulation game designed to teach social skills to elementary school pupils. The major purposes of this man machine social system are to develop in students the ability to: (1) observe pupil behaviors in group problem-solving situations, (2) identify and analyze the relationship of these behaviors to the success of the group in its problem-solving task, and (3) generalize the implications of these observed behaviors to other settings. The game consists of three stages which correspond to the above objectives and represent an integrated instructional system in which pupils, counselors, and media components interact. In the first stage the pupil views video tapes which present a wide range of pupil behavior types in a group setting. The second stage requires the pupil to analyze his observations by interrogating a computer system. In the final stage students meet with a counselor in a group discussion to evaluate the information they have individually acquired. They examine alternative solutions to the problem and a concensus is achieved through an exchange of various socio-cultural views held by the participants. Implications of such a system for elementary school counseling are discussed.

72. Budke, W. E. Review and synthesis of information on occupational exploration. Columbus: ERIC Clearinghouse on Vocational and Technical Education. The Ohio State University, 1971.

The method is a review and synthesis of significant research and information available concerning occupational exploration in K–12th grade. Its purpose is to provide a useful reference for educators who will be developing systematic programs of occupational exploration in elementary and secondary schools. It includes interdisciplinary approaches to occupational exploration programs. In addition to programs, it contains relevant information concerning terminology, history and development of programs, legislature, theories of career development and evaluative statements.

73. Buffalo Board of Education. School to employment program: district progress report—1963–1964. Buffalo, N.Y.: BBE, 1964. (ED 001 439)

   Part-time work experience and modification of curriculum were designed to help prevent students from dropping out of school. Concern was focused on the satisfactory placement of students in full-time employment if they should leave school. The program was coordinated by the Bureau of Guidance of the State Education Department. Financial assistance was granted by the state on a matching basis to enable communities to continue the project. The annual report covers all aspects of the program: pupils involved; facilities utilized; specifics, including classes taken, work experience provided, employing firms and field trips; advisory council selection and participation; parental contacts; outcomes; comments by the students, teachers, parents, and employers; general comments; follow-up of the previous year's student participants; and expenditures involved. The program has demonstrated that potential school dropouts can be retained, if offered a program especially designed to meet their educational needs. Appended are records, forms, letters, and curriculum outlines utilized in the administration and promotion of the program.

74. Bunda, R. & Mezzano, J. A study of the effects of a work experience program on performance of potential dropouts. *The School Counselor,* 1968, 15(4), 272–274.

   The purpose of this study is to determine the effectiveness of a work experience program in modifying the academic achievement, school attendance, and attitudes of the potential dropout.

75. Burchill, G. W. Work-study programs for alienated youth. Chicago: SRA, College and Professional Publications, 1970.

   Descriptions of nine work-study programs are presented in this casebook. They are presented as examples illustrating what is being done in schools utilizing work-study programs to prevent students from developing predelinquent tendencies or to rehabilitate students who have already manifested such tendencies.

76. Bureau of Employment Security. Counselor's desk aid eighteen basic vocational direction. Summary information. Washington, D.C.: Department of Labor, BES, 1967. (ED 027 379)

   Each of the 18 basic vocational directions (occupational clusters) has a general role description, relevant personality traits, and types of interests generally considered to be compatible with that occupational cluster. The Branch of Counseling and Testing Services developed the "Counselor's Desk Aid" to facilitate use of the "Counselor's Handbook" (ED 023 857) by employment counselors in state employment offices. Vocational counselors in schools, rehabilitation agencies, etc., should also find these publications useful. In addition to occupational information in capsule form, the "Desk Aid" contains sample worksheets and checklists for use with individual counselees.

77. Bureau of Employment Security. Dictionary of occupational titles, 1965. Volume I, definitions of titles. Washington, D.C.: Department of Labor, BES, 1965. (ED 013 963)

   The occupational definitions present considerably more information than those in previous editions (1939 and 1949), and a new classification system reflects relationships among occupations not only in terms of work involved but also in terms of worker characteristics required such as training time, aptitudes, interests, temperaments, physical demands, working conditions, industry, and work performed. There are 21,741 separate occupations defined which are known by 13,809 additional titles, making a total of 35,550 titles. This edition contains 6,432 jobs new to the "dictionary." Definitions are arranged alphabetically and include information on what gets done, how it gets done, and why it gets done. In Volume 2 (ED 013 964) the occupations have been incorporated into a classification structure in which the individual occupations are identified by 6-digit code numbers and arranged by the occupational group and the worker traits. This document is available as GPO L7.2—OC1/965/V.I for $5.00 from Superintendent of Documents, U.S. Government Printing Office, Washington, D.C. 20402.

78. Bureau of Employment Security. Dictionary of occupational titles, 1965. Volume II, occupational classification and industry index. Washington, D.C.: Department of Labor, BES, 1965. (ED 013 964)

Volume 2 complements Volume 1 (ED 013 963) by providing a classification structure which groups jobs having the same basic occupational, industrial, or worker characteristics. The sections are (1) the occupational categories, divisions, and groups, (2) an alphabetic arrangement of occupational divisions and groups, (3) the occupational group arrangement of titles and codes, (4) an alphabetic arrangement of areas of work, (5) an alphabetic arrangement of worker trait groups, (6) the worker trait groups within areas of work, (7) the worker traits arrangement of titles and codes, (8) the industry arrangement of titles, which lists jobs by industries in which they are usually found, (9) the industry index, (10) a glossary, which defines many technical terms used in the definitions found in Volume 1, (11) Appendix A, which identifies the three digits of a code reflecting jobs' relationships with data, people, and things, and (12) Appendix B, which explains the worker trait components—general educational development, specific vocational preparation, aptitudes, interests, temperaments, physical demands, and working conditions. This document is available as GPO L7.2—OC1/965/V.II for $4.25 from Superintendent of Documents, U.S. Government Printing Office, Washington, D.C. 20402.

79. Bureau of Employment Security. Selected characteristics of occupations (physical demands, working conditions, training time), a supplement to the dictionary of occupational titles. Washington, D.C.: Department of Labor, BES, 1966. (ED 013 965)

This supplement lists individual physical demands, working conditions, and training time data for each job defined in Volumes 1 and 2 (ED 013 963 and ED 013 964). It was published in response to the special needs of organizations and individuals concerned with manpower utilization who require more specific occupational characteristics data than that presented in the "Dictionary of Occupational Titles" (DOT) itself and provides additional source material for determining job relationships in such activities as worker mobility, training, and rehabilitation. The data were collected and developed according to job analysis techniques established by the U.S. Employment Service, and reflect the findings from approximately 75,000 studies of individual job situations. Information for each job is presented in columns—(1) DOT code number, (2) page number in Volume 2 for worker trait group in which job appears, (3) industry designation, (4) job title, (5) code for physical demands such as strength, climbing and balancing, talking and hearing, and seeing, (6) code for working conditions such as inside or outside location, temperature and moisture extremes, hazardous, and toxic, and (7) code for training time by general educational development and specific vocational preparation. This document is available as GPO L7.2—OC1/965/Supp. for $2.75 from Superintendent of Documents, U.S. Government Printing Office, Washington, D.C. 20402.

80. Bureau of Employment Security. Training and reference manual for job analysis. Interim revision. Washington, D.C.: Department of Labor, BES, 1965. (ED 024 769)

Devoted to an explanation of the procedures used to analyze jobs and to record the analyses using the format of the Job Analysis Schedule of the U.S. Employment Service, this manual may be used in formal training courses or for self-training in job analysis. The categories necessary for a complete analysis of a job are what the worker does, how he does it, why he does it, and the skill involved in doing it. This information is used in such activities as recruitment and placement, vocational counseling, job and employee evaluation, training, and labor relations. The job analysis schedule is divided into informational areas of (1) identification data, (2) work performed, (3) sources of workers, (4) performance requirements, (5) comments, and (6) physical demands. A description of items within each informational area includes a discussion of procedures and methods used to secure detailed, valid, and authoritative occupational information. A narrative report accompanies the analysis schedule and offers the analyst an opportunity to present such information as purpose of the plant, plant environment factors, plant placement policies, and plant organization. Examples of completed job analysis forms are given in the appendixes.

81. Bureau of Employment Security. Interest check list. Washington, D.C.: BES, Department of Labor, 1967. (ED 068 584)

The original edition of the Department of Labor Interest Check List aims at helping students decide what kinds of work they would like and lists activities that are found in a broad range of industries and occupations. The student is advised to read each of approximately 175 items and indicate how he feels about the activity described by placing a check under "like," "uncertain," or "dislike." He is further advised to then go back and indicate at least three activities that he would most like to do, even if he has no training or experience for them. Responses are evaluated with the student by a counselor. This document is available from Superintendent of Documents, U.S. Government Printing Office, Washington, D.C. 20402.

82. Bureau of Employment Security. Guide to local occupational information. Washington, D.C.: BES, Department of Labor, 1966. (MP 000 217)

Under the United States Employment Service's job opportunities information program, state Employment Service agencies have surveyed and reported on job opportunities and other manpower information for their areas. This directory lists two principal types of studies developed as a part of this program—occupational guides and area skill surveys.

83. Bureau of Employment Security. Counselor's handbook: I, counselor's interviewing guides in individual appraisal; II, counselee appraisal patterns related to fields of work. Washington, D.C.: BES, Department of Labor, 1967. (ED 023 851)

Part I includes guides for appraising individual characteristics such as interests, temperament, educational development, and aptitudes, to help the counselee learn about himself. Part II includes guidelines for appraising individual characteristics as they relate to the 18 fields of work (occupational clusters) which help the counselee learn about the world of work. Some of the occupational clusters are: (1) engineering and related, (2) clerical, (3) service, (4) mechanical and electrical, and (5) graphic arts. Comparable information in capsule form is given in the "Counselor's Desk Aid" (VT 006 359), which also includes sample forms for use with individual counselees. The Branch of Counseling and Testing Services developed the "Counselor's Handbook" and the "Counselor's Desk Aid" for the use of employment counselors in state employment offices, but it should also be useful to vocational counselors in other settings such as schools and rehabilitation agencies.

84. Bureau of Labor Statistics. Occupational outlook handbook 1966–1967. Report number bulletin 1450. Washington, D.C.: Department of Labor, BLS, 1965. (ED 015 269)

The employment outlook, nature of the work, training and other qualifications needed for entry, lines of advancement, job location, earnings and working conditions, and sources of additional information are provided for over 700 occupations. Introductory chapters suggest supplementary sources of occupational information, describe State Employment Office services and give a general picture of employment trends and opportunities. Major divisions are (1) professional, managerial, and related occupations, (2) clerical and related occupations, (3) sales occupations, (4) service occupations, (5) skilled and other manual occupations, (6) some major industries and their occupations, (7) occupations in agriculture, and (8) occupations in government. Within each of these major divisions, occupations are grouped into related fields. General information on many fields of work not covered in the individual occupational reports is given in the introductions to the major divisions. The table of contents, in most cases, and an index at the back of the book list occupations and industries alphabetically. The technical appendix contains a discussion of the sources and methods used in analyzing the occupational outlook in different fields of work and an explanation of the "Dictionary of Occupational Titles" numbers used in the reports. Availability information for reprints of the descriptions of individual occupations is given. This document is available as GPO L2.3—1450 for $5.00 from Superintendent of Documents, U.S. Government Printing Office, Washington, D.C. 20402.

85. Bureau of Labor Statistics (DOL). Occupational outlook handbook, 1970–71 edition. Washington, D.C.: BLS, 1970. (ED 044 513)

Developed for counselors and students, this handbook contains descriptions and occupational trends of over 700 occupations which are categorized according to: (1) professional and related occupations, (2) managerial occupations, (3) clerical and related occupations, (4) sales occupations, (5) service occupations, (6) skilled and other manual occupations, and (7) occupations of major industries. Included in the descriptions are nature of the work, places of employment, training, qualifications, advancement, employment outlook, earnings, working conditions, and sources of additional information. Several introductory chapters tell how the handbook is organized, give suggestions for supplementary information, and describe some of the most important occupational and industrial employment trends. Additional technical information is appended, and an index to the occupations and industries is included.

86. Bureau of Occupational Education Research. A demonstration system of occupational information for career guidance. Final report. Albany: State University of New York, BOER, 1968. (ED 024 838)

The purpose of this project was to test the effectiveness of a cooperative arrangement between the New York State Education Department and the New York State Employment Service, undertaken to produce and disseminate up-to-date information about local entry occupations for use in the career guidance of students. In a sampling of high schools and 2-year colleges in Nassau and Suffolk counties of the New York metropolitan area, four page descriptions of 200 entry occupations were prepared in two forms: (1) a looseleaf binder and (2) a deck of microfilm aperture cards. Three comprehensive high schools, three academic high schools, three area vocational technical programs, and three 2-year colleges were supplied with the 200 occupational guides. Of the students who use the guides, 92 percent said they would recommend the guides to other students; 75 percent wanted to keep copies of the guides they had read. In proportion to enrollment, students in area vocational technical educational programs made twice as much use of the guides as did the students in either academic or comprehensive high schools, and 13 times as much use as students in 2-year colleges.

87. Burton, J. R. (et al.) A study of the opportunities for, requirements of, and knowledges, abilities, and related characteristics needed by beginning office workers, with implications for business and office education. Hartford: Connecticut State Department of Education, Division of Vocational Education; Storrs: Connecticut University, School of Education, 1967. (ED 022 864)

This study was designed to obtain detailed information on the qualifications and needs of young people seeking employment in Connecticut business offices. Survey forms were mailed to every fifth Connecticut company listed in the 1966 "Dun and Bradstreet Reference Book" and other companies recommended by the Connecticut State Employment Service. Of 1,226 firms contacted, 824 responded providing the data requested. Research teams conducted 522 interviews with beginning office workers and 353 supervisors of these workers in 130 firms which employed 5 or more beginning workers. Among the many findings were: (1) Most of the major employers were located in the metropolitan areas of the state, (2) Some firms carried on active recruitment programs and the high school was the main target for recruitment, (3) The tests most relied upon as selective devices were the aptitude test and a straight-copy typing test, (4) Nearly two-thirds of the workers held jobs that would be classified in the clerical job family, a sixth in machine operation jobs, and the remainder in secretarial, bookkeeping, and customer contact families, and (5) Nearly all workers had graduated from high school and only 1 in 4 had taken training beyond high school.

88. Bush, D. O. (et al.) Between education and the world of work; the image of the world of work. Occupational education program. Greeley, Colo.: Rocky Mountain Educational Laboratory, Inc., 1969. (ED 032 582)

The activity Image of the World of Work, part of the Occupational Education Program of the Rocky Mountain Educational Laboratory, RMEL, is designed to influence and nurture positive work relevant attitudes of seventh grade pupils as well as to increase pupils' knowledge of occupational information and career alternatives. The workshops designed to help teachers carry out this program are described in this report. Several instruments were used to measure attitude change, first of teachers and later, of their pupils. These instruments and results are thoroughly examined. Extensive data are included. Some of the results of the workshop were: (1) teachers became more favorable to an integrated study approach to occupational education after the workshop, and (2) teachers did not show increased insight into viewing occupational choice in relation to self as a result of the workshop. Exhibitions are given, including those on content, manpower, correspondence, and opinions.

89. Bush-Goenner Associates. Career opportunities through organized research. Mt. Pleasant, Mich.: BGA; Roscommon, Mich.: Kirtland Community College, 1967. (ED 021 992)

A study was undertaken to improve the occupational training programs for youth and adults in the four counties of Crawford, Vogemaw, Oscoda, and Roscommon, Michigan, which made up the COOR Intermediate School District and the geographical area of Kirtland Community College. A rationale, based upon literature in the field, was developed for vocational education at each level of the educational system. A student occupational inventory determined high school students' career interests in eight occupational categories. Of these students, 46 percent expressed interest in community college or vocational-technical school. Upon the basis of this interest, Kirtland Community College and the high schools might consider programs for drafting, chemical distribution, law officer training, carpentry, and computer operation. The jobs mentioned most often on 704 questionnaire returns (78 percent) from businesses were retail salespeople, waiters, bus drivers, bookkeepers, janitors, cashiers, nurse aides, auto mechanics, assemblers, and secretaries. Some recommendations were to (1) provide an area vocational-technical program, (2) provide programs cooperatively between the high schools and the community college, and (3) emphasize work attitude development.

90. Byerly, C. L. (et al.) Preparing pupils for the world of work. Detroit: Detroit Public Schools, 1962. (ED 001 452)

A committee was assigned to evaluate the programs preparing students for employment. Major criticism was leveled at both the inconsistency and inadequacy of many school programs.

One of the most critical needs was the improvement of counseling and guidance services available to students. Schools tended to downgrade vocational courses and create poor attitudes by differentiating between college preparatory and vocational courses. Some students felt encouraged to drop out because they were not academically inclined.

It is recommended that all curricula recognize those elements which have significant bearing on employability and effective performance in job situations. Efforts should be made to bridge the gap between academic and vocational curricula. Ability grouping is necessary for challenging the needs of every student.

Guidance should be intensified and expanded. Case work in elementary schools and complete records would help prevent later school dropouts. The junior high student should be allowed to explore many experiences and should have regular counseling. Senior high students need complete information on career opportunities and preparation. World-of-Work Services, including vocational education and work-study plans, need to be expanded to include girls and mentally retarded students. Adult education programs in high school and post-high school technical training programs should be initiated.

91. California Coordinating Unit for Occupational Research and Development. Vocational choice and job satisfaction. 1967. (ED 013 958)

Vocational guidance can be employed by education as one means of effecting school adjustment to industrial change. The 115 recent (1960–1966) studies reviewed in this publication have implications for vocational guidance. Five projections of employment which indicate future job needs are reviewed. Studies of vocational choice are classified on the basis of choice—(1) interests, (2) parents, (3) aspiration, (4) maturation, (5) attitudes, (6) prestige, (7) values, (8) achievers, (9) motivation, (10) self-concept, (11) stages of occupational choice, (12) vocational training, (13) individual counseling, (14) group counseling, (15) guidance and college, and (16) roles. Studies of job satisfaction are classified as follows—(1) working conditions, (2) attitudes, (3) measurement, and (4) demography. A bibliography of the studies is included.

92. California State Advisory Council on Vocational Education and Technical Training. Feasibility study of career ladder curriculum and guidance and counseling. Sacramento: CSACVETT, 1971. (ED 050 260)

Discussions with council members, a review of relevant documents, contacts with legislative personnel, and interviews with vocational personnel in the California State Department of Education were the sources of information used to determine the feasibility of a "career ladder" curriculum. It was concluded that the career preparation of all people must be developed on a broad basis, that vocational education must be introduced at the kindergarten level and carried through the community college level, and that the career ladder concept may be the most desirable curriculum to achieve these results. Recommendations are that steps be taken to implement this program and to provide funds and a plan for the training of counselors to meet the needs of this program.

93. California State Department of Education. A proposed system for reporting job placement follow-through data. Sacramento: CSDE, Bureau of Industrial Education, 1968. (ED 022 916)

A model was prepared for an information storage and retrieval system for reporting job placement follow-through data of persons trained in industrial education programs in the state public schools. Recommendations for application of the model are made on a statewide basis to serve the information needs of local, state, and federal industrial education agencies. New forms are recommended, using standardized codes and reporting procedures to provide data of job placements for required reports. The prescored card was selected for the questionnaire instrument with responses read directly by various electronic data processing techniques. The registration forms and the in-class follow-through forms are completed by all industrial students while in school. The out-of-class follow-through form is mailed to students after they leave school. Samples of the forms are included in this report. From the data collected many types of directories could be compiled, estimates could be made of when the students in any particular training program would be ready for employment, the students' major could be identified, individual dropouts could be identified early, and job placements could be accounted for, thereby evaluating certain industrial education programs and classes. The system may stand alone, operate in conjunction with other projects, or become a part of a larger information storage and retrieval system.

94. California State Department of Education. Selected entry office jobs for the high school student, report of conferences with

government, business, and industry. Sacramento: CSDE, 1965. (ED 018 563)

Fifty-three representatives from government, business, and industry participated in three conferences to discuss present and future opportunities for high school students in office occupations and to review a synthesis of entry requirements for office jobs for high school students. The synthesis, made by the Bureau of Business Education, utilized results of two procedures—(1) job descriptions for stenographers, clerk-typists, and general office clerks gathered from the state personnel board, other governmental agencies, and business and industry, and (2) the descriptions were analyzed to determine the knowledge and abilities needed, duties performed, personality traits and attitudes needed, work habits and grooming desired, and speed requirements in shorthand and typewriting. Summaries of remarks by Wesley Smith and R. C. Wagenen and comments of conferees on (1) job opportunities in entry office jobs, (2) application blanks, job interviews, requirements, and preparation, and (3) personality traits, attitudes, work habits, and grooming are included. Conference participants agreed that there were job opportunities for high school students in entry office jobs and that the bureau's synthesis of job descriptions was very complete. Observations, recommendations, and plans of the bureau concerned the need for fundamentals, curriculum improvement, job-oriented course sequences, specific courses, tests, standards, advisory committees, and additional workshops. The job descriptions are included.

95. Campbell, G. C. The organization and implementation of an occupational information service program in the high school. Frankfort: Kentucky State Department of Education, 1965. (ED 010 695)

Occupational information service in guidance focuses on the differing needs of high school students for knowledge of occupations. Occupational information is defined as accurate, up-to-date treatment and interpretation of data important to the process of occupational selection, preparation, placement, and adjustment. To meet the need for such information, a well-organized occupational information service should be planned and implemented and become an integral part of the school curriculum. Organization of the collection of material as a whole, in terms of worth, frequency of items, and coverage and authenticity should be the guiding principles rather than mere accumulation. This presentation sets forth an information service for students as well as suggesting sources and criteria for evaluation of information. It was recommended that needs of users are best served by material organized and filed according to interest and ability areas. An outline for preparation of occupational information and suggested methods and teaching aids to help students utilize it is included.

96. Campbell, R. E. (et al.) The systems approach: an emerging behavioral model for vocational guidance. A summary report. Research and development series number 45. Columbus: Ohio State University, Center for Vocational and Technical Education, 1971. (ED 047 127)

The primary purpose of this project was to develop a procedural model for improving vocational guidance programs in senior high schools. Using a systems approach, the model: (1) emphasizes student behavioral objectives, (2) gives alternative methods for accomplishing these objectives, (3) provides program evaluation strategies, (4) incorporates guidelines for program change adjustments, and (5) can be operationally demonstrated in pilot locations and subsequently replicated in other locations. The 10 procedural phases of the model were developed over a 2-year period in cooperation with a comprehensive high school, although the basic model is flexible enough for use at many levels such as the state guidance system or local school systems. Each phase is independent, allowing the adoption of the combination best suited to individual needs. A revised model will be published following extensive field testing.

97. Campbell, R. E. (et al.) Systems under development for vocational guidance, a report of a research exchange conference. Columbus: Ohio State University, Center for Vocational and Technical Education, 1966. (ED 011 039)

Purposes of the conference were to (1) review experiences, problems, and insights developed by the individual participants through research and operational use of new technologies, (2) review the relation of these technologies to vocational education, vocational counseling, and guidance, and (3) arrange for continued communication among participants as they use systems analysis and technology in vocational guidance research and practice. Three areas were discussed—(1) projects devoted to the study of careers, (2) projects for the development and presentation of material for the enhancement of career decisions but not involving the computer, and (3) projects devoted to the development of material and the presentation and assessment of presentation with the assistance of time-shared computers. Summaries are given for (1) project TALENT, (2) exploratory study of information processing procedures and computer-based technology in vocational counseling, (3) a Harvard-needs-Newton information system for vocational decisions, (4) a study of intellectual growth and vocational development, (5) the development and evaluation of a pilot computer-assisted vocational guidance program, (6) clear language printout of demographic and psychometric data regarding college students, (7) a multimedia approach for communicating occupational information to noncollege youth, (8) vocational orientation systems, and five other projects.

98. Campbell, R. E. (et al.) Vocational guidance in secondary education. Results of a national survey, Research 36. Columbus: Ohio State University, Center for Vocational and Technical Education, 1968. (ED 026 534)

A national survey of vocational guidance in secondary education was conducted in the fall of 1966. The purposes of the survey included: (1) to describe the present status of guidance in public secondary schools in terms of services, functions of counselors, and student contact, (2) to provide a reference point for future surveys, (3) to compare the viewpoints of school administrators, counselors, teachers, students and parents on guidance issues, (4) to compare guidance programs by type of secondary school, (5) to identify needed changes in the professional education of the counselor, and (6) to identify needed research in program planning. Six types of public secondary schools were surveyed: urban comprehensive, rural comprehensive, urban general academic, rural general academic, urban vocational, and area vocational-technical. Principals, counselors, teachers, parents, and students representing 355 schools from 48 states returned a total of 6,484 completed questionnaires. The survey findings were reported in 62 tables. Detailed comparisons were made both by type of respondent and type of school, as well as broader analyses of major issues.

99. Cangemi, J. P. A school to employment program in Syracuse, New York. Syracuse, N.Y.: City School District. (ED 001 677)

STEP, the School-to-Employment Program, is a state-supported experimental project to help pupils in grades 7 through 10 who have been identified as potential dropouts. It is designed to put into effect a program of instruction and school-supervised work-experience that will develop habits, attitudes and skills enabling students to obtain suitable employment when they leave school, or, to increase their interest in completing their education. In the morning, pupils meet with a coordinator for home-room and two instructional periods. Emphasis is on job guidance and related subjects. They report for work experience in the afternoon with private industry or the school system and are paid the prevailing wage stipend. The work experience is fully supervised and rated for school credit. Students carry 5 subjects, two given by the coordinator, two in a regular school program and one in job experience. Specific screening and testing procedures record pupil experiences. The organization of the program, including the flow and organizational charts of the different phases of the STEP operation, is presented. Sample reports, forms, and questionnaires for teachers, pupils, industry and parents conclude the report.

100. Career Information Center. The Career Information Center, a working model. Boston, Mass.: CIC, 1969. (ED 039 359)

Information about careers is an essential ingredient in the process of career choice. This model program of career information services was developed for junior and senior high school students. The services include informative assemblies, conferences, radio and television programs, tape recordings, and filmstrips. The objectives, rationale, and development of each type of service are described in detail. The Northeastern University Career Information Center serves guidance counselors, teachers, youth workers, club advisors, secondary school students—individually and in groups, and the general public.

101. Careers Research and Advisory Centre. An introduction to the design and use of the Connolly Occupational Interests Questionnaire. Cambridge, England: CRAC, 1968. (VT 007 305)

The development and use of the Connolly Occupational Interests Questionnaire are discussed. The two instruments most used today are the Strong Vocational Interests Blank and the Kuder Preference Record, both developed in America and not particularly applicable to Great Britain. For this reason, the Connolly Occupational Interests Questionnaire was designed for British use, providing an instrument to (1) show the quality and relative strengths of an individual's interest, and (2) allow comparison between the interest pattern of an individual and that of a selected population. A survey of previous work indicated a general agreement upon seven interests: (1) in things, such as natural phenomena, (2) in people as individuals, (3) in the manipulation of people, (4) in the use of verbal concepts, (5) in the arts, (6) in data classification, and (7) in manual activities. Twelve occupations and 12 activities were chose for each interest. From these, a questionnaire was constructed in which the individual chooses the activities and occupations he prefers. Profiles drawn up from responses to the questionnaire after being administered to a random sample of the general population as well as to specific occupational groups showed significant differences between the various groups. Definitions of the occupations used and suggestions for administering and interpreting the questionnaires are given.

102. Career selection education for students attending small isolated schools. Salt Lake City, Utah: Western States Small Schools Project, 1967. (ED 010 964)

This document lists the assumptions upon which the career selection education project is based and the criteria for a school's participation in the project, as developed by the Western States Small Schools Project. The objectives of the project are to aid students make realistic career selections, develop skills and competencies useful in many careers, and develop specific job entry skills. A career selection agent administers the program and coordinates the general education and vocational education divisions of each student's program. An integral part of the program is the effective use of community resources for work experience, exploration, observation, and analysis. Attached appendixes include a specific outline of the career selection education projects at Virgin Valley High School, Mesquite, Nevada, and Patagonia High School, Patagonia, Arizona, and an outline of the test battery used in the project.

103. Carey, N. E. Vocational guidance for all; is differentiated staffing the answer? *American Vocational Journal,* 1970, 45(4), 68–69.

In an attempt to provide vocational guidance services to all students, a differentiated staffing pattern is recommended. This program would use the services of four categories of personnel: (1) paraprofessional; (2) guidance teacher; (3) school counselor; and (4) specialist/coordinator.

104. Case Western Reserve University. A working curriculum paper on technology and the world of work and careers. Cleveland, Ohio: CWRU, 1970. (ED 052 359)

This paper is concerned with technology as an area of study in education and how children might learn about technology. The curriculum strategy is intended to help the student gain the skills needed to enable him to earn his way in society, to understand his part in the work force, to understand how technology affects his life, to try out tentative career directions, and to find out about his skills, abilities, interests, beliefs, and values as they apply to technology, the "world of work," and "self." At first, the child will study jobs that are thing-centered or people-centered, then jobs that are product-centered or service-centered. In other words, he will classify jobs according to this continuum. During 3 years the student can study within the major subdivisions of technology, which are communications, construction, manufacturing and service. Also, he will have the opportunity to work within a small student-directed company so that he may apply his knowledge.

105. Chalupsky, A. & Koff, T. P. Job performance aids and their impact on manpower utilization. Washington, D.C.: Manpower Administration, Office of Manpower Policy Evaluation and Research.

The purpose of the study was to review and synthesize the results of research on job performance aids and explore their current and potential on industrial manpower utilization. Job performance aids are auxiliary information storage devices which present job instructions or reference data for use by the employee during the course of his job performance. An underlying assumption was that the job performance aids could be viewed as a major tool for matching job requirements with available manpower resources. Findings were derived from a review of the literature and from a field study of performance aid utilization in 12 electronics assembly organizations and patient care areas of 12 hospitals. The results showed that depending upon their design and usage, job performance aids could compensate for lack of training and experience, improve job quality, and increase productivity. The impact of job aids was particularly apparent in complex or lengthy tasks, diminishing in effectiveness as tasks were subdivided into short cycle, repetitive operations. A basic framework for advancing the field of job performance aids was proposed, and a series of research questions was listed. It was recommended that the Department of Labor consider the role it might play in overcoming the lack of communications which up to now has hindered the development of the job performance aid field.

106. Chancey, G. E. Career development unit—job interview. Lexington: Kentucky University, College of Education, 1966. (ED 012 780)

The major teaching objective of this unit is to develop in the students the effective ability to be successful on a job interview.

107. Chau, L. C. An econometric model for forecasting income and employment in Hawaii. Honolulu: Hawaii University, 1970. (ED 048 466)

This report presents the methodology for short-run forecasting of personal income and employment in Hawaii. The econometric model developed in the study is used to make actual forecasts through 1973 of income and employment, with major components forecasted separately. Several sets of forecasts are made, under different assumptions on external conditions, demonstrating the model's value in comparing the effects of different government policies. Sample forecasts for the 1966–68 period which were made as a test of the model's predictive powers show that the model is quite accurate, especially in projecting employment.

108. Chicago Urban League. Jobs, now, a project to find employment for 3,000 young men and women, provide a unified approach to employment of the disadvantaged and to operate a seminar center for personnel involved in recruiting, training, and employment, status report, number 3. Chicago: CUL; Young Men's Christian Association; Illinois State Employment Service, 1967. (ED 016 125)

The general objective was to help the clients attain employment readiness. Two-week workshops were held on each of the following—transportation and orientation to the city, grooming and personal hygiene, money management, and human relations training and job orientation. Daily lesson plans with objectives specifically related to the world of work and the clients' personal management were developed for each workshop. Teachers concentrated on concrete experiences expressed in simple quantitative language free of abstractions. Questions and answer sessions, role playing, problem solving, discussions, and field trips were the instructional methods used. Client growth was judged on the basis of teacher observation and the client's response to work experiences. Of 1,218 clients enrolled, 831 completed orientation, and 48 percent of those were either employed or enrolled in other programs. Clients who retained jobs were compared to those who lost them on the basis of sex, age, education completed, I.Q., marital status, police record, work history, and the degree of high support (personalized concern for the client) present in the job situation. There was no significant difference between the two groups of clients except on the factor of high support present in the job situation. It seemed to contribute to job retention. A study of 10 participating companies providing high support and 10 providing little or no high support showed that the former retained 82 percent of the clients while the latter retained only 28 percent of the clients employed.

109. Chronical Guidance Publications. Chronical plan for filing unbound occupational information. Moravia, N.Y.: CGP, 1966.

The "Chronical Plan" is a collection of 550 occupational briefs, reprints and posters arranged in a file that can be transferred from one place to another. The plan is based on the D.O.T., using code numbers and occupational titles closely similar to those used in the D.O.T. The number of folders under each title can be increased, so that this filing system is both economical and flexible. The folders are readily available for placing in a counselor's file drawer or box. For your information on the plan and any other supplementary material available on a commercial basis, contact the publisher.

110. Cincinnati Public Schools. Man: his life and work. A career orientation manual for teachers of seventh and eighth grade social studies. Ohio: Cincinnati Public Schools, 1970. (ED 050 005)

Among the challenges facing the U.S. as it enters the 1970s has been one to public education to adapt its program to technological change and its social effects; this manual deals with a limited aspect of this problem. Seventh and eighth grade social studies instruction is the focal point of the effort, and career orientation is the theme by which adaptation will be approached whether a pupil is interested in pursuing a liberal arts, vocational, or technical program. This project was started in the summer of 1969 as an interdisciplinary effort including art, English, home economics, industrial education, mathematics, science, and social studies. This approach contributes to the following specific goals: 1) provide meaningful career information in the context of specific subject matter instruction; 2) strengthen pupil interest in all subject areas; 3) provide a classroom atmosphere which would foster pupil motivation and encourage learning by discovery; 4) encourage pupil investigations which would lead to greater self understanding; and, 5) provide activities for pupil participation which simulate many roles in careers. This activity manual includes more than 100 career activities related to American history, urban living, Ohio history, and the social sciences.

111. Circle, D. F. (et al.) The career information service. A guide to its development and use. Newton, Mass.: Newton Public Schools, 1968. (ED 021 300)

This volume emerges from three collaborative projects developed in the Newton, Massachusetts public schools. The Career Information Project attempted to develop improved procedures for acquiring, processing, and disseminating career information. The Follow-Up Program designed and implemented as system for conducting comprehensive follow-up studies of Newton students. A third project developed a job placement service for Newton secondary-school students. Because of the strong interrelationships of these three projects, in 1967–1968, they were coordinated in a single Career Resource Center. This document provides theoretical background for the services, describes briefly the projects as developed in Newton, and presents guidelines for the development of similar services in other school systems. A major bibliographic index of materials assembled and used in the Career Resource Center is also included.

112. Civil Service Commission. Job briefs, selected federal jobs—duties, qualification requirements, sample test questions. Washington, D.C.: CSC; Office Economic Opportunity, 1966. (ED 019 434)

Information about jobs in the federal government for persons with limited work experience or education is provided. Job briefs describing the work, opportunities, number employed, employing agencies, and qualifications are given for (1) 19 white collar and post office jobs such as clerk-typist, clerk-stenographer, nursing assistant, soil conservation aid, and mail handler, and (2) 27 wage board jobs such as apprentice, agricultural research helper, animal caretaker, carpenter, forklift operator, food service worker, laundry worker, machinist, packer, painter, plumber, truck driver, warehouseman, and welder. Also included are (1) sample test questions for both white collar and wage board examinations, (2) policies relative to hiring, wages, and qualification examinations, (3) a list of civil service regional offices, and (4) classification act salary rates for March, 1966.

113. Civil Service Commission. Youth opportunity campaign—summer 1966, a report of training conducted by federal agencies for non-college youths employed during the summer of 1966. Washington, D.C.: CSC, 1967. (ED 013 961)

Agency programs varied with the mission and size of the agency and with the number and dispersion of noncollege youth employees. The great majority of the employed were appointed under the economic and educational need criteria of the special authorities available for the purpose. On-the-job training was the educational method most extensively used but other methods such as lectures, discussions, role playing, question-and-answer sessions, films, and slide presentations were utilized. Most of the skills training was in the office skills areas common to all federal agencies but a majority of the agencies provided a variety of other learning experiences in addition to training in specific skills. Agencies provided individual and group counseling and many trained supervisors especially for the program. New and different training approaches were attempted by some of the reporting agencies. Some implications were—(1) guidelines and training materials should be developed earlier in the year to allow agencies more time for planning, (2) consideration of individual needs and problems is of special importance, and (3) the work experience was particularly valuable in preparing the youths for the business world.

114. Clark County School District. Shared services: opportunities for small schools. Las Vegas: CCSD, 1968. (ED 027 132)

An approach used in the Virgin Valley High School, a small, rural school in Mesquite, Nevada, in finding the solution to shortages of personnel created by involvement in educational changes is discussed. Shared services in a small school are described with relationship to school personnel, community personnel, and other governmental agencies. The major portion of the document is devoted to excerpts from the Clark County School Board Policy Manual on items such as pupil personnel services, school health services, dental hygiene, medication during school hours, guidance programs, special education, speech therapy, and programs for children who are homebound, neurologically impaired, emotionally disturbed, mentally retarded, orthopedically handicapped, visually handicapped, or acoustically handicapped. A concluding section includes records (forms) utilized in several of the programs. This report is disseminated under Title III funds of the Elementary and Secondary Education Act.

115. Clary, J. R. & Westbrook, B. W. The construction and validation of a measure of vocational maturity. Raleigh: North Carolina University, 1967. (ED 018 837)

This report deals with the organization, rationale, methods and expected end-products of a research project (scheduled for completion on June 23, 1970) for the construction and validation of a reliable vocational maturity measure (VMM). The project's eight phases and activities are explained. The project assumes—(1) the individual and society as a whole suffer from unwise educational and vocational choices, (2) these choices are related to vocational maturity, and (3) a need exists for better measures of vocational maturity. The project staff will administer, to representative samples of Southern public school pupils in grades eight–12, three tests—(1) the tryout form of the VMM, (2) the preliminary form, and (3) the final form. After all the data is analyzed, a final report will give an account of the project and will include the VMM. An administrator's manual, and a technical manual of normative data for the VMM. It is expected that the VMM will aid in—(1) evaluating educational programs which include vocational exploration as a major component, (2) increasing understanding of the construct of vocational maturity, (3) identifying pupils who need special assistance in vocational development, and (4) evaluating programs designed to provide students with vocational exploratory experiences.

Compendium of Abstracted Methods

116. Cogswell, J. F. (et al.) The design of a man-machine counseling system. A professional paper. Santa Monica, Cal.: Systems Development Corporation, 1966. (ED 014 781)

> Two projects on the design, development, implementation, and evaluation of a man-machine system for counseling in the Palo Alto and Los Angeles school districts are reported. The earlier Philco 2000 computer programs simulated a counselor's work in the educational planning interview by accepting inputs such as school grades, test scores, and biographical data. It analyzed data according to an inferred model of the counselor's decision-making rules, and printed out evaluative statements. An automated educational interview program now reviews student progress, collects comments from the student, reacts to student plans, and helps plan a high school course schedule. The current project, in the initial design phase, included a survey of counselor practices, selected an experimental field site, analyzed counseling operations in the field site, and trained counselors in systems technology and lab development of limited software systems. A plan was formulated to computerize the major information-processing tasks in the counseling operation. The development, implementation, and evaluation phases will follow. A sample interview is included. This paper was presented at the American Psychological Association Convention, New York, N.Y., September 4, 1966.

117. Cogswell, J. F. & Estavan, D. P. Explorations in computer-assisted counseling. Santa Monica, Cal.: Systems Development Corporation, 1965. (ED 010 582)

> Models of a school counselor's cognitive behavior in the appraisal of student information and of his overt verbal responses in the "educational planning interview" were made with computer programs and computer-controlled equipment. The verbalizations of the counselor while reviewing the records of 20 ninth-grade students prior to interviews and while conversing with the students during the interviews were used to construct the model. The automated interview is conducted by a teletype under control of a Q-32 computer in a time-sharing mode. This automated interview program was planned to review student progress, collect comments from the students, react to student plans, and help the student plan a schedule of high school courses. To assess the validity of the model, the automated systems were compared to the responses of the original human counselor with a new sample of 20 students from the same population. The study indicated the potential value of the automated procedure for both research and field application.

118. Cogswell, J. E. (et al.) Exploratory study of information—processing procedures and computer-based technology in vocational counseling. Final report. Santa Monica, Cal.: System Development Corporation, 1967. (ED 017 710)

> As a preliminary to designing a man-machine counseling system, the guidance practices in 13 schools distributed through seven states were surveyed to study the variations in counseling practices.

119. Cohen, K. C. Effects of the 'consumer game' on learning and attitudes of selected seventh grade students in a target-area school. Baltimore: Center for the Study of the Social Organization of Schools, Johns Hopkins University, 1970. (ED 038 733)

> The following report describes one teacher's use of the Consumer Game in a class of seventh grade students in a target area school. These students were not highly motivated and displayed poor attitudes toward school, and it was hoped that a game experience might interest them. Despite unusual administrative conditions, the game appears to have taught the students important concepts. Their behavior in school and attendance records also showed improvement during the time they used the game, and as a group they sought an additional opportunity to play it.

120. Cohn, B. (et al.) The effects of group counseling on school adjustment of under-achieving junior high school boys who demonstrate acting-out behavior. Bedford Hills, N.Y.: Board of Cooperative Educational Services, 1964. (ED 003 370)

The application of group counseling was investigated with respect to its effect on underachieving, acting-out, junior high school boys. In addition, two other effects were studied—(1) that of involving teachers in discussion groups and (2) that of these discussions groups on teacher attitudes. Three counselors from different schools in similar socioeconomic areas participated. Each conducted two experimental counseling groups and a teacher discussion group. Students in the seventh and eighth grades of all three schools were tested for project selection. Evaluative instruments were used with the selected sample before and after counseling during 1 academic year for purposes of pre- and post-testing. Followup testing was accomplished 1 year after counseling to determine what changes were maintained by the student population. All student and teacher meetings (25 and 13, respectively) were tape recorded. (Evaluative instruments used with students and teachers, and how they were used, are described in the report text.) As a direct result of counseling, the experimental groups improved in self-concept, leaned more toward nonconforming behavior, felt they had difficulty accepting their peers, and were poorly motivated toward academic work when compared with control groups. After 1 year these experimental students became more delinquency-prone than their counterparts. The effects of teacher discussion groups and the results of a parent survey were discussed also.

121. College Entrance Examination Board. A chance to go to college. A directory of 800 colleges that have special help for students from minorities and low-income families. New York: CEEB, 1971. (ED 047 636)

The first section of this document relates information useful to high school students who are interested in going to college, such as the reasons for going or not going, applying for admission, and financial aid. This section also includes titles of other related books. Section 2 lists colleges by state that have many black students. Section 3 lists the 829 colleges included in this Directory, by state, and some pertinent information about the availability of special services, and programs for minority-group or disadvantaged students. The last section, the bulk of the report, presents a brief description, by state, of the special services and programs available at each of the 829 colleges.

122. College Entrance Examination Board. Comparative guidance and placement program (CGP). Princeton, New Jersey: CEEB, 1971.

The CGP program is a comprehensive information system composed of questionnaires, tests, and services designed to meet the unique guidance and placement needs of two year college and vocational-technical institutes and students entering these institutes. Since the program was launched in 1969, more than 150 institutes and approximately 150,000 students have taken the CGP battery of tests and questionnaires.

The program helps students learn more about themselves, critically evaluate their career goals and make wiser decisions. It helps institutions to guide and place students in appropriate courses or remedial programs, identify student needs, such as for financial aid and evaluating and improving academic and administrative programs and relating to community needs.

123. College Entrance Examination Board. Deciding, A decision-making program for students. Princeton, New Jersey: Publications Order Office, CEEB, Box 592, 08540

Deciding is a decision-making program in the form of a course of study. It encourages the development of decision-making skills in junior and senior high school students. The program, through student and leader materials, provides a course of study that can be taught in group or classroom settings. Program includes exercises, group activities simulations and discussion guides aimed at helping students learn and apply the decision-making process to the personal, educational and vocational decisions they face in the early secondary school years.

124. Colorado State University. Occupational education program. Image of the world of work. Description and analysis of teacher orienta-

tion activities (August, 1968). Fort Collins: CSU; Greeley, Colo.: Rocky Mountain Educational Laboratory, Inc., 1969. (ED 029 993)

A project was conducted to determine the relationship between changes in attitudes toward work of seventh grade pupils and specified instructional practices of their social studies or language arts teachers. The study encompassed: (1) developing and administering instruments to students and instructors to assess attitudes toward work, (2) conducting a workshop to change teacher attitudes toward work, and (3) changing pupil attitudes toward work by specified instructional practices and through changing the attitudes of their language arts and social studies teachers. Approximately 60 language arts and social studies teachers participated in a 1-week workshop to learn the skills necessary to integrate occupational education into their subject matter presentation and to define the pupil attitudes toward work to be strengthened through their courses. Benefits of the workshops included an increased understanding and appreciation for educational objectives, modern concepts of occupational education, and modern theories of occupational choice. The document contains instruments, tabulated results, related correspondence, a list of participants and scheduling details.

125. Colorado State University. Occupational education programs; image of the world of work, volume III. Lesson plans: resource file. Fort Collins: CSU; Greeley, Colo.: Rocky Mountain Educational Laboratory, Inc., 1960. (ED 034 884)

This third volume of the Image of the World of Work program presents guidelines for the development of lesson plans by participating teachers and representative lesson plans which were developed. Lessons were planned within the existing content of seventh grade language arts and social studies—35 lesson plans for language arts, 20 for social studies, and 4 miscellaneous. The components of these lessons were to include cognitive objectives, occupational information, attitudinal objectives, student tasks, and evaluation of lesson effectiveness. Volumes I and II are available as VT 009 939 and VT 009 986 respectively. "The World of Work and Learning," a position paper which provides an overview of all three phases of the project, is available as VT 009 940.

126. Comics make the job scene. *Training in Business and Industry,* 1970, 7(6), 27–30.

A pilot program to use comic books which supply occupational information to youths at the state employment agencies.

127. Council for Exceptional Children. Behavior modification and related procedures. Exceptional children bibliography series. Arlington, Va.: Information Center on Exceptional Children, CEC, 1969. (ED 036 025)

Contained in the bibliography are 55 abstracts and descriptive terms of documents concerned with all aspects of vocational education, work study programs, and rehabilitation techniques for use with virtually all handicapping conditions. Also included are a subject and author index, user information, and information on ordering specific documents or the entire collection.

128. Council for Exceptional Children. Vocational education and work study programs. Papers presented at the annual international convention of the Council for Exceptional Children (48th, Chicago, Illinois, April 19–25, 1970). Arlington, Va.: Council for Exceptional Children, 1970. (ED 039 386)

The implementation of a work-study program in a rural, depressed area, the operation of the program, and evaluation are discussed in the first of six papers on vocational education for the retarded. The sheltered workshop at the Kurtz Training Center in Pennsylvania is described with a focus on promoting self image and adjustment. A 6-year secondary program for students with IQ's of 80 and below, located in a self-contained high school, is considered. Also examined are two aspects of work aptitudes and prevocational evaluation in work-study programs.

129. Cromer, C. A. Procedure for determining vocational education needs through community analysis. Lincoln: Nebraska Occupational Needs Research Coordinating Unit. (ED 023 916)

Designed as a model for determining vocational education needs, the procedures recommended in this publication were tested in 20 Nebraska communities during 1965, 1966, and 1967. Data gathered by a study of local vocational needs can be beneficial to policy making groups in evaluating the entire educational program and in determining demographic patterns. Some major objectives of local community analysis are to: (1) evaluate existing vocational courses and determine needed additional offerings, (2) focus attention on the development of quality comprehensive community programs, (3) summarize occupational opportunities within a community, (4) assist local schools in establishing the type of vocational offerings which will generate a desirable curriculum balance, (5) determine the need for supplemental education and training or retraining, and (6) supplement local data with area and state data to project a regional picture of employment opportunities. The document content includes: (1) philosophy, (2) purpose, (3) objectives, (4) benefits, (5) model, (6) a 7-step outline for determining vocational education needs, (7) determining multi-county vocational education needs, and (8) problems in compiling area data. The appendixes contain sample forms for use in a survey.

130. Cross, W. C. A career guidance program for small rural high schools. *Vocational Guidance Quarterly,* 1970, 19(2), 146–150.

Advanced graduate students in counseling, through "circuit riding" services to two rural high schools, raised substantially the number of graduating seniors continuing their education.

131. Cuony, E. R. Post-secondary counseling in junior high school. *The School Counselor,* 1968, 15(3), 227–229.

A junior high school program is discussed which provides group guidance for prospective college students. Its objectives are to: 1) aid students in making curricular and cocurricular choices, and 2) to aid students in choosing a post-secondary school.

132. Daane, C. J. (et al.) Developments in counseling. Tempe: Arizona State University, College of Education, 1965. (ED 017 949)

The purpose of this collection of articles is twofold—(1) to help fulfill the need for the training of professional counselors, and (2) to disseminate information about research in the field. The first of the seven articles presents an overview of the state of counseling in 1964. The next three articles deal with various new thoughts on counseling in the schools—(1) elementary school counseling, (2) the junior college transition function, and (3) counseling and careers. The last three articles deal with specific aspects of counselor education at Arizona State University—(1) growth of the department, (2) practicum training, and (3) research in the department. All the articles are based on the assumption that counseling improves individual dignity, growth, and adaptation to a world of rapid social change because it reduces the number of drop-outs, helps youth reach their full potential, and leads to well-adjusted and happy workers. This publication may be obtained through the Bureau of Educational Research and Services, College of Education, Arizona State University, Tempe, Arizona for $1.50.

133. Dailey, C. A. Project gatekeeper. The reduction of job discrimination by the use of self-confrontation and feedback to the discriminator. Washington, D.C.: American University, Research Center in Policy and Behavioral Sciences. (VT 004 318)

The main objective of this pilot study was to design a program for training decision-makers (employers) to interact with disadvantaged persons and to evaluate their "career potential" more appropriately. Training methods include

Compendium of Abstracted Methods 251

the use of videotape recordings and playback, audiotape recordings of interviews and playback, sensitivity training, role-playing (simulated interviewing), programed cases, programed personnel data, and traditional methods of training such as lecturing and case studies. Findings of earlier studies and experiments of this study are included in the evaluations of the project. Findings included—(1) The social distance desired by the applicant with the interviewer is correlated with the understanding the applicant believes the interviewer has for him, (2) The social distance viewed by the applicant is related inversely to the qualification rating of the applicant by the interviewer, (3) Interviewers do a better job when applicants feel qualified, (4) Interviewers do a better job when they regard applicants as qualified, and (5) Interviewers do a better job when the applicant's rating of social distance indicates greater intimacy and understanding.

134. Darcy, R. L. & Powell, P. E. A basic manpower economics library. Revised 1970. Arkadelphia, Ark.: Henderson State College, M. H. Russell Center for Economics Education, 1970. (ED 045 475)

The 33 publications included in this annotated bibliography are intended to serve as a basic list for a small, but authoritative and balanced library. The materials included run from 1963 to 1970, and in addition to the books, a few appropriate periodicals are included. Selections were made on the basis that junior and senior high school teachers, and vocational counselors would be the users. The selections include current and historical information, statistical data, problem identification, and analysis. It should be useful in explaining the major dimensions of the work system, and the broader economic and social world to students. A list of 11 selected sources of free and inexpensive materials is also included.

135. Darcy, R. L. An experimental junior high school course in occupational opportunities and labor market processes. Final report. Athens: Ohio University, Center for Economic Education, 1968. (ED 022 056)

An experimental project was initiated to provide the schools with instructional materials, evaluation instruments and a realistic classroom educational program for bridging the gap between school and work. Some major objectives were to: (1) identify appropriate course content for economic and manpower education, (2) develop instructional materials, and (3) develop evaluation instruments and procedures. Eighth, 9th and 10th grade classes in three school systems within a 75-mile radius of Athens, Ohio were selected for the pilot project. Pre- and posttests designed to measure understandings and attitudes were administered to treatment and control groups matched on mental ability and socioeconomic characteristics. Some conclusions were: (1) Eighth graders enrolled in the experimental course increased their test scores by 33.4 percent more than the control group, (2) The experimental course did not induce changes in student attitude toward manpower and economic issues, and (3) Students enrolled in the experimental course reflected more interest in school and a lower dropout rate. The appendixes contain 316 pages of textual material, the 140-page teacher manual, and evaluation instruments.

136. De Hoyos, A. Occupational and educational levels of aspiration of Mexican-American youth. East Lansing: Michigan State University (Doctor's dissertation), 1961. (ED 044 208)

Studies of levels of aspiration have made some important contributions to the understanding of the relationship between social structure and personality. In this type of study, however, minority groups have almost been neglected. The present study was designed to investigate the differentials in levels of occupational and educational aspiration of Mexican American youths in Lansing, Michigan. Of great importance to the study of the social structure of the target population are the changes (1) from mostly rural to mostly urban environment; (2) from seasonal, agricultural work to industrial, urban employment; and (3) from a position of subordination typical of the Southwest to one of greater social equality in the North. The main proposition, in the form of 11 hypotheses, was that the level of occupational and educational aspiration of Mexican American youths was positively correlated to the acculturation to the dominant society. At the conclusion, it is noted that the data are not sufficient to determine whether the high level of social aspiration of the sample is a manifestation of their identification with the values of the dominant society or a manifestation of external imitation of those values.

137. Delaware Occupational Research Coordinating Unit. Concept of a total program in education for the world of work. Dover: DORC. (VT 007 273)

The concept of "education for the world of work" has for its objective the preparation of each individual to meet successfully the problems of life in his physical, social and political environment. This concept is concerned with the total program of education, not only for persons in school, but for those out of school and unemployed, for those already in the labor market but who need training or re-training, and for those who are emotionally, economically or physically handicapped. Only 76 out of every 100 entering students complete high school and, of these, 40 will enter college but only 20 will finish a 2- or 4-year program. This means that approximately two-thirds of the original 100 ninth graders are left untrained for productive work of any kind. In this context, the secondary school must fulfill its responsibility by providing (1) an academic program for college entrance, and (2) a practical arts or technical program, either in the high school or in a separate vocational-technical high school.

138. Delta County Joint School District 50. Development of social and occupational perception in rural areas. Delta County, Colorado: DCJSD. (ES 002 308)

Occupational information and guidance will be offered to high school students in a rural 4-county area. Emphasis will be placed upon introducing vocational awareness into the traditionally oriented curriculum. A professional staff will collect films, slides, and related data and will assemble this material into instructional presentations. New curricular additions in the areas of social studies, mathematics, psychology, and speech will be designed to fill the needs of both education and business. Visitations and inservice workshop sessions will be instituted for teachers and counselors so that they may be exposed to the philosophies and immediate needs prevalent in the world of work. Through the cooperative efforts of business, industry, and community service groups, links of communication will be established between the rural areas and the highly industrialized metropolitan areas. Parental understanding and participation in the vocational development program will be stressed. Informal lectures and audiovisual presentations by business and industries will be used to introduce the parents to the complexities of cybernetic society. Small groups of parents will meet with school teachers and counselors to discuss the role of the school in preparing the students for a place in industry. A business and industrial day, similar to the college day, will be instituted, so that students and parents may discuss job opportunities with representatives from business and industry. A resource directory, containing data on organizations and personnel grouped according to occupational area, will be compiled for teacher use. Approximately 3,651 high school students and parents will be served. For further information, contact M. C. Kreutz, Route 1, Box 66, Delta, Colorado 81416. (303) 874-4438.

139. Denues, C. Career perspective: your choice of work. Worthington, Ohio: Charles A. Jones Publishing Co., 1972.

Career Perspective is a guide to individuals seeking a place in the world of work and proposes to instruct these individuals in the processes of making career decisions, self-analysis and evaluation. Career Perspective is organized into three basic parts: (1) The World of Work, (2) The Basis of Choice and (3) Making the Choice. This book provides a comprehensive view of work as a way of life, not merely a job and the career path as a developmental process, not one single decision.

140. Department of Labor. Bridging the gap from school to work. Washington, D.C.: DL, 1968. (ED 021 144)

High rates of youth unemployment, especially for those in low-income minority group families, and underemployment, despite the fact that the United States keeps larger proportions of its children in school longer than does any other nation, give some indication of why the school-to-work problem commands public attention. Some of the variables considered to affect the process of transition, and requiring intensive review, are counseling and placement by schools and other agencies, work experience programs in schools, occupational information in schools, work-oriented curriculums, specific and general occupational training, cooperative education in this country with that experienced in Europe sug-

Compendium of Abstracted Methods

gests that the school-to-work gap in the United States is largely a result of the high educational and flexible career sights that have been set while available job opportunities have not been at as high a level. While recognizing an insufficiency of relevant research, certain general conclusions can be reached on the basis of present knowledge concerning the character of the steps that can be taken to narrow the gap between school and work. Among these steps are (1) increasing student knowledge about the environment of work while in school, (2) increasing opportunity for students to gain actual work experience, (3) increasing participation of business and other private groups in the education world, and (4) providing improved knowledge and training at the point of entry into the job market. This chapter appears in "Manpower Report of The President and Report on Manpower Requirements, Resources, Utilization, and Training" (1968). Available as VT 001 025.

141. De Santalo, R. Field trips for Guidance? *School Counselor,* 1963, 15(5), 183–185.

Field trips give high schoolers a helpful opportunity to become acquainted with various aspects of college life. The system used by the author at Sachem High School, Lake Ronkonkoma, New York, is described in this article.

142. DesRoches, D. L. Occupations for you. Part one. Washington, D.C.: George Washington University, 1965. (ED 017 704)

This book was designed to stimulate interest and answer questions about vocational choice, stimulate interest in reading, and provide content to relate to academic study.

143. Detroit Public Schools. Evaluation of the project in-school youth work training program for fourteen and fifteen year old youth. Program evaluation section. Detroit: DPS, 1968.

A project to provide in-school work experiences for 14 and 15 year old junior high school students was conducted for the purpose of: (1) encouraging them to remain in school after the age of 16, (2) improving their school attendance and scholastic achievement, (3) providing opportunities for growth in the ability to work and explore aspects of the world of work, and (4) providing income, sound work habits, work training, and salable skills for pupils from low income families. Data from the fall term of 1966 on 140 pupils who had participated in the program were compared with data from the fall term of 1965. A follow-up was conducted on 42 students who had participated in the project. The chi-square test of significance shows no statistically significant changes in the frequency counts of absences or tardiness or changes in the distribution of academic grades or citizen marks. Case studies indicate that individual students did show progress in academic performance, in attitude toward school, and in social demeanors. In general, the program met only the objectives of providing earned financial assistance to needy pupils and providing pupils with supervised work experiences which will better prepare them for entry into the world of work.

144. Digneo, E. H. & Shaya, T. (Eds.) Career selection education program, 1965–1968. Report. Santa Fe: New Mexico Western States Small Schools Project, 1968. (ED 029 725)

Career Selection Education Programs were conducted during the 1965–66 school year at Cloudcroft and Weed High Schools under the direction of personnel from New Mexico State University, and at Cliff High School under the direction of personnel from Western New Mexico University. These programs were designed specifically to enable young people in small, rural schools (1) to have an opportunity to gain information about job opportunities and (2) to assess more adequately their own individual capacities to fit into the world of work. Some sources of vocational information were field trips, interviews, films, tape recordings, and group guidance sessions. A series of reports were submitted annually by staff personnel at each operating location. The programs at Weed and at Cloudcroft High Schools were continued during the 1966–67 and 1967–68 school years; the program at Cliff High School had to be discontinued at the conclusion of the first year because of lack of funds.

145. Dilley, J. S. Counselor actions that facilitate decision-making. *The School Counselor,* 1968, 15(4), 247–252.
Discussed are five counselor actions that facilitate decision-making.

146. Doerr, J. J. Individualized vocational guidance: a new look. Final report. Kansas City: Missouri University, 1970. (ED 042 928)
This study was conducted to evaluate the usefulness of discriminant analysis in classifying vocational and technical curricular groups in a single secondary school setting. The researchers compared scores on the Dailey Vocational Test and the Minnesota Vocational Interest Inventory in terms of the selection of vocational and technical courses by 585 Grade 11 and 12 students in Kansas City, Missouri. After finding a statistically significant difference between vocational groups, the study concluded that discriminant analysis can be valuable in classifying students with aptitude and interest variables.

147. Dolan, E. F. (et al.) Counseling techniques for mature women. Report of the adult counselor program (June 14–August 6, 1965). Washington, D.C.: American Association of University Women, 1966. (ED 014 106)
This project determined successful counseling techniques and the length of time necessary to prepare employment counselors to work with women 35 to 54 years old, and presents a guide to help others interested in such a program. Research was carried out by a director, three faculty members who planned and presented the eight week curriculum, consultants for special topics, and 20 women students. These participants had classes in the morning and counseling experience with adult women in the afternoon. The first curricular area explored the history, place in society, psychology, and education of the adult woman. In all areas, comparisons with men and women of other age groups were provided. Principles basic to counseling were presented in "Counseling Techniques and Practicum." Conclusions from taped interviews between participants and counselees indicated—(1) there was no difficulty in establishing rapport, (2) the two major counselee problems were lack of self confidence and lack of information, and (3) most women did not respond well to the exclusive use of the client-centered approach. Group methods were investigated, and are seen as an adjunct, rather than substitute, for individual counseling. Occupational and related information, health, relevant legislation, and volunteer jobs are also discussed. Recommendations for future programs are presented.

148. Drews, E. Counseling for self actualization in gifted girls and young women. *Journal of Counseling Psychology,* 1965, 12(2), 167–175.
Although intellectually superior young women are more highly "growth motivated" than average or slow girls, few are able either to develop or to use their potentialities. Various approaches to counseling and curriculum which emphasize "being and becoming," show that gifted girls are helped to break through restraining social sanctions and to move toward greater self-actualization.

149. Drews, E. M. The effectiveness of special training with audio-visuals in changing aspirations in intellectually superior students. Draft of final report. East Lansing: Michigan State University, College of Education, 1964. (ED 001 304)
An attempt was made to determine the effectiveness of specially prepared audiovisual materials for changing the aspirations of the students selected to participate in the study. The 243 subjects, chosen on the basis of their high reading comprehension scores on the California Reading Test, Advanced Form, were divided into experimental and controls group at random. Controls received the standard guidance program offered in the Lansing, Michigan, junior high schools while the experimental group viewed a series of specially prepared movies in which gifted college students discussed ways in which intellectual and creative activities held excitement for them. The film served to demonstrate how they posed questions and arrived at original answers. The discussion was amplified in later films and each of the eight models later appeared in a documentary, a

biographical style-of-life film designed to introduce the students not only to high level technical and professional careers, but also to the growing edge of knowledge, to the changing nature of each career and to topics of crucial interest in our times. Specially prepared "textbooks" were provided along with extensive magazine and newspaper clippings which were relevant to and correlated with class discussions. Extensive testing and evaluation of the students' self-images, goals and aspirations were performed before and after the experiment. It was found that the experimental girls increased their acceptance of women who advance themselves and enter high level careers and also increased their own expectancies more than did the control girls. The boys followed a similar trend, but to a lesser degree; the experiment increased the social concern and humanitarianism of the girls, though apparently not of the boys. In general the girls were more concerned with social problems than were the boys.

150. Drier, H. N. & Jepsen, D. A. The use of television and video tape compared to researching printed career information as a means of assisting rural 9th grade youth career decision making process. Research report. Iowa City: Iowa University, 1971. (ED 053 561)

A study was devised to test the hypothesis that rural ninth grade students viewing videotaped field trips as part of vocational group guidance classes will exhibit greater occupational knowledge than similar groups who do not view the videotapes. Subjects were 262 ninth grade students from four rural high schools; the schools were paired to form a control and an experimental group. Both groups met for a class period twice weekly for 14 weeks. The experimental group centered discussions and reading around 20-minute videotapes which portrayed a variety of occupations such as paper industry, machine trade, communication, office, and public utility occupations, while the control group read and discussed the same occupations using commercially produced reading materials. Responses from three questionnaires which were administered at the end of the 14-week period were analyzed. Limited positive results obtained showed that videotapes appear to influence the accuracy of stereotypes reported and to stimulate a wider range of occupational possibilities in schools where counselors are employed. Also, it appears that girls are more likely to present scattered occupational choices and less likely to seek occupational information or state positive occupational stereotypes.

151. DuBato, G. S. A feasibility study to investigate the structure and operation of a model occupational information dissemination unit which would operate between the New York State Employment Service and the New York State Education Department. Albany: New York State Education Department, Bureau of Occupational Education Research, 1967. (ED 032 382)

The possibility was explored of greater cooperation between the New York State Employment Service and the secondary schools and 2-year colleges of New York in the production and dissemination of improved occupational information for students and counselors. To compile data on present practices and opinions of counselors and administrators, responses were obtained from 740 elementary and high school counselors, 52 2-year college counselors, 44 high school administrators, and 26 administrators in 2-year colleges. The responses indicated that counselors felt less well prepared in occupational information than in other aspects of their work and that both counselors and administrators valued highly the kinds of information which the Employment Service could supply. As a result of this study, a pilot project will be undertaken in Nassau and Suffolk Counties in 1967–68. A list of 212 local occupations has been prepared with the help of Employment Service occupational analysis. Guides on these occupations will be prepared and distributed to secondary schools and 2-year colleges as a part of the pilot project. A summary report is available as VT 005 799.

152. DuBato, G. S. VOGUE: a demonstration system of occupational information for career guidance. *The Vocational Quarterly,* 1968, 17(2), 117–119.

A major feature of this New York State study was an occupational information utilization survey. Questionnaires were administered personally to guidance counselors with the threefold purpose of determining (1) the occupational information needs of counselors, (2) the occupational information resources available to and used by counselors, and (3) the changes in occupational information which might be desired by counselors in order to make it more useful in career guidance.

153. Dunlop, R. S. & Hintergardt, B. C. Innovation in guidance: implications of flexible-modular scheduling. *Personnel and Guidance Journal,* 1967, 45, 812–817.

Numerous American high schools are turning to flexible-modular scheduling as one means of freeing educational programs from the rigid demands of traditional programs. Advantages include far more student contacts, greater availability of counselees, increased drop-in traffic, improved team relationships with teachers, and greater accessibility of guidance library materials to students. Among disadvantages are a greatly increased workload, student truancies, necessity for counselor involvement in supervisory activities, excessive professional time devoted to clerical tasks, and initially negative lay reactions.

154. Dunn, J. A. The 1970 PLAN guidance program. Washington, D.C.: American Institutes for Research, 1970. (ED 038 677)

This paper describes the first component of PLAN'S guidance program. The five basic assumptions underlying Phase I concern the role of guidance within PLAN's educational system. In line with these assumptions, direct attention is being focused on seven goals: (1) orienting new students to PLAN and orienting current PLAN students to operational changes in PLAN when they occur; (2) assisting students in improving their listening, study, and test taking skills; (3) providing students with a broad base of information regarding the nature of the working world; (4) helping students determine their personal interests and abilities; (5) assisting students and parents in more effective formulation of their goals; (6) developing individualized programs of study for students; and (7) providing for the transition from high school with basic military, college, and post-high school counseling. Each of these objectives is thoroughly discussed.

155. Dunn, J. A. Project PLAN: guidance through the instructional process. The accommodation of individual differences in the development of personal programs of study. Washington, D.C.: American Institutes for Research, 1969. (ED 035 907)

Project PLAN is designed to make educational programs fit the needs of individual learners, and the problem of how such a curriculum can be implemented is discussed. In addition to individualization of what is to be learned and amount of exposure to learning matter, individualization must also be based on the student's learning style; for example, on the various ways in which the content to be learned may be studied. This imposes a massive monitoring task which must be computerized. The paradigm for the development of a PLAN program of studies for secondary school is summarized. PLAN education, however, is designed to be more than a program of academic instruction, and guidance is an integral part of the project. The guidance program will be developed over the next few years and prototype I will implement the educational and vocational counseling effort by attempting to make the educational system vocationally and learner relevant. It calls for experiences which will increase the child's knowledge and skill in the areas of: (1) independent learning, (2) rational decision making, (3) the assessment and implication of individual differences for vocational, avocational and social choice, (4) vocational information, and (5) leisure and citizenship opportunities.

156. Dworkin, E. P. and Walz, G. R. An Evaluation Model for Guidance. In: Cook, D. Guidance for education. Boston: Allyn & Bacon, Inc., 1971 (Chapter 14).

The Evaluation Model for Guidance was developed based on a conceptual framework which is carefully defined and specified in a collection of eight assumptions. The development of a conceptual framework is considered by the authors to be the first step in translating the model into practice, although the use of the model does not require the adoption of the basic assumptions.

Built on the conceptual framework is a network of strategies, tactics and procedures related to the adoption and implementation of the model, which is designed as a model for evaluating career guidance. However, the structure of the model and its systematic procedural guidelines make the model a highly flexible one, and one which can be adopted for any kind of guidance program.

157. Dyste, R. The Los Angeles City College mobile advisement center: a study of its operation. Los Angeles, Cal.: Los Angeles City College, 1970. (ED 046 369)

Los Angeles City College in 1969-70 successfully conducted an experimental study on the Mobile Advisement Center (MAC) as an effective means of enhancing the extent and quality of information on the college reaching low-income communities. MAC is housed in a modified mobile home, 28 feet long and eight feet wide, containing four counseling cubicles, lounge, small library, and bath. The author discusses the background, implementation, findings, and future of the program. MAC's effectiveness is directly proportional to: (1) geographical area covered by: MAC; (2) amount of time MAC is in a given area; (3) number and quality of personnel working on MAC; (4) frequency of visits to each designated target community; and (5) extent of dissemination to the residents of information that could come only from a program like MAC. MAC diminishes dependency on chance and word-of-mouth communication and brings the college catalog to the community. Counseling is available to those who otherwise would not have the opportunity to discuss educational and vocational goals. MAC provides an important paraprofessional career service to those who man it. Several recommendations were made: (1) MAC and its funding should be continued and expanded into other service areas; (2) program details should be reviewed; (3) MAC should be integrated into other campus activities; and (4) it should communicate with similar out-reach agencies.

158. Economic Development Administration. Vocational guidance institutes 1966. Evaluation. Washington, D.C.: Department of Commerce, EDA, 1966. (ED 022 218)

Presented here is a detailed summation of the evaluation of 17 Vocational Guidance Institutes initiated, promoted, and supported by Plans for Progress. The data used for evaluation included an analysis of proposals and other pre-institute material, survey data from trainers and participants in the institute, and material resulting from on-site visits by the evaluators. Recommendations are made on: (1) the role of business and industry in promoting counselor training institutes, (2) the nature of the relationship between local and national Plans for Progress offices, (3) the selection of institute directors and staff, (4) the use of indigenous persons as program participants, (5) the Vocational Guidance Institute in the community context, (6) institute, structure and content, and (7) participant selection.

159. Ehling, W. Development of a computer model of the factors which influence school students to continue or discontinue their education. Syracuse, N.Y.: Syracuse University, 1966. (ED 010 094)

The problem of this effort involved—(1) the development of a workable and empirically grounded theory of communication and decision-making relative to student transition from high school to college, and (2) the design and empirical testing by computer manipulation of a formal model to characterize this theory, using the "Markov Chain Process." An empirical setting, a conceptual framework, and term definitions were provided in describing the communication-decision behavior among high school students. Given the conceptual framework, the next step was to choose an "optimal" strategy (in relation to the state of information) for the model design. Next, the "time-dependent" communication behavior of students in relation to the state of decision was examined in terms of two possible solutions—(1) a communication-decision model with constant transition matrices or incremental behavior in a sequence over time, and (2) a model with time-varying parameters or transformational information over time. From this activity, a Markovan time-varying, communication-decision model was developed. A digital computer program, using Fortran language and providing random outputs, was then developed for model simulation. The computer generated a number of outcomes which showed how long it took a student to arrive at a "decision" and what kind of decision was made, namely, to go or not go to college.

160. Elliot, D. S., Voss, M. L. & Wendling, A. Capable dropouts and the social milieu of the school. San Diego, Cal.: San Diego State College, 1964. (ED 001 466)

It was maintained that socialization in middle-class families prepared youth to compete successfully in school while in lower-class families, children were not trained to conform to academic (formal) and social (informal) requirements of the school.
Frustration arose from status deprivation among the lower classes in their activities in both the formal and informal aspects of the school. The student had two basic alternatives, depending on his attitude towards his failure. If he blamed the system, he would most likely join a delinquent gang. If he blamed himself he would drop out. When an adolescent assumed personal responsibility for his status deprivation, the probability of dropping out was maximized, especially if there was significant contact with other dropouts and little educational support from his family.

161. Elliott, R. D. (et al.) Economics education: a guide for New York schools. Grades K–6. Project PROBE. Oneonta: State University of New York, College at Oneonta, 1970. (ED 042 668)

A series of inquiry plans for the systematic development of learning and thinking skills are provided in this teaching guide. The materials for each grade level include: 1) a summary of the plans, justification of them, identification of the concepts and content that the students will explore, and an outline of the instruction strategy; 2) a statement of the objectives of each topic concerning skill development and the level of performance expected at the close of a planned activity; 3) a description of strategy including specific activities, a questions that should be used, and the inquiry model or plan to be applied to a series of events or situations throughout the year. Since the student is expected to identify the content he needs, in most cases the content is not described. In addition, the selection of instructional materials is left to the teacher based on what is available and the media the students need. Evaluation techniques can be translated from the descriptions of the performance objectives. This guide is not intended as a total program for social studies in any grade. The second part of the guide (ED 042 669) contains the materials for grades 7 through 11.

162. Elliott, R. D. (et al.) Economics education: a guide for New York schools. Grades 7–11. Project PROBE. Oneonta: State University of New York, College at Oneonta, 1970. (ED 042 669)

This is the second part of a teaching guide described in ED 042 668. "A series of inquiry plans for the systematic development of learning and thinking skills are provided."

163. Ellis, A. B. (et al.) A rudimentary demonstration for the information system for vocational decisions—orientation, guidance scripts, test of occupational knowledge, and a script writing language. Information system for vocation decisions, project report number 11. Cambridge, Mass.: Harvard University, 1967. (ED 014 110)

A computerized information system for vocational decisions is described and demonstrated. Demonstration materials include an introduction to the system, six scripts, a test of occupational knowledge, and a script writing language. The inquirer's name is first requested by the system. The inquirer decides whether he wishes to choose a specific script, take the test of occupational knowledge, or write a script himself. The script, "Naming and Collecting Job Preferences," elicits appropriate data, collects job preferences, and calls up other scripts. "Exploration" collects data and directs users to other scripts. "Learning The Roe Categories" is for those who have not thought about future occupation, and "Choosing Further Education" presents educational opportunities. "Choosing a Job by Characteristics" elicits preferences and dislikes about job characteristics using a base of 11 occupations. "Getting Specific Job Descriptions" uses the information collected to provide specific information. The six part occupational knowledge test deals with particular job classifications and the inquirer's occupational choice. The Minorca scriptwriting language is discussed and explained. Script copies are appended.

Compendium of Abstracted Methods 259

164. Ellis, B. W. & Swan, R. (Eds.) NVGA bibliography of current career information: 1969. Washington, D.C.: American Personnel and Guidance Association Publications, 1970.

This classified compilation of career literature and alphabetical listing of career films reviews and rates materials over a three year period.

165. Englander, M. E. Influencing vocational choice: a pilot study. *Vocational Guidance Quarterly,* 1966, 14(2), 136–140.

This pilot study explored the effect of a career day which was designed to encourage subjects to consider mathematics teaching as a possible vocation. Data from pre- and post-testing show that perception of mathematics teaching and respective self concepts became significantly more congruent although attitudes of mathematics teaching *per se* were unchanged.

166. Epstein, C. F. Woman's place; options and limits in professional careers. Berkeley: University of California Press, 1971. (ED 047 249)

The author contends that, despite the struggle for equal participation with men in all social and economic spheres, most American women have not adequately exploited their rights and talents. Beginning with a survey of the cultural themes and values that profoundly affect how women's career decisions are made, she gives detailed attention to the socialization process from which individuals derive their self-identity and the sense of personal limits and options. Six major categories of role conflict are then identified and discussed, each deriving from the ambiguities and contradictions associated with being both a female and a professional. Paths and obstacles to the reconciliation of such conflicts are described, along with effects which typically follow from such decisions as marriage or childbirth. Finally, different professions (including law, medicine, engineering, and teaching) are examined in terms of how women's participation is shaped by structural factors, behavioral norms, and tendencies toward change in each field. Problems encountered by poor women—a major part of the work force—are also touched on.

167. Ewing, T. N. & Gilbert, W. M. An investigation of the importance of the personal relationship and associated factors in teaching machine procedures. Urbana: Illinois University, 1965. (ED 003 604)

A "self-counseling manual" was developed to replace the standard personal pre-college counseling interview. A branching programed text presented the following topics to high school seniors who had taken a battery of admissions, guidance, and placement tests—(1) your test results and scholastic achievement, (2) areas of specialization within the university, (3) summary of interpretation of your test results, (4) study habits and reading, (5) information about the university, (6) your personality characteristics and success, and (7) areas of interest. A total of 391 males were divided into groups which received normal counseling, programed counseling, or simulated programed counseling. Participants completed a pre-counseling questionnaire, a post-counseling questionnaire, a similar questionnaire at the end of their first semester, and a post-counseling interview when it was requested after programed counseling. Findings indicated that counseling carried out by a programed book was as effective as or more effective in changing self-concepts than normal counseling. It was implied that a programed counseling book such as that developed in this study could do much to alleviate the critical shortage of trained counselors at the national level. Future research was suggested on an investigation of programed psychotherapy as compared with normal psychotherapy.

168. Farlow, B. A. An equal chance: handbook for counseling Indian students. Stevens Point: Wisconsin State University, 1971. (ED 050 364)

This handbook provides educational, vocational and resource information to aid teachers, advisors, and counselors in guiding Indian students. Information presented includes the cultural dilemma, Wisconsin's Indians today, Wisconsin Indian tribes, counseling techniques, economic assistance, educational opportunities, state resources and books representing true Indian culture. Essentially, the handbook is a resource of contextual insight into the world of the Indian, in order that the counselor, teacher or advisor may be better equipped to understand the world of the Indian, his needs, and his perceptions of a white socioeconomic world. Only with this degree of understanding of the Indian can the counselor attempt to counsel the Indian justly and benefit both Indian and counseling interests. In effect, the handbook gives the view that the Indian is a member of our American culture and, simultaneously, a member of a unique, valued sub-culture.

169. Farmer, H. S. Helping women to resolve the home career conflict. *Personnel and Guidance Journal,* 1971, 49(10), 795–800.

Counselors can no longer dodge the special demands of vocational decision-making with women by saying either "Sooner or later she will settle down and get married" or "A woman can do anything a man can do." Counselors and educators can help to clarify the factors involved in the vocational choice process with high school and college girls, particularly where these factors differ from those affecting men. There is no need to wait for a woman to seek counseling in order to expose her to these factors; such clarification should be built into high school and college guidance programs for girls. Society will gain if women choose careers at a level commensurate with their potential.

170. Feck, V. What vocational education teachers and counselors should know about urban disadvantaged youth. Columbus: Ohio State University, Center for Vocational and Technical Education, 1971.

This publication is designed to serve teachers and counselors interested in reviewing the key concepts relative to working with disadvantaged youth in urban areas. The compact nature of the review and its organization into guideline format should provide a ready reference for the practitioner seeking to improve his instruction. Major sections of the document include: (1) Characteristics of Urban Disadvantaged Youth and Their Environment, (2) Guidance and Counseling, (3) Curriculum Design and Content, (4) Teaching Techniques, (5) Teacher Characteristics, and (6) Placement of Students.

171. Ferguson, E. T. Education program of the 70's. *Balance Sheet,* 1970, 51(5), 208–212.

Methodologies are presented for improving distributive education programs through assessment of student's occupational choices, parental aspirations and local manpower needs within the context of national manpower needs and employment opportunities.

172. Ferman, L. A. Operation retrieval. Disadvantaged youth: problems of job placement, job creation, and job development. Ann Arbor: Institute of Labor and Industrial Relations, University of Michigan, 1967. (ED 033 211)

Operation Retrieval is a research project designed by the Department of Labor to review and assess the experiences of 55 experimental and demonstration projects for disadvantaged youth conducted during the period 1963-65, and to assess the impact of strategies in job placement, job creation, and job development. Job placement and development units are discussed in terms of their relationship to other project components, the structure of the staff, and the location of the job placement unit. Methods used to obtain jobs for disadvantaged youth include: (1) applying traditional techniques, (2) developing new jobs, (3) working with employers to modify job requirements, and (4) developing youth potential to meet employer standards. Five types of problems and possible approaches to job placement are: educational deficiencies, arrest records, and physical, emotional, and resource problems. Follow-up is discussed in connection with supportive services and employment experiences. Recommendations relate to retrieval and use of information, research, inter-agency relations, and follow-up activities.

173. Ferris State College. Perspectives on vocational guidance. Big Rapids, Mich.: FSC, 1969. (ED 036 842)

A workshop on vocational guidance was conducted to meet a continuing counselor-teacher-administrator need for assistance in identifying and encouraging students in technically oriented careers. The following presentations are reported in their entirety: (1) Vocational Rehabilitation Program; (2) Students with Special Needs; (3) Basic Elements of Career Guidance; (4) Vocational Opportunities for the Technical Trained Individual in Conservation and Outdoor Education; and (5) Excerpts of a Discussion on Vocational Guidance between Trade-Technical Students and Workshop Participants. Also included is an evaluation of the workshop by the participants and the director and a summary of recommendations.

174. Fibkins, W. A different approach to sharing occupational information. *The School Counselor,* 1969, 16(5), 390–393.

Discusses use of contemporary music on life's meanings to initiate discussion among low-achievers regarding relationship between background, education and job opportunities.

175. Fielstra, C. Work experience education program in Santa Barbara County High School districts. Report of an evaluative study. Santa Barbara, Cal.: Work Experience Education Program, 1961. (ED 001 667)

The program has operated since 1953 in five communities. High School personnel have developed a work-study program in an attempt to help students: (1) make better occupational choices, (2) gain the necessary preparation for their chosen work, (3) find placement on the job and (4) adjust to and grow on the job.
Three forms of work education are offered. Exploratory work experience education is intended to help the student discover his aptitudes and interests through a variety of work situations. General work experience offers financial remunerations and school credit and is related to a student's proposed career. Vocational work experience education is a program of paid work directly related to the occupation the student expects to enter.
It is recommended that the schools, the employment service, and the employers work closely together and that each school district employ a coordinator to help with the effort.
Parents', students', employers', faculties' and principals' program evaluations reveal that the program is judged to be successful and of much value. The work experience education program was found not to interfere with regular school work, and participants compared favorably with non-participants.
Recommendations given are applicable to any work-study program and include the formation of advisory committees and the careful supervision and assignment of students. A selective bibliography is appended.

176. Fine, S. A. Guidelines for the design of new careers. Staff paper. Kalamazoo, Mich.: Upjohn (W.E.) Institute for Employment Research, 1967. (ED 024 762)

The design of new careers involves technical and strategic considerations and commitment on the part of employers that transforms dead-end jobs into opportunities for growth and makes the technical and strategic guidelines relevant. Technical guidelines include (1) titling positions to reflect commitment to a career, (2) using selection procedures that recognize the range and development of potential, (3) structuring tasks to allow for higher functional attainment and increased discretionary functioning, (4) providing supervision that implements the growing of people as well as the achieving of production standards, (5) providing regular increases in compensation to correspond with increased experience and competence, and (6) providing training and growth opportunities for those who can and need to achieve higher functional performance. Strategic guidelines include: (1) directing opportunities for new careers primarily at the poor and disadvantaged, (2) developing new careers primarily in the newly emerging community and health services work fields, and (3) initiating new careers by resorting to both short- and long-term approaches, and, especially, by avoiding assumptions that ignore the realities of professionalization.

177. Fishman, J. R. (et al.) Training for new careers. The community apprentice program. Washington, D.C.: Howard University, Institute for Youth Studies; President's Committee on Juvenile Delinquency and Youth, 1965. (ED 025 472)

The Community Apprentice Program, developed by the Howard University Center for Youth and Community Studies, was an exploratory attempt, through combined rehabilitation, vocational education, and supervised work experience, to train disadvantaged youth as human service aides in child care, recreation, and social research. Seven boys and three girls, ranging in age from 16 to 20, who were currently unemployed and lacked education beyond high school were selected. The 12-week program consisted of three related parts: the "core group," in which members learned to analyze personal, social, and job-related problems, make decisions, and relate more effectively to others; specialty workshops and seminars; and supervised on-the-job experience. Consisting of experimentation with data gained from observation and tape recordings and attempts to develop instruments for more refined and controlled future studies, evaluation of the project focused on delineation of the characteristics of the youths who volunteered for the program, analysis of reasons for their identification and affiliation with or alienation from the program, and description and evaluation of the group process. (Also included are comments of aides, results, curriculum outlines, sample position descriptions, and a 19-item bibliography.)

178. Fishman, J. R. & Terris, S. Procedural guide for program development in new careers. Washington, D.C.: University Research Corporation, Information Clearinghouse, 1968. (ED 022 925)

This manual is intended to provide general guidelines and assistance to staff participating in the organization and development of a New Careers Program in a community. These activities are supported through contract with the Bureau of Work Programs, U.S. Department of Labor, as part of the New Careers Program, Section 123(a)(4) of the Economic Opportunity Act of 1964 as amended (Scheuer Amendment). The program is structured around the development of new jobs, training, employment, and career development at the nonprofessional levels in public services: health, public education, social service, law enforcement and public safety, child care, and community development. The manual includes: (1) an outline or checklist of steps and components to be followed in proposal and program development, (2) a narrative discussing in greater detail several of the key items listed in the outline, (3) a brief description of a job development model being used in a community mental health center, (4) a sample proposal which was developed by an urban community under the auspices of the New Careers Program, and (5) a selected bibliography of available references.

179. Flanagan, J. C. Individualizing education. Palo Alto, Cal.: American Institutes for Research in the Behavioral Sciences, 1968. (ED 040 566)

Various attempts have been made in the past to improve the quality of American education by individualizing instruction. The most common method of individualizing instruction has been by varying the rate of progress or the type of assignment. Perhaps a more important and little used method is that of adapting education to individual differences with respect to the goals of the educational program. An effective program for individualizing instruction must be based on extensive additional psychological research and development in (1) formulating the functions of an educational system, (2) achieving the individual's educational goals, (3) monitoring the individual's progress, (4) formulating goals and planning individual development, and (5) preparing the teacher for individualizing education. Using the knowledge now available, a program known as Project PLAN (Program for Learning in Accordance with Needs) is being developed and tested. Project PLAN attempts not only to utilize knowledge about the learning process itself and about instructional materials, but also to help the individual student to know his strengths and weaknesses and, with the help of guidance and counseling, to select his educational objectives. A list of references is appended.

180. Flanagan, J. C. Project PLAN: the basic role of guidance in individualizing education. Washington, D.C.: American Institutes for Research, 1970. (ED 038 676)

The inadequacy of the traditional educational program has been clearly shown in the results of Project TALENT. To remedy these defects, the Project PLAN educational system includes six principal components: (1) an extensive informational program describing the opportunities, roles, and activities for which the student might prepare; (2) ability and interest testing and interpretation of these in relation to the available opportunities; (3) a series of units and practical exercises designated to develop the student's skill in decision making; (4) a means to the information and skills gained in the three activities mentioned above to assist the student in formulating his personal goals; (5) a way of helping each student plan an educational program to enable him to achieve these goals; and (6) a system to develop the student's skill in managing the program of development which will enable him to carry out his educational plans and achieve his life goals. Experience with this program in PLAN during the past year suggests that this type of computer-supported individualized education, based on an effective set of guidance procedures, offers much promise in enabling each of our young people to achieve personal fulfillment.

181. Flanagan, J, C. Project TALENT, the identification development, and utilization of human talents, the American high school student. Pittsburgh, Pa.: Pittsburgh University, 1964. (ED 002 224)

An intensive study of the American high school was made to survey available talent identify interests, aptitudes, and background factors determine effects of lack of interest and motivation; identify factors affecting vocational choice; identify predictors of creativity and productivity; determine the effectiveness of various types of educational experience; and study procedures for realizing individual potential.

In the spring of 1960, a two-day test battery was given to about 440,000 students in the 9th, 10th, 11th, and 12th grades in 1,353 public, private, and parochial schools in all parts of the country. They constituted approximately 5 percent of the population of the high schools in the United States.

Included is detailed information about the achievement, aptitude, interests, and personality characteristics of these students. Most of the data pertains to students who were in grade 12 in the Spring of 1960. Detailed tables are included.

182. Flicker, B. A school and work program in an adult manpower setting for potential dropouts needing educational redirection. Evaluation of state urban education programs in New York City. New York: New York Educational Research Committee, Center for Urban Education, 1969. (ED 036 579)

The objectives of this high school redirection project were to redirect potential dropouts to continue full-time education and training with an educational-vocational plan, to provide high school dropouts with job skills that will enable them to enter the labor market on the highest possible level while continuing to upgrade their skills on a part-time basis, and to test a curriculum designed for out-of-school youths and adults in which the skills of training, basic education, and job orientation (group counseling) are directly related to the skills needed for success on the job. This project functioned with the Manpower Development Training Program (MDTP) in a cooperative school and work program. The basic education curriculum included English, general mathematics, civil service preparation, job skills, and a group guidance session. Students' jobs fell into three categories: clerical, health occupations, and maintenance. Evaluation was based on questionnaires, interviews, observation visits, and examination of school records.

183. Flint Board of Education. Mott program summaries (title supplied). Flint, Mich.: FBE. (ED 002 402)

The Better Tomorrow for the Urban Child program (BTU) attempts to help inner-city children become more effective citizens, both educationally and socially, through the use of additional human and material resources. The goals are to raise the level of school readiness, to develop a greater motivation for learning, and to improve student self-image and performance. Involved are a pre-kindergarten program, in-service training, a health program, curriculum development, enrichment through the community-school program, and the improvement of instructional materials.

The Community School Director is responsible for after-school activities. Serving as a part-time teacher in most schools, he begins his day at noon and continues through the evening hours. He is involved with the areas of juvenile delinquency, adult education, area improvement, enrichment courses, retraining for job upgrading, interracial harmony, and recreation and service organizations for students and adults.

The Personalized Curriculum Program encourages students to remain in school, introduces them to employment opportunities and improves their basic academic skills. The Regional Counseling Team (the principal, deans of students and counseling, visiting teachers, the nurse counselor, police counselor and the community school director) unite their abilities to help students having academic, personal or social problems.

The Stepping Stone Program encourages informal discussions among girls from the fifth grade through senior high school. The Police School Liaison Program attempts to detect and prevent crime and to identify and help students with special academic, health, social or moral problems.

Other programs described are the Big Brother Program, the Mott Summer Camp, the School Health and Safety Program, and the Physical Fitness Program. General descriptive statistical data of Flint, Michigan, are appended.

184. Flowers, S. H. A project to demonstrate the effectiveness of unstructured group counseling in developing in disabled persons insights and positive attitudes. Final report. Group counseling as an aid in the employment of hard-to-place rehabilitation clients. Research brief. Baltimore: Maryland State Department of Education, Division of Vocational Rehabilitation, 1970. (ED 044 750) (Not available from EDRS)

The project attempted to learn whether group counseling could be used effectively to move into employment, or into training for employment, hard core clients of a state vocational rehabilitation agency who, though apparently ready for employment consistently failed to obtain or retain satisfactory employment. A sample of 99 clients were involved in small group meetings aimed at helping them overcome obstacles which had prevented them from becoming employed. Early sessions were totally without structure. It was later found that better results were obtained when the therapists structured and directed the group discussions. The report includes a discussion of instruments which were devised to show what happens to certain attitudes of individuals who participated in group counseling sessions, and to observe and analyze the content and interaction of the groups as they developed. Results indicate that 69 out of 99 obtained employment, or were active in training programs, at or soon after the end of the group sessions.

185. Frank, R. L. & Matthes, W. A. Strategies for implementation of guidance in the elementary school. Five monographs. Des Moines: Iowa State Dept. of Public Instruction, 1970. (ED 048 602)

A series of five monographs comprises this document. The overall concern is with elementary school guidance and each monograph which is complete within itself deals with a specific aspect of this topic: (1) Models and Directions; (2) Role of the Superintendent and School Board; (3) Role of the Principal; (4) Role of the Teacher; (5) Role of the Secondary School Counselor. They are designed to assist all personnel of local schools in establishing organized guidance programs at the elementary school level.

186. Frank, R. L. & Paten, B. A three-way occupational file. *Vocational Guidance Quarterly,* 1960, 8(3), 171–172.

Where to file unbound occupation materials containing information on more than one occupation is a common problem for most counselors. This calls for a simple cross-reference filing system which makes provision for all types of occupational information. This article proposes such a filing system.

187. Frankel, E. Attendance task force to strengthen high school attendance programs. Evaluation of state urban education programs in New York City. New York: Educational Research Committee, Center for Urban Education, 1969. (ED 036 580)

This report evaluates a demonstration project attempted for the first time in

New York City schools in 1969 which was designed to remediate absenteeism in the high schools. The project was to provide individualized attention and concentrated services for 16-year-old and older chronic absentees and their parents. Other objectives included the development of a referral service for job counseling and evening education programs, and assistance to principals with their school registers. The evaluation design was based on: (1) comparisons of school attendance records before and after implementation of the project, (2) surveys of opinions about the reasons for chronic absenteeism; and (3) assessment of the strengths and weaknesses of the project. The data were gathered through interviews and questionnaires. Recommendations and sample questionnaire forms used are included.

188. Franklin County Schools. Area education information center. A systems summary description. Columbus, Ohio: FCS, 1968. (ED 027 571)

The pupil personnel accounting system developed and used by Ohio's Franklin County schools is presented. Three main areas are described: (1) the construction, use, and maintenance of the student data base; (2) input, school and center processing, and output routines involved in progress reporting, and (3) procedures for dealing with pupil class assignment (scheduling) functions in secondary schools. Examples of materials and outputs obtained are provided. This study was funded under a Title II, Elementary and Secondary Education Act grant.

189. Franklin County Board of Education. Operation DIRECT—developmental itinerant rural elementary counseling teams. Carnesville, Ga.: FCBE. (ES 002 430)

Mobile student-personnel teams will be formed to serve a four-county rural area. Emphasis will be placed upon providing guidance and counseling services to K-3 students in scattered small schools. Five teams will be formed, each composed of an elementary counselor and a paraprofessional working in conjunction with the classroom teacher. Support personnel for the teams will include a psychologist and a psychometrist. The counselor will work in a classroom on a scheduled basis to identify—(1) children with learning difficulties or motivational problems, and (2) students with social adjustment problems, especially those caused by cultural/subcultural dissonance. Counselors will strive to develop in teachers an increased sensitivity to classroom dynamics and will aid teachers in the administration and interpretation of sociometric devices.

190. Freedman, M. Part-time work experience and potential early school leavers. *American Journal of Ortho-Psychiatry,* 1963, 33, 509–514.

Work-study programs for potential dropouts rest on assumptions about the value of work in improving adolescent motivation and adjustment. Data from recently completed research by the author on urban, early school-leavers raises serious questions concerning these assumptions. Many new programs are not designed either to test specific hypotheses or to differentiate the effect of diverse program factors. The assumptions underlying work-study for potential dropouts and the need to refine criteria for judging the effectiveness of such programs are discussed.

191. Friesen, D. D. The validation of an automated counseling system. Santa Monica, Cal.: System Development Corporation, 1965. (ED 016 262)

The validity of a computer based counseling system was tested by comparison of its effectiveness with that of two counselors in—(1) pre- and post-interview pupil appraisal, (2) student educational decisions, and (3) the completeness of educational plans.

192. Friesen, J. D. Computer based systems in guidance and counseling. An annotated bibliography. Vancouver: British Columbia University, 1970. (ED 046 006)

This bibliography is divided into three general categories: (1) information storage and retrieval theory; (2) computer-based systems in education; and (3) computer-based systems in guidance and counseling. The latter comprises, by far, the bulk of the bibliography and contains general works, monographs, periodicals, microprints, government publications, and unpublished works. In addition, there is a separate section of entries published by the Information System for Vocational Decisions (ISVD) which is a project under the combined direction of the Harvard Graduate School of Education, the New England Educational Data System, and the Newton (Mass.) Public School System. Thirty-six project reports are included.

193. Ganschow, L. H. (et al.) Stimulating educational information—seeking and changes in student attitude toward vocational education by videotape and film presentations. Final report. Palo Alto, Calif.: American Institutes for Research in the Behavioral Sciences, 1970. (ED 043 778)

To help counselors develop appropriate models for students with different characteristics, this investigation involved two studies using films and videotapes in an effort to stimulate individuals to explore and to gather information on vocational educational opportunities. The key experimental phases of the two studies compared the relative influence of Mexican-American and non-Mexican-American social models on Mexican-American and non-Mexican-American 10th grade subjects. Among the findings in Study A was that subjects who saw social models of an ethnic group like their own scored higher on the measure of the subject's interest in occupations and related activities than did subjects who saw models of an ethnic group unlike their own. In Study B it was found that Mexican-American subjects who saw the Mexican-American social models performed slightly more information-seeking behaviors, and made slightly more favorable attitude changes than did Mexican-American subjects who viewed non-Mexican-American models. Study B further suggested that films rather than written presentations are more favorably reacted to by all subjects and that female subjects responded to the treatment suggestions to engage in information seeking significantly more than did male subjects.

194. Garbin, A. P. (et al.) Problems in the transition from high school to work as perceived by vocational educators. Columbus: Ohio State University, The Center for Vocational and Technical Education, 1967. (ED 016 811)

As a part of a large project to develop and test solutions to alleviate adjustment problems and to encourage the adoption of new instructional materials and other programatic solutions, this study explored the factors related to the transition of modern youth from school to work with the intention of identifying specific impediments to a smooth and lasting adjustment. Through the use of interviews and open-ended questionnaires, a "purposive" (nonrandom) sample of 69 respected vocational educators from cities in representative geographic areas provided data identifying social and psychological problems faced by youth adjusting to the work world, the specific curriculum materials and other devices used to alleviate some of the most crucial problems, and additional suggestions or recommendations.

195. Garrison, T. G. Vocational guidance manual for counselors, teachers, and educators. Terre Haute: Indiana Research and Development Coordinating Unit for Vocational and Technical Education, 1969.

The purpose of this document is to bring an awareness to counselors, teachers, educators, and parents of those vocational education programs now available, not only for persons in school, but also for those out of school and unemployed, for those already in the labor market who need training or retraining, and for those persons who are emotionally, economically, or physically handicapped. Programs are discussed for each of the vocational education service areas as well as for students with special needs, that is, academic, socioeconomic, or other handicaps preventing them from succeeding in regular on-going programs of vocational education. Vocational youth organizations are discussed as an important component in the training and development of the students as he engages in both individual and group activities connected with his career objective.

196. Gartland, T. C. & Carmody, J. F. Practices and outcomes of vocational-technical education in technical and community colleges. Iowa City: American College Testing Program, 1970. (ED 049 360)

> A study of 2-year post secondary institutions was conducted to provide more adequate information about institutional guidance and research programs. A questionnaire was sent to 351 vocational-technical schools that offered no transfer programs, and a slightly different version was sent to 689 community or junior colleges offering both college transfer work and vocational-technical programs. Data were requested on counseling, research, data collection, program completion, transfer rates, and graduates' employment experiences. The results showed that vocational schools collected more extensive standardized data for selection purposes, whereas community colleges provided more comprehensive counseling. Research by community colleges was oriented toward demographic studies, unlike the vocational schools, which mainly conducted studies of student satisfaction and success both in school and after leaving. Vocational school graduates were less likely to transfer or drop out.

197. Gelatt, H. B. A decision-making approach to guidance. *NASSP Bulletin,* 1968, 52(324), 88–98.

> Decision-making, as a model for building a guidance program and for training guidance counselors, is presented.

198. Gentile, F. D. & Houseman, R. A development project in self and home employment for the homebound. Rehabilitation series 1. Albertson, N.Y.: Human Resources Center, 1970. (ED 043 993)

> Reported is a project designed to explore the feasibility of establishing a self and home employment program for disabled homebound persons in clerical, business, and service occupations. The local homebound population was surveyed, businesses contacted, jobs studied, and five clients trained and placed. Results were successful and the jobs showed a potential for regional development. The jobs developed were insurance teleservice claims representative, bank credit collection clerk, and school substitute acquisition clerk. Companies involved were satisfied with the quality of work and interested in hiring more homebound.

199. Gerstein, M. & Hoover, R. Regional center for collection, synthesis and dissemination of career information for schools of San Diego County. Paper presented at the meeting of the American Psychological Association, Washington, D.C., April, 1966. (ED 011 382)

> The purpose of this regional center is to develop an efficient system of providing career information to San Diego county schools. Six junior colleges are participating in the pilot project. The program is divided into two phases. The first is the collection and synthesis of occupational information based upon student and counselor perceptions of which occupational information is most valuable, the preparation of data about 55 occupations in hospital careers, the development of a workable, efficient, economical system of dissemination and retrieval, and the preparation of auxiliary materials. The second is the evaluation of the efficacy of the "viewscript" material in order to refine the content of the card material, and to test the ease of use and acceptance by students and faculty. A description of the equipment, materials, instructions for their usage, and evaluation in the schools participating in the pilot project is included. The future activities of the center will include expanding the "viewscript" approach to many occupations, following-up of graduates of local secondary school technical and vocational programs, and selecting of secondary schools to receive the "viewscript" materials. This speech was presented at the American Personnel and Guidance Association Convention (Session 266, New York, April 6, 1966).

200. Gerstein, M. & Hoover, R. VIEW-vocational information for education and work. *Personnel and Guidance Journal,* 1967, 45(6), 593–596.

A Career Information Center is described that provides restructured occupational information in a microfilm format that is readily kept current and is instantly accessible. The information is based upon what students and counselors feel is occupational information of the most worth. The Career Information Center also provides counselor in-service education in the belief that the principal rationale for counseling in the secondary schools is educational and career development activities for all students.

201. Geteles, F. (et al.) A cooperative vocational pattern for in-school mentally retarded youth. Orange, N.J.: Occupational Center of Essex County. (ED 054 344)

This project was established to experiment with a work-study program for mentally retarded youth in the hope that it would improve the vocational functioning of these adolescents. The 300 male students, aged 14 to 18 with IQs ranging from 43 to 83, were divided into an experimental group and a control group for the purpose of the project. The experimental group was treated in a program where the following changes were instituted; the time spent in academic pursuits was reduced from 5 days to 3 days; the school curriculum was modified to include a greater emphasis on vocationally-related material; and the students were assigned to a community workshop for additional training and rehabilitation services on the 2 days they no longer attended school. The control group remained in school for the full 5 days per week. Results showed that more of the experimental group completed their year in school than did the control group. Fewer of the experimental group were institutionalized during or after the project, and some showed signs of personal growth.

202. Glassman, A. I. (et al.) Summer work-study program on urban problems for secondary school youth from inner-city communities. Final report. Philadelphia: Philadelphia School District, 1968. (ED 028 226)

During the summer of 1968, 625 inner-city secondary school youth, ages 14–18, participated in a work-study program. Objectives were: (1) to involve inner-city youth in the development and interpretation of open-ended urban problems study programs: (2) to determine the effects of involvement in a variety of study and employment experiences related to the identification and amelioration of urban problems on individual and group behavior of inner-city youth; and (3) to determine the extent to which project activities implemented in the program can be diffused into the regular school program. Trainees, organized into teams of 10–13, each led by a young adult team leader, engaged in a daily 2-hour classroom session and a daily 4-hour work session. In many cases, they designed their own afternoon work projects in the community. The project was characterized by intensive community involvement. The findings of a questionnaire evaluation showed that the trainees were interested in a wide range of occupations, including nonprofessional jobs, and that they disliked occupations associated with the opposite sex.

203. Glatthorn, A. A. (et al.) On their own. (A handbook of independent study.) Pa.: Abington Township School District, 1966. (ED 011 132)

The responses of 741 ninth-grade students to the Independent Study Program (ISP) were recorded from homeroom discussions and the Independent Study Questionnaire (ISQ). The ISP provided time blocks, special facilities, and minimal rules and regulations for a high school student's day. Basic content courses (departmental centers) and skill improvement areas (independent study centers) were organized with structured and unstructured learning experiences, using teachers, aides, and student leaders. The principal selected and trained a student discussion leader for each homeroom. A student recorded summarized student responses to each discussion question and submitted a resume to the principal. The summary compiled from the resumes listed (1) the discussion questions, (2) a consensus of student responses, and (3) a sample of the most interesting responses. Responses were tabulated by (1) failure notices, (2) periods spent in department centers and ISP centers, (3) materials and equipment used, (4) type of ISP, and (5) weekly attendance in each center. Recommendations included (1) greater use of the ISP for basic course content, (2) more materials and equipment for ISP centers, (3) more space for ISP centers, and (4) the addition of a full-time ISP program coordinator. The appendix included (1) form letters to students and parents explaining the ISP and scheduling procedures. (2) student and teacher ISP guides, (3) teacher reporting forms for ISP and (4) the ISQ.

204. Glenn, M. Student placement and follow-up services in the junior college. 1968. (ED 022 443)

A placement service may make higher education possible for certain students by providing on- or off-campus jobs for them while they attend college. It also helps graduates and former students find jobs related to their study areas, keeps the institution in touch with employers so that the adequacy of course content can be evaluated, and interprets college purposes to business and industry. To do these things, the placement service must (1) solicit jobs, (2) handle student applications, (3) interview and refer applicants, (4) keep recommendations and records on file, (5) give vocational counseling to applicants, (6) interpret college programs to employers, (7) schedule student and recruiter interviews, (8) keep referral and placement records, (9) evaluate the college program in relation to community needs, (10) compile reports and studies on working students and full-time placements, and (11) work in coordination with state employment agencies. The placement service should also give time and effort to followup. Ideally, this would (1) measure transfer success by comparison of pre- and post-transfer grade point averages, (2) supply this information to accrediting associations, (3) obtain data from senior colleges on academic and career success of transfers, (4) keep track of vocational graduates' success in finding and holding jobs, (5) hold exit interviews with withdrawing students, and (6) determine reasons for dropout or withdrawal.

205. Goetz, W. & Leach, D. The disappearing student. *Personnel and Guidance Journal,* 1967, 883–887.

359 randomly selected freshmen (1962) at the University of New Mexico were sent a questionnaire related to college attrition, and the attitudes of withdrawees and continuers were compared regarding teachers, counselors, facilities, and various personal experiences and conditions that might lead to withdrawal. The results failed to support reasons for attrition commonly cited in the literature. Only 5 items distinguished the groups' reaction to the college environment. In fact, the continuers were more negative toward the college environment than the withdrawees. Only 3 reasons generally related to attrition differentiated the groups: withdrawees felt that problems of marriage, family finance, and general unhappiness were somewhat more important than did the continuers. These findings indicate that the real causes for college withdrawal have yet to be discovered.

206. Goff, W. H. Vocational guidance in elementary schools. Columbus: Ohio State University, 1967.

An experimental program of vocational guidance in the elementary school was designed and activated to determine if measurable increments in occupational knowledge, vocational aspiration and realism in occupational choice could be achieved in predetermined situations in two different elementary schools.

207. Goff, W. Widening occupational horizons kit. Our working world kit. Preparing aspiring career exploration. Dayton, Ohio: Dayton City School District, 1967. (ED 012 934)

Certified school counselors were assigned to two elementary schools to develop, use, and test vocational and occupational materials. Aspiration levels of students in one class each in the second, fourth, and sixth grades in each school were also explored and related to occupational potential. Methods of using occupational materials effectively were also tested. Pre- and post-tests were given to assess pupil knowledge of occupations, achievement and ability measures were obtained early in the school year. Questionnaires were given to teachers and parents of children in the experimental groups. Some findings were—(1) the students assimilated vocational and occupational information, (2) older elementary students exhibited greater vocational awareness, (3) changes in level of aspiration as a function of learning potential were not differentiated between the experimental and control groups, (4) the dictionary of occupational titles was used successfully by the counselor and older elementary student, and (5) parents and teachers were enthusiastic about the program.

Career Guidance

208. Goldberg, G. S. (et al.) New careers: the social service aide. A manual for trainees. Washington, D.C.: University Research Corporation, Information Clearinghouse, 1968. (ED 025 467)

This manual is intended for use by social service aide trainees in the New Careers Program and provides description and explanation of the history and background of social welfare, social services, skills important in individual services, clerical and administrative activities connected with social services, and procedures for working with community groups and organizations. An accompanying manual for trainers of social service aides (SP 002 031) is also available from the New Careers Institute.

209. Goldhammer, K. (et al.) Career oriented relevant education (CORE). Corvallis: Oregon State University, 1968. (EP 011 687)

The primary objective of this project is to develop the basis for a total state program of curriculum revision based upon a careers centered approach. A statewide planning center for this project will be established in order to effect a close working relationship with the State Board staff. The state center's functions will be to develop the master plan, establish regional coordinating centers to serve the needs in local school districts, and mobilize local, state, and national resources to support the project. This center will also develop evaluation and adaptive processes and ensure their being conducted. During the initial planning phase, the state planning center will develop and synthesize a sound theoretical base for modifying the total curriculum in Grades K–14 in such a way as to achieve the project's primary objective.

210. Goldstein, G. (Ed.) College bound: a directory of special programs and financial aid for minority group students. White Plains, N.Y.: Urban League of Westchester, Inc., 1970. (ED 045 776)

This directory of special programs and financial assistance for black and other minority group students is designed for guidance counselors and college-bound students. The information was obtained directly from the colleges, and describes programs, assistance, and admission policies for the disadvantaged. The description of each school is only as complete as the information received in reply to the questionnaire sent would provide. All of the schools that showed an interest are included in the directory. The counselor is urged to use this book as an introduction, but not as a substitute for his concern, commitment, and skill.

211. Goodson, S. Children talk about work. *Personnel and Guidance Journal,* 1970, 49(2), 131–136.

The children disclosed their knowledge, interests, and attitudes related to various occupations and reasons for working. Some children were well informed and had specific vocational goals, while others were quite unaware of work. The data from the study were used to develop telecasts and other modes of presentation for occupational information.

212. Goodson, S. Occupational information materials in selected elementary and middle schools. *The Vocational Guidance Quarterly,* 1968, 17(2), 128–131.

The data collected in this survey of a small sample indicate a preponderance of occupational information material at third-grade reading level, tapering to kindergarten and to sixth grade with relatively little material for upper elementary grades. This suggests that the child approaching high school has less career information available at his reading level than he had at a younger age.

213. Gordon, A. T. Evaluation of the second year of operation of the Contra Costa Mobile Counseling Center. San Pablo, Cal.: Contra Costa College, 1970. (ED 043 332)

Second year operations of this mobile center have validated many of the assumptions on which it was founded (see ED 031 243), including a reduction in the communications gap between Contra Costa College and the community at large. While attempts to compare this year's results with last year's can be considered premature, some findings may be of interest. During the preceding 9-month period, over 700 hours of service were provided. This includes individual and small group counseling for 150 people. Of these 150, approximately 50 per cent had an annual family income of $4000 or less, and over half had left high school by the eleventh grade. Sixty-five per cent of the 150 were also either too young to work, or experienced employment difficulties due to a lack of education. Of these, 29 per cent were subsequently placed in college, 11 per cent in job training, and 30 per cent referred to other agencies for counseling or job placement. Of those not placed, many had come to the center only for information, and could not have been placed anyway. A questionnaire completed by 80 counselees indicated that 80 per cent came to the counseling center to receive college or career planning information, 93 per cent felt they were helped there, and 100 per cent would not only use the center again, but would also recommend that their friends use it.

214. Gordon, J. E. (et al.) Role modeling and role playing in employability development agencies. A manual for vocational development and employment agencies. Ann Arbor, Mich.: Manpower Science Services, Inc., [1969]. (ED 035 030)

This manual is the result of an effort designed to solve the problems of the unemployed poor. A total of six agencies participated in this project and designed this manual with focuses on role modeling and role playing. The manual is directed toward the unsophisticated client who has had too little experience to be able to understand the fairly common signals which people use to guide their behavior in new situations. The manual has six sections dealing with the following areas: (1) an introduction which includes selecting behaviors to be modeled, (2) drawing attention to the model's performance, (3) role playing, (4) rewards, (5) characteristics of good models, and (6) conclusions. Each section provides principles involved on the left side of the page, and examples for each principle on the right. At the bottom of the page, relevant literature is identified.

215. Gorman, R. E. A guidance project to investigate characteristics, background, and job experiences of successful and unsuccessful entry workers in three selected industries. Final report. Missoula: Montana University; Helena: Montana State Department of Public Instruction, 1966. (MP 000 094)

Fifteen certified secondary school counselors participated in an on-the-job investigation of three selected industries in Montana—mining, lumbering, and construction. The purposes were to (1) provide the participating counselors with on-the-job knowledge essential for engaging in more effective vocational counseling of secondary school students, and (2) present recommendations for personnel management in the cooperating industries for increasing the chances for success among entry workers.

216. Greater Hartford Chamber of Commerce. Project Inspire: vocational guidance institute. Conn.: GHCC, 1971. (ED 052 472)

Two introductory speeches suggest the general social and interracial climate in the United States. It is against this backdrop that Project Inspire is described. Its purpose is the development of a vocational guidance component within the broader school curriculum. Its major objective is elevating the awareness level of students to the work world through the establishment of a comprehensive Human Resources Library. Specific institute materials included in this booklet are: (1) sample educational projects and techniques, including an educational simulation; (2) a listing of specific career orientation program objectives; (3) sample forms and letters for program participants; (4) a Connecticut task force report on manpower needs; and (5) the results of an end-of-the-first week evaluation of institute participants' knowledge and feelings about minority youth, employment, and poverty.

217. Greenfield, R. An experimental and demonstration manpower program for disadvantaged youths. Final report. Brooklyn: New York City Board of Education, 1966. (ED 019 518)

The Job Counseling Center initiated an experimental and demonstration program to test the thesis that an urban school could provide a manpower training program to out-of-school unemployed, and disadvantaged youth.

218. Griessman, B. E. (Ed.) The concerted services approach to developmental change in rural areas: an interim evaluation. Raleigh: North Carolina Research Coordinating Unit in Occupational Education.

In 1965 Concerted Services in Training and Education (CSTE) began operation in three selected rural counties of New Mexico, Arkansas, and Minnesota with objectives of: (1) developing general operational patterns for alleviation and solution of occupational education problems, (2) identifying employment opportunities and occupational education programs for low income youth and adults, (3) developing ways for providing services needed to help people become employable, (4) demonstrating that occupational education programs can significantly increase employment opportunities, (5) demonstrating that a cooperative occupational effort based on local involvement will result in continuing community development, and (6) determining the relationship of educational and occupational patterns to the present and emerging needs of communities and making recommendations for adjustments. Some tentative conclusions pending full analysis of data are: (1) the program has created a vehicle for communication between agencies, (2) the program should be inaugurated in one county with future expansion to surrounding areas, (3) the local coordinator should have approval of area leaders, (4) many trainees have secured employment, (5) no marked increase in available jobs is evident, and (6) both obscurity and excessive publicity can be detrimental to program success.

219. Grossmont Union High School District. Studies in success. A promising approach to the vocational guidance of average high school students. Grossmont, Cal.: GUHSD, 1964. (ED 010 703)

This report describes an educational plan to improve the vocational guidance of average or noncollege preparatory high school students. The program is designed to create a positive attitude on the part of the student toward formal education, the world of work, and the means for succeeding in one's vocation through experiences which will provide a positive and realistic self-concept in reality testing situations. A complete unit of study for use in the classroom is presented and includes a listing of all materials needed for implementation as well as classroom methods which were utilized. The rationale employed in developing the unit and implication for teachers and guidance personnel are discussed. Preliminary research findings support the methodology of this program.

220. Gueder, B. (Ed.) Handbook for elementary school guidance. Texas: Edinburg Consolidated Independent School District, 1969. (ED 048 603)

This handbook is divided into three parts: (1) a statement of the philosophy and objectives of the program with aids to the teacher for its proper utilization, (2) a handy reference of child development and educational principles covering areas in which teachers frequently request advice; and (3) a catalog of materials available from the Guidance Department for use with children or as aids to professional growth. Part two deals with both academic and behavioral needs: (1) learning disabilities; (2) underachievement; (3) creativity; (4) intellectual brightness; (5) sex differences in learning; (6) types of behavior problems and suggested teacher responses; (7) conferences; (8) home visits; and (9) test interpretation. The format in this second part consists of definitions, identification tools, suggested activities, etc. References are provided for those who wish to delve more deeply.

221. Guidance Associates. Guidance catalogue. Volume 11. Pleasantville, New York: Guidance Associates.

Catalog provides a listing of sound filmstrip programs available from this company. All sound filmstrips are in full color, with few exceptions. Filmstrips include such titles as: Job Attitude Series; Career Discoveries, Choosing Your Career, Job Hunting: Where to Begin, and so on. Filmstrips may be ordered on-approval for 30 days. Projectors and other equipment are also available.

222. Gutcher, D. G. Determination of occupational skill level. Research report. Fort Collins: Colorado Research Coordinating Unit, 1968. (ED 024 804)

Compendium of Abstracted Methods

The purpose of this study was to develop a measurement technique for determining skill levels required for various occupations for use in training, counseling, job placement, and measuring labor force quality. Measures related to income and educational levels of workers were selected. It was assumed that higher earnings reflected a higher skill requirement. Data were collected from census information and "The Dictionary of Occupational Titles." Only those mutually exclusive occupations were selected which contained 50,000 workers in a 1960 census and which were clearly defined in "The Dictionary of Occupational Titles." Some of the information collected included: general educational development, specific vocational preparation, aptitude, interest, temperament, physical demands, percent of workers with less than a high school education, percent of workers with 4 years or more of college, median school years by worker in each occupation, median income by worker in each occupation, and median wage and salary. Intercorrelations were obtained and a model for use of canonical correlations with multiple criteria and predictors was developed. Variables were assigned to groups arbitrarily in the model. A list of the references and occupations selected is included.

223. Gutsch, K. U. & Logan, R. H. Newspapers as a means of disseminating occupational information. *Vocational Guidance Quarterly,* 1967, 15(3), 186–190.

This study was designed to explore: (1) the amount and type of occupational or career information currently being published through this medium; (2) the level of readability of this career information; and (3) the suitability of this information in terms of the NVGA criteria for evaluating career information.

224. Haettenschwiller, D. L. Counseling black college students in special programs. *Personnel and Guidance Journal,* 1971, 50(1), 29–35.

The black college student's encounter with special programs creates special counseling needs. In effect, the counselor's task is to assist the student to cope with institutional demands and overcome the alienating effect of the impersonal, white, middle class institution by establishing a unique relationship with the student at a critical moment through an outreach approach. Subsequently, the counselor will also be called upon to assist the student in the resolution of an identity crisis. White counselors are not disqualified, but they may need to modify their style of counseling.

225. Hale, R. N. Teaching the talented. Slippery Rock, Pa.: Slippery Rock State College, 1964. (ED 001 314)

The 1964 Workshop on the Academically Talented at Slippery Rock State College was given graduate credit. The participants of the session wrote articles on the proceedings that were compiled into a booklet to help administrators and teachers develop educational programs for the gifted.

One of the areas discussed was identification. Some of the criteria suggested included group tests, individual intelligence tests, peer and teacher recommendation, achievement tests, reading readiness, and aptitude tests. Another area, creativity, involved four steps—awareness or sensitivity to an area of knowledge, organization of information, illumination or development, and evaluating and setting of new goals. In regard to counseling and guidance, the roles of the teacher and parent should be dealt with as well as that of the pupil. Administration of programs included segregation, partial segregation, acceleration, and enrichment.

Two programs described were The Colfax Plan and The Cleveland Major Works Classes. The Colfax Plan placed gifted children in workshops for half a day after attending heterogeneous homerooms. The Cleveland Major Works Classes segregated gifted pupils for everything except such activities as physical education, orchestra, and clubs.

Suggestions for teaching creative writing and drama, language, mathematics, reading and English, science, and social studies were given.

226. Hall, L. G. An occupational orientation inventory. A preliminary investigation. *Dissertation Abstracts,* 1967, 27(12A), 4126–4127.

The purpose of this study was to design, construct and refine an occupational orientation inventory which would include and incorporate those characteristics common to most jobs. It was hoped that such an instrument would provide youth with a systematic structure of information about job characteristics that would enable them to assess their implicit vocational values in terms of occupational characteristics and provide a guide from which the counselor could initiate and sustain occupational counseling.

227. Haller, A. O. (et al.) The occupational aspirational scale—theory, structure, and correlates of an instrument designed to measure differential levels of occupational aspiration, final report. East Lansing: Michigan State University, 1961. (ED 002 868)

A study was made to develop a quick and accurate method for measuring occupational aspirations, adding to known explanatory and predictive techniques concerning the occupational selection process. "Level of Occupational Aspiration" (LOA) was the conceptual focal point of this project. Subjects of the project, approximately 450 17-year-old boys, were tested using the "Occupational Aspiration Scale" (OAS). In addition, they were administered the following instruments— (1) "16 Personality Factor Test" (Form B), (2) Cattell's "Test of G-Culture Free," (3) "California Test of Personality," (4) "MSU Work-Beliefs Check-List," and (5) a questionnaire on educational and occupational aspirations, family background, and sociometric data. The OAS was also administered to approximately 110 junior and senior high school boys twice about 10 weeks apart to provide statistics for a test-retest reliability analysis. Results of these samples were then correlated, and evaluation techniques were employed for the OAS in terms of— (1) reliability and validity, (2) factorial structure, and (3) correlation with selected personality variables, parental social class status, ambition for youth, and level of occupational aspiration of a youth's best friends. It was found that OAS has a structure which does justice to the various elements of the LOA concept and has a design which makes it a practicable instrument for research and for counseling when evaluated specifically for this latter purpose. The most pressing unresolved problem of the OAS was that of its unknown prediction validity.

228. Hallworth, H. J. (et al.) A computer assisted vocational counseling system. Alberta, Canada: Faculty of Education, Calgary University, 1970. (ED 038 686)

The development of a counseling system designed for a small computer, although limited in both scope and objectives, appears to be practicable and economical. Described herein is a program intended to perform some of the functions performed by a counselor. It is merely a tool to be used by counselor, not a replacement for him. The program described applies to vocational counseling. Keeping data current is simplified by using a computer. The main object of such a program is to promote the decision making ability of the student by making information available to him, and by giving him the opportunity for vicarious experiences in making occupational choices. A total of three precise tasks in the design of this exploration system are indicated: (1) the development of interest categories; (2) the development of categories of educational aspirations; and (3) the classification of a given set of occupations in terms of the specified interest and educational categories. The system may then be used by students or counselors in any of three modes: (1) exploration, (2) index, or (3) guidance. This program has been implemented on a DEC TSS-8 system, for reasons described in another paper. It is being used in the Faculty of Education, The University of Calgary.

229. Hamburger, M. The significance of work experience in adolescent development. Washington, D.C.: Office of Education, Division of Adult and Vocational Research. (ED 019 403)

Research evidence on the efficiency of work experience as educational or therapeutic is lacking. It is the connection, the relationship, or the fact of life which gives the experience meaning, not the task which has inherent meaning. Coordinators and job supervisors need to receive special training.

230. Hamilton, J. A., and Jones, G. B. Individualizing educational and vocational guidance designing a prototype program. *Vocational Guidance Quarterly*, 1971, 19(4), 293–299.

A primary aim of individualized career guidance programs should be to assist each student to formulate educational and vocational goals that will serve to

Compendium of Abstracted Methods 275

direct his performance both within and outside the school environment. To select (and to manage his progress toward achieving) both immediate and long-range goals, each student must have specific and accurate information obtained from reliable sources to help him relate his own personal characteristics to the wide variety of educational and vocational opportunities.

231. Hamilton, J. A. & Jones, G. B. Integrating and evaluating career information in a developmental guidance program. Palo Alto, Cal.: American Institute for Research in Behavioral Sciences, 1970. (ED 039 587)

Three specific student needs are initially discussed: (1) the need to assess personal abilities, aptitudes, interests, job and college characteristic preferences, and physical and social characteristics (2) the need to acquire information about educational and occupational alternatives; and (3) the need to learn and apply a strategy for processing this information into personal goals, plans, and actions. Throughout the program, students are seen as problem-solvers, partners in the process of education. The Developmental Guidance Program presented in this paper was designed to facilitate the student in this role of exploration and the formation of tentative decisions about long range educational and occupational goals. The program, however, is only prototypical and intended to stimulate the design of a broad program of educational and vocational information to meet student career needs. Evaluation instruments designed to assess the success of such programs were mentioned and the need for further evaluative procedures stressed.

232. Hamilton, J. A. & Webster, W. J. Occupational information as an integral strand in the PLAN social studies curriculum. Washington, D.C.: American Institutes for Research, 1970. (ED 038 666)

Project PLAN, a system of individualized education designed to adapt the curriculum to the specific needs of each student, has as one of its principal objectives the assistance of young people in exploring and reaching tentative decisions about long range occupational goals. PLAN charges each student with the responsibility for formulating his personal goals, for making decisions and plans with respect to his educational development, and for the management of his learning in such a manner that his goals will be achieved. Through the economics strand in the social studies curriculum, PLAN provides students with a broad program of occupational education. The program consists of approximately 30 individualized learning units distributed across all levels of instruction. The primary level is the introduction to work, the intermediate covers practice in decision making, the secondary level concentrates on exploration and making specific post high school plans.

233. Hamilton, J. A. Video group social models, group stimulus materials and client characteristics in vocational counseling: an experimental study. Washington, D.C.: American Educational Research Association, 1969. (ED 028 475)

Eleventh grade male students participated in this study designed to promote career information-seeking and information-processing behavior. Three experimental treatments were administered: (1) structured group stimulus materials, (2) group social modeling, and (3) group social modeling combined with discussion. Three control procedures were employed: (1) insight group counseling, (2) wait control, and (3) no-interest control. Planned stimulus materials were used in four group counseling sessions. Four video presented group social models were used in four sessions. This sequence and content was followed in the modeling-discussion treatment. Group social-modeling and modeling-discussion treatments were found to promote significantly more knowledge of and ability to stimulate career decision-making at one school. Structured stimulus materials and modeling-discussion were found to stimulate significantly more subject performance of actual career decision-making behaviors at a secondary school.

234. Hamilton, J. B. Youth with special needs in non-metropolitan Ohio high schools. 1967. (ED 023 897)

To determine characteristics of students and aspects of vocational education programs essential to the serving of youth with special needs in rural Ohio high schools, 154 ninth grade youths with special needs were compared with 169 other ninth grade students. Analysis of variance and coefficient of correlation "t" test and chi square were used to establish significant differences and to examine relationships. Some findings were: (1) One of seven ninth grade students in rural Ohio high schools was considered to have special educational needs, (2) Boys identified as disadvantaged outnumbered girls by a ratio of three to two, (3) The greatest numbers of students were considered to be intellectually handicapped, educationally deprived, economically deprived and socially disadvantaged, (4) Very few students were considered to be ethnically disadvantaged or physically handicapped, (5) Youth with special needs were found to have larger families, more broken homes, and lower education and occupational levels of parents. (6) Youth with special needs had lower grades, high rates of absence, lower reading levels, lower intelligence test scores, and lower educational and occupational aspirations, and (7) No significant differences were found in terms of race, place or origin, or whether or not the mother worked outside the home.

235. Hansen, J. & Cramer, S. Group guidance and counseling in the schools. New York: Appleton Century Crofts, 1970.

This book provides a perspective of group guidance and counseling in the school setting as well as practical applications for working with groups.

236. Hansen, L. S. (et al.) Career guidance practices in school and community. Ann Arbor, Mich.: ERIC Clearinghouse on Counseling and Personnel Services, 1970. (ED 037 595)

This monograph is designed to determine what is being done in the nation's schools in the area of career guidance. From a survey of state departments of education, professional journals, research reports, colleges and universities, conference reports, vocational guidance specialists, and individual school systems; an attempt has been made to select proven programs and techniques related to the school curriculum. The monograph is organized into six chapters. Chapter One summarizes principles and trends of career development. Chapter Two describes current practices and programs. Chapter Three presents school community projects. Chapter Four discusses computer oriented systems. Chapter Five concerns guidance and vocational education and examples of programs. Chapter Six presents issues and challenges for the future. Included are chapter summaries, supplementary references and a subject index.

237. Hansen, L. S. Description of an emerging developmental career guidance program at Marshall-University High School utilizing volunteer paraprofessionals. Minneapolis: University of Minnesota.

Program utilizes volunteers who undergo an intensive training program. They learn about such areas as the counseling and guidance functions, scope and range of volunteer's duties, goals of the career information program and resources and media available to students in their planning and decision-making. Trained volunteers then staff the Career Resource Center as guidance assistants. They make educational-occupational-personal-social information available, and work with counselors, students and teachers in developing programs and organizing tours and visits to sources of direct occupational information.

238. Hansen, L. A learning opportunities package. Minneapolis, Minn.: Department of Counseling and Student Personnel Psychology, 1970.

The Learning Opportunities Package is a collection of some 29 individual packages on various topics ranging from "Life Style and Work" and "Self Concept Exploration" to "Planning an Education" and "Vocationally Relevant Behavior" all designed to become part of a career development curriculum.

Each individual topic package provides instructions and guidelines for teachers, to help them initiate and organize activities and learning experiences which will be useful for students' growth and development in the area of career choice and occupational participation.

239. Harding, F. D. What can happen when there are enough coun-

selors. One approach at a two-year technical institute. Washington, D.C.: Washington Technical Institute, 1969. (ED 031 761)

Washington Technical Institute (WTI) presents an opportunity to structure a two-year technical education program which will effectively serve the needs of an urban population. The guiding philosophy of the school is that it be student centered with learning objectives stated in measurable behavioral terms. The school is staffed with one instructor to every 16 students and one counselor to every 40 students. To emphasize the developmental aspects of the educational efforts, counselors are called development advisors. The development advisors have three facets to their job: (1) aiding the vocational or career development of their advisees, (2) facilitating the learning activities that their advisees are undergoing, and (3) providing necessary supportive counseling in the emotional and psychological areas. Students are encouraged to work part time at a job that has some relevance to their program. The development advisor assists students in getting these jobs. The development advisor is also responsible for: (1) understanding his advisee and his background in relation to the learning aspects of his program, (2) assessing progress so that goals are reasonable, and (3) helping the student to assess his own progress. No statistics are available now, but plans are to develop evaluative techniques for this program at WTI.

240. Harkness Center. Multi-occupations at Harkness Center. Progress report number 1. Buffalo: HC, Board of Cooperative Education Services, 1968. (ED 021 289)

The Multi-Occupations Program was developed to help the general high-school student to explore vocational areas. The program included seven exploratory vocational offerings, remedial reading, extensive counseling, and a teacher workshop. This progress report deals with program and scheduling procedures, materials covered in the teacher workshop, group counseling, current status of remediation work, and progress being made on the development of instructional aids for use with multi-occupations classes.

241. Harris, J. Computerized vocational information system project. Villa Park, Ill.: Willowbrook High School. (ED 019 840)

A computer based storage and retrieval system has been developed for use with vocational testing and occupational descriptive data, by high school students. Occupations are classified by level of training and categories of interest, compared with student, class rank, composite, test battery, and preference scores. The system provides for student-computer conversations in locating occupational data. Student, counseling, and research benefits are described. Hardware, data, content, and research information are briefly indicated.

242. Harvard University. Annual report. Information system for vocational decisions; June 1, 1967 to May 31, 1968. Cambridge: HU, Graduate School of Education; New England Education Data Systems; West Newton: Newton Public Schools, 1968. (ED 031 928)

The Information System for Vocational Decisions (ISVD) helps a person make decisions in choosing a vocation by collecting and processing data which include the following areas of information: college, career, military service, family, and the user's responses. It is vital that the machine be made to understand English— the natural language of the user. Of the several computer programs that are designed to do this, ELIZA met the needs of this system. By "recognizing" key words and "decomposing" what the user says, it can analyze the sentence and thereby understand it. It is the user that makes the decision, not the machine. The machine relentlessly displays all the relevant facts (as far as is possible) so that the user is guided to consider them in his decision making, even if it means doubting a preconceived purpose. The user is provided with opportunities to analyze and harmonize disconnected sections in his vocational development. The ISVD data are somewhat like ERIC abstracts. There is a full report of the Harvard Project, and five appendices provide information relevant to the project.

243. Harvard University. The world across the street. Cambridge, Mass.: HU, 1966. (ED 018 452)

This article consists of excerpts from taped interviews with two groups of five 14-year-old youths, one Negro and one white, who lived in different parts of the same public housing project and were not acquainted with each other. The interviews focused on the boys' educational and vocational aspirations. Then, without knowing the identity of the other group, each group of boys listened to recordings of the other's discussion and commented on their differing characteristics and expectations. As members of the dominant society, the white boys expressed greater certainty about their futures and the value of an education. The Negro youths were skeptical about their own school achievements and about the possibility of realizing their vocational goals, but they responded sympathetically and somewhat admiringly to the other group's confident self-presentations. The white boys reacted to the Negro youths' discussion by negatively stereotyping them. The article contains the comments of the interviewers on the discussions and on the psychological impact of membership in the black community. This article is a reprint from the "Harvard Graduate School of Education Association Bulletin," Volume 11, Number 2, Fall 1966, and is also available from the Publications Office, Longfellow Hall, Appian Way, Cambridge, Massachusetts 02138.

244. Hedges, J. N. Future jobs for high school girls. Washington, D.C.: Department of Labor, Womens Bureau, 1966. (ED 014 575)

Girls must prepare themselves for both marriage and a career. Statistics showed that a girl's chances of marrying were almost 10 out of 10 and of being engaged in paid employment were eight or nine out of 10. In 1966, about 27 million women were working in all occupations. This document explores occupational opportunities for girls beyond high school. It discusses (1) obtaining more education by utilizing low cost arrangements, scholarships, part-time jobs, and loan funds, (2) obtaining training and job experience, and (3) becoming a worker. Short descriptions including duties, aptitudes, educational or special training requirements, place of training, advancement opportunities, licensing requirements, and special related legislation are given for 44 specific occupations in the areas—health services, clerical occupations, retailing, food services, factory work, technical work in engineering and science, miscellaneous services and government careers. A list of publications giving further occupational information and a suggested form of application for specific jobs are included. This document is also available as GPO L13F9—7 for 30 cents from Superintendent of Documents, U.S. Government Printing Office, Washington, D.C. 20402

245. Heiner, H. G. (et al.) A forced-choice procedure for measurement of pupil's attitudes toward major dimensions of work, report number 3. (ED 010 654)

An instrument was developed and pilot tested for measuring occupational attitudes of secondary school students toward component dimensions of nonprofessional-level work involved in office, retail, health service, and construction vocations. The dimensions measured were tools, materials, nature of tasks, personal relationships, and physical environments. The instrument provided a means of confronting subjects with theoretically "total" work situations and measuring their preferences for "total" situations over reservations they would have about some dimensions. A total of 153 subjects from the seventh, eighth, and ninth grades were used for testing. A reliability measure for the student tests was obtained by using the instrument to interview 20 adults with several years of work experience. Test results indicated the instrument's potential counseling suitability for helping students better analyze and understand their occupational interests. The authors suggested that the instrument might also be useful in determining the ways which vocational attitudes of individuals and groups are influenced by socioeconomic status, age, and sex differences. Plans for further validation and standardization were recommended. This volume represents part 3 of the 13-part final report on the vocational-technical education research and development project of Washington State University. Related volumes are ED 010 652 through ED 010 664.

246. Helm, C. Computer simulation techniques for research on guidance problems. *Personnel and Guidance Journal,* 1967, 46, 47–52.

The possibilities of the use of a computer to facilitate the clarification and testing of counseling theory is discussed. Test interpretations by a psychologist and by a computer are presented.

247. Herr, E. L. Guidance of the college bound: problems, practices, perspectives. New York: Appleton-Century Crofts, 1969.

The text offers the counselor research-based aids for helping young people choose realistically among academic alternatives in light of their personal characteristics.

248. Herr, E. L. Review and synthesis of foundations for career education. Columbus: Ohio State University, Center for Vocational and Technical Education, 1972. (ED 059 402)

To identify conceptual elements and trends leading to career education so that assumptions which the term represents are clear to program developers and decision-makers, an analysis was made of available historical, philosophical, conceptual, and theoretical literature. The analysis offers substantiation that the antecedents of career education reside in both vocational education and guidance, and that the term "career education," so far as it is presently articulated, does have significant support from these knowledge domains. During the past century, much of the support for the antecedents to career education has come from the needs of a labor market changing from an agricultural to a technical character. A review of existing projects reveals that only a few meet the levels of integration, synthesis, or longitude now expected of career education. There has been more emphasis on career programs at the elementary and junior high levels than at the senior high school level or beyond. The evolution of career development theories has stimulated programs of a prevocational character placed earlier in the life of children. Many research requirements are stimulated by career education, and these needs are listed.

249. Hershenson, D. B. Techniques for assisting life-stage vocational development. *Personnel and Guidance Journal,* 1968, 47(8), 776–780.

Since vocational development processes are not synonymous with psychopathology, the techniques for assisting vocational development must be conceptualized as distinct from psychotherapy. Two levels of assistance are suggested: facilitation (promoting normal development) and remediation (actively removing serious blocks to development. Utilizing the author's earlier formulation of five vocational development life stages, four transitions exist: (a) social amniotic to self-differentiation; (b) self-differentiation to competence; (c) competence to independence; and (d) independence to commitment. Procedures required for making these transitions involve, respectively: (a) determining the program; (b) information in-put; (c) information processing; and (d) information utilization. Techniques for assisting these procedures involve, respectively: (a) facilitation—life style analysis, remediation—environmental manipulation and psychotherapy; (b) facilitation—guidance, remediation—skill training; (c) for content—client-centered approach for process—training in decision-making; and (d) for intrapsychic difficulties—existential approaches, for situational difficulties—job matching. For c and d, facilitation and remediation differ in degree, not in kind.

250. High School District A. Pilot project—mobile vocational guidance services. Havre, Mont.: HSDA. (ES 002 070)

A mobile center will provide vocational guidance services to high school students in six counties. The mobile center will be scheduled to visit each high school in the six-county area for a designated number of days, prorated over the period of one school year on the basis of school enrollment. During each visit, the center's guidance counselor will organize students to visit the mobile center in small groups representing their various vocational interests. Each group of students will be exposed to generalized group counseling, including the utilization of 16mm film, slides, blackboard presentations, and other related methods. In addition, each student will have the opportunity to view 8mm single-concept film strip film, and transparency presentations related to his specific field. Students will also have the opportunity to view model displays, pamphlets, and brochures in a browsing situation. Finally, each student will have a chance to meet individually with the counselor to discuss matters of particular interest to him.

251. Hillinger, Yvonne M. When you go to work. A book for the needle trades. Trenton: New Jersey State Department of Education, Division of Vocational Education, 1968. (ED 026 508)

Instructional materials for student use were developed by the author and a state-level committee of teachers to be used in a vocational school for the deaf, slow learner, or near illiterate. The program was tested at the State School for the Deaf. The book presents the non-technical information that the students will need to have as employees. Unit topics are: (1) The Factory, (2) A Good Worker, (3) The Job, (4) Shop Mathematics, (5) Clothing for Women, and (6) Clothing for Men. Objectives are stated for each lesson. Boldly printed vocabulary lists, cartoons, drawings, assignments, as well as forms and facsimiles for employment, interviews, warnings, checks, social security applications, and time cards are distributed liberally throughout. The workbook type format contains answering space. Exemplary lesson topics are the production line, paycheck, work habits, grooming, first day on the job, time-piecework, and the yardstick.

252. Hillson, H. T. The demonstration guidance project, 1957–1962. Pilot program for higher horizons. New York: Board of Education of the City of New York. (ED 001 785)

Identification and stimulation were attempted for disadvantaged students whose deprivation would tend to keep their abilities from being recognized. It was hoped that the program would make it possible for many more such young people to go on to higher education.

A major program of cultural enrichment was planned for the project students and included such activities as visits to museums and libraries, attendance at concerts and the theater, and a trip to Washington, D.C. Because all students were aiming toward college, at least in theory, they were placed in academic courses at the beginning; every effort was made to meet their needs within this framework. To provide the most favorable learning conditions, students were grouped homogeneously in all major subject areas on the basis of test scores and school records. The heart of the guidance program was individual counseling. For students with complex and severe problems, clinical services under a psychologist and social worker were also available.

Based on the number of project students who received diplomas, those who went on to higher institutions, those who received top scholastic honors, and the favorable opinion of both students and teachers, the project was considered highly successful. Although the problem of dropouts and underachievers still existed, the project demonstrated that many underprivileged children with mediocre records can, under proper conditions, reach high academic levels.

253. Hilverda, E. & Slocum, W. L. Vocational guidance through the curriculum in a small rural school system. *Vocational Guidance Quarterly,* 1970, 19(1), 65–71.

Teachers and students in elementary and secondary grades participated in a broad program of vocational guidance; the rationale for the program is explained and its major features identified.

254. Hoeltzel, K. E. Evaluating short-term guidance programs through site visits. *Vocational Guidance Quarterly,* 1971, 20(1), 15–20.

One way practicing counselors have been able to update and improve their vocational guidance programs is through participation in short-term in-service seminars and workshops. Vocational guidance seminars have been offered in many areas of the country with program improvement and development as desired ends.

A primary question which needs to be answered is, "What actual guidance program changes are precipitated by these in-service seminars?" Granted, most seminars use some sort of post-session questionnaire which asks participants questions such as: "What did you like most about the workshop?," "What changes are needed in program format?," or "What changes did you make in your program as a result of the seminar?" Even though the latter asks for a listing of definite changes, there is no way to know whether the seminar was even indirectly related to any changes made. Often, rating scales accompany or substitute for the questionnaire. Participants are asked to rate such workshop aspects as facilities, materials, teaching staff, consultants, field trips, and program format.

In the spring of 1970, the writer surveyed guidance supervisors from State Departments of Education to ascertain how they evaluated any short-term guidance workshops or seminars in their states. Of the 44 replies, few state departments did any evaluation at all and those that did used methods similar to those described in the preceding paragraph.

255. Hoeltzel, K. E. (et al.) Papers presented at the workshop on the development of guidelines for planning career development programs K–12 in Ohio. Columbus: Ohio State Dept. of Education. (ED 053 313)

> The purpose of this workshop, held June 8, 1971, was to develop guidelines for planning career development programs for Grades K–12. Seven persons from various universities throughout the United States presented papers. The presenters, their positions, and their topics were: (1) Kenneth E. Hoeltzel, Assistant Professor of Education at State University of New York, "Change and Introduction of Career Development Innovations in the School," (2) Kenneth B. Hoyt, Professor of Education at the University of Maryland, "The World of Work: A Component in Career Development Programs," (3) Lorraine S. Hansen of the University of Minnesota, "Identifying, Organizing, and Using Resources in a Career Development Program," (4) George E. Leonard, Project Director at Wayne State University, "Career Guidance for Inner-City Youth in Action: The Developmental Career Guidance Project," (5) Harry N. Drier, Guidance Consultant for Wisconsin Public Schools, "Implementing Career Development Programs in Senior High Schools," (6) Juliet V. Miller, University of Michigan, "Career Guidance Methods," and (7) Robert L. Darcy, Colorado State University, "Introduction to the Economics Component."

256. Hoffnung, R. T. & Mills, R. B. Situational group counseling with disadvantaged youth. *Personnel and Guidance Journal,* 1970, 48(6), 458–464.

> Male adolescents in a job training program were provided 14 weeks of on-the-job Situational Group Counseling (SGC), supplementing casework. Interdisciplinary teams of leaders met with work-training crews for discussions. Trainees meeting twice weekly showed greater improvement in job performance and adjustment than others.

257. Hollis, J. W. & Hollis, L. U. Organizing for effective guidance. Chicago: SRA, College and Professional Publications, 1970.

> This book deals with the major considerations in organizing an efficient and effective guidance program to the needs of the individual community and school.

258. Hollis, J. W. & Hollis, L. U. Personalizing information processes: educational, occupational, and personal-social. New York: MacMillan Co., 1969.

> The authors have drawn from theories of both counseling and communications to construct a new and dynamic theory to assist counselors in obtaining, utilizing, and personalizing information.

259. Holt, F. D. Short course for counselors on vocational-technical training and opportunities. Athens: Georgia University, College of Education, 1965. (MP 000 019)

> A short-term training program to improve the effectiveness of school counselors was initiated.

260. Hoover, R. & Whitfield, E. A. Regional center for collection, synthesis and dissemination of career information for use by schools of San Diego County (developmental), July 1, 1966–June 30, 1967. San Diego, Cal.: San Diego City Board of Education, 1967. (ED 015 513)

> The provision of occupational information on microfilm aperture cards (VIEW) is valuable to both students and counselors. This system can increase the effectiveness of the school vocational guidance service because the materials are easy to read with current, well-organized information. Counselors perceive VIEW materials as an aid which saves time and increases the amount of information available.

The VIEW system attracts students, who had not used occupational information frequently, to the use of occupational files. Student reaction to the project is favorable. The VIEW system also increases interstaff participation. Activities of the career information center during the 1966-67 year have shown that—(1) a summer workshop for counselors which provides instruction in vocational guidance and experience in entry level occupations is valuable, (2) positive community reaction to the VIEW project and to a summer workshop exists, and (3) vocational training provided by the junior colleges is perceived by the students as necessary and valuable in their chosen career.

261. Hopfengardner, J. D. (Ed.) Sources of occupational information. Columbus: Ohio State Department of Education, 1966. (ED 020 398)

The 150 annotated references in this bibliography meet one or more of the objectives—(1) present sources of available occupational information, (2) identify materials presenting occupational information for students, counselors, and others involved in educational services, and (3) describe techniques for gathering, organizing, and using occupational information. All references have been recently published and are grouped according to the sources—(1) U.S. government publications, (2) state publications, (3) armed forces publications, (4) commercial publications, and (5) professional publications and periodicals. A list of popular periodicals which frequently contain articles about occupations or vocational choice, a list of organizations representing the occupations most frequently inquired about, and a list of local sources of occupational information are included. A subject and a title index are provided.

262. Hopke, W. E. A new look at occupational literature. *Vocational Guidance Quarterly,* 1966, 15(1), 18–25.

This discussion reviews some of the major developments in the field of occupational literature since 1950. It then examines a number of current developments and looks into the future of occupational literature as it may evolve during the next two decades.

263. Hoppock, R. How to conduct an occupational group conference with an alumnus. *Vocational Guidance Quarterly,* 1970, 18(4), 311–312.

A complete guide to conducting a group conference concerning occupational information.

264. Horyna, L. L. (et al.) Working, learning and career planning: a cooperative approach to human resource development. Greeley, Co.: Rocky Mountain Educational Laboratory, Inc., 1969. (ED 034 874)

As an approach to solving the problem of under-utilization of human resources, the Cooperative Career Planning (CCP) concept stresses the role of the public school system in the coordination of available educational resources with potential job-training work stations in a given community or geographic area. In this way the community could become a laboratory for learning experiences available to everyone, regardless of age or socioeconomic condition. This position paper presents a brief review of existing manpower programs and policies, proposed objectives and organizational structure of the CCP, a model for evaluation, and a selected bibliography. A related document is available as VT 009 940.

265. Hosford, R. E. Product or process-implications for decision-making. Paper presented at the American Psychological Association Convention, Washington, D.C., September 1967. (ED 014 111)

The importance of assisting students in the decision-making process is explored. Counselors assist students in learning how to make decisions. A decision should be evaluated in terms of the process used to arrive at it rather than in terms of the resulting choice. Knowledge of alternatives, possible outcomes, and the probability for success of each of the outcomes are necessary for scientific decision-making. New counseling procedures have been proposed and experimentally studied to promote this type of behavior. Model-reinforcement and reinforcement counseling have been shown to be effective in motivating students to seek and use information prior to making decisions. Results of several research studies utilizing such procedures are presented. Other studies using counseling techniques derived from research in learning have also proved effective in promoting good decision-making procedures. These techniques include verbal reinforcement, use of programmed booklets, and participation in simulated experiences. These techniques have also helped students gain skills necessary for meeting decision-making problems.

266. Houston vocational guidance project. *American Vocational Journal,* 1972, 4(4), 54–57.

Produced as a step by step "how-to" operation, the project was aimed at: (1) helping youth stay in school, (2) helping youth plan realistically for achieving occupational or post-high school training goals, and (3) helping youth make an easier and more positive transition from school to work. The program was developed within a school system. It centered primarily on the counseling sector for operations, and a viable plan was worked out for a counselor based program, with specific details about individual and group programs. In addition, an operations manual was developed in detail in curriculum and resource development, including utilization of external community resources and occupational resources.

267. Howell, K. M. Teaching vocational and citizenship education in social studies, final report. East Lansing: Michigan State University, 1967. (ED 022 022)

A pilot project was conducted to determine if there was evidence to support an experimental program for comparison with the current, conventional programs of 9th grade social studies in the East Lansing, Michigan schools. The experimental program was one in which students were introduced into the world of work and spheres of the citizen within the broad context of "man and society" by use of a comparative cultures approach. Forty-four students were subjected to the experimental program and 50 to the conventional program. Pre-post measures of attitudes considered basic to citizenship behavior and several other instruments were administered to both groups. Data indicated relevant attitudinal change for both experimental and conventional programs. Data from a social distance scale favored the experimental with respect to increased acceptance of racial and nationality groups. Tests of student self-concept of academic ability and self-identity indicated no differential effectiveness. Subjective student judgments indicated that the experimental program was more interesting. The results of the pilot study were considered sufficiently promising to warrant the recommendation that a more comprehensive study be initiated.

268. Hoyt, K. B. Pupil personnel service for the speciality oriented. *National Association of School Principals Bulletin,* 1968, 52, 66–75.

High school counselors and counselors in area vocational schools need to maintain a close relationship and serve as consultants for each other. Specific activities which encourage a good professional relationship are listed.

269. Hoyt, K. B. The speciality oriented student research program: a five year report. *The Vocational Guidance Quarterly,* 1968, 16(3), 169–176.

The program is aimed at the collection, analysis, and dissemination of new knowledge to allow counselors to perform better the guidance function with students headed toward trade, technical, or business school settings after high school. This summary refers readers to specific documents containing reports of analyses.

270. Hudak, V. M. & Butler, F. C. Development and evaluation of an experimental curriculum for the New Quincy (Mass.) vocational-

technical school, development and tryout of a junior high school student vocational plan, ninth quarterly technical report. Pittsburgh, Pa.: American Institutes for Research, 1967. (ED 024 767)

Significant characteristics of the guidance program are reviewed and materials developed, staff preparation, tryout procedures, and implementation and evaluation plans are described. To try out evaluation procedures, a random sample of 505 students in grades 7, 8, and 9 in six schools provided data for (1) measuring student choices relative to educational and vocational planning, the extent of student ability to make these choices, and the extent to which the student ability to make these choices, and the extent to which the student displayed positive attitudes relative to these choices, and (2) evaluating program activities in each grade. Four instruments were used to gather data: (1) a four-part Educational and Vocational Inventory, (2) Parent Information Questionnaire, (3) Indices of Choice Quality, and (4) Implementation Record for Guidance Activities. The results suggested that the program had considerable potential and that students would increase their capabilities to make appropriate educational and vocational decisions by completing the program. The appendixes include (1) outlines of the Student Vocational Plans, (2) samples of Activity Forms for student use, material from the "Counselor Handbook," a job description, a job chart, and occupational analysis chart, and a McBee card for occupational analysis, and (3) the instruments used in this phase of the program. Other reports are available as VT 001 392–001 397 and ED 013 318.

271. Huff, E. E. (et al.) Dropout follow-up: a report of a summer project in guidance. South Bend, Ind.: South Bend Community School Corporation, Guidance Department, 1964. (ED 001 732)

With six persons to staff the summer camp, the following objectives were set: 1. to gain additional information about dropouts; 2. to provide counseling services for students no longer in contact with the school: 3. to provide educational and occupational information for dropouts: 4. to provide a liaison between the dropout, the school, and the community; 5. to encourage further education of dropouts; and 6. to gain information to help identify potential dropouts. A job counseling center was established, and the staff developed an occupational-educational information library. In counseling the dropouts the approach was that of trying to provide the student with a better understanding of himself and the world around him. 70% out of 121 actually interviewed responded to counseling sessions. It was discovered that family attitude contributed to the student's dropping out. The majority of dropouts are academic dropouts long before they actually drop out physically. Help for dropouts must be provided by the school. A look at the total group of 225 boys showed that 104 were no longer in the community. Of the boys counseled 15 made arrangements to go back to a full-time school program and 13 to complete their high school programs.

A handbook on employment and educational assistance for out-of-school youth is given, designed to help the dropout. It shows how and where to look for a job, and was given to all students.

272. Iadipaoli, M. V. Projects for group guidance. New Brunswick, N.J.: Rutgers, The State University, 1965. (ED 012 789)

The purpose of this resource unit is to aid guidance functions of the homeroom and planned group guidance program. The ultimate objective is to help the student to understand himself by focusing in group situations on problems common to teenagers and then to seek additional counseling when necessary. It was developed by the Guidance Department at the Essex County Vocational-Technical High School in New Jersey. Units are—(1) Educational Guidance, (2) Personal Guidance, (3) Social Guidance, (4) Vocational Guidance, and (5) Civic Guidance. The organization of each project includes objectives, an outline of information, suggested procedures and activities, and some resources for the teacher and the student. The material is for use by certified teachers with any high school homeroom group, especially those in a vocational program. A general outline for the course and teacher references are included. This document is also available from the Vocational-Technical Curriculum Laboratory, Rutgers University, 10 Seminary Place, New Brunswick, New Jersey 08903, for $2.00.

273. Impellitteri, J. T. The computer as an aid to instruction and guidance in the school. Ithaca: State University of New York, 1967. (ED 020 529)

Compendium of Abstracted Methods

Computer applications in education are discussed in terms of (1) a description of Computer-Assisted Instruction (CAI) and counseling, (2) the number and types of computer-assisted developments, (3) the nature of the Penn State University program, (4) tentative results of experimentation using CAI, and (5) implications and projections for the future.

274. Impellitteri, J. T. Exploration with a computer assisted occupational information system. *Educational Technology,* 1969, 9(3), 37–38.

Exploration describes a system whose purpose is threefold: to provide easily updated individualized occupational information retrieval; to develop an approach whereby youth could develop their own individualized frameworks of occupational structure; and to provide experiences for youth to acquire operational strategies in relating abilities and interests to occupational opportunities.

275. Impellitteri, J. T. The development and evaluation of a pilot computer-assisted occupational guidance program. Final report and appendices A–E. University Park: Pennsylvania State University, Vocational Education Department, 1968. (ED 029 095)

The purpose of this system is three fold: (1) to provide an easily updated individualized occupational information retrieval system, (2) to develop a process whereby youth can develop an individualized framework of the occupational structures, and (3) to provide an experience for youth to acquire operational opportunities by simulated practice. When a student working at a computer terminal requests information on a specific occupation, four operations are activated in the following order: (1) discrepancies which may exist between the student's ability-preference profile and the requirements for the particular occupation are typed out, (2) a 2-minute taped interview with a worker in the occupation is played, (3) an image is projected on the slide projector screen depicting the worker undertaking four typical tasks in the occupation, and (4) a 150- to 200-word description of the occupation is typed out for the student to read and to keep for later use. Appendixes include computer printouts of job descriptions for 80 occupations, types of student preference items, and taped interviews with workers. Also included are a bibliography of sources of occupational information, selected dissemination papers, and instruments developed during the course of the project.

276. Implementing an occupational and exploratory program related to the world of work in the modern junior high school. (ES 002 580)

A model program providing occupational and exploratory experiences and information related to the world of work will be established at the junior high school level. The instructional program will incorporate the latest technological advances in all areas with special emphasis on industrial arts and homemaking. All areas of the junior high school program, with assistance from the guidance department, will provide educational and occupational information to assist students in planning a realistic high school program of studies. The on-the-job work experience program will be a cooperative effort with all segments of the work community, and will function concurrently with the school instructional program. Approximately 58,057 students, grades 7–9, will be served. For further information, contact Connell Ward, 1309 Ferry Street S.E., Salem, Oregon 97310. (503) 585-6166.

277. Independent School District Number 742. Evaluation of a comprehensive planning unit for development of an educational and occupational planning program for out-of-school youth. St. Cloud, Minn.: ISD, 1967. (ED 027 586)

The primary purposes of this project were to provide data for developing operational proposals and programs for dealing with the dropout problem. Information and statistics were gathered about school dropouts in St. Cloud, Minnesota; age and grade, type of student, current functioning and future plans, expressed reasons for leaving, etiological factors, agency information and attitudes, and committee recommendations. Following each section of data and interpretation are recommendations relevant to that information. Recommendations include: (1) the need for more parental involvement and for continuing curriculum and grade study; (2) the importance of reading problems, (3) broadening the function of the guidance program and counseling services, (4) part-time programs, and (5) inter-agency involvement. The direct service aspect of the program is also discussed.

278. Indiana Research and Development Coordinating Unit for Vocational and Technical Education. Vocational guidance seminar. A report of a summer project for administrators, counselors, and teachers. Terre Haute: IRDCUVTE, 1968. (ED 029 972)

Four regional workshops in vocational guidance were designed to inform and update school counselors, teachers, and administrators concerning the working conditions, requirements, and opportunities in business, industry and the service occupations for certain industrial areas in Indiana, namely Evansville, Hammond, New Albany, and Wabash. Each seminar consisted of a 3-week intensive course in which businesses, industries, and various services were visited and discussions were held with management, personnel directors, and on-the-job personnel. The specific objectives included: (1) to help counselors more fully understand the relationship between the school curriculum and vocational opportunities in the community, (2) to acquaint counselors with occupational information materials, the sources and effective utilization of such materials, and (3) to prepare school counselors to relate understandings of vocational offerings and vocational opportunities to students—thereby providing sound vocational counseling.

279. Institute for Educational Development. Industry and education, study no. 2/partnerships: "partnership" high schools: the search for new ways to cooperate. New York: IED, 1969. (ED 038 534)

A new phenomenon in American education is the working relationship of "high school partnerships." These commitments between a corporation and an urban school pledge cooperation over a period of years in an organized group of projects intended to improve education and benefit the students. To determine the problems, risks, and potentials of high school partnership programs, representatives of 10 partnership programs were interviewed and completed questionnaires. Although it is too soon to expect conclusive evaluation of the partnership programs, some patterns have emerged which should prove valuable to future associations. This report covers: (1) history of the cooperative school, (2) what partnerships are, (3) what happens to a partnership, (4) how to start a partnership, (5) evaluation of programs, and (6) some preliminary conclusions. A summary of projects in 30 partnerships, catalog of companies and schools, a company's agreement, a partnership plan, methods of study, an interview guide, and a sample questionnaire are appended.

280. Institute for Educational Development. "Partnership" high schools: the search for new ways to cooperate. Industry and education, study no. 2/partnerships. New York: IED, 1969. (ED 039 273)

Industry-school partnerships are needed to help students, especially urban youth, become acquainted with the realities of preparing for employment and with the processes of finding a job, staying employed, and moving on through training to improved productivity and earning power. This report suggests considerations for organizing such partnerships and also presents estimates on costs and risks of such enterprises. Summaries of some of the important projects now underway are included. These projects cover work study, job placement and career guidance, basic skills training and remedial education, curriculum development and evaluation, administrative services, community relations, health services—with an emphasis on drug problems, interactions between school and business personnel, and material and financial resources. An index of alliances between companies and schools, a Chrysler Corporation proposal, and a New York City High School proposal for partnership plans are appended.

281. Interactive computer system will help students make career decisions. *Vocational Guidance Quarterly,* 1971, 20(1), 61–62.

A community college vocational guidance office may have hundreds of books and pamphlets of occupational information and a counselor who, if he is lucky, has to serve not more than 300 students. If a student has a small number of possible careers in mind, he can make good use of this service in the short time that is available, but what about a student who has only vague ideas of what he wants to do? How can he explore possibilities that are in line with his values, interests, and abilities to a point where the counselor and the books can help him most efficiently?

This is a problem on which a computer can help, and in a way that is the very opposite of the stereotype of feeding in test scores and getting back a prescription. Instead, Martin Katz and his associates at Educational Testing Service (ETS) are developing a "System of Interactive Guidance and Information" (SIGI) that actually teaches the student how to think about vocational choices rationally and systematically. Although the system is still far from operational, both the hardware and the software have developed far enough to show how it will work.

282. Isaacson, L. E. Career information in counseling and teaching. Boston: Allyn and Bacon, 1970.

This text is intended for the guidance and counseling major who has finished an introductory course in the area. The author highlights the broad relationships which exist between the individual and the world of work.

283. Ivey, A. E. & Morrill, W. H. Career process: a new concept for behavior. *Personnel and Guidance Journal,* 1968, 46, 644–649.

Vocational guidance has been traditionally too concerned with helping individuals choose an occupation. There is need for more awareness of change in vocational life. The concept "career process" stresses the continual changes and the varied developmental tasks in occupational life.

284. Jackson, J. S., Jr. (et al.) Evaluation of the career development laboratory Sayre Junior High School. Philadelphia, Pa.: Office of Research and Evaluation, Philadelphia School District, 1969. (ED 035 942)

The Career Development Laboratory is a program of vocational orientation for junior high school students which was conducted at Sayre Junior High School, Philadelphia. To determine the program's success three instruments were administered: a Career Plan Survey showing students' present career plans and their present knowledge about the career, a Career Information Survey indicating students' information about careers in the six major career areas covered by this program, and a Semantic Differential to determine the program's effect on students' attitudes toward certain careers. Findings indicated: (1) no increase in knowledge of careers in which students were interested. (2) a significant increase in knowledge about certain aspects of the six major career areas, and (3) no significant attitude changes. Recommendations were made to place greater emphasis on concrete activities in planning by the staff. Also recommended was a reevaluation of the time spent in various activities in terms of program priorities and further evaluation of the program when its offerings have stabilized.

285. Jeffery, R. C. Development of a program to prepare delinquents. Disadvantaged youths and slow learners for vocational education. Washington, D.C.; Washington School of Psychiatry, 1967. (ED 019 498)

The social and educational rehabilitation of high school dropouts with delinquent records was attempted by reinforcing behavior associated with academic remediation, work preparation, and social conduct, of the 163 Negro youths who participated at some time during the program, only 42 were actively participating when the program terminated, and the range of participation for this latter group was from 16 weeks to 130 weeks. Subjects were enticed to the project by offers of food and refreshment and, once there, were offered a system of rewards, including money, for completing educational and occupational tasks. Weekly earnings ranged up to $40 for successful participation in remedial programmed instruction ranging from third to 12th grade levels and classroom and work activities. academic progress was achieved in Mathematics, English, Social Studies, Science, and Reading and 13 of 22 participants who took the general educational development test passed, thus being certified as high school graduates. Work crews of eight to 10 participants were supervised in refurbishing slum housing as general work preparation. A recreation program for students was a total failure. There was little success in efforts toward employment or job training, and there was no evidence that the antisocial or delinquent behavior of the group was diminished to any significant extent. The participants were primarily interested in "beating the system." It was concluded that delinquency, under-education, and unemployment are related to each other and to other variables in such a way that a change in one variable will not necessarily produce a change in others.

286. Jeffs, G. A. (et al.) Group counseling and personal development. Las Vegas: Edward W. Clark High School, 1968. (ED 024 096)

Some 23 11th-grade underachievers were exposed to group counseling sessions once each week for a period of about eight months during the 1967-68 academic year. The purpose of the investigation was to determine if group counseling could produce changes among underachievers in motivation toward school, acceptance of self, and realism of occupational and educational aspirations. No significant difference in academic motivation scores between the counseled and noncounseled groups was found. The results of this investigation revealed that the counseled group made a significant change in mean self-acceptance score when compared to the gain made in self-acceptance by the noncounseled group. The counseled group at the termination of the program was selecting educational and occupational goals more in accord with their potential or more realistically, while the reverse was true of the noncounseled group. It may be concluded that group counseling might well promote more positive student acceptance of self as well as greater realism in occupational and educational goal selection.

287. JOBS NOW Project. JOBS NOW project—second year. Final report for phase one. Chicago: Jobs Now Project, 1969. (ED 053 264)

This multifaceted, large-scale E and D project in Chicago is based on the much-emulated "hire now, train later" concept which has become a force in the Concentrated Employment Program. During the second year of operation, JOBS NOW was redesigned to become a four-component program, stressing brief (2 week) orientation for disadvantaged youth and heavy involvement and cooperation of private industry. An outline elaborates the methodology of contacting, involving, and developing capability on the part of business and industry so that movement from disadvantaged status to meaningful employment can be facilitated. Two sections of the report are handbooks on coaching and counseling. Statistical tables provide analysis and evaluation of enrollment, placement, test scores, enrollee profile, and industry involvement. Tables are shown correlating post-placement high support and job retention. Rather than a detailed diary of JOBS NOW, this report is a delineation of what the project personnel believe has been done to accomplish important goals and what they think others can do. The first year report is available in "Manpower Research," 1969, as MP 000 818.

288. Johnson, D. & Burham, R. Computer based guidance system. Rochester, N.Y.: City School District; Eastman-Kodak Co.

The Rochester system is a multimedia support system to improve educational and career exploration and planning. The system includes a computer-based index of career-planning information and an adjunct perceptual resources file in which career-planning information and materials are stored. The fully developed file will include books, periodicals, microfilms, movies, tapes, and slides. These materials will be available for independent use as well as for use within a system framework.

While a fully developed system will be appropriate for all Rochester secondary school students, the target population for the prototype is eighth-grade students. The system will include a large component of nonverbal materials and, therefore, will have special relevance for the disadvantaged. The system will facilitate role model identification among students by utilizing audio-visual materials showing real people performing a variety of major life roles.

289. Johnson, R. G. Difficulty level of simulated vocational problems in encouraging career exploration. *Dissertation Abstracts,* 1968, 28(4A), 4448A.

The majority of the studies related to vocational choice have provided counselors with many factors related to vocational choice but with very little that they can do to encourage young people to explore opportunities, broaden interests, and see the alternatives available. Recent research has demonstrated that procedures which provide young people with realistic though simulated occupational experiences do generate vocational interest and stimulate exploration. This present study attempted to determine the optimal difficulty level of the occupational problems for students with varying interests and ability levels.

290. Johnson, R. G. Job simulations to promote vocational interests. *Vocational Guidance Quarterly,* 1971, 20(1), 25–30.

Research studies directed by John Krumboltz at Stanford University have developed and tested a series of simulated job experience kits for stimulating interest in particular occupations and for increasing vocational exploration. These kits actively engage students in realistic though simulated problems typical of those encountered on the job by workers in occupations in which the students before the experimental procedures had no special interest. As a result of working on these simulated occupational problems, students demonstrated increased interest in the particular occupations. The simulated job experiences were found to be more interest-promoting than informational monographs in the same occupations.

The research reported here is a continuation of the above studies. In this study simulated problems in x-ray and medical laboratory technology were tested with a group of 9th and 11th grade girls to determine whether or not the simulations would generate interest in learning more about these two health service occupations. Of special interest in this research was whether or not simulated experiences in specific occupations would also motivate interest in learning more about occupations in general. Quite obviously if job simulations not only arouse interest in specific occupations as indicated in previous research but also stimulate interest in general vocational exploration, their value would be increased considerably.

291. Johnson, R. G. Simulated occupational problems in encouraging career exploration. Paper presented at the meeting of the American Personnel and Guidance Association, Detroit, April, 1968. (ED 021 284)

The present study attempted to determine the optimal difficulty level of some occupational problems for students with varying interests and ability levels. Some 288 high school boys were presented with simulated vocational problems in sales, medical laboratory technology, and x-ray technology. The criterion for a successful performance was set at three levels of difficulty. Each subject was assigned at random a problem in one occupation and at one of the three levels of difficulty. Subject variables were grade level, grade point average, and initial occupational interest as measured on the Holland Vocational Preference Inventory. Criterion measures of three types were taken: expressed interest in the occupation, scores on an information test covering the occupation simulated, and incidents of information seeking during the week following treatments. Analysis of variance was used to test the main effects and all interactions. Difficulty level was not found to produce differences on the measures used, but did significantly interact with initial vocational interest pattern. The simulated problems in each occupation did generate interest and exploration in that occupation. Most students reacted favorably to the experience.

292. Joint Council on Economic Education. Economics in the elementary school; who, what, where? A handbook for teachers. New York: JCEE; Minneapolis: Minneapolis Citizens Committee on Public Education, 1967. (ED 028 839)

Economic education is needed. Elementary school children should be taught the following concepts of economics: that economics is concerned with the problem of deciding how to make the best use of resources to satisfy human wants; that production and consumption are functions of any economic system; that in America competition in a market is the system whereby consumer and producer goods and services are allocated; that the federal government helps to regulate the system and participates in the allocation of goods and services through its spending; that economic growth depends on the quality and quantity of productive resources; that money is a medium of exchange, a measure for comparing all economic goods, and a store of value; that specialization leads to interdependency locally and internationally; and that other nations have the same basic economic considerations. The kindergarten should be concerned with the home and school; the first grade, with the home and neighborhood; the second grade, with the neighborhood; the third grade, with the city—past and present; the fourth grade, with the state; the fifth grade, with the nation; and the sixth grade, with the western hemisphere.

293. Joint District 8. Prevocational thrust in general education. Madison, Wis.: JD8. (ES 002 286)

Vocational development will be introduced into the general-education curriculum for high school students in an urban area. Emphasis will be placed upon integrating the study of occupations into the total educational program to make academic work more meaningful to terminal students. Occupational themes will be developed and incorporated into all academic courses for noncollege-bound youth, occupational materials will be used in all classes. Field trips into the business world will be arranged. Group and individual guidance will be offered to students to provide —(1) information about jobs and careers so that students can make wise decisions regarding their future, (2) assistance in determining types of jobs best suited to individual abilities and aptitudes, (3) awareness of the entry-level requirements of various industries, (4) training on the procedures to be followed in securing and maintaining employment, (5) training in human relations necessary for the world of work, and (6) understanding of the relationship of academic skills to future success in employment. Approximately 400 students, grades 10–12, will be served initially. For further information, contact Dr. Carl Waller, 545 West Dayton St., Madison, Wisconsin 53703. (608) 256-1911.

294. Jones, G. B. Handbook for enhanced individual learning program. Sunnyvale, Cal.: Fremont Union High School, Curriculum and Research Department, 1964. (ED 001 148)

The Fremont Union High School District's program's aims were to identify gifted students, encourage them toward maximum intellectual growth, challenge them by enriching their learning experiences, require of them more self-direction, and help them develop a growing understanding of their own capabilities and major interests.

Identification of the student should be by a score of 130 or above on an individual intelligence test and by a score at or above the 98th percentile on group intelligence or achievement tests. The program should be limited to 3% of the participating minors, by judgments of teachers and school administrators.

The role of the counselor was important because he initiated, organized, regulated, and sustained the program. He should keep record's for each child.

The types of state-identified programs included enrichment in the regular classroom, correspondence courses or special tutoring, and placement in advanced grades or classes. Also recognized were attendance in college classes and special counseling or instruction outside regular classes.

Certain procedures should be carried out for each student. He should give his consent and he should have a sponsoring committee. Also, individual case study records should be kept on him.

Some suggestions for specific activities in enhancing the individual learning program included special counseling, a teacher-student project, individual study, and student seminars. Also important were personal contacts, field trips, and special school facilities.

A bibliography and forms were included.

295. Jones, G. B. Using project TALENT to improve vocational guidance. Washington, D.C.: American Institutes for Research, 1968. (ED 034 242)

The problem of assisting students to consider vocational-educational opportunities is discussed. To meet the needs of prospective vocational education students, a guidance system must help them in educational and vocational planning; interest them in the exploration of training opportunities, and motivate them to seek information and pursue enrollment at the appropriate institutions. Since there are many negative attitudes (parents' and students') toward vocational education, it is recommended that parents become involved in the processes which are part of a vocational guidance system. Twelve possible components of a comprehensive vocational guidance system are outlined. It is stressed that in order to be comprehensive the system must complement the other activities of the educational program so that the total program attempts to meet all the needs of all the students. Examples which illustrate how the findings of Project TALENT can contribute to the improvement and development of a guidance system are also included.

296. Jones, G. B. & Krumboltz, J. D. Stimulating vocational exploration through film-mediated problems. *Journal of Counseling Psychology,* 1970, 17(2), 107–114.

Two-hundred-and-seventy subjects were randomly assigned to seven treatments within each of two schools in different socio-economic neighborhoods. Findings: (1) experimental treatments were more effective; (2) active participation generated more interest in banking occupations; (3) a precise decision favoring overt over covert responding in the active participation film versions cannot be made on many criteria.

297. Jones, G. B. & Nelson, D. E. Elements of a comprehensive guidance system integrated in the instructional process. Washington, D.C.: American Personnel and Guidance Association, 1969. (ED 033 398)

This study describes a current attempt to design a comprehensive guidance system which will be an integral part of a program of individualized education and which serves the needs of all students at each academic level. Preliminary investigation has led to tentative specification of 12 components comprising the guidance system, five involving indirect intervention on behalf of the students, and seven presenting guidance experiences directly through the instructional process. Basic objectives are to encourage problem solving behaviors among the students involved, and to create greater awareness of career information in order to enable students to make better decisions for their own futures. Programmatic research and development activities to assist individuals to acquire and perform behaviors which will result in their solving real-life problems wisely is also currently underway. The ultimate training program must specify behaviors included in solving real-life problems wisely, and reliable criterion measures for assessing students' abilities to perform these behaviors must be developed. Hopefully, findings from this research will point the way toward discovering a superior problem-solving training approach, including the cost in time and money for such a program in a school setting.

298. Jones, M. & Kandel, D. Work adjustment as a function of occupational therapy, study course V. New York: American Occupational Therapy Association, 1964. (ED 015 602)

Resulting from one of six 1-week study courses following the third international congress of the world federation of occupational therapists in 1962, this manual presents a broad review of the philosophy, role, and techniques of occupational therapy in the field of prevocational evaluation, vocational training, and sheltered workshops. Nineteen lectures by therapists from several countries describe occupational therapy programs related to work adjustment for the physically handicapped and for the former psychiatric patient, forms used in performance testing, photographs of skill testing and work situations, and a listing of appropriate films are included. A final lecture summarizes content of the study course. Some lectures cite references. This document is available from Wm. C. Brown Book Company, 135 South Locust Street, Dubuque, Iowa 52001, for $2.25.

299. Joseph, M. P. (et al.) Work Opportunity Center for Minneapolis, Minnesota. Twelfth quarterly technical report, 1 Feb. 1969–30 April 1969. Minneapolis, Minn.: Work Opportunity Center, 1969. (ED 035 005)

Skill training, related academic subjects, job orientation, counseling, and attitudinal modification are at the core of the Work Opportunity Center (WOC) program. All energies are focused on assisting each person as an individual deserving of every opportunity for success. Specific procedures to carry out this goal include personalized scheduling, motivational devices, and skill training. The methods and materials used are illustrated through the presentation of two case studies. The results of a WOC Student Follow-up Questionnaire are given. Data indicates that most participants felt that the WOC provided valuable experiences. The measurement and modification of attitudes as done in the WOC is discussed. Results of a study utilizing an adjective checklist are given. Seven areas of concern regarding student attitude are discussed: (1) need for clear goals, (2) social problems, (3) emotional problems, (4) specific personal needs, (5) classroom oriented needs, (6) school oriented needs, and (7) pace. The observations and procedures of the WOC in the areas above are listed. The report ends with plans for the following quarter. The research reported herein was funded under Title III of the Elementary and Secondary Education Act.

300. Joslin, L. E. (Ed.) Proceedings of the national seminar on vocational guidance in the preparation of counselors held at the University of Missouri in Columbia, August, 1967. (ED 024 826)

The major emphases of the seminar were: (1) programs and services needed to facilitate vocational development of youth and adults, (2) the preparation of personnel to staff these programs and provide these services, and (3) available and potential resources to enhance the vocational aspects of counseling and counselor education programs.

301. Kagan, N. Multimedia in guidance and counseling. *Personnel and Guidance Journal,* 1970, 49(3), 197–203.

The author describes his own research and use of affect simulation and videotape recall to accelerate the usual counseling processes and to better assure that traditional goals in counseling will be achieved. He examines the potential of multimedia for allowing a client to view objectively his own "inner" reactions as well as his "outer" behaviors to himself and his environment.

302. Kaiser, R. S. Educational and vocational guidance in a summer camp setting. *Vocational Guidance Quarterly,* 1967, 16,(1), 56–58.

There are many programs serving youth in age groups where career planning is a stated concern but where guidance services are typically not available. This study focuses on one of these youth serving programs: a summer camp. It is an attempt to determine the response of high school students to the addition of group guidance and individual counseling to a regular summer camp program. It represents a look at the practicality and effectiveness of having an agency counselor leave his office and conduct guidance activities in a camp environment.

303. Kaltsounis, G. L. (et al.) The national aptitude survey. Formal report and test manual. Ann Arbor: Michigan University, School of Education, 1968. (ED 018 835)

The National Aptitude Survey attempted to provide a high school guidance instrument to identify potential automotive repairmen.

304. Katz, J. (et al.) Educational and occupational aspirations of adult women. Report to the College Entrance Examination Board. Calif.: Stanford University, Inst. for Study of Human Problems, 1970. (ED 045 005)

The first chapter of this report, "Career and Autonomy in College Women," by Joseph Katz deals with the career choice of undergraduate women at San Jose City College and Stanford University. Chapter 2, "Adult Women at Work and at Home," by Joseph Katz, and Chapter 3, "Career-Oriented versus Home-Oriented Women," by Marjorie M. Lozoff, present data based on questionnaire responses from alumnae of Santa Rosa Junior College and Stanford University who were between 26 and 50 years old in 1968, from hour-by-hour diaries of two full days in the lives of 17 college educated adult women in the San Francisco Peninsula area, and from interviews with 27 of the women who had completed the questionnaires. Chapter 4, "Images of Women in Women's Magazines," by Peggy Comstock, presents a content analysis of a selected number of women's magazines in terms of the attitudes toward education, career, and home that are held or presumably held, by middle-class adult women. Chapter 5, "Selected Bibliography on Women: 1950–1969," by Peggy Comstock, presents a survey of an annotated bibliography of the literature on the educational and occupational situation of adult women. The questionnaire results, the questionnaire form, and the interview protocol are presented in the appendix.

Compendium of Abstracted Methods

305. Katz, M. A model of guidance for career decision-making. *Vocational Guidance Quarterly,* 1966, 15(1), 2–10.

This model of guidance for career decision making first assists the student in taking full cognizance of the range of values in the culture and encourages him to make his own values explicit. The next task is to convey appropriate information about the opportunity or strength of return inherent in each option. Then it is time to harness relevant predictive data and to show how these three systems can be combined in a rational process.

306. Kay, E. R. Vocational education: characteristics of teachers and students, 1969. Washington, D.C.: National Center for Educational Statistics (DHEW/OE), 1971. (ED 050 297)

Despite the long existence of vocational education in the school system, very little is known about the characteristics of the participants. Thus, this report presents the findings of a study of the characteristics of vocational education teachers and students. Information on the professional qualifications and teaching experiences of teachers is examined in relation to other characteristics and to the types of vocational education programs being taught. Information on students includes individual and family characteristics, program and labor force activity, and plans for the future. Among the findings of this report are: (1) the typical vocational education teacher is a male in his early 40's, (2) median earnings of vocational education teachers are approximately $8,700 for a contract year, and (3) there are slightly more female vocational students than male students. However, males outnumber females at the postsecondary level.

307. Kellogg, F. Computer-based job matching systems: an exploration of the state of the art and the proposed nationwide matching system. Washington, D.C.: Office of the Manpower Policy, Evaluation and Research, Department of Labor, 1967. (VT 007 083)

In its report to the President and the Congress, the National Commission on Technology, Automation, and Economic Progress recommended "... that a computerized nationwide service for matching men to jobs be established." Such a service was expected to improve and extend labor market information, and thereby help to reduce unemployment and underemployment. But even as the Commission advanced the proposal, companies, professional associations, and public organizations had started to design and operate a variety of computer-based "matching systems." In short, many systems, local and national in scope, were operating or in advanced stages of design. In the spring of 1966, the United States Employment Service awarded a contract to a consulting firm for help in designing a national system and in developing several operational pilot projects. Against this background a 2-day workshop was planned. It was intended to accomplish several purposes. First it would bring together people involved in the operation and design of a variety of different kinds of matching systems to describe what they were doing. Second, the workshop was planned to bring the "doers" in matching systems operation and design together with people from the academic community with backgrounds in manpower research—especially the operation and structure of both internal and external labor markets. This report is the product of the workshop.

308. Kemp, C. G. Foundations of group counseling. New York: McGraw-Hill, 1970.

Theories, techniques, and uses of group counseling are all presented in this book whose purpose is to describe the process, clarify the underlying theory, and present the purposes and skills necessary to make it effective.

309. Kemp, C. G. (Ed.) Perspectives on the group process: a foundation for counseling with groups. Boston: Houghton Mifflin, 1970.

This book offers an interdisciplinary approach, relevant to group counseling in many professions. Attention is paid to the biological, philosophical, and religious bases of human interaction, as well as to group dynamics and leadership.

310. Kendall, M. A trip to the Statler Hilton Hotel. The special education curriculum series. Marshfield, Mass.: Project Lighthouse, 1969. (ED 031 843)

A program designed for high school level work-study classes for students of limited mental ability presents specific curriculum methods and materials to teach information regarding positions available in the hotel industry. A field trip tour of the Boston Statler Hilton Hotel is the focal activity of the unit, and is accompanied by a history of the hotel industry, job descriptions and employee qualifications, activity sheets which test facts about the Statler Hilton, understanding the floor plan, and requirements and characteristics of the jobs. In addition to the content material and activity pages, the kit contains student booklets, teacher's manual, a brochure and 15 slides depicting the Statler Hilton, and a field trip permission slip.

311. Kersch, S. F. Personnel services review. Series 1: innovations in the training and supervision of counselors. Simulation gaming. Ann Arbor, Mich.: ERIC Clearinghouse on Counseling and Personnel Services, 1970. (ED 036 671)

This is one of a series which focuses on innovations in the training and supervision of counselors. It discusses simulation gaming by providing: (1) a definition of the procedure; (2) a description of models of practice; (3) a discussion of the effects of using simulation gaming; (4) suggestions for possible applications of the procedure; and (5) questions to consider when designing or using simulation gaming experiences. A bibliography is included.

312. Kilpatrick, G. Choosing an occupation wisely—a proposal to take the guesswork out of future vocational guidance. 1968. (ED 020 718)

A systems approach is proposed to assess the student's abilities and interests by a battery of tests. The profile of his test scores is compared mathematically for best fit with statistical renditions of profiles of job requirements as determined by the test scores of successful practitioners in many jobs.

313. Klaurens, M. K. Occupational experience and career development training for distributive educators and vocational counselors. Final report. Minneapolis, Minn.: College of Education, University of Minnesota, 1969. (ED 036 649)

A seminar program was held during the summer of 1968 at the University of Minnesota to improve the preparation of vocational counselors and distributive educators in helping students in career development and occupational adjustment. A total of 36 counselors and educators who had at least 1 year of experience were selected for the project. They participated in a variety of activities during the 6-week project which included human relations training, directed occupational experience at a local firm, lectures, seminars, and materials development in small groups. The participants evaluated the human relations training lab and the directed occupational experience as the most useful part of the program.

314. Klein, W. (et al.) New careers. A manual of organization and development. Washington, D.C.: University Research Corporation, Information Clearinghouse, 1968. (ED 025 471)

Based upon material drawn from experimental programs at Howard University Institute for Youth Studies (1964–67), this manual is intended for those wishing to train workers as nonprofessionals in the human services (health, education, mental health, recreation, child care, research, and community organization) and is designed to be used with SP 002 003, SP 002 034, SP 002 035, and other related curriculum manuals on specific occupational and skill areas. While the manual is predicated upon core-group training, i.e., all trainees receive a base of common generic training, the authors nonetheless recommend the manual, on the basis of its generic approach, for training programs not using the core-group model. Five major topics are covered: (1) the nonprofessional worker in human services; (2) job development; (3) qualifications, recruitment, and selection (trainee qualifications and the recruitment and selection processes); (4) training (training content, relationships with employing agencies, duration and completion of training, training guidelines, and training problems); and (5) research and program evaluation (the purposes and nature of evaluation, the duration of evaluative studies, and the research staff). Included is a 17-item bibliography.

315. Knaus, W. J. An experimental study of three methods of programmed vocational instruction presented to mentally retarded adolescent females. *Dissertation Abstracts,* 1967, 28(3), 965-A.

The investigation involved comparing three methods of presenting programmed vocational materials to mentally retarded adolescent females. The three methods were: (1) *automated method* refers to exclusive use of an automated teaching aid and programmed materials; (2) *integrated approach* refers to a method where the teacher used the teaching aid as an adjunct to a partially programmed lecture, discussion and demonstrations; (3) *sequence control* refers to a method which involved teachers using partially programmed lectures with discussions and demonstrations.

316. Korim, A. S. Government careers and the community college. Washington, D.C.: American Association of Junior Colleges, 1971. (ED 052 775)

This document is intended to serve as a planning tool for public service education, and is to be used jointly by community colleges and public agencies (local, state, and federal). With the growing need for well qualified personnel at mid-entry or paraprofessional levels, agencies are abandoning their internal training programs in favor of cooperative programs with community colleges. The training consists of in-service or pre-employment education, the latter composed of career categories either identical with the private employment sector or unique to the public sector. The basic public service career families are in: community development; educational, human, and judicial services; public finance; resource management; and transportation. Government programs in the Department of Housing and Urban Development or Department of H.E.W., for example, enable community colleges to be extensively involved in community affairs. Challenges to be considered are: identification of distinct career families; need for data; improvement of student services; faculty shortage; and hurdles in government hiring practices. Public service education is analyzed; examples of organization and administration of career education are offered. Suggested curriculum patterns are presented for air traffic controller, child care, corrections, fire science, law enforcement, recreation, teacher aide, traffic engineer, pollution, library technology, and urban planning technology.

317. Krumboltz, J. D. (et al.) Nonverbal factors in the effectiveness of models in counseling. *Journal of Counseling Psychology,* 1967, 14(5), 412–418.

The degree of model counselor attentiveness and prestige in increasing later Information-Seeking Behavior (ISB) was tested experimentally. 1 of 2 video taped interviews, in which the model counselor was either attentive or non-attentive, was presented to 56 female high school juniors in 7 schools. 4 treatment combinations were arranged by introducing each of the 2 interviews with a statement attributing either high or low prestige to the model counselor. Active and inactive control groups (n = 56 each) were randomly constituted. Exposure to the video taped model interviews produced more ISB than did either control procedure. Hypothesized differences attributable to levels of prestige and attentiveness were not found.

318. Krumboltz, J. D. & Schroeder, W. W. Promoting career planning through reinforcement. *Personnel and Guidance Journal,* 1965, 19–25.

54 11th grade volunteers for educational and vocational counseling were randomly assigned to three treatments: (a) reinforcement counseling (information-seeking responses reinforced), (b) model-reinforcement counseling (tape-recording of a male counselee played to each client prior to reinforcement counseling), and

(c) control. Findings: (a) Experimental groups engaged in more information-seeking behavior outside the interview (external ISB) than control; (b) Reinforcement counseling produced significantly more external ISB than control for females but not males; (c) Model-reinforcement counseling produced significantly more external ISB than control for males but not females; (d) The ratio of information-seeking responses to other responses in the interview was positively correlated with external ISB.

319. Krumboltz, J. D. (et al.) Vocational problem-solving experiences for stimulating career exploration and interest. Final report. Stanford: Stanford University, School of Education, 1967. (ED 015 517)

To motivate interest in career exploration, five sets of job simulation materials were developed and tested for accounting, x-ray technology, medical laboratory technology, sales, and banking. Each "career kit" presented problems representative of each occupation and the background information needed to guarantee that most subjects could solve them.

320. Krumboltz, J. D. (et al.) Vocational problem-solving experiences for stimulating career exploration and interest: phase II. Final report. Stanford, Cal.: Stanford University, School of Education, 1968. (ED 029 101)

This project was composed of two major research experiments and four subsidiary experiments, designed to test alternative ways of constructing and applying occupational problem-solving materials. In Part I, Difficulty Level of Simulated Vocational Problems in Encouraging Career Exploration, it was found that the difficulty level did significantly interact with initial occupational interest when knowledge of the occupations studied was used as a measure. Part II includes four subsidiary studies: (1) Simulated Work Experience: An Attempt To Encourage Career Exploration, (2) An Optimal Grade Level for Career Exploration?, (3) Vocational Information-Seeking Behavior as Affected by a Problem-Solving Work Kit and Set Establishment, and (4) Simulated Work Experience: How Realistic Should It Be? Results from Part III, Orienting Stimuli in Vocational Problem-Solving as Factors in Promoting Career Information Seeking, indicate that subjects who receive their first choices of vocational stimulation kits reported varied information-seeking activities more than did subjects who were denied their first choices. Also, subjects who receive specific questions comparing occupations achieved higher scores on occupational information tests than did subjects who received general questions.

321. Krumboltz, J. D. Vocational problem-solving experiences for stimulating career exploration and interest, phase II. Mid-project report, December 1, 1966–April 30, 1967. Stanford: Stanford University, School of Education, 1967. (ED 016 265)

New occupational career kits are designed to provide realistic occupational experiences in the fields of appliance repair, law enforcement work, and electronics. The two major experiments designed to test hypotheses about the optimal use of these kits are described.

322. Kunze, K. R. Overview of needs, programs and implementations of vocational counseling and guidance. Paper presented at the Regional Conference on Career Guidance, Counseling and Placement in Burbank, Calif., 1970. (ED 049 499)

The author begins by overviewing some recent criticisms of the vocational guidance field: (1) too little collaboration with industrial personnel; (2) an emphasis on processing masses of people rather than on the individual; and (3) the need for a systems approach to counseling. His impressions, from the vantage point of industry (i.e. the placement end of the vocational counseling sequence), suggest flaws in the educational-counseling system, resulting in inappropriate, inexperienced and unqualified job applicants. The differences between a counseling approach and the industrial personnel approach to job seekers/holders are enumerated. Trends and circumstances which may affect the infusion of counseling into industrial relations systems are discussed. The paper concludes with a consideration of "lifelong counseling" wherein adults would have vocational counseling throughout their work histories and even into retirement.

323. Landers, J. Higher horizons program. Brooklyn, N.Y.: Board of Education, 1961. (ED 001 757)

The Higher Horizons Program grew out of the Demonstration Guidance Projects, a six-year program to help prevent dropouts. Extension of the services to other junior high and elementary schools of various economic standing and to all students within these schools was planned. The program in 1960–61 involved 13 junior high schools and 52 elementary schools. The entire program was under the direction of the superintendent of schools and an advisory committee. A larger staff was required to provide curriculum assistants, subject area specialists and special teachers.

Objectives include: identifying and stimulating students' interests and abilities; helping students obtain better cultural experiences; helping children aspire to high goals in education and occupations; fostering greater teacher and parent participation and understanding; encouraging the community to provide assistance for education; developing better trained teachers, better techniques, better organization, and better guidance and counseling procedures.

324. Laramore, D. Jobs on film. *Vocational Guidance Quarterly,* 1968, 17(2), 87–89.

The author wrote, in the fall of 1966, a vocational education project aimed at utilizing both visual and audio effects of job interviews. The hypothesis, at this time, is that this is a more effective way of disseminating job information than written and taped materials which are presently in use. .

325. Laws, L. Elementary guide for career development grades 1–6, Austin, Texas: Education Service Center, Region XIII, 1970.

This study is designed to investigate the area of career guidance at the elementary level. The study further suggests and outlines a developmental program of career guidance which can be implemented within the existing framework of the school. Activities and materials for the program are designed to (a) promote the student's understanding of various vocations, (b) provide occupational information, (c) explore the world of work, and (d) assist the student in finding out about himself as part of the preparation for decision making. The study is confined to the elementary school, grades one through six. A central theme of "Careers of the Month" spotlights careers associated with various areas, of the curriculum, e.g., mathematics, science, health and physical education.

326. Leach, A. Syllabus for pre-vocational and vocational education programs for the disadvantaged. Monmouth: Oregon College of Education, 1966. (VT 004 184)

This extensive course outline is for teacher use in a course for adults or college students who plan to work with disadvantaged persons. It was developed by the author. The content objective is to present information about pre-vocational and vocational education programs.

327. Leachen, S. & Lipschitz, B. School service agency. *School Counselor,* 1970, 17(5), 370–371.

Describes school "employment" agency to secure school jobs for interested students. They filled out applications, had interviews and secured recommendations. Program attempted to relieve hall congestion and improve tone of school.

328. Lecznar, W. B. Vocational-technical education: new horizons. *Vocational Guidance Quarterly,* 1970, 18(4), 242–263.

The symposium reported is intended to give guidance counselors a view of present developments and trends in disciplines related to vocational counseling. Summarized are some innovations in curriculum, test development, application of research to curriculum development, and how a new technical institute in the inner city treated the vocational guidance program. A summary offers implications for secondary school guidance counselors.

329. Lee, E. R. & Walch, J. L. Career guide for demand occupations. Washington, D.C.: Department of Labor, Bureau of Employment Security, 1965. (ED 015 252)

This publication updates the "Career Guide for Demand Occupations" published in 1959 and provides counselors with information about occupations in demand in many areas which require preemployment training. It presents, in column form, the education and other training usually required by employers, high school subjects of particular pertinence to the occupation, special characteristics inherent in the job, and selected reference materials. Space is provided for adding local training and employment opportunities. The occupations, arranged by part IV of the dictionary of occupational titles classification structure, are translator, librarian, teacher, occupational therapist, economist, clinical psychologist, social and welfare workers, patrolman, mathematician, dental hygienist, dentist, registered nurse, physical therapist, physician, veterinarian, X-Ray technician, agronomist, bacteriologist, chemist, dietitian, entomologist, medical technologist, parasitologist, pharmacist, pharmacologist, soil scientist, metallurgist, physicist, accountant, statistician, meteorologist, professional engineer, production planner, city planner, programer, systems analyst, systems engineer, draftsman, general office clerk, clerk-typist, typist, secretary, stenographer, insurance salesman, central-office operator, airplane hostess, ward attendant, machinist, tool-and-die maker, engine-lathe operator, turret-lathe operator, milling-machine operator, millwright, airplane mechanic, automobile mechanic, electrician, electrical repairman, electronics mechanic, pipe fitter, plumber, carpenter, bricklayer, welder, instrument repairman, sheetmetal worker, dental technician, tailor, baker, and automobile-body repairman. An alphabetical index is included. This document is available as L7.25/3—C18/965 for 30 cents from superintendent of documents, U.S. Government Printing Office, Washington, D.C. 20402.

330. Lee, S. L. (et al.) High school senior girls and the world of work: occupational knowledge, attitudes and plans. Columbus: Ohio State University, 1971. (ED 047 155)

In an effort to provide educational planners and counselors with information related to the educational and vocational needs of girls, this study of the plans, aspirations, and work knowledge and attitudes of female high school seniors analyzes the effects of community size, type of school, and social status. A questionnaire was administered to 365 senior girls from six vocational, comprehensive, and general academic schools in Michigan, Kentucky, and Ohio. Questions were included on work attitudes, work knowledge, and personal and family characteristics. Analysis of variance and an intercorrelation matrix were used to determine interrelationships between variables. The results show that social status and community size have positive effects on knowledge and negative effects on plans for full time work. Vocational school girls showed more interest in financial rewards of work and in early marriage than did graduates of other types of schools. Recommendations for further research and for possible changes in educational programs are made. The findings of this study will be used to develop a curriculum unit, "Planning Ahead for the World of Work," designed to assist girls in preparing more adequately for their probable futures.

331. Lelevier, B., Jr. A portfolio of outstanding Americans of Mexican descent. 1970. (ED 045 245)

A cross section of Mexican American achievement is presented in a portfolio of 37 portraits of outstanding Americans of Mexican descent. Drawn in black and white on heavy paper stock by Mr. David L. Rodriguez, the sketches are suitable for display purposes. With the likenesses are biographical sketches in both English and Spanish which were researched by Mr. Benjamin Lelevier, Jr. through personal contact with the subjects. Among the subjects are Cesar Chavez, U.S. Senator Joseph M. Montoya, Dr. Julian Nava, George I. Sanchez, Lee Trevino, and Armando M. Rodriguez.

332. Le May, M. An inexpensive address file for occupational information. *Vocational Guidance Quarterly,* 1965, 14(1), 55.

The most popular (in our school) occupations were selected and typed one job name and the D.O.T. classification at the top of loose-leaf notebook paper. Addresses of recommended information sources for that job were then typed on the

Compendium of Abstracted Methods

page. These pages were then placed in a loose-leaf notebook in alphabetical order and an index was typed. In the index, each job was given a page number and the standard DOT classification.

333. Leonard, G. E. Developmental career guidance in action, the first year. Detroit: Wayne State University. (ED 013 465)

The Developmental Career Guidance in Action (DCGA) Project sought to: (1) broaden and raise the educational-occupational levels of aspiration of a selected group of Detroit inner-city public school students, (2) develop a pilot program to better meet their needs through emphasis on developmental educational-occupation career guidance in grades one through 12, and (3) to involve the staffs of the participating schools in the program through cooperative planning and development.

334. Leonard, G. E. (et al.) The developmental career guidance project: an interim report. Detroit, Mich.: Wayne State University, Detroit Public Schools, 1968. (ED 035 031)

The Developmental Career Guidance Project objectives are: (1) to aid a selected group of inner-city high school students to raise and broaden their educational and occupational aspirations, (2) to develop a pilot program designated to better meet the needs of inner-city youth, (3) to involve the staffs of the participating schools in the program, and (4) to systematically evaluate the program. The first phase of the project involved a two-week workshop for school personnel. The main goal was to encourage these participants to look critically at their school program with an eye toward utilization of occupational and career as a focus for helping inner-city youth to raise their level of aspiration. The setting in Detroit, the personnel involved, the rationale and broad objectives for activities are discussed at length. Data tables are found throughout the booklet. Activities are described, including counseling and guidance, curriculum, community contacts, parent involvement, broadening perceptions, and dissemination of information. Three external evaluations of the program are given together with future plans.

335. Leonard, G. E. & Stephens, E. Elementary school employment service. *Vocational Guidance Quarterly,* 1967, 16(1), 13–17.

A program was organized so that fifth and sixth graders would be encouraged to apply for and be able to obtain various jobs that were available. The jobs were those that are available in almost any elementary school: senior and junior safety squad boys, audio-visual aides, library helpers, service squad helpers, auditorium assistants, office helpers, etc.

336. Leonard, G. E. Vocational planning and career behavior, a report on the developmental career guidance project. *Educational Technology,* 1969, 9(3), 42–46.

Presents goals, activities, and evaluation of project designed to widen opportunity horizons for inner city youth, to help them plan realistically for the future rather than seek immediate gratification, and to provide better role-models with whom the youth can identify.

337. Leonard, R. S. Vocational guidance in junior high: one school's answer. *Vocational Guidance Quarterly,* 1969, 17(3), 221–222.

Describes year-by-year program to provide vocational exploration through community work models, film presentations, field trips and career days.

338. Lesh, S. The recruitment and training of automobile mechanics. New York: National Committee on Employment of Youth, 1965. (ED 015 246)

A survey of 20 employers, association representatives, and union leaders indicated that difficulties in recruiting capable youth for the automobile mechanics trade are caused by (1) a chaotic structure, including unclear definition of function, variety of places of employment, and size of the employing units, (2) the complexities of training and standard setting in the rapid but unplanned growth of the occupation, and (3) the variation in response of employers to alleged shortages of competent and skilled workers. Training programs sponsored by the armed forces, government, and vocational schools are asked by industry to provide broad background and by local businessmen to provide specialized training. Programs probably need to be revised to prepare two levels of workers, the auto technician and the auto mechanic. Jobs need to be restructured so that the highly qualified can diagnose and the lower skilled can do manipulative tasks. The movement toward specialization in repair and standardization of training probably is an attempt to upgrade the whole field and lead to some form of certification of skill. Licensing has many disadvantages, however, and could possibly discourage instead of encourage prospective trainees. Capable youth will be attracted to the field if the industry provides such conditions as job security, a fair assignment of work, a logical system of promotion, a fair wage policy, adequate space and tools, a clean shop, and long range planning. This document is available as FS14.2—AU8 for 15 cents from Superintendent of Documents, U.S. Government Printing Office, Washington, D.C., 20402.

339. Letson, J. W. Formulation of models for preparing occupational materials for pupils from various socio-economic levels in grades three through eight. Atlanta: Atlanta Public Schools, 1969. (ED 043 063)

This document accompanied a request from the Atlanta Public Schools to the United States Office of Education for a Title III continuation grant which would enable that school system to continue an innovative program intended to develop, compile and disseminate appropriate occupational information for elementary school age children. The report is comprised of four sections, two of which constitute its bulk: (1) a narrative account of the rationale behind, purposes of, and planning which went into the program design, a summary of its accomplishments to date in the area of materials compiled and developed, and an exposition of the evaluative techniques utilized; and (2) an informational run-down of projected activities and anticipated needs, should the grant be continued. All budgetary expenditures and needs are included. In the appendices, the accomplishments, summarized in the body of the report, are presented in their actual form. The research reported herein was funded under Title III of the Elementary and Secondary Education Act.

340. Leubling, H. E. Counseling with dropouts: a three-year study. *Vocational Guidance Quarterly,* 1967, 15(3), 173–180.

In an effort to bridge the gap between the dropout's unsuccessful school experience and his subsequent attempts to find a place for himself in the world of work, the Vocational Advisory Service (VAS) initiated a three-year Youth and Work Program in May 1962 on Manhattan's Upper West Side. The services available to the experimental group consisted of counseling, social casework, prevocational training, remedial education, and job placement. The control group received only job placement assistance.

341. Likert, J. G. (Ed.) Conversations with returning women students. Ann Arbor: Michigan University, Center Continuing Education for Women, 1967. (ED 017 815)

In the spring of 1967, the University of Michigan's Center for Continuing Education of Women held a series of four discussions, "Women in School and at Work," to give women who are continuing their education or thinking about it an opportunity to talk to each other. At each session, two or three women who had returned to college began a general conversation by discussing their own return and some of their initial fears, handicaps, and rewards. They compared notes on coping with their multiple obligations and gave advice to the newcomers. Members of the university faculty, administration, and staff, and the center staff also took part. This booklet reproduces the conversations arranged under the general points covered—returning to school, anxieties such as attitude of husbands, faculty, and other students, fear of failure, finances, and discrimination, and ways of managing at home, school, and work. This document is available for $1.00, from the University of Michigan Center for Continuing Education of Women, 330 Thompson St., Ann Arbor, Mich. 48108. 55 pages.

342. Lindquist, E. F. (et al.) Educational information project. Iowa City: Iowa University, 1966. (ED 010 033)

>To aid data collection analysis, storage, and dissemination, instruments and procedures were developed for collecting information on all aspects of the educational program for a large population of schools, including information on individual pupils, school personnel, schools, and school districts. Computer programs and data-processing techniques and systems for transcribing, integrating, and storing this information had to be developed, along with a system to sort and disseminate the needed information to schools and other agencies upon request. The beginning phase of the project involved determining what information about individual pupils, professional school personnel, and school districts was to be collected and the development of data collection instruments. This included reviewing the related research and collecting available materials for gathering such data. Pilot tests were made of the stencil card method of preparing input. The tests were successful in grades 3 through 12. Primary children exhibited difficulty in keeping the cards aligned for stenciling. A thorough analysis of the elements of the information system indicated that the success of the system would rest largely in the hands of individual school principals and that each of them must thoroughly understand its basic principles and procedures if it is to succeed.

343. Link, A. D. The VIEW of Texas. *Vocational Guidance Quarterly,* 1970, 19(2), 134–139.

>The State of Texas has piloted a modified VIEW program under the name, "Vital Information for Education and Work."

344. Litzinger, W. & Visser, C. Closing the vocational counseling realities gap. *Personnel and Guidance Journal,* 1968, 46(7), 650–654.

>A two-week summer institute sponsored by Plans for Progress, encompassing company visitations and scheduled campus speakers augmented by seminar discussions, provided significant improvement in counselors' perceptions of industry expectations and requirements.

345. Lloyd, B. J. A conference to enlist the participation of fifty institutions of higher education in specific research and developmental programs to prepare women for productive employment. Pittsburgh, Pa.: Carnegie Institute of Technology, 1964. (ED 003 416)

>Conference objectives were threefold—(1) the preparation of plans to reach the undergraduate woman and motivate her to plan realistically for combining family and work in the successive phases of her life, (2) the development of a mechanism for cataloging existing part-time courses on campus and existing materials for home use so that this information can be disseminated for institution development of experimental materials and courses, and (3) procedure design for incorporating in the placement offices three pilot college vocational advisers. Conference discussion groups were formed to review the latest thinking from 50 institutions concerning these problems. Major findings were (1) on-campus administrative and academic efforts should be conducted to reach and motivate the undergraduate in liberal arts, (2) on- and off-campus efforts should be planned and implemented to offer intellectual stimulation and direction to graduates during the early "family years," (3) continuing education for credit should be offered on campus and in extension programs, (5) a counseling service should include continued counseling in the academic and vocational realm as well as a reciprocal placement service, and (6) a clearinghouse operation should be established for communication between institutions in the dissemination of information.

346. Lockett, R. E., Davenport, L. F. Review and synthesis of research on vocational education for the urban disadvantaged. Columbus: Ohio State University, Center for Vocational and Technical Education. Washington, D.C.: National Center for Educational Research and Development, November 1971.

>The document includes: (1) Historical Perspective of Vocational Education for the Disadvantaged, (2) Rationale for and Characteristics of the Disadvantaged, (3)

Research on Vocational Education Programs for the Disadvantaged, (4) Evaluation and Discussion of the Research Effort Related to the Disadvantaged, and (5) Important Considerations in Developing and Operating Vocational Education Programs for the Disadvantaged.

347. Lockwood, O. (et al.) Four worlds: an approach to occupational guidance. *Personnel and Guidance Journal,* 1968, 46(7), 641–643.

A vocational guidance approach used by a teacher team instructing a vocational guidance course in a junior high school was to broaden a student's understanding of the world, rather than specific career areas. Areas introduced were the Natural, the Technological, the Aesthetic, and the Human World.

348. Lofquist, L. H. A system for predicting outcomes of vocational counseling. 1967. (ED 015 511)

The Theory of Work Adjustment (TWA), which provides a conceptual framework for research in work adjustment, has been tested, criticized, and recently restated. TWA assumes that each individual seeks to achieve and maintain correspondence with his environment. Correspondence is defined as a harmonious relationship and mutual suitability between the individual and his environment. In the case of work, correspondence is described in terms of the individual fulfilling the requirements of the work environment, and the work environment fulfilling the requirements of the individual. The stability of this correspondence is manifested as job tenure. The levels of satisfactoriness and satisfaction (SS), for individuals with substantial tenure in a specific work environment, establishes the limits of SS from which tenure can be predicted for other individuals once their necessarily stable work personalities have been assessed. Instruments were developed to measure—(1) work relevant needs of individuals, (2) occupational reinforcer systems of jobs, (3) intermediate work adjustment short of tenure, and (4) satisfactoriness scales. The vocational counselor can now more precisely determine what jobs are most likely to facilitate client SS. A list of the formal propositions of TWA are included. This paper was presented at the American Psychological Association Convention, Washington, D.C., September 5, 1967.

349. Lorber, F. & Schrank, R. The Bloomingdale project, report of a demonstration on-the-job training program. New York: Mobilization for Youth, Inc., 1964. (ED 012 290)

An experimental training program tested two hypotheses—(1) unemployed minority group youth with training and reinforcement could succeed in jobs in middle-class settings and (2) high school graduates would be more successful than dropouts in competing for jobs, but dropouts also would benefit from the training program. In New York City, Mobilization for Youth (MFY), Bloomingdale's Department Store, and a local union cooperated in this project for 29 young people, aged 17 to 22, who were literate at the seventh-grade level. A 3-month training period consisted of orientation to department store work, specific formal skill training, and direct supervision by a MFY staff member who had supportive, counseling, and liaison functions. Orientation meetings included role playing and instruction on how to act while applying for a job. One important feature of the project is its salary-sharing plan—one half paid by MFY, the other half by the store. This scheme helps to open up the job market for MFY's program and enables MFY to act as a bargaining agent. The success of the project was shown by followup figures—(1) 14 of the ultimate trainees were regularly employed 6 months later and (2) among dropouts, only one person who wanted a job was unemployed. The six trainees who were school dropouts and who would not normally have qualified for jobs were either working or back in school.

350. Los Angeles City Schools. Careers related to industrial education: a collection of career guidance outlines to assist with planning and preparation for occupations with industry. Los Angeles, Cal.: LACS, Evaluation and Research Section, 1964. (ED 001 623)

The guidance format for each occupation includes five major topics: Personal Requirements, Education and Training Opportunities in Junior and Senior High School, Opportunities Beyond High School, Advancement and Outlook, and Related and Specialist Occupations.

The outlines are intended to help the student identify and appraise his own pattern of aptitudes, interest, and other personal qualifications. They serve to acquaint him with available industrial education programs and employment possibilities.

The outlines include: auto mechanic jobs; drafting jobs—architectural, industrial and electrical; electronics positions; graphic arts occupations—book binder, linotype operator, and photoengraver; industrial crafts—camera repairs, leather worker, optician and shoe repairman; metal working jobs; and finally, woodworking occupations such as carpentry and cabinet making.

351. Los Angeles City Schools. A guide: a work experience education and employment placement program. Los Angeles: LACS, 1960. (ED 001 031)

This guide contains the basic principles, general policies, educational objectives, and minimal standards of the work experience education course and employment placement program in Los Angeles. This program enables students to have a part-time job supervised and coordinated by the school and given course credit.

352. Los Angeles County Superintendent of Schools. Portraits: the literature of minorities: an annotated bibliography of literature by and about four ethnic groups in the United States for grades 7–12. Los Angeles: LACSS, 1970. (ED 042 771)

Intended to aid the secondary school teacher in recommending appropriate works to students, this annotated bibliography by and about black Americans, North American Indians, Mexican Americans, and Asian Americans gives detailed information and evaluations on themes. literary quality, and intellectual and emotional levels of materials. The bibliography, based on the standards of the booklist "We Build Together," is organized according to literary types—novels, short stories, poetry, drama, folk tales and legends, biographies, autobiographies, essays, letters, speeches, and anthologies—with every selection intended to foster the development of better self-concepts for minority group students and to contribute to a greater understanding for majority culture students. Availability of paperback editions is noted. A separate bibliography for teachers and suggestions for thematic units are included.

353. Losi, C. R. Guidance practices for improving school holding. Annual report. (title supplied) Newark, N.J.: Board of Education, 1963. (ED 001 424)

Many procedures were utilized for checking symptoms and causes of behavior common to potential dropouts. such as failure, truancy, apathy, disinterest, poor reading, lack of adjustment, and non-participation in activities. Cumulative records, teacher observation and counselor contacts helped to identify these students. Students were interviewed every term. Group guidance was conducted in educational, vocational, personal and social matters. Orientation and testing were given to all new students. Individual programs were adjusted where courses seemed to be the possible cause of failures and dropouts. Non-academic students were allowed to explore in shop experiences. Potential dropouts were carefully interviewed. Case conferences including teachers and counselors helped to solve individual problems. If all efforts failed to keep a student in school, follow-up conferences helped to guide the student into evening classes and employment situations. Plans are underway to initiate a work-study program to bridge the gap between school and employment.

354. Loughary, J. W. & Tondow, M. Computers as substitute counselors: some possibilities. Paper presented at the meeting of the American Psychological Association, San Francisco, September, 1968. (ED 022 228)

A three-level classification for describing computer assisted counseling systems is proposed. The first level consists of computer assisted systems which are information processing tools. Second level computer systems go beyond information processing and substitute for counselors in performing certain tasks. These systems, and those on the first level, are totally controlled by the counselor. The memories of such systems are completely available to the controlling counselor.

Computer systems at the third level could be described as substitute counselors. Their significance is that their designers and operators would attribute to them certain characteristics found in human counselors, e.g., privileged communication or privacy. Examples of systems at the first two levels are mentioned to provide an operational definition. A rationale is given for the tri-level systems classification. Some suggested uses of third-level substitute computer systems include: (1) a catharsis system, (2) a system permitting dialogue, (3) a behavior reinforcement system, and (4) a developmental monitor system. The question of whether these systems should be developed and, if so, by whom is discussed.

355. Loughary, J. W. Man-machine systems in education. New York: Harper, 1966. (ED 014 888)

This book includes 5 parts. The first, background, provides a theoretical and conceptual base for the man-machine systems described later. It defines man-machine systems, describes computers, and discusses the relationships between media technology and learning processes. Part 2, instruction, describes advanced systems in education which are concerned primarily with instruction as such. Part 3, administration, examines applications of systems at 3 management and executive levels—the school, the district, and the state and national levels. Part 4, pupil personnel services, describes computer systems in counseling and other areas. Requirements for implementing man-machine systems are discussed in part 5. This document is available from Harper and Row, Publishers, Inc., 49 East 33rd Street, New York, N.Y. 10016.

356. Lux, D. G. and Ray, W. World of construction: industrial arts curriculum project. Bloomington, Ill.: McKnight and McKnight Publishers, 1971.

The World of Construction is the first year course in a two-year program designed for junior high students. The second year course is in manufacturing technology. The two-year sequence is designed to provide an introductory study of industrial technology.

The course is a total educational package. It provides the teacher with all that is needed to operate the program, for example, textbooks, laboratory manuals, a teacher's guide, visual aids and devices, & lectures. This one-year course is divided into three major sections: an analysis of the managed-personnel-production system of construction, a synthesis of housing construction practices, and a synthesis of city and regional planning practices.

357. Lux, D. G. and Ray, W. World of manufacturing: industrial arts curriculum project, 4th edition. Bloomington, Ill.: McKnight and McKnight Publishers, 1970.

The World of Manufacturing is a total educational package. It provides a comprehensive and innovative one-year junior high school course in manufacturing technology. The course is divided into three major sections: (1) an introduction providing a brief history of manufacturing and an overview of the major concepts of the course, (2) an analysis of the managed-personnel-production system of manufacture, and (3) a synthesis of manufacturing practices applied to the corporation. *The World of Manufacturing* is the second part of an integrated two-year program; the first course is in construction technology. This two year program is designed to provide an introductory study of industrial technology.

358. Madison Junior High School. Madison area project. Suggested typical content outline for junior high school group guidance. Appendix E. Syracuse, N.Y.: MJHS, 1964. (ED 001 672)

The suggested outline begins with an orientation to group guidance, an attempt to help the student understand the functions of group guidance and of the guidance personnel (the counselor, social worker, psychologist, and psychiatrist). The outline also suggests the discussions deal with problems faced in adjusting to school, in getting along with parent and in overcoming prejudicial attitudes. Such topics as dating, sex, smoking, and alcohol are recommended in consideration of the special world of the 7th grade student. Occupational information and academic planning should be included in group guidance at this level.

At the 8th grade level it is suggested that group guidance begin with helping each student to know himself and others. He should begin to consider the process of social interaction taking place in the community. A study of occupations and of teenage problems such as sex, alcohol, and race is recommended.

Group guidance for the 9th grade is composed of four major units. The first deals with study skills, attempting to reinforce good study habits and to activate motivation. The second unit is entitled Personality-School and Community Adjustment. The purpose is to strengthen values of self-worth, to realize personal assets and liabilities, and to develop social skills. Vocational and occupational information is the subject of Unit III. The final unit, orientation and preparation for transition, is designed to help students adjust to now situations.

359. Mahler, C. A. & Caldwell, E. Group counseling in secondary schools. Chicago: SRA, College and Professional Publications, 1970.

This book discusses coordination and initiation of group counseling and the skills needed by the counselor, including suggestions for evaluation of group counseling.

360. Mahler, C. A. Group counseling in the schools. Los Angeles: Western Psychological Services, 1970.

A step-by-step description of group counseling in the schools is presented.

361. Maley, D. & Mietus, W. S. The implementation and further development of experimental cluster concept programs through actual field testing and evaluation at the secondary school level. The cluster concept project. Phase III. Interim report. Washington, D.C.: Office of Education, 1968. (ED 022 965)

The Cluster Concept Program in vocational education, a program for the 11th and 12th grades, is designed to prepare youth for entry level capability in a variety of related occupations rather than a specific occupation. Phase III of research with the program was the evaluation of the first year of experimentation with the programs for the 11th grade. A pretest-post test research design with four control and four experimental construction cluster groups, four control and three experimental metal fabrication cluster groups, and three control and three experimental electromechanical cluster groups was used to estimate the program effectiveness. Newly developed measurement instruments and standardized tests were used to estimate changes in selected cognitive, affective, and psychomotor behaviors. Objectives were attained in varying degrees with significant gains in cognitive abilities in eight experimental groups and modest gains in two groups. Increased flexibility of occupational preferences and broadened interests were found in the experimental groups. Inadequacies identified from the evaluation will serve to establish a list of realistic recommendations for the further development of the programs. The appendixes contain measurement instruments and achievement tests used in program evaluation. Related documents are VT 002 356, VT 002 254, and VT 004 162-VT 004 165.

362. Manpower Administration (DOL). Interviewer's handbook for selection and referral to training and placement. Washington, D.C.: MA, 1970. (ED 052 368)

This handbook is designed to assist local employment service personnel in effective selection and referral of applicants to training and job opportunities. Guidelines for placement are combined with detailed information on training programs. General guidelines for the identification of disadvantaged applicants are supplemented with a discussion of the outreach, motivation, and special assistance available to this group, within the Human Resources Development framework. The guidelines for job placement are followed by procedural modifications to meet the needs of special groups or situations.

363. Manus, G. I. & Manus, M. Educational and vocational guidance for the handicapped student. Washington: American Personnel and Guidance Association, 1971. (ED 051 525)

Gross deficiencies in educational and vocational counseling of handicapped students are examined. The authors' major thesis concerns the one-sided stress which has been placed on personal factors, to the ignoring of situational and environmental factors, as the focus of intervention efforts. Noting that, by and large, vocational information, vocational self-concept, and career patterns and choices are the product of previous experiential, exploratory opportunities, and further that most handicapped persons do not pass through this stage, the authors conclude that our society has not been concerned with or effective in guaranteeing the essential component of vocational maturity. A counseling model for handicapped persons is proposed which would require counselors to become advocates for equalizing experiences for handicapped students.

364. Margolin, J. B. & Misch, M. R. Education in the seventies. A study of problems and issues associated with the effects of computer technology on education. Washington, D.C.: George Washington University, 1967. (ED 022 361)

To aid policy development for the utilization of computers in education, a panel of 10 scientists and educators formed a traveling seminar that actually inspected the state of the art of computer-assisted instruction at seven research and development centers throughout the U.S. The panel agreed on four principles. First, a systematic approach to the achievement of educational goals is required. Second, the development of models is useful for the synthesis, presentation, and testing of new systems. Third, the computer has vast potential as an administrative aid to education. And finally, the panel agreed that the introduction of computers into the schools to deal with clerical and administrative problems will lead to their use in an instructional capacity. The main area of disagreement was over the nature and specific objectives of the optimal CAI system. In addition, the panel expressed a general concern over the effect of the computer on human values. Topics covered in the panelists' papers are learner needs and systems requirements, the hardware-software disparity, decision making in education, social change, urban education, public policy, school architecture, economics of education, teacher education, educational administration, computer languages and applications of the computers in the classroom, in the library, in research, and in counseling.

365. Margulis, J. G. Progress report for 1963–1964 describing the project ABLE program. Buffalo, N.Y.: Board of Education, 1964. (ED 001 515)

Project ABLE is an experimental program designed to identify and to encourage potentially able pupils from culturally deprived or low socio-economic backgrounds to complete appropriate programs of secondary education.
Students from the seventh and twelfth grades from culturally poor or unhappy homes were selected by principals and faculties of schools in the Buffalo School District. The selection was based on such criteria as school records, teacher recommendations, and intelligence tests. The staff of the project (teachers, counselors, and psychologists) met with groups of students before and after school. The project provided various remedial and advanced courses and language courses, and formed clubs of interest to the students. Counseling was undertaken in group sessions, on an individual basis, and with the parents of the students. The last session was carried out by a home-school coordinator who had achieved some success in convincing parents of the value of higher education. The community was enlisted for aid, and many outside lectures and tours were organized. The project has led to some positive results, especially in instilling a regard for education among the students. Project ABLE, with expanded facilities and modifications, will continue in 1964–65.

366. Martin, A. M. A multimedia approach to communicating occupational information to noncollege youth. Technical report. Pittsburgh, Pa.: Pittsburgh University, 1967. (ED 026 544)

A behavioral model on which to base guidance materials was developed by the project. This model includes three components that ought to be considered in conjunction with one another and are dependent upon one another, namely, an informational component, a behavioral component, and a media component.

367. Martin, A. M. A multimedia approach to communicating occupational information to noncollege youth. Interim technical report. Pittsburgh: Pittsburgh University, Graduate School Library and Information Science, 1967. (ED 017 005)

This project's primary concern has been the design of new types of guidance materials and new instructional approaches centering upon educational-vocational aspirations of students, particularly the noncollege bound and culturally disadvantaged.

368. Massachusetts State Labor Council, AFL-CIO. The role of organized labor in the vocational training and placement of hardcore youth. Boston, Mass.: MSLC. (ED 028 299)

This is a report of a training project conducted in Massachusetts to explore mechanisms through which organized labor might involve itself more fully in new and existing programs for preventing and controlling youth crime. Specifically, the objectives were: (1) to explore the problem of the young offender, (2) to explore what is being done for the young offender and by whom, and (3) to explore what might be the role of labor in these existing programs or what new programs labor might develop. The training project became operative in July 1966 and was subsequently continued until March 15, 1968. This report concerns itself with the following areas of the project: (1) planning, (2) conference, (3) workshops and training sessions, (4) impact and recommendations. Recommendations include: (1) a program of trained, on-the-job counselors, (2) creation of skill centers, and (3) active support by organized labor of legislation pertaining to progressive correctional matters.

369. Mawby, R. G. Adult education programs and parents' roles in career plans of rural youth. Washington, D.C.: National Committee for Children and Youth, 1963. (ED 002 540)

The role of parents in the occupational choices of rural youth is discussed. Conclusions are based on information gathered from nine previous studies and from a limited survey of adult education programs. Consideration is given to parental influences in vocational choice of rural inhabitants, to programs to improve parental roles in occupational choice of rural youth, and to implications for future action.

Educational and occupational counseling of rural parents is less effective than that of urban parents; there are few adult education programs to improve this function. Helpful programs include home visits of a 4-H Club agent with interested farm families to discuss occupational plans, joint meetings of parents and youth in rural communities to provide information on college opportunities, a parents' night in 4-H Clubs to present career information, for the special career problems of rural youth, as reflected in action programs, is limited. Rural parents' aspirations for their children are low. Mothers' educational and occupational aspirations for their children are higher than are fathers'. Recommendations are made for adult education programs to improve the occupational and educational counseling functions of rural parents. Rural and professional leaders should be made aware of the disadvantaged situation of rural youth in competition for jobs before successful programs can be implemented. Once the need is realized, programs can be designed to help rural parents appreciate the value of education and the importance of their counseling role. Maximum effectiveness depends on the stimulation of community as well as of individual parental response.

370. McBee, M. L. A career development program for select freshmen: a pilot project. *Journal of the National Association of Women Deans and Counselors,* 1970, 33(3), 131–133.

Program objectives were to give undecided students a chance for self-exploration as well as familiarization with academic program and vocational possibilities.

371. McBride, C. A. The Cleveland job development service. Quincy-Woodhill Center, 10600 Quincy Avenue, Cleveland, Ohio. Bureau of National Affairs, Inc. Case Study, Public Schools, *Manpower Information Service,* Washington, D.C., Vol. 3, Number 17, 1972.

The Job Development Service, established in 1966 by the Cleveland Board of Education with federal funding under Title I of the Elementary and Secondary Education Act and now financed by The Ohio State Department of Education, provides a variety of services to assist inner-city high school students in finding gainful, full-time employment after graduation. Going beyond the traditional functions of the high school, the program offers job development and placement services, vocational counseling, interviews with area businesses, orientation to the world of work, and referral to educational and training opportunities.

372. McDaniels, C. How to develop better career films. *Vocational Guidance Quarterly,* 1970, 19(1), 56–60.

Specific factors are delineated toward the provision of films maximally responsive to the need youth have for career information.

373. McGovern, L. & Hansen, L. S. National vocational guidance week: a post-mortem. *Vocational Guidance Quarterly,* 1967, 16(1), 31–33.

A description and evaluation of the projects and procedures tried at University High School, University of Minnesota. This "post-mortem" is offered in the hope that it will be of use to other counselors and schools concerned about doing a better job of career guidance with youth.

374. McPherson, H. & Stephens, T. M. Developing a work-experience program for slow learning youth. A report of a three year extension and improvement project. Dayton, Ohio: Dayton Public Secondary Schools; Ohio Bureau of Vocational Rehabilitation, 1964 (ED 027 649)

A work experience program for educable mentally handicapped youth in special classes included 215 students, 138 of them in 11th grade (105 boys, 33 girls) and 77 in 12th grade (47 boys, 30 girls). Their mean chronological age was 18.6 years and their mean IQ was 73 with a range of 52 to 82. The program coordinator of the Ohio State Department of Special Education developed the work study program; coordinated it with the Bureau of Vocational Rehabilitation, the Citizens' Advisory Committee, and the Technical Advisory Committee; obtained job placement; and shared supervisory responsibilities with the teacher-counselors, who were assigned to participating schools. Of the unskilled job placements obtained, 50% were in food service areas and 30% in porter or custodial areas. Hospital placements were also recommended; service stations and domestic homes were not. The gross annual earnings of students were $118,000. Success was related to on the job supervision, and the teacher-counselor's interview with each student on pay day was important. In a followup study of 73 graduates of the special classes, 89% of the 44 who had participated in the program were working while only 35% of the 29 who had not participated were working.

375. Meade, M. E. STEP—school to employment program, school year: 1963–1964. New York: Board of Education of the City of New York, High School Division. (ED 001 436)

Emphasis was placed on strengthening instructional plans by development of special resource materials and encouragement of coordinators to consult more frequently with subject teachers to plan cooperatively for the progress of students. STEP remained effective in motivating students to continue their schooling to graduation, as well as in upgrading those students who leave before graduation so that they may be better prepared for the world of work. The budget was $65,745.98, well below the estimated $85,075.

Materials distributed during the year included: job orientation and guidance content outlines, job guides, civil service material, job referrals and placements, lesson planning and instruction, maps, cartoons, and economic graphs. The Advisory Council functions in an important consultant capacity.

Of 577 individuals enrolled, 28.4% were discharged, 36.4% resumed the regular program, 27.5% continued in the program, and 7.7% graduated. Of the discharged group, 57.3% were discharged for full-time employment. Over 80% of the total were employed in private industry.

376. Melnotte, J. M. The application of project TALENT and project PLAN data to goal-oriented curriculum. *California Personnel and Guidance Association Journal,* 1970, 2(2), 22–26.

Describes individualized process whereby student proceeds at his own rate with materials geared to his ability and, in part, to his media preference. Participation by both parent and student in decision making is also discussed.

377. Mercer County Board of Education. The bold new venture-school dropout training program. Mercer County, W. Va.: MCBE, 1962. (ED 001 431)

Investigated was the question why boys of 16 and 17 years of age drop out of school and what can be done to help prepare them for a productive and satisfactory life in society.

The job preparation program began with Bill #72 of the West Virginia legislature. It included shop training in various vocations such as radio-TV repair, industrial and household painting, carpentry, auto repairing, sheet metal, etc. The students were all boys and were bused from various home locations to the work shops throughout the county.

Material is included in its original form, as spoken or written by the 150 members of the classes, parents, teachers, and visitors to the program.

Some observations made were: (1) dropouts are out of school as a result of the failure of the home and the school; (2) the period of intensified training was too brief; (3) all youth should be required to remain in school until they are 17 or have completed high school; (4) all school systems should provide vocational or job training; (5) the tendency to drop out may begin in the third, fourth, or fifth grade; laxity on the part of teachers toward such students contributes to dropout problems.

The program motivated most of the 150 boys to consider their futures and take positive steps toward completing their educations.

378. Mezzano, J. Group counseling with low-motivated male high school students; comparative effects of two uses of counselor time. *Journal of Educational Research,* 1968, 61, 222–224.

The experiment compared group-individual (GI) and group (G) counseling groups with a control (C) group. The groups were equal in ability and initial grade point averages. Results indicate that those S's in the G groups had an observably larger GPA ten weeks following the completion of the experiment than the S's in the C group. It was suggested that a period of incubation is necessary before the insights gained during group counseling are translated into action.

379. Miami-Dade Junior College. Career college: a report of the first year (August 1968—June 1969). Miami, Fla.: MDJC, 1969. (ED 038 119)

Career College (originally known as Cooperative Education Program for Dropouts was set up under the auspices of Title I of the Higher Education Act. The grant for the pilot project specified a two-thirds federal contribution and a one-third contribution from the South Campus of Miami-Dade Junior College. Program objectives included identifying 60 young male school dropouts and enrolling them in a program of full-time study alternated with full-time work. Counseling services, developmental activities, cooperative work experiences, and relevant learning experiences were provided to encourage ghetto youths, who left school early, to pursue their interests and improve their academic and vocational skills. This report of Career College's first year of operation describes some of the problems and difficulties encountered by the staff in setting up the program.

380. Michigan State Department of Education. A vertically integrated occupational curriculum for schools in Michigan. Lansing: MSDE, 1969.

A vertically integrated occupational curriculum that extends from the elementary through the post-secondary education levels is needed. This integrated curriculum should develop positive attitudes about work, create an awareness of the vast occupational opportunities and provide knowledge and skill sufficient to meet the demands of a constantly changing society.

This publication was prepared to stimulate the study of occupational education curriculum which ultimately could lead to the development of effective occupational education in all regions of the State of Michigan. Further information can be obtained from the State of Michigan, Division of Vocational Education, Box 928, Lansing, Michigan, 48904.

381. Mihalka, J. A. Job hunting course. Columbus, Ohio: College of Education, 1972. (To be published by NVGA as part of their "How to . . ." series).

The rationale behind the Job Hunting Course is that success in obtaining employment depends in large part on the skill of the applicant to use certain techniques and methods that can be clearly identified.

The suggested curriculum involves approximately 15 hours of instruction and activity with a group of 12 to 15 students. The program stresses learning by doing. Topics for each session are outlined in detail, and additional references are provided. Appendices include: A. A self-scoring survey entitled "How to Find a Job"; B. Personal Assessment Checklist; and C. New Worker Orientation Checklist.

382. Miller, C. H. A pilot project in vocational counseling in economically underdeveloped areas. De Kalb: Northern Illinois University, 1970. (ED 035 950)

The general purpose was to demonstrate by means of a pilot project what could be accomplished by providing guidance and counseling services conducted by itinerant counselors. A total of nineteen schools located in twelve counties participated. These counties are the southernmost counties in Illinois. A total of 432 boys and 397 girls were reached by the project, either through individual counseling interviews, or through group activities. Two custom designed walk-in buses were purchased, each equipped with a counseling office, work space around a table, and storage space for tests and occupational information materials. Two counselors were employed, both qualified according to Illinois standards for certification. Three principal criteria were employed in evaluation of the project: the degree of acceptance by school administrators, stimulation provided to participating schools, and the impact made upon state level guidance services in Illinois. On the basis of all three criteria the project was judged to be definitely successful.

383. Miller, C. H. A pilot project for vocational guidance in economically underdeveloped areas. Springfield: Illinois State Office of the Superintendent of Public Instruction, Department of Guidance Services, 1968. (ED 026 527)

The purpose of this project was to establish a demonstration program to provide guidance services for: (1) non-college bound high school seniors, (2) recent high school graduates currently unemployed, and (3) former high school students who had dropped out of school within 3 years of initiation of the project. Specific objectives included: (1) provision of information regarding jobs and training opportunities, as well as sources of assistance, (2) personal counseling interviews to assist in developing an understanding of the labor market, and (3) assistance in the vocational development of the individual. The project was implemented in the 12 southern-most counties of Illinois and was extended over a 3-year period. An evaluation of the project indicated definite success in stimulating leadership for the schools involved, and adoption of selected practices by other counties and other states; however, the influence of the project upon the lives of individual students could not be quantitatively described. A 5-year follow up is considered.

384. Miller, J. G. Predictive testing for entrance in vocational-technical schools; a study of the predictive values of a pre-selected battery of standardized tests as a tool for the selection of entering students in certain trade programs offered in the vocational-technical schools of the state of Connecticut. New York: New York University, Center for Field Research and School Services, 1968. (ED 024 813)

This study was organized for the purpose of determining the validity of any part or parts of a pre-selected battery of standardized tests as predictors of success in secondary school trade programs. The study was limited to the trade areas of machine shop and electrical wiring in 14 state vocational schools in Connecticut. A battery of pre-selected standardized tests was administered to approximately 200 entering pupils in Bullard-Havens Technical School. The tests were also administered to about 200 grade 12 pupils who were completing programs in trade machine shop and trade electrical shop in six pilot schools. Achievement tests were developed and administered to these same 12th grade pupils. As a result of this pilot study, the original standardized test battery was reduced from 30 variables (sub-tests) to 15 variables, thus decreasing the testing time from the original 21 hours to 14 hours on the reduced battery. Subsequent research indicated that a reduced number of selected variables would yield almost as high a correlation as the original number of variables. A related document is ED 019 437.

385. Miller, K. L. Adapting the WIN employability orientation program to the needs of a medium-sized community: Bellingham, Washington. *Journal of Employment Counseling,* 1970, 7(1), 9–12.

Describes program instituted to fulfill "Orientation" component of Work Incentive Program (WIN), but adapted to meet realities and needs of the community. Certain elements of group counseling have been incorporated. Salient features are identified for purpose of illustrating what can be done at local level.

386. Miller, S. M. & Saleem, B. Two years in the Syracuse labor market—work experiences of dropouts. Syracuse, N.Y.: Syracuse University Youth Development Center, 1964. (ED 001 662)

The aim was to discover what kinds of problems dropouts face in the labor market, the kinds of training and/or guidance of benefit to them and whether the school system should provide special training and guidance facilities. Only a few research efforts have studied in depth the post-dropout experience of school-leavers. Forty-one boy and forty-six girl dropouts were located and interviewed two years after leaving school. The sample included only those who did not complete the 12th grade and who did not transfer to another school.

Detailed information is provided in the following areas: description of the sample, marriage after leaving school, dropouts in the labor market, delinquency among dropouts, characteristics of dropouts with favorable employment experience, and the post-dropout experiences of girls. Jobs secured by dropouts were not compared with those secured by graduates over the same time span.

Some of the conclusions drawn were that: (1) social background did not seem to affect the type of entry job secured by dropouts, but did affect rate of job instability; (2) juvenile delinquency was not found to be a general characteristic of dropouts; (3) only low level jobs are available to dropouts; (4) boy dropouts seemed not to have been as handicapped by their aborted education as girl dropouts; (5) the type of job secured was generally limited with respect to advancement opportunities; (6) many jobs were automatically closed to dropouts; (7) most dropouts did not have serious difficulty in securing jobs for which they were eligible though the public employment service was not an efficient means of finding jobs. It was suggested that a much closer relationship between educational processes and available work opportunities is needed. A re-evaluation of the educational system, a reconsideration of employment qualifications by industry, and training programs by industry are called for.

387. Miller, W. R. and Blankenbaker, E. K. Annotated bibliography of publications and reports of research dealing with the interpretation of the world of work to elementary children. Columbia, University of Missouri: Department of Practical Arts and Vocational-Technical Education, 1970.

This annotated bibliography contains 50 annotations of references. These sources of information deal with such topics as: (1) Rationale, (2) Experimental Research, and (3) Pilot and Developmental Projects, of the general area of interpreting the "World of Work" to elementary children. Most references in the bibliography contain their respective ERIC number. References are arranged by topic.

388. Mink, O. G. & Kaplan, B. A. (Eds.) America's problem youth: education and guidance of the disadvantaged. Scranton, Pa.: International Textbook Company, 1970. (ED 044 467)

This book is the result of a series of workshops designed for school personnel desiring to improve educational programs for disadvantaged youth and potential dropouts. The workshops were conducted at Cornell University during the summer of 1964 through 1967. The chapters in this book on milieu, basic issues, dropout problems, counseling the disadvantaged, and action projects represent, in part, papers presented during the Cornell workshops. The problems discussed are generally concerned with disadvantaged youth in urban areas. This book is intended to be a basic text on education and guidance of the disadvantaged; it is also directed to public school educators at all levels and all varieties of assignment.

389. Minneapolis Public Schools. World of work: grade nine. Teacher's guide for the school year 1967–1968. Minneapolis: MPS, 1968. (ED 031 723)

This manual is designed to serve the classroom teacher as a guide to the accompanying televised series of programs on the world of work. The television series is designed to give a broad overview of many occupations, by bringing into the classroom more than fifty "guests" from all levels of preparation: the semi-skilled, the skilled, the technical, and the professional. The lessons employ familiar classroom techniques in bringing guidance information to the students, not from professional entertainers, but from people actually working in the community. The prime objectives of the series are: (1) to present information on occupation areas, job families, and related types of work possibilities; (2) to stimulate further investigation by the students into the world of work, and (3) to provide a basis for program planning for the senior high years. Lessons have been based upon the interest categories found in the Kuder Preference Record, and are prepared by the Radio—Television Department of the Minneapolis Public Schools.

390. Minnesota University. Suggested teaching-learning approaches for career development in the curriculum. Minneapolis: MU, 1968. (ED 053 289)

Recognizing the need to provide classroom teachers with teaching aids usable in career development, a federally subsidized project was conducted by the University of Minnesota during the summer of 1968. Resulting from this conference were teacher formulated behavioral objectives and activities that should prove useful in needed program development. In most instances the stated objective is followed by a statement of rationale, enabling objectives, and innovative teaching-learning approaches. It should be noted that these behavioral objectives represent only a beginning in relation to the need for career development programs and are in need of refinement. Also included in this document is a self-appraisal form for the job ahead.

391. Mitchell, E. F. (et al.) A comprehensive orientation to the world of work through industrial arts and vocational education (grades 1–12). Miss.: Greenwood Public Schools, 1970. (ED 049 361)

In response to the philosophy of vocational education outlined by the National Advisory Council, the Greenwood Public School Administration drew up this proposal for a new educational structure. Designed to prepare students for the world of work through a comprehensive orientation process involving practical arts, vocational education, and guidance, the program is justified by the cultural and economic deprivation, and the high dropout rate in Greenwood schools. The purpose of the elementary industrial arts phase is to introduce pupils to the world of work. Grades 7–8 provide students with exploratory experiences and are prevocational in nature, and the high school offers a complete vocational education program. A comprehensive study of modern industry and occupational orientation is provided for in Grade 9, followed by mechanical drawing in Grade 10. Vocational part-time cooperative education and vocational counseling are integral parts of the program. It is recommended that as much of the program be put into effect each year as qualified staff, facilities, and finances will allow. A detailed course sequence is provided in the appendixes.

392. Mitchell, F. H. Implementing a vocational guidance program. *The School Counselor,* 1968, 15(3), 223–227.

The program synthesizes placement in part-time jobs and guidance in employee behavior, with a variety of opportunities to investigate those adult careers in which the students express interest.

393. Modern Language Association of America. Guidance packet. New York: MLAA, 1967. (ED 012 577)

This packet provides vocational and academic advice to the language learner and useful information about language learning to teachers, counselors, and administrators. The documents, published from 1963 to 1967, are—(1) "Vocational Opportunities for Foreign Language Students" by Gilbert C. Kettelkamp, (2) "Advice to the Language Learner" by Donald D. Walsh, (3) "A Handbook for Guiding Students In Modern Foreign Languages" by Ilo Remer, and (4) "Translating Foreign Languages into Careers" compiled by Richard T. Hardesty of the Indiana Language Program. This document is available as Packet B51 for $1.25 from the MLA Materials Center, 62 Fifth Avenue, New York City, New York, 10011.

394. Modesto Junior College. Review of Stanislaus County multi-occupational vocational training project, 1964–1965. Modesto, Cal.: MJC, 1965. (ED 011 997)

This report outlines problems encountered and progress made in the Stanislaus County, California, training project. Initial difficulty in securing federal approval and funds for prevocational or basic education was ended by the amended Manpower Training and Development Act. However, difficulties, mainly in reorienting prevocational and vocational instructors, obtaining suitable materials, setting up courses, and selecting trainees, and the medical, emotional, financial, and other problems of trainees, still had to be met. Projects, in basic reading and arithmetic and in reading above grade 4 level used Readers' Digest materials, the science research associates reading laboratory kit, "News for You" (Level B), and local newspapers, and stressed practical activities and exercises, tests and drills, audiovisual aids, and discussion and counseling. Community resources (field trips, work experience, resource persons, cultural enrichment) supplemented the classes. Vocational and prevocational programs and auxiliary services come under the Yosemite Junior College board. Placement followups showed gains in employment, wage scales, job tenure, and training related work. The document includes personnel requisites. test results, employment data, patterns of local and state cooperation, the overall status of projects, and the community service role of the junior college.

395. Mohs, M. C. Service through placement in the junior college—the organization and operation of a junior college placement bureau. Washington, D.C.: American Association of Junior Colleges, 1962. (ED 014 968)

The placement service, recognized as an important junior college function, (1) assists students in relating their qualifications to occupational requirements, (2) assists students in their search for part-time and full-time employment, (3) cooperates with employers in the induction of students into part-time and career positions, (4) screens and refers qualified applicants, and (5) serves as liaison in acquainting college personnel with needs of business and industry in curriculum development. Organizational patterns vary with types of institutions, size, complex of courses, amount of departmental autonomy, faculty desire to place their own students, relationships with employers, and administrative support. Central to the success of the service is the selection and allocation of professional staff. The report includes descriptions of personnel duties and qualifications, types of operational procedures, a collection of typical placement office forms, sample policy statements, and a reading list. This document is also available for $1.25 from the American Association of Junior Colleges, 1315 Sixteenth Street, N.W., Washington, D.C. 20036.

396. Molen, R. L. V. Student placement by means of a flexibility rigidity score—a design. Detroit: Wayne State University, 1963. (ED 002 272)

Some cases of emotional maladjustment and underachievement have been a result of poor student placement with certain types of teachers. If students and teachers could be tested through the use of a flexibility-rigidity score, their behavioral characteristics could be matched and the classroom environment improved. Flexibility in a classroom environment, is the ability to adjust rapidly to changing conditions; rigidity is a form of negative transfer. Experimental tests could be administered to sixth-grade students and seventh-grade teachers to properly place the students in the seventh grade.

The tests would utilize subject matter rules to solve problems, and norms of flexibility-rigidity would be established. Some of the problems on the tests could be solved if the rules were not applied; the persons who did apply rules to these problems would be exhibiting rigid behavior. An experimental classroom could be established. The upper and lower 20 percent of the pupils, as measured by the flexibility-rigidity norms, would be assigned to the teachers receiving corresponding scores.

A prognostic instrument would be developed as a result of the proposed experiment. Pupil placement would become more logical, and cases of underachievement and/or emotional maladjustment would be corrected. A bibliography of references is given.

397. Monroe School District 103. An exemplary cooperative in elementary school guidance for small school districts. Final evaluation report. Monroe, Wash.: MSD 103, 1969. (ED 048 605)

This project was designed to provide a new comprehensive, and sophisticated guidance program to meet the needs of pupils and teachers in nine school districts. The major purpose of the program was to maximize the development of each child, and broadly stated its functions included the following: (1) inservice activities to extend and enrich teachers' understanding of areas such as changing goals and behavior and diagnostic cues, (2) counseling with groups and individuals, (3) working with parents of problem children, (4) arranging for referrals to other community agencies when necessary, (5) evaluating the program, and (6) disseminating information concerning the program. The common philosophical core that undergirds the entire counseling program was that the role of the elementary counselor was that of a facilitator of the learning process; consequently, the central role of the teacher was constantly kept in mind. In order to assess the effects of the program, a descriptive model was utilized. At the conclusion of the program, after federal funds were no longer available, only two of the participating districts dropped elementary school counseling. The research reported herein was funded under Title III of the Elementary and Secondary Education Act.

398. Montgomery, G. W. G. Vocational guidance for the deaf; a classified guide to the basic requirements for occupations open to the profoundly deaf. Baltimore: Williams & Wilkins, 1967. (ED 026 755)

Published in Britain for use by counselors and placement officials, the book offers a systematic attack on occupational placement problems of the prelingually deaf. The system is based on a vocational guidance profile, which is developed from intelligence and achievement test scores. The vocational guidance profile is explained, and occupational prospects for the deaf and general considerations for placement are treated. The classified list of occupations and its use in placement are described as follow: test scores from the profile are categorized into P (performance), I (written intelligence), N (written tests of numerical ability), L (written tests of language skills), O (tests of oral skills). Following each occupation listing is the code letter with the estimated standard score of the average worker in the occupation named; other notations indicate special physical or ability requirements and/or hazards of particular jobs, and possible financial or training demands. The classified list of occupations is recommended for use only in conjunction with individual vocational guidance profile scores and knowledge of local employment conditions. Profiles are provided as normative information in the areas of scientific, professional and office workers, skilled and unskilled, tradesmen, and unemployed. Listings are given of agencies and services for the deaf, mostly in Britain, and of 35 references.

399. Moore, J. W. How high schools can reduce their dropout rate—an action guide. Albany: State Education Department of New York, 1964. (ED 001 691)

After the school has committed itself to reducing the number of dropouts, personnel must formulate a plan of action. The following suggestions are made: "start small, work together, take your time, meet regularly, get outside help, report progress and evaluate results." The program for regular students should not be neglected. A checklist is included to help in identifying the scope of the problem. A second evaluation checklist may be used to aid in the systematic identification of potential dropouts.

Because the cause of dropping out varies with each student, each case must be treated individually. An understanding of student problems is necessary for better counseling. A work-study program and extracurricular activities are suggested. Parents should be informed and consulted about their children. If a student leaves school despite efforts to retain him, job advice and counseling should be made readily available to him. Dropouts should be convinced of the continuing interest of the school in their progress. School personnel should make clear their readiness to readmit dropouts without censure.

400. Morrill, W. H. & Forrest, D. J. Dimensions of counseling for career development. *Personnel and Guidance Journal,* 1970, 49(4), 299–305.

Four types of career counseling are described: a traditional vocational counseling approach which helps the client with a specific decision; teaches decision making skills; one which views career development as a process rather than an endpoint; and one which focuses on creating the ability to utilize one's own strengths to achieve self determined objectives.

401. Mullen, M. J. A volunteer program in vocational information and career guidance for secondary schools. A handbook. Redwood City, Cal.: Sequoia Union High School District, 1968. (ED 024 809)

Presented as a record of volunteer activities, this handbook is intended for the use of school administrators, teachers, and/or counselors who may wish to use volunteers in a school-community, career-guidance program. Possible activities may range from a simple vocational information center to a multi-faceted year-round program. The purpose of the school resource and career guidance program is to provide volunteer service which will supplement the effectiveness of school personnel in the fields of vocational information, career guidance, and cultural and educational enrichment. Among the conclusions are: (1) Relationships with community parents, consultants, and volunteer workers give high school students more than vocational enrichment, and (2) Such a program can provide the community with the kind of information which leads to active efforts in support of public education.

402. Munger, D. I. The occupational information speakers' bureau. *Vocational Guidance Quarterly,* 1967, 15(4), 265–266.

Each participating student (about half of 250 students in a team teaching speech program [1]) chose an occupation to study in depth. His research included observations and interviews as well as printed materials from counseling offices, libraries, and professional agencies. He then prepared a 7–10 minute speech based upon his study. The design of this speech was to generate audience interest in the occupation, to describe the nature of the work, to portray a "typical" day in the life of such an individual, and to close with an appeal to look further into the vocational area.

403. Muro, J. J. Evaluation of a comprehensive guidance and counseling service for rural Maine communities. Camden: Maine School Union 69, 1970. (ED 046 561)

Career Guidance

An evaluative report of a single school guidance counselor's professional efforts as an itinerant rural school counselor in four rural Maine schools is presented. Findings are limited to the following areas: counseling, use of media, vocational guidance, community agencies, working with teachers, working with children, research, public relations, testing, and general evaluation of the itinerant counselor. Recommendations for each area are given. Survey results for 1967–70 describe the feelings of students, principals, and teachers as related to the "oneman" guidance program, which was funded under Title III of the Elementary and Secondary Education Act.

404. Muskegon Public Schools. The effect of additional counseling on the able student's vocational and educational planning. A report of the Muskegon guidance project. Muskegon, Mich.: MPS, 1965. (ED 024 959)

In a three-year study to determine the effectiveness of additional counseling and guidance in aiding realistic educational and occupational choice by junior high school students, the 721 members of the seventh-grade classes of three Muskegon junior-high schools were randomly assigned to experimental and control groups. The Ohio Student Inventory of Guidance Awareness, Stanford Achievement Test Battery, Illinois Inventory of Parent Opinion, and Science Research Associates' Youth Inventory, and data on failures, honor rolls, disciplinary actions, and dropouts were used to compare results. Experimental students received both home visits by counselors and group counseling. No statistical difference was found between experimental and control groups in numbers of students receiving failing grades, being on the honor roll, or dropping from school. Experimental group students were reported for disciplinary action at a significantly higher rate in both the seventh and ninth grades. Experimental group students received higher grades, showed increased interest in educational and vocational planning, and developed more awareness of the need for early economic planning. It was not evident that families increased planning for future educational and vocational goals or consciously created an environment conducive to optimum development.

405. Myers, R. A., Lindeman, R. H., Forrest, D. J., and Super, D. E. Preliminary report: assessment of the first year of use of the educational and career exploration system in secondary schools of Genessee County, Michigan. New York: Teachers College, Columbia University, 1971.

This document presents a preliminary report of an evaluation of Educational and Career Exploration System (ECES), a program initially launched in 1969 and recently revised and evaluated in Genessee County, Michigan.

The present program contains three sections: Occupations (400 occupations representing many fields and levels), Majors (300 post-high school, college and other training programs), and Charts, summarizing and comparing information about the student and his exploration. These sections are available to the student through a computer terminal which the student uses to obtain a film image display unit which presents relatively individualized information to the student. A post-high school program locator called College Finder, is available without the use of a terminal.

406. Myers, R. A. Career development in the college years. New York: Columbia University, 1971. (ED 050 372)

This paper concerns itself with two relatively central issues in career development, life stages and choice behavior and focuses on the tasks of the college counselor in regards to them. Life stages refer to sequential series of tasks to be accomplished within time periods that can be specified. Choice behavior is the on-going process of making a realistic career choice. Three implications derived from the material surveyed are offered: (1) a counselor can arm himself with a knowledge of what kinds of characteristics indicate one's degree of vocational maturity; (2) counselors can develop expertise in promoting, eliciting and teaching clients how to profit from exploratory behavior; and (3) counselors can talk to educational policy makers about the importance of restructuring the college or university in ways that better fit the realities of student development.

Compendium of Abstracted Methods 317

407. National Center for Career Information Services. Bloomington: NCCIS, Indiana University.

The National Center for Career Information, located at 715 East Seventh Street, Bloomington, Indiana, 47401, is both a clearinghouse and coordinating agent for a series of related vocational and career development programs operating throughout the nation. It is a cooperative effort on behalf of almost 30 states to operate microfilmed career information programs such as VIEW, VITAL, WISC and WORK. These programs provide information on jobs and career fields and each is designed primarily for non-college bound high school students. NCCIS is also coordinating the design of career development and career awareness programs for the educable mentally handicapped and elementary students, mainly through the use of microfilmed job information.

408. National Institutes of Health. Graduate, then what—jobs in health. A report on the use of radio as a recruitment tool for the health occupations. Bethesda, Md.: NIH, 1970. (ED 050 230)

To evaluate the use of radio as a means of recruiting minority students into the health fields, 11 schools in the San Francisco Bay Area were selected to participate in a program of weekly radio broadcasts studying 11 health professions with manpower shortages. A combination panel and question and answer format was used for the broadcasts. Meetings were held with school representatives before the program began to discuss topics, objectives, and other technical matters as well as after the fourth broadcast to assess reactions and difficulties encountered. A followup survey was conducted after the series ended. Although attendance figures and other statistical data were incomplete, the project staff reported that the programs were effective in producing interest and enthusiasm, particularly in schools in which faculty and administrators took a personal interest in helping disadvantaged students examine their interests and capabilities. Results demonstrate that two-way radio broadcasts are a promising means of recruiting disadvantaged students into the health professions. Recommendations are provided for planning, staff, physical arrangements, criteria for panelists, student participation, publicity, followup coordination, and reporting procedures.

409. National Vocational Guidance Association. Washington, D.C.: NVGA, Commission on Computer-Assisted Guidance Systems, 1971. Toward guidelines for computer development in guidance. JoAnn Harris, Chairperson.

This report summarizes the observations, conclusions and recommendations of the Commission on Computer-Assisted Guidance Systems. In February 1970, the Trustees of the National Vocational Guidance Association empowered the Commission to study the issues involved in the development, implementation and use of computer-assisted guidance systems. The report includes information on types of computer-assisted guidance systems, guidelines for computer-assisted guidance systems, conclusions including a collection of questions and issues that must be faced by administrators or counselors as they approach the decision regarding the inclusion of a computer-based system, and a description of guidance as a system.

410. Nelson, D. E. An experimental evaluation of methods of teaching students to consider alternative problem solutions. Stanford, Cal.: American Institutes for Research in the Behavioral Sciences, 1970. (ED 040 475)

A problem solving skill was investigated to provide direction for training strategies for a proposed personal problem solving training program. There were eight treatment groups utilized including video-tape modeling, audiotape modeling, social modeling through means of a written booklet, parallel treatments for each of these using social reinforcement of desirable verbal responses, and a control group designed to yield baseline data. There were nine criteria derived from three criterion devices which encompassed two problem solving simulations and a self assessment device. Conclusions were: (1) no one strategy proved optimal; (2) social reinforcement did have an effect upon some problem solving behaviors examined; (3) no training medium was found completely effective; (4) audiotape and written booklet procedures were not significantly different in their effect; (5) the oral lecture was no more effective than the baseline control treatment; and (6) the measures may have lacked the necessary sensitivity to discriminate between problem solvers.

411. Nelson, D. E. & Krumboltz, J. D. Encouraging career exploration through "simulated work" and "vocational detective" experiences. *Journal of Employment Counseling,* 1970, 7(2), 58–64.

This study tested two alternative ways of stimulating non-college bound youth to explore career opportunities: (1) a problem solving simulated occupational experience in appliance service; and (2) a general career kit. Behavioral criteria were measured for both methods. Results show little differences in the way each method inspired exploration.

412. New Hampshire Health Careers Council. A guidance counselor's handbook to career opportunities in the health field. Concord: NHHCC, 1968. (ED 036 620)

Intended for use by all persons in New Hampshire involved in occupational guidance, this looseleaf manual presents information about 35 health occupations at all levels. For each occupation, information is included about the nature of the work, employment opportunities, income potential, educational requirements, schools offering programs, and sources of additional information.

413. New Hampshire State Department of Education. An annotated bibliography of resources in the fields of vocational-technical education and vocational guidance. Concord: NHSDE, Division of Instruction. (ED 038 513)

Twenty-nine annotated bibliographies on vocational-technical education and vocational guidance are presented in this report. They are divided into five sections which provide information on trade and industrial education, the disadvantaged child, work experience programs, the dropout, and vocational guidance. The annotations contain information about publisher, author, date of publication, number of pages, and an abstract and indexing terms. All the documents have ED numbers and are available on microfilm from the ERIC Document Reproduction Service.

414. New Jersey State Department of Education. Teacher's guide for a model program on introduction to vocations. Trenton: NJSDE, Division of Vocational Education. (VT 001 455)

This pilot program, developed by the New Jersey Division of Vocational Education and tried in 14 school districts, is to assist teachers in guiding students in their choice of educational and vocational career objectives. The course, intended for students who are non-college bound and will terminate their formal education upon completion of high school, is designed to coordinate those areas of school (vocational guidance, industrial education, business education, and home economics) closely allied to the world of work. The major units are: (1) Introduction to the Course, (2) Understanding Yourself—Individual Characteristics, Interests, and Abilities as They Relate to Occupations, (3) The Economics of Industry, (4) Exploring Occupations (Mechanical, Science Laboratory, Home Economics and Office), and (5) Evaluating Your Experience and Planning Ahead. Included in each unit are concepts, objectives, suggested time allotment, class discussion topics and activities, learning experiences, and references.

415. New Jersey State Education Department. The world of work: increasing the vocational awareness of elementary school children. A guidebook for teachers and guidance counselors. Trenton: NJSDE, Division of Vocational Education, 1969. (ED 038 511)

The development of a person's perception of himself in a career role is a continuing process which requires constant focus on relevant experiences throughout his entire life. This guidebook was developed to enhance teaching techniques and related media for expanding the vocational awareness of elementary school children. The emphasis is placed on approaches that should enrich the child's understanding of work as a function of man, the importance of the development of man's abilities in relation to the progress of his civilization, and on how the child may relate these to his own individuality. Although this project has been placed within the social studies subject matter area, this approach may be easily adapted to any other area of instruction. A conceptual model of vocational awareness, sample survey questions, instructional units, and activities are included in the guidebook.

416. New Mexico State Department of Public Instruction. Books to give vocational information to grade school children; western states small schools project. Santa Fe: NMSDPI. (VT 007 434)

This bibliography lists the title, author, publisher and grade level of 49 books selected for the purpose of providing vocational information to school children in kindergarten through Grade 8.

417. Newton, G. E. A report of the elementary school guidance project —Centennial and Irving Schools. Bloomington, Ill.: Bloomington Public Schools, 1966. (ED 026 677)

The Bloomington, Illinois public schools recognized the need for a developmental and continuous guidance program from grades kindergarten through 12. During 1965–66, an elementary school guidance pilot project was initiated in two schools. This report provides information about the implementation of the program and role and functions of the counselor working with the children, parents, and teachers. An evaluation of the year's program is made by the counselor with the assistance of pupils, teachers, and principals in both schools, and the program is seen to have been moderately to very successful in meeting its various objectives. Recommendations are also made relative to future program development.

418. New York City Board of Education. Guidance and job placement. Career guidance series. *Curriculum Bulletin,* 1967, 8. (VT 004 657)

The career guidance program utilizes specialized and intensive guidance and a curriculum centered around the world of work to accomplish its objectives, namely, an increased level of educational and vocational aspiration within junior high school students. This specially designed teaching guide in guidance and job placement is one of a series designed for use with junior high school pupils who are in general over age, frustrated, retarded in most school subjects, and indifferent to education. The guide is organized in two parts. Part I, Organization and Implementation of the Program, includes scope of the program, criteria for the selection of pupils, the testing program, high school placement, job placement services, and working with the individual pupil. Part II, Suggested Group Guidance Units includes: What can the career guidance program do for me? What can school do for me? What is the job for me? How do I get the job? The bibliography lists resources in the areas of occupational information, testing, and counseling information.

419. New York State Commission for Human Rights. Expanding opportunities through guidance. New York: NYSCHR. (ED 002 030)

The effective guidance program is committed to the principle that all people are ethically equal, though personally and culturally different. It inter-relates the needs and abilities of the individual with the social situation of which he is a part. One of the basic needs of students is preparation for entering the job world. Often, however, students lower their vocational sights because of limited knowledge of expanding opportunities based on merit and thereby encourage the student to choose a career in accordance with his true interests and aptitudes.

There are four major goals for the guidance worker in fulfilling his responsibility. First, he must accept responsibility to help all students realize their full potential. Inservice teacher training, intercultural extracurricular activities, fundamental and remedial instruction in basic skills, and curriculum development are several suggested programs for implementing such a goal. Becoming well informed on the behavioral and social sciences as they relate to guidance programs is the second major goal. To know the changing job world and its occupational needs and expectations is another guidance objective. After acquiring such knowledge, the guidance worker must use the information imaginatively in assisting the student to determine his vocational goals. Finally, the guidance counselor must seek to utilize community resources for cooperative planning to provide greater opportunities for those who have been limited because of social and economic groupings.

420. New York State Education Department. Developing work-study programs for potential dropouts—a manual STEP: the school to employment program. Albany, N.Y.: NYSED, Bureau of Guidance, 1965. (ED 001 426)

A work-study program was designed to motivate and train potential dropouts for employment. A teacher-coordinator conducted orientation classes, supervised STEP pupils on the job, visited parents, employers and resource personnel, counseled students, followed up pupil progress with subject teachers, maintained contacts with community employment resources and prepared special teaching materials.

Students were selected on the basis of familial environment and poor school records. They were interviewed at length and placed in the work-study programs of orientation classes, regular subject classes, and afternoon on-the-job training. Students were permitted to transfer to other jobs if they did not do well. Classes made use of group discussion, role playing, field trips, guest speakers, materials from work stations, and library materials on the world of work. Parent meetings sought to encourage them to cooperate in motivating their children.

Lesson plans included provided educational experience to train youth in applying for jobs, to initiate proper attitudes and provide vocational guidance. Students studied why they should stay in school, how to use the newspaper in looking for a job, good grooming, opportunities in the armed services, and other vocational information. A list of audio-visual aids in vocational education is given. An extensive professional bibliography of vocational publications for pupils accompanies the text.

421. New York State Education Dept. Elementary school guidance. Program development suggestions. Albany: NYSED, 1969. (ED 044 725)

This paper deals with suggestions for elementary school guidance program development. (1) The guidance program should be constructed on the needs of the individual school and its unique attributes. Stereotyped programs should be avoided. (2) The counselor's most important attributes are knowledge and skill in the art of human relations. (3) The initiation phase, including the development of program labels, is all important since the expectations for the program are set at that time. (4) The counselor should approach the staff with the philosophy that other personnel are to be accepted as they are, and that the counselor's purpose is that of service and assistance, rather than expert supervision. (5) Decision making with regard to objectives and program directions should be a cooperative venture in which administration, school staff, and the counselor participate together. (6) The counselor should avoid being identified with either the administration or the instructional staff. (7) A communication system which effectively interprets the guidance program operation, its purposes, and its goals is essential for program development and progress.

422. New York State Education Department. Guided occupational training. A vocational work experience program for intellectually limited and educationally handicapped students. Final report. Albany: NYSDE, Bureau of Occupational Education Research, 1969. (ED 034 042)

Twenty-four intellectually limited and educationally handicapped 10th grade students participated in the first year of the Guided Occupational Training program of the Oceanside Senior High School. An academic core of English, citizenship, and mathematics was blended with classes in one of the following areas: (1) business education and office skills, (2) home economics and food trades, (3) pre-

Compendium of Abstracted Methods

vocational-industrial education, and (4) distributive education. Depending on their age, interests, and aptitudes, students also worked in private employment or some unit of the school system related to the occupational courses they were studying. In addition, each student attended weekly group counseling sessions and individual sessions as needed. There were no dropouts from the experimental group, compared to a 25 percent rate in the control group. While academic growth was limited, there was significant growth of employer satisfaction with gains in the areas of motivation and attitudes toward self, peers, and society. School attendance and in-school behavior improved. Implications for educating other youths with special needs are suggested.

423. New York State Education Department. A manual for guidance personnel in area occupational centers and in all occupational education settings. Albany: NYSDE, Bureau of Guidance, 1970. (ED 041 120)

To make this manual useful in understanding required counselor functions in occupational education and how to apply them, data were obtained by questionnaire from administrative personnel and guidance staff in New York State Area Occupational Centers and from 45 out-of-state persons in comparable positions. Guidelines for specific service areas of occupational guidance cover selection and admission, counseling, student appraisal, coordination, student and public information, job placement, and evaluation and research. In each of these areas, guidance personnel will find objectives, needed aids and activities for accomplishing objectives, current and suggested offerings by New York State Area Occupational Centers, suggestions or comments for performance, and useful forms and materials.

424. New York State Education Department. Planning models for group counseling. Albany: NYSDE, Bureau of Continuing Education Curriculum Services, 1969. (ED 045 934)

This publication provides planning models for counseling with groups of disadvantaged adults; the models are focused on the vocational success of the individual. The trainee is helped to perceive his role realistically and to plan his future place in society. Self-evaluation and planning for future employment are major themes running through the sessions. Through the sessions the counselor can teach significant items of information regarding work and self. Although this material is especially designed for adult groups preparing to enter the labor force, the techniques may be modified somewhat for use with non-college-bound secondary students. The materials do not constitute a sequential course of study, nor do they encompass all the problems encountered by the disadvantaged worker. Rather they are planning models that counselors will want to adapt to the needs of their own clientele and the local conditions prevailing in their area.

425. New York State Education Department. Project ABLE: descriptive summaries of project ABLE programs. Albany: NYSDE, Division of Pupil Personnel Services, 1969. (ED 038 737)

Project ABLE is a series of demonstration educational programs initiated in 1961 for the purpose of identifying and encouraging potential abilities among pupils from culturally deprived groups and low socioeconomic backgrounds. The word ABLE was chosen to indicate a belief that, given adequate resources, schools are ABLE to devise educational procedures which insure equality of educational opportunity for all pupils including those identified as "disadvantaged." In order to participate and receive financial support from state funds, school systems in Cooperation with the Project Unit of the Division of Pupil Personnel Services developed demonstration programs to meet identified educational needs at the local level. A wide variety of techniques with observable positive results were utilized by the participating school districts.

426. New York State Education Department. School to employment program (STEP)—second annual report, 1962–1963: Albany: NYSED, Bureau of Guidance, 1963. (ED 001 440)

STEP is a part-time school, part-time work program designed to meet the needs of potential school dropouts 15 years of age or older. Pupils attend school in the morning and work in the afternoons. The teacher-coordinator plays a crucial role and meets with a group of 15 to 20 pupils daily to "orient" them to school and work experiences. The coordinator counsels his pupils individually, places them, and supervises their work experience. A typical day includes a period each of English, social studies, an elective, STEP orientation in the morning, and work as a clerk, messenger, stock boy, custodian, or general helper in the afternoon. The majority of students were placed with private agencies, but some were assigned to work stations in tax-supported agencies.

Cases presented show these results: in 1962–63, 27% of the pupils were returned to a normal school program, 11% entered full-time employment, 13% were removed for lack of progress, 44% completed the year in STEP, and 5% became school dropouts.

A substantial number of participants in the follow-up study are reported in the "no information" category, 66% of the active but only 48% of the control group were either in school or employed in June 1963.

427. New York State Education Department. Vocational guidance models. A review. Albany: NYSDE, Bureau of Guidance, 1969. (ED 038 533)

The five projects presented in this report illustrate different approaches to vocational guidance. (1) An occupational survey of St. Lawrence County was undertaken to determine the curriculum needs of the vocational centers. Secondary objectives were to determine employment needs and opportunities and to provide improved occupational information, placement, and public relations, (2) The establishment of District Vocational Guidance Centers provided a broad-based model program of information and guidance services, (3) While enrolled in an inservice course which integrated career information and counseling techniques, counselors developed a curriculum guide designed to help students make a smooth transition from school to work and to develop a realistic understanding of their role in life, (4) The Rochester Career Guidance Project developed an electronic counseling system to enable students to learn how to make effective plans and decisions, (5) A model vocational guidance program featured group guidance sessions for occupations and careers in grades 7 and 9, and job placement with supportive counseling in grades 11 and 12. A followup study is included for graduates of two area vocational centers, classes of 1963–1966.

428. Niles Community Schools. Occupational education for all students. Niles, Mich.: NCS. (ES 001 777)

Occupational education will be offered to college-bound and prevocational students in grades 1–10. Emphasis will be placed upon helping each student to develop—(1) proper attitudes toward the world of work, (2) an appreciation of the tools of work, (3) a knowledge of the many families of work, and (4) an understanding of the free enterprise system. Occupational counselors will work with sixth grade students and their parents to assure that students are working toward realistic goals. In the seventh and eighth grades, students will have 9 weeks of occupational courses in home economics, business, and industrial arts. The units will be designed to help the student develop insight into how people get their work done. The student will have the opportunity to work in many different phases of a specific occupational area. Ninth grade students, in addition to occupational arts unit, will be offered a course entitled "Occupational Information," to create an awareness of clusters of occupations. During the final week, students will be required to develop a tentative schedule of goal-oriented courses for the next three grades. All 10th grade students will be required to enroll in a junior achievement program. Representatives from local business and industry will consult with the staff and students on their projects. Approximately 2,626 public and nonpublic school students, grades 6–10, will be served. For further information, contact Daniel Stevens, 720 East Main St., Niles, Michigan 49120. (616) 683-0731.

429. Oakland Unified School District. A bold venture, integration in depth with student populations. Oakland, Cal.: OUSD, 1965. (ED 001 598)

This project will focus on increasing the quality of education and human relations to foster real understanding across racial lines. A series of closely related programs will attempt to help disadvantaged children develop the skills, knowledge and attitudes necessary for future success. Integration in depth will be fostered by common social activities and educational activities, among students, school personnel and parents.

Included are inter-school activities, teacher in-service education, and cooperative projects with community agencies. A regional demonstration laboratory will be set up to conduct experimental programs in educating disadvantaged students, with the assistance of the University of California. Full-time planning personnel who are specialists in urban affairs will be assigned to schools. Emphasis will be on technical and vocational education, use of teaching fellows, and in-service education. A Parent Education Experimental Program will include training teachers to work with parents. The Scholarship Development Program will work to identify students with potential, assist them in educational and career planning and in finding scholarship assistance.

Development of mass communication services will include education via closed circuit television and video tape recorders. The Basic Educational Skills Training Center will serve recent or potential high school dropouts, offering intensive vocational guidance and a core curriculum on a part time basis. An intensive attack on the dropout problem will consist of curricular experimentation and improved counseling systems. Massive health services will conduct educational health and referral services in and out of school sites.

430. Oakland Unified School District. Summary digest of the interagency school project. Oakland, Cal.: OUSD. (ED 001 600)

Programs included in the Interagency School Project were listed and described. They included Kindergarten-Primary Grades, Language Awareness Program, Madison Junior High School Special Instructional Program, Youth Study Centers, Adult Education, Curriculum Material Development, a program for school-age pregnant girls, Associated Agencies (Elementary School Program, Group Counseling for Boys in Elementary Schools, Special Assignments to augment the Project Operations such as reading consultants, librarians, guidance and psychometric testing, school-community workers, reading specialists, and research assistants), Youth Employment Project, and a Preschool Project.

431. Odgers, J. G. Placement: a counselor's job. *School Counselor,* 1968, 15(5). 398–400

Only to the extent that the guidance program identifies and tackles pupil needs, sometimes in cooperation with other school staff and non-school resources, will it get the support it needs. One of the significant guidance needs faced by all pupils is help in placement in that first step beyond high school.

432. Odle, S. G. The student information center as an educational resource. *Vocational Guidance Quarterly,* 1967, 15(3), 217–220.

This article records how the College of Idaho, Caldwell, Idaho, has integrated educational and occupational information with a multi-purpose information center as a service to the college community. Two principles were applied. The first was that students are more likely to make meaningful use of educational-vocational and related guidance materials when they are individually motivated. The second was that these materials would be utilized most effectively by constant exposure in a variety of settings to a number of people at their individual convenience.

433. Ofman, W. Evaluation of group counseling procedures. *Journal of Counseling Psychology,* 1964, 11(2), 152–159.

In evaluating the effectiveness of a group counseling procedure five groups of 60 students each were compared. Results indicated that the groups, while comparable in ability, differed in initial GPA. As a function of counseling, the Experimental Group's GPA became comparable to the Baseline Group's, and significantly higher than the Control and Dropout Group's GPA. The Wait Group did not improve until after counseling. GPAs of the Control and Dropout Groups did not improve at all.

Since this investigation stressed the control of relevant baseline, temporal (criterion measures were taken over eight semesters) and critical motivational variables, it was concluded that the group counseling procedure described was effective in improving scholastic behavior.

434. Ohio Department of Education. Ohio vocational interest survey. Columbus, Ohio: Ohio Testing Services, Division of Guidance and Testing, 751 Northwest Boulevard, Columbus, Ohio 43212.

The OVIS contains 24 interest scales which encompass all jobs in the world of work, from "manual work" to "medical." The inventory consists of 280 job activity items and students response to each item in terms of "like," "neutral to," "dislike," and "dislike very much." The student information questionnaire gathers background information about the student's expressed vocational plans, subject area preferences, high school program plans, post-high school plans and vocational education course interests. By combining information from the inventory and the questionnaire, a comparison can be made to check the consistency between measured interests and expressed interests, subject area preferences and educational plans.

435. Ohio State Department of Education. Student vocational survey. Columbus: OSDE, 1965. (ED 014 532)

Procedures for determining student interest in a vocational education program are described. A planning check sheet, an orientation check sheet, a tabulation procedure, and a report form are included for use of school system personnel engaged in a vocational survey. The appendix includes a student vocational interest questionnaire, an interpretation key, suggestions for using the questionnaire, and an overview of the procedures for conducting a vocational education community survey. A newspaper article, an announcement, and speech outlines are included for use in promoting and administering a survey.

436. Ohio State Department of Education. Vocational home economics curriculum guide for Ohio, grades 7–12. Columbus: OSDE, Division of Vocational Education, 1966. (ED 034 024)

Developed by teachers, supervisors, and teacher educators, this guide is designed to aid teachers and administrators in planning and implementing effective junior and senior high school home economics education programs. The first section of the guide covers general background information such as the purpose and role of home economics, teacher views on homemaking, definitions, and a suggested subject matter, sequence, and time allotment per unit for grades 7–12. The major portion of the guide is comprised of resource units for each of the subject areas listed on the scope and sequence chart: (1) Home Management, Family Finance, and Consumer Buying, (2) Personal, Family, and Community Relations, (3) Child Development, (4) Foods, Nutrition, and Health, (5) Clothing, Textiles, and Related Art, and (6) Housing, Home Furnishings, and Equipment. Units contain generalizations to be developed, content, learning activities, suggested resources, and bibliographies. The material should be adapted to meet local needs.

437. Ohlsen, M. M. Counseling children in groups. Springfield: Illinois State Office of the Superintendent of Public Instruction, 1966. (ED 010 890)

Counseling is an accepting, trusting relationship dealing with normal children and emphasizing the counselor's special ability to listen, empathize, and understand. The setting of group counseling provides excellent conditions for learning. Effective group counseling involves treatment by the group as well as individual treatment within the group. Counselors must be aware of how group members' comments and actions influence other members. The selection of youngsters for group counseling should be based upon the type of problem (students with similar problems should not be placed in the same group), readiness for counseling, the child's impact on other group members, and his parents' support. Group counseling methods must be modified for use with elementary school children (fourth, fifth and sixth graders). Such groups require more structure and should be more limited in time and number of participants. The counselor plays a more active role, and support and assistance from teachers and parents are needed outside the group. Role-playing is an effective method for this age level. As verbalization is difficult for primary school-age children, more play material is necessary. Teachers may use group techniques to motivate learning and to provide individuals with an opportunity to relieve a special problem through role-playing. This is one of the reports from the Zion Conference and the Elementary School Demonstration Centers included in "Elementary School Guidance in Illinois."

438. Ohlsen, M. M. & Proff, F. C. Response patterns associated with group counseling. Urbana: Illinois University, College of Education, 1960. (ED 002 993)

Further analyses of data collected in an earlier study (ED 002 992) were conducted to determine effects of selected group counseling factors including (1) relationships between client growth and topics discussed in group counseling sessions, (2) effects of group composition on counseling group interpersonal behaviors, and (3) ways of measuring changes in clients' behavior. Interactions among ninth graders and prospective counselors were classified in terms of effect, referent, and topic. Four psychologists (not previously connected with the study) arranged protocols obtained from a picture-story test in order from pretest to followup tests for the ninth graders and their prospective counselors. Then the effect of change on protocol arrangement was determined. Interpersonal behaviors of clients and prospective counselors were then grouped under the categories of approach, attack, and withdrawal. Analysis of variance, chi square, and rank order correlations were then performed. Major objectives of the study were not achieved. Cues used to arrange protocols, however, suggested meaningful questions for subsequent analysis.

439. Oklahoma State Department of Education. A guide for developmental vocational guidance. Grades K–12. Oklahoma City: OSDE, 1968. (ED 026 532)

The purpose of this guide is to share with teachers, administrators, and counselors recommendations involving some facets of child development and some basis for vocational decision making. Vocational guides are presented for Grades K–3, Grades 4–6, Grades 7–9, and Grades 10–12. Elements of each guide include: introduction; objectives of vocational guidance, both general and specific; suggested activities; activity models including goals, activities, and resource materials; descriptive information on occupational clusters; periodicals and journals, and additional resources.

440. Oklahoma State Dept. of Education. A guide for elementary guidance and counseling in Oklahoma schools. Oklahoma City: OSDE, 1970. (ED 049 475)

Starting from the premise that guidance is a technique for facilitating learning and the development of youth, this booklet represents the thinking of teachers, administrators and college personnel about guidance related concepts. The guide deals with a comprehensive range of topics: (1) the history, needs and trends of elementary guidance in Oklahoma, (2) the philosophy, principles and objectives of elementary school guidance, (3) the developmental aspects and special needs of elementary school children, and (4) the responsibilities and competencies of the elementary school counselor. The bulk of the guide delineates the essential components of elementary school guidance programs. A short bibliography is included.

441. Oklahoma Vocational Research Coordinating Unit. A guide for teachers of a course in career exploration, grades 8–9–10. Stillwater: OVRCU, 1970. (ED 049 356)

Developed by counselors and teachers in a workshop setting, this teaching guide should be of value in planning and implementing a course in career exploration. Designed for use in grades 8, 9, and 10, the guide presents creative ideas for the following units: (1) Know Yourself, (2) World of Work, (3) Use of Occupational Information, and (4) Career Educational Planning. Each unit includes stated objectives, suggested activities, evaluation techniques, and sources of recommended instructional materials. Arranged in a four-column format, the guide also includes check lists, illustrations, sample forms, and a publisher index.

442. Olsen, L. C. & Venema, W. H. Development of a projective technique for obtaining educationally useful information indicating pupil's attitudes toward work and occupational plans, Report number 21. Final report. Pullman: Washington State University, Department of Education, 1968. (ED 022 960)

The purpose of this study was to develop a projective technique which would (1) identify youths' attitudes toward certain distributive, construction, service, and agricultural occupation, and (2) identify factors associated with occupational aspirations. Interviews were conducted with 88 Caucasian and Negro Job Corps enrollees and 91 Caucasian and Negro ninth grade pupils using 10 drawings representing work typical of the occupations. Results indicated the nature of subjects' occupational preferences and ways these are influenced by factors such as socioeconomic status and self concepts. Practically all subjects aspired to occupational levels higher than the occupations of their parents. Perceptions of parental feelings only slightly affected the occupational interests of the subjects. Most subjects seemed to view work largely from a basic need level—food, shelter, clothing, etc.—with relatively little concern for satisfying higher needs. Few subjects expressed concern about abilities and aptitudes necessary for various jobs. This suggests that more knowledge of occupations and one's abilities and aptitudes are necessary for adequate occupational choice making decisions. Further research might focus on modifying this technique for use with groups.

443. Oregon State Board of Education. Guidelines: elementary school Guidance and Counseling. Salem: Oregon State Board of Education, 1972.

The Guidelines was developed for use by school administrators, teachers, counselors, parents and others who want to establish or improve a program of guidance services for elementary school children. Guidelines is based on the philosophy that guidance services should focus upon not only educational and career awareness of the child, but also provide activities that build personal and social awareness.

This monograph provides guidelines for establishing and/or evaluating a school guidance program at the elementary level.

444. Oregon State Department of Education. Guide to structure and articulation of occupational education programs (grades 7 through 12 and post-high school). Salem: OSDE, Division of Community Colleges and Vocational Education, 1968. (ED 023 856)

Intended as a flexible instrument, this guide suggests approaches for providing (1) meaningful occupational education throughout the junior high and high school structure, (2) opportunities for attaining entry level occupational competency in the secondary education complex, and (3) occupational education at the high school level which is appropriate to continuation beyond high school. On the basis of (1) the adoption of the occupational cluster concept which involves its grouping of occupations with identical or similar skill and knowledge requirements, (2) the implementation of a program of occupational exploration in grades 7 through 10, (3) the availability of adequate guidance and counseling, and (4) the provision of introductory courses at the ninth and 10th grade levels, a pattern of occupational education for secondary schools is suggested and approaches to organization, content, scope, and sequence of 12 cluster-based occupational curriculums are presented. The roles of high school occupational programs are identified as providing specific preparation for those who drop out and those who do not continue their occupational education. The alignment of the 12 curriculums with typical community college programs is illustrated, and the development of agriculture education from grade 9 through the community college program is presented schematically.

445. Oregon State Department of Education. Teacher's guide to: self understanding through occupational exploration (SUTOE). Salem: Oregon State Department of Education, Division of Community Colleges and Vocational Education, 1968. (ED 024 965)

Self Understanding Through Occupational Exploration (SUTOE) is a one year course designed to assist ninth graders with educational and career planning. SUTOE aims at enabling students to gain knowledge and understanding of possible future goals and job opportunities, to develop social skills in applying for work via application and job interviews, to gain understanding of employers' viewpoints and requirements, to broaden knowledge of the general economic structure as related to labor force needs, to understand the importance of opportunities offered through high school and post-high school training programs, and to assess one's own strengths and weaknesses. The course, individually tailored, includes evaluation of goals via investigation, idea exchanges in groups, role playing, interviewing, letter writing, reporting, visitations, speakers, films, appropriate research exercises, and testing. A teacher's guide accompanies the course description.

446. Osipow, S. H. & Alderfer, R. D. The effects of a vocationally oriented speech course on the vocational planning behavior of high school students. *Personnel and Guidance Journal,* 1968, 47(3), 244–248.

> A sample of 407 tenth, eleventh, and twelfth grade students took a speech course oriented toward assignments concerning career development and decisions. The vocational attitudes and behaviors of the students at the completion of the course indicated that both male and female students were engaging in more frequent informal discussions about career development following the course than they had preceding it.

447. Overs, R. Covert occupational information. September, 1967. *Vocational Guidance Quarterly,* 1967, 16(1), 7–12.

> Covert occupational information includes occupational information which is generally unwritten and modifies, amends, or contradicts overt occupational information. The authenticity of covert information may be denied publicly by responsible authorities although its validity may be high as measured by administrative actions. The counselor who achieves practical results in helping the client make realistic occupational choices which culminate in the client getting into school or getting a job usually collects and uses this covert information.

448. Overs, R. P. & Deutsch, E. C. Sociological studies of occupations; abstracts. Milwaukee, Wis.: Curative Workshop of Milwaukee, 1968. (ED 027 397)

> One hundred abstracts of sociological studies of occupations are collected in this volume, designed primarily as a vocational guidance counseling tool. Taken mainly from journal articles, the studies usually relate to the subtle social characteristics of jobs, such as cultural pressures, role identities, role conflicts, prestige, and differential social situations. The occupations range from janitor to physician and musician to city-manager. The abstract format for each of the studies included: (1) a brief description of the article and its major findings, (2) the author's own abstract (when available), (3) a description of data gathering and treatment methods, (4) methodological cautions to heed when interpreting findings (when relevant), (5) a general statement of theoretical orientation, (6) an indication of scope, whether the article refers to a job or an occupational field, (7) implications for counseling, emphasizing the study's significance in the area of vocational counseling, written by an experienced psychologist (vocational counselor), and (8) the pertinent Dictionary of Occupational Titles classification and code. A subject and an author index are included.

449. Palo Alto Unified School District. Conference summary—from theory to practice. The description and demonstration of a guidance program in one district K–12. Palo Alto, Cal.: PAUSD, 1968. (ED 020 535)

> Various aspects of the Palo Alto guidance program were presented at the conference. The objectives of the program were based on the belief that guidance should foster individualization in the development of all children by providing conditions which would ensure this individualization. These two theoretical constructs, reinforcement theory and decision-making process, have directly affected the development of the Palo Alto guidance program, and have contributed to its framework. The abstracts presented, which describe particulars of the program, can be divided into three general categories—(1) the role and function of guidance workers, (2) some guidance programs and practices, and (3) research and evaluation activities. The concluding section examines areas of future concern. This paper was presented at the Palo Alto Guidance Conference (Palo Alto, California, January 20, 1968).

450. Paniagua, L. & Jackson, V. C. Role play in new career training. New York City: New York University, School of Education, 1968.

> Role play is discussed as an aid to the implementation of New Careers programs in human service agencies. Goals of the New Careers programs include: (a) expansion of health, education, and welfare institutions, (b) meaningful jobs for the

underemployed, (c) advancement opportunities for all human service agency employees through in-service training, and (d) development of new skilled and professional manpower. Role play is defined in context, and its functions discussed. Consideration is given to (a) the protected environment of role play, (b) role play as an aid to group process and increased self-knowledge, (c) implications for learning new ideas, teaching new communications, and leadership skills, (d) dealing with ambiguity, and (e) modification of behavior through role playing. A second section is a manual on how to conduct role playing sessions. It discusses the role of the trainer, techniques and methods for stimulating interest, and incidental learnings in the process.

451. Parker, P. Characteristics of full-time public community junior college instructors; the Kansas profile. Kansas State College of Pittsburg, 1970. (ED 052 777)

A 10-page questionnaire was used to determine the characteristics of Kansas junior college personnel. The data collected were to provide a profile of the teachers and to be available in detail to anyone interested. The four categories of inquiry were: (1) biographical data on age, sex, marital status, residence, schooling, education and occupation of parents, etc.; (2) teaching experience such as kind and number of previous positions, early career pursuits, and out-of-state jobs; (3) professional qualifications, including degrees and where earned, special areas of preparation, certification, teaching assignments and the time devoted to them; and (4) community activities and membership in professional organizations. Fourteen significant findings of the survey are listed with comments. This type of descriptive research, by its nature, cannot pin-point cause and effect and their use in long-range planning, but it can nevertheless make a great contribution when combined with other objectively derived information. After further research, administrators may eventually discover, for example, the relationship of an instructor's preparation and experience to his teaching productivity, or even how to measure the productivity of the instructor. A copy of the questionnaire, its cover letter, and a list of Kansas junior colleges are appended.

452. Parr, C. Student's personal adjustment to work suggested plans for group discussions in vocational industrial education, volume I. Austin: Texas University, Department of Industrial Education, 1963. (ED 016 764)

Vocational teachers may use this guide as a source of appropriate discussion topics and methods in student discussions relative to job orientation in cooperative part time classes. It was developed by an instructor-coordinator and an advisory committee. Textual material covers the purpose of group discussions, how to plan a discussion, suggestions on leading a discussion, reminders on the use of the chalkboard, do's and don'ts on the use of questions, and master outline of discussion topics. Nineteen lesson guides and information sheets cover actual subjects for discussion—introduction to vocational education, safety, vocational guidance, and job attitudes and relations. Each lesson guide contains the aim, reference, materials or aids, introductory information, correlated points to be covered and methods, group participation, and summarization. The teacher of the 2-year program should be a qualified coordinator, and students should be juniors or seniors. This guide and volume II (VT 000 268) are available for $6.00 from Industrial Education Department, Division of Extension, The University of Texas, Austin, Texas 78712.

453. Parry, K. & Burch, J. An instrument for measuring the "need to work." *Vocational Guidance Quarterly,* 1968, 16(4), 264–268.

An instrument capable of measuring individuals' need-to-work was constructed following the model of the Edwards Personal Preference Schedule, using items that corresponded to Super's description of the three basic needs-to-work. An item analysis and consequent improvement of item discrimination were performed on several populations. The need-to-work patterns were then investigated and differences were demonstrated congruent with Super's hypothesis. This can be used to execute carefully controlled studies.

454. Patten, R. J. & Steinmetz, L. L. Enthusiasm, interest, and learning, the results of game training. A study of simulation. Boulder: Colorado University, 1967. (ED 012 405)

At the University of Colorado's School of Business, an evaluation was made of gaming as an effective training device for lower ranking management and rank-and-file personnel. Participants were college students and part-time students, believed to be like persons involved in management training programs and programs for rank-and-file employees. The course was introductory accounting, decisions being made on finance and distribution functions of a business firm. Through an accounting feedback system, these decisions resulted in financial data to be used in making further decisions. Learning and attitudes were compared with those of students taught the same material by the same professors using the traditional practice set. The game participants tended to surpass their expectations, appeared to learn more, like the course, and seemed to be influenced toward choosing a business career. The nongame participants' experience failed to meet their expectations of the course. Companies interested in training employees in mechanistic routine work would do well to consider the use of games to stimulate interest and reduce the expense of training (by reducing the number of dropouts and from the economies of the self-teaching aspects). This article was published in "Training and Development Journal," April 1967, a monthly journal of the American Society for Training and Development, 313 Price Place, P.O. Box 5307, Madison, Wisconsin 53705.

455. Paulson, B. B. (et al.) Group guidance for high school. Chicago: Board of Education, 1964. (ED 001 052)

A group guidance program is designed to assist the student in the development of realistic ideas about himself and to help him promote plans for himself within this context. Emphasis on the needs for the individual to make his own decisions increases from age/grade level to age/grade level. Many of the practicalities of such decision-making are best served in group guidance sessions. The sessions have the advantage of sharing with others, providing inescapable guidance services and structure for the counselor.

Modular materials have been developed to assure guidance service of over a four-year period with weekly regularity. The units provided are: Ninth grade: "Getting the Most Out of High School"; Tenth grade: "Developing Myself for the Future"; Eleventh grade: "Taking a Long Look Ahead"; Twelfth grade: "Living in an Adult World."

Session management suggestions are provided for use in planning and operating a group guidance program. A bibliography is provided by grade level unit.

456. Pearce, F. C. Continuing employment through training. Modesto, Cal.: Modesto Junior College, 1966. (ED 011 357)

The effectiveness of Modesto Junior College's Multioccupational Training Project at New Hope School was evaluated on the basis of subsequent employment of trainees. Data on the current employment statuses of trainees and dropouts, reasons for being out of the labor force, anticipated employment, employment patterns and earning power of employed trainees, sources of present jobs, referral patterns, and assessments of the value of training were obtained with a post-training report, generally in conjunction with interviews, 3, 6, and 12 months after training. New Hope Project employment rates for any given week ran between 55 and 60 percent. The actual unemployment rate for the project was between 10 and 19 percent. Eight percent of the trainees were out of the labor force. Trainees tended to enter training-related jobs, and those who did so overwhelmingly found their training of value. Job placement was done more successfully by the training project than by employment services. The average earning power was listed as $1.82 per hour and compared favorably with the earning power of others in the subculture. Prevocational training or lack thereof appeared to have little bearing on subsequent employment. A comprehensive followup study of trainees and evaluative studies of training programs, training needs, participant characteristics, and reasons for nonparticipation were recommended. The document includes 13 tables.

457. Pennsylvania Advancement School. Group counseling for urban schools: a handbook. Philadelphia: PAS, 1971. (ED 048 411)

Established in September 1967 and funded under ESEA Title I and Title III, the Pennsylvania Advancement School (PAS) is a non-profit corporation under contract to the School District of Philadelphia. Funds from the Education Professions Development Act and from private foundations have been used to support small projects initiated by the school. About 200 underachieving boys, were selected from the fifth, sixth, seventh, and eighth grades of Philadelphia public and parochial schools. During the first two years of PAS, boys remained for a 14-week term; currently the students attend for an entire school year. The PAS program also includes curriculum development, intern training, and staff development activities. During 1970–71, PAS is helping to prepare a core staff group for the opening of a new middle school in September of 1971. In its external staff development program, PAS works closely with groups of teachers and administrators in six Philadelphia public schools, helping each to plan and operate semi-autonomous units called "minischools." PAS conducts an intensive summer program for these groups and several PAS staff members are assigned full-time to help the minischools during the school year.

458. Perrone, P. A. & Gross, L. A national school counselor evaluation of occupational information. Madison: Wisconsin University, 1968. (ED 019 717)

A comprehensive survey of occupational information literature and an evaluation of its use by secondary school personnel were conducted. Analysis showed that the evaluations and recommendations held true for all regions of the United States. Further analysis indicated that counselors' responses were not affected by such situational variables as student destination after graduation, time spent in counseling, and pupil-counselor ratio. The responses by the librarians showed that —(1) senior boys made the greatest use of occupational information and ninth- and 10th-grade boys the least, (2) the Occupational Outlook Handbook, pamphlets from private publishers, and general books were the most common sources, and (3) accuracy and readability were the reasons given for students' use of these sources. The vocational instructors mentioned textbooks, periodicals, and the Dictionary of Occupational Titles as other frequently used sources. The counselor's responses to the questionnaire suggested that counselors are generally satisfied with the available information if they feel college-bound students have the greatest information need, while counselors who feel terminal high school students have the greatest need are generally dissatisfied. The Occupational Outlook Handbook was the primary source of information. The major criticism of both descriptive and outlook sources was that not enough aspects of the job were covered, and those aspects which were covered lacked detail.

459. Perrone, P. A. Use and evaluation of occupational information materials. 1967. (ED 013 462)

Of 18,000 secondary schools contacted, 30 percent responded to a questionnaire on occupational information materials. Occupational literature was obtained by counselors 80 percent of the time. On the average, $178.00 is available yearly for this purpose. The facilities available for displaying materials are described. The circumstances under which students use occupational information and the kinds of students who use these materials are discussed. The information sources used most frequently are rated and explained. Counselors were asked to evaluate two types of occupational literature (description and outlook) for (1) terminal students, (2) students planning post high school, vocational, or technical training, and (3) students planning to enter junior college or college. A summary of the information is presented in percentages. No conclusions are drawn because of the low percentage of returns. Another survey of schools not previously contacted is underway. This speech was presented at the American Personnel and Guidance Association Convention, Dallas, Texas, March, 1967.

460. Perry, P. Tommy's career choice. *School Counselor,* 1970, 17(3), 182–188.

Presents skit designed to help students open doors to exploration of job possibilities.

461. Peterson, N. D. A pilot project in vocational guidance. Placement and work experience for youth for whom existing work experiences are not appropriate. Livonia, Mich.: Livonia Public Schools, Department of Secondary Education. (ED 021 970)

Twenty-five sophomore students recommended by their school principal or counselor participated in a pilot educational program designed to be appropriate to the interests and needs of potential high school male dropouts. Test scores, inventories, student records, office files, and employment analyses of the participants were examined to determine similarities of those students who showed some or little success in school, on the job, or in school and on the job. The students were provided with some form of low-level community work experience and 1 hour per day in the classroom. Some findings were (1): The boys participating in the project had a mean IQ of 88 with a range of 82 to 99 for 95 percent of the group, (2) 82 percent of the participants scored below the 50th percentile on the Iowa Silent Reading Test, (3) All of the students tended to score low in mental ability and achievement tests, and (4) The boys as a group had a dislike for academic subjects before and during the study. The objectives of the project were generally met, and the majority of the boys were retained for the 1965-66 school year. Although the project had its impact and served a good purpose, it was concluded that the progress made by the participants was not commensurate with the time, effort, and money invested in their interests.

462. Peterson, R. A. Rehabilitation of the culturally different: a model of the individual in cultural change. *Personnel and Guidance Journal,* 1967, 1001–1007.

Services of rehabilitation agencies and facilities tend to be structured to the needs of the larger American culture. It is important, however, to reconsider our social service programs in view of the needs of different cultural groups when providing services that will aid these individuals to move across cultural boundaries. An attempt is made in this paper to develop a model of the individual who undergoes such cultural transition. Such a model should help define problems in service programs, assess the value of current service activites, and identify areas for developing new services that will aid the overall process of cultural transition. A model of behavior development is outlined, followed by a formulation of a model of the individual in cultural change.

463. Pettit, M. L. & Robinson, H. G. A study of methods designed to improve the relationships between parents' attitudes and the underachievement of their elementary school children. Ellensburg: Central Washington State College, 1966. (ED 012 809)

This study was designed to test the differential effectiveness and interaction effects of several methods designed to improve the relationship between parents' attitudes and the underachievement of their elementary school children. The investigation also attempted to extend an earlier study of the effects brought about in children by emphasizing psychological changes in parents. Two groups of probable underachieving students who were soon to be fourth graders were identified. The mothers of these children were then asked to an orientation meeting, and a self-analysis form was administered to those mothers who returned to the second meeting. The scores were rank-ordered and the mothers assigned to one of three groups according to anxiety level. An interpersonal check list was also administered, where the mothers sorted on self, spouse, child, and self-ideal. After 11 sessions in three experimental groups which either emphasized group dynamics, group guidance, or a combination of both, the mothers were retested. The children were retested also to determine if benefits accruing to the mothers from their group experiences had become manifest in the children. Although there were changes in academic performance in the direction predicted, the study could not determine the differential effectiveness of the group methods used to involve the mothers. Nevertheless, it was concluded that the mothers' group involvement was a beneficial experience and that further studies should include the fathers of underachievers.

464. Philadelphia Public Schools. Evaluation of the Harrison Heights Program. Philadelphia, Pa.: PPS, Great Cities School Improvement Program, 1961. (ED 001 639)

The program was designed for children of limited background. It attempted to discover and develop to the fullest, visible, or latent talents of the children. Its goals were to raise the aspirations of the pupils. By exposing all of the children to many kinds of experience, the attempt to interest them early in their career choices was successful.

Pupil talent was identified by the use of the Verbal Ability Test, Iowa Test, Lorge-Thorndike Test, and City Standardized Tests. The pupils were rated according to their physical, social, emotional and mental characteristics, as well as by teacher-counselor referrals.

In the language arts program, homogeneous grouping was used but individual differences were not ignored. Small groups and individual instruction were used to provide for various rates of progress and differences in achievement within the grade level. Within the language arts program, emphasis was placed on phonics, spelling, handwriting, creative writing, and speech. A language laboratory was used, and in-service education was provided for teachers. The other programs included arithmetic, social studies, science, and physical education.

The counselor worked with teachers in handling problem children. The school-community coordinator maintained communications with parents; some of her activities included assisting and training the families in domestic duties.

465. Phillips, P. B. The guidance of Negro students in northern secondary schools: a source book. *Dissertation Abstracts,* 1967, 27(8), 2617A.

The development of this source book was based on an attempt to study in depth the present principles and techniques of guidance as they relate to the stated and implied needs of Negro youngsters, and to offer a conceptual scheme for the focus and clarification of guidance theory and program.

466. Phillips, P. B. (et al.) How high school counselors can assist students to successfully enter government and industry. Paper presented at the meeting of the Workshop on Vocational and Occupational Guidance in the Sixties and Seventies, May, 1964. (ED 015 250)

Approximately 200 counselors and principals from 85 high schools enrolling 76,610 pupils throughout seven southern states attended a 2-day conference to examine and evaluate guidance programs and to suggest improvements. A followup study of the conference, indicated that 88 percent of the respondents had improved their vocational guidance programs through a greater variety of informative materials and that 67 percent had better accessibility to such materials. Texts of the major speeches are given—(1) "The Role of the High School in Preparing Students for Employment," by Samuel Danley and Hugh Ryals, (2) "Career Outlook," by Brunswick Bagdon, (3) "Management Looks at Employment Possibilities," by Howard Lockwood, (4) "Opportunities for Women in the Sixties and Seventies," by Rose Terlin, (5) "The College Placement Office and the High School," by Anthony Rachel, (6) "Tasks for Today, Goals for Tomorrow," by Arthur Chapin, (7) "Motivation—A Realistic Approach by Schools in Urban and Rural Communities in Relation to Employment," by William Johnston, and (8) "Recent Developments in Employment Trends for Youth," by Eli Cohen. Comments by other speakers, a conference summary, a summary of grassroots reports from the participating states, and a statement ("Employment Trends and School Enrollment") by Willard Wirtz are included. The appendixes consist of sources of resource materials, evaluation instruments, a list of participants, and an extensive bibliography.

467. Pierson, G. N. (et al.) A regional career information center, development and process. 1967. (ED 015 260)

The Center was established to collect, abstract, synthesize, produce, store, and disseminate career information to high schools and junior colleges in San Diego County, California.

468. Platt, A. H. Room to grow: "something special for all kids." Philadelphia: Philadelphia School District, 1969. (ED 033 403)

Room to Grow, an elementary school career guidance program grew out of frustration with urban problems of education and was shaped by contemporary research in career development theory. Career choice is viewed as developmental. It is also believed that life histories cannot be predicted and that a career is something that gives purpose to life. Experiences are provided which give more attention to the elementary school child's perception of himself and the image of the person he would like to become. Aspects taken into consideration are: (1) attitudes and values toward work, (2) socio-economic level, (3) educational expectations, and (4) self-concept. Room to Grow is conducted once a week for 7,000 fifth and sixth graders in Philadelphia. The program, supervised by three guidance consultants, consists of 25–30 weekly sessions of 45 minutes to an hour and a half. Some sessions are teacher-led, some have guest speakers, some are tours, and others are guidance sessions. The objectives of the program are: (1) to improve self-confidence, (2) to provide a wide range of career experiences, and (3) to develop a desirable approach to the process of career choice.

469. Ploughman, T. L. Project: Pontiac vocational career development program; evaluation report. Pontiac, Mich.: Educational Services and Products, Inc., 1971. (ED 053 331)

During the 1970–71 school year the Pontiac School District operated a vocational career development program to increase the occupational knowledge and self-concept of students. Evaluation of that first year pertained to context, input, process, and product. A description of the program, its results, and research procedures is included. Three major findings were: (1) Students showed significant gain in their level of occupational knowledge, (2) Upper elementary children showed greater gain in occupational knowledge than did lower elementary children, and (3) At the end of the program students selected occupations of higher rank than they did at the beginning of the program.

470. Poppel, N. Summer activities for students. *Vocational Guidance Quarterly,* 1964, 12(2), 99–103.

The summer months have always been an ideal time for high school students to experiment with new experiences. It is the purpose of this article to discuss some of the activities high school and college students can engage in which will be of benefit to them.

471. Powell, P. E. Implementing the manpower and economic education program. Arkadelphia, Ark.: Henderson State College, 1970. (ED 045 472)

The Manpower and Economic Education Program (MEE) is an occupational orientation course at the secondary level. Experiences in implementing MEE are discussed. The strategy used involves doing everything possible to promote programs that help youngsters prepare for effective participation in the manpower market. School districts are encouraged to develop occupational orientation programs. The three key words in this strategy are communicate, cooperate, and coordinate. It must include a delivery system providing results similar to those indicated in promotional activities. Schools must be provided with a complete package of materials and services, including text, teaching manual, evaluation instruments, personnel, etc. Television lessons have also been developed. Training the personnel is one of the most valuable services provided. Included with the speech is a handout summary of 82 lessons learned in implementing MEE, including categories for innovators, teachers, administrators, materials, students, and the community. Included is a list briefly describing some of the 75 television programs that are utilized.

472. Prediger, D. J. Converting test data to counseling information: system implementation in a vocational school. Iowa City, Iowa: American College Testing Program, 1971.

General objectives were to develop and implement computer-based procedures for obtaining validated data on the characteristics of vocational school students and to convert this data into counseling information. Two types of data-information conversion procedures were field-tested: similarity scores based on discriminant analysis, and success estimates on regression analysis. Scores from 36 aptitude, interest, and personality measures were accumulated for approximately 1600 prospective area vocational school students. A progress record was kept for each of these students after vocational school enrollment. Multivariate analyses conducted on antecedent and criterion data formed the bases for data-information conversion procedures used in the field tests. It is concluded that: (1) successful and satisfied students enrolled in diverse vocational programs can be differentiated by aptitude, interest, or personality measures obtained prior to or shortly after entry into the programs; (2) similarity scores and profiles represent effective techniques for translating data on these differences into useful counseling information; (3) useful estimates of vocational program success can be conveyed to students in the form of experience tables based on the best predictors in a comprehensive battery of aptitude measures; and (4) the development of a generalized system of computer-based procedures for data-information conversion is both feasible and desirable.

473. President's Council on Youth Opportunity. Manual for youth coordinators. Washington, D.C.: PCYO, 1969. (ED 038 496)

This manual was designed primarily for use by coordinators responsible for developing comprehensive community youth opportunity programs of employment, education, and recreation, but the material may also be of assistance to community and business leaders, educators, and others involved in expanding local opportunities for young people. Contents consist of five sections, covering (1) Planning, (2) Employment, (3) Education, (4) Recreation, and (5) Transportation, with each section providing information on the role of the coordinator within that facet of the program, funding and resources, reference materials, and program examples. Listings of various contacts helpful to youth coordinators are appended, including: (1) voluntary organizations, (2) local contacts and labor unions, (3) regional contacts in the Department of Health, Education and Welfare, (4) recreation and parks consultants, (5) Bureau of Outdoor Recreation state liaison officers, (6) National Forest camps, (7) 4-H youth camps, (8) state distributing agencies of the consumer food program, and (9) State Councils on the Arts.

474. Pressman, H. Enrichment program for academically talented junior high school students from low income families. Medford, Mass.: Tufts University, Lincoln Filene Center for Citizenship and Public Affairs, 1964. (ED 002 291)

A proposal for an enrichment program for academically talented junior high school students from low-income families in certain areas of Boston is presented. Basic assumptions are that there is an obvious and pressing need to give extra help to the able student from a disadvantaged background, and that a relatively brief enrichment experience for such students can produce substantial results in terms of future educational opportunities.

Some specific objectives are to identify academically talented junior high school students in the districts involved; to provide supplementary educational, cultural, and recreational experiences for these students; and to provide each student with useful guidance information about his immediate educational choices, special opportunities for future educational assistance, and part-time earning opportunities.

The program began during the spring semester of the school year 1964-65, and will run for 14 to 16 months thereafter. It involves 75 junior high school students who are predominantly boys. The program provides such services to students and parents as an evaluation and assessment of academic talent that is based on school records and that is followed by a series of tests; a full introduction and orientation to the project for the selected students and their parents; and a series of motivational initial experiences that include recreational exposures, general guidance sessions, discussion meetings with "hero" figures, and introductory student-parent meetings. Personnel include a director, a part-time associate director, a half-time secretary, five experienced teachers, and seven after-school guidance people. Preliminary budget estimates total $84,185.

475. Prince George's County Board of Education. Guidance guidelines: a handbook for secondary school counselors. Upper Marboro, Md.: PGCBE, 1964. (ED 001 140)

Directional procedures and techniques for administering the overall program of secondary school guidance is presented. The major emphasis of this guidance program is upon occupational, educational and social adjustment of all the pupils.

Services of the guidance program are described at length. The key is counseling, of individuals or groups. Referrals may be necessary to the various pupil personnel service which are ennumerated. The appraisal service is concerned with gathering and evaluating data about each pupil. The administration of both local and national test programs is the responsibility of the guidance service. Administrative procedures and hints for interpretation as described. Cumulative records are kept by guidance personnel; examples of various necessary forms are included. Other services are information, placement and in-service training. The clerical responsibilities described are often carried out by a guidance clerk.

A concluding analysis of this county's program indicates that growth of services and number of personnel have enabled counselors to concentrate more directly on counseling.

476. Pruitt, A. S. Plans for progress: vocational guidance institutes. *Counselor Education and Supervision,* 1968, 7(3), 292-298.

This article describes nine institutes held in 1965 which were designed to study the employment problems of disadvantaged youth. This description includes implications for these institutes in further counselor education efforts.

477. Pruitt, A. S. Teacher involvement in the curriculum and career guidance. *Vocational Guidance Quarterly,* 1969, 17(3), 189-193.

Discusses need for educational change to enable teacher to have planned impact on vocational decisions through curriculum.

478. Pruitt, R. E. (et al.) The career information center: a working model. Boston: Career Information Center, Northeastern University, 1969. (ED 037 772)

Northeastern University has, through its Career Information Center, developed a variety of career information programs and services for junior and senior high school students. The various services developed by the Career Information Center include the following: (1) providing career information services, (2) career assembly programs, (3) career conferences, (4) career radio programs, (5) career tape recording services, (6) career filmstrip services, and (7) career television programs. This pamphlet is a guide to the development and use of the above seven ideas. Each is explained, objectives are given, organization methods are suggested, and techniques for successful results are included. Each of the seven services are thoroughly explained and easily understood. Examples are used in each section.

479. Pucel, D. J. & Nelson, H. F. Project MINI-SCORE: some preliminary implications for vocational guidance. Washington, D.C.: Office of Education, Division of Comprehensive and Vocational Education Research, 1968. (ED 023 658)

The purpose of the 6-year Minnesota Student Characteristics and Occupationally Related Education Project (MINI-SCORE) is to identify criteria which are useful to counselors and others in the selection and counseling of post-high school vocational-technical students as they choose specific vocational-technical curriculums. Data were collected on 6,400 applicants with a variety of instruments, and three preliminary analyses were conducted. Descriptive data and implications for vocational guidance are reported. Project MINI-SCORE is scheduled for completion in 1970.

480. Quey, R. L. Structure of work as purposeful activity. *Vocational Guidance Quarterly,* 1971, 19(4), 258-265.

Work in its most universal aspect represents man's attempt to impose human purpose on his environment. Work is purposeful physical and mental activity oriented to the future and designed to produce economic goods and values to satisfy man's needs. It requires us to notice and respond actively to those aspects of the world that will serve our purposes directly and, indirectly. Consequently, the parameters of work are unusually broad, and it assumes many different forms resulting in thousands of distinct job titles. Certain recurring regularities of content, process, and function help to organize this otherwise confusing variety of work activity into a discernible essential structure, the consideration of which can greatly enhance our understanding of work and its significance for vocational guidance.

481. Rector, W. H. & Shaw, M. C. Group counseling with parents: feasibility, reactions, and interrelationships. Monograph number 5. Chico, Cal.: Chico State College, Western Center of the Interprofessional Research Commission on Pupil Personnel Services (IRCOPPS). (ED 022 235)

This monograph reports upon data collected and analyzed in connection with a research project testing the feasibility of group counseling with parents. The group counseling was a part of the school guidance services. Data were collected in six school districts and based upon the experiences of 38 counselors and 53 parent counseling groups. An analysis of the parent post-series reaction sheet showed a highly positive attitude in parents participating in group counseling. This attitude was strengthened after a second year of counseling in the same district. An analysis of the written "counselor reactions to specific groups" (CRSG) showed that counselor responses became more positive the longer parents remained in their respective groups. The correlations between parent and counselor responses suggest that parents' enjoyment of the group experience and the benefits they gain from it may not necessarily be related. Attendance patterns were also analyzed.

482. Reinhart, B. A. Toward a vocational student information system: a progress report. Los Angeles: California University, Division of Vocational Education; Sacramento: California State Department of Education, 1969. (ED 039 320)

An information storage and retrieval system has been developed for reporting job placement and followup data of persons trained in industrial education programs in California public schools. The system is built around five forms: (1) school registration, (2) verification of enrollment, (3) verification of address, (4) in-class follow-through, and (5) out-of-class followup. Eventually the system calls for all data to enter a central, state-wide electronic data processing center; however, the emphasis in this report is on the data collection system, not the storage and retrieval system. Prescored cards are prescribed for data collection along with the consideration of mark sensing and optical character scanning when their use is perfected. Field tests emphasized the necessity of having all data processed at the state level, and the importance of a good public relations program to gain faculty cooperation. The tests also resulted in the modification of some forms and the elimination of the verification of address forms. The complete illustrated text for the proposed system including modified and recommended forms is appended.

483. Research Council of the Greater Cities Program for School Improvement. Promising practices from the projects of the culturally deprived. Chicago: RCGCPSI, 1964. (ED 001 633)

In the survey taken of 14 urban school districts, successful special projects include: in-service education and recruitment, reading programs, summer programs, community school relationships, guidance activities, early admissions programs, team-teaching programs, special placement classes and job retraining programs. All practices are intended to serve as compensatory education for disadvantaged youth.

Each school district described briefly a few of its successful programs. Baltimore's "Early Admissions" seeks to give children the ability to compete successfully in school. Enriched reading is part of the Buffalo elementary school program for the culturally different. Fourteen year olds are specially grouped in non-graded classes to build reading skills in programs that provide compensatory education in the language arts, special textbooks giving attention to the American Negro, library services in the elementary schools, and summer school and demonstration laboratory schools. Houston has initiated a back-to-school drive, while Los Angeles is providing tutorial services and a work-study program for potential dropouts. Orientation is provided in Milwaukee for immigrant and transient children. New York's Demonstration Guidance Project is attempting to prevent dropouts with pre-employment education, night school, career guidance classes and the school-to-employment programs. In-service education, school-community coordinating teams, and language arts are given emphasis in Philadelphia. Pittsburgh uses team-teaching for more able students. By using tutoring, counseling and work-study programs, St. Louis has fought the dropout problem. San Francisco has a Youth Opportunities Center to train youth for jobs and to help them find employment.

484. Reswick, J. The effectiveness of full time and coordinated guidance services in the high school. Project ABLE, fourth annual report. Brooklyn: New York City Board of Education, 1966. (ED 011 663)

This annual report is an interim review for the school year 1964–65 of a 5-year project with the 1965 graduating classes of three New York City high schools. The project was concerned with (1) identifying the potential abilities of the culturally disadvantaged students, (2) studying the effectiveness of increased guidance time with such students, and (3) assessing the use of full-time counselors and specialized personnel such as a psychologist and a social worker in the high schools. One high school was the control with a grade adviser system of counseling and no increased services. One of the experimental schools had a full-time coordinator and part-time counselor. The other experimental school had full-time counselors and specialized personnel on a part-time basis. Both experimental schools had an equal amount of increased guidance time. A random sample of 570 and matched samples (sex, age, and mental ability) of 192 were selected. The project hypothesis was that increased motivation, improved scholastic achievement and lower attrition would result in the experimental schools with increased guidance time. In this 4th year of study, the criteria of course selection, course load, term averages, attendance records, and dropout rate showed no significant effect of Project ABLE.

485. Rhodes, J. A. A vocational education and guidance: a system for the seventies. Columbus, Ohio: Charles Merrill Publishing Co., 1970.

This book proposes a system of vocational guidance and vocational education to be established at the core of the curriculum starting with kindergarten. The system is developed to serve as a means of changing the direction of the massive public education system in this nation without attempting to duplicate that system. The "System for the Seventies" seeks to prepare youth for choice in training of his plan for employment and a concept for implementing that choice through vocational, technical or professional preparation.

486. Rich, J. V. The use of information in personnel services. CAPS current resources series. Ann Arbor: Michigan University, Counseling and Personnel Services Center, 1968. (ED 017 036)

This publication is one of a series on current research and resources compiled by the Counseling and Personnel Services Information Center. Resumes of selected literature on new information techniques applicable to personnel work are presented. Computer systems for processing and using information, applications and standards for new information systems, and specific personnel areas affected by such developments are among the topics covered. Subject and author indices on the abstracted literature are included, as well as information on obtaining complete documents.

487. Ritter, T. Project VISION: an approach to a model system of occupational employment information. Indianapolis: Indiana Manpower Research Association, 1967. (ED 021 258)

The aim of Project VISION (Vocational Information System Involving Occupational Needs) is the development of a model system of local occupational and employment information involving current and prospective manpower resources and requirements. Discussed in this presentation are the background and environment of the project, and some past, current, and future research activities. Although the project had, as its only basic guideline, the development of a model system of local occupational employment information to meet the needs of vocational education in Wisconsin, other areas of research were identified through reviewing existing information, defining the needs of vocational education, and answering problems referred by others in the field. During the early part of Project VISION, attention was focused on the language problem existing between vocational educators and employment service personnel. Current research projects include: (1) reviewing population and labor force data to build a data system on future supply, (2) identifying patterns of occupational mobility, (3) determining occupational needs on the basis of new and expanding industries, (4) working with the Medvin Technique, and (5) doing a comprehensive employer survey.

488. Rivera, F. A Mexican American source book with study guideline. Menlo Park, Calif.: Educational Consulting Associates, 1970. (ED 045 244)

The source book is designed as a guideline for all persons who wish to have a better knowledge of the history of the Mexican American people in the United States. The author states that the guideline is not intended as a history per se; therefore, the usefulness of the book depends upon how well the reader uses the bibliography and suggested reference materials. The Table of Contents lists the following major units: (1) Introduction to "North from Mexico," by Carey McWilliams; (2) a Study Guideline of the History of the Mexican American People in the United States; (3) Selected Bibliography; (4) Missions of California; (5) A Portfolio of Illustrations; (6) A Portfolio of Outstanding Americans of Mexican Descent; (7) The Treaty of Guadalupe Hidalgo; (8) A Critical Commentary on the Treaty of Guadalupe Hidalgo; and (9) Appendix. The selected bibliography includes a list of approximately 120 books, articles, magazines, and newspapers; 33 films; and 24 filmstrips.

489. Roberts, T. L. & Frederick, F. J. Computer assisted counseling progress report number 1. Stillwater: Oklahoma State University, Stillwater Research Foundation, 1967. (ED 017 016)

Discussed here are the theoretical concerns and levels of system development of an Oklahoma State University project involved with using a computer or rapid access information retrieval system to provide access data required for formulation of "intelligent" student decisions.

490. Roberts, T. L. & Keahey, S. P. Gaming for vocational awareness: a systems approach. The Bartlesville system. Stillwater: Oklahoma State University, 1970. (ED 037 754)

The total systems approach to guidance and counseling is an attempt to help the student understand the personality of the environmental systems in relation to his own personality. Such an approach would provide for integration of the two personalities leading to productive behavior and individual goal achievement. This objective can be approached by teaching the student how to become aware of himself as a "human system" in terms of "system logic." For the Bartlesville System (Total Guidance Information Support System) is proposed that game models be constructed to teach systems logic and concepts. By providing the student with a chance to experience concepts of importance in the economic world, the student has an opportunity to experience how his own personality might react. The gaming approach emphasizes the responsibility of the individual in constructing his personal value and moral system in relationship to his environment. The game development process is discussed. The report concludes with a description of various game models which can be used at various points within the system.

491. Roberts, T. L. (et al.) Software documentation for the Bartlesville Public Schools: part one. The Bartlesville system total guidance information support system. Bartlesville, Okla.: Bartlesville Public Schools, 1970. (ED 038 704)

The Total Guidance Information Support System (TGISS), is an information storage and retrieval system for counselors. The total TGISS, including hardware and software, extends the counselor's capabilities by providing ready access to student information under secure conditions. The hardware required includes: (1) IBM 360/50 central processing facility; (2) IBM 2314 mass storage device; (3) IBM 2260 remote video display terminal; (4) IBM 2848 display controller; (5) IBM 1053 Printer for hard copy; and (6) a modem for sending or receiving data communications to and from the central site. The TGISS software system includes: (1) IBM 05 Operating System; (2) a Type III IBM Information and Data Retrieval System called FASTER; (3) the Load; (4) an Update and File Management subsystem; and (5) the FASTER Application Programs. The program is designed to facilitate future expansion. The software functions are discussed: (1) input format and definition; (2) load and input verification program; (3) data update and revision routines and specifications; and (4) FASTER access and retrieval routines. Concluding the document is a readily understandable TGISS users' guide. The research reported herein was funded under Title III of the Elementary and Secondary Education Act.

492. Roeber, E., Walz, G., & Smith, G. A strategy for guidance. New York: Macmillan Co., 1969.

The basic aim of this book is to present a viable approach to developing and implementing an effective school guidance program.

493. The role of guidance services in community action programs combating poverty. (ED 002 129)

Guidance objectives to be included in a community action program combating poverty are presented. The objectives include early adjustment of students, early identification and interpretation of abilities, educational and career plans based on abilities and skills, parent understanding of opportunities, encouragement of realistic goals in line with potential, healthy school attitudes, teacher understanding of each student, continuous revisions of programs to meet student needs, and utilization of community resources and guidance services.

Guidance services should be provided for preschoolers, adults, and school-age youths, and should be offered in an accessible location. A year-round professional staff with each member holding at least a master's degree, nonprofessional people, and volunteers are necessary.

Community programs which offer intensive educational services to the disadvantaged are illustrated. They include: the Early School Admissions Project in Baltimore, Maryland; New York City Preschool Program; the Doolittle Project in Chicago, Illinois; An Adventure in Human Relations in Wilmington, Delaware; New York City's Higher Horizons Program; the Project ABLE in New York State; The Talent Preservation of the Junior High Schools Program in Houston, Texas; the Macfarland-Roosevelt Guidance Project in Washington, D.C.; the Carrollton School Project in Baltimore, Maryland; the Dunbar Vocational High School Program in Chicago, Illinois; the Syracuse Action for Youth Program in Syracuse, New York; the Action for Appalachian Youth Program in Charleston, West Virginia; and A Future for Jimmy Program in Washington, D.C.

494. Roman, R. A. Implementation of a career decision game on a time shared computer: an exploration of its value in a simulated guidance environment. Information system for vocational decision. Cambridge, Mass.: Harvard University, 1969. (ED 052 497)

The Information System for Vocational Decisions (ISVD) places Boocock's (1967) Life Career Game in the core of its operating system. This paper considers the types of interaction that will be required of the system, and discusses the role that a career decision game might play in its total context. The paper takes an into-the-future look at the day when an artificial intelligence system guiding simulated counselor, teacher, and career generator systems becomes a feasible programing task. Toward this ultimate goal, the author proposes to start with the career decision game, and to develop the full system as a series of increasingly complex modifications of its basic format. The game in its present form is described and its use as a miniature model for the entire system of interacting simulations (teacher-student, counselor-client) is discussed.

495. Rose, S. D. A behavioral approach to group treatment of children. 1967. (ED 013 464)

A behavioral approach was used to treat small groups of children in an inner city setting. The groups were organized under the auspices of the Hartwig Project of the Neighborhood Service Organization of Detroit and consisted of children with school adoption problems, delinquent gangs, and children from disadvantaged sections of the community. Groups contained three to seven children between the ages of eight and 15. They were homogeneous in regard to sex, age, and socioeconomic background and heterogeneous in regard to problems presented. Behavioral assessment determined the nature, frequency, and conditions of the maladaptive behaviors. On the basis of the maladaptive behaviors, goals were set for each group member. A baseline was determined for each maladaptive behavior so that subsequent behavior after intervention by the worker could be monitored for change. Means of intervention included reinforcement, token economy, group activities, behavioral assignments, model presentation, and systematic desensitization. Treatment was terminated on the basis of achievement of treatment goals. To date, results appear promising. Changes in the desired direction have been observed in a large majority of the male clients, behavioral assignments have been favorably received, and group workers are enthusiastic about the approach.

496. Rossman, J. E. & Prebomics, E. M. School counselor employment service relations; the Minnesota report. *Vocational Guidance Quarterly,* 1968, 16, 258–263.

An eight-page questionnaire was sent to 258 Minnesota high school counselors and the 33 local offices of the Minnesota State Employment Service. The resulting data suggested a good foundation for cooperation between the schools and the employment service offices, although there were a number of areas in which communications between the two institutions could be improved.

497. Rothney, J. W. Adaptive counseling in schools. Englewood Cliffs, New Jersey: Prentice-Hall, 1972.

Adaptive counseling is a completely new system of guidance techniques which combine present methods with tested procedures and strategies for varying these in more complex situations. The book illustrates some specific problems and shows the reader some innovative procedures of how to deal with it. The book provides techniques for coping with a large heterogeneous student body and case loads found in a typical school. The book is designed for use by counselors and includes coverage of such topics as: Individual differences in counselors; foundations of adaptive counseling, techniques of adaptive counseling; procedures in adaptive counseling and evaluation of counseling.

498. Rothstein, H. J. Problems and issues in the counseling of the disabled disadvantaged patient. Washington, D.C.: American Psychological Association, 1970. (ED 043 896)

In the counseling phase which is imbedded in the global vocational rehabilitation process, the primary challenge, in dealing with the disabled disadvantaged client, is viewed as being the disadvantagement rather than the disability per se. A multitude of factors and interacting clusters of variables that influence the counseling process with these persons are identified: (1) the negative, resistive attitude, or, at least, the unenthusiastic and guarded orientation; (2) the usually alien and unfamiliar qualities (to the disadvantaged client) of agencies; (3) the social, cultural, educational and emotional gaps between the middle-class counselor, black or white, and his disadvantaged client; and (4) the foreign quality of a verbal, interpersonal model of transaction. Suggestions for improving counselor effectiveness with the disabled disadvantaged are offered: (1) minimizing the effects of unfamiliar settings and procedures; and (2) altering the counselor's basic orientation where style, content, goals, and evaluation are concerned. Qualities of counselors who would work most effectively with these clients are delineated. In conclusion, the author notes that the above efforts would have an ameliorative effect, but that only significant social, economic and political changes will truly alter the condition of the disabled disadvantaged.

499. Rowe, F. A. Foundation for a seventh grade guidance unit: an analysis of the developmental level of the seventh grade student and nationally current occupational guidance classes. Final report. Salt Lake City: Utah State Dept. of Public Instruction, 1970. (ED 052 492)

This is a review of the relevant literature and current practices in the field of occupational guidance. Because it was prepared in connection with the beginning of a seventh grade occupational guidance class in Utah, it deals, in the first part, with the vocational-maturational level of seventh graders. The second part summarizes contemporary efforts and practices throughout the nation for occupational guidance on this level. Several guidance approaches are considered, but the developmental approach utilized by the New England School Development Council is included in its entirety because of its comprehensiveness. The report concludes with: (1) a list of guidance objectives; (2) activities and projects geared toward meeting those objectives; (3) a short bibliography of relevant educational materials; and (4) brief comments about guidance program evaluation.

Compendium of Abstracted Methods

500. Ryan, C. W. & Whitman, R. A. Video aides in school counseling—some practical innovations. Orono: Maine University, 1969. (ED 036 819)

This paper examines the potential of video tape and closed-circuit television as an addition to a counseling and guidance program. A review of literature in this area is given. The technical competence for operating the equipment is limited. Suggestions for the use of extra equipment (wide angle zoom lens) in special situations are given. Confidentiality must be considered when using video tape equipment. Suggestions for the use of video equipment are given. The counselor, as an information resource, provides data on tests, colleges and jobs. Standardized materials on these subjects could be stored on video tape thereby reducing time needed for this activity. A table of school applications of video tape potential users of video tape is given along with references.

501. Ryan, T. A. Effect of an integrated instructional counseling program to improve vocational decision-making of community college youth. Final report. Corvallis: Oregon State University, 1968. (ED 021 132)

A planned vocational guidance program incorporating instructional and counseling components in a community college setting was evaluated. The primary purpose of the program was to improve occupational choice-making of post-high school youth. Three hundred community college students whose verbal and quantitative scores on college entrance examinations fell below the 50th percentile and who had not made firm vocational choices were included in the study. A post-test control group design was implemented which included active and inactive control groups with subjects assigned randomly to five different treatment conditions. Results supported the major hypothesis—(1) reinforcement counseling techniques are effective for improving students' vocational decision-making, (2) reinforcement counseling techniques are effective for helping students acquire knowledge of sources of personal data and occupational information, (3) simulation materials are effective in improving students' vocational decision-making, and (4) simulation materials are effective for helping students acquire knowledge of sources of occupational information. The experimental program which incorporated testing, counseling, and occupational information services in a coordinated package was found to be effective for improving occupational choice-making of community college youth. An extensive appendix includes data, a typescript of a counseling session, information-gathering instruments, and occupational information.

502. Sandhofer, R. G. & Nichols, J. L. (Eds.) The development of specialized educational programs for poor learners for use in non-educational settings, final report. Minneapolis, Minn.: Minneapolis Rehabilitation Center, Research and Development Division, 1968. (ED 029 973)

Automated audio visual vocational training courses for duplication machine operator and janitor occupations were developed for poor learners to use in rehabilitation centers, state hospitals, etc. Program development included: (1) surveying pertinent literature in the field of program learning of occupations, (2) visiting business and industrial concerns to determine trainee responsibilities, (3) training curriculum development personnel, (4) preparing, testing and revising subject matter, (5) selecting a presentation system, (6) integrating the content and presentation system, and (7) monitoring trainee performance in the completed program. The teaching system used programmed question and response booklets, tape recordings, color slides, structured practice, and human supervision. It was concluded that the programs imparted the necessary skills to poor learners, and could be effectively used in non-educational settings. Individualized vocational training for poor learners has some distinct advantages, and the techniques can be used with similar job training programs for other occupations. The development and reproduction of the programs proved to be time-consuming, difficult and costly.

503. San Diego Unified School District. Supplementary educational services—instructional television educational experience development and distribution. San Diego, Cal.: SDUSD. (ES 000 395)

An instructional television broadcasting station will be established to serve identified educational, cultural, and informational needs of students in San Diego County and possibly Baja, California. Educational programming will be designed to promote new instructional classroom projects including—(1) specialized instruction for preschool children, (2) exploration of career-vocational opportunities for secondary pupils, (3) programs of an advanced and scientific nature, and (4) development of creativity in the learning process as applied to problem solving, idea evaluation, and self-motivation at all levels of instruction. Evaluation will involve pre- and post testing of students, comparing those who have used instructional television with others who have not. Approximately 1,213,000 persons will be served, excluding potential citizen participants of Mexico. For further information, contact Dr. Harmon Kurtz, Special Projects Administrator, San Diego Unified School District, 4100 Normal St., San Diego, California 92103. (714) 298-4681.

504. San Mateo Union High School District. Toward a comprehensive district in a "know and care" community. San Mateo, Cal.: SMUHS. (ED 001 871)

The comprehensive high school should provide a broad general education for all, with a phased curriculum centered on major, serviceable ideas. It should also provide vocational training and guidance. In a comprehensive district, it can truly individualize instruction.

Specific considerations on which the need for a comprehensive district are based included: The need of school youth to be introduced to the world of work as well as to the professions and culture; adults and out-of-school youths should be provided with the opportunity for general education as well as technical-vocational training; the total system should be flexible; large high schools should be required to afford diversified and well-balanced programs; school districts should be large enough to provide a sufficient tax base; a phased curriculum is more appropriate than a tracked curriculum; and special high schools should be designated to serve special needs.

A guidance center should be planned and developed where personnel would administer and coordinate the separate entities. It would serve secondary youth, drop-outs, adults returning to the labor force, and adults needing retraining. A schedule of basic studies in an extended day and evening program is also proposed, and technical courses would be included.

A system of chairs to be held by master teachers is proposed and the holders would constitute a District Academy of Instruction. Fellowships would be available to faculty members who have tenure status, and the holders would have the opportunity to teach in unique summer programs, to enroll in graduate school, to prepare classroom projects, and to draw a special stipend. Projects would be monitored by the Academy.

505. Santa Fe Junior College. One paradigm for vocational-technical counseling (Santa Fe Junior College Workshop, Gainesville, Florida, June 1969). Gainesville, Fla.: SFJC, 1969. (ED 042 884)

The purpose of this summer workshop was to enhance communication channels between the public school and college personnel, to acquaint public school personnel with resources for enlarging their counseling programs, and to expand upon the concept of vocational counseling. Presentations included (1) "New Dimensions/Problems in Secondary School Counseling" by Clifford R. LeBlanc, (2) "Future Dimensions in Vocational-Technical Education" by E. L. Kurth, (3) "Introduction to Growth Group Experiences" by Tal Mullis, (4) "New Perspectives in Group Work" by Richard Blouch, (5) "Counseling the Disadvantaged" by J. D. Beck, (6) "Counselor Use of Tests" by Marlin R. Schmidt, and (7) Summary and Conclusions by April O'Connell.

506. Saskatchewan NewStart, Inc. Life skills: a course in applied problem solving. Prince Albert: SNS, 1971. (ED 049 353)

The Life Skills course of Saskatchewan NewStart represents a serious attempt to integrate educational and psychotherapeutic principles and techniques for the development of personal competence in many areas of life. This is the third in a series of program approaches being tried on disadvantaged youth, and emphasizes the problem-solving process in skill objectives for manpower training. Course outlines, theoretical models, lesson plans, and evaluation techniques are included.

507. Scates, A. Y. Research on career development and vocational guidance. Paper presented at the meeting of the National Conference on Development of State Programs for Vocational Guidance, January, 1968.

Due to an increasing interest in the applications of technology in solving guidance problems, the fourth Symposium for Systems under Development for Vocational Guidance, held in March 1968, was devoted to computer-based vocational guidance systems. This publication is a compilation of the papers presented at the symposium. They have been divided into two categories: theoretical considerations in developing systems for vocational guidance and problems of implementation. Some brief descriptions of systems currently under development are presented in a third part.

508. Schauble, P. G. Emotional simulation in personal counseling: an application of research innovations in counseling to accelerate client movement. Paper presented at the meeting of the American Personnel and Guidance Association, Detroit, 1968. (ED 022 204)

The influence of stimulated recall and emotional simulation films on client growth in short-term personal counseling was evaluated at Michigan State University with nine clients from vocational rehabilitation caseloads. The two experimental groups (stimulated recall and simulated film treatment) and one control group with traditional counseling met for six, one and one-half hour sessions. Pre- and post-treatment videotapes rated by judges indicate that clients exposed to simulated treatments made significantly more progress in characteristics of client growth (owning of discomfort, commitment to change, differentiation of stimuli and different behavior); had more positive change in client behavior and therapeutic process changes (client insight, lessening of defenses, ability to experience feeling and relate to counselors, and overall therapeutic relationships); and, therefore, made more movement within counseling than did the control subjects. Subjective reports on all clients tentatively indicate that experimental subjects made better adjustments outside counseling situations and, on the basis of vocational placement rates, had a better placement prognosis than control subjects.

509. Schill, W. J. & Nichols, H. E. (Eds.) Career choice and career preparation. Danville, Ill.: Interstate Printers, 1970.

This programmed self-study guide is designed as a counseling aid for students faced with the problem of planning their educational and vocational future.

510. Schissel, R. F. Development of a career-orientation scale for women. *Journal of Counseling Psychology,* 1968.

The present study developed a Career-Orientation Scale (COS) that discriminates between career- and non-career-oriented women on the basis of interests.

511. School Districts of Cochise County. Pilot program (demonstration project) of an experimental method for providing occupational education to youth in small schools. Bisbee, Ariz.: SDCC. (ES 022 372)

Mobile units will be used to bring vocational education to isolated rural high schools. Five multidistrict groups will be formed, and in each group one school will serve as the site for training in a given curriculum. To implement the program, four itinerant teachers will provide intensive instruction for students and training for resident instructors to insure the continuity of instruction during the absence of the specialized personnel. Two itinerant vocational guidance counselors will serve the participating schools on a scheduled basis to—(1) provide information about jobs and training opportunities, (2) conduct counseling interviews with students, and (3) provide testing services which are not available in the smaller schools. Adult vocational education programs will also be established, in cooperation with the itinerant staff and with the local junior college. Approximately 200 secondary students will be served. For further information, contact Keith Jackson, Superintendent, Cochise County Schools, Bisbee, Alizona 85603. (602) 432-5381.

512. Schreiber, D. (et al.) Dropout studies, design and conduct. Washington, D.C.: National Education Association, 1965. (ED 002 199)

Although the dropout problem is one of great concern at both local and national levels, it is readily apparent that the problem is not the same everywhere in the country. Dropout rates vary considerably from one community to another, and even differ between high schools in the same school system. Limitations in previous studies of the problem have been in terminology, research initiation, data determination, data collection, and data interpretation.

The NEA Dropout Study was perceived as a significant guidance tool and as a reliable annual index against which renewal or extended guidance efforts might be reviewed. It was also seen as a tool for the acquisition of pertinent data on pupil needs to which school guidance services could address themselves, and for the establishment of effective early identification procedures. Interpretation of results may lead to changes in school organization and curriculum development.

The study should provide possibilities for standardizing dropout studies in American schools by aiding in policy development, program planning, and guidance and counseling. The guidance form for dropouts and potential dropouts should request easily accessible information, require exact answers, include a built-in system of double-checking responses, and be economically feasible to reproduce. All information gathered should lend itself to comparability. Methods of combining dropout data for analysis and calculating rates of pupil mobility are presented. Numerous tables and charts are included.

513. Scoggins, W. Labor in learning: public school treatment of the world of work. Los Angeles: California University, Center for Labor Research and Education, 1966. (ED 023 787)

The purpose of this study was to determine what 11th and 12th grade students in social studies classes in Los Angeles County are being taught about what it means to be an employee, i.e., the responsibilities, regulations, problems, rights, and benefits of being a wage or salary earner. Personal interviews, questionnaires, check lists, and tally sheets were used with teachers, publishing company salesmen, and others to obtain responses to questions such as: (1) How is the American labor movement, its history, contributions, problems, and ambitions, presented in the required textbooks and courses of social studies in public high schools? and (2) Are adequate space and explanation devoted to the legislation regulating labor-management relations at the present time? The conclusion of the study was that youth are being taught what it meant to be an employee in the crafts or laboring class up to 1935; however, within the limits of this study, they are not being realistically oriented to the contemporary world of work. The appendixes include data such as the evaluation of 35 labor topics as presented in current textbooks.

514. Sears-Roebuck Foundation. Directory of post-secondary retailing and marketing vocational programs. Skokie, Ill.: SRF, 1968. (ED 032 390)

This directory lists 357 general and 135 special retailing and marketing vocational programs at the post secondary level. Institutions vary somewhat in the identification of general programs; for example, they may be called retailing, merchandising, marketing, mid-management, or distributive education programs. Specialized programs offered by institutions are reported, including such areas as advertising, air transportation, banking and finance, credit management, and petroleum marketing. When available, the following information is presented for each program: institutional name and address, enrollment figures, cooperative training required, associative degree programs, accreditation or approval, resume availability, career clinics, and contact personnel.

515. Segel, D. & Ruble, R. A. The Lincoln project: a study of the educational program of a junior high school in a transitional neighborhood. A report of the Lincoln guidance research project. Albuquerque, N.M.: Albuquerque Public Schools, 1962. (ED 023 494)

The Lincoln Guidance Research Project, funded by the National Defense Education Act studied a group of junior high school students in a transitional neighborhood with major emphasis on educational needs of students who will find employment in service occupations. Recommendations included intensive remedial work at the seventh grade level, continual evaluation of students' progress throughout the junior high grades, increased guidance and counseling staff, and a third curriculum choice at the tenth grade level, in addition to college preparation and vocational education. It was proposed that students with less than high school capabilities enter a two-year intensive work-experience training program in preparation for vocational opportunities which do not require high school graduation for employment. Test results, questionnaires, and rating forms used in the study are included as appendices.

516. Severinsen, K. N. Vocational-educational information workshop for rural guidance workers. Macomb: Western Illinois University, 1967. (ED 015 042)

The objectives of this project were to up-date counselors concerning occupational information and to develop new approaches for disseminating vocational information.

517. Severson, R. A. A comprehensive early intervention program employing behavior modification techniques. Paper presented at the Annual Meeting of American Orthopsychiatric Association, San Francisco, California, March, 1970.

This paper describes an application of behavior modification techniques and new means of presenting academic materials to the 450 children in the kindergarten and first grade of a small semi-urban community. Four years of research on behaviors useful in educational diagnosis and prediction of future success revealed two tests highly related to the achievement goals of the first grade; these are knowledge of vocabular and visuoperceptual memory. Screening is the program's first phase: the second is establishment of intervention strategies with regard to children diagnosed as highly susceptible to academic failure. The lowest children were initially treated individually by paraprofessionals trained to be instructional aides. Academic materials were often presented in a gamelike format to provide continuing reinforcement of learning. Techniques with a lower cost per pupil were selected for learning enhancement at other levels. These included cassette programming, the training of individual classroom teachers in behavior modification, the modification of the curriculum format, and the active involvement of parents in their children's education.

518. Shappell, D. L. (et al.) An application of Roe's vocational choice model. *School Counselor,* 1971, 19(1), 43–48.

By utilizing occupational inventories and counseling strategies as presented, counselors can apply Roe's vocational choice model to the counseling setting. Practicum supervisors might also assist counselors-in-training via small group procedures, using selected items from such an inventory to stimulate counselees' thinking about untapped needs.

519. Shatz, E. (et al.) New careers: generic issues in the human services. A sourcebook for trainers. Washington, D.C.: University Research Corporation, Information Clearinghouse, 1968. (ED 025 468)

Designed for use by trainers in preparing unskilled workers with minimum education (at least fourth grade reading ability) for entry as non-professionals in human services, this manual is organized around the core of understanding of individual and group behavior and needs and of methods of interviewing or obtaining and recording information needed by all social service aides; it is intended as a basis for small group discussions occurring simultaneously with the speciality skill and on-the-job training components of the New Careers program. (An accompanying manual for trainees is also available.) The generic issues presented concern individual growth and development (practical skills including remediation and interviewing skills) and the individual and his relationship to work, people (human growth and development, human behavior and needs, communication skills, and group process), and the community (community structure, poverty, the Negro, law and society, and consumer education). The topics are accompanied by objectives, content outlines, and bibliographies. Also included are a glossary, explanation of the New Careers approach with suggestions for using the manual and for operating a program, training tips, and sections on field trips and development of attitudes and responsibilities. Appended are a basic bibliography and list of materials for trainers and an explication of the fundamentals of the New Careers model.

520. Shaw, G. H. Essential vocational guidance services and their implementation in the public junior colleges of California. Los Angeles: California University, 1968. (ED 024 385)

The purposes of this dissertation were (1) to identify vocational guidance services and practices considered essential by authorities in the field for provision by the public junior colleges of California, (2) to determine the extent of their current implementation in these institutions, (3) to report the factors judged by certain administrators in the colleges to have been the most helpful and the most retarding to the implementation of these essentials, and (4) to assemble a set of guidelines for establishing and developing meaningful vocational guidance programs in these institutions. Based primarily on a review of the literature and on discussions with junior college personnel and guidance leaders, the study involved a compilation of items describing specific vocational guidance services and related practices. Of these, 70 were incorporated into an appraisal instrument that was submitted to a select panel of experts for critical review. A revised questionnaire was mailed to all public junior colleges in the state. A 92% return was obtained. Among the conclusions reached were: (1) a critical requirement exists for effective vocational programs; (2) a large number of vocational services considered essential for institutions were identified; (3) the statewide survey of essentials showed that very few were judged to be implemented at a very high or very low level; and (4) considerable improvement can be made in the implementation of essentials by most colleges and in most areas of service.

521. Shaw, M. C. & Tuel, J. K. Guidance research in action, group counseling with parents, monograph 2. Chico, Cal.: Chico State College, 1965. (ED 012 077)

The second phase of a 3-year study to define an objective for guidance services is primarily concerned with the inclusion of teachers in group counseling and the continued development of group counseling with parents. The 22 participating schools from six school districts in California and New Mexico included K-12 from all socioeconomic levels. To facilitate both the research procedure and the data processing, 10 data-collection instruments were developed, refined, and used with individuals, groups, and schools. A wide variety of data ranging from expression of attitude to ratings of overt behavior was collected and stored on punch cards. The analysis of these data was conducted according to the pattern set by the specific major hypotheses regarding correlations of the perceptions of students, teachers, and parents concerning aptitudes, vocational interests, and student scholastic performance as well as the relationship of educational attitudes, community attitudes, and parental participation in the study. Eleven variables were considered in the hypotheses. One major hypothesis was concerned with the effects counseling with parents and teachers has on students. The preliminary findings, although primarily actuarial in nature and not complete, provide some indication that the group approach is feasible from both the point of view of the pupil personnel specialist and the degree of parent participation.

522. Sheppard, L. E. Effects of a problem-solving procedure for stimulating vocational exploration. *Dissertation Abstracts,* 1967, 28(3), 943-A.

This study was designed to test the effect of a set of simulated occupational problems on the occupational attitudes and information-seeking of young people. It was hypothesized that eleventh-grade students who were given an opportunity to solve some simulated occupational problems would engage in more interest-indicative activities than would equivalent subjects given either information about the same occupations or general occupational information.

523. Sherman, V. S. Guidance curriculum for increased self-understanding and motivation for career planning. Planning and develop-

ment of research programs in selected areas of vocational education, volume III. Palo Alto: American Institute for Research in Behavioral Sciences, 1966. (ED 010 625)

The methodology used in developing experimental curriculum materials (ED 010 626) for an innovative guidance program in career planning was presented. Research data, gathered during a questionnaire survey of student attitudes and interests relevant to career planning, were used for the curriculum content. The content format was organized to provide a framework of relevant and meaningful information for youths to use in gaining perspective on themselves and in acquiring appreciation and understanding of the decision-making processes involved in career planning. The theoretical construct of developmental tasks (Tryon and Lilienthal, 1950) was used as one basis for curriculum planning. A taxonomy for educational objectives in the affective domain (Krathwohl and others, 1964) was used for defining curriculum objectives, the nature of desired learning experiences, and means of evaluation. Although the curriculum was developed for junior high school guidance sessions, a preliminary tryout indicated that it could be readily adapted for use with upper elementary and senior high school students as well. Students exposed to the curriculum during the tryout appeared to (1) respond favorably to the novelty of content, as it was directly related to their plans and personal concerns, and (2) use an open-ended, scientific approach in relating the content to their own experience. Related reports are ED 010 623 through ED 010 626.

524. Sherman, V. S. Guidance curriculum for increased self-understanding and motivation for career planning. Planning and development of research programs in selected areas of vocational education, volume III, appendix. Palo Alto: American Institute for Research in Behavioral Sciences, 1966. (ED 010 626)

Experimental materials that were developed for the vocational guidance of junior high school students were presented in this appendix to ED 010 625. These materials were planned to enable students to thoroughly and systematically explore their own self-perceptions, attitudes, personal values, achievement, abilities, and diverse career possibilities. Development of the materials was guided by the hope that they would enable the students to emerge from learning experiences with clearer conceptions of who they are and where they are going. Sample student work sheets. questionnaires, and reading and writing materials were included for all lessons. The questionnaire responses of approximately 100 boys and girls (grades 6, 8, 10, and 12) were presented in graph form to allow students using these study materials to look at the career plans and attitudes of a sample of their peers while simultaneously viewing and evaluating their own. Although developed for use with junior high school students, the author suggested the materials were also suitable for use by students in the upper elementary grades or at the senior high school level. Included with the materials were teaching guidelines and evaluation sheets for a recommended followup evaluation of the empirical effects of the curriculum materials. Related reports are ED 010 623 through ED 101 625.

525. Sherman, V. S. Trial and testing of an experimental guidance curriculum. Final report. American Institute for Research in Behavioral Sciences. Palo Alto: 1967. (ED 020 554)

Innovative vocational guidance curriculum materials were designed to increase self-understanding and motivation relative to career exploration and planning.

526. Shirts, R. G. Career simulation for sixth grade pupils. San Diego, Cal.: San Diego County Department of Education, 1966. (ED 010 076)

This was a pilot project designed to develop a modified version of the "Life Career Game" developed for high school use and explore its potential use at the sixth-grade level. The project was divided into a developmental phase and a research phase. In the development phase the "Life Career Game" developed by Mrs. Sarane Boocock of Johns Hopkins University was modified and simplified in an effort to make it appropriate to the intellectual and interest level of sixth-grade pupils. In the research phase the mean scores on the "Vocational Development Inventory" and the "Vocational Information Achievement Test" of three sixth-grade classes of pupils randomly selected from two school districts were compared to the mean scores on the same tests of three randomly selected control groups. The treatment groups played the modified game for 15 hours over a period of a month. The control groups received the regular curriculum which did not include any systematic study of career development. No significant differences between treatment and control groups were found. It was evident, however, that the game evoked a high degree of pupil interest. Because of this fact, further classroom study concerning the use of the game was felt to be warranted. For further information on the "Life Career Game," see Accession Number ED 010 077.

527. Shirts, R. G. Life career game, players manual. San Diego, Cal.: San Diego County Department of Education. (ED 010 077)

This report presents a modified (sixth-grade) version of the "Life Career Game," developed previously for high school use by Mrs. Sarane Boocock of Johns Hopkins University. Included are manuals for teacher and pupil (showing how to organize, supervise, and play the game) as well as the game material itself. The game is an activity which requires pupils to simulate making some of the decisions a person would make as he progresses through school, prepares for a job, and enters marriage and family life. The purposes of the game are to give pupils some understanding of educational and career choices, provide experiences in planning for their own future, and provoke thought about the nature of the "Good Life." The game is presented as a supplement to the final report of OEG-HRD-131-65, accession number ED 010 076, entitled "Career Simulation for Sixth-Grade Pupils."

528. Silverman, A. Projected design for the higher horizons program in selected schools. Bronx, N.Y.: Board of Education of New York City, Districts 17–18, 1961. (ED 001 750)

The purpose is to raise the educational, cultural, and vocational sights of all pupils in order that they may have better opportunities for advancement in social and economic life. The project aims are carried out through emphasis in the following areas: curriculum enrichment; cultural experiences; remedial instruction; teacher workshops, and seminars; identification and encouragement of talent; pupil counseling; group guidance; testing; and parent workshops and counseling.

Districts 16 and 17 (Bronx), employ the services of a number of specialized personnel. Everything related to the project is cleared and coordinated through the office of the assistant superintendent. Under the guidance of the assistant superintendent, the project coordinator acts as liaison between the district office and the schools, and visits schools to observe the program in action. The school project teacher acts in a consultative capacity, works with teachers, coordinates trips, gives demonstration lessons, and acts as liaison between school and community. The district guidance coordinator is responsible for assisting teachers in the interpretation of test data, making guidance materials available to school counselors and helping tap community resources. Other special personnel involved in implementing the aims of Higher Horizons are: the district community coordinator, attendance teachers, auxiliary teachers, corrective reading teachers, district staff coordinators, and teacher training consultants.

529. Sloan, N. E. Personnel services review. Series 3: human resources in the guidance programs. Family counseling. Ann Arbor, Mich.: ERIC Clearinghouse on Counseling and Personnel Services, 1970. (ED 036 674)

Descriptions of family counseling programs in schools and other settings are presented. The program models include different group and individual counseling structures and different goals in work with families. Guides to the development of a program within the school guidance setting are included.

530. Smith, G. C. Counselor's guide to manpower information; and annotated bibliography of government publications. Washington, D.C.: Bureau of Labor Statistics (DOL), 1968. (ED 037 559)

This selected bibliography of materials published by all Federal and many state agencies from 1962 to 1968 is divided into four sections. One deals with occupational and industry manpower literature, including occupational outlook service information, occupational and industry manpower studies, job descriptions, and

Federal government careers. The second part discusses education, financial assistance, and placement information. The next section examines manpower problems in relationship to depressed areas, defense expenditures, labor standards, technological change, and worker mobility. The last part cited studies concerning problems of such special groups in the labor forces as agricultural migrants, apprentices, older workers, women, and youth. Information on sources of statistics useful to counselors and a section on broad-scope directories, catalogs, and bibliographies is also provided. Appended are: (1) addresses of Federal agencies, (2) a 2-year cumulative index to the "Occupational Outlook Quarterly" by article title, (3) a section on how to obtain government publications, (4) a listing of Federal Government periodicals and how to obtain them, and (5) a listing of Federal Depository Libraries.

531. Smith, T. W. Development of a research-based and computer-assisted guidance program. *California Personnel and Guidance Association Journal,* 1970, 2(2), 27–32.

Innovative program aids counselors to ensure that students' activities are congruent with their professional goals.

532. Snellgrove, C. E., Jr. The effects of counselor reinforcement on a student's negative responses. Tallahassee: Florida State University, 1966. (ED 010 437)

The simulation of a desirable counseling process with emphasis on systematic counselor reinforcement of negative self-reference statements by students was reported. The objective was to demonstrate that definite measurable counseling procedures could be experimentally tested and have practical consequences. The verbal operant conditioning paradigm was employed in an attempt to answer several questions—(1) can the frequency of negative self-reference statements be modified by verbal reinforcement in a quasi-counseling situation, (2) will schedules of reinforcement produce different effects, and (3) would subjects respond differently to the same schedule of reinforcement. A functional research design permitted a focus on individual behavior of subjects. Results after 3 months indicated that reflection (paraphrasing) was not a reinforcing stimulus when made contingent upon a negative self-reference. It was shown that counselor reflection of negative statements had no undesirable effect and seemed to contribute to a decline of such statements.

533. Soong, R. K. Career ladders and core curriculum in human services. Phase II. Final report. Chicago: YMCA of Metropolitan Chicago, 1970. (ED 047 141)

This portion of Phase II of the Social Service Aide Project, a program of exemplary education for the career development of paraprofessionals in social and/or human services, represented an attempt to boaden the career ladders developed during Phase I and to extend the core curriculum above and below the Associate in Arts degree. The scheme of the career ladders was broadened by standardizing the six levels of occupational status (Professional, Technologist I and II, Technician I and II, and Trainee) in terms of educational achievement and/or life/work competency, ultimately gauged by the worker's range of functions in dealing with people, data, and things. This information is provided in chart form, and each occupational status category is described in terms of functions with people, data, and things. In addition the core curriculum for each occupational status category was developed for secondary and postsecondary levels, and these outlines are included in the report. Phase I is available as ED 035 062 (RIE, May 1970), and related documents are available as VT 012 530-012 532 and VT 012 535 in this issue.

534. South Central Educational Service Unit. Pupil personnel services program. Bloomington, Ind.: SCESU, 1968. (ED 026 685)

This report presents a narrative and evaluative description of the operations of South Central Educational Service Unit's (SCESU) pupil personnel services, serving 36 secondary schools in southern Indiana. The main topics discussed include (1) the history of SCESU's mobile counseling services, (2) a description of the geographical area, (3) the development of procedures prior to, and during, the presence of the mobile counseling center at a particular school, and (4) the feedback procedures utilized. A summary is given of pupil personnel services in the mobile counseling center. Discussed are the impact of mobile counseling units and psychometric services and an evaluation thereof. A summary of recommendations and comments from the overall evaluation is followed by examples of evaluation instruments. This program was funded under a Title III Elementary and Secondary Education Act grant.

535. Staley, E. Planning occupational educational and training for development. Stanford, Cal.: Stanford University, Stanford International Development Education Center, 1967. (ED 029 943)

This preliminary essay was designed to raise issues for discussion in the International Workshop on Occupational Education and Training for Development held at Stanford Univerity, August 1967, and participants were asked to test and challenge all propositions. The essay offers a conceptual framework and a rational procedure for the planning of occupational education and training in relation to the needs of economic, political, and social development, and gives attention to the following topics: (1) new concepts that appear to be promising and to challenge some old concepts, (2) emerging "best practices," with respect to such things as ways of determining the content of occupational education and training, relations between general and occupational education, respective responsibilities of schools and employers, and provision for feedback between the employment system and the education system, and (3) unsettled issues, key problems and opportunities, and important directions for research and development. While conceived primarily to help development planners in the newly modernizing countries, the essay deals for the most part with principles thought to have wide applicability at nearly all levels of development.

536. State University of New York. A demonstration system of occupational information for career guidance. Final report. Albany: SUNY, Bureau of Occupational Educational Research, 1968. (ED 024 838)

The purpose of this project was to test the effectiveness of a cooperative arrangement between the New York State Education Department and the New York State Employment Service, undertaken to produce and disseminate up-to-date information about local entry occupations for use in the career guidance of students. In a sampling of high schools and 2-year colleges in Nassau and Suffolk counties of the New York metropolitan area, four page descriptions of 200 entry occupations were prepared in two forms: (1) a loose-leaf binder and (2) a deck of microfilm aperature cards. Three comprehensive high schools, three academic high schools, three area vocational technical programs, and three 2-year colleges were supplied with the 200 occupational guides. Of the students who use the guides, 92 percent said they would recommend the guides to other students; 75 percent wanted to keep copies of the guides they had read. In proportion to enrollment, students in area vocational technical educational programs made twice as much use of the guides as did the students in either academic or comprehensive high schools, and 13 times as much use as students in 2-year colleges.

537. Steinberg, S. S. & Fishman, J. R. New careers: the teacher aide. A manual for trainers. Washington, D.C.: University Research Corporation, Information Clearinghouse, 1968. (ED 025 470)

This manual is intended for use by trainers of teacher aides in New Careers programs (which focus on training the unemployed and/or underemployed for entry-level placement as nonprofessionals in human service occupations). An introductory chapter considers the qualifications of the training team, qualifications of the trainee, the function and job description of the teacher aide in both elementary and secondary schools, and the need for realistic career mobility. Chapter 2 describes typical problems encountered in teacher aide training and outlines possible solutions. In Chapter 3, the organization and structure of the New Careers Training Model are explained, including the rationale for curriculum content areas, points to stress during training, articulation of program components, and program scheduling. Chapter 4 presents a basic curriculum in education, complete with suggested discussion units and activities, consisting of selected resource material for the trainer to use in enabling the teacher aide trainer to develop insight into education in general as well as his local school system. Also included are a glossary of New Careers terms, a list of audiovisual aids (and their distributors) and basic training materials, and an explication of the basic concepts of the New Careers Training Model.

538. Stetter, R. A group guidance technique for classroom teachers. *The School Counselor,* 1969, 16(3), 179–184.

In order to increase the communication between young people and to remove their negative self-concept, a technique for revealing to the group the personal-social problems and worries of individual group members was developed. The technique was tested in a controlled experiment.

539. Stevens County Board of Education. To provide experience to broaden the occupational horizons of rural high school age youth. Colville, Wash.: SCBE. (ES 001 970)

Vocational counseling will be offered to high school juniors and seniors in a rural, isolated area. Emphasis will be placed upon offering students sufficient knowledge of the world of work outside their immediate environment to enable them to make an informed choice on—(1) the kinds of work available, or (2) ways in which to prepare themselves for careers or occupations. Group guidance will be used for career development sessions. Grouping will be based on the counselor's analysis of each student's Kuder Interest Profile and the Strong Vocational Interest Blank, as well as on the student's considered evaluation of his own interests. Three vocationally-oriented guidance groups will be established for—(1) people-minded students who are interested in working with people, (2) data-minded students who are interested in ideas, facts and figures, and (3) thing-minded students who have good manipulative skills. Students will be free to attend two of the three groups. The counselor, through group guidance techniques, will help students to become increasingly aware of their aptitudes and qualifications for success in particular vocational fields. Students will visit business and industries throughout the state, and representatives from industry will conduct school seminars. A mobile library of films and printed materials related to occupational alternatives will be developed. Approximately 698 students, grades 11 and 12, will be served. For further information, contact Robert Price, 151 South Oak St., Colville, Washington 99114. (509) 684-6500.

540. Stevenson, W. W., and Sandline, B. E. Evaluating careeer guidance, counseling and placement—state level. Identifying areas of concern and determining evidences needed for evaluation: career guidance, counseling and placement—state level. Oklahoma City: Oklahoma State Department of Education, 1970. (ED 046 009)

The overall purpose of these papers is to provide a background working paper to serve as a basis for developing a system for evaluating states' programs in Career Guidance, Counseling and Placement. An extensive review of published materials is summarized into three areas: (1) the accomplishments, limitations and trends of the current guidance effort; (2) the major concerns of guidance people; and (3) criteria for evaluating programs and identifying methods of improving vocational guidance services. Taking this information as a point of departure, the second paper recommends a procedure for securing the information, within a state, about major areas of concern and about evaluative criteria, i.e. evidences which show a program to be effective. A sampling of pertinent state level personnel as well as local administrators, students, teachers, and teacher- and counselor-educators were presented lists of identified items under each classification and asked to rank them. Results were presented.

541. Stogdill, R. M. & Bailey, W. R. Changing response of vocational students to supervision: the use of motion pictures and group discussion. Columbus: Center for Vocational and Technical Education, The Ohio State University, 1969. (ED 032 430)

This study was designed to determine whether viewing and discussing five movies, each depicting a different pattern of supervisory behavior, would enable maladjusted students to react more favorably to supervision. Patterns of behavior were: (1) consideration of employees, (2) structuring expectations, (3) tolerance of freedom of action, (4) production emphasis, and (5) representation of the interests of the group. Small groups composed equally of well-adjusted and poorly-adjusted high school students viewed the movies and then engaged in free discussion without any attempt by researchers to influence student attitude towards the supervisory role being discussed. Approximately 8 weeks after discussing the movies, the students were rated again by the teachers on adjustment to supervision. Poorly-adjusted boys in the experimental group gained more in ratings of adjustment to supervision than did poorly-adjusted control groups that did not see the movie. Teachers tended to adjust their second ratings downward, however the experimental groups lost less than the control groups. The results for all groups, except well adjusted girls, favored the experimental groups that saw and discussed the movies. It was recommended that the movies be used further in training and research.

542. Stone, P. J. An interaction inquirer. Paper presented at the Invitational Conference on Testing Problems, New York City, October, 1966. (ED 012 499)

Automated language processing (content analysis) is engaged in new ventures in computer dialog as a result of new techniques in categorizing responses. A computer "need-achievement" scoring system has been developed. A set of computer programs, labeled "The General Inquirer," will score computer inputs with responses fed from its memory bank. These responses, drawn from some 17 different dictionaries, will contain approximately 6 million words on International Business machines (IBM) cards. When a subject writes a story, the computer will immediately give a summary of the amount of "need-achievement" present and also a sentence-by-stentence analysis showing where "need-achievement" is found. In another system, called the "Eliza," developed by J. Weizenbaum, the computer plays the role of a psychotherapist. It has been tested experimentally by Abelson and McGuire, and reveals that subjects could not consistently identify whether responses were being made by the computer or a person. More complex and continuous computer dialogs will become possible. This paper was presented at the Invitational Conference on Testing Problems (New York City, October 29, 1966) and is available from the Educational Testing Service, Rosedale Road, Princeton, New Jersey 08540, 17 pages, for $1.50.

543. Sturges, J. C. Assisting vocational development through a unit in civics: a comparison of two techniques. New Orleans, La.: Educational Systems Development Corp., 1969. (ED 036 845)

An experimental classroom instruction program in vocational information was conducted as a six-weeks civics unit in 12 selected secondary schools in New Orleans. Field trips, career days, and viewing specifically constructed television programs were the experimental activities, while the control treatment consisted of the textbook approach to providing vocational information. The results were examined in an attempt to determine the effectiveness of the two treatments. They indicated that neither method was superior in helping the student learn the textbook material, modifying his attitude toward work, self and education and effecting his willingness to seek out or become involved with vocational information. However, open-ended responses showed that the experimental activities were relatively more appealing to students.

544. Sturges, J. C. (et al.). A comparison of two methods of providing information to ninth grade students about the world of work. New Orleans, La.: Educational Systems Development Corp., 1969. (ED 044 722)

During the 1967–1968 academic year an experimental program of classroom instruction in vocational information and career selection was introduced in selected secondary schools. Data were obtained by testing students in the experimental and control groups by administering pre- and post-test instruments which focused on four major areas: (1) knowledge concerning occupations and related information; (2) level of occupational aspiration; (3) perceptions of the degree of importance of certain job factors; and (4) student attitudes toward work, self, and education. Analysis of the data revealed that no significant differences in knowledge existed between the experimental and control groups. However, the fact that the experimental group performed equally well on a textbook oriented test suggests that the field experience compensated for the lack of study time normally devoted to study of the textbook. Career aspirations of students in both groups were higher following the treatment.

545. Stutz, R. C. Promising practices for small schools' improvement. Annual progress report. Salt Lake City, Utah: Western States Small Schools Project, 1965. (ED 020 065)

Meeting the unique problems of providing quality education in small schools calls for special programs. The Western States Small Schools Project has compiled 9 promising program practices which capitalize upon the potential strengths inherent in smallness—individualized instruction in high school language arts, individualized English in a small high school, individualized instruction in a small elementary school, individualized and non-grade math in a small high school, modern mathematics in an individualized program, and expanding mathematic study opportunities in small high schools. Each practice is described by the participating school, with an account of the desired outcomes, preparation, practice, and evaluation. (SF)

546. Sullivan, H. J. The effects of selected film and counseling experiences on capable girls' attitudes toward college. Monmouth: Oregon State System of Higher Education, Teaching Research Division, 1964. (ED 003 224)

A sample of approximately 200 high-ability girls who indicated that they were unlikely to attend college, were screened from approximately 2,000 senior girls in 8 high schools. The experimental treatments employed were (1) a counseling interview, (2) an interview plus the showing of a film designed to change attitudes toward college, and (3) two showings of the film. Several variations of the treatment groups were made, and a no-treatment control group was selected. Criterion measures consisted of (1) attitudes toward college, as assessed by a questionnaire, and (2) applications for admission following the treatment phase. It was discovered that—(1) girls who indicated that lack of money was their primary deterrent were more favorable in attitude than those who indicated that motivational factors were the chief obstacle, and applied for college in greater numbers, and (2) girls with low-motivation who saw the film and were individually counseled scored greater on the attitude scale than those who were group-counseled. Actual applications for admission were not significantly different. Implications are discussed, along with other findings.

547. Summers, R. Methods and techniques for improving the educational aspirational level of senior high school students. Columbia: Missouri University, 1970. (ED 044 746)

This paper presents methods and techniques for improving the educational aspirational level of disadvantaged senior high school students. The objectives of the program are listed, followed by a list of ten activity areas within which the substance of the motivational thrusts of the project are to be implemented. The activity areas are discussed. These include general orientation activities, exploration of the worlds of beauty and work activities, motivation through models using resource people, reward activities, cleanliness and orderliness activities, counseling services, student participation and publicity, extended day activities, and motivation through films. Both specific objectives and a plan for action are given for each of the above activities. A basic organization for the program is then explained, as well as the various methods of evaluation which will be used.

548. Super, D. E. and Forrest, D. J. Career development inventory, form 1, preliminary manual for research and field trial. New York, N.Y.: Teachers College, Columbia University, 1972.

This preliminary draft relates information regarding the Career Development Inventory (CDI), a paper and pencil, objective, multifactor inventory measuring the vocational maturity of adolescents. This measure yields three scale scores, two of them affective and one conative, in addition to a total score. Names of scales and number of items contained in each are: A. Planning Orientation (Affective, 33 items); B. Resources for Exploration (Affective, 28 items); C. Information and Decision Making (Cognitive (30 items). The overall readability of the measure is at the sixth grade level.

549. Super, D. E. Using computers in guidance: an experiment in a secondary school. *Canadian Counselor,* 1970, 4(1), 11–20.

Describes the Educational and Career Exploration System (1969), its use in one school, some results of a current evaluation study. Basic computer involved is the IBM 360.

550. Super, D. E. Work values inventory. New York: Houghton-Mifflin, 1964.

The Work Values Inventory is an instrument designed as one of the basic instruments of the career pattern study and consisting of 210 diads which provide scores for 15 work values: Altrusim, Creativity, Independence, Intellectual Stimulation, Esthetics, Achievement, Management, Way of Life, Security, Prestige, Economic Returns, Surroundings, Associates, Supervisory Relations and Variety. In each diad, the two statements are keyed to different work values, and the examinee chooses the one which he considers as more important to him. Research on the relationship between the WVI and vocational success and satisfaction has not been extensive.

551. Syracuse City School District, School-to-employment program journal. Syracuse, N.Y.: SCSD, 1964. (ED 001 685)

Twenty students at Central High School who participate in the School to Employment Program share their thoughts and experiences. Comments by the students indicate the friendliness of employers, the success of the STEP program, and a gratefulness for being involved in a job training experience.

The following are among the many different jobs which students gained through the work-study program: office assistant to a professor at Syracuse University, page at the Public Library, cook's helper in a university kitchen, saleslady at a department store, school office aid, typist at the City Hall, and stockboy at a general store.

552. Tarrier, R. (Ed.) Sources of occupational information. Columbus: Ohio State Department of Education, Division of Guidance and Testing, 1968. (ED 024 810)

This publication identifies some of the many sources of occupational information and describes representative publications. All references cited have been published recently, contain general sources of information, and meet one or more of the following criteria: (1) present sources of available occupational information, (2) identify materials presenting occupational information for students, counselors, and others involved in educational services, or (3) describe techniques for gathering, organizing, and using occupational information. References are grouped according to source in order to eliminate duplication in listing publishers. Two separate indexes have been prepared—one by title and one by supplier—in order to provide easy access to the information.

553. Taylor, J. E., Montague, E. K., and Michaels, E. R. An occupational clustering system and curriculum implications for the comprehensive career education model. Human Resources Research Organization, Alexandria, Virginia 22314, January 1972. Prepared for The Center for Vocational and Technical Education, The Ohio State University, Columbus, Ohio 43210.

This project report is aimed at contributing to the school-based model of career preparation as developed by The Center for Vocational and Technical Education of The Ohio State University, by proposing a clustering system that will help integrate the world of work with a career education system.

The clustering system serves as a planning model, integrated with the progression of career development goals: Awareness, Orientation, Exploration and Selection. The clustering system can serve as the basis for arranging instructional objectives, content, and methods that guide and inform students about the world of work.

554. Tennyson, W. W. (et al.) The teacher's role in career development. Washington, D.C.: National Vocational Guidance Association, 1965.

Tennyson stresses the importance of the teacher in an effective school guidance program. This booklet provides bibliographies of occupational information and charts that demonstrate how school subjects such as art, mathematics, and music relate to careers. In addition, information is provided concerning post high school education opportunities such as on-the-job training, government training programs, and private trade and correspondence schools.

This book also contains important discussions of the structure of occupations and the meaning of work in our present society.

555. Tennyson, W. W. & Meyer, W. G. Pilot training project for teachers of distribution and marketing, focusing on responsibilities for career development. Minneapolis: Minnesota University, College of Education, 1967. (ED 027 383)

This pilot training project conducted during the summer of 1967 was Phase I of a two-phase training program. Phase I (ED 016 805) was conducted during the summer of 1966 and provided a group of 30 distributive education teacher-coordinators with distributive occupational experience in two business firms. The purpose of Phase II was to increase teacher effectiveness in encouraging self-exploration and developing judgement and decision-making skills in students. General approaches followed were: (1) consideration of instructional content and methods appropriate to the career development of the distributive education student, and (2) group experiences designed to focus on the career and personal development of the coordinators and distributive teachers enrolled in the workshop. The instructional program was conducted within a 5-week schedule and consisted of three courses: (1) didactic instruction, 25 class hours, (2) group process, 30 class hours, and (3) integrative seminar, 35 class hours. Fifteen graduating seniors from local schools were selected for the demonstration class. The program was evaluated through: (1) studies of behavioral and performance change during the time the teacher was enrolled in the training program, (2) the effect on the career and self-development of the participant in the demonstration class, and (3) the quality of teaching materials that were developed.

556. Terlin, R. Jobfinding technique for mature women. Washington, D.C.: Women's Bureau, 1970. (ED 050 229)

Written by the Chief of Special Projects of the Women's Bureau as a guide for assisting the mature woman in preparing for and finding employment, this pamphlet contains sections on: (1) How to Do a Self-Inventory, (2) How to Prepare a Resume, (3) The Jobhunt, (4) How to Prepare a Letter of Application, (5) Guides to an Effective Interview, and (6) Training Opportunities. Selected readings and addresses of agencies and organizations are appended.

557. Texas Board of Education. Texas occupational orientation program, Austin, Texas: TBE 1972.

The Texas Occupational Orientation Program was initiated through the authorization by the State Board of Education of 18 pilot projects for the implementation of career education.

The Occupational Orientation Program consists of three sequential parts: (1) Occupational awareness, (2) Occupational investigation, (3) Occupational exploration. These parts are aimed at developing worthwhile attitudes toward work in students, assisting students in discovering occupational interests, opportunities and requirements, narrowing occupational-career choices, and so on. The program serves students in grades K–9 with the aid of specially developed curriculum materials and in-service training for teachers.

558. Thomas, A. H., and Stewart, N. R. Counselor response to female clients with deviate and conforming career goals. *Journal of Counseling Psychology,* 1971, 18(4), 352–357.

This study was designed to determine whether secondary school counselors respond more positively to female clients with traditionally feminine (conforming) goals than those with traditionally masculine (deviate) goals. Five stimulus interviews with high school girls elicited information concerning their home, school, self-description, and personal values. These were presented on audiotape to 64 practicing counselors and their responses were analyzed by sex and experience. Results were as follows: (a) Female counselor gave higher acceptance scores to both deviate and conforming clients than did male counselors; (b) counselors, regardless of sex, rated conforming goals as more appropriate than deviate; (c) counselors, regardless of sex, rated female clients with deviate career goals to be more in need of counseling than those with conforming goals.

559. Thompson, A. S. (et al.). The educational and career exploration system: field trial and evaluation in Montclair High School. New York: Columbia University, Teachers College, 1970. (ED 046 005)

This is the report of the field trial and evaluation of an experimental computer-assisted guidance system designed for use by junior and senior high school students. This trial was designed to determine the system's applicability and feasibility in a secondary school setting. It sought also to obtain information on the outcome of its use, both in terms of possible changes in vocational developmental behavior patterns of the students using the system and in attitudes and opinions toward the system by students and their parents and teachers. Included in the report are: (1) a general introduction; (2) a description of the system; (3) the field trial, methods and procedure; (4) effects of the system usage on student vocational development; (5) results: attitudes toward the system; and (6) summary, conclusions, and implications.

560. Thompson, J. M. & Laramore, D. The relative effectiveness of two types of media in the dissemination of vocational information. *California Personnel and Guidance Association Journal,* 1970, 3(1), 27–35.

The relative effectiveness of "VIEW" and "Film Loop" in the dissemination of vocational information was investigated. The results indicated no general superiority for either medium. Results support the use of VIEW as a differential approach to career guidance while FL is seen as a nondiscriminatory technique for a wide range of students.

561. Thoreson, C. E. (et al.) Behavioral school counseling: a demonstration of the Stanford career planning project. Washington, D.C.: American Personnel and Guidance Association, 1969. (ED 031 721)

The Stanford Career Planning Project designed and tested the effectiveness of three competing experimental treatments for promoting career exploration in adolescents. They were: (1) group structured stimulus materials, (2) group social modeling, and (3) a combination of the two. Planned stimulus materials were prepared and used in four group counseling sessions with eight subjects per counseling group. Four video-presented group social models were developed and used in four sessions paralleling the content of the structured stimulus materials. The sequence as well as content of these first two treatments were followed in the third treatment. A variety of learning activities and suggested counselor comments are included in the report to help achieve the following behavioral objectives: (1) given a small group of between four and eight high school students, it will be possible to identify student verbal responses demonstrating career information-seeking behaviors; (2) given the same type of group, it will be possible to use four types of verbal and nonverbal reinforcers immediately after students' verbal demonstrations of above-indicated behaviors; (3) it will be possible to use at least one method of determining how effective the group counseling program actually was.

562. Tiedeman, D. V. The cultivation of careers through guidance and vocational education. Information system for vocational decisions. Project report no. 18. Cambridge, Mass.: Graduate School of Education, Harvard University, 1969. (ED 034 212)

The enlargement of the understanding of the career for the individual is necessary in order to put the imperative need of work for everyone more into perspective. First, secondary education in 1980 needs to be taken, not as a high school education but rather as an educational process reserved for those in need of an interdependent, not completely independent, learning experience in order to progress in the expansion of their intelligence and career according to their own purposes. It is proposed that this secondary education take place in a Learning Resource Center (LRC) with the basic instructional aid being an Educational Machine. Counselors at the LRC would help the individual to convert his learning into real life experiences. The education machine would provide the series of "dress rehearsals" which a person needs in career in order to achieve realization of self processes in the choice processes of career. The ultimate goal for this program includes the integration of community resources for the common good, individualization of instruction, and education for individuality (including therapy or education for the mentally ill) leading to the fostering of identification, the fundament of identity.

563. Tiedeman, D. V. Economic, educational, and personal implications of implementing computerized guidance information systems. Information system for vocational decisions. Cambridge, Mass.: Harvard University, 1967. (ED 053 402)

The author asserts that financial support of guidance activities, the job of the counselor, and counselors themselves will all have to change if computerized guidance support systems are to come into widespread use. The potential costs, benefits, and operating economics are discussed. Needed educational reorganization is dealt with on several levels: (1) the Information System for Vocational Decisions (ISVD) which is basically an inquiry system, will function optimally only in a school climate where inquiry is the major pedagogy; (2) an ISVD program will require that books, films and computer console arrangements be effectively coordinated; and (3) an ISVD program ideally will be available to people other than students in places other than schools. Counselor attitudinal changes needed for effective implementation of a computerized guidance program, as well as the resultant demands on counselor training, conclude the paper.

564. Tiedeman, D. V. (Ed.) Eighth invitational conference on systems under construction for career education and development, report of proceedings. Palo Alto, California: American Institutes for Research, 1972.

Among the topics covered during the conference were: (1) Models for Career Education, examples included school-based model, employer-based models and home-community-based model, (2) A report on the Program in Career Research, Education and Development at the American Institutes for Research (Projects TALENT, PLAN and CCGS), (3) Reports on Status and Progress of Various Guidance Systems, (4) The basic functions of an effective program for career guidance and counseling, (5) The relative advantages of available procedures, and (6) Implementation problems.

565. Tiedeman, D. V. (et al.) An information system for vocational decisions. Sixth quarterly report. Cambridge, Mass.: Harvard University, 1967. (ED 018 825 MF $.50 HC $3.20)

The purpose of this report is to outline the major activities and accomplishments of the information system for vocational decisions during its sixth quarter (1 September 1967 to 30 November 1967) at Harvard University.

566. Tiedeman, D. V. (et al.) Thought, choice and action: processes of exploration and commitment in career development. Volume I. Cambridge, Mass.: Harvard University, 1967. (ED 050 293)

This document, the first of two volumes, contains papers that represent recent work in career development research at Harvard University. The purpose of the papers is to review, clarify, and offer a critical commentary on several issues crucial to current research and to emphasize a point of view from which important resources of conceptual analysis can be brought to bear on the issues.

Section I, Developmental Context, and Section II, "Stock Taking" include the following chapters: (1) The Harvard Studies in Career Development: Retrospect and Prospect, (2) Decision and Vocational Development: a Paradigm and its Implications, (3) The Self-Concept: A Critical Analysis, (4) Self as Process, (5) The Self-Concept: A Construct in Transition, (6) From Self-Concept to Personal Determination in Career Development, (7) Occupational Psychology and Guidance in Education; Foundations For a Language Career in Development, (8) Personally Determined Career and Entrepreneurial Behavior: Annotated Texts and Contexts, (9) Current Findings: Precursors of New Directions, and (10) Creativity and Career. Volume II, a continuation of these papers, is available as ED 050 294.

567. Tiedeman, D. V. (et al.) Thought, choice, and action: processes of exploration and commitment in career development. Volume 2. Cambridge, Mass.: Harvard University, 1967. (ED 050 294)

This document, the second of two volumes, is a continuation of papers that represent work in career development research at Harvard University. Section III, Choosing as Figure in the Styling of Life, Section IV, Conceptual Integration, and Section V, Professional Implications, include the following chapters: (11) A Return to Models: Differentiation and Integration in Personality Development, (12) The Organization and Intention of a Proposed Data and Educational System for Vocational Decisions, (13) Aspects of Imagination in the Learning Process, (14) Recent Developments and Current Prospects in Occupational Fact Mediation, (15) The Forms of Language and the Forms of Life in the Conduct of Inquiry, (16) Vocational-Technical Education and Occupational Guidance, (17) Liberation Through Education, and (18) Predicament, Problem, and Psychology. Three appendixes and a 33-page reference list are included. Volume I of these papers is available as ED 050 293.

568. Tillery, D. (et al.) SCOPE: grade eleven profile 1968 questionnaire selected items. Berkeley, Cal.: Center for Research and Development in Higher Education, University of California, 1969. (ED 035 000)

The primary research emphasis of School to College: Opportunities for Post Secondary Education (SCOPE) is to analyze and report the inter-relationships of yearly data in such ways as to help answer questions about why different students behave and believe as they do, and how these actions and attitudes influence the decision-making process. For this study, eleventh grade students from four states completed a questionnaire. Several new areas of student life were investigated in this report. Among these are guidance contacts with counselors and teachers about work, and information about counselors and teachers. Students also used a series of 20 role behaviors to describe themselves in three different situations: (1) at home, (2) at school, and (3) with friends. For each item response in this grade 11 report, it is possible to observe similarities and differences between the sexes, across aspiration groups, and among the four states. One noted conclusion was that grades as an incentive to learning are more attractive to girls than to boys. Complete data tables are presented according to student response to the questionnaire.

569. Todd, R. D. & Todd, K. P. A prospectus for the development of a career-development and technology program for elementary school children. Cleveland, Ohio: Case Western Reserve University, 1968. (ED 053 311)

The Career Development and Technology Program will help elementary school children examine various occupations, the world of work, technology, and their own interest and abilities in relation to possible career directions. Specifically it will: (1) provide learning activities that engage the learner in experiences suited to his interests, (2) interrelate areas through jobs and activities that cross disciplines, (3) help pupils develop an understanding of self, technology, and the world of work, and (4) provide a foundation for later study of technology and continued career exploration. The materials will be packaged so that they can be used in spontaneous as well as planned activities. A Technology Resource Kit contains a variety of games, simulation and reading materials, role playing props, tools, and construction materials. It is anticipated that the student will develop in the following way: (1) The elementary child will look at the basic elements of "man and things," (2) The middle grades students will gain an understanding of self and the dimension of "products and services," and (3) The high school student will gain information necessary to develop a career plan.

570. Todd, V. E. & Bates, Z. Development of a junior high school instrument for appraising social readiness for employment. Long Beach: California State College, 1967. (MP 000 008)

Two appraisal devices were developed to measure social readiness for employment. The devices are direct means for a student to record his thoughts about work and school situations so that he and others can observe the veracity of his responses.

571. Tonkin, W. J. Vocational guidance through videotaping and television. 1967. (ED 036 047)

The research study described here was designed to provide vocational guidance through student involvement in the videotaping of live occupational situations and later showing in the classroom. A major goal of the program was to identify the factors involved in student dropout situations.

572. Traux, C. B. The use of supportive personnel in rehabilitation counseling: process and outcome. Fayetteville: Arkansas State Rehabilitation Research and Training Center; Evanston, Ill.: Association of Rehabilitation Centers, Inc. (ED 022 217)

The following issues are discussed in relation to counseling and vocational rehabilitation: (1) the process and outcome of counseling and therapeutic practice, (2) selection of effective counselors, (3) effective counselor training, (4) the role of untrained supportive personnel in the role of counselor aids; and (5) guidelines for the most effective use of supportive personnel in rehabilitation counseling.

573. Tuckman, B. W. The development and testing of an evaluation model for vocational pilot programs. New Brunswick, N.J.: Rutgers, The State University, 1967. (ED 014 567)

A progress report on the development of a "Curriculum Hierarchy for the Evaluation of Course Knowledge," the "Check" technique, is presented. The technique is based upon a model which initially necessitates translating the learning processes and objectives into easily identifiable behavioral responses. The process of translating vague course goals into precise behavioral ones is described. After behavioral goals have been translated, they can be analyzed into a sequence of prerequisite behaviors by task analysis. This sequence of prerequisite behaviors is then used as a frame of reference for the development of content valid test items. In the final phase, not described in this report, content valid test data can be analyzed, and results can be used for pinpoint location of course strengths and weaknesses. A sample check test for data processing—key punching is included.

574. Tuckman, B. W. A study of curriculum for occupational preparation and education. (SCOPE program: phase I.) Progress reports I and II. New Brunswick, N.J.: Rutgers, The State University, 1969. (ED 027 438)

The major objective of the Study of Curriculums for Occupational Preparation and Education (SCOPE) is to coordinate and contribute to national curriculum development effort at the secondary school level aimed at increasing the relevance of high school education for the large majority of our youth who must seek employment or further job training upon graduation. The first phase of the SCOPE program is Coordination and Non-occupational Curriculums and Technology (CONECT). The objectives of this first phase are: (1) to establish communication among the state-supported vocational curriculum development centers, (2) to assist center directors in becoming aware of behavioral approaches to curriculum development, devices, and evaluation, (3) to refine and test a scheme for classifying educational objectives in terms of performance requirements and objectives, and (4) to develop a detailed plan of activity for Phase II of the

SCOPE program. These two progress reports outline major accomplishments and developments during the first two quarters of SCOPE's first year of existance.

575. Tunker, J. A. Pre-high school vocational group guidance for potential dropouts and noncollege bound students. Tracy, Cal.: Tracy Elementary School District, 1967. (ED 012 944)

The purpose of this study was to determine the effects of small group guidance sessions and industrial tours on an experimental group of male, eighth grade students deemed lacking in academic interest and/or ability who were classified as potential dropouts and non-college-bound students.

576. Turpeau, A. B. (et al.) A program for the rehabilitation of dropouts. A planning project. Washington, D.C.: Washington Urban League, 1963 (ED 002 468)

A project to develop a program of rehabilitation that would guide school dropouts back to school or into a learning situation that would provide them with basic educational and job skills was described. The procedures of the project included: developing a pilot program for the rehabilitation of dropouts: renting an office; hiring administrators, counselors, and caseworkers; formulating a list of dropouts; formulating and testing interview forms; locating and interviewing dropouts; holding followup meetings with counselors and the caseworker; and collecting, analyzing, and recommending for revision the findings of the three-month pilot program. The program was based on four assumptions: each year a million boys and girls drop out of school; there should be an early identification of potential dropouts and the initiation of steps by schools and other community agencies to prevent dropouts; when a pupil drops out of school, a rehabilitation agency working in concert with the public schools should take the initiative in recruiting the dropout into a continuous program of guidance and counseling; and a good relationship between a dropout and competent counselor should be established to help the dropout develop high aspirations and a positive self-concept.

Characteristics of dropouts were determined. Personal characteristics included age, sex, marital status, number of own children, and the support of such children. Home characteristics included family size, mobility, support, and health conditions. Emotional characteristics included last grade completed in school, reasons for leaving school, and general attitude toward school. Delinquent characteristics included involvement with police and incarcerations. Most dropouts wanted either to return to school or to obtain job training.

577. Tuttle, D. C. A follow-up study of graduates' and employers' opinions of a cooperating training program. Research study number 1. Greeley: Colorado State College, 1965. (ED 024 012)

Interviews collected information from 135 graduates of the trades and industrial cooperative education training program, and 30 employers in Des Moines, Iowa, to appraise the effectiveness of training in relation to post high school employment. Graduates and employers commented on the value of core area training, school counseling, and different phases of the training program. It was found that the primary reasons for enrolling in the program were to gain work experience and earn extra money. Personal feelings and family influenced choice of core area. Sixty-two percent of the graduates were working at, or in, areas related to their high school training. Satisfaction was expressed with training, present job, and the school counseling and coordinating service. Employers felt training helped graduates secure employment and receive promotions. Graduates felt core area training could be improved by more production training and wider experience on shop equipment, while employers thought additional training in production work, business ethics, and employment procedures should be included in the core area training.

578. Ulibarri, S. R. Learn, amigo, learn. *Personnel and Guidance Journal,* 1971, 50(2), 87–89.

The authors of this first article relate their thoughts about ethnic conflicts in general. They confront guidance personnel with their dealing with culturally different clients. The articles that follow consider distinct ethnic groups more specifically.

579. Ullery, J. W. & O'Brien, R. K. Testing of the guidance program. Project ABLE; development and evaluation of an experimental curriculum for the New Quincy (Mass.) Vocational-Technical School. Pittsburgh: American Institutes for Research, 1970. (ED 048 487)

> The Project ABLE Guidance Program was designed to prepare junior high school students for making an appropriate and stable choice of a high school program. To determine the success of the program, an experimental and a control group were administered the Project ABLE Career Development Inventory prior to and after implementation of the guidance plan. The results of the testing program were inadequate, with many inconsistencies occurring in the data and on the student score sheets. Serious questions can be raised about proper administration of the pre- and post-test and use of the student kit materials, required reference, and multi-media support materials. Funds for the support of staff for the proper revision of the student kit materials have not been readily available. It is felt that further refinement of the materials and administrative procedures, better implementation, and a more exhaustive investigation of student performance will lead to more positive results. The Career Development Inventory and summary of test scores are appended. Related reports are available as ED 024 752 and ED 024 767.

580. University of Texas. Student's personal adjustment to work, suggested plans for group discussions in vocational industrial education. Volume II. Austin: UT, Department of Industrial Education; Texas Education Agency, Industrial Education Division, 1963. (ED 016 765)

> Vocational teachers can use this study guide as an organized plan of developing appropriate discussion topics relative to job orientation in 2-year part-time classes. It was developed by an instructor-coordinator and an advisory committee. Major divisions are (1) Personal Traits, (2) Money and Banking, (3) School Relations, (4) Civic Responsibilities, (5) Records and Reports, (6) Applying and Interviewing for Jobs, (7) Facts About Narcotics, and (8) Public Relations. Lessons within each section include Topic, Aim, References, Introductory Information, Procedures, Group Participation, Teaching Methods, and a Summary. Information sheets supplement other references. The teacher should be a qualified coordinator, and students should be juniors or seniors. A bibliography includes booklets, pamphlets, books, and 58 films. This guide and a companion Volume I (VT 000 267) are available for $6.00 from Industrial Education Department, Division of Extension, The University of Texas, Austin, Texas 78712.

581. Upcraft, M. L. Undergraduate students as academic advisers. *Personnel and Guidance Journal,* 1971, 49(10), 827–831.

> An experimental college tried to solve its academic advising problems by employing undergraduate students to advise freshmen. The evaluation of faculty, freshmen students, and the undergraduate students themselves was generally positive, although some problems arose.

582. Ury, C. M. Books in the field: career-related guidance for youth. *Wilson Library Bulletin,* 1970, 44(6), 621–631.

> Counselors, in general have too little knowledge of vocational education and the labor market. This literature review covers many aspects of career guidance and suggests that the librarian should have an important role in providing reference help in this area. Includes extensive bibliography.

583. U.S. Dept. of Health, Education and Welfare. The career information center: a working model. Washington, D.C.: DHEW, Office of Education, 1969. (ED 039 359)

> Information about careers is an essential ingredient in the process of career choice. This model program of career information services was developed for junior and senior high school students. The services include informative assemblies, conferences, radio and television programs, tape recordings, and filmstrips.

584. Usitalo, R. J. Elementary counseling and guidance. A second year's report on the operation of a laboratory. Olympia, Wash.: Olympia School District, 1968. (ED 022 216)

An evaluation of the elementary counseling program in the Olympia, Washington schools is presented. The emphasis is upon counselor role as seen by the counselors, teachers, and principals. Models of counelor role in intervention and change are developed. Case examples further explain the models. Evaluative comments by teachers and principals on counseling effectiveness are quoted, and the results of a questionnaire are described.

585. U.S. Office of Education. World of work curriculum (PM400-7). Instructors manual. Washington, D.C.: OE, Jobs Corps, 1967.

The *World of Work* Curriculum is a program specifically designed for training Job Corpsmen. The goal of the Job Corps program is to help young men and women become employable and able to meet their adult responsibilities. While adequate training in basic educational and vocational skills is necessary for achieving this goal, it is not sufficient. The *World of Work* Curriculum is designed to supplement both basic and vocational education curricula by developing additional skills, work habits and attitudes. The curriculum provides Corpsmen with information on getting a job, meeting on-the-job responsibilities, managing money and getting along with other workers.

586. Utah Research Coordinating Unit for Vocational and Technical Education. V.I.E.W., vocational information for education and work. Salt Lake City: Utah State Department of Employment Security, URCUVTE. (ED 021 068)

The purpose of this volume is to provide a readily accessible source of vocational information which acquaints the high school student with a wide variety of jobs available in Utah, gives basic information about a given job, and is easily read.

587. Utah State University. Proposal for a mobile assisted career exploration unit. Logan: USU, 1968. (ED 042 179)

A pilot program is proposed to determine if a mobile guidance unit operating on a limited time schedule can provide a feasible means for increasing maturity of rural ninth grade students. The program is based on the hypothesis that students interacting for a short period of time with a counselor and a counselor aid will enhance their vocational development as measured by an increase in vocational maturity. Two samples of ninth grade rural students who are generally without full time counseling service are to be used (one as a control group). The program is designed to help the student acquire experience in two basic areas: (1) knowledge of self and the world of work and (2) practice in utilizing this knowledge in prevocational decision making. The student will be exposed to career information, given aptitude and interest tests and interact with the counselor in individual and group sessions. The proposal is designed to involve parents. Also included are outlines for career exploration schedules, evaluation designs and cost estimates.

588. Varenhorst, B. B. Information regarding the use of the life career game in the Palo Alto Unified School District guidance program. Palo Alto, Cal.: Palo Alto Unified School District. (ED 012 939)

A program to teach decision-making skills to ninth and 11th grade students using local research data, visual aids, and other materials was undertaken. In group guidance sessions, these problems were discovered—(1) some decisions are never consciously made, (2) the emotional bases of decisions are not considered, (3) many students avoid making decisions because they fear lasting consequences, and (4) provisions for practice in decision-making are needed. To alleviate some of these problems, the Life Career game developed by Boocock and Coleman, was employed. Using two groups comprised of 10 and 18 students respectively, teams of two students were formed. Each team planned a fictitious student's life for 20 years, including education, occupation, family life and leisure time. Teams competed for the highest number of points in the game. The games were successful because they provided motivation and involvement, illustrated future factual realities, and led to discussion. Since the game meets some needs which were lacking in group guidance sessions, it can be used in conjunction with the sessions. Plans call for its extended use in the high schools as well as implementation in junior high schools.

589. Varenhorst, B. B. How students use values in decision making. 1966. (ED 012 483)

High school students are examining and internalizing values. Their fear of commitment to anything deviating from accepted values may hinder their clarification of personal goals and values. The decision-making process should be an important part of the guidance program. Standard questionnaires do not provide information about specific factors which affect personal decisions such information is more effectively obtained through evaluation of spontaneous samples of students in a decision-making situation. Related questions include—(1) whether only the mature, independent student can effectively examine subjective desires, (2) whether counselors should use students' affective reactions to alternatives as a basis for working with them, (3) whether the high school student is able to distinguish personal values from peer, community, or school values, and, if not, should the counselor work with the student toward clarifying and distinguishing the two, and (4) whether the limited life experience of the high school student also limits rational utilization of values in decision making. Experiences with group counseling, group experiences with a simulation life career game, group guidance sessions on decision making, and individual counseling which helped students develop values and make decisions are described. Suggestions for further research are given. This speech was presented at the American Personnel and Guidance Association Convention (Washington, D.C., April 6, 1966).

590. Varenhorst, B. B. Innovative tool for group counseling: the life career game. *The School Counselor,* 1968, 15(5), 357–362.

The Life Career Game is the focus of this article. It is a simulation technique whereby teams of students attempt to plan the most satisfying life for a hypothetical student. Its adaptation for guidance purposes in group settings is described, and advantages of group counseling are delineated.

591. Vetter, L. & Sethney, B. J. Planning ahead for the world of work: research report abstract, teacher manual, student materials. Transparency master. Columbus: Ohio State University, 1971. (ED 050 272)

Expanding educational and occupational opportunities for girls and women have occurred as attitudes toward women workers have become more liberalized and as legislation has provided for such opportunities and changes. However, research has indicated that many secondary-school-age girls have unrealistic educational and vocational plans and incomplete knowledge of relevant facts about the world of work. Therefore, the purpose of this project was to develop a package of curriculum materials designed to aid girls in considering future alternatives in terms of labor force participation and adult female roles. Curriculum materials and a questionnaire consisting of attitude, objective, and demographic items were developed and pilot tested at the seventh, ninth, and eleventh grade levels. It was found that students at all grade levels gained information about the world of work and women's roles in employment through the use of these materials. A major recommendation was that, with slight revisions, the materials would be appropriate to use with classes of boys and girls.

592. Viernstein, M. C. The extension of Holland's occupational classification to all occupations in the dictionary of occupational titles. Baltimore: Johns Hopkins University, 1971. (ED 051 420)

Two methods are presented for extending Holland's occupational classification to include all occupations in the Dictionary of Occupational Titles (DOT). Holland's classification is based on a theory of personality types, with occupations in the classification organized into major categories (Realistic, Investigative, Artistic, Social, Enterprising, and Conventional) and subcategories using the same concepts. The two conversion methods enable translation from any DOT occupational code (a six digit number) into the corresponding Holland Occupational code. The first method is essentially an application of Bayesian statistics to 399 occupations in Holland's Occupational Classification, while the second method was developed by using the definitions of each DOT group (first three DOT digits) and assigning the Holland code which seems theoretically consistent with the DOT definition. Testing and comparisons with four occupational samples revealed that Holland's classification could be extended to all DOT occupations.

593. Vocational Guidance Service. Career guidance through groups. A job placement and group vocational guidance program for high school youth. Phase II July 1, 1969 through August 15, 1970. Houston, Tex.: Vocational Guidance Service, 1970. (ED 050 362)

The first two operational years of the Houston area Vocational Guidance Service's Group Guidance Program for minority high school youth who live in economically disadvantaged urban areas is described. The program is experimental and is designed to prepare youth to make a positive transition from high school to suitable employment or post high school training. Objectives include: (1) exposing students to national and local labor market information and manpower trends; (2) helping students learn and implement techniques for employment and career planning; and (3) facilitating job-seeking techniques. Complete program activities are described for both years. First year results indicate that participants were more aggressive in the labor force, were better equipped to enter the labor force and earned higher wages. A second year evaluative summary points to success in respect to knowledge and motivational effects on participants, staff adequacy, program-school relationships, and program relevance to the target population. Plans for the third year are discussed.

594. Von Stroh, G. E. A socio-economic study of vocational-technical education students. 1968. (ED 047 122)

To isolate certain socioeconomic and academic characteristics of postsecondary vocational and technical education graduates and dropouts, which should enable students to receive more effective counseling and training, 210 graduates of Oklahoma State Tech were sent questionnaires before and after graduation. Questionnaires were returned by 187 prior to graduation and 153 after graduation. In addition, the student file of 223 dropouts was examined. The majority of the graduates and dropouts were male Caucasians, had a mean age at matriculation of 22-23 years, and were from rural Oklahoma areas. Of the jobs held by graduates at graduation, 51.1 percent were found through the school, while other important methods were the state employment service, friends and relatives, and direct application. Graduates employed out-of-state received higher monthly incomes than those employed in the state. The educational attainment of parents appeared to have an effect on whether or not their children sought higher education. This Ph.D. dissertation was submitted to the University of Oklahoma.

595. Walker, M. B. The remunerative work experience program. *Canadian Counselor,* 1970, 4(3), 205-206.

Briefly describes a program which acquaints students with what employers expect of them, helps develop techniques for job interviews, and presents possibility of permanent employment.

596. Walker, R. W. What vocational teachers should know about disadvantaged youth in rural areas. Columbus: Ohio State University, Center for Vocational and Technical Education, 1971.

Because of poor attitudes toward educational involvement and a lack of basic scholastic skills, some students do not succeed in the regular programs offered in the high schools. Intended to be an authoritative analysis of the literature in the field, this "state-of-the-art" paper should serve as a guideline for teachers concerned with the development of programs at the local level to meet the needs of students identified as academically disadvantaged. The paper focuses on rural academically disadvantaged students the factors which contribute to their maladjustment, and their personal characteristics. Conclusions reveal that programs must be student-centered and designed to meet individual needs. Successful programs can be developed for students through the total involvement of the school staff and the community.

597. Walsh, G. A. A study of a new and dramatic approach to vocational guidance through the use of exhibits and displays. National Education Industrial Foundations, Inc., 1966. (ED 003 107)

This is a description of a new approach to vocational guidance through the use of exhibits and displays. The choice of approximately 150 specific occupations to be exhibited was based on such criteria as (1) projected number of workers in each occupation, (2) appeal of selected occupations to secondary, trade, and technical schools, (3) appeal of selected occupations to potential dropouts, and (4) exhibit possibilities of selected occupations. Students from grades 7 through 12 served as the optimum experimental group to attend the exhibition. Plans were initiated for exposure of the exhibition to college students and interested adults. The exhibit design provides an interesting layout as well as an excellent traffic flow. In addition, it provides maximum flexibility for adaptation to various room sizes and shapes as well as the addition or deletion of display material without adding major alteration costs. An evaluation of the approach was not presented.

598. Walz, G. R. & Urbick, T. The design and implementation of information systems for pupil personnel services. Final report. Paper presented at the meeting of the American Personnel and Guidance Association, Washington, D.C., July, 1967. (ED 022 205)

Student personnel workers and services have increased without parallel increase in research in this area. To update and augment existing research skills, including knowledge of computers and computer language, to work toward a more adequate interdisciplinary conceptual base, and to encourage the establishment of information centers in the participants' own locales, an intensive, workshop on information systems was sponsored the week of March 13-17 in Dallas, Texas, prior to the National Convention of the American Personnel and Guidance Association. Some 54 participants representing a diversity of student personnel positions attended in teams of two to four members. Team attendance was used to increase the likelihood that the workshop participants would organize their own information systems and undertake needed research. Among the means used to reach the instructional goals were: large and small group information sessions, opportunities to hear and confer with consultants, a counselor's information game, and orientation on methods used by the Educational Research Information Centers (ERIC). Followup studies will attempt to evaluate the workshop approach in stimulating the establishment of information systems in local areas.

599. Ware, C. & Gold, B. K. The Los Angeles City College peer counseling program. Washington, D.C.: American Association of Junior Colleges, 1971. (ED 047 688)

The Los Angeles City College Peer Counseling Project report is the second in the Urban Community College Project Series. The project was based on two assumptions: (1) peer counselors from the same ethnic and socio-economic background as the counselee can uniquely contribute to behavioral growth in meeting student needs; and (2) the result of such contributions could reduce the drop-out rate among minority students as well as relieve pressures on the professional counseling staff. The training program was evolved for and by students. Training consisted of 40 hours one week before the beginning of each semester, plus two hours a week in-service training for four semesters. The average caseload was 12-15 counselees per peer counselor. The program, ideally, was staffed by professionals from the psychology department, but had the cooperation and support of the entire institution. Two program objectives were: familiarize the peer counselor with the factual information most needed by students; and enable the counselor to be confident of his ability to function at an effective level. Although there are several areas of difficulty for implementation of a peer counseling program, the evaluation of the Los Angeles Project indicates peer counseling on academic and subjective grounds is very effective. It is hoped that the project will stimulate experimentation and replication by other colleges.

600. Warner, J. F. R. The role of the guidance coordinator as consultant in the inservice education of teachers in Alabama. New York: Columbia University, 1963. (ED 016 920)

Ways in which guidance counselors can help teachers develop ability in guidance were assessed in this study, primarily based on data collected during 1957–58, with recent pertinent data added. Descriptions and evaluations were made of such service education methods as staff meetings, conferences, professional reading and associations, team teaching, work experiences, and travel, and for lectures, films and film discussions, demonstrations, television, case studies, critical incidents, and manuals. Tape-recorded interviews, made with over 100 Alabama administrators, supervisors, guidance workers, and classroom teachers, indicated several changes needed in Alabama schools. Activities appropriate for guidance coordinators in in-service teacher education include assisting with a child's problems, creating and maintaining services in which teachers are co-workers, providing opportunities for conferences and casual contacts, participating in curriculum and administrative planning, evaluating guidance services and facilities, and keeping informed of avenues of in-service growth. This document, Order No. 64–1509, is available from University Microfilms, Ann Arbor, Mich.

601. Warren, M. A. (et al.) Generalizations related to concepts important for youth orientation to the world of work. Norman: Oklahoma University, Research Institution, 1967. (ED 029 998)

A basic first step in building a curriculum contributing to the orientation of youth to world of work is identification of concepts important to that orientation. In this study, the generalizations within the concept framework were identified through a developmental process of analysis and synthesis, including a review of current literature, a review of the findings of the earlier concept conference, an evaluation conference, and a compilation of findings by project staff, and an individual and group study of materials by national, state, and local consultants, and by youth. The concept and generalization framework was divided into three areas: (1) personal influences which include human needs, values and individual personalities, (2) environmental influences which include technology, automation, economic framework and work opportunity, and (3) personal-environmental influences which include vocational plans and work attitudes. Through use of this framework, equality of opportunity for students of varying abilities and socioeconomic levels is possible.

602. Warren, M. A. (et al.) Identification of concepts important for youth orientation to the world of work. Norman: Oklahoma University, School of Home Economics, 1965. (ED 003 103)

An attempt was made to identify concepts and to develop effective materials and media which could be important to high school students in guiding them to a personal awareness of the demands of the "World of Work" for the purposes of successful attainment, retention, and advancement in employment. Selected teachers, representing the various vocational education areas, participated in a 10-day conference. Consultants from business and industry, government, agriculture, and welfare gave presentations. Prior to the conference, identification of concepts was facilitated by a research team through the evaluation of relevant resource materials. The topics receiving consideration during the conference were classified as (1) Socioeconomic Factors Related to the World of Work, (2) Psychological Factors Related to the World of Work, (3) Individual and Family Management Concepts Related to Work, and (4) Communication Concepts Related to Work.

603. Washington Township Board of Education. Adventures in occupations. Robbinsville, N.J.: WTBE. (ES 002 197)

Vocational development experiences will be offered to junior high school students in a three-county rural area. Emphasis will be placed upon developing proper attitudes toward the world of work. Occupational clusters will be defined in the areas of industrial arts and home economics. Participation will be required of all seventh and eighth grade students. Social histories will be made by qualified personnel to afford teachers an opportunity to study the background pressures, deficiencies, and strengths of project students. Students with severe learning disabilities will be provided with additional opportunities for rewarding supplementary experiences. Full articulation will be maintained between the regular instructional program and the prevocational studies. A summer workshop will be conducted for staff members who will be directly involved in the prevocational program. To implement project goals, two industrial arts teachers, two home economics teachers, and a vocational guidance teacher/counselor will be engaged. An existing building will be remodeled to serve as headquarters for the project, and students

Compendium of Abstracted Methods 367

from outlying districts will be bussed to the Center twice a week. Approximately 515 students, grades 7–8, will be served. For further information, contact Melindo A. Persi, Sharon Rd., Robbinsville, New Jersey 08691. (609) 259-7607.

604. Waterloo, G. E. A guide to pupil personnel services for schools in the state of Illinois. Springfield: Illinois State Office of the Superintendent of Public Instruction, 1965. (ED 010 893)

Pupil personnel services are essential for a broadly based, comprehensive program of instruction for all children. The basic considerations related to the coordination and effectiveness of pupil personnel services, as defined in the policy statement of the Council of Chief State School Officers, are outlined. Both the superintendent and the principal play a vital role in the development of pupil personnel services. Administrators must evaluate the facilities of the community and the needs of the students, and then develop guidelines of organization for pupil personnel services. Pupil personnel services must be carefully interpreted, integrated into, and accepted in the interdisciplinary pattern of the school. Some devices which help establish and strengthen interprofessional relationships are meetings (case conferences, orientation meetings), written materials (manuals of rules, written job analyses), and research. Close coordination of pupil personnel services with community agencies and professional individuals is imperative. The functions and objectives of attendance, guidance, school health, school psychological, and school social work services are described. The main aims of the recently created Interprofessional Research Commission of Pupil Personnel Services are discussed.

605. Watson, W. S. Logical analysis skill as a tool for career guidance. Final report. New York: Cooper Union, 1969. (ED 026 978)

The report describes a new kind of psychological testing machine, the Logical Analysis Device (LAD), and the attempts to use it for predicting academic grades of 97 freshmen engineering students at The Cooper Union in 1958, 77 of whom were re-tested in 1962. The LAD system allows a subject to proceed in his own way and at his own pace to solve problems which increase in complexity, while recording how the subject solves a problem and the level of difficulty he has mastered. As problems increase in complexity, the subject must develop a logical procedure for arriving at an effective solution. The research was based on two hypotheses, that freshman LAD scores would not change significantly during 4 years of college, and that freshman or senior scores could probably predict career choices within occupations followed by engineering graduates of The Cooper Union (electrical, chemical, mechanical, and civil engineering). A correlation of .14 between freshman LAD scores and 4-year college grades was too low to add to usual grade predictors. A correlation of .39 between senior-year LAD and college grades showed that there was a significant relationship between senior year and scores and grades. No significant differences in mean LAD scores of those preferring more theoretical careers as opposed to less theoretical careers was found in the 1967–1968 career reports. A later career follow-up is planned.

606. Watuaga County Board of Education. Showcase for vocational guidance and occupational education. Boone, N.C.: WCBE. (ES 002 516)

A sequential vocational education program will be developed for students in a rural area. Emphasis will be placed upon providing disadvantaged students with guidance toward an attainable occupational goal. Four certified vocational guidance teacher-counselors will be employed in the elementary schools. The elementary counselors will provide—(1) occupational group guidance classes on a periodic basis developed by grade level, (2) occupational information, orientation, and exploration, and (3) early identification of academically handicapped students with special needs. Two additional counselors will be engaged at the high school level to provide—(1) articulation with the elementary programs, (2) group and individual vocational guidance, (3) articulation with post-high school institutions with technical education programs, and (4) placement services for graduates and dropouts. A comprehensive construction project will be implemented to combine the efforts of all advanced vocational education classes. A small dwelling unit will be constructed within the vocational center, and carpentry, masonry, plumbing, heating, and electrical classes will be responsible for construction relating to their particular area. Agriculture students will landscape the property, and home economics students will perform interior decorating. Approximately 4,126 students, grades 1–12, will be served. For further information, contact Robert D. Danner, P.O. Box 112, Boone, North Carolina 28607. (704) 267-2121.

607. Wayne State University. Project pit: a summer industrial work experience and occupational guidance program. Detroit: WSU, Department of Industrial Education, 1967. (ED 024 755)

Project PIT (Program of Industrial Training) was a pilot and demonstration program of industrial training for Detroit's inner city youth. Its major aims were to provide youth with occupational information and guidance, to help youth see the need for a good education, to provide these youth with financial means to return to school, and to make useful goods for non-profit organizations. Those aims were fulfilled through a simulated industrial setting and an intensive guidance program. Questionnaires and analyses of the Detroit high school population have shown that most youths either have not selected an occupational goal or have selected a goal that is unrealistic for their abilities and potentials. Project PIT's most important aim, the upgrading of the employee's goals and aspirations and the acquisition of a sound background of the occupations available to them, is an intangible that is difficult to measure in a short-range program; however, results were obtained which indicated a significant shift in educational and occupational aspirations to both a high and more realistic level.

608. Weals, R. & Johnson, E. Doubled and vulnerable: a sociodrama on vocational decision making. *Vocational Guidance Quarterly,* 1969, 17(3), 198–205.

Presents short play intended to stimulate discussion among both parents and students on how to understand processes of decision making.

609. Weaver, C. E. Orientation to work for the students in the junior high school. Paper presented at the Institute on Occupational Analysis as a Basis for Curriculum Development, Fort Collins, Co., August, 1968. (ED 024 990)

The junior-high school lends itself readily to innovative approaches in preparing youngsters to meet the challenge of the work world. The junior-high years are important because 30% of those who drop out of schools drop out during this period. Ohio has taken steps to provide continual updating of the vocational information held by its counselors, under the impetus of the 1968 Vocational Education Act. Workshops and summer guidance seminars are held at approved Ohio counselor education institutions, with additional advanced workshops being held for those counselors who have already attended at least one seminar. Realizing that a good vocational guidance program is dependent on a good attitude toward technical education, Ohio educators are attempting to devise a completely new program for vocational and technical educational studies, for presentation to the next session of the Ohio General Assembly. The targets of the program are the 30,000 dropouts and 60,000 graduates with so general an education that they have no marketable skills. The aim of the program is to eradicate the stigma which has long been attached to vocational education, and raise the status of technical education, so that parents and students alike will have a healthier outlook toward the work world.

610. Webster, W. J. Occupational information and the school curriculum. *Vocational Guidance Quarterly,* 1971, 19(3), 215–219.

Occupational information is an integral part of the PLAN curriculum, through which the student learns about occupations by active participation in the occupational education portion of the social studies and language arts program.

611. Weiss, D. J. Computer-assisted synthesis of psychometric data in vocational counseling. Washington, D.C.: Social and Rehabilitation Service (DHEW), 1968. (ED 025 787)

This paper proposes computer assistance in the synthesis operation of vocational counseling. The goal of vocational counseling is to match the client with a vocation in which he will be both satisfied and satisfactory. The computer would, through its rapid scanning and computation, produce probabilities of satisfactoriness based on (1) the individual's unique pattern of vocational abilities, and (2) individual differences in ability requirements of various occupational environments. Probabilities of satisfaction would be based on (1) the individual's vocational needs, and (2) information on the reinforcer characteristics of various occupational environments. These four lists of potential jobs would result: those in which the client would be (1) satisfied and satisfactory, (2) satisfied and unsatisfactory, suggesting training, (3) unsatisfied but satisfactory, and (4) unsatisfied and unsatisfactory. The computer could also be used in individualizing assessment techniques which provide the banks of data on which the probabilities are constructed. The advantages would be time saving, increased motivation, simultaneous prediction, clarification of reliability, and the greater amount of information at the counselor's disposal.

612. Wellman, F. E. Training institute for vocational guidance and counseling personnel. Columbia, Mo.: Missouri University, 1966. (ED 011 614)

A multidisciplinary training institute was provided for a select group of 40 state and local vocational guidance and counseling personnel employed in leadership positions. The design of the institute emphasized the development of understandings knowledges, and professional materials related to (1) economic factors influencing vocational education needs and the vocational decision-making process, (2) social and cultural factors of vocational counseling, (3) psychological factors related to career development and vocational choices, and (4) administrative considerations in the evaluation of multidisciplinary factors in vocational program organization as well as in the coordination of guidance and counseling activities at all organizational levels. The format of the institute provided for 30 hours of scheduled activities in each of 4 weeks. One-half of this time was devoted to lecture and discussion of the dimensions of vocational counseling in the four areas of economics, sociology, psychology, and administration. The balance of the time was devoted to small-group work sessions in the preparation of professional working papers on assigned topics related to the major areas. The overall evaluation of the institute by the trainees and the staff was favorable to the multidisciplinary curriculum approach used and to the high degree of trainee involvement which the institute's format required. A followup was recommended to determine the long-term training effectiveness.

613. Westervelt, E. M. & Fixter, D. Women's higher and continuing education: an annotated bibliography with selected references on related aspects of women's lives. 1971. (ED 053 375)

This document is principally an annotated bibliography of works dealing with women in higher education. A total of 290 annotations are included. Twenty additional annotations are contained concerning related aspects of women's lives.

614. Whitfield, E. A. & Glaeser, G. A. A demonstration of a regional career information center; the VIEW system. A summary of research results 1967–1968. San Diego, Cal.: San Diego County Department of Education, 1968. (ED 029 318)

The demonstration phase of Project VIEW (Vital Information for Education and Work) was designed to enable school counselors and administrators to familiarize themselves with the operation of the Regional Career Information System. VIEW provides information on 200 occupations requiring less than a baccalaureate degree. Objectives of the study were: (1) to provide occupational information on local job opportunities, (2) to show how students can utilize information, (3) to illustrate how one system can meet the needs of rural and urban youth, (4) to encourage students to discuss career information at home, (5) to demonstrate a process by which counselors can use information to aid noncollege bound youth, (6) to disseminate information detailing the services and results of this project, and (7) to demonstrate the services of this system to other areas. Data was obtained from three experimental and three control groups. Conclusions indicate that: (1) providing good information does not assure its effective use by counselors and staff, (2) the approach, utilized by this system, to information dissemination is well liked by students, and (3) parents play a major role in students' educational and career planning. This project was founded under provisions of Title III of the Elementary and Secondary Education Act.

615. Whitfield, E. A. & Glaeser, G. A. Project VIEW. History and development. San Diego, Cal.: San Diego County Department of Education, 1968. (ED 026 675)

The Regional Center for the Collection, Synthesis, and Dissemination of Career Information for Schools in San Diego County was established as a pilot project (VIEW) in 1965. Participating institutions included the county department of education, colleges located in the county, and the California State Department of Employment. The present paper gives a history of VIEW through its pilot, developmental, and demonstration phases. Evaluation procedures and results involving students and counselors are presented. A junior college follow-up study and summer training workshop are discussed, with evaluations of these project components also included. A discussion of limitations and an outline of 1968–69 operations follow.

616. Whitfield, E. A. & Hoover, R. Regional center for collection, synthesis and dissemination of career information for use by schools of San Diego County. San Diego, Cal.: San Diego County Department of Education, 1967. (ED 015 513)

Activities of the Career Information Center during the 1966–67 year have shown that—(1) a summer workshop for counselors which provides instruction in vocational guidance and experience in entry level occupations is valuable, (2) positive community reaction to the VIEW Project and to a summer workshop exists, and (3) vocational training provided by the junior colleges is perceived by the students as necessary and valuable in their chosen career.

617. Whitfield, E. A. Vocational guidance in the elementary school: integration or fragmentation? *The School Counselor,* 1968, 16(2), 90–93.

To provide integrated vocational guidance in the elementary school will require that the elementary school counselor have not only a thorough knowledge of vocational and child development theories but also an understanding of the elementary school curriculum and its relation to the above theories.

618. Whitlock, J. W. Development of a plan for an intensive study of automation and its implications for education. Nashville, Tenn.: George Peabody College for Teachers. (ED 003 475)

A detailed study model was developed for community use in studies of automation and its implications for the educational process. Three specific steps were involved in developing this model—(1) a comprehensive study plan was developed which included the specific data to be collected, and design and analytical procedures for the collection process, (2) the study plan was tried out in a pilot situation and location, namely, the Nashville-Davidson County metropolitan area in Tennessee, and (3) the study plan was then revised on the basis of pilot experiences. Four major facets of investigation to be considered were included in the final study plan or model—(1) basic background information on the community, (2) the extent to which community industries are automating, the nature of automated jobs in the community, and the educational and training requirements of these automated jobs, (3) the status of elementary, secondary, out-of-school, and adult education programs and personnel in the community and of current vocational and technical educational opportunities in the community, and (4) the changes in the program of education which are dictated by the changing requirements of automation.

619. Wigderson, H. The name of the game—simulation. Research brief 4. Visalia, Cal.: ADAPT, a PACE Supplementary Educational Center, 1968. (ED 028 647)

Simulation games are a recent innovative technique that can be used in the classroom. In the past these games have been used by the military, by industry, and by social scientists. Simulation emphasizes the inquiry approach to learning. Each student is an independent and individual learner who can interact with others and react to different situations. Advantages claimed for simulation include added motivation, improvement of problem-solving ability, emphasis on communication, and an interdisciplinary approach rarely achieved otherwise. Objections to the use of these games include fear that they breed conformity, emphasize winning over learning, and threaten discipline. An appendix lists 85 commercially produced games with the academic use of the game and the grade level to which it applies and the manufacturer from whom it can be obtained. A bibliography of 48 items covers many approaches to simulation games.

620. Wilkinson, R. D. Student campus employees. *Education,* Oct. 1965, 86(2). (ED 015 743)

Campus employment is offered to needy students at a community college in a large urban center, where both terminal and transfer programs in nine major study areas are offered to its 1,000 day and 3,000 evening students. Not created especially for these students, jobs represent needed services for which the college would otherwise hire outside help (e.g., operation of audiovisual equipment, clerical functions, and laboratory assistance). The program receives funds from a private foundation, the college budget, and money raising efforts. In making work assignments, a faculty committee considers students' financial needs and scholastic performance. A survey of students led to the conclusions that (1) many families cannot completely finance an education even at a community college, (2) average students can work a few hours weekly without academic loss, (3) students benefit financially, socially, and academically from work experience, and (4) the college benefits from the program. This article is published in "Education," Volume 86, Number 2, October 1965.

621. Willowbrook High School. A report on project CVIS (computerized vocational information system). Villa Park, Ill.: WHS, 1969. (ED 029 331)

The Computerized Vocational Information System (CVIS) team, has designed a system utilizing a computer as a tool to help students explore occupations in the light of their own student records. This system aims at teaching a decision-making process in a way that interests students and allows counselors more time for counseling functions. The project was developed in five phases. Using Poe's two-dimensional classification, occupations were divided into six levels by amount of training and responsibility required. These six levels were then divided into eight categories of interest. Student records in computer storage include cumulative class rank, composite score on battery of tests, and interest inventory scores. Students use the system voluntarily and during a sophomore vocational unit. Each counselor also has a display terminal in his office. Student attitude is highly positive. Appended is the script, beginning list of occupations, sample brief, student-record displays, and an evaluation questionnaire.

622. Wilmington Public Schools. Closed circuit TV—A tool for guidance. Wilmington, Del.: WPS, 1968. (ED 026 663)

Educational television (ETV) has been explored fairly widely as a tool in supplementary or large scale curriculum presentation, but relatively little work has been done using it as a guidance tool. This paper presents Delaware's Alfred I. du Pont School District's program using the district and state closed-circuit television network. The major contribution television can make to the counselor's efforts is to instruct and monitor the large-group testing and information giving functions. This frees the counselor for more individual and personal contacts. This district has found it very successful in pre-college, high school, and junior high orientation programs. Intercom systems allow two-way communication. Several scripts are described briefly, and an evaluation study discussed. High-school vocational guidance use of the Delaware ETV series "It's about Work" is presented in some detail.

623. Wilson, E. H. A task oriented course in decision-making. Information system for vocational decision, project report number 7. Cambridge: Harvard University, Graduate School of Education, 1967. (ED 014 119)

A course in decision-making, built around the Tiedeman-O'Hara Paradigm, was taught at a junior high school to test materials. The three essential aspects of teaching decision-making are—(1) learning the language of the decision-making process, (2) practicing decision-making while under supervision, and (3) formulating criteria for a decision. A booklet, "You, The Decider," containing relevant theory, activities, tasks, and cases resulting in explicit criteria for choice was given to students. Weekly workshops for teachers were held six weeks before the course began. A sharing of competencies by research personnel, counselors, and teachers took place at the workshops, which were continued through four weeks of actual teaching. Resource materials included the "Occupational Outlook Handbook" and Katz's "You, Today and Tomorrow." Results of the evaluation of the course are not presented, although a definite research program has been designed. A copy of "You, the Decider" and various evaluation instruments are included.

624. Wilson, P. C. New directions in vocational guidance. Flushing: City University of New York, Queens College, 1965. (ED 003 099)

An institute for counselor education was conducted to provide counselor educators with new knowledge of employment trends and major issues in the world of work. This information would assist them in arriving at an initial statement of criteria to be met in revising vocational guidance to meet current needs. Representatives from government, industry, labor, and counselor education gave presentations which were followed by group discussions. The counselor educators concluded—(1) that some educational and vocational choice is possible for everyone and the ability to choose is a precious freedom, (2) that educational and vocational planning must command the major attention of school counselors and guidance workers, (3) that counselors and guidance workers must be better trained than they now are, (4) that counselor educators have failed to come to grips with two major issues—the place of educational and occupational information in guidance and how vocational counselors can help meet the need for more talented and better educated workers, and (5) that counselor educators need help from experts in related academic and professional fields.

625. Winborn, R. & Martinson, W. Innovation in guidance: a mobile counseling center. *Personnel and Guidance Journal,* 1967, 45(8), 818–820.

A mobile counseling center staffed by 4 counselors serves high schools in 4 counties of southern Indiana. The operation of the center is designed to enrich, supplement, and improve the quality of counseling services for secondary students of the area. The mobile center also serves as a model to stimulate the development of exemplary and innovative guidance services in regular school programs.

626. Winefordner, D. W. Orienting students to the world of work using the data-people-things conceptual framework and the Ohio vocational interest survey. Paper presented at the meeting of he American Personnel and Guidance Association, Las Vegas, April, 1969. (ED 029 343)

The Ohio Vocational Interest Survey (OVIS) has two aims: (1) to assist youth in understanding themselves in relation to the world of work and, (2) as a result, to provide a background for career choice. To do so, OVIS provides a functional system for relating an individual's interests into broad homogeneous clusters of jobs. OVIS consists of a six-item Student Information Questionnaire and a 280-item Interest Inventory, and is appropriate for use at the eighth grade level and above. A unique value of OVIS lies in its compatability with the following occupational information and guidance tools: (1) Dictionary of Occupational Titles, (2) The Occupational Outlook Handbook, (3) National and state labor market and occupational information publications and (4) the General Aptitude Test Battery. It is concluded that OVIS is an important tool for school guidance and counseling programs.

627. Witczak, L. A. & Ehlers, D. Project: occupational orientation. *School Counselor,* 1970, 17(5), 362–363.

Describes project undertaken during school year in an attempt to help students better identify with the world of work while still in high school. Students explored entry job opportunities and requirements in the metropolitan Washington area. The object was to show them job possibilities they never dreamed of.

628. Witherspoon, F. D. Group guidance in junior college—a frame of reference. St. Louis, Mo.: St. Louis Junior College District; Forest Park, Mont.: Forest Park Community College, 1967. (ED 016 487)

This group guidance program is designed to provide (1) a chance for self-assessment of personal strengths and weaknesses, (2) improvement of attitudes in human relations, (3) improvement of study habits and techniques, and (4) realistic assessment of vocational abilities. Group guidance is intended to supplement, not supplant, individual counseling. This monograph suggests certain organized group experiences, particularly for use with under-or nonachievers, whenever enough students have a common problem to be solved. The counselor must understand the dynamics of group behavior, must be a skillful discussion leader, must be alert to both the individual's and the group's reactions, and may choose to be directive or non-directive. Some techniques for conducting the sessions are (1) discussion, (2) sociometric (role-playing), (3) case conference, and (4) self-appraisal. Each technique is explained, with examples of its use. Ways of evaluating the success of the guidance sessions are (1) continuous appraisal (in both group and individual situations), (2) terminal review (at the end of a semester or year), and (3) a controlled study (of those with and without group guidance or under various procedures). All methods of evaluation make use of a simple questionnaire to analyze the reactions of the group members to the various activities.

629. Wisconsin State Employment Service. Career without college. Madison: WSES, Program Development and Research Bureau. (ED 029 135)

The purpose of this booklet is to acquaint students as well as school counselors and teachers with the major occupations providing opportunities for non-college bound youth. The occupations listed were selected from a number of occupational surveys conducted by the Wisconsin State Employment Service. Occupations chosen are those in which the number of opportunities are expected to increase and, more importantly, those which provide opportunity for the high school graduate to get a start without going to college. Certain other occupations are omitted, either because the number of job openings each year are relatively insignificant, or because they fail to offer career potential. As a whole, occupations listed in this publication constitute approximately 80 percent of the jobs for which a recent high school graduate could qualify. Occupational areas include automobile mechanics, building trades, drafting, fire and police protection, health services, machine operators—skilled and semi-skilled, office occupations, supervisory occupations, and a career in government.

630. Women's Bureau (DOL). Expanding opportunities for girls: their special counseling needs. Washington, D.C.: WB, 1970. (ED 052 315)

This brochure describes the changing social patterns which have resulted in increased female labor force participation. Educational counseling is necessary to develop a woman's talents for a rewarding career.

631. Woody, R. H. Vocational counseling with behavioral techniques. *Vocational Guidance Quarterly,* 1968, 17(2), 97-103.

This paper reviews the various behavioral techniques that seem appropriate for counseling, and discusses their application to vocational guidance. These behavioral techniques seem especially well suited to vocational counseling.

632. Wright, G. N. (et al.) An expanded program of vocational rehabilitation: methodology and descriptions of client population. Madison: Wisconsin University, Regional Rehabilitation Research Inst., 1970. (ED 046 012)

The purposes of this report are to provide: (1) an overview of the Wood County, Wisconsin Project methodology, including a description of the experimental and control areas, the research design, and the instrumentation used to assess the impact of services; and (2) a description of the client populations in terms of selected pre-rehabilitation demographic variables and other information. This project is the first large-scale attempt to examine the feasibility of and guidelines for the expansion of rehabilitation to serve not only the medically disabled but also the culturally disadvantaged. It was discovered that certain characteristics differentiated the culturally disadvantaged clients from other subgroups: (1) sex; (2) age; (3) source of referral; (4) marital status; (5) onset of disability; (6) automobile licensing and possession; (7) employment status; (8) highest grade completed; and (9) educational achievement.

633. Wrightstone, J. W. (et al.) Assessment of the demonstration guidance project. New York: Board of Education, Bureau of Educational Research. (ED 001 752)

The purpose was to identify able students from disadvantaged urban areas and to stimulate them through cultural experiences, special classes, and guidance to seek higher educational and vocational goals. A primary objective was to refine the methods and techniques for prediction of academic potential, through aptitude testing, achievement testing, and counselor and teacher ratings in junior high school. In an overall sense, pupils who received academic diplomas and went on to college scored higher on each of these initial criteria than did students who did not complete high school.

In addition to the intensive counseling services for students involved in the project, there was remedial instruction in reading and arithmetic in the junior high school and special enriched instruction in small homogeneously grouped classes in high school, including a double period daily in English. The cultural enrichment program included visits to museums, libraries, colleges, plays, films, concerts, and places of historical interest.

Standardized tests in academic subjects show that project students made a greater gain in academic areas than had previous classes. Their greatest gain was in reading. Using a chronological age of 15 for the I.Q. score base there were appreciable gains in I.Q. among project students. There was positive peer acceptance among project and non-project students. Of the 329 project students, 21.3 dropped out of school and 51 entered some kind of post high school training, a major increase over comparable groups. Students emphasized the helpfulness of guidance services in the project, while teachers stressed the gains in student desires for higher education to be the project's greatest asset.

634. Wurtz, R. E. Vocational development: theory and practice. *Vocational Guidance Quarterly,* 1966, 15(2), 127–130.

The two school practices of occupational filing and curricular organization will be examined against the concept of vocational development. The purpose is to investigate the meaning of vocational development and to illustrate how these school practices might hamper or foster the vocational development of high school students.

635. Yabroff, W. W. An experiment in teaching decision making. Sacramento: California State Department of Education, 1964. (ED 010 701)

Two hundred forty-eight ninth-grade students were given 4 weeks of daily intensive group guidance on vocational and educational planning prior to experimental treatment. Students were randomly divided into three ability groups and three treatment groups. The control group received no further treatment. Group 1 received training using local probability data (experience tables). Group 2 received instruction in decision-making using general probability data similar to that presented in the first 4 weeks. Group 1 scored significantly higher (beyond .01 level) than groups 2 and 3 at all ability levels in (1) knowledge about the process of decision-making, (2) awareness of high school and college alternatives, and (3) knowledge of the probabilities involved in these alternatives. No significant differences between sexes were found. This experiment suggests that in helping ninth-grade students learn decision-making, local probability data can be meaningful to students at all ability levels, equally effective with boys and girls, and more effective than general data or structured guidance units on general information. The author suggests that using local data and allowing the student to make his own tentative interpretation makes the data more personal and stimulates intensive group discussion about educational plans and personal values.

636. Yinger, J. M. (et al.) Middle start: supportive interventions for

higher education among students of disadvantaged backgrounds. Final report. Ohio: Oberlin College, 1970. (ED 047 659)

Since 1964, Oberlin College has conducted a "special opportunity program" for post-seventh graders from deprived backgrounds. Each year approximately 65 students have been brought to the campus for an intensive period of educational, artistic, and recreational experience. This report concerns the post-program educational attainments of the first three summer groups, a total of 195 students. Schools in St. Louis, Mo., and Cleveland, Lorain, Elyria, and Oberlin, Ohio were asked to nominate twice as many individuals from culturally deprived or poverty backgrounds who had some likelihood of success as the program was able to accept. From each school's list pairs were matched as closely as possible, and one from each pair was randomly selected to participate in the program. This study tried to determine whether the summer experience, plus the follow-up contacts with the Special Opportunity staff, significantly improved the likelihood of a person staying in school, attaining good grades, and for the 1964 group, of entering college. Significance was measured against the performance of the randomly selected controls. This report also describes the method that was used for taking account of the equality of the match and examines the importance of networks of "significant others."

637. Young, E. Counseling without offices: guidance in a new context. Englewood, Colo.: Cherry Creek High School, 1967. (ED 022 224)

The counseling center at Cherry Creek High School was moved from a remote part of the high school to one of the busiest areas, across from the library and student lounge. The physical facilities consist of a large, open and carpeted area with desks, comfortable chairs, tables, and bookshelves filled with material related to counseling. Conference rooms for privacy, group work, or teacher-counselor group meetings were provided. Each counselor was, and is, scheduled out of the office for one-half day a week on a regular basis. The counselors are thus free to work with students elsewhere. Noticeable differences were observed in the frequency of student visits to the center and in the open and spontaneous nature of student-counselor interaction. Students seemed to feel much more free to congregate in the center to talk, look through materials, and to engage counselors in casual conversation. Teachers also frequented the center. The use of radically different physical facilities and the development of new attitudes toward counselor involvement in the total student life helped to dissolve the idea of the "problem centered counselor."

638. Youst, D. B. A comprehensive micro-image file for occupational information. Final report. New York: Rochester City School District, 1970 (ED 047 335)

The report describes the activities which comprised the design, implementation and evaluation of a Micro-Image System for occupational information, which is one component of a comprehensive career guidance program. The location of the film equipment in the Frederick Douglass Junior High in Rochester, New York is discussed in terms of the amount of use it received by students. A data gathering phase, during which students using the equipment filled out a questionnaire, is elaborated in detail and the results presented. The rationale underlying the Rochester Career Guidance Project's development of the Micro-Image File is explained and actual steps in the development are enumerated. Appendices include: (1) further theroetical and practical career guidance considerations, (2) a description of a Career Guidance Laboratory where students participate in simulated work situations, and (3) actual career guidance materials focused on the work of X-ray technologists.

639. Youst, D. B. The Rochester career guidance project. *Educational Technology,* 1969, 9(3), 39-41.

A short explanation of the project development and utilization of a system approach is presented.

640. Zaharevitz, W. & Marshall, J. N. Aviation—where career opportunities are bright, counselor's guide. Washington, D.C.: National Aerospace Education Council, 1968. (ED 026 481)

This aviation occupations guide is designed for use as a unit as well as in conjunction with an aviation careers package of material that contains a film strip and recording. Chapter One contains the script of the film strip, Aviation—Where Career Opportunities are Bright, and includes all photographs used in the film strip plus numerous amplifying statements. Chapters Two through Nine present information on occupational clusters within aviation: Aircraft Manufacturing Occupations, Career Pilots and Flight Engineers, Aviation Mechanics (Including Repairmen), Airline Careers, Airline Stewardesses or Stewards, Aviation Careers in Government, Airport Careers, and Aviation Education and Other Aviation Related Careers. Each chapter includes general information about an occupational cluster, specific jobs within that cluster, description of the nature of work, working conditions, wages and benefits, and identifies where the jobs are as well as the schools or sources of training.

641. Zimpel, L. (Ed.) The disadvantaged worker: readings in developing minority manpower. 1971. (ED 053 344)

This document examines the efforts made by American business to make employment opportunities available to the disadvantaged minority worker. Ten major areas are discussed, including the following: changing social attitudes, Negro work attitudes, patterns for disadvantaged programs, management views of hard-core hiring, testing the disadvantaged, training the unemployed, company experience with the disadvantaged, the role of the unions, upgrading and job mobility, and job programs during business slowdowns. Forty readings are included. The point of this collection is to bring together some of the lessons learned over the past few years about how best to fit the disadvantaged jobless into the country's employment pattern.

642. Zweibelson, I. Guiding parents and motivating talented students who live in low-rent neighborhoods. New Rochelle, N.Y.: New Rochelle Public Schools, 1962. (ED 001 763)

The first of a series of three projects was designed to study the responses of children and their parents in an effort to formulate an experimental guidance program. A group of 111 ninth grade students who live in low-rent districts was studied. In addition to the analysis of the students, school records, aptitude tests, and preference tests, the parents were interviewed. Findings suggest that short-term efforts to help parents of students with higher aptitudes motivate their children might be effective if the parents have a generally high educational level and if the student has high vocational aspirations; efforts to guide parents of students with below average scores would require longer term, more extensive services. Student preference tests indicated that the guidance programs should influence the talented youngster to improve his school performance.

The second project was a guideline program designed, in light of information obtained in the first study, to help parents develop the talents and abilities of their ninth-grade children. Each family received one to six individual conferences and six two-hour group information sessions.

The third project was similar to the second with the exception that it was aimed at the families of seventh-grade students.

643. Zweibelson, I. Motivating and educating the student living in a poor neighborhood, a school-family approach. 1965. (ED 011 396)

The New Rochelle Talent Search Project attempted to involve parents and students in a family counseling program in order to stimulate motivation for improved school performance and improved planning for the future. The report summarizes 6 years of experience, experimentation, and study, and is a compilation of the findings of six different projects with a common set of purposes and goals. For the preliminary survey, a sample consisting of 81 ninth-grade students from four neighborhoods were given the Differential Aptitude Tests (DAT), and their parents were interviewed by a counselor using a standard interview schedule to obtain data on family statistics, student characteristics, and parents' opinions. The families of 40 youngsters who received high DAT scores participated in a program consisting of an "intake" interview, an orientation session, one to six individual conferences, and seven group sessions. Talent Search Projects for the following 4 years continued to utilize the same general project approach. Program results and program evaluation are discussed and bibliographies, parental interview schedules, tables, and evaluation sheets are included in the report.

ABSTRACT METHOD INDEX

Adults: 287, 341, 424
American Indians: 67, 168, 352

Behavior Change: 127, 318, 495, 532, 561, 631
Bibliotherapy: 44

* Career Days: 165
* Career Development Programs: 165, 214, 219, 230, 236, 248, 255, 284, 313, 325, 333, 334, 390, 545, 554, 555, 564, 569, 634
* Career Guidance: 42, 57, 60, 63, 64, 65, 70, 91, 92, 96, 97, 98, 103, 122, 130, 138, 154, 156, 158, 173, 180, 192, 195, 197, 206, 216, 219, 228, 230, 236, 246, 247, 249, 250, 252, 271, 275, 283, 295, 297, 300, 322, 328, 347, 363, 373, 382, 383, 392, 398, 401, 403, 413, 417, 418, 419, 427, 439, 449, 461, 468, 469, 477, 479, 485, 493, 499, 505, 507, 520, 540, 562, 571, 582, 593, 605, 612, 617, 624, 628, 631, 633, 639

Career Planning: 155, 166, 169, 180, 207, 244, 264, 266, 277, 305, 312, 318, 319, 320, 321, 336, 345, 369, 370, 400, 404, 442, 446, 464, 509, 523, 524, 525, 561, 579, 591, 606
Computer Oriented Programs: 29, 30, 52, 71, 93, 97, 116, 117, 118, 159, 163, 188, 191, 192, 228, 236, 241, 242, 246, 273, 274, 275, 281, 288, 307, 342, 354, 355, 364, 405, 409, 482, 487, 489, 490, 491, 494, 531, 542, 549, 559, 563, 564, 565, 566, 567, 611, 621
Counseling: 21, 39, 45, 47, 52, 55, 61, 83, 118, 130, 131, 132, 147, 148, 157, 168, 187, 189, 191, 213, 224, 301, 302, 317, 340, 353, 354, 362, 378, 400, 404, 497, 498, 500, 501, 508, 532, 546, 561, 572, 578, 625, 630, 637
Counselor Role: 3, 14, 18, 65, 103, 117, 145, 154, 185, 195, 239, 268, 423, 496, 558, 584, 600
Counselor Training: 22, 132, 158, 216, 259, 278, 300, 311, 313, 344, 476, 505, 516, 518, 598, 612, 624
Curriculum: 2, 4, 8, 9, 18, 23, 35, 37, 51, 59, 90, 92, 104, 106, 110, 123, 125, 135, 155, 209, 216, 230, 253, 293, 325, 326, 347, 356, 357, 376, 380, 381, 387, 389, 390, 391, 402, 414, 415, 441, 445, 446, 477, 499, 501, 504, 523, 524, 525, 543, 553, 557, 569, 573, 574, 579, 585, 591, 601, 602, 603, 606, 609, 610, 623

Decision Making: 123, 145, 155, 159, 163, 197, 231, 265, 270, 281, 305,

377

400, 410, 449, 501, 506, 526, 527, 588, 589, 590, 608, 623, 635
Disadvantaged Youth, 20, 35, 42, 45, 108, 113, 121, 133, 140, 170, 172, 183, 202, 210, 216, 217, 243, 252, 256, 285, 323, 326, 333, 334, 339, 346, 349, 365, 368, 371, 375, 382, 383, 388, 419, 424, 425, 429, 462, 464, 473, 474, 476, 483, 484, 493, 498, 506, 515, 528, 547, 596, 606, 607, 633, 636, 641, 642
Dropouts: 14, 50, 51, 54, 64, 73, 74, 99, 160, 182, 187, 190, 205, 266, 271, 277, 323, 340, 353, 365, 377, 379, 386, 399, 420, 426, 461, 512, 575, 576

Elementary Schools: 2, 9, 26, 33, 42, 53, 72, 104, 161, 211, 212, 292, 325, 333, 334, 335, 387, 391, 416, 417, 463, 468, 469, 526, 527, 569
Elementary School Guidance: 184, 189, 206, 207, 220, 397, 421, 440, 584, 617
Employment Services: 83, 86, 107, 108, 126, 151, 172, 214, 307, 316, 327, 335, 362, 371, 473, 496, 536, 629

Females: 39, 40, 147, 148, 166, 169, 244, 304, 330, 341, 345, 510, 546, 556, 558, 591, 613, 630
Field Trips: 141, 310, 372
Films: 47, 61, 193, 296, 324, 541, 546, 560

Group Counseling: 21, 32, 45, 120, 184, 235, 256, 286, 308, 309, 359, 360, 378, 385, 424, 433, 437, 438, 443, 457, 481, 521, 529, 590
Group Guidance, 233, 235, 263, 272, 302, 309, 358, 452, 455, 538, 541, 575, 580, 593

Handicapped: 3, 127, 128, 174, 184, 198, 234, 298, 310, 363, 398
High Schools: 3, 4, 5, 8, 19, 25, 28, 32, 33, 38, 42, 43, 44, 52, 59, 61, 66, 69, 72, 89, 95, 96, 123, 146, 151, 159, 162, 175, 187, 194, 219, 229, 244, 247, 250, 268, 279, 318, 330, 359, 361, 378, 436, 444, 446, 455, 504, 513, 547, 593, 602
Higher Education: 1, 33, 121, 131, 141, 205, 224, 341, 345, 370, 406, 432, 444, 568, 581, 594, 613, 636

Individualized Instruction: 11, 12, 53, 153, 154, 155, 167, 179, 180, 203, 230, 294, 297, 315, 376, 509, 523, 524, 525, 545, 564, 605, 623
Industry: 94, 158, 215, 236, 278, 279, 280, 287, 338, 344, 349, 350, 368, 385, 466, 476, 607, 624, 641

Instructional Media: 9, 20, 68, 86, 100, 149, 221, 223, 270, 301, 366, 367, 408, 410, 502, 508, 597, 602, 638, 639
Interest Tests: 6, 28, 81, 101, 146, 226, 434, 472, 510, 626

Job Skills: 94, 105, 106, 108, 133, 215, 217, 222, 240, 256, 280, 299, 307, 327, 338, 377, 381, 452, 456, 513, 541, 570, 576, 595
Junior Colleges: 21, 46, 49, 62, 122, 151, 157, 196, 199, 204, 213, 281, 316, 379, 394, 395, 451, 456, 501, 520, 599, 620, 628
Junior High Schools: 3, 6, 8, 27, 33, 42, 59, 72, 88, 99, 110, 119, 120, 123, 124, 131, 135, 162, 203, 267, 270, 276, 284, 337, 347, 358, 389, 396, 404, 428, 436, 441, 444, 445, 474, 499, 515, 544, 570, 575, 579, 603, 609

* Manpower Education: 134, 135, 161, 162, 171, 292, 471, 530, 618
Mentally Handicapped: 36, 201, 315, 374, 422
Mexican Americans: 67, 136, 331, 352, 488, 578
Mobile Educational Services: 157, 189, 213, 218, 250, 382, 383, 403, 511, 534, 587, 625

Negroes: 67, 121, 210, 224, 352, 465

Occupational Aspiration: 1, 136, 149, 207, 227, 304, 547
* Occupational Classifications: 77, 78, 79, 80, 186, 222, 226, 258, 282, 329, 339, 518, 592, 621, 626
Occupational Clusters: 4, 5, 20, 25, 37, 76, 347, 361, 553
* Occupational Exploration: 8, 59, 72, 102, 175, 207, 209, 240, 274, 276, 289, 290, 291, 293, 296, 405, 411, 414, 415, 441, 445, 460, 503, 522, 557, 559, 587, 621, 626, 627
Occupational Information: 5, 10, 13, 20, 34, 46, 57, 69, 76, 77, 78, 79, 80, 82, 84, 85, 112, 126, 139, 142, 150, 151, 164, 174, 211, 212, 221, 223, 231, 232, 244, 251, 258, 261, 262, 282, 324, 329, 337, 339, 350, 366, 367, 372, 393, 401, 402, 408, 412, 416, 447, 448, 458, 459, 514, 530, 544, 552, 560, 597, 610, 629, 640
* Occupational Information Systems: 86, 95, 100, 109, 111, 152, 163, 186, 199, 200, 237, 241, 258, 260, 269, 274, 284, 332, 343, 407, 432, 467, 478, 486, 536, 560, 583, 586, 592, 598, 614, 615, 616, 638

Compendium of Abstracted Methods

Paraprofessional School Personnel: 103, 176, 177, 178, 208, 237, 314, 316, 401, 450, 519, 533, 537, 572
Parents: 369, 463, 481, 521, 529, 608, 642, 643
* Peer Counseling: 581, 599
Placement: 7, 87, 93, 94, 122, 140, 172, 204, 287, 351, 362, 368, 375, 395, 396, 418, 431, 466, 482, 487, 540, 556, 593
Prevocational Education: 326, 340, 380, 391, 394
Program Development: 96, 114, 129, 185, 218, 220, 248, 254, 255, 257, 282, 322, 392, 421, 423, 430, 439, 444, 465, 475, 484, 485, 492, 520, 534, 604, 637
Program Evaluation: 89, 98, 156, 196, 246, 254, 257, 348, 359, 458, 459, 492, 497, 521, 540, 573, 584, 604

Role Playing: 26, 41, 214, 450, 460, 608
Rural Schools: 102, 114, 130, 138, 144, 150, 189, 218, 253, 369, 382, 383, 397, 403, 511, 516, 539, 545, 596, 606

Simulation: 27, 55, 56, 71, 119, 246, 289, 290, 291, 301, 311, 319, 320, 321, 411, 454, 490, 494, 522, 526, 527, 588, 590, 619
* Social Modeling: 26, 233, 317, 410, 631
Social Studies: 110, 124, 232, 267, 543
Systems Approach: 96

Teacher Education: 16, 48, 600
Teacher Role: 12, 18, 70, 170, 185, 195, 306, 313, 390, 445, 477, 538, 554, 555
Television: 25, 34, 150, 211, 503, 622

Testing: 6, 54, 83, 88, 115, 181, 222, 227, 245, 295, 303, 312, 384, 399, 435, 442, 453, 479, 548, 550, 568, 570, 611

Underachievers: 120, 286, 396, 463
Urban Schools: 24, 170, 183, 202, 243, 252, 280, 333, 334, 336, 457, 468, 483, 528, 599

Videotape Recordings: 193, 233, 301, 500, 571
Vocational Adjustment: 66, 194
Vocational Development: 19, 22, 23, 33, 41, 49, 57, 63, 91, 98, 139, 144, 249, 283, 330, 406, 507, 518, 543, 558, 634
Vocational Education: 16, 17, 24, 36, 48, 50, 51, 69, 87, 88, 89, 90, 92, 97, 102, 128, 129, 171, 193, 196, 198, 209, 234, 248, 267, 306, 315, 328, 338, 346, 356, 357, 368, 379, 385, 413, 428, 436, 444, 456, 485, 502, 511, 535, 553, 557, 562, 574, 577, 580, 594
* Vocational Maturity: 115, 548
Vocational Rehabilitation: 184, 198, 256, 285, 298, 462, 498, 502, 572, 632
Vocational Schools: 60, 239, 240, 259, 264, 266, 268, 269, 272, 299, 384, 423, 479, 514, 577

Work Experience Programs: 3, 15, 31, 35, 38, 43, 62, 73, 74, 75, 99, 113, 128, 143, 175, 182, 190, 201, 202, 229, 276, 386, 420, 422, 426, 461, 470, 551, 595, 607, 620
* World of Work: 88, 104, 124, 125, 137, 245, 276, 285, 330, 349, 351, 356, 357, 374, 387, 389, 414, 415, 418, 480, 513, 539, 585, 601, 602, 603, 609, 627

AVAILABILITY OF METHODS

To order from the ERIC Document Reproducton Service:

References in this publication that have an ED (ERIC Document) number may be ordered from the ERIC Document Reproduction Service (EDRS). Copies are available in either hard (photo) copy or in microfiche form. The microfiche require a special machine for use. To order any of the ED materials, the following information must be furnished.

The ED number of the document.
The type of reproduction desired—photo copy (HC) or microfiche (MF).
The number of copies being ordered.

All orders must be in writing. Payment must accompany orders under $10.00. Residents of Illinois and Maryland should pay the appropriate sales tax or include a tax exemption certificate. There is no handling charge. Book rate or Library rate postage is included in the price. The difference between Book Rate or Library Rate and first class or foreign (outside the continental U.S.) postage rate will be billed at cost. Send orders to ERIC Document Reproduction Service, P.O. Drawer O, Bethesda, Maryland 20014.

To use ERIC collection in geographic region:

LOCATION OF ERIC MICROFICHE COLLECTIONS

ALABAMA
2) Ralph Brown Draughon Library
   Auburn University
   Auburn 36830
1) University of Alabama in Birmingham
   College of General Studies Library
   1919 Seventh Avenue, South
   Birmingham 35233
1) Ramona Wood Library
   Jacksonville State University
   Jacksonville 36265
1) Julia Tutwiler Library
   Livingston University
   Livingston 35470
1) University of South Alabama Library
   307 Gaillard Drive
   Mobile 36688
3) Troy State University Library
   Troy 36081
2) College of Education Library
   University of Alabama
   University 35486

ALASKA
1) University of Alaska Library
   College 99701

ARIZONA
1) Northern Arizona University
   Flagstaff 86001
1) Arizona State University Library
   Tempe 85281
1) Pima College
   Tucson 85543
2) University of Arizona Library
   Tucson 85721

ARKANSAS
1) Riley Library
   Quachita Baptist University
   Arkadelphia 71923
1) University of Arkansas Library
   Reference Department
   Fayetteville 72701
3) Arkansas Polytechnic College Library
   Russellville 72801

1) Dean B. Ellis Library
   Arkansas State University
   State University 72467

CALIFORNIA
3) Far West Laboratory for Educational Research and Development-Library
   2180 Milvia Street
   Berkeley 94705
1) Chico State College Library
   Chico 95926
1) Honnold Library
   Government Publications
   Claremont 91711
3) California State College Library
   1000 East Victoria Street
   Dominquez Hills 90246
2) Fresno State College Library
   Fresno 93710
1) California State College at Fullerton, Library
   8000 North State College Boulevard
   Fullerton 92631
1) Fullerton Junior College Library
   321 East Chapman Avenue
   Fullerton 92632
2) Southwest Regional Laboratory for Education Research & Development
   11300 La Cienega Boulevard
   Inglewood 90304
3) University of California
   Serials Acquisitions
   The University Library
   La Jolla 92037
1) Education and Curriculum
   California State College Library
   6101 East 7th Street
   Long Beach 90801
1) John F. Kennedy Memorial Library
   California State College,
   Los Angeles
   5175 State College Drive
   Los Angeles 90032
1) Education Library
   University of Southern California
   University Park
   Los Angeles 90007

AVAILABILITY CODE:
1) Collection open to public
2) Collection limited to organizational use only
3) Information not available

1) ERIC Clearinghouse on Jr.
   Colleges
   University of California
   Education-Psychology Library
   Powell Library Building
   Los Angeles 90024
1) San Fernando Valley State
   College
   18111 Nordhoff Street
   Northridge 91324
2) Ambassador College Library
   300 West Green Street
   Pasadena 91105
1) Contra-Cost County
   Department of Education
   75 Santa Barbara Road
   Pleasant Hill 94523
1) California State Polytechnic
   College, Reference Library
   Pomona 91766
2) San Mateo County Information
   and Library Resources
   Dissemination Ctr.
   Office of Education
   590 Hamilton Street
   Redwood City 94063
3) University of California Library
   Government Publications Dept.
   Riverside 92507
1) Sonoma State College Library
   1801 East Cotati Avenue
   Rohnert Park 95928
1) California State Dept. of
   Education
   Bureau of Program Planning and
   Research, Room 455
   721 Capitol Mall
   Sacramento 95814
1) Sacramento State College Library
   6000 J Street
   Sacramento 95819
2) San Diego County Dept. of
   Education
   6401 Linda Vista Road
   San Diego 92111
2) Education Resource Center
   San Diego State College Libary
   5402 College Avenue
   San Diego 92115
3) U.S. International University
   Elliott Campus Library
   8655 Pomerado Road
   San Diego 92124
1) Education Library
   San Francisco State College
   1630 Holloway Avenue
   San Francisco 94132
1) U.S. Office of Education/DHEW
   Federal Office Building
   50 Fulton Street
   San Francisco 94102
1) College Library
   California State Polytechnic
   College
   San Luis Obispo 93401
1) University of California Library
   Santa Barbara 93106
1) University of Pacific Library
   Stockton 95204
1) ERIC Clearinghouse on
   Educational Media and
   Technology
   Institute for Communication
   Research
   Stanford University
   Stanford 94305

COLORADO
1) ERIC Clearinghouse for
   Social Studies
   Social Science Education
   University of Colorado
   970 Aurora Avenue
   Boulder 80302
1) Information Retrieval Center
   North Colorado Education
   DOCES
   1750 30th Street, Suite 48
   Boulder 80301
1) Education Library
   University of Colorado
   Boulder 80302
1) University of Denver Library
   University Park
   Denver 80210
1) U.S. Office of Education,
   Region VIII
   9017 Federal Office Building
   19 and Stout Streets
   Denver 80202
1) University of Northern
   Colorado Library
   Greeley 80631
3) Western State College
   Gunnison 81230

CONNECTICUT
3) University of Bridgeport Library
   Bridgeport 06602
3) H. C. Buley Library
   Southern Connecticut State
   College
   501 Crescent Street
   New Haven 06515
3) Area Cooperative Education
   Services
   Village Street
   North Haven 06473
1) Wilbur Cross Library
   University of Connecticut
   Storrs 06268

Compendium of Abstracted Methods

DELAWARE
1) Departmental Library
   State Department of Public Instruction
   John G. Townsend Building
   Dover 19901

DISTRICT OF COLUMBIA
1) American University Library
   Massachusetts & Nebraska Ave., N.W.
   Washington 20016
1) Mullen Library—Room 203 A
   Catholic University of America
   Washington 20017
3) District of Columbia Public Schools
   412 12th Street, NW, Suite 1013
   Washington 20036
1) D.C. Teachers College Library
   1100 Harvard Street, NW
   Washington, D.C. 20009
1) Educational Materials Center
   Federal City College
   425 Second Street, NW
   Mailing address:
     U.S. Office of Education
     Washington, 20202
1) Center for Applied Linguistics
   1717 Massachusetts Avenue, NW
   Washington, 20036
1) ERIC Clearinghouse on Higher Education
   One Dupont Circle, Suite 630
   Washington 20036
1) ERIC Clearinghouse on Library and Information Sciences
   1440 Connecticut Avenue, NW
   Washington 20036
1) ERIC Clearinghouse on Teacher Education
   One Dupont Circle
   Washington 20006
1) Library of Congress
   Microfilm Reading Room
   (Deck 38)
   Washington 20540
1) National Education Association
   NEA Staff Library—Room 527
   1201 16th Street, NW
   Washington 20036
3) National Reading Center
   1776 Massachusetts Avenue NW
   Washington 20036
2) U.S. Dept. of Health, Education & Welfare-Dept. Library
   Room 1436 North Building
   330 Independence Avenue, SW
   Washington 20201
2) U.S. Office of Education/DHEW
   Bureau of Adult, Vocational, and Technical Education
   GSA Regional Office Building
   7th and D Streets, SW
   Washington 20202
1) U.S. Office of Education/DHEW
   Educational Reference Center
   400 Maryland Avenue-Library
   Washington 20202

FLORIDA
1) Florida Atlantic University Library
   Boca Raton 33432
2) Otto G. Richter Library
   University of Miami
   Coral Gables 33124
1) Professional Library
   Board of Public Instruction of Broward County
   1320 S.W. 4th Street
   Fort Lauderdale 33310
3) Indian River Community Coll Library
   South 35th Street and Cortez Blvd.
   Fort Pierce 33450
1) Education Library
   University of Florida
   341 Norman Hall
   Gainesville 32601
3) Dade County Public Schools
   Professional Library
   1410 N.E. 2nd Avenue, Room 800
   Miami 33132
1) Florida International University
   Tamiami Trail
   Miami 33144
1) Professional Library
   Marion County Public School System
   406 S.E. Alvarez Avenue
   Ocala 32670
1) Florida Technological University Library
   Orlando 32816
3) University of West Florida
   Library Building
   Pensacola 32504
1) Documents-Map Division
   Florida State University Library
   Tallahassee 32306
1) Florida Educational Resources Information Center, Division of Vocational, Technical and Adult Education
   Knott Building, Room 258
   Tallahassee 32304

1) University of South Florida
Tampa 33620

GEORGIA
1) Albany Junior College Library
2400 Gillionville Road
Albany 31705
1) Main Library
University of Georgia
Athens 30601
2) Augusta College Library
2500 Walton Way
Augusta 30904
3) Department of Education
156 Trinity Avenue S.W.
Room 318
Atlanta 30300
1) U.S. Office of Education,
Region IV
50 Seventh Street, NE Rm 404
Atlanta 30323
1) West Georgia College
Sanford Library
Carrollton 30117
3) North Georgia College Library
Dahlonega 30533
2) Savannah State College
Savannah 31404
2) Georgia Southern College Library
Statesboro 30458
1) Richard H. Powell Library
Valdosta State College
Valdosta 31601

HAWAII
1) Hamilton Library
University of Hawaii
2880 The Mall
Honolulu 96822
3) Honolulu Community College
874 Dillingham Blvd.
Honolulu 96817
1) Ralph E. Woolley Library
The Church College of Hawaii
Laie 96762

IDAHO
1) Professional Library
Idaho State Department of Education
200 State Office Building
Boise 83702

ILLINOIS
1) Education-Psychology Library
Southern Illinois University
Carbondale 62901
1) Booth Library
Eastern Illinois University
Charleston 61920
1) Northeastern Illinois State
College Library
Bryn Mawr at St. Louis Avenue
Chicago 60625
1) U.S. Office of Education,
Region V
226 W. Jackson Blvd., Room 406
Chicago 60606
3) University of Illinois at Chicago
Circle Library
Chicago 60680
1) University of Chicago Library
Chicago 60637
1) Swen Parson Library
Northern Illinois University
DeKalb 60115
3) Lovejoy Library
Southern Illinois University
Edwardsville 62025
1) Northwestern University Library
Evanston 60201
1) Memorial Library
Western Illinois University
Macomb 61455
1) Milner Library
Illinois State University
Normal 61761
3) Governors State University
Library
Park Forest South 60466
2) Cullom-Davis Library
Bradley University
1501 West Bradley Avenue
Peoria 61606
2) Klinck Memorial Library
Concordia Teachers College
7400 Augusta Street
River Forest 60305
1) Sangamon State University
Library
Springfield 62703
1) Education and Social Science
Library
University of Illinois
100 Library
Urbana 61801
1) ERIC Clearinghouse on Early
Childhood Education
University of Illinois
805 W. Pennsylvania Avenue
Urbana 61801
1) ERIC Clearinghouse on Teaching
of English, 1111 Kenyon Road
Urbana 61801

INDIANA
1) ERIC Clearinghouse on Reading
200 Pine Hall
Indiana University
Bloomington 47401

Compendium of Abstracted Methods

1) School of Education,
   Education Library
   Indiana University
   Bloomington 47401
1) Saint Francis College Library
   2701 Spring Street
   Fort Wayne 46808
1) Phi Delta Kappa
   School Research Information
   Service
   8th and Union
   Bloomington 47401
1) Purdue University Library
   Lafayette 47907
1) Educational Resources Division
   Ball State University Library
   Muncie 47306
1) Memorial Library
   University of Notre Dame
   Social Studies Division
   Notre Dame 46556
1) Indiana State University Library
   Terre Haute 47809

IOWA

1) Iowa State University Library
   Ames 50010
1) University of Northern Iowa
   Library
   Cedar Falls 50613
1) Cowles Library
   Drake University
   28th and University
   Des Moines 50311
3) Department of Public
   Instruction
   Gremes State Office Building
   Des Moines 50319
2) American College Testing
   Program
   Iowa City 52240
2) Education—Psychology Library
   University of Iowa
   Iowa City 52240

KANSAS

1) William Allen White Library
   Kansas State Teachers College
   Emporia 66801
3) Forsyth Library
   Fort Hays Kansas State College
   Hays 67601
1) Kansas State University Library
   Education Division
   Manhattan 66502
1) Education Media Center
   Johnson County
   Community College
   57th and Merriam Drive
   Shawnee Mission 66203
1) Wichita State University Library
   Wichita 67208

KENTUCKY

1) Margie Helm Library
   Western Kentucky University
   Bowling Green 42101
1) Kentucky Department of
   Education Library
   State Office Building
   Frankfort 40601
2) University of Kentucky
   Education and Curriculum
   Library
   205 Dickey Hall
   Lexington 40506
1) University of Louisville Library
   Louisville 40208
1) Johnson Camden Library
   Morehead State University
   Morehead 40351
1) Murray State University
   Murray 42701
1) John Grant Crabbe Library
   Eastern Kentucky University
   Richmond 40478

LOUISIANA

1) Louisiana State Department
   of Education
   Office of Asst. Deputy for
   Vocational Education
   Baton Rouge 70804
3) Sims Memorial Library
   Southeastern Louisiana
   University
   Hammond 70401
1) Dupre Library
   University of Southwestern
   Louisiana
   Lafayette 70501
3) Louisiana State University in
   New Orleans
   Earl K. Long Library
   Lake Front New Orleans 70122
1) Sandel Library
   Northeast Louisiana University
   Monroe 71201
2) Polk Library
   Francis T. Nicholls
   State University
   Thibodaux 70301

MAINE

1) Planning & Evaluation Unit
   ERIC Office

Maine Department of Education
Augusta 04330

1) Raymond H. Fogler Library
University of Maine
Orono 04473

MARYLAND
1) Loyola College Library
4501 North Charles Street
Baltimore 21210

1) Maryland State Department
of Education
301 West Preston Street
Baltimore 21201

1) Albert S. Cook Library
Towson State College
Baltimore 21204

2) ERIC Processing and Reference
Facility, 4833 Rugby Avenue
Bethesda 20014

2) McKeldin Library
University of Maryland
College Park 20742

3) Montgomery County
Public Schools
550 Stonestreet Avenue
Rockville 20850

3) Blackwell Library
Salisbury State College
Salisbury 21801

MASSACHUSETTS
1) University of Massachusetts
Library
Amherst 01002

1) Boston Public Library
Boston 02117

3) Boston University
School of Education
765 Commonwealth Avenue
Boston 02215

1) Educational Reference Center
Massachusetts Department of
Education
182 Tremont Street
Boston 02111

1) U.S. Office of
Education/Region I
J.F. Kennedy Federal Building
Boston 02203

3) Maxwell Library
State College of Bridgwater
Bridgewater 02740

3) Massachusetts Board
of Education
Southeast Regional Center
Buzzards Bay 02532

2) Harvard University
Graduate School of
Education Library
Longfellow Hall, 13 Appian Way
Cambridge 02138

2) Merrimack Educational Center
101 Mill Road
Chelmsford 01824

1) Boston College Library
Chestnut Hill 02167

3) School Committee Supply Room
1216 Dorchester Avenue
Dorchester 02125

1) Fitchburg State College Library
Fitchburg 01420

3) Lowell State College Library
Rolfe Street
Lowell 01854

3) Education Development Center
55 Chapel Street
Newton 02160

3) Massachusetts Board of
Education
Pittsfield Regional Center
Pittsfield 01202

3) Department of Library Services
Quincy Public Schools
Coddington Street
Quincy 02169

3) Massachusetts Board of
Education
Northeast Regional Center
555 Chickering Road
North Andover 01845

3) Springfield College Library
Springfield 01109

3) Massachusetts Board of
Education
Springfield Regional Education
Center
2083 Roosevelt Avenue
Springfield 01104

3) Massachusetts Board of
Education
Worcester Regional Center
Worcester 01600

MICHIGAN
1) Education Library
University of Michigan
Ann Arbor 48104

1) ERIC Clearinghouse on
Counseling and Personnel
Services
The University of Michigan
School of Education Building,
Rm 2108
East University Street
Ann Arbor, Michigan 48104

1) University of Michigan
Dearborn Campus Library
4901 Evergreen Road
Dearborn 48128

Compendium of Abstracted Methods

2) Professional Library
1068 School Center Building
Detroit 48202
3) Professional Library
Detroit Public Schools
1032 School Center Building
Detroit 48202
1) Education Division
Wayne State University Library
Detroit 48202
1) Michigan State University
Library
East Lansing 48823
1) Educational Resources Center
Western Michigan University
Kalamazoo 49001
1) Bureau of Library Services
Michigan Department of Education
785 East Michigan Avenue
Lansing 48913
1) Oakland Schools Resource Center
2100 Pontiac Lake Road
Pontiac 48054
1) University Library
Eastern Michigan University
Ypsilanti 48197

MINNESOTA
1) Bemidji State College
Bemidji 56601
3) Memorial Library
Mankato State College
Mankato 56001
1) Education Library
University of Minnesota
Minneapolis 55455
2) Moorhead State College Library
Moorhead 56560
1) Learning Resources Services
St. Cloud State College
St. Cloud 56301
2) Maxwell Library
Winona State College
Winona 55987

MISSISSIPPI
2) W. B. Roberts Library
Delta State College
Cleveland 38732
1) University of Southern
Mississippi Library
Hattiesburg 39401
3) Mitchell Memorial Library
Mississippi State University
State College 39762

MISSOURI
1) University of Missouri Library
Columbia 65201

2) State Department of Education
Division of Public Schools
Jefferson Building—7th Floor
Jefferson City 65101
1) Missouri Southern College
Library
Newman and Duquesne Roads
Joplin 64801
1) Resource Center
Mid-Continent Regional
Education Laboratory
104 East Independence Avenue
Kansas City 64106
1) Pickler Memorial Library
Northeast Missouri State College
Kirksville 63501
1) Southwest Missouri State
College Library
Springfield 65802
1) Central Midwestern Regional
Educational Laboratory
10646 St. Charles Rock Road
St. Ann 63074
3) University of Missouri Library
St. Louis Campus
8001 Natural Bridge Road
St. Louis 63121
2) Audio Visual Department and
Photo Publication Service
Laboratory
Washington University
St. Louis 63130
1) Wards Edwards Library
Central Missouri State College
Warrensburg 64093

MONTANA
1) Eastern Montana College Library
Billings 59101
1) Northern Montana College
Library
Havre 59501

NEBRASKA
3) Reta King Library
Chadron State College
Chadron 69227
1) Kearney State College Library
Kearney 68847
1) University of Nebraska Library
Lincoln 68508
2) Gene Eppley Library
University of Nebraska at Omaha
Omaha 68101

NEVADA
1) Nevada Southern University
Library
Las Vegas 89109
1) University of Nevada Library
Reno 89507

NEW HAMPSHIRE

3) State Department of Education
64 North Main Street
Concord 03301

1) University of New Hampshire
Library
Durham 03824

1) Herbert H. Lamson Library
Plymouth State College
Plymouth 03264

NEW JERSEY

1) Occupational Research and
Development Center
Building 871, R.M.C.
Plainfield Avenue
Edison 08817

3) Savitz Library
Glassboro State College
Glassboro 08028

3) Jersey City State College
Forest A. Erwin Library
2039 Kennedy Boulevard
Jersey City 07305

1) Government Publications Dept.
Rutgers University
New Brunswick 08901

1) Phillipsburg Free Public Library
Phillipsburg 08865

1) ERIC Clearinghouse on Tests
Measurement and Evaluation
Educational Testing Service
Princeton 08540

1) Monmouth County Library
Eastern Branch
N.J. Highway 35
Shrewbury 07701

2) Roscoe L. West Library
Trenton State College
Pennington Road
Trenton 08625

2) Newark State College Library
Union 07083

1) Paterson State College Library
300 Pompton Road
Wayne 07470

NEW MEXICO

1) Zimmerman Library
University of New Mexico
Albuquerque 87106

3) Southwestern Cooperative
Education Laboratory
117 Richmond, N.E.
Albuquerque 87106

1) ERIC Clearinghouse on Rural
Education and Small Schools
New Mexico State University
Las Cruces 88001

1) New Mexico State
University Library
Las Cruces 88001

NEW YORK

1) State University of New York
at Albany
1400 Washington Avenue
Albany 12203

1) New York State Library
Albany 12224

3) Board of Cooperative
Educational Services
6th South Street
Belmont 14813

1) Drake Memorial Library
State University College
at Brockport
Brockport 14420

3) Brooklyn College Library of the
City University of New York
Brooklyn 11210

1) Edward H. Butler Library
State University College
at Buffalo
Buffalo 14222

1) Lockwood Memorial Library
State University of New York
at Buffalo
1300 Elmwood Avenue
Buffalo 14214

1) Teaching Materials Center
Cornish Hall, D-206
State University of New York
Cortland 13045

2) Paul Klapper Library
Queens College
City University of New York
Flushing 11367

1) Reed Library
State University College
Fredonia 14063

2) Adelphi University Library
Garden City 11530

1) Milne Library
State University College
Geneseo 14454

1) C. W. Post College Library
Long Island University
Greenvale 11548

2) Hofstra University Library
Hempstead 11550

3) Albert R. Mann Library
Cornell University
Ithaca 14850

3) La Guardia Community College
Long Island City 11101

1) State University College Library
New Paltz 12561

Compendium of Abstracted Methods

3) Bank Street College of Education
610 West 112th Street
New York 10025

1) Center for Urban Education
Library
105 Madison Avenue
New York 10016

3) Baruch School Library
The City College
17 Lexington Avenue
New York 10010

1) City College Library of the
City University of New York
Convent Avenue a W. 135th
Street
New York 10031

2) Fordham University Library
at Lincoln Center
Columbus Avenue and 60 Street
New York 10023

2) Graduate Studies Division
Library
City University of New York
33 West 42nd Street
New York 10036

1) ERIC Clearinghouse on
Languages and Linguistics
Modern Language Assoc.
of American
62 Fifth Avenue
New York 10011

1) Education Library
New York University
4 Washington Place
New York 10003

1) ERIC Information Retrieval
Center on the Disadvantaged
Teachers College
Columbia University
New York 10027

1) Teachers College Library
525 West 120th Street
New York 10027

1) U.S. Office of Education,
Region II
26 Federal Plaza, Room 1013
New York 10007

1) Penfield Library
State University of New York
College at Oswego
Oswego 13126

2) Suffolk County Regional
Education Center
20 Church Street
Patchogue 11772

3) State University of New York
College of Arts and Science
Plattsburg 12901

1) Frederick W. Crumb
Memorial Library
State University College
of New York
Potsdam 13676

2) Education Library
University of Rochester
Rochester 14627

1) The-MAD-Her-On, Inc.
200 East Garden Street
Rome 13440

2) Northern Colorado Educational
Board of Cooperative Services
Essex Col Area Education Center
Mineville 12956

3) Richmond College Library
130 Stuyvesant Place
Staten Island 10301

1) State University of New York
at Stony Brook Library
Stony Brook 11790

3) Film Library
Board of Cooperative
Educational Services
145 College Road
Suffern 10901

1) Educational and Cultural Center
700 East Water Street, Rm 213
Syracuse 13210

1) ERIC Clearinghouse on
Adult Education
107 Roney Lane
Syracuse 13210

1) Syracuse University Library
Carnegie Building, Rm 210
Syracuse 13210

2) Nassau Regional Education
Resource Center
1196 Prospect Avenue
Westbury 11590

1) Board of Cooperative
Educational Services
845 Fox Meadow Road
Yorktown Heights 10598

3) U.S. Dept. of Schools
European Area
Professional Library
APO New York 09164

NORTH CAROLINA

1) Appalachian State University
Library
Boone 28607

1) University of North Carolina
Library
Chapel Hill 27514

1) Hunter Library
Western Carolina University
Cullowhee 28723

1) Learning Institute of
North Carolina
1006 Lamond Avenue
Durham 27701
1) National Laboratory for
Higher Ed.
Mutual Plaza
Durham 27701
3) Walter C. Jackson Library
University of North Carolina
at Greensboro
Greensboro 27412
1) J.Y. Joyner Library
East Carolina University
Greenville 27834
1) D. H. Hill Library
North Carolina State University
Raleigh 27607
1) Research and Information Center
North Carolina State Department
of Public Instruction
Education Building, Room 252
Raleigh 27602

NORTH DAKOTA
1) Chester Fritz Library
University of North Dakota
Grand Forks 58201

OHIO
1) University of Akron Library
Akron 44304
3) Ohio University Library
Athens 45701
Bowling Green State
University Library
Bowling Green 43403
3) Main Campus Library
University of Cincinnati
Cincinnati 45221
3) Cleveland State University
Library
Euclid Avenue at E. 24th Street
Cleveland 44115
1) Ohio State Department of
Education
Department of Research,
Planning and Development
781 Northwest Boulevard
Columbus 43212
1) ERIC Clearinghouse on
Vocational and Technical
Education
The Ohio State University
1900 Kenny Road
Columbus 43210
1) ERIC Clearinghouse for Science
Mathematics and Environmental
Ed.
1460 West Lane Avenue,
2nd Floor
Columbus 43221

1) Education Library
Ohio State University
060 Arps Hall
1945 North High Street
Columbus 43210
1) Wright State University Library
Serial Records Section
Colonel Glenn Highway
Dayton 45431
1) Kent State University Library
Kent 44242
2) Alumni Library
Miami University
Oxford 45056
1) University of Toledo Library
Toledo 43606
3) Central State University
Wilberforce 45384
1) Youngstown State University
Library
410 Wick Avenue
Youngstown 44503

OKLAHOMA
3) East Central State College
Ada 74820
1) Acquisitions Department
Central State College Library
Edmond 73034
2) University of Oklahoma Library
401 West Brooks, Rm 130
Norman 73069
1) Oklahoma State University
Library
Stillwater 74074
2) John Vaughn Library
Northeastern State College
Tahlequah 74464
1) Harwell Library
University of Tulsa
Tulsa 74104
1) Southwestern State College
Library
Weatherford 73096

OREGON
1) Southern Oregon College
Library
Ashland 97520
1) William Jasper Kerr Library
Oregon State University
Corvallis 97331
1) ERIC Clearinghouse on
Educational Management
University of Oregon Library
South Wing
Eugene 94703
1) Northwest Regional Educational
Laboratory
400 Lindsay Building

Compendium of Abstracted Methods

    710 S.W. 2nd
    Portland 97204
1) Portland State University Library
    Portland 97207
2) Oregon State Library
    State Library Building
    Salem 97310

PENNSYLVANIA
3) Bloomsburg State College
    College Library Department
    Bloomsburg 17815
1) California State College Library
    California 15419
3) Research and Information Services for Education
    117 West Ridge Pike
    Conshohocken 19428
2) Kemp Library
    East Stroudsburg State College
    East Stroudsburg 18301
2) Hamilton Library
    Edinboro State College
    Edinboro 16412
2) State Library of Pennsylvania
    Education Building
    Harrisburg 17126
1) Rhodes R. Stabley Library
    Indiana University of Penn.
    Indiana 15701
2) Regional Resources Center of Eastern Pennsylvania Special Education
    443 South Gulph Road
    King of Prussia 19406
1) Kutztown State College
    Kutztown 19530
2) Ganser Library
    Millersville State College
    Millersville 17551
1) Bucks County Community College Library, Swamp Road
    Newtown 18940
1) Samuel Paley Library
    Temple University
    Philadelphia 19122
1) Pedagogical Library
    School District of Philadelphia
    Parkway and 21st Street
    Philadelphia 19103
1) Research for Better Schools
    1700 Market Street, Suite 1700
    Philadelphia 19103
1) U.S. Office of Education, Region III
    401 North Broad Street
    Philadelphia 19108
1) Hillman Library C-16
    University of Pittsburgh
    Pittsburgh 15213
2) Shippensburg State College Library
    Shippensburg 17257
1) Maltby Library
    Slippery Rock State College
    Slippery Rock 16057
1) Pattee Library—205
    The Pennsylvania State University
    University Park 16802
1) Documents Department
    Francis Harvey Green Library
    West Chester State College
    West Chester 19380
1) Eugene Shedden Farley Library
    Wilkes College
    Wilkes-Barre 18703

RHODE ISLAND
3) University of Rhode Island Library
    Kingston 02881
1) Rhode Island College
    Providence 02908

SOUTH CAROLINA
2) Charleston County School District
    67 Legare Street
    Charleston 29401
1) Clemson University Library
    Clemson 29631
1) South Carolina State Library
    1500 Senate Drive
    Columbia 29201
2) Dacus Library
    Winthrop College
    South Carolina College for Women
    Rock Hill 29730

SOUTH DAKOTA
2) South Dakota State Library
    322 South Fort Street
    Pierre 57501
3) Southern State College Library
    Springfield 57062
1) I. D. Weeks Library
    University of South Dakota
    Vermillion 57069

TENNESSEE
1) Jere Whitson Memorial Library
    Tennessee Technological University
    Cookeville 38501
3) University of Tennessee
    Research Coordinating Unit
    909 Mountcastle Street
    Knoxville 37916

1) John Brister Library
   Memphis State University
   Memphis 38111
1) George Peabody College for
   Teachers, Library
   Nashville 37203

TEXAS

2) Southwest Educational
   Development Laboratory
   800 Brazos Street
   Austin 78701
3) Texas Education Agency
   Resource Center Library
   201 East 11th Street
   Austin 78711
1) Educational Psychology Library
   OLB 200
   University of Texas at Austin
   Austin 78712
1) West Texas State University
   Library
   Canyon 79015
1) Texas A & M University Library
   College Station 77843
2) East Texas State
   University Library
   Commerce 75428
1) U.S. Office of Education,
   Region VI
   1114 Commerce Street
   Dallas 75202
1) Special Materials Section
   North Texas State University
   Library
   N.T. Station
   Denton 76203
1) Texas Women's University
   Library
   Box 3715, TWU Station
   Denton 76201
2) Educational Service
   Region XIX
   6501-C Trowbridge
   El Paso 79905
1) Pan American University
   Library
   Edinburg 78539
1) Sam Houston State University
   Huntsville 77340
1) Texas A & I University Library
   Kingsville 78363
3) Texas A & I University at
   Laredo Library
   Laredo 78040
2) Texas Technological University
   Library
   Lubbock 79409
3) Education Service Center
   Region XVII
   713 Citizens Tower
   Lubbock 79401
2) Education Service Center
   Region VIII
   100 N. Riddle Street
   Mount Pleasant 75455
3) Stephen F. Austin State College
   1534—Library
   Nacogdoches 75961
1) Ector County Independent
   School District,
   Curriculum Library
   Odessa 79760
3) Education Service Center
   Region X
   Richardson 75080
1) Our Lady of the Lake College
   411 S.W. 24th Street
   San Antonio 78207
2) Education Service Center
   Region IX
   2000 Harrison Street
   Wichita Falls 76309

UTAH

1) Utah State University
   Logan 84321
1) Weber State College
   Ogden 84403
1) Brigham Young University
   Library
   Provo 84601
1) Marriott's Library
   University of Utah
   Salt Lake City 84112
2) Technical Assistance Reference
   Center
   Utah State Board of Education
   1400 University Club Building
   136 East South Temple
   Salt Lake City 84111

VIRGINIA

3) Alexandria School Board
   418 S. Washington Street
   Alexandria 22313
3) T. C. Williams High School
   33 King Street
   Alexandria 22312
2) Arlington County Public
   Schools Professional Library
   1426 North Quincy Street
   Arlington 22207
2) ERIC Clearinghouse on
   Exceptional Children
   Council for Exceptional Children
   1411 South Jefferson Davis
   Highway
   Arlington 22202
1) Carol M. Newman Library
   Virginia Polytechnic Institute
   and State University
   Blacksburg 24061

Compendium of Abstracted Methods

1) Adlerman Library
   University of Virginia
   Charlottesville 22903
1) Fairfax County Public School
   Administration Building
   10700 Page Avenue
   Fairfax 22030
1) George Mason College of the
   University of Virginia Library
   Fairfax 22030
1) Johnston Memorial Library
   Virginia State College
   Petersburg 23803
2) Virginia Polytechnic Institute
   and State University
   Extension Division
   12100 Sunset Hills Road
   Reston 22070
1) James Branch Cabell Library
   Virginia Commonwealth
   University
   901 Park Avenue
   Richmond 23220
3) State Board of Education
   1312 East Grace Street
   Richmond 23216
3) College of William and Mary
   Earl Gregg Swem Library
   Williamsburg 23185

WASHINGTON
1) Bellevue School District
   310 102nd Avenue, N.E.
   Bellevue 98004
1) Education-Curriculum Division
   Wilson Library
   Western Washington State
   College
   Bellingham 98225
1) Kennedy Library
   Eastern Washington State
   College
   Cheney 99004
1) Central Washington State
   College Library
   Ellensburg 98926
1) Office of Superintendent of
   Public Instruction,
   Professional Curriculum Library
   Old Capitol Building
   Olympia 98501
1) U.S. Office of Education,
   Region X
   Arcade Plaza Building
   1321 Second Avenue
   Seattle 98101
1) Social Science Reference Library
   University of Washington
   Library
   Seattle 98105

WEST VIRGINIA
1) Research and Evaluation
   Division
   Appalachia Educational
   Laboratory, Inc.
   Charleston 25325
2) West Virginia Research
   Coordinating Unit on
   Vocational Education
   Marshall University
   Huntington 25701
1) West Virginia University
   Library
   Downtown Campus
   Morgantown 26506

WISCONSIN
3) William D. McIntyre Library
   Wisconsin State University
   Eau Claire 54701
1) Wisconsin Board of Vocational
   and Technical and Adult
   Education
   137 East Wilson Street
   Madison 53706
1) Instructional Materials Center
   154 Education Building
   University of Wisconsin
   Madison 53706
1) Wisconsin Department of Public
   Instruction
   Professional Library
   126 Langdon Street
   Madison 53706
1) The Robert L. Pierce Library
   Stout State University
   Menomonie 54751
3) University of Wisconsin—
   Milwaukee
   UWM Library
   2311 East Hartford Avenue
   Milwaukee 53201
1) Forrest R. Polk Library
   Wisconsin State University—
   Oshkosh
   Oshkosh 54901
1) Chalmer Davee Library
   Wisconsin State University
   River Falls 54022
1) Waukesha County Technical
   Institute
   222 Maple Avenue
   Waukesha 53186
1) Wisconsin State University
   Whitewater 53190

WYOMING
1) Wyoming Research
   Coordinating Unit
   State Department of Education
   Capitol Building
   Cheyenne 82001

AMERICAN SAMOA
3) Community College Office
Government of American
Samoa
Pago Pago 96920

PUERTO RICO
1) Catholic University of
Puerto Rico
Encarnacion Valdes Library
Ponce 00731
1) University of Puerto Rico
Biblioteca General
Rio Piedras 00931

CANADA
1) University Library
The University of Calgary
Calgary 44, Alberta
3) University of Alberta Library
Edmonton, Alberta
1) Microfilm Division
University of British Columbia
Library
Vancouver 8, British Columbia
3) Department of Education
Library
Room 206
1181 Portage Avenue
Winnipeg 10, Manitoba
1) Education Library
The University of Manitoba
Winnipeg, Manitoba
2) Bibliotheque Champlain
Universite de Moncton
Moncton, New Brunswick
3) Memorial University of
Newfoundland
Education Library
St. John's, Newfoundland
3) Douglas Library
Queen's University
Serials Department
Kingston, Ontario

2) Althouse College of Education
University of Western Ontario
Lawson Memorial Building
London 72, Ontario
1) Faculties and Psychology
Library
University of Ottawa
Ottawa 2, Ontario
3) Education Centre
155 College Street
Toronto 28, Ontario
3) Ontario Institute for Studies
in Education
252 Bloom Street, West
Toronto, Ontario
2) The F. W. Minkler Library
Education Administration
Centre
Board of Education for the
Borough of North York
5050 Young Street
Willowdale, Ontario
3) University of Saskatchewan
Acquisitions Department Library
Saskatoon, Saskatchewan
3) Sir George Williams University
Library
Montreal 25, Quebec
3) Department of Education
Bibliotheque de L'Univ.
du Quebec
1180 Rue Bleury, Montreal
3) University de Montreal
Bibliotheque
Montreal 101, Quebec
2) Bibliotheque Generale
University Laval
Ste-Foy, Quebec
3) University de Sherbrooke
Bibliotheque
Sherbrooke, Quebec

REFERENCES

Abington School District. Career development activities. Grades 5, 6, 7, Abington, Pa.: ASD, 1968.

Abt. C. C. Games for learning. In S. S Boocock and E. O. Schild (Eds.) *Simulation Games in Learning.* Beverly Hills, California: Sage Publications, Inc., 1968.

Akron-Summit County Public Schools Placement Department, Akron, Ohio, Raymond A. Wasil, Director, 1972.

Albracht, J. (et al.) Using existing vocational programs for providing exploratory experiences. Carrollton: West Georgia College, 1968.

Anderson, A. R. Group counseling. *Review of Educational Research,* 1969, 30(2), 209–226.

Anderson, C. S. Young men ten years after leaving Pennsylvania rural high schools. University Park: Pennsylvania Agricultural Experiment Station, Bulletin 468, September 1944.

Anderson, R. N. Educationally disadvantaged youth. In R. E. Campbell (Ed.) Guidance in vocational education. Guidelines for research and practice. Columbus: Center for Vocational and Technical Education, Ohio State University, 1966.

Angel, J. L. *Employment opportunities for the handicapped.* New York: World Trade Academy Press, 1969.

Arffa, M. S. The influence of volunteer experience on career choice. *The Vocational Guidance Quarterly,* 1966, 14(4), 287–289.

Arkansas State Department of Education. *Guidebook for classes in special education.* Little Rock: Division of Instructional Services, 1969.

Armstrong, H. Place of values in American education. *California Journal of Educational Research,* 1955, 23, 141–154.

Arthur, J. K. *Employment for the handicapped.* Nashville: Abington Press, 1967.

Ashcroft, K. B. (Ed.) Implementing career development theory and research through the curriculum. Report of conference sponsored by the National Vocational Guidance Association, August 1966.

Aubrey, R. F. The counseling of underachievers. *Focus on Guidance,* 1970, 2(5).

Baer, M. F. & Roeber, E. *Occupational information: the dynamics of its nature and use.* Chicago: Science Research Associates, Inc., 1964.

Bancroft, J. & Lawson, W. H. Project NOTIFY—Needed occupational television instruction for youth. San Bernardino: San Bernardino Valley College, 1966.

Barbula, P. M. & Isaac, S. W. Career simulation for adolescent pupils. Final Report. San Diego: County Department of Education, 1967.

Baumgartner, Bernice B. *Guiding the retarded child.* New York: John Day, 1965.

Baymur, F. B. & Patterson, C. H. A comparison of three methods of assisting underachieving high school students. *Journal of Counseling Psychology,* 1960, 7, 83–89.

Beilin, H. & Werner, E. Sex role expectations and criteria of social adjustment for young adults. *Journal of Clinical Psychology,* 1957, 13, 341–343.

Beltz, S. E. Some gentle comments on Dr. Hosford's review of behavioral counseling. *The Counseling Psychologist,* 1969, 1(4), 40–44.

Bender, L. & Silver, A. Body image problem of brain damaged child. *Journal of Social Issues,* 1948, IV, 84–89.

Bender, R. E. Role of high school vocational agriculture in occupational decision making. Paper presented at a meeting of the North Central Regional Research Committee #86, Chicago, October, 1969.

Benson, C. S. The efficient allocation of educational resources. In Committee for Economic Development (ED.) *The schools and the challenge of innovation,* Supplementary paper No. 28. New York: Author, 1969. Pp. 57–73.

Bertrand, A. L. and M. B. Smith. Environmental factors and school attendance: A study in rural Louisiana. Baton Rouge: Louisiana Agricultural Experiment Station, Bulletin 533, May, 1960.

Bishop, C. E. The changing educational needs of rural people. Fayetteville: Department of Vocational Teacher Education, College of Education, University of Arkansas, 1970.

Bishop, J. R. Work experience program for upper junior high and senior high school. In F. Bottoms and W. R. Cleere (Eds) *Report of a one-week institute to develop objectives and models for a continuous exploratory program related to the world of work from junior high through senior high school.* Carrollton: West Georgia College, 1969.

References

Bitter, J. *Training guide for vocational rehabilitation.* St. Louis: Jewish Employment and Vocational Service, 1966.

B'nai B'rith Vocational Service. Catalog of publications, 1970–1971. Washington, D.C.: BBVS, 1971.

Boocock, S. S. From luxury item to learning tool: an overview of the theoretical literature on games. In S. S. Boocock and E. O Schild. (Eds.) *Simulation Games in Learning.* Beverly Hills, California: Sage Publications, Inc. 1968a.

Boocock, Sarane S. The life career game. *Personnel and Guidance Journal,* 1967, 45, 328–334.

Boocock, S. S. & Schild, E. O. (Eds.) *Simulation games in learning.* Beverly Hills, California: Sage Publications, Inc., 1968b

Bottoms, G. and Cleere, W. R.: A one-week institute to develop objectives and models for a continuous exploratory program related to the world of work from junior high through senior high school—final report. Paper presented at the West Georgia National Conference, Carrollton, September, 1969.

Bottoms, J. E. Overview of student personnel services in Georgia's area vocational-technical schools. Atlanta: Georgia State Department of Education, 1967.

Bottoms, J. E. *Student personnel services in Georgia's area vocational-technical schools.* Atlanta: Georgia State Department of Education, Vocational Education Division, 1966–1967.

Bowman, P. H. & Matthews, C. V. *Motivations of youth for leaving school.* Quincy, Il.: University of Chicago, Quincy Youth Development Project, 1960.

Brain, G. B. Administrative and supervisory practices affecting the school dropout. In R. Schasre & J. Wallach (Eds.), *Readings in dropouts and training.* Los Angeles: The Delinquency Prevention Training Project, Youth Study Center, University of Southern California, 1965.

Brazziel, W. F. & Gordon, M. Replications of some aspects of the Higher Horizons program in a Southern junior high school. *NASSP Bulletin,* 1963, 47, 135–143.

Broedel, J., Ohlsen, M., Proff, F., & Southard, C. S. The effects of group counseling on gifted underachieving adolescents. *Journal of Counseling Psychology,* 1960, 7, 163–170.

Broedel, J., Ohlsen, M., & Proff, F. The effects of group counseling on gifted adolescent underachievers. Paper read at American Psychological Association Convention in 1958.

Brough, J. R. A profile of junior high school counseling. *The School Counselor,* 1969, 17(1), 67–72.

Brown, B. R. The assessment of self concept among four-year-old Negro and white children: a comparative study using the Brown-IDS Self Concept Reference Tests. New York: Institute for Developmental Studies, New York University, 1966.

Buck, R. C. & Bible, B. L. Educational attainment among Pennsylvania rural youth. University Park: Pennsylvania Agricultural Experiment Station, Bulletin 686, November 1961.

Bugg, C. A. Implications of some major theories of career choice for elementary school guidance programs. *Elementary School Guidance and Counseling,* 1969, 3(3), 164–172.

Bunda, R. & Mezzano, J. A study of the effects of a work experience program on performance of potential dropouts. *The School Counselor,* 1968, 15(4), 272–274.

Bundy, R. F. Computer-assisted instruction—where are we? *Phi Delta Kappan,* 1968, 49(8), 424–429.

Burchinal, L. G. Differences in educational and occupational aspirations of farm, small-town, and city boys. *Rural Sociology,* 1961, 26, 107–121.

Burchinal, L. G. ERIC and dissemination of research findings. *Theory into Practice,* 1967, 4(2), 77–84.

Burma, J. *Spanish-speaking groups in the United States.* Los Angeles: University of Southern California Press, 1944.

Bushnell, D. S. A systems approach to curriculum change in secondary education. *Educational Technology,* 1970, 10(5), 46–47.

Calia, V. The culturally deprived client: a reformation of counselor's role. *Journal of Counseling Psychology,* 1966, 13, 100–105.

Campbell, R. E., Dworkin, E. P., Jackson, D. P., Hoeltzel, K. E., Parsons, G. E., Lacey, D. W. *The systems approach: An emerging behavioral model for career guidance* Columbus, Ohio: The Center for Vocational and Technical Education, The Ohio State University, January, 1971.

Campbell, R. E. (et al.) Vocational development of disadvantaged junior high school students. Final report Research series number 41. Columbus: Ohio State University, Center for Vocational and Technical Education, 1969.

Campbell, R. E. Vocational ecology: A perspective for the study of careers? *The Counseling Psychologist,* Vol. 1, No. 1, 1969, pp. 20–23.

Campbell, R. E. *Vocational guidance in secondary education. Results of a national survey.* Columbus: Center for Vocational and Technical Education, Ohio State University, 1968.

Cervantes, L. F. *The dropout.* Ann Arbor: University of Michigan Press, 1965.

Chaloupka, D. W. An analysis of factors related to early school leaving of Nebraska City High School, Nebraska. Ann Arbor, Mi.: University Microfilms, Inc., 1958.

Chance, June E. Independence training and first graders' achievement. *Journal of Consulting Psychology,* 1961, 65, 337–347.

Chu, G. C. & Schramm, W. Learning from television: what the research says. Final report. Stanford, Ca.: Institute for Communication Research, Stanford University, 1968.

Circle, D. F. *The career information service: a guide to its development and use.* Newton, Ma.: Newton Public Schools, 1968.

References

Coers, W. C. Comparative achievement of white and Mexican junior high school pupils. *Peabody Journal of Education,* 1935, 12, 157–162.

Cogswell, J. F. The design of a man-machine counseling system, a professional paper. Paper presented at the annual meeting of the American Psychological Association, New York, September 1966.

Cohn, Benjamin (Ed.) *Guidelines for future research on group counseling in the public School setting.* Washington, D.C.: American Personnel and Guidance Association, 1967.

Coleman, J. S. Academic games and learning. *The Bulletin of the National Association of Secondary School Principals,* 1968a, 52(325), 62–72.

Coleman, J. S. Social processes and social simulation games. In S. S. Boocock & E O. Schild (Eds.) *Simulation Games in Learning.* Beverly Hills, California: Sage Publications, Inc., 1968b.

Coleman, S. J. The adolescent subculture and academic achievement. *American Journal of Sociology,* 1960, 65, 337–347.

Combs, C. F. (et. al.) Group counseling: applying the technique. *The School Counselor,* 1963, 11(1), 12–18.

Cook, J. C. Intelligence ratings for 97 Mexican children in St. Paul, Minnesota. *High School Journal,* 1955, 38, pp 24–31.

Cooley, W. W. Computer systems for guidance. Paper presented at the annual meeting of the American Educational Research Association, Chicago, February 1968.

Cooley, W. W. & Lohnes, P. R. Prediction development of young adults: project TALENT five-year follow-up studies. Interim report 5. Palo Alto, Ca.: American Institutes for Research, 1968.

Cooley, W. W. & Hummel, R. C. Systems approaches in guidance. *Review of Educational Research,* 1969, 30(2), 251–262.

Cottingham, H. F. Rationale for elementary school guidance. Final report. Tallahassee: Florida State University, 1967.

Coulson, J. E. *Programmed learning and computer-based instruction.* New York: John Wiley and Sons, Inc., 1962.

Council for Exceptional Children. Reading methods and problems (Handicapped children). *Exceptional Children Bibliography Series.* Arlington, Virginia: Information Center on Exceptional Children, November 1969.

Counseling technology. *Educational Technology,* Special Issue, Saddle Brook, New Jersey: Educational News Service, 9(3), March, 1969.

Cowhig, J. D. (et al.) Orientations toward occupations and residence: a study of high school seniors in four rural counties of Michigan. East Lansing: Michigan Agricultural Experiment Station, Special Bulletin 428, 1960.

Cox, R. F. & Herr, E. L. *Group techniques in guidance.* Harrisburg, Pa.: Pennsylvania State Department of Public Instruction, 1968

Crawford, W. L. & Cross, J. L. *Guidelines, Work study program for slow learning children in Ohio Schools.* Columbus: Columbus Blank Book Company, 1967.

Crites, J. O. *Vocational psychology.* New York: McGraw-Hill, 1969.

Cruickshank, W. M. (Ed.) Psychological consideration with crippled children. In *Psychology of exceptional children and youth*. Englewood, N.J.: Prentice-Hall, 1955.

Cruickshank, W. M., et al. *A Teaching method for brain-injured and hyperactive children*. A demonstration—pilot study. New York: Syracuse University Press, Syracuse, New York, 1961.

Cushman, H. R. (et al.) The concerns and expectations of prospective participants in directed work experience programs. Ithaca: State University of New York, 1967.

Darcy, R. L. An experimental junior high school course in occupational opportunities and labor market processes. Final report. Athens: Ohio University, Center for Economic Education, 1968.

D'Costa, Ayres and Winefordner, David W. A cubistic model of vocational interests. *The Vocational Guidance Quarterly*, 17: 242–49, June 1969.

Dela-Dora, D. Culturally disadvantaged: Educational implications. *Exceptional Children*, 1963, 29, 226–236.

Demsch, B. & Tracy, M. Using small groups as a tool in pupil personnel services. *The Journal of the International Association of Pupil Personnel Workers*, 1968, 12(3), 118–121.

Department of Labor. Manpower report of the President. Washington, D.C.: U.S Government Printing Office, March, 1970.

DePianta, H. J. Work experience: the necessary link. *The Bulletin of the National Association of Secondary School Principals*, 1969, 53(338), 71–79.

Detroit Public Schools. Project PIT: a summer industrial work experience and occupational guidance program. Detroit: DPS, 1967.

Dinkmeyer, D. Group counseling theory and techniques. *The School Counselor*, 1969, 17(2), 148–152.

Dinkmeyer, D. Elementary school guidance: principles and functions. *The School Counselor*, 1968, 16(1), 11–16.

Drasgow. *Journal of Counseling Psychology*, 1957, 4, 210–211.

Drews, E. M. Career considerations in junior high school. Paper presented at the Third Annual All Ohio Junior High School Guidance Conference, Willoughby, 1965.

DuBato, G. S. VOGUE: a demonstration system on occupation information for career guidance. *Vocational Guidance Quarterly*, 1968, 17(2), 117–119.

Duncan, J. A. & Gazda, G. M. Significant content of group counseling sessions with culturally deprived. *Personnel and Guidance Journal*, 1967, 46, 11–16.

Dunn, J. A. The development of procedures for the individualization of educational programs. Paper presented at the American Psychological Association Convention, Miami Beach, Florida, September 5, 1970.

Dworkin, E. P. & Walz, G. R. An evaluation model for guidance. In D. Cook (Ed.) *Guidance for Education in Revolution*. Boston: Allyn and Bacon, Inc., 1971.

References

Dye, H. A. *Fundamental group procedures for school counselors.* Guidance Monograph Series, Series II: Counseling. New York: Houghton Mifflin Co., 1968.

Edling, J. V. A basic reference shelf on instructional media research. Stanford, Ca.: Stanford University, Institute for Communication Research, 1967.

Elliott, R. D. (et al.) Economics education: a guide for New York school. Grades K–6. Project PROBE. Oneonta: State University of New York, College at Oneonta, 1970.

Elliott, R. D. (et al.) Economics education: a guide for New York schools. Grades 7–11. Project PROBE. Oneonta: State University of New York, College at Oneonta, 1970.

ERIC Clearinghouse on Vocational and Technical Education. Characteristics of disadvantaged groups. Columbus: The Center for Vocational and Technical Education, The Ohio State University, July, 1970.

Ellis, G. G. Pupil information and records systems. *The Bulletin of the National Association of Secondary School Principals.* 1968, 52(324), 99–109.

Eshelman, W. M. Disabled workers. In R. E. Campbell (Ed.) *Guidance in vocational education, guidelines for research and practice.* A report of a National Interdisciplinary Seminar. Columbus: Center for Vocational and Technical Education, Ohio State University, 1966.

Fernberger, S. W. Resistance of stereotypes concerning sex differences. *Journal of Abnormal Social Psychology,* 1948, 43, 97–101.

Fielstra, C. Work experience education program in Santa Barbara County. Santa Barbara, California, 1961.

Fine, B. *Underachievers—How they can be helped.* New York: Dutton and Co., 1967.

Fink, M. B. Objectification of data used in underachievement self concept study. *California Journal of Educational Research,* 1962, 13, 105–112. (b).

Fink, M. B. Self concept as it relates to academic underachievement. *California Journal of Educational Research,* 1962, 13, 57–62. (a)

Flanagan, J. C. *Developing a functioning model of an educational system for the 70's.* Pittsburgh: American Institutes for Research, 1967.

Frank, D. S. *Three cities job clinic and services system manual.* Washington, D.C.: Epilepsy Foundation of America, February 1968.

Flanagan, J. C. The PLAN system for individualizing education. *National Council on Measurement in Education* (NCME), 1971, 2(2).

Flanagan, J. C. Project PLAN: The basic role of guidance in individualizing education. Paper presented at the Annual Convention of the Association for Measurement and Evaluation in Guidance, New Orleans, Louisiana, 24 March, 1970.

Frankel, E. A comparative study of achieving and underachieving high school boys of high intellectual ability. *Journal of Educational Research,* 1960, 53, 172–180.

Franklin County Schools: Area education information center. A systems summary description. Columbus, Oh: FCS, 1968.

Franks, C. M. & Susskind, D. J. Behavior modification with children: rationale and technique. *Journal of School Psychology,* 1968, 6(2), 75–88.

Gagne, R. M. *The conditions of learning.* New York: Holt, Rinehart and Winston, Inc., 1965.

Gallington, R. O. *Basic criteria for identifying potential high school dropouts.* Carbondale, Il.: Southern Illinois University, 1965.

Gallington, R. O. *High school dropouts: fate—future—identification.* Carbondale, Il.: Southern Illinois University, 1966.

Garbin, A. P. and Vaughn, D. *Community-junior college students enrolled in occupational programs: Selected characteristics, experiences, and perceptions.* Columbus, Ohio: The Center for Vocational and Technical Education, The Ohio State University, September 1971.

Garbin, A. P. (et. al.) Worker adjustment problems of youth in transition from high school to work. Columbus: Center for Vocational and Technical Education, Ohio State University, 1970.

Gazda, G. M. Group approaches to guidance. *Focus on Guidance,* 1970, 3(3), 1–16.

Gazda, G. M. Group psychotherapy and group counseling: definition and heritage. In G. M. Gazda (Ed.) *Basic approaches to group psychotherapy and group counseling.* Springfield, Illinois: Charles C. Thomas, Publisher, 1968.

Gelatt, H. B. & Varenhorst, B. A decision-making approach to guidance. *The Bulletin of the National Association of Secondary School Principals,* 1968, 52(324), 88–109.

Ginzberg, E. (et. al.) Occupational choice: an approach to a general theory. New York: Columbia University Press, 1951.

Glenn, Hortense. Attitudes of women regarding gainful employment of married women. *Journal of Home Economics,* 1959, 51, 247–52.

Ginzberg, E. *Career Guidance.* New York: McGraw-Hill Book Co., 1971.

Goldhammer, K. and Taylor, R. E. Career education Perspective and promise. Columbus, Ohio: Charles E. Merrill Publishing Company, 1972.

Goldman, L. Group guidance: content and process. *Personnel and Guidance Journal,* 1962, 40, 518–522.

Gordon, A. T. Evaluation of the second year of operation of the Contra Costa Mobile Counseling Center. San Pablo, Ca: Contra Costa College, 1970.

Gordon, J. E. Testing, counseling, and supportive services for disadvantaged youth; experience of MDTA experimental and demonstration projects for disadvantaged youth. University of Michigan, Ann Arbor, Michigan, 249 pages, 1969.

Gowan, J. C. Factors of achievement in high school and college. *Journal of Counseling Psychology,* 1960, 7, 91–95.

Gowan, J. C. The underachieving gifted child—A problem for everyone. *Journal of Exceptional Children,* 1957, 24, 98–101.

References

Grams, A. Facilitating learning and individual development, toward a theory for elementary guidance. Elementary guidance series, Minnesota guidance series. St. Paul: Minnesota State Department of Education, 1966.

Griessman, B. E. & Densley, K. G. Review and synthesis of research on vocational education in rural areas. Las Cruces: ERIC Clearinghouse on Rural Education and Small Schools, New Mexico State University; Columbus: ERIC Clearinghouse on Vocational and Technical Education, Ohio State University, 1969.

Gulick, M. C. Nonconventional data sources and reference tools for the social science and humanities. *College and University Libraries,* 1968, 29(3), 224–234.

Hacker, H. Women as a minority group. *Social Forces,* 1951, 30, 60–69.

Hall, D. T. A Theoretical model of career sub-identity development in organizational settings. *Organizational Behavior and Human Performance,* 6, 50–76, 1971.

Hamburger, M. The significance of work experience in adolescent development. Washington, D.C.: Division of Adult and Vocational Research, Office of Education, 1967.

Hamilton, J. A. Video group social models, group stimulus materials and client characteristics in vocational counseling: an experimental study. Washington, D.C.: American Educational Research Association, 1969.

Hansen, D. Computer-assisted instruction and individualization process. *Journal of School Psychology,* 1968, 6(3), 177–185.

Hansen, J. C. & Stevie, R. R. *Elementary school guidance.* London: The MacMillan Co., Collier-MacMillan Limited, 1969.

Harrison, Don K. Role modeling with the disadvantaged. In Judith Mattson (Ed.), CAPS capsule, Volume 4, Number 2. Ann Arbor, Mi.: ERIC Clearinghouse on Counseling and Personnel Services, 1971.

Havelock, R. G. & Benne, K. D. An exploratory study of knowledge utilization. In G. Watson (Ed.) *Concepts for social change.* Washington, D.C.: National Education Association, 1967.

Havelock, R. G. *Planning for innovation through dissemination and utilization of knowledge.* Ann Arbor: Center for Research on Utilization of Scientific Knowledge, University of Michigan, 1969.

Havighurst, R. *Developmental tasks and education.* New York: Longmans, Green & Co., 1962.

Havre High School District A. Pilot project mobile vocational guidance services. Havre, Mt.: HSDA.

Hechlik, J. E. & Lee, J. S. *Small group work and group dynamics.* CAPS Current Resources Series. Ann Arbor: ERIC Counseling and Personnel Services Information Center, University of Michigan, 1968.

Hedlund, D. E. Cornell study of placement services in New York State two year colleges (study in progress). Ithaca, New York: Department of Education, Cornell University, [Personal communication], 1972.

Herr, E.L. and Cramer, S.H. *Vocational guidance and career development in the schools: toward a system approach.* Boston: Houghton Mifflin, 1972.

Hewett, Sheila. *The family and the handicapped child.* Chicago: Aldine, 1970.

Hill, G. E. *The guidance of elementary school children.* Albany: New York State Education Department, Bureau of Guidance, 1968.

Hill, H. S. Correlation between IQ's of bilinguals at different ages on different intelligence tests. *School and Society,* 1936, 44, 89–90.

Hoffer, J. R. A national communication system in social welfare. Paper presented at the 95th annual forum of the National Conference on Social Welfare, San Francisco, 1968.

Hosford, R. E. Behavioral counseling: a contemporary overview. *The Counseling Psychologist,* 1969, 1(4), 1–32.

Hoyt, K. B. The specialty oriented student research program: a five year report. *Vocational Guidance Quarterly,* 1968, 16(3), 169–176.

Hudak, V. M.; Butler, F. C. Development and evaluation of an experimental curriculum for the New Quincy (Mass.) vocational-technical school. Development and tryout of a junior high school student vocational plan. Pittsburgh: American Institutes for Research, 1967.

Huffman, H. *Guidelines for cooperative education and selected materials from the national seminar held August 1–5, 1966. A manual for the further development of cooperative education.* Columbus, Ohio: The Ohio State University, Center for Vocational and Technical Education, 1967.

Hyman, I. & Feder, B. Instituting group counseling in the public school. *Psychology in the Schools,* 1964, 1(4), 401–403.

Impellitteri, J. T. The computer as an aid to instruction and guidance in the school. A paper prepared for the Regional Seminar and Research Conference in Agricultural Education, Cornell University, November, 1967.

Impellitteri, J. T. and Kapes, J. T. The measurement of occupational values. University Park, Pennsylvania: The Pennsylvania State University, 1971.

Ivey, A. E. & Morrill, W. H. Career process: a new concept for vocational behavior. *Personnel and Guidance Journal,* 1968, 644–649.

Ivey, A. E. The intentional individual: a process-outcome view of behavioral psychology. *The Counseling Psychologist,* 1969, 1(4), 56–60.

Jaffee, A. J. (et al.) *Disabled workers in the labor market.* Totowa, N.J.: Bedminster Press, 1964.

Jeffrey, C. R. *Development of a program to prepare delinquent, disadvantaged youths and slow learners for vocational education.* Washington, D.C.: U.S. Department of Health, Education and Welfare, Office of Education, June, 1967.

Jensen, A. R. Learning abilities of Mexican-American and Anglo-American children. *California Journal of Educational Research,* 1961, 12, 147–59.

Johnson, G. O. *Education for the slow learners.* Englewood Cliffs, N.J.: Prentice-Hall, 1963.

Johnson, M.; Busacker, W. E. & Bowman, F. Q. *Junior high school guidance.* New York: Harper & Brothers, 1961.

Johnson, R. G. Simulated occupational problems in encouraging career exploration. Paper presented at the convention of the American Personnel and Guidance Association, Detroit, April 1968.

References

Joint Council on Economic Education. Economics in the elementary school: who, what, where? A handbook for teachers. New York: JCEE; Minneapolis: Minneapolis Citizens Committee on Public Education, 1967.

Joslin, L. C. Proceedings of the national seminar on vocational guidance in the preparation of counselors. Report of a conference held at the University of Missouri, Aug. 20-25, 1967.

Kennedy, D. A. A behavioral approach to elementary school counseling. In H. J. Peters & M. J. Bathory (Eds.) *School counseling: perspectives and procedures.* Itasca, Illinois: F. E. Peacock Publishers, Inc., 1968, Pp. 125-130.

Kersch, S. F. Innovations in the training and supervision of counselors: simulation gaming. Personnel Services Review. Ann Arbor: ERIC Counseling and Personnel Services Information Center, University of Michigan, March 1970.

Kimbrell, G. and Vineyard, B. S. *Succeeding in the world of work.* Bloomington, Ill: McKnight and McKnight Co., 1970.

Kinnane, J. F. & Suziedelis, A. *Work values of the handicapped.* Washington, D.C.: Catholic University of America, 1966.

Kinnick, B. C. Group discussion and group counseling as applied to student problem soving. *The School Counselor,* 1968, 15(5), 350-356.

Kornrich, M. A note on the definition of underachievement. In M. Kornrich (Ed.), *Underachievement.* Springfield, Il.: Charles C. Thomas, 1965.

Kriger, Sara Finn. n Ach and perceived parental child-rearing attitudes of career women and homemakers. *Journal of Vocational Behavior,* 1972, 2.

Kroll, A. M. The career information library. In D. F. Circle (Ed.) *Career information service.* Newton, Ma.: Newton Public Schools, 1967.

Kroll, A. M. Improving counselor effectiveness on the pupil services team: Planning for the future. *Focus on Guidance,* June, 1971, 3(10).

Krumboltz, J. D. & Thoresen, C. E. (Eds.) *Behavioral counseling: cases and techniques.* New York: Holt, Rinehart and Winston, Inc., 1969.

Krumboltz, J. D. Behavioral counseling: rationale and research. In H. J. Peters & M. J. Bathory (Eds.) *School counseling: perspectives and procedures.* Itasca, Illinois: F. E. Peacock Publishers, Inc., 1968. Pp. 118-124.

Krumboltz, J. D. Vocational problem-solving experiences for stimulating career exploration and interest, Phase II. Mid-Project Report. Stanford: Stanford University, 1967b.

Krumboltz, J. D. Vocational problem-solving experiences for stimulating career exploration and interest. Final Report. Stanford: Stanford University, 1967a.

Krumboltz, J. D. & Sheppard, L. E. Vocational problem-sovlng experiences. In J. D. Krumboltz & C. E. Thoresen (Eds.) *Behavioral counseling: cases and techniques.* New York: Holt, Rinehart and Winston, Inc., 1969.

Kuvlesky, W. P. Implications of recent research on occupational and educational ambitions of disadvantaged rural youth for vocational education. Paper to Meet the Needs of Disadvantaged Youth and Adults in Rural Areas." State College: National Inservice Training Multiple Institutes for Vocational and Related Personnel in Rural Areas, Mississippi State University, July, 1970.

Kuvlesky, W. P. & Ohlendorf, G. W. Occupational status orientations of Negro boys. Paper presented at the Rural Sociological Society Annual Meeting, Miami Beach, August, 1966.

Kuvlesky, Wm. P., Wright, E. D., & Juarez, R. X. Status projections and ethnicity; a comparison of Mexican-American, Negro and Anglo youth. Paper read at the annual meeting of the Southwestern Sociological Association, New Orleans, April 1969.

Laramore, D. Jobs on film. *The Vocational Guidance Quarterly,* 1968, 14(2), 87–90.

Law, Gordon F. A regular place for guidance. *American Vocational Journal,* March 1969, 44(3), 27–28, 60–62.

Laws, Lee. Elementary guide for career development grades 1–6. Austin, Texas: Education Service Center, Region XIII, 1970.

Leonard, G. E. Developmental career guidance project: career guidance manual for teachers. Detroit: Detroit Public Schools, 1968a.

Leonard, G. *Developmental career guidance in action, the first year.* Detroit: Wayne State University, 1968 b. An interim report.

Leonard, G. E. Vocational planning and career behavior; a report on the developmental career guidance project. *Educational Technology,* 1969, 9(3), 42–46.

Leonard, G. E. The developmental career guidance project: 1965–1970. Detroit: Wayne State University, 1972.

Leonard, R. S. Vocational guidance in junior high: one school's answer. *The Vocational Guidance Quarterly,* 1969, 17(3), 221–222.

Lewis, E. C. *Developing woman's potential.* Ames: Iowa State University, Press, 1968.

Ley, R. Labor turnover as a function of worker difference. *Journal of Applied Psychology,* 1966, 50.

Lieberthal, M. Labor: neglected source of support. *American Vocational Journal,* December 1967, 42(9), 49–52.

Life career Game. Player's manual. San Diego: San Diego County Department of Education.

Lifton, W. M. *Working with groups: group process and individual growth.* New York: John Wiley and Sons, Inc., 1967.

Lockwood, O. (et al.) Four worlds: an approach to occupational guidance. *Personnel and Guidance Journal,* 1968, 46(7), 641–643.

Lodato, Francis S. and Kosky, Elizabeth M. A multi-leader approach in group counseling as a method of modifying attitudes toward school in slow learners. Proceedings of the 75th Annual Convention of the American Psychological Association, 1967, 2, 343–344.

Los Angeles City Schools. A guide: a work experience education and employment placement program. Los Angeles, California, 1960.

Loughary, J. W. & Tondow, M. Computers as substitute counselors: some

References

possibilities. Paper presented at the annual meeting of the American Psychological Association, San Francisco, 1968.

Loughary, J. W. The computer is in. *Personnel and Guidance Journal,* 1970, 49(3), 185–192.

Loughary, J. W. & Tondow, M. (Eds.) *Educational information system requirement: the next two decades.* Eugene: University of Oregon, 1967.

Love, H. D. *Exceptional children in a modern society.* Dubuque, Iowa: Kendall Hunt Publishing Company, 1967.

Lux, D. G. and Ray, W. World of construction: industrial arts curriculum project. Bloomington, Ill.: McKnight and McKnight Publishers, 1971.

Lux, D. G. and Ray, W. World of manufacturing: industrial arts curriculum project, 4th edition. Bloomington, Ill.: McKnight and McKnight Publishers, 1970.

Lynn, D. B. Sex-role and parental identification. *Child Development,* 1962, 33, 555–64.

McCracken, D. *Work experience for broadening occupational offerings: a selected bibliography for use in program development.* Columbus: The Ohio State University, Center for Vocational and Technical Education, 1969.

Madsen, W. *The Mexican-Americans of South Texas.* New York: Holt, Rinehart and Winston, Inc., 1964.

Mahler, C. A. *Group counseling in the schools.* Boston: Houghton Mifflin Co., 1969.

Marland, S. P., Jr. Career education now. Address at the 1971 convention of the National Association of Secondary School Principals, Houston, 1971.

Marsh, R. E. Geographic labor mobility in the United States, Recent findings. *Social Security Bulletin,* No. 30, 1967, pp. 14–20.

Martin, A. M. Guidance, the learning process, and communication media. A paper presented at the annual meeting of the American Educational Research Association, Los Angeles, 1969.

Martin, A. M. Occupational information and vocational guidance for non-college youth. Proceedings of a conference held at the University of Pittsburgh, March 11–13, 1966.

Mathis, H. The disadvantaged and the aptitude barrier. *Personnel and Guidance Journal,* 1969, 47, 467–472.

Merrell, R. G. (Director) An integrated career development curriculum for small rural schools. Salt Lake City, Ut.: Western Small Schools Project, 1970.

Miller, A. J. The philosophy and challenge of career education, paper presented to local boards of education, American Vocational Association Convention, Portland, Oregon, December 6, 1971.

Miller, J. V. Information retrieval systems in guidance. *Personnel and Guidance Journal,* 1970, 49(3), 212–218.

Miller, S. M. School dropouts and American society. *New Society,* 1963, 58, 18–20.

Minneapolis Public Schools. World of work: grade nine. Teacher's guide for the school year 1967–1968. Minneapolis: MPS, 1968.

Minnesota State Department of Education. An elementary guidance bibliography of books and journal articles. St. Paul: MSDE, Pupil Personnel Services Section, 1968.

Mitchell, F. H. Implementing a vocational guidance program. *Vocational Guidance Quarterly,* 1968, 15(3), 223–226.

Moore, P. L. Factors involved in student elimination from high school. *Journal of Negro Education,* 1954, 23, 117–122.

Moullette, J. B. New philosophies; renewed efforts; and improved strategies, paper presented to members of the local boards of education, American Vocational Association Convention, Portland, Oregon, December 6, 1971.

Muskegon Public Schools. The effect of additional counseling on the able student's vocational and educational planning. Muskegon, Mi.: MPS, 1965.

National Committee for Children and Youth. *Guidelines for consideration of the dropout and unemployment problems of youth.* Washington, D.C.: NCCY. 1961.

Nelson, R. C. Knowledge and interests concerning 16 occupations among elementary and secondary school students. *Educational and Psychological Measurement,* 1963, 23, 741–754.

Nelson, R. C. Opening new vistas to children through career exploration. Paper presented at the Eighth Annual All Ohio Elementary School Guidance Conference, Dayton, November, 1968.

New Jersey State Department of Education. Teacher's guide for a model program on introduction to vocations. Trenton: NJSDE, Division of Vocational Education.

Nixon, R. A. Federal legislation for a comprehensive program on youth employment. New York: New York University, 1966.

O'Dell, F. L. Where the challenge is met: a handbook for guidance in grades seven, eight, and nine. Columbus: Ohio State Department of Education, Division of Guidance and Testing, 1968.

Odgers, J. G. *Proceedings of a national seminar on vocational guidance, August 21–26, 1966.* Washington, D. C.: American Vocational Association and the American Personnel and Guidance Association.

Office of Education. *Computer-based vocational guidance systems.* Washington, D.C.: U.S. Government Printing Office, 1969.

Ohio Department of Education. *Teaching home economics to the slow learning student.* Columbus: Home Economics Service, ODE; Athens: School of Home Economics, Ohio University, 1961.

Ohlsen, M. M. Counseling children in groups. *The School Counselor,* 1968, 15(5), 343–349.

Oklahoma State Department of Education. A guide for developmental vocational guidance. Grades K-12. Oklahoma City: OSDE, Department of Vocational Technical Education, 1968.

Oregon State Department of Education. Teacher's guide to: self under-

References

standing through occupational exploration (SUTOE). Salem: OSDE, Division of Community Colleges and Vocational Education, 1969. Draft.

Osipow, S. H. & Walsh, W. B. *Behavior change in counseling: readings and cases.* New York: Appleton, Century, Crofts, 1970a.

Osipow, S. H. & Walsh, W. B. *Strategies in counseling for behavior change.* New York: Appleton, Century, Crofts, 1970b.

Osipow, S. H. *Theories of career development.* New York: Appleton-Century-Crofts, 1968.

Ozoglu, S. C. A comparison of occupational choices of achieving and underachieving high school juniors. Unpublished doctoral dissertation, University of Illinois, 1964.

Perrone, P. A. & Thrush, R. S. Vocational information processing systems: a survey. *The Vocational Guidance Quarterly,* 1969, 17(4), 255–267.

Peters, H. J. and Shertzer, B. *Guidance: program development and management.* Columbus, Ohio: Charles E. Merrill, Inc., 1963.

Petersen, N. D. A pilot project in vocational guidance placement and work experience for youth for whom existing work experiences are not appropriate. Livonia, Michigan: Livonia Public Schools, 1967.

Petry, D. W. Vocational students' perception of guidance needs. St. Paul: Pupil Personnel Section, Minnesota Department of Education, 1969.

Phelps, M. C. An analysis of certain factors associated with underachievement among high school students. *Dissertation Abstracts,* 1957, 306–307.

Picou, J. S. & Campbell, R. E. (Eds.) Career behavior of special groups. Columbus, Ohio: Charles E. Merrill, in process.

Portland Public Schools. *The gifted child in Portland.* Portland, Or.: PPS, 1959.

Powell, P. E. Implementing career development programs in the junior high school. Paper prepared for Workshop in Developing Guidelines for Planning Career Development Programs K-12 in Ohio, June 7, 1971, Columbus, Ohio. Paper may be obtained by writing the author at M. H. Russell Center for Economic Education, Henderson State College, Arkadelphia, Arkansas, 71923.

Pruitt, A. S. Teacher involvement in the curriculum and career guidance. *The Vocational Guidance Quarterly,* 1969, 17(3), 189–193.

Pucel, D. J. & Nelson, H. F. Project mini-score: some preliminary implications for vocational guidance. Washington, D.C.: Office of Education, 1968.

Raph, J. B., Goldberg, M. I. & Passow, A. H. *Bright underachievers.* New York: Teachers College Press, Columbia University, 1966.

Rappaport, S. R. *Childhood aphasia and brain damage: Volume II, Differential diagnosis.* Narberth, Pennsylvania: Livingston Publishing Company, 1965,

Rector, W. H. & Shaw, M. C. Group counseling with parents: feasibility, reactions and interrelationships. Monograph number 5. Chico, Ca.: Chico State College, Western Center of the Interprofessional Research Commission on Pupil Personnel Services, 1966.

Riccio, A. C. and Quaranta, J. J. *Establishing guidance programs in secondary schools.* New York: Houghton Mifflin Company, 1968.

Riessman, F. *The culturally deprived child.* New York: Harper, 1962.

Riessman, F. *Helping the disadvantaged pupil to learn more easily.* Englewood Cliffs, N.J.: Prentice-Hall, 1966.

Roberts, R. L. & Frederick, F. J. Computer assisted counseling. Progress report 1. Project 336. Stillwater: Research Foundation, Oklahoma State University. 1967.

Roberts, R. W. *Vocational and practical arts education.* 2nd ed. New York: Harper & Row, 1965.

Rossi, P. H. & Biddle, B. J. (Eds.) *The new media and education.* Chicago: Aldine Publishing Co., 1966.

Roth, R. M. & Meyersberg, H. A. The nonachievement syndrome. *Personnel and Guidance Journal,* 1963, 41, 535-546.

Rousseve, R. J. Teachers of culturally disadvantaged American youth. *Journal of Negro Education,* 1963, 32, 114-121.

Rowan, Helen. The Mexican American. Paper prepared for the U.S. Commission on Civil Rights, 1968.

Ryan, C. Innovations in career development. *American Vocational Journal,* 1963, 44, 63-65.

Ryan, T. A. Systems techniques for programs of counseling and counselor education. *Educational Technology,* 1969, 9(6), 7-17.

Samler, J. Vocational counseling: a pattern and a projection. *The Vocational Guidance Quarterly,* 1968, 17(1), 2-11.

Schasre, R. & Wallach, J. (Eds.) *Readings in dropouts and training.* Los Angeles: The Delinquency Prevention Traning Project, Youth Study Center, University of Southern California, 1965.

Schiffman, J. Employment of high school graduates and dropouts in 1961. Special Labor Force Report No. 21. *Monthly Labor Review,* 1962.

Schild, E. O. Interaction in games. In S. S. Boocock and E. O. Schild (Eds.) *Simulation games in learning.* Beverly Hills, California: Sage Publications, Inc., 1968.

Schill, W. J. Concurrent work-education programs in the 50 states. 1965-1966. Washington, D. C.: Office of Education, 1966.

Schramm, W. Science and the public mind. In E. Katz (et. al.) (Eds.) *Studies of innovation and of communication to the public.* Studies in the utilization of behavioral sciences. Vol. 2. Stanford, Ca.: Institute for Communication Research, Stanford University, 1962.

Schreiber, D. L., Kaplan, B. A., & Strom, R. D. *Dropout studies: Design and conduct.* Washington, D.C.: National Educational Association, 1965.

Schreiber, D. (Ed.) *Profile of the school dropout.* New York: Random House, 1967.

Sewell, W. H. & Ornstein, A. M. Community of residence and occupational choice. *American Journal of Sociology,* 1965, 70, 557-563.

Shaw, F. Educating culturally deprived youth in urban centers. *Phi Delta Kappan,* 1963, 45, 91-97.

References

Shaw, M. C. & Wurstein, R. Research on group procedures in schools: a review of the literature. *The Personnel and Guidance Journal,* 1965, 44, 27–34.

Sherman, C. N., Lewis, E. R. & Wanger, J. *The educational information center: an introduction.* Los Angeles: Tinnon-Brown, Inc., 1960.

Sherman, V. S. Trial and testing of an experimental guidance curriculum. Final Report. Palo Alto: American Institutes for Research in the Behavioral Sciences, 1967.

Sherriffs, A. C. & Jarrett, R. F. Sex differences in attitudes about sex differences. *Journal of Psychology,* 1953, 35, 161–168.

Simpson, G. E. & Yinger, T. M. *Racial and Cultural minorities.* New York: Harper, 1958.

Skinner, B. F. *Science and human behavior.* New York: Macmillan Co., 1953.

Slocum, W. L. Occupational and educational plans of high school seniors from farm and non-farm homes. Pullman: Washington Agricultural Experiment Station, Bulletin 564, February, 1956.

Soares, A. T. & Soares, L. M. A comparative study of the self perceptions of disadvantaged children in elementary and secondary schools. Paper presented at the annual convention of the American Psychological Association, Washington, D.C., September, 1969.

Somora, J. The Spanish speaking groups in the American society. San Jose, Ca.: Community Council of Central Santa Clara County, Santa Clara County Welfare Department, 1964.

Straus, M. A. Societal needs and personal characteristics in the choice of farm, blue collar, and white collar occupations by farmers' sons. *Rural Sociology,* 1964, 29, 408–425.

Stubbins, J. & Hadley, R. G. *Workshops for the handicapped.* An annotated bibliography. Washington, D.C.: National Association of Sheltered Workshops and Homebound Programs, Inc., October, 1967.

Super, D. E. (et al.) Floundering and trial after high school. New York: Teachers College, Columbia University, 1967.

Super, D. E. *The psychology of careers.* New York: Harper & Row, 1957.

Super, D. E. & Overstreet, P. L. *The vocational maturity of ninth grade boys.* New York: Columbia University, Teachers College, Bureau of Publications, 1960.

Suppes, P. Computer-based instruction. *Electronic Age,* 1967, 26(3), 2–6.

Suppes, P. Computer technology and the future of education. *Phi Delta Kappan,* 1968, 49(8), 420–423.

Suppes, P. The uses of computers in education. *Scientific American,* 1966, 215(3), 207–220.

Sutton, J. *Revised instructional program for "slow learners" to improve their job placement opportunities: a three phase study.* Washington, D.C.: U.S. Department of Health, Education and Welfare, Office of Education, 1967.

Tennyson, W. W. (et al.) *The teacher's role in career development.* Washington, D.C.: National Vocational Guidance Association, 1965.

Thompson, J. M. Career development in the elementary school: rationale and implications for elementary school counselors. *The School Counselor,* 1969, 16(3), 208–210.

Thorndike, R. L. *The concepts of over and underachievement.* New York: Bureau of Publications, Teachers College, Columbia University, 1963.

Tiedeman, D. V. (Project Director) Information system for vocational decisions. Annual report. Cambridge: Graduate School of Education, Harvard University, 1967.

Tiedeman, D. V. Information system for vocational decisions: the cultivation of careers through guidance and vocational education. Project report 18. Cambridge: Harvard University, 1969.

Tiedeman, D. V. The role of decision-making in information generation: an emerging new potential in guidance. Project report no. 12. Cambridge, Ma.: Harvard University, 1968.

Tolor, A. & Griffin, A. M. Group therapy in a school setting. *Psychology in the Schools,* 1969, 6(1), 59–62.

Trow, W. C. *Teacher and technology: new designs for learning.* New York: Appleton, Century, Crofts, 1963.

Twelker, P. A. (Ed.) *Instructional simulation systems.* Corvallis, Oregon: Continuing Education Publication, 1969.

Ulibarri, H. Educational needs for the Mexican-American. Paper presented at the National Conference on Educational Opportunities for Mexican-Americans, Austin, Texas, April, 1968.

Ullmann, L. P. & Krasner, L. (Eds.) *Case studies in behavior modification.* New York: Holt, Rinehart, and Winston, 1965.

U.S. Bureau of Labor Statistics. *Factbook on the school dropout in the world of work.* New York: U.S. Department of Labor, Bureau of Labor Statistics, 1962.

U.S. Department of Health, Education, and Welfare. Career Education. Washington, D.C.: U.S. Government Printing Office, 1971.

U.S. Dept. of Health, Education & Welfare. *Career opportunities in service to the disadvantaged and handicapped.* Washington, D.C.: OE (Department of Health, Education and Welfare), 1969.

U.S. Dept. of Health, Education & Welfare. *The educational problems of the Mexican American.* Washington, D.C.: OE (Department of Health, Education and Welfare), 1962, p. 2.

U.S. Department of Labor. Manpower Report of the President. Washington, D.C.: April 1968.

U.S. Department of Labor. *Sheltered workshops: a pathway to regular employment.* Manpower research bulletin 15. Washington, D.C.: Manpower Administration, 1967.

Van Hoose, W. H. *Counseling in the elementary schools.* Itasca, Il: F. E. Peacock Publishers, Inc., 1968.

Van Hoose, W. H. Guidance for the total development. Detroit: Wayne State University, 1969.

Varenhorst, B. B. Innovative tool for group counseling: the life career game. *The School Counselor,* 1968, 15(5), 357–362.

References

Varenhorst, B. B. Learning the consequences of life's decisions. In J. D. Krumboltz & C. E. Thoresen (Eds.) *Behavioral counseling: cases and techniques.* New York: Holt, Rinehart and Winston, Inc. 1969.

Veldman, D. J. & Menaker, S. L. Computer applications in assessment and counseling. *Journal of School Psychology,* 1968, 6(3), 167–176.

Vontress, C. E. Our demoralizing slum schools. *Phi Delta Kappan,* 1963, 45, 77–81.

Vriend, J. Report on the Harvard invitational conference on computer assisted systems in guidance and education. *Educational Technology,* 1970, 10(3), 15–20.

Wages, S. (et al.) Mexican American teenage school dropouts; reasons for leaving school and orientations toward subsequent educational attainment. Paper presented at the Southwestern Sociological Association Meeting, Houston, April, 1969.

Wagner, B. A. The responses of economically advantaged and economically disadvantaged sixth grade pupils to science demonstrations. Ann Arbor, Mi.: University Microfilms, 1967, No. 68–1421.

Walker, R. Guidance in grades seven, eight, and nine: a report of a study work conference conducted at Kent State University. Columbus: Ohio State Department of Education, Division of Guidance and Testing, 1960.

Walz, G. R. Technology in guidance: a conceptual overview. *Personnel and Guidance Journal,* 1970, 49(3), 175–184.

Warner, T. (Ed.) Needed concepts in elementary guidance. Columbus: Ohio State Department of Education, Division of Guidance and Testing, 1969.

Wells, Jean. Labor turnover of women factory workers, 1950–55. *Monthly Labor Review,* 1955, 78, 889–94.

Westfall, R. L. Selected variables in the achievement or nonachievement of the academically talented high school student. Unpublished doctoral dissertation, University of Southern California, 1958.

Whitfield, E. A. & Glaeser, G. A. *A demonstration of a regional career information center: the VIEW system. A summary of research results, 1967–68.* San Diego, Ca.: San Diego County Department of Education, 1968.

Whitfield, E. A. Vocational guidance in the elementary school: integration or fragmentation? *The School Counselor,* 1968, 16(2), 90–92.

Wichita Unified School District. *Special education and resource center project, 1966–1969. ESEA Title III final evaluation report.* Washington, D.C.: Office of Education (DHEW), 1969.

Willingham, W. W., Ferrin, R. I. & Begle, E. P. *Career guidance in secondary education.* New York: College Entrance Examination Board, 1972.

Wilson, E. H. A task oriented course in decision making. Information system for vocational decision. Project report no. 7. Cambridge: Harvard University, 1967.

Winborn, R. & Martinson, W. Innovation in guidance: a mobile counseling center. *Personnel and Guidance Journal,* 1967, 45(8), 818–820.

Winefordner, D. W. A suggested model for the full-time counselor who conducts and coordinates an exploratory program in grades 7–9. Report of a conference to Develop Objectives and Models for a Continuous Exploratory Program Related to the World of Work from Junior High through Senior High at West Georgia College, Carrollton, Georgia, August 18–23, 1968.

Wolpe, J. *Psychotherapy by reciprocal inhibition.* Stanford: Stanford University Press, 1958.

Women's Bureau. Nineteen sixty-two handbook on women workers. Washington, D.C.: Government Printing Office, Bulletin No. 285, 1963.

Women's Bureau. Women workers and their dependents. Washington, D.C.: WB (DOL), Bulletin No. 239, 1952.

Woods, B. G. Curriculum implications for career development. In K. B. Ashcraft (Ed.) *Implementing career development theory and research through the curriculum.* Report of a conference sponsored by the National Vocational Guidance Association, August 1966.

Woody, R. H. Vocational counseling with behavioral techniques. *The Vocational Guidance Quarterly,* 1968, 17(2), 97–103.

Zeran, F. R. and Riccio, A. C. *Organization and administration of guidance services.* Chicago: Rand McNally & Co., 1962.

Zimpfer, D. G. (et al.) A comparison of approaches to group counseling. Paper presented at the annual meeting of the American Personnel and Guidance Association, Dallas, Texas, March 1967.

Zimpfer, D. G. Some conceptual and research problems in group counseling. *The School Counselor,* 1968, 15(5), 326–333.

Zinn, K. L. & McClintock, S. A guide to the literature on interactive use of computers for instruction. (2nd ed.) Stanford, Ca.: ERIC Clearinghouse on Media and Technology, Stanford University, 1970.

INDEX

Abington School Districts, 20, 27, 147
"Access," 209
Accountability, 188
Adams County Board of Education, 27
Adoption concerns, 205
Akron-Summit County Public Schools, 35
Approaches. *See* Career guidance approaches
Arkansas Educational Television Commission, 136
Arkansas State Department of Education, 73
Atlanta Board of Education, 20, 27
Audio-Visual media, 89

Behavior Model for Career Guidance (BMCG), 173-76, 190, 191, 193, 194
Behavior modification, 150-54
Behavioral objectives, 15
Behavioral techniques, 79-80; characteristics, 78; defined, 77; implications, 80; method applications, 81; types of, 79-80
B'nai B'rith, 192
Bureau of Employment Security, 35, 43
Bureau of Labor Statistics, 35, 43

CAPS/Capsule, 209
"Career Development Activities," 147
Career guidance: basic questions, 9; trends, 2; what we need, 206-11; where we are, 201-6
Career guidance approaches: career information systems, 123-28; classroom activities, 160-65; designing, 122, 126-28; developmental program, 128-31; implementation, 122; manpower

Career guidance (continued)
and economic education, 135-39;
media, 160-65; mobile career
guidance services, 139-42; parent
involvement, 131-35; simulation,
154-60; special curricula, 146-50;
teaching decision making, 143-46;
use of models, 150-54
Career guidance goals. *See* Goals
of career guidance
Career guidance implications. *See*
Implications of career guidance
Career guidance method applications:
behavioral techniques, 81;
career relevant curricula, 111-14;
computer-assisted guidance,
85-87; disadvantaged, 59-60;
dropouts, 50; educational media,
90-91; elementary schools, 20-22;
group procedures, 96-98; handicapped youth, 74; high school,
35-37; information-retrieval
systems, 101-2; junior high schools,
27-30; Mexican-American youth,
67; post high school, 42-43; rural
youth, 64; simulation gaming,
106-7; slow learners, 53; underachievers, 56; women, 70; work
experience programs, 119-20
Career guidance methods: behavioral
techniques, 77-81; career relevant
curricula, 107-14; checklist, 197;
computer-assisted, 81-87;
considerations, 18-19; 25-26,
33-34, 40-42; defined, 1;
educational media, 87-91;
elementary schools, 18-19; group
procedures, 92-98; high schools,
33-34; information-retrieval
systems, 98-102; junior high
schools, 25-26; limiting and
modifying, 46; post high school,
40-42; selection of, 76-77; sharing,
205, 208; simulation gaming, 102-7;
size and cost, 46; survey of, 10;
unique methods, 47; work

experience program, 114-20
Career guidance programs: basic
questions, 9-12; implementation,
195-99
Career guidance rationale: *See*
Rationale for career guidance
Career Information Center, 35
Career information systems, 123-28;
basic principles, 126; designing
and implementing, 126-28; as
developed by others, 124-26
Career relevant curricula, 107-14;
characteristics, 108; defined,
107-8; implications, 110-11;
method applications, 111-14; types
of, 109-10
Carey, Richard, 143
Center of Economic Education, 136
Checklist in selecting methods, 197
Chicago Urban League, 35, 43
Cincinnati Public Schools, 28
Civil Service Commission, 35, 43
Classroom activities, 160-65; basic
principles, 161-62; design and
implementation, 162-65; as
developed by others, 160-61
Client role, 78
College Entrance Examination
Board, 28, 143
Colorado State University, 28
"Communique," 209
Community participation, 210
Community resources, 162
Comprehensive Career Guidance
Program (CCGS), 181-84, 194
Computer-assisted guidance, 81-87;
characteristics, 82-83; defined,
81-82; implications, 84-85; method
applications, 85-87; types of, 83-84
Congruent practices, 205
Contra Costa College, 140
Cooperative education programs, 117
Cornell Study, 42
Council for Exceptional
Children, 73
Counseling: defined, 77; group, 94

Index

Counseling and Personnel Services Information Center, 209
Counselor: defined, 2; needs, 204; role of, 78, 209; training, 127, 159
"Counselor Six-Pack," 209
Counterconditioning, 80
Credibility, 193
Crystallization, 14
Curricula to motivate career exploration, 146-50; basic principles, 148; design and implementation, 148-50; as developed by others, 147-48

"Deciding," 143
Decision making, 25, 143-46; basic principles, 144-45; designing and implementing, 145-46; as developed by others, 144
Detroit Public Schools, 118
Developmental career guidance curricula, 109
Developmental Career Guidance Program, 129
Developmental Career Guidance Project (DCGP), 132, 179-81, 189, 191, 192, 194
Developmental-maturational factors, 33
Developmental programs, 128-31; basic principles, 129-30; designing and implementing, 130-31; as developed by others, 129
Dialogue systems, 84
"Dictionary of Occupational Titles," 171
Disadvantaged, 56-60; defined, 56; implications, 58; method application, 59-60; research, 57-58
Dropouts, 48-50; defined, 48; implications, 49-50; method applications, 50; research, 48-49

Economic education, 25
Economic Opportunity Act, 117
Educable mentally retarded. *See* Slow learners
Education and training, 25
Education levels. *See* Elementary, Junior high, High school, Post high school
Educational development and planning systems, 99
Educational media, 87-91; characteristics, 87-88; defined, 87; implications, 90; method applications, 90-91; types of, 88-89
Educational Resources Information Center (ERIC), 6, 100
Educational technology, 207
Elementary and Secondary Education Act, 126
"Elementary Guide for Career Development," 187
Elementary school, 17-20; career guidance methods, 18-19; goals of career guidance, 17; implications, 19-20; rationale for career guidance, 16
Employability skills, 25
Environmental input evaluation, 195
Evaluation, 12, 194; of career guidance approaches, 135, 142, 146, 150, 154, 159, 164
"Evaluation Model for Guidance," 194
Extension programs, 208

Fantasy stage, 14
Flexibility, 190-91
Follow up, 128, 164
"Four Worlds," 161
Franklin County Board of Education, 140
Future shock, 211

Gelatt, H. B., 143
Georgia's Student Personnel Services, 194
Goals of career guidance: decision making experiences, 145; elementary school, 17; high school,

Goals of career (continued) 31-32; individual differences, 46; junior high, 24; mobile career guidance service, 141; parent involvement program, 134; post high school, 38
Group counseling, 94, 151
Group guidance, 94
Group procedures, 92-97; characteristics, 92-93; defined, 91; implications, 95-96; method applications, 96-97; types of, 93-95
Group therapy, 95
"Guidance for Education in Revolution," 194
Guidance point of view, 149

Handicapped youth, 71-74; defined, 71; implications, 73; method applications, 74; research, 71-73
Hardware, 207
Harkness Center, 36, 43
Havre High School District A, 140
High School, 30-36; career guidance methods, 33-34; goals of career guidance, 31-33; implications, 34-36; rationale for career guidance, 30-31
Houston Vocational Guidance Project, 36
Hoyt, Kenneth, 44, 125

"Impact," 209
Implementation concerns, 205
Implementing career guidance program, 195-99
Implications for career guidance: behavioral techniques, 80; career-relevant curricula, 110; computer-assisted guidance, 84-85; disadvantaged, 58-59; dropouts, 49-50; educational media, 90; elementary schools, 19-20; group procedures, 95-96; handicapped, 73-74; high schools, 34-35; information-retrieval systems, 100-101; junior high schools, 26-27; Mexican-American youth, 67; post high school, 42-43; rural youth, 62-64; simulation gaming, 105-6, slow learners, 52-53; underachievers, 55-56; women, 69-70; work experience programs, 118-19
Indiana Career Resource Center, 36
Indiana county program, 139
Individual differences, 45-46
Individual input evaluation, 194
Individual skill simulations, 105
Information-processing systems, 83
Information retrieval systems, 98-102; characteristics, 98; defined, 98; implications, 100-101; method applications, 101-2; types of, 99-100
Information System for Vocational Decisions, 144
"Introductions to Vocations," 147

Job experience kits, 155-56, 158
Joint Council on Economic Education, 136, 137
Joint vocational school, 62
Junior high school, 22-30; career guidance methods, 25-26; goals for career guidance, 24-25; implications, 26-27; method applications, 27-30; rationale for career guidance, 22-24

Kuder Preference Record Manual, 55

Large group instruction, 93-94
Leonard, George, 179
"Life Career Game," 12, 104, 156, 158
Life Styles, 206
"Little Annual," 209

Madison Junior High School, 29
Manpower Development Training Act, 117

Index

Manpower and economic education, 135-39; basic principles, 137-38; as developed by others, 136-37
Media, 160-65; basic principles, 161-62; design and implementation, 162-65; as developed by others, 160-61
"Mental Measurement Yearbook," 7
Method applications. *See* Career guidance method applications
Method types. *See* Career guidance methods
Mexican-American youth, 65-67; defined, 65; implications, 67; method applications, 67; research, 65-67
Michigan Community Schools, 36
Michigan State Department of Education, 36, 44
Minneapolis Public Schools, 29, 137, 161
Mobile career guidance services, 139-43; basic principles, 141; designing and implementing, 141-42; as developed by others, 139-40
Models, 150-54; basic principles, 151; design and implementation, 152-54; as developed by others, 151
Monroe School District, 21
Muskegan Public Schools, 29, 132

Need-press factors, 33
New Hampshire State Department of Education, 36
New Jersey State Department of Education, 21, 37, 147
New York State Education Department, 21
Newton Public Schools, 125
Niles Community Schools, 29
Northern Systems Company, 151

Objective evaluation, 195
Office of Education, 37, 44

Ohio State Center, 176
Oklahoma State Department of Education, 21, 29, 37, 129
Oklahoma Vocational Research Coordinating Unit, 29
"Operation Guidance," 176
Oregon State Department of Education, 29, 37, 44, 147, 169, 189
Organizational-administrative management, 168
Organizational structures, 211
Outreach programs, 208

Palo Alto Unified School District, 21, 29, 37
Paraprofessionals, 141
Parental involvement, 131-35; basic principles, 133; designing and implementing, 134-45; as developed by others, 132
Parents, 207
Pennsylvania Advancement School, 21, 29
Physical facilities, 142
Placement, 202
Population: defined, 45; disadvantaged, 56-60; dropouts, 48-50; handicapped youth, 71-74; Mexican-American youth, 65-67; rural youth, 60-65; slow learners, 51-53; underachievers, 53-56; unique, 203; women, 68-71
Post high school, 38-43; career guidance methods, 40-42; goals for career guidance, 38-40; implications, 42-43; rationale for career guidance, 38
Powell, Phillip, 136
President's Council on Youth Opportunity, 37, 44
Problem-solving orientation, 198
Procedural parsimony, 189-90
Process evaluation, 195
Product evaluation, 195
Program design, 188-89

Program mission and accountability, 188
Programmed instructional materials, 89
Project MINI-SCORE, 144
Project PROBE, 137
Project VIEW, 7, 124, 127

Rationale for career guidance: elementary schools, 16; high schools, 30-31; junior high schools, 22-24; post high school, 38
Realistic stage, 14
Reaves, Lee, 136
Reinforcement, 79
Research, 210; disadvantaged, 57-58; drop-outs, 48-49; handicapped, 71-73; Mexican-American youth, 65-67; rural youth, 61-62; slow learners, 51-52; underachievers, 54-55; women, 68-69
Resources, 191-92
Rural youth, 60-65; defined, 60; implications, 62; method applications, 64; research, 61

San Diego County Career Information Center, 124
San Diego Unified School District, 22, 29
School Districts of Cochise County, 29
School Research Information Service (SRIS), 100
Science Research Associates, 156
Self, 24
Self Understanding Through Occupational Exploration (SUTOE,) 169-73, 189, 194
Setting evaluation, 195
Simulated work experience programs, 117
Simulation, 154-60; basic principles, 157; design and implementation, 157-60; as developed by others, 155-57

Simulation gaming, 102-7; characteristics, 103-4; defined, 102; implications, 105-6; method applications, 106-7; types of, 104
Slow learners, 51-53; defined, 51; implications, 52; method applications, 53; research, 51-52
Social interaction games, 104
Social interaction orientation, 198
Social modeling, 79
Social skill seminar, 151
Societal forces, 2
Socio-economic conditions, 206
Special career guidance curricula, 109
Specialty-Oriented Student Research Program (SOS), 125
Specification, 12
Staff training, 100
Staffing of career guidance approaches, 134, 141
Student development, 168
Student Personnel Services (SPS), 176-79
Students, 10; needs, 163; as resources, 162
Supportive services, 12
"Synthesis," 209

Team teaching, 161
Technological innovation, 2
Tentative stage, 14
Texas Board of Education, 22, 30
Theoretical advancements, 2
Theory of career development, 186-87
Therapy, 95
Training designs, 206
Tutorial systems, 83

Underachievers, 53-56; defined, 53; implications, 55-56; method applications, 56; research, 54-55
United States Bureau of Labor Statistics, 49
University of Minnesota, 144

Index

Urban League, 62

Varenhorst, Barbara, 143
Viability, 190-91
Video tape, 160
Vocational Education Act, 9, 117, 126
Vocational maturity, 14
Vocational Rehabilitation Law, 71
Volunteer work experience programs, 117

Washington Township Board of Education, 30
Western States Small Schools Project, 62

Whitfield, Edwin, 125
Wichita Unified School District, 73
Wilmington Public Schools, 37
Women, 68-71; implications, 69-70; method applications, 70-71; research, 68-69
Work experience programs, 114-20; characteristics, 115-16; defined, 114-15; implications, 118-19; method applications, 119-20; types of, 116-18
Work-study programs, 117
"World of Work," 161
World of work, 24

"You, the Decider," 144

HF
5381
.C2657

CAMPBELL

CAREER GUIDANCE

DATE DUE		
OCT 23 1979		

556432 M
08486